Competition Policy and Intellectual Property Rights in the Knowledge-Based Economy

GENERAL EDITORS:
ROBERT D. ANDERSON AND NANCY T. GALLINI

Competition Policy and Intellectual Property Rights in the Knowledge-Based Economy

The Industy Canada Research Series

University of Calgary Press

© Ministry of Supply and Services Canada 1998

ISBN 1-895176-97-2
ISSN 1188-0988

University of Calgary Press
2500 University Dr. N.W.
Calgary, Alberta, Canada T2N 1N4

Canadian Cataloguing in Publication Data (Canada)
Main entry under title:
Competition Policy and Intellectual Property Rights in the Knowledge-Based Economy

(The Industry Canada research series, ISSN 1188-0988; v.9)
Issued also in French under title: La politique de concurrence et les droits de propriété
intellectuelle dans l'économie du savoir.
Includes bibliographical references.
ISBN 1-895176-97-2

1. Competition.
2. Intellectual property.
3. Industrial policy.
I. Anderson, Robert D.
II. Gallini, Nancy T.
III. Series.

HF1414.C67 1998   338.6'048   C98-910527-X

EDITORIAL & TYPESETTING SERVICES: CIGC Services conseils inc.
COVER DESIGN : Paul Payer/ArtPlus Limited.

Printed and bound in Canada

∞ This book is printed on acid-free paper.

a121066   NOV 23 1998 gft

Table of Contents

Preface

ENSURING A HIGH RATE OF INNOVATION AND PRODUCTIVITY IMPROVEMENT is at the core of the challenges facing the Canadian economy as we approach the next century. Meeting this challenge requires, among other tasks, that the design and application of micro-economic framework policies such as competition policy and intellectual property rights be up to date and in line with current economic thinking and analysis. These policies play a vital role in setting the framework for innovation and the rapid diffusion of new technologies and information, and are particularly important in the context of network industries and the knowledge-based economy of the late 1990s.

The application of competition policy vis-a-vis intellectual property rights and innovation poses particularly complex challenges for policy makers and administrators. While competition policy has traditionally focused on maintaining rivalry and maximizing efficiency primarily in a static sense, increasingly, scholars and administrators recognize the need for consideration of the dynamic effects of framework policies on innovation and the diffusion of new technology. The purpose of this volume is to assess and reflect on the application of competition policy toward intellectual property in Canada, to help ensure an appropriate balance between the provision of incentives for innovation and the maintenance of vigorous inter-firm rivalry in markets for goods and services.

This volume is the outcome of a research exercise initiated by the Competition Bureau in cooperation with the Canadian Intellectual Property Office and the Micro-Economic Policy Analysis Branch of Industry Canada. The volume includes ten substantive papers authored by leading scholars of the law and economics of competition policy and intellectual property from Canada, the United States and Europe, in addition to select government policy analysts with experience working in competition agencies in Canada and the U.S. The volume also incorporates: (i) perceptive (and sometimes dissenting) comments prepared by knowledgeable discussants at a Symposium held to review the initial drafts of the papers, in Aylmer, Québec, in May 1996; (ii) the Summary of a Roundtable Discussion at the Symposium on the subject of Competition Policy, Intellectual Property and Innovation Markets; and (iii) an

Introduction and Conclusions for the volume prepared by the General Editors. This volume will contribute to improved understanding of the important role of competition policy and intellectual property rights in promoting an efficient, innovative economy, in Canada and abroad.

The research incorporated in this volume was planned and overseen jointly by the General Editors, Robert Anderson, formerly with the Competition Bureau and now at the World Trade Organization in Geneva, and Professor Nancy Gallini, Chair of the Department of Economics at the University of Toronto. I would like to take this opportunity to thank them, as well as the authors and discussants of the various papers, for their valued role in this project.

JOHN MANLEY
MINISTER OF INDUSTRY

Robert D. Anderson & Nancy T. Gallini
Competition Bureau Department of Economics
Industry Canada, and University of Toronto
World Trade Organization[1]

1

Competition Policy, Intellectual Property Rights, and Efficiency: An Introduction to the Issues

COMPETITION POLICY AND INTELLECTUAL PROPERTY (IP) RIGHTS are key instruments of government policy, providing incentives for innovation and the rapid diffusion of new technology. More specifically, intellectual property rights (IPRs) – particularly patents and copyrights – prevent the widespread copying of new inventions or creative works, which undermines the returns from innovation. Competition policy, on the other hand, seeks to prevent restrictive commercial practices that impede the efficient production and diffusion of goods and technologies. Ensuring an appropriate balance between IP protection and competition policy is vital to providing optimal incentives for innovation and efficiency in a knowledge-based economy. Consequently, the interplay between these two instruments is a central focus of ongoing debates and scholarly analysis of economic policies in advanced industrial economies[2] – and forms the subject matter of the present volume.

The relationship between competition policy and intellectual property rights was a central consideration in the early development of Canadian competition legislation.[3] The current *Competition Act* contains several specific provisions relating to IP.[4] In addition, issues relating to IP rights and/or proprietary information have figured prominently in several recent enforcement cases brought under the *Competition Act*.[5] However, no systematic analytical framework exists for applying the relevant statutory provisions in such cases.

Over the past few years, both the United States and the European Union have issued new policy guidelines pertaining to the application of competition policy vis-à-vis IPRs.[6] These rights have played a major role in several important cases in these jurisdictions.[7] Japan also has in place a set of antitrust guidelines for technology licensing.[8] Moreover, policies relating to the interface between competition policy and intellectual property rights have been the subject of international deliberations at both the multilateral and regional levels in recent years.[9]

The interplay between competition policy and IP is the subject of an extensive body of economic and legal literature. This literature provides many useful insights into the pro- and anti-competitive effects of licensing arrangements and related aspects of firm behaviour.[10] However, the optimal stance of competition policy towards IP rights remains the subject of vigorous debate among competition policy scholars and practitioners.[11]

The current high level of interest in this subject among scholars and policymakers reflects important tensions in economic theory. Economists today recognize that the accumulation of knowledge and innovation is central not only to growth but to the process of competition in a market-based economy.[12] There is also a consensus that interfirm rivalry plays an important role in fostering innovation and productivity improvement. Considerable diversity of opinion exists, however, on the specific market configurations and institutional structures that are optimal for fostering the development and diffusion of new technology. There is also extensive debate regarding the impact of the firm's organization (e.g., the degree of vertical integration) and the implications of IP licensing arrangements for the competitive process.[13] The positions taken by scholars on these basic issues carry important implications for the application of competition policy and related microeconomic framework policies.

Without purporting to resolve all of the underlying theoretical issues, this volume seeks to provide practical advice on the application of competition policy vis-à-vis IP rights, while drawing on, summarizing, and (where possible) extending existing theoretical contributions and empirical analysis. The focus of the volume is on competition issues relating to patents, although aspects of the analysis may be applicable to other forms of intellectual property. We set out below relevant information on the respective roles of competition and IP rights in relation to innovation and growth, outline the broad issues addressed in the volume, and provide an overview of its contents.

THE NATURE AND ROLE OF INTELLECTUAL PROPERTY RIGHTS

INTELLECTUAL PROPERTY RIGHTS – patents, trademarks, copyrights, registered industrial designs, integrated circuit topographies, etc. – are a key factor in fostering innovation and growth in today's economy. By providing a limited ability to exclude others from making, or enjoying the benefits of, the protected ideas/materials, IPRs provide vital incentives for research and development leading to new products and production processes, and facilitate the diffusion of new technology or creative works.[14] The precise terms of protection vary with the particular type of IPR.[15]

Intellectual property rights are extensively employed by firms in Canada and other countries that view them as important strategic assets.[16] The use of IPRs, however, varies considerably across industries and firms.[17] The role of IP in fostering innovation is complemented by other incentives, such as first-mover advantages, which exist independently of IP legislation.[18]

The legal and institutional framework for the enforcement (and nullification) of IPRs is an important factor bearing on their overall impact.[19] In the United States, the courts will not protect a patentee against infringement where a patent has been "misused." The grounds for a finding of misuse include, but are not limited to, possible antitrust violations. The scope for use of alleged competition law violations (or other alleged misuses) as a defence in patent infringement suits is considerably narrower in Canada.[20] Moreover, whereas treble damage claims for some types of competition law violations are possible in the United States, there are no provisions for them in Canada, thus limiting the incentive for private parties to allege violations of competition law in the context of patent litigation.

Recently, a spirited debate has arisen in the scholarly literature over issues relating to the optimal length and breadth (i.e., scope) of patents and other forms of IPRs.[21] The scope of a patent refers to the range of products that are deemed to infringe it. The broader the scope of IP protection, the more difficult it will be for other firms to "invent around" it, and therefore the greater will be the returns to the rights holder. Clearly, concerns about "over-breadth" of IPRs, where they exist, reinforce the need for effective competition policies. Such concerns appear to be particularly relevant in the context of network industries, where the combination of IP protection and substantial (positive) externalities associated with the size of a network can create or entrench substantial market power.[22] In the majority of cases, however, it is doubtful that the mere existence of IPRs confers significant market power on their owners.[23] This reflects the fact that the actual product "space" covered by a particular IP right is usually smaller than a "relevant market" in an antitrust sense.[24]

THE ROLE OF INTERFIRM RIVALRY IN FOSTERING INNOVATION AND TECHNOLOGICAL DIFFUSION

STARTING WITH SCHUMPETER'S PATH-BREAKING ANALYSIS in *Capitalism, Socialism and Democracy*, theoretical economic research has emphasized the overall importance of interfirm rivalry to the innovation process. While Schumpeter argued that competition in *innovative activity* is the driving force of a capitalistic economy, he also asserted that some degree of market power in *product markets* may be necessary to achieve this.[25]

In a recent contribution, Aghion and Howitt expand upon Schumpeter's analysis, arguing that competition in product markets as well as in R&D activities is likely to promote innovation and growth.[26] This viewpoint reflects three underlying considerations. First, unlike the case of a monopolist, R&D efforts by competitive firms do not pose the risk of eroding ("cannibalizing") profits from existing products.[27] Second, a higher degree of competition in the product market, by making survival more tenuous for individual firms, will encourage them to innovate in order to gain (or preserve) a significant lead over their rivals. Third, Aghion and Howitt argue that competitive firms, because they are more adaptable, are more likely to transfer workers quickly to sectors with the greatest scope for the development and commercialization of new ideas.

These theoretical developments highlight an important distinction in recent economic literature – namely, the distinction between competition in product markets and in innovation activity *per se*. Promoting competition in product markets, which until recently has been the traditional focus of competition policy, does not necessarily ensure competition in *innovation markets*. The latter concept, which is highlighted in the recently released *Antitrust Guidelines for the Licensing of Intellectual Property* in the United States, refers to "research and development directed toward particular new and improved goods and processes, and the close substitutes for that research and development."[28] This approach complements conventional product market analysis, where the focus is on the degree of potential or actual competition in markets for final goods and services.[29]

While empirical studies corroborate the overall importance of interfirm rivalry as a spur to innovation and productivity improvement, they do not support robust relationships between the rate of innovation and particular market structures.[30] The business literature, however, does provide strong confirmation of the positive relationship between competition and innovative activity. Most notably, Michael Porter finds that interfirm rivalry, particularly in *domestic* markets, contributes directly to the international competitiveness of a nation's firms:

> Among the strongest empirical findings from our research is the association between vigorous domestic rivalry and the creation and persistence of competitive advantage in an industry . . . Domestic rivalry not only creates pressures to innovate but to innovate in ways that *upgrade* the competitive advantages of a nation's firms.[31]

Similar findings are reported in the U.S. Federal Trade Commission's 1996 *Study on Competition Policy and the New High-Tech Global Market Place*. The study notes that "Business participants . . . were emphatic that competition is a primary incentive for innovation, and that continuous innovation is critical for success in increasingly global markets."[32]

In this context, the challenge for competition policy is to ensure a high degree of interfirm rivalry in markets without jeopardizing business arrangements that are reasonably necessary to achieve desirable efficiencies. Indeed, the competition policies of most industrialized countries seek to provide the necessary scope for efficient interfirm arrangements – for example, by providing special treatment for R&D joint ventures.[33] The application of competition policy vis-à-vis intellectual property rights, however, raises particularly challenging issues – issues that are the subject of the present book.

THE ISSUES

THE VOLUME EXAMINES THE APPROPRIATE ROLE of competition policy in relation to the exercise of IP rights and innovative activity. It does so by focusing on a number of important issues, outlined below.

How should specific IP licensing and R&D practices be treated under competition law?

The IP practices that are contentious in relation to competition policy objectives can be divided into three main categories: 1) the acquisition of patents; 2) the transfer of technology through licensing arrangements; and 3) cooperative arrangements among innovating firms. These practices raise concerns when they are seen as attempts to extend market power, by excluding entry into the market, suppressing innovation or charging excessive prices, beyond those provided by the patent right. In varying degrees, however, these types of practices may also serve legitimate, efficiency-related purposes. A central goal of many of the papers in the volume is to assist competition authorities in striking the appropriate balance between the adverse and beneficial effects of these practices in their analysis of individual cases.

Should competition policy attempt to correct for perceived excesses/deficiencies in the protection of intellectual property rights?

For example, competition policy might attempt to counterbalance strong IP protection in network industries by imposing strict constraints on restrictive licensing practices; alternatively, it might compensate for weak patent protection by allowing firms to impose private restrictions in licensing contracts. The challenge here is to evaluate whether competition policy should attempt to influence R&D activity in this way or whether it should restrict itself to concerns not related to the creation of innovations.

Finally, the papers in the volume delve into a wider range of questions relating to the interface of competition policy and intellectual property in different jurisdictions. Among the issues addressed are: the potential benefits of guidelines on the competition policy treatment of intellectual property for firms' incentives to innovate and diffuse their technologies; special considerations relating to consumer protection in the context of emerging technologies; and the implications of using patents to segment international markets.

Organization of the Volume and Overview of Individual Papers

THE PAPERS PRESENTED IN THIS VOLUME are organized into four parts:

Part I: Intellectual Property, Competition Policy and Economic Efficiency: Framework Issues

Nancy T. Gallini and Michael J. Trebilcock,
"Intellectual Property Rights and Competition Policy:
A Framework for the Analysis of Economic and Legal Issues"

This paper provides an overview of key economic issues pertaining to the interface between competition policy and intellectual property in Canada. In particular, the paper identifies and evaluates distinguishing characteristics that could be argued to justify differential treatment under competition policy. Alternative frameworks for the application of competition policy to IPRs are presented. The paper also examines the laws and jurisprudence relating to particular licensing practices in Canada, the United States, and the European Union. A proposed economic framework is applied to various competition cases involving intellectual property.

Donald G. McFetridge,
"Intellectual Property, Technology Diffusion, and
Growth in the Canadian Economy"

This paper examines the implications of intellectual property rights for the diffusion of innovations and discusses the relationship between technology diffusion and economic growth in the Canadian economy. The paper also provides an analysis of the Canadian experience with compulsory licensing as a tool for promoting the rapid diffusion of new technologies.

Robert P. Merges,
"Antitrust Review of Patent Acquisitions:
Property Rights, Firm Boundaries, and Organization"

This paper analyzes several issues relating to the acquisition and transfer of IPRs, focusing on patents and copyrights. The author emphasizes the threat to competition that may be posed by the strategic acquisition of patents as well as the implications of IP protection for the organization of production. Competition policy is highlighted as an important instrument for balancing the effects of patent accumulation in appropriate cases.

Part II: Contractual Practices and Organizational Arrangements

William F. Baxter and Daniel P. Kessler,
"The Law and Economics of Tying Arrangements:
Lessons for the Competition Policy Treatment of Intellectual Property"

This paper examines the efficiency and competitive implications of tying arrangements that involve intellectual property. A tying arrangement exists when a producer makes the purchase of one product, the tying product, conditional on the purchase of another product, the tied product. The authors comment on various rationales for tying that have been identified in the literature, and particularly on the use of tying as a means of extending the life of a patent in time or product space.

Patrick Rey and Ralph A. Winter,
"Exclusivity Restrictions and Intellectual Property"

This paper provides an analysis of exclusivity provisions in IP licensing contracts. These may include exclusive rights to the use of a particular technology, the assignment of exclusive territories to particular licensees, exclusive grant-backs, and exclusive dealing arrangements. These practices raise concerns when they facilitate the extension of market power by excluding entry into a market, suppressing innovation or facilitating excessive prices. On the other hand, in varying degrees these types of practices may also serve legitimate, efficiency-related purposes. The paper identifies various criteria that can assist in distinguishing harmful from benign manifestations of such practices.

Suzanne Scotchmer,
"R&D Joint Ventures and
Other Cooperative Arrangements"

The author analyzes the application of competition law to R&D joint ventures, cross-licensing, patent pools, and other types of horizontal arrangements – i.e., arrangements involving firms that would otherwise be in competition with each other. As in recent economic literature, the paper emphasizes both the potential efficiency-enhancing and anticompetitive implications of the sharing of technological information and related aspects of such arrangements. The paper discusses a number of policy and enforcement issues, with particular reference to biotechnology industries.

7

Jeffrey Church and Roger Ware,
"Network Industries, Intellectual Property Rights and
Competition Policy"

This paper examines the interaction of competition policy and IPRs in network industries, where issues of standardization and compatibility of technologies are important. Examples of such industries include telecommunications, information processing, and electronic funds transfer, where IP protection has been expanded to cover software, operating systems, chips, and other information technologies. In these industries, a degree of cooperation among firms (for example, in the setting of standards) may be necessary to the provision of efficient service. However, it is important that such cooperation not go so far as to facilitate collusion or deter the introduction of more efficient technologies. The authors explore these issues from a positive perspective, but also discuss the normative aspects: when are these practices efficient and when should they be discouraged through the application of competition policy?

Part III: Policy Issues and Comparative Perspectives

Derek Ireland,
"Competition Policy, Intellectual Property and the Consumer"

This paper reflects on the implications of adopting a consumer perspective for the design of IPRs and the application of competition policy, especially in an environment with asymmetric information. One issue raised is whether current policy has been effective in addressing consumer concerns regarding, for example, safety and the environment. These issues are particularly relevant in the context of biotechnology. The authors note that, to some extent, the concerns developed in the paper can be addressed by competition authorities applying a broader, more flexible interpretation to the concepts of consumer welfare and productive efficiency gains.

Willard K. Tom and Joshua A. Newberg,
"U.S. Enforcement Approaches to the
Antitrust-Intellectual Property Interface"

This paper examines the implications and intellectual underpinnings of the *Antitrust Guidelines for the Licensing of Intellectual Property* recently established by the U.S. Department of Justice and the Federal Trade Commission (FTC), and of related enforcement developments. It comments, in particular, on the concept of innovation markets and alternative approaches for evaluating the competitive effects of IP licensing arrangements. The paper also reviews various contributions to the recent FTC hearings on globalization and antitrust, which provide insights into the interaction between competition policy, IP, and international economic policy.

Robert D. Anderson, Paul M. Feuer,
Brian A. Rivard and Mark F. Ronayne,
"Intellectual Property Rights and International Market Segmentation in the North American Free Trade Area"

This paper examines the use of intellectual property rights to facilitate the international segmentation of markets. Special attention is given to the "exhaustion" principle, which provides that intellectual property rights may not be used to restrict the movement of goods internationally once they have been legitimately put on the market in one country. The paper also considers issues relating to international licensing agreements and technology transfer.

Each of the papers described above is followed by a critical commentary that expands upon the analysis presented in the paper and/or provides a contrasting viewpoint.

Part IV: Roundtable Discussion and Conclusions

"Roundtable Discussion on Competition Policy,
Intellectual Property and Innovation Markets"

A unique feature of the volume, found in Part IV, is a roundtable discussion in which most of the authors and discussants expand on and debate the issues developed in the papers. The roundtable provides a lively exchange of viewpoints regarding the optimal application of competition policy in information-based industries.

Robert D. Anderson and Nancy T. Gallini,
"Summary and Conclusions"

In this paper, we summarize the principal findings of the various contributed papers and discuss their implications for policy development and application.

NOTES

1   Robert Anderson's input to this chapter was substantially completed while he was on the staff of the Competition Bureau, at Industry Canada.

2   The application of competition policy vis-à-vis IP rights was a central consideration in a wide-ranging study of the role of competition policy in the current economic environment conducted by the U.S. Federal Trade Commission in 1995-96. See Federal Trade Commission, *Anticipating the 21st Century: Competition Policy in the New High-Tech, Global Marketplace*, May 1996. See also *Antitrust, Innovation and Competitiveness*, edited by Thomas M. Jorde and David J. Teece, New York: Oxford University Press, 1992.

3   Remedies to deal with alleged abuses of IP rights were a key element of amendments made to the then *Combines Investigation Act* in 1910 and 1946. IP issues also figured in debates regarding attempted further changes to the legislation in the 1970s. See R. D. Anderson, S. D. Khosla and M. F. Ronayne, "The Competition Policy Treatment of Intellectual Property Rights in Canada: Retrospect and Prospect," in *Canadian Competition Law and Policy at the Centenary*, edited by R. S. Khemani and W. T. Stanbury, Halifax: Institute for Research on Public Policy, 1991, chapter 15, pp. 497-538.

4   For a discussion, see Nancy Gallini and Michael Trebilcock, "Intellectual Property Rights and Competition Policy: A Framework for the Analysis of Economic and Legal Issues," chapter 2 of this volume.

5   See, for example, *Canada (Director of Investigation and Research) v. The NutraSweet Co.* (1990) 32 C.P.R. (3d) 1 (Competition Tribunal, October 4, 1990); and *Director of Investigation and Research v. The D&B Companies of Canada Ltd.* (Competition Tribunal, August 30, 1995).

6   See U.S. Department of Justice and Federal Trade Commission *Antitrust Guidelines for the Licensing of Intellectual Property*, Washington, D.C.: U.S. Government Printing Office, April 6, 1995, and European Commission, *Block Exemption Regarding Technology Transfer*, Brussels: EC, January 31, 1996.

7   For example, in *Dell Computer Corp.*, the U.S. Federal Trade Commission alleged that Dell had restricted competition regarding certain design standards for computing systems by threatening to exercise patent rights. In the *Pilkington* case, the Department of Justice charged that Pilkington, a firm that had developed a revolutionary float-glass process, had monopolized the world market for float glass through patent and know-how licensing arrangements limiting the territories in which licensees could compete. For discussion and citations, see Federal Trade Commission, *Anticipating the 21st Century*, supra, note 2.

8   See Hideki Ogawa, "New Technology Licensing Guidelines in Japan," *World Competition Law and Economics Review*, 13, 2 (December 1989).

9   Both the multilateral agreement on trade-related intellectual property rights (TRIPs) and the North American Free Trade Agreement (NAFTA) embody significant new provisions regarding competition and IP. In particular, article 40 of the TRIPs agreement allows member states to adopt measures to deal with restrictive licensing practices and requires that contracting parties extend "sympathetic consideration" to requests for consultation by other contracting parties regarding the effects of such practices in particular cases. In the North American context, chapter 15 of the NAFTA provides that each party to the agreement will adopt or maintain measures to deal with anti-competitive business practices generally. chapter 17 contains precedent-setting

provisions pertaining to standards for protection. Article 1704 of the agreement stipulates that parties to the agreement may adopt or maintain appropriate measures dealing with anticompetitive abuses of intellectual property rights.

10   Classic contributions to the literature include William Baxter, "Legal Restrictions on the Exploitation of the Patent Monopoly: An Economic Analysis," *Yale Law Journal*, 76 (1966): 267; Ward S. Bowman, *Patent and Antitrust Law: A Legal and Economic Appraisal*, Chicago: University of Chicago Press, 1973; and Louis Kaplow, "Extension of Monopoly Power Through Leverage," *Columbia Law Review*, 85 (1985): 15. A useful survey of practical enforcement issues reflecting the theoretical perspectives of the 1980s is provided in Organisation for Economic Co-operation and Development, Committee on Competition Law and Policy, *Competition Policy and Intellectual Property Rights*, 1989. For highlights of recent theoretical contributions, see Gallini and Trebilcock, chapter 2 of this volume.

11   See *Anticipating the 21st Century*, *supra*, note 2, for a discussion of the wide spectrum of scholarly opinion in this area.

12   Howitt observes that "the essence of the competitive struggle in a free economy has little to do with whether or not firms take prices as parametric, as in textbook price theory. Instead, it involves the very innovative process that gives rise to creative destruction. The firms that survive this struggle do not respond to adversity by reallocating resources and manipulating prices within known technological parameters. They respond by innovating, by finding previously undiscovered ways to trim costs and open up new markets, and by creating new products that can be sold even in hard times." Peter Howitt, "On Some Problems in Measuring Knowledge-Based Growth," in *The Implications of Knowledge-Based Growth for Micro-economic Policies*, edited by Peter Howitt, Calgary: University of Calgary Press, 1996, chapter 1, pp. 9-29.

13   For a useful overview of the issues, see A. L. Keith Acheson and Donald G. McFetridge, "Intellectual Property and Endogenous Growth," in *The Implications of Knowledge-Based Growth*, *ibid*.

14   *Ibid*; and Donald G. McFetridge, "Intellectual Property, Technology Diffusion and Growth in the Canadian Economy," chapter 3 of this volume.

15   More specifically, patents, which are the principal focus of analysis in this volume, are a property right in new inventions, including both products and processes. They allow their owners (the patentees) to exclude others from making, using or selling the invention for a period of up to 20 years from the date on which an application is filed. In return for the right to exclude, a patentee must disclose the essence of his invention in the patent application, thereby making it available for others to copy upon expiration of the patent. Copyright differs from patents in several key respects. First, it applies to fixed expressions of ideas rather than to the underlying ideas themselves. Rather than being obtained through formal application, it arises automatically when a work is embedded in a physical medium. Two other types of IP rights should be noted. First, in Canada, the *Integrated Circuit Topography Act* protects original-design semiconductor chips. Similar legislation, the *Semiconductor Chip Protection Act*, has been in place in the United States since 1984. The term of protection is 10 years. Second, new plant varieties in Canada are protected by another special IP statute, the *Plant Breeders' Rights Act*. The term of protection in this case is 18 years. Finally, it should be noted that the law of trade secrets provides a kind of intellectual property protection. Unlike a patent, however, this legislation does not provide protection against independent discovery of a process or of another invention. For a useful

elaboration on the roles and distinguishing characteristics of the various kinds of IP rights, see Acheson and McFetridge, "Intellectual Property and Endogenous Growth," *supra*, note 13.

16   *Intellectual Property and Canada's Commercial Interests: A Summary Report*, Ottawa: Consumer and Corporate Affairs Canada, 1990.

17   John Baldwin, *The Use of Intellectual Property Rights by Economic Sector*, Working Paper, Industry Canada, Ottawa, 1996.

18   Wesley M. Cohen and Richard C. Levin, "Empirical Studies of Innovation and Market Structure," in *Handbook of Industrial Organization*. Edited by Richard Schmalensee and Robert D. Willig, 1990.

19   Gordon F. Henderson, *Intellectual Property: Litigation, Legislation and Education. A Study of the Canadian Intellectual Property and Litigation System*, Ottawa: Consumer and Corporate Affairs Canada, 1991.

20   *Ibid.*; and Anderson, Khosla and Ronayne, *supra*, note 3.

21   For a review of the literature, see Gallini and Trebilcock, *supra*, note 4.

22   See Jeffrey Church and Roger Ware, "Network Industries, Intellectual Property Rights and Competition Policy," chapter 8 of this volume.

23   The concept of market power relates to the ability of a firm (or a group of firms acting together) to maintain prices above competitive levels, without losing sales so rapidly that the price increase is unprofitable. Market power may also be manifested through an adverse impact on service quality, innovation or other relevant variables. See Director of Investigation and Research, *Merger Enforcement Guidelines*, March 1991, p. 3.

24   See J. Paul McGrath, "Patent Licensing: A Fresh Look at Antitrust Principles in a Changing Economic Environment," *Patent and Trademark Review*, 82, 9 (September 1984): 355-65.

25   Joseph A. Schumpeter, *Capitalism, Socialism and Democracy*, 3rd ed., New York: Harper and Row, 1950. Reflecting this viewpoint, Schumpeter asserts that "perfect competition is not only impossible but inferior, and has no title to being set up as a model of ideal efficiency" (p. 106).

26   Philippe Aghion and Peter Howitt, "A Schumpeterian Perspective on Growth and Innovation," in *Advances in Economics and Econometrics: Theory and Applications*, edited by David Kreps and Ken Wallis, Cambridge: Cambridge University Press (forthcoming).

27   This effect was initially identified by Kenneth J. Arrow, "Economic Welfare and the Allocation of Resources for Invention," in *The Rate and Direction of Economic Activity*, edited by Richard R. Nelson, Princeton: Princeton University Press, 1962.

28   U.S. Department of Justice and Federal Trade Commission, *Guidelines*, *supra*, note 6. See also Richard N. Gilbert and Steven C. Sunshine, "Incorporating Dynamic Efficiency Concerns in Merger Analysis: The Use of Innovation Markets," *Antitrust Law Journal*, 63, 2 (Winter 1996): 569-601.

29   Gilbert and Sunshine, *ibid.*

30   Relevant studies include Cohen and Levin, *supra*, note 18; M. Baily and H. Gersback, "Innovation and the Nature of Competition," *Brookings Papers on Economic Activity: Microeconomics*, 1992; and F. M. Scherer, "Schumpeter and Plausible Capitalism," *Journal of Economic Literature*, 30, 3 (September 1992): 1416-33.

31   Michael Porter, *The Competitive Advantage of Nations*, New York: Free Press, 1992, p. 121. Porter also establishes an explicit link between the need for interfirm rivalry

and the importance of competition (antitrust) policy. He argues that "a strong antitrust policy . . . is essential to the rate of upgrading in an economy."

32   U.S. Federal Trade Commission, *Anticipating the 21st Century, supra*, note 2.

33   See R. D. Anderson and S. D. Khosla, *Competition Policy as a Dimension of Economic Policy: A Comparative Perspective*, Occasional Paper no. 7, Industry Canada, Ottawa, May 1995.

ACKNOWLEDGMENTS

A LARGE NUMBER OF PERSONS CONTRIBUTED TO THE PREPARATION of this volume. In addition to the various authors and discussants, the General Editors wish to express their thanks to the following individuals: Paul Feuer and Brian Rivard of the Competition Bureau, and Douglas Cumming, a student at the University of Toronto, for able assistance in reviewing the papers and related editorial tasks; Denis Gauthier, Someshwar Rao and Gilles Mcdougall of the Micro-Economic Policy Analysis Branch of Industry Canada for excellent collaboration and helpful suggestions throughout the project; Derek Ireland, formerly with the Competition Bureau and now at the Office of Consumer Affairs, for his help in initiating the project; and Claire Rock and Nicole Vézina of the Competition Bureau for cheerful and efficient word-processing services. Finally, we wish to record a special note of appreciation to Val Traversy, formerly Director-General of Economics and International Affairs at the Competition Bureau, for his valued guidance and encouragement in the early and middle stages of the project, and to Patricia Smith, the current Director-General, for supporting it through to its completion.

Part I
Intellectual Property, Competition Policy and
Economic Efficiency: Framework Issues

Nancy T. Gallini   &   Michael J. Trebilcock
Department of Economics   Faculty of Law
University of Toronto   University of Toronto

Intellectual Property Rights and Competition Policy: A Framework for the Analysis of Economic and Legal Issues

INTRODUCTION

THE LEGAL AND POLICY ISSUES RAISED BY INTELLECTUAL PROPERTY have attracted increasing attention from policymakers around the world. Modern advances in technology have created classes of products and processes that present new challenges for patent and competition authorities. Moreover, markets have changed. With the elimination of many barriers to trade, survival in highly competitive global markets depends on the development or adoption of state-of-the-art technologies. These changes have necessitated a reevaluation of the laws that impact on the development and diffusion of innovations – namely, intellectual property (IP) laws and competition laws.

From the point of view of maximizing social welfare, an inherent tension exists between competition and patent laws, which Kaplow has described as follows: "A practice is typically deemed to violate the antitrust laws because it is anticompetitive. But the very purpose of the patent grant is to reward the patentee by limiting competition, in full recognition that the monopolistic evils are the price society will pay."[1]

This tension can be traced to the familiar public-good problem. Intellectual property embodies information that is a public good: an inventor's consumption of the information does not preclude others from consuming it and so, in the absence of property rights, an innovation will be imitated. In recognition of the public-good nature of IP, patent law provides intellectual property rights (IPRs) in innovations; without IPRs, the incentive to invest in innovation would be diminished. The law also recognizes that the dynamic benefits from IPRs come at an allocative cost, in that the use of the innovation will be suboptimal: information is relatively costless to transmit, and its efficient price is therefore zero; exclusionary rights, on the other hand, enable the patentee to set a positive price for the information, thus reducing the output and flow of that information. By giving rights to an innovation that are exclusive but limited in scope and duration, an IPR awarded under patent law attempts to strike the appropriate balance between these competing concerns.[2]

Competition law impacts on the exercise of the innovator's rights – and therefore on its reward – by restricting certain practices involving the IPR. The dynamic-allocative efficiency trade-off that underlies patent law also applies to competition law, and here again the tension between the two approaches is evident. Simply put, the IP grant seeks to protect property rights, and, in so doing, limits competition. In contrast, competition law generally reflects the premise that consumer welfare is best served by removing impediments to competition. However, this previous short-run view of competition authorities has been replaced by a longer-run view, which acknowledges that technological progress contributes at least as much to social welfare as does the elimination of allocative inefficiencies associated with non-competitive prices.[3] There is, therefore, a growing willingness to restrict competition today in order to promote competition in new products and processes tomorrow.[4] Thus IPRs and competition policy are now seen as complementary ways of achieving efficiency in a market economy.[5]

The problem of coordinating patent and competition policy is subjected to economic analysis in the next section. First, a brief review of the relevant patent and licensing economic literature is provided, followed by alternative economic proposals for competition policy treatment of IPRs, especially with respect to licensing contracts,[6] which form the largest proportion of patent-competition cases.[7]

We then provide a comparative analysis of the laws reflecting the interface between IP and competition law in the United States, Canada, and the European Union (EU), with a view to identifying major similarities and differences among the regimes. As in the economic review, the legal analysis focuses on licensing arrangements for patented innovations – both unilateral restrictions by a dominant firm (e.g., resale price maintenance, package licensing, exclusivity, grantbacks, output royalties) and multilateral agreements among competitors (e.g., patent pooling and cross-licensing).[8] The economic and legal discussions are brought together in a subsequent section where our economic analysis is applied to particular licensing restrictions and their treatment by competition authorities. Our conclusions close the paper.

THE ECONOMICS OF THE INTELLECTUAL PROPERTY/ COMPETITION INTERFACE

A S DISCUSSED IN THE INTRODUCTION, the challenge facing policymakers is to coordinate patent instruments (patent scope[9] and duration) and competition instruments (contractual restrictions) so as to achieve an efficient allocation of resources directed towards the development and use of new products and processes. We analyze this problem after a brief review of the economic literature dealing with these issues.

ECONOMIC LITERATURE ON THE INTELLECTUAL PROPERTY/ COMPETITION INTERFACE

BEGINNING WITH NORDHAUS,[10] A NUMBER OF AUTHORS have examined the problem described above. In this literature, two patent instruments are considered:[11] the length (or duration) of the patent grant, and the scope (or breadth) of the patent. While patent length establishes the extent to which firms have exclusive rights over their own inventions, patent scope establishes the extent to which a pioneer has property rights over related inventions. In other words, scope dictates how similar imitations may be to the original innovation without infringing the patent grant. If patent scope is narrow, then firms may develop a close substitute – for example, through small chemical changes in a drug's composition.

Tandon and Gilbert and Shapiro[12] model the social planner's problem in two stages. In the first stage, the level or amount of the reward to the innovator is determined, while in the second stage the problem is to design the structure of the patent policy – that is, the combination of patent length and patent scope that provides an incentive to engage in a desired level of research.

In their model, a striking result emerges: the socially efficient way to optimize the innovator's reward is through a patent policy that entails infinite patent lives, but with a narrow scope[13] that effectively constrains that reward. Both papers show that a small reduction in the patentee's monopoly price, compensated by an extension in patent life that preserves the firm's incentive to innovate, enhances social welfare. In other words, a reduction in scope contributes more to a reduction in dead-weight loss than to the innovator's profits, thus calling for long, narrow patents.

These results are not robust, however, to changes in the assumption of competition in the market. If the innovator faces competition from firms that produce their own differentiated products or imitations of the patented product, as is typically the case, the optimal policy may be one that provides for a large profit flow (broad patent) over a short patent life.

For example, in Klemperer,[14] scope is defined by the set of products close to the innovation that is protected by the patent. In this model, the original innovator sets the price so that consumers will buy some variety of the product, although they may switch to less-preferred varieties at that price. Although less-preferred varieties (or imitations) are costless to develop in this model, a transport cost is incurred when consumers purchase inferior products. The trade-off in the model lies in the fact that wide patents raise prices but reduce the dead-weight loss (relative to profits) that arises from consumers switching to inferior products. If switching costs are similar among consumers, then the innovator can set a price that keeps inferior imitators out of the market, which makes long, narrow patents desirable. However, if consumers have identical reservation prices for the most preferred variety, then short, broad patents are efficient because a narrow patent would result in a social cost from consumers switching to other brands.

Gallini[15] extends the analysis to allow for imitation responses to patent policy by rivals. As in the other papers, a patent confers a monopoly over the patented drug for a given duration. Although *duplication* (e.g., producing the same drug) is prevented during the patent life, firms may *imitate* a product or process in such a way that the result is different in some way. For any patent duration and scope, a rival can either wait for the patent to expire to begin producing the product, or it can attempt to develop one of its own. The longer the rival must wait for the innovation, the greater is its incentive to imitate. There will be some "critical" patent length for every level of imitation costs that will trigger entry by the first rival. As patent life increases beyond that critical patent life, further imitators will enter until profits are dissipated. Increasing patent life, then, encourages wasteful imitation; to prevent this, a broad-scope patent with patent life adjusted to achieve the desired return to the innovator becomes the optimal policy.

In these models, competition policy is absent or, in some cases, redundant, given the availability of patent scope. For example, in the Gilbert and Shapiro paper, patent scope and competition policy are perfect substitutes for constraining the innovator's profits in each period: patent scope is defined as the profit that the innovator is allowed to earn (or equivalently, the price it is allowed to set) in each period. Hence the socially efficient profit level derived in their model can be achieved either through a narrow scope or a strict antitrust policy. In contrast, the substitutability between patent and antitrust policy is not perfect in the Klemperer and Gallini papers in that price can be controlled only indirectly by narrowing the scope of patent protection. But an attempt to reduce price by narrowing the scope may result in inefficient imitation, suggesting that both policies are necessary to achieve an efficient allocation of resources toward development and use of innovations.[16]

In reality, patent and competition policy are complementary instruments for rewarding the innovator most efficiently: patent scope, by preventing imitation; and antitrust, by affecting price through constraints on contracts for transferring technology. Green and Scotchmer[17] recognize this distinction. In their paper, the incentive to conduct research depends not only on patent policy but also on the ability of firms to cooperate through licensing arrangements. Two types of cooperative arrangements are considered: 1) *ex ante* licensing or joint ventures between the pioneer and a subsequent innovator, prior to making R&D investments in the second stage; and 2) *ex post* licensing after the second-stage investment has been sunk. The breadth of patent claims establishes whether or not *ex post* licensing takes place: if the claims are broad, then the second-generation "innovation" infringes and the firms enter into an *ex post* licensing agreement; if the claims are narrow, then the two firms compete in the market.

A subtle interaction is identified between patent and antitrust policies: patent scope fixes the bargaining strength of the innovator in its negotiations with the licensee. Hence patent scope and competition policy are distinct instruments with different impacts on the incentives to research and to transfer technologies: one sets the "threat points" or the opportunity cost of entering into the licensing agreement (e.g., whether or not a rival can introduce an imitation), and the other establishes the feasible set of legal licensing contracts. Green and Scotchmer conclude that, in a situation in which innovation is sequential – i.e., in which innovations build upon each other – the best allocation of resources is ensured by a competition policy that allows joint ventures and *ex post* licensing and a patent policy that grants a broad scope to the initial innovator.

Chang[18] follows Green and Scotchmer by examining the optimal policy regarding price-fixing between the innovator and potential entrants under different patent regimes. In particular, four cases are considered in which patents are broad or narrow, and antitrust policy towards price-fixing is strict or lenient. For these policy parameters, Chang shows that broad protection should be available for innovations that either are very valuable or have very little value relative to subsequent improvements, whereas antitrust policy should restrict price-fixing between the innovator and entrants so as to reduce incentives for inefficient entry by imitators.

While this literature is illuminating, the results are not robust, nor do they go far enough in suggesting an appropriate competition policy towards IP; for example, the papers by Green and Scotchmer and Chang restrict attention to only joint ventures and price-fixing.[19] Perhaps a greater concern with this analysis is the formidable task assigned to competition policy: in coordination with patent policy, it must determine the flow of patent profits that will induce the firm to make the desirable R&D investment. In an environment of technological and market certainty and low transaction costs for coordination, such a task is not insurmountable. In less ideal conditions, this task would be difficult at best. As discussed below, the analysis in this literature represents only one of several alternative approaches that competition policy might adopt towards IP. For our part, we argue that, compared to alternatives that place less emphasis on R&D, competition policy towards IP, as modelled in the literature, is neither practical nor socially efficient in more complex environments.

ALTERNATIVE APPROACHES FOR
COMPETITION TREATMENT OF IPRs

WE BEGIN OUR QUEST FOR AN EFFICIENT COMPETITION POLICY towards IP by identifying three effects that competition policy can have on social surplus generated by innovation. Competition policy:

- provides *ex ante* incentives to innovate;
- affects *ex post* incentives to transfer new technologies and products; and
- promotes price competition in product markets that use the new products and processes.

Hence competition policy affects welfare through its effects on R&D, licensing and prices. Competition policy typically concerns itself with the third of those effects – namely, anticompetitive effects on prices and output. We propose here that competition policy towards IP should also centre its analysis around the pro-competitive effects of diffusion – the second type of impact mentioned above. The role that competition policy should play in fostering R&D (the first effect) is more contentious, as discussed below.

A Framework for Competition Policy in IPRs

Given these initial observations, we believe that the following set of principles should guide competition policy towards intellectual property:

P1: There should not be a presumption that an intellectual property right creates market power.

P2: Competition policy should acknowledge the basic rights granted under patent law.

P3: A licensing restriction should be permitted if it is not anticompetitive relative to the outcome that would result if the licence were proscribed; otherwise, an evaluation of the potential efficiency effects of the restriction on the pricing and diffusion of the intellectual property should be made.

The first principle (P1) makes the important, well-known point that the scope of a patent is not commensurate with an antitrust market; that is, most products and processes face a large number of substitutes. For example, in a survey of licensors, there were no close substitutes in only 27 percent of cases; whereas in over 29 percent of cases, they had more than 10 competitors.[20]There should be no presumption that a patent grants market power but, where it does so, it is not in violation of antitrust laws. This principle is consistent with that followed in the general enforcement of competition policy: market power acquired through "superior skill, foresight, and industry" should not be condemned,[21] although the anticompetitive exercise of this right may be prevented.

The second basic principle (P2) is not as straightforward as it may seem. For patented innovations, patent law ensures the *existence* of property rights, while antitrust policy restricts the *exercise* of those rights. In Canada, for example, this principle appears in section 79(5) of the *Competition Act* (a qualified exemption of IPRs from the abuse of dominant-position provisions), yet compulsory licensing is believed to have a role to play when the exercise of the property right raises anticompetitive concerns.

In the United States, the innovator's "right to exclude others from making, using, or selling the invention" under the *Patent Act* is respected by antitrust courts. However, beyond this right to "refuse to license," not much more is explicitly guaranteed. For example, while the right to grant an exclusive licence of the entire bundle of rights is inherent in the patent, that right does not allow assignment to anyone; nor does it allow partial restrictions – for example, the right to make and use but not to sell, or to license with price, quantity, or use restrictions. Moreover, where the exclusion of others from using the property right extends market power beyond that intended by the patent right, antitrust policy may intervene – for example, when patents are accumulated for the purpose of eliminating competition. In other words, recognition of the existence of the right does not imply that the exercise of that right will escape antitrust scrutiny.

The third basic principle (P3) acknowledges the roles that competition policy must play in promoting the efficient diffusion of technology and in setting prices for the goods that use the technology. Note that the principle evaluates the impact of a licensing restriction relative to a benchmark situation in which the restriction is prohibited. For example, if the licensor and licensee were horizontal competitors prior to licensing, then an innovator may choose not to license its competitor if restrictions in the contract are prohibited. In this case, the benchmark against which to compare the licence is the situation with no licensing. When the transfer of technology generates social benefits relative to the exclusive exploitation of the patent, this principle permits such restrictions, even when they have anticompetitive effects.

But licensing may not always be socially desirable – for example, licensing "sham agreements" that transfer technologies of little value for the purpose of dividing the market among competitors. Other contentious restrictions include those which foreclose the market to competing technologies (exclusive dealing), and patent-pooling arrangements that facilitate a cartel, unless diffusion by this means generates offsetting efficiencies and a less harmful arrangement is not feasible.

Moreover, if the restriction in the licence is not necessary to encourage diffusion – in the case of vertically related firms, for example – then the analysis would be similar to that in non-IP cases: anticompetitive effects would be weighed against possible efficiency benefits in order to determine the social merits of the restriction.

While these rules or guidelines for competition policy explicitly acknowledge the rights provided by patents and the diffusion benefits associated with particular licensing restrictions, as well as the possible adverse effects on prices, they are silent on whether competition policy should evaluate the impact that the licensing restriction may have on incentives to innovate. The role that competition policy should play in promoting research and development is more contentious, as will be evident from the different positions adopted by the authors in this volume and in the court cases discussed later in this paper. Three different views might be adopted in answer to the question, How important should R&D considerations be in competition cases?

Approach 1: Competition policy should intervene to correct perceived excesses or deficiencies in the IP protection provided under patent policy.

This approach mirrors that taken in the economic literature summarized above, whereby both policies are coordinated to provide the correct incentives for conducting research and for using society's resources in the most efficient manner. On this view, competition policy plays a direct role in ensuring that an innovator receives an adequate return on its R&D investment. For example, if patent policy is perceived as providing inadequate incentives for research, competition policy should be more lenient; where it is too generous and rival firms are discouraged from innovating, it would intervene in certain licensing arrangements.

Approach 2: Competition policy should determine whether a licence reduces competition in innovation markets.

This approach echoes that proposed in 1995 by the U.S. Department of Justice and Federal Trade Commission in their *Antitrust Guidelines for the Licensing of Intellectual Property* (hereafter, 1995 Guidelines):[22] restrictions that reduce innovation of future products and processes or, in the language of the *Guidelines*, competition in "innovation markets," should be prohibited.[23] The innovation market is a forward-looking concept defined as "the research and development directed to particular new or improved goods or processes, and the close substitutes for that research and development."[24] The policy is similar to the first approach in that R&D considerations are taken into account; however, the focus is on the effect of contractual restrictions on future innovation, not on the return to past innovation efforts. Several types of arrangements would be challenged under this approach: mergers between firms capable of developing similar technologies; exclusive-dealing restrictions that prevent a licensee from using the technologies of the licensor's rival; and patent-pooling arrangements that are perceived as suppressing future innovation.

Approach 3: Competition policy should determine whether a licence reduces potential competition in product and/or technology markets.

In contrast to the previous two approaches, this view argues that the paramount concern of competition policy should not be R&D but the allocative effects of a contract on diffusion and pricing. In terms of the effects of competition policy identified above, this approach focuses on providing incentives for transferring technology and ensuring that product markets operate efficiently, and defers the problem of providing incentives to innovate to patent law.[25] Note that this approach, while avoiding innovation market analysis, does rely on the more conventional "potential competition" doctrine. That is to say, if a licence restriction is perceived as reducing potential competition in product or technology markets, then it should be proscribed.[26]

Comparison of Approaches

Each of the three approaches attracts support from authors in this volume: the Church and Ware and Merges papers favour the first approach; the Rey and Winter paper, the second; and Scotchmer, the third. In fact, all three approaches may be appropriate, depending on the particular market or technological conditions. For example, the competition agency might decide that it will generally follow the second or third approach, in most instances, while still allowing itself the flexibility to follow the first approach if there is strong evidence that IP protection is too broad and unnecessarily stifles competition.

We recommend, as a general policy, that competition policy follow the third approach: this second-best policy has the advantage of dividing responsibilities according to the comparative advantages of the two legal institutions. The task of patent policy is to define those rights which encourage innovation (in terms of duration and protection from imitation); the task of competition policy is to prevent the anticompetitive transfer and use of technology while respecting the basic exclusive rights as laid out by patent law. Indeed, this policy will affect the innovator's overall return, and therefore the incentive to innovate in the first place, but the decision to allow the licence will be based on the *ex post* incentives to license, not on the *ex ante* incentives to innovate.[27] As shown later on (in the Economic Analysis section), attempts by competition authorities to play a more direct role in ensuring an innovator's return have resulted in confusing decisions.

Even if R&D considerations are not explicitly taken into account, as recommended by the first approach, competition policy has a built-in mechanism for fine-tuning patent policy indirectly. For example, if patent protection is weak, then imitation is easy, leaving the innovator with minimal market power. In contrast, where patents are strong and effective, restrictions (such as tying) would be more carefully scrutinized. In other words, to the extent that the effectiveness of patent policy in protecting property rights is correlated with the degree of market power acquired, a competition policy that is sensitive to market power may indirectly "fine-tune" the protection granted under a patent.

Similarly, conventional potential-competition analysis appears to be adequate for addressing the concerns of the second approach. For example, if rival innovators who are affected by a licensing restriction are also potential competitors in the product market, then the expected deleterious effect on prices in the product market of a reduction in potential competition may be sufficient to proscribe a particular restriction without appealing to innovation market analysis. If competitors in innovation are not competitors in the product market, potential competition analysis may continue to be adequate, in contrast to the recommendation made by the Federal Trade Commission.[28] In this case the relevant market will be the technology market rather than the product market. In other words, a reduction in innovation competition implies a reduction in potential competition in technology markets, and conventional potential-competition analysis can be applied to address concerns of contentious licensing restrictions.[29]

In summary, we recommend that competition authorities give only limited attention to the R&D effects of licensing restrictions. Extensive economic investigations have not uncovered a causal link between innovation and competition; to expect more success from competition authorities in predicting the social harm to innovative activity that can result from certain arrangements is impractical at best. Indeed, failing to make the correct prediction "could inhibit or deter innovation rather than further it."[30] Moreover, some restrictions, while they have the potential to suppress competition in future R&D, may be necessary to induce the patentee to transfer the innovation in the first place (e.g., in the case of grantbacks), thus rendering the concerns of future R&D less important.

Whether R&D considerations are explicitly taken into account by competition authorities or not, an important distinction exists between IP and other forms of property, as implied by the above framework: IP can be used by many individuals at the same time, unlike tangible property, which, if transferred, merely changes hands. Since the social cost of transferring innovations is effectively zero, it is socially efficient for the innovation to be freely available. However, a patentee may be reluctant to license its competitors unless it can impose some restrictions on the use of the innovation. This distinction may call for a different application of competition law towards IP.[31]

A second important distinction between IP and other property should be mentioned here as it has important implications for the evaluation required under principle P3: in many licensing contracts, the relationship of the parties to the contract is both horizontal and vertical. The licensor and licensee are horizontally related if they would have been competitors in the product market without licensing; they are vertically related if the IP represents an input used in the production of the licensee's product. Examples of this "mixed" relationship are developed in the Economic Analysis section later in the paper.

We turn now to a review of patent and competition law and the jurisprudence related to intellectual property in Canada, the United States, and the European Union.

COMPETITION LAW TOWARDS INTELLECTUAL PROPERTY

THE LAW IN CANADA

Overview

In Canada, both the *Patent Act* and the *Competition Act* check the abusive exercise of patent rights and provide remedies for such practices.[32] A third body of law has also been used sparingly in IP cases – namely, the common-law doctrine on restraint of trade.[33] As in the United States, IPRs were viewed with suspicion in Canada prior to the 1980s. In contrast to what occurred in that country, however, this suspicion was reflected more in legislative attempts to limit the exercise of patent rights than in jurisprudence.[34] The 1980s saw policymakers adopt a more positive view of IPRs, recognizing their importance to Canada's economic growth and its ability to compete in world markets. The *Competition Act, 1986*, as well as recent patent policy, incorporate this new attitude. Given the paucity of Canadian case law in this area, it is particularly important to analyse the legislative provisions.

The Patent Act

The *Patent Act* designates both the life and the scope of a patent right, restricts the exercise of the patent, and provides for compulsory licensing and for the removal of patent rights. Practices that constitute abusive behaviour under the *Patent Act* are set out in section 65(2). These abuses include: the failure to meet the demand for the patented article in Canada to an adequate extent or on reasonable terms; the refusal to license on reasonable terms when it is in the public interest to do so; and unfair hindrance of trade or industry in Canada through unfair conditions for licensing. These provisions include the review of certain "competition-related" restrictions, such as tie-ins and field-of-use restrictions where they have been used to unfairly prejudice the manufacture, use, or sale of unpatented materials.[35] Moreover, compulsory licensing may be invoked under the *Patent Act* in some cases where a firm refuses to license. The jurisdiction to oversee these provisions of the *Patent Act* is vested in the Commissioner of Patents and the Attorney General: any person may apply to the Commissioner of Patents alleging an abuse. If the Commissioner is satisfied that there has been an abuse, he or she may order that the patentee license the patent, pursuant to section 66.

The Competition Act

The *Competition Act* also covers IPR holders by either exempting them from its provisions or ensuring that they fall within its purview. Two sections provide specific exemptions from parts of the *Competition Act*.

First, subsection 79(5) creates an exemption from the abuse of dominance provisions in sections 78 and 79 of the *Competition Act*. This exemption is limited to acts engaged in, pursuant *only* to the exercise of any right or the enjoyment of any interest derived under IP statutes. This should not be read as a blanket exemption: if the exercise of the IPR goes beyond the purposes contemplated in the statutes, violations of sections 78 and 79 may occur.[36]

Second, section 86(4), which deals with specialization agreements, provides for a specific exemption from scrutiny under section 45 (conspiracies) and section 77 (exclusive dealing) in the case of agreements that, for example, ration output so that firms may meet international competition more effectively, or that involve the cross-licensing or pooling of patents. The latter agreements must first receive the approval of the Competition Tribunal, which may require widespread licensing of the patents throughout the industry as a condition for the registration of a specialization agreement.

Two sections of the *Competition Act* specifically ensure that IP holders fall within its purview. First, section 32 allows the Attorney General to apply to the Federal Court of Canada for various remedial orders in order to address the abuse of IPRs.[37] The remedial powers of the Federal Court are broad and include powers to revoke the patent, to declare the contractual arrangement void, or to impose compulsory licensing.[38] It is worth noting, however, that while section 32 specifically addresses IPRs, it has rarely been invoked.[39] Furthermore, as with any allegation of abuse under section 32, the Attorney General must establish that the practices in question have led to an *undue* lessening of competition. Second, section 61, which prohibits resale price maintenance, contains a specific "no exemption" clause for IPR holders so that if they attempt to influence prices in the downstream market they may be held criminally liable.

In addition to the explicit reference to IPRs in these four sections, several other sections of the *Competition Act* contain provisions that affect the exercise of those rights, as in U.S. antitrust law. In particular, section 77 (reviewable vertical restrictions) includes licensing practices of IPRs such as tied-selling, exclusive-dealing, and territorial-market restrictions; section 75 covers refusals to deal, which may be relevant to refusals to license intellectual property; and section 45 covers conspiracies, which are subject to criminal sanctions. A licensee choosing to challenge a potential abuse of IPRs may do so directly only under the *Patent Act*. Complaints under the *Competition Act* must, in most cases, be made through the Director of the Bureau of Competition Policy, although section 36 provides for a private right of action for single damages in the case of violations of the criminal provisions of the act. This contrasts with the U.S. legislation, where the scope for private action is much greater.

Unilateral Licensing Practices by a Dominant Firm

Tied Sales and Extension of IPRs

The paucity of case law makes a detailed analysis of the Canadian law on tied selling extremely difficult. To date, there have been only four tying cases in which charges have been laid. Only two of these proceeded to trial, and neither resulted in conviction.

Complaints under section 32 of the *Competition Act* were filed in two cases against Union Carbide. In the first of these, the licensee used patented machines that extracted polyethylene film from resin and was required to purchase resin from the licensor and a particular group of suppliers.[40] Licensees were forced to pay higher royalties if they imported polyethylene resin from other suppliers. The Crown contended that this practice caused an undue lessening of competition in the market for resin. In the settlement, Union Carbide agreed to abandon this practice. In the second case, several of Union Carbide's practices involving process and machinery patents for polyethylene film were alleged to be anticompetitive. These practices included sliding-scale royalties believed to be discriminatory against small suppliers, royalty payments beyond the patent life, restraints on patent challenges, and field-of-use restrictions. Union Carbide agreed to cease all of these practices, and the complaint was dropped.

The first of the two cases regarding an allegation of tying in the IP area to proceed to trial was the *NutraSweet* case.[41] NutraSweet was accused of giving buyers a lower price in the United States, where its patent on aspartame (an artificial sweetener) was still in effect, if they also purchased their aspartame from NutraSweet in Canada, where the patent had expired, thus effectively tying sales in the United States to those in Canada. The Tribunal did not find evidence of this alleged practice. The second case, a patent extension decision – *Culzean Inventions Ltd. v. Midwestern Broom Company Ltd. et al.*[42] – was heard under the common law of restraint of trade. In this case, the patentee attempted to obtain royalties from the licensee after patent expiration. The licensee argued that this was illegal and an attempt to extend the patent life. However, since the agreement was freely made between the parties and the respondent had failed to demonstrate "unreasonableness," the court concluded that the royalties were not in violation of the doctrine.

Refusal to License

The patentee's exclusive right to use and work the innovation is not as extensively recognized under the Canadian *Patent Act* as it is in the United States. Compulsory licensing is an instrument that can be, and has been, used if the innovation is not being worked to an adequate degree, especially when licensing (on reasonable terms) would be in the public interest (including the benefit of consumers).

The courts have found royalties to be "unreasonable" under patent law if they were so high that the patent could not be worked. In some cases, this was seen as a "refusal to license" and compulsory licenses were issued.[43] This diverges dramatically from U.S. jurisprudence, where the courts have indicated that an innovator does not have to offer a royalty that is acceptable to a licensee.[44] In Canada, a showing of anticompetitive effects is not necessary to establish this "abuse" under the *Patent Act*. It is unclear if section 75 (refusal to supply under the *Competition Act*) applies to IPRs. Most likely, unless the practice were a part of a conspiracy, licensing-refusal cases would not be reviewed under competition laws.[45]

Resale Price Restrictions

There have been no cases regarding price restrictions on the resale of licensed products, but section 61 of the *Competition Act* states clearly that IP will be treated no differently than other forms of property.

Exclusivity Restrictions

Territorial Restrictions

In international territorial division, restrictions on a foreign licensee's territory of production/sale are dealt with under both the *Competition Act* and the *Patent Act*. The *Patent Act* allows the patent holder to claim infringement against the parallel importation of goods embodying the IP, whereas the *Competition Act* is the vehicle by which territorial arrangements are challenged. There have been few cases on the parallel importation of patented goods in Canada to test whether exclusive territories will be challenged, although cases on trademarked goods abound, as discussed in Anderson et al. in this volume.[46] The ability of a patentee to segment international markets extends to the domestic market. For both international and domestic market segmentation, when territorial restrictions used by major suppliers have the effect of lessening competition, they will not escape the scrutiny of competition law and are subject to a case-by-case review under section 77 of the *Competition Act*.[47]

Exclusive Contracts

The exclusive transfer of patent rights is not necessarily an offence under either patent or competition law. For example, in *E.C. Walker and Sons, Ltd. v. Lever Bras Machine Corporation*,[48] the court permitted the licensor's refusal to license because it had already licensed the patented machine on an exclusive basis.

However, since the *Patent Act* prohibits the suppression of innovations, an exclusive contract, especially with a potential competitor of the licensor, will be viewed with suspicion if the licensee does not work the invention because such exclusivity might imply cartelization.

Exclusive Dealing

The only case in this area is *NutraSweet*,[49] an abuse-of-dominance decision involving an exclusive dealing arrangement. The Director applied to the Tribunal for remedial orders on the grounds that NutraSweet was blocking its competitor from the market through rebates to customers who used the NutraSweet trademarked logo, as a result of most-favoured-customer and meet-or-release clauses in NutraSweet's agreements with its customers.[50] The Tribunal concurred with the Director in holding that NutraSweet was not "entitled to any more protection against competition than it was able to obtain through patent grants that provided it with a considerable head start on potential competitors,"[51] and prohibited the use of related, most- favoured-customer, meet-or-release, and exclusivity provisions.

Multilateral Agreements: Pooling and Cross-Licensing

Patent pools that do not enhance efficiency and have the effect of eliminating competition between members of the pool, or of fixing or restricting prices, will be treated like any other collusive agreement to eliminate competition.[52] The only Canadian horizontal IPR case was an unsuccessful attempt by an alleged infringer to declare "patent misuse" through conspiracy.[53] In contrast to the United States, this defence is rare in Canada because of the courts' view that even if patent misuse is found, the patent would not be revoked if it had been acquired legally prior to the anticompetitive offense and thus the court would allow the patentee to retain its patent.[54]

THE LAW IN THE UNITED STATES

Overview

In the United States, the patent and antitrust laws define and govern the extent of IPRs. The *Patent Code* of 1952 is a federal statute that defines the patent right as "the right to exclude others from making, using or selling the invention throughout the United States."[55] The exercise of IPRs is subject to private and public enforcement under two bodies of law – patent law's doctrine of "misuse"; and antitrust laws.

Patent-misuse cases arise when a patentee sues for infringement of its IPR and the responding party claims that there has been no infringement because the patent has been misused, usually in violation of the antitrust laws.[56] If the defence prevails, the patent is void, thereby eliminating the possibility of infringement. Although antitrust jurisprudence has influenced the law in this area, in many cases "antitrust-related" misuse has been shown when such acts would not have violated the antitrust laws.[57] In 1988, the *Patent Misuse Reform Act* was passed; although this legislation does not resolve the conflict, it does add the antitrust requirement of market power in tying cases under the patent-misuse doctrine.[58]

The antitrust statutes that are relevant to the anticompetitive exercise of IPRs include sections 1 and 2 of the *Sherman Act* and sections 3 and 7 of the *Clayton Act*.[59] Explicit reference to IPRs, however, is not contained in any of those laws. In applying antitrust law to IP, antitrust authorities adopt two principles derived from the exclusive right granted in the *Patent Code*. First, the patentee is not obligated to use or license its innovation. Second, the patentee can grant exclusive licences for particular territories in the United States.[60]

In addition to the antitrust statutes, the U.S. Department of Justice (DOJ) and the Federal Trade Commission (FTC) have released guidelines regarding their view of enforcement in the IP area. In 1988, the DOJ published the *Antitrust Enforcement Guidelines for International Operations* (1988 *Guidelines*).[61] According to these guidelines, the IP owner is "fully entitled" to exploit the market power derived from the protected property unless a licensing arrangement is "likely to create, enhance, or facilitate the exercise of market power beyond that which is inherent in the IP itself." The *Antitrust Guidelines for the Licensing of Intellectual Property* released by the DOJ and the FTC in 1995[62] echo three main principles from the 1988 *Guidelines*: first, IP is comparable to other forms of property; second, IPRs do not necessarily imply market power; and third, the licensing of IP may have pro-competitive effects, particularly when combined with complementary factors of production. In contrast to the 1988 *Guidelines*, which applied merger law to most licensing agreements, the 1995 *Guidelines* provide a much more comprehensive application of the law on specific practices adopted by IPR holders, such as horizontal market division, price fixing, and resale price maintenance. In this respect, the 1995 *Guidelines* attempt to conform the DOJ and FTC's approach to that of the courts.

The 1995 *Guidelines* identify a "safety zone" within which IP practices will not be challenged: an agreement is free from scrutiny if the restraint is not typically *per se* illegal and if the parties to the contract account collectively for no more than 20 percent of each type of market (technology, product, innovation) affected by the restraint. These agreements will be subject to a rule-of-reason analysis. In contrast, agreements that fall outside the safety zone and generate no efficiency-producing benefits will be challenged under the *per se* rule (for example, sham agreements). The former scenario represents the majority of cases.[63]

Unilateral Licensing Practices of a Dominant Firm

Application of the Patent-Misuse Doctrine

Tying Restrictions and Extension of IPRs

In general, tying two products together, or refusing to sell them separately, is only unlawful if the seller has market power in the tying product or if substantial anticompetitive effects result from the tie. Historically, however, ties in the patent area have often been found to entail patent misuse even though neither requirement was shown.[64] In *Motion Pictures Patents Co. v. Universal Film Manufacturing Co.*,[65] the Supreme Court invalidated a licence restriction stipulating that only movies leased from the patent owner could be shown with the patentee's projector. This decision was not based on antitrust laws but rather on general patent policy against using tying requirements to extend the scope of the patent monopoly. This reasoning was affirmed and followed in a number of subsequent cases where economic power was presumed.[66]

Recent cases have reached divergent results. The Court adopted a permissive approach in the 1980 decision on *Dawson Chemical Co.*[67] but acknowledged that "misuse of a tie-in would substantially reduce the incentives for firms to invest in research."[68] Conversely, however, the most recent tying case, while not a patent-licensing decision, contains elements that echo the stricter position of earlier cases. In *Jefferson Parish*,[69] the Court upheld the tie unanimously but was split on how tie-ins generally should be treated. Following prior case law, the majority held that a tie should receive *per se* treatment because of the market power implied by a patent. Consistent with current thinking, however, the minority argued that this view was misguided and that market power cannot be assumed.[70] Although the law still remains confused on this issue, there exists a growing consensus amongst economists and policymakers that the existence of a patent ought not to lead inexorably to a presumption of market power.[71]

Package Licensing and Royalty Terms – Licensing a bundle of products or setting royalties on the total sales of the licensee, as opposed to the use of the licensed input, are alternative forms of tying, and there have been several cases involving these practices. Where the granting of a licence is conditional on the acceptance of a package by a firm with market power, the agreement may be disallowed.[72] When the agreement, however, is mutually agreed upon for any one of the following reasons, a royalty on total sales may be permitted: if the royalty represents "the most convenient method" of payment;[73] if it avoids costly monitoring of output produced with the innovation;[74] if the licensee can terminate the agreement after some of the patents expire;[75] or if the patented product is used in fixed proportions with other inputs. In the 1988 *Guidelines*, the DOJ indicated that it would take a different approach from the courts with respect to the enforcement of tying arrangements, and generally would not be concerned with the "basis upon which license royalties are measured."[76] That having been said, the settlement that the DOJ attempted to make in the *Microsoft* case indicates that it will not tolerate such arrangements by dominant firms when they are perceived to foreclose the market to competitors. In that case, the DOJ argued that the royalty that Microsoft placed on total computer sales foreclosed the market to competitors because a manufacturer that included a rival's system would have to pay royalties to both Microsoft and the competitor. A consent decree that would have ended this practice was initially rejected by the Court but has now been approved.[77]

Grantbacks – Another practice that has been interpreted as a form of tying in licensing contracts is the inclusion of grantbacks – a restriction in which the licensor requires that the licensee transfer the patent, or grant a licence to the licensor, on any improvement of the original innovation that it may develop. The approach taken by the courts in this area has been much stricter than that of the DOJ. In the *TransWrap* case,[78] the licensee refused to "grant-back" licenses for its patents on improvements of the original machines. The Supreme Court decided against the licensor, noting that the grantback created a "double monopoly" and expressing concern that the "fruits of invention of an entire industry might be systematically funnelled into the hands of the original patentee."[79] In contrast, the DOJ views grantbacks as an arrangement that can "promote innovation and subsequent licensing of the results of the innovation."[80] However, the 1995 *Guidelines* caution against such arrangements if competitors' incentives to research are reduced or if rivalry in innovation markets is limited.

Application of Antitrust Laws

Refusal to License

Court decisions have generally recognized that a patentee is under no obligation to use its patent or to license it to others.[81] This view, however, has not gone unchallenged. For example, in 1975, the FTC brought an action against Xerox for refusing to license high-speed plain-paper copiers. As part of an out-of-court settlement, Xerox and foreign joint-venturers were obligated to license the technology and knowhow in the United States.[82]

If the refusal to license other parties is seen as part of a conspiracy between the licensor and a licensee,[83] or used to enforce illegal restrictions on licensees (e.g., resale price maintenance), it will be contested. More generally, competitors cannot agree to refuse to license or to refrain from practising a patent as part of a conspiracy or anticompetitive arrangement.[84] Such refusals to license are often the consequence of exclusive licensing arrangements, which are discussed below.

Resale Price Restrictions

In *United States v. General Electric Co.*,[85] the Supreme Court held that a patentee should be able to place reasonable price restrictions on a licensee in order both to achieve the profits it would obtain if it produced the product exclusively and to secure pecuniary reward for its monopoly.[86] Since *General Electric*, the courts have taken a stricter approach to resale price maintenance restrictions on IP. Fifteen years later, the Supreme Court, in *Univis Lens*,[87] ruled that Univis' patent rights were exhausted after the first sale of its lenses, making further price restrictions unlawful under section 1 of the *Sherman Act*. The Court drew a distinction between *General Electric* because the licensee in *Univis Lens* was not a producer of the innovation. In later cases in which price restrictions were proscribed, the courts have also distinguished *General Electric* on various grounds, noting that the licensor was not a manufacturer of the product,[88] that there were multiple licences,[89] that a large proportion of firms in the industry were licensed,[90] that the price restriction was on an unpatented product produced from a patented process,[91] and that the licensor and licensee cross-licensed competing patents.[92] Despite this series of negative decisions on resale price restrictions, *General Electric* may still re-emerge as the governing precedent, as the courts become more lenient towards resale price maintenance on non-patented products.[93]

Exclusivity Restrictions

Exclusive Territories – The "exclusive territories" restriction is a vertical restraint that limits the territory in which the licensee may produce and sell. This typically entails a restriction on both the licensor, who is constrained from licensing others in the specified territory, and the licensee, who is restricted from operating outside the designated area. A similar restriction is on the "field of use," where the licensee is restricted to a particular use of, or market for, the innovation.[94]

The *Patent Code* explicitly recognizes the right to establish territorial restrictions in licensing agreements and sanctions such restrictions on the first sale of the product. After the good has been placed on the U.S. market, however, it is no longer *per se* legal for an IPR holder to use its patent right to restrain trade in its good.[95] Even so, territorial restrictions may be permitted under a rule of reason.[96] In addition, leniency has been extended towards international territorial restrictions that prevent the importation of the patented goods into the United States from other countries (parallel importation),[97] especially when they are seen as a way "to secure the pecuniary reward for the patent monopoly."[98]

More generally, the 1988 *Guidelines* note that while the licensor has no obligation to "create competition in its own technology," exclusive territories may be challenged where the licensee is a competitor or potential competitor, markets are concentrated, or barriers to entry are high. Similarly, for unpatented products produced from patented processes, licences that include exclusive territorial restrictions are examined under a rule of reason.[99]

Exclusive Contracts – In an exclusive contract, the patentee undertakes not to license the patent to anyone but the licensee. While the patentee has the right exclusively to transfer its innovation, the identity of the licensee is important to the legality of the transfer. If the licensee is a competitor, the transfer is viewed as an asset acquisition, and therefore will be evaluated under the Merger Guidelines.[100] In addition, section 2 of the *Sherman Act* may be implicated if a firm has a policy of acquiring exclusive licences in an area and then not practising the patents.

Exclusive Dealing – Exclusive dealing will be found when there is a requirement that the licensee not engage in the use or sale of the technology or products of the licensor's rivals. Although there is relatively little jurisprudence on exclusive dealing, the courts have prohibited such restrictions when they affect a significant proportion of buyers or sellers, and deprive either other suppliers of a market for their goods or other buyers of a source of supply.[101] The courts have condemned this practice because it is seen as one where "the lawful monopoly granted by the patent [is used] as a means of suppressing the manufacture and sale of competing unpatented articles."[102] In addition to explicit exclusive dealing contracts, firms can arrange royalty payments to achieve the same effect.[103]

Multilateral Agreements: Pooling and Cross-Licensing[104]

In an approach analogous to decisions involving information exchange in non-patent cases, the courts treat patent pools and cross-licensing under a rule of reason where the reduction of litigation costs in patent infringement litigation is seen as one legitimate use of a pool.[105] Similarly, the 1995 *Guidelines* take the view that while cross-licensing and pooling arrangements are not intrinsically anticompetitive, attendant restrictions may raise antitrust concerns. The *Guidelines* caution against agreements with horizontal competitors, especially where they comprise exclusive pools involving a large proportion of market participants, involve joint coordination of substitute innovations,[106] or appear to suppress innovation,[107] unless there are offsetting efficiencies.[108]

The Law in the European Union

Overview

In the European Union (EU), competition policy towards IP, particularly the licensing of patents and knowhow, is governed by article 85 (addressing anti-competitive agreements) and article 86 (addressing abuse of dominance) of the Treaty of Rome. The primary goal of the Treaty is market integration.[109] Article 85 prohibits and voids all agreements that may affect trade between member states and that have as their object or effect the prevention, restriction, or distortion of competition within the common market. However, article 85(3) provides an exemption for agreements that contribute either to improving the production or distribution of goods, or to promoting technical or economic progress. For a practice to be exempted, it must leave consumers with a fair share of the benefits; it must be indispensable towards achieving the benefits; and it cannot have the effect of eliminating competition.[110] The block exemptions for patent licence and knowhow, issued in 1984 and 1987,[111] respectively, identify the patent and knowhow[112] practices exempted under article 85(3).[113]

Although the protection of national IPRs is discussed in other articles of the Treaty, the free movement of goods is paramount. In most cases, the Treaty supersedes national laws, although article 36 explicitly recognizes national IPRs. The potential conflict between the two bodies of law is resolved in that, while the Treaty respects the *existence* of IPRs[114] as recognized under national IP laws, it regulates the *exercise* of those rights. However, the European Commission and the Court of Justice do not always agree about when "existence" rights end and anticompetitive "exercise" begins. As noted above, practices that impede the free flow of goods across borders are particularly suspect. In contrast to Canada and the United States, this places territorial segmentation by country high on the list of suspect practices. In general, exclusivity in contracts appears to be a central concern of the Commission.

Unilateral Licensing Practices by a Dominant Firm

Tying and Extension of IPRs

Tie-in clauses are illegal pursuant to article 85 unless they are indispensable to successful exploitation of the patent. Exemptions under article 85(3) are rarely granted for tie-ins.[115] In addition, neither of the block exemptions includes tying unless it is "necessary for a technically satisfactory exploitation of the licensed invention" or to ensure high quality.[116] Forcing the purchase of an unwanted product on the licensee falls outside the exemptions.[117] An approach similar to package licensing is followed.

Package Licensing and Royalty Terms

The Commission has found that royalty arrangements on expired patents or on patents that are not being used are in violation of article 85(1) and without "economic justification," especially if the licensee cannot terminate such a contract.[118] As in the United States, the Commission has expressed concern that this practice could result in reduced incentives to research or to use competitors' innovations. In contrast to patent royalties, royalties on non-public knowhow collected after patents expire are sanctioned under the knowhow block exemption. However, restrictions are placed on extensions of contracts achieved through the transfer of additional knowhow beyond that in the original contract. Additional contraventions include royalties on unpatented products as well as products produced either with an unpatented process or with public knowhow.

Grantbacks

The Commission has generally allowed grantbacks on improvements of the original innovation and on patents not related to the original invention, especially when the licence is non-exclusive and either party can terminate the agreement after the original patent expires.[119] Consistent with this view, the patent block exemption includes a "mutual exchange."[120] Similarly, the knowhow block exemption calls for non-exclusive contracts but provides for the protection of the licensor's trade secrets; it also stipulates that the grantback cannot continue beyond the length of the basic licence. Exclusive grantbacks are not exempted.

Refusal to License

The leading case in this area is *Volvo/Weng*,[121] in which Volvo had refused to license its patented car parts to Weng; the issue was whether the refusal to license implied an abuse of dominant position granted by the patent right. The Court of Justice ruled that forcing a firm to license its invention, even when the potential licensee is prepared to pay reasonable royalties, would eliminate the existence of the exclusive right. Thus there was no abuse of dominance. The Court did, however, add that the exercise of the exclusive right may be regulated by article 86 if a firm with a dominant position in the market takes "unfair advantage" by arbitrarily refusing to deliver spare parts to independent repairers, setting spare part prices at inequitable levels, or terminating the production of spare parts for specific car models that are in demand, where these practices "affect the trade among EC members."[122]

Resale Price Restrictions

For both patents and knowhow, there is no block exemption on contracts that restrict the price of products under licence. Similarly, output restraints do not receive a block exemption for patented goods, but knowhow may benefit from such an exemption, under certain conditions.[123] Although not benefiting from the block exemption, output restrictions may be exempted from article 85(1) under article 85(3).[124]

Exclusivity and Extension of IPRs

Exclusive Contracts

Exclusive contracts have been found to restrict intra-Community trade since the licensor is restricted from competing with the licensee or from adding licensees. While exclusive contracts have been held to violate article 85(1), they have usually been exempted under article 85(3) because they were "indispensable" for the licensee to invest in the technology. This reasoning and conclusion changed in *Maize Seed*, where the court noted that exclusivity is permitted, except when used to restrict trade within the Community.[125] Exclusivity once again became contentious in *Boussois/ Interpane*,[126] where the Commission departed from *Maize Seed* and found a violation of article 85 but granted an exemption under article 85(3) because of redeeming benefits from the exclusive territory restriction.

Exclusivity provisions on knowhow that prevent competition in research are not covered by the block exemption, although a licensor may withhold information and ensure that the knowhow is not being used in competing products. This parallels attempts by the DOJ and the FTC in the United States to preserve competition in innovation markets.

Exclusive Territories

The largest proportion of exclusivity cases involve territorial restrictions. Territorial restrictions that prevent parallel imports are not allowed when the imports originate in an EU member state.[127] As long as goods have been placed in the common market with the authorization of the IP holder, the location of the resale of those goods embodying the IP cannot be restricted;[128] in order words, the doctrine of exhaustion prevails throughout the Union.[129] However, in *Maize Seed*[130] an important distinction was made between "open" and "closed" or "absolute" exclusive licensees.[131] The Court disagreed with the Commission on the exclusivity of the contract awarded to a German importer and noted that an "open exclusive licence" does not restrict competition under article 85, since it does not block parallel imports from other member states of the EU. Furthermore, there was no exemption under article 85(3) because the facts did not "justify a special system for breeders' rights"[132] and the agreements were neither justified nor "indispensable" for economic progress.

The "open" vs. "absolute" distinction of *Maize Seed* was adopted in the patent licensing block exemption that was issued two years later. "Open" territories – in which licensors agree not to sell in a designated area and licensees agree not to "manufacture or use" licensed products or processes in territories reserved for the licensor or other licensees – are exempted, whereas "absolute" territories (which restrict parallel imports) fall under the black list. The regulation also distinguishes between "active" and "passive" sales; restrictions on an "active policy of putting the licensed product on the market" in other licensees' territories are exempted, but restrictions on passive sales (e.g., not selling to third-party importers) would impede parallel imports within the EU and are therefore prohibited.

Furthermore, when the agreement "contributes to improving the production or economic progress, while allowing consumers a fair share of the benefits" and the restriction is "indispensable" to encourage the licensee to adopt and promote the technology; when goods originate outside of the EU; or when goods originate within the EU under a compulsory licence,[133] then parallel goods may be excluded from importation into any member state. Moreover, the Commission may allow territorial restrictions that prevent exports from countries outside the Community into the EU when "practical barriers to such exports were likely to be insurmountable"[134] or when they do not affect intra-Community trade.[135] If the exclusive territories do not involve inter-state trade, then national competition laws, which are generally permissive towards vertical market restraints, are allowed to prevail.[136]

Multilateral Agreements: Pooling and Cross-Licensing

Both pools and cross-licensing agreements fall outside the block exemption, but stricter treatment is applied to patent pools in which a group of firms make available their patents to other members of the pool.[137] Pools are condemned when they create a "monopoly bottleneck" and offer no pro-competitive ancillary benefits. In contrast, a cross-licensing agreement may be allowed if "the parties are not subject to any territorial restriction within the common market on the manufacture, use or putting on the market of the products covered by these agreements or on the use of the licensed processes."[138]

Summary of the Legal Analysis

There are sharp differences between the competition laws of the three jurisdictions with respect to IPRs. In the United States, the statutes are broadly worded and subject to judicial interpretation, whereas in Canada, the *Competition Act* includes specific provisions that apply directly to IPRs. However, the DOJ and FTC provide guidelines as a framework for challenging IPR practices, in contrast to Canada, where no guidelines presently exist. In the EU, the block exemptions on patent and knowhow licensing provide explicit lists of practices that are condemned, exempted, or subject to the rule-of-reason analysis. These detailed guidelines provide a clear but more restrictive framework under which licensors operate relative to the other two jurisdictions. A review of comparative legislative and judicial experience with IPRs is a first step in formulating coherent rules that might guide the courts and enforcement agencies.

Economic Analysis of Specific Contractual Restrictions

In this section, we analyze particular licensing restrictions using the general framework outlined earlier in this paper. We do not examine all the benefits and costs of certain restrictions but focus on those distinguishing features of IP that may imply differential treatment under IP law. Relevant competition cases, reviewed in the preceding section, are revisited to determine whether the decisions in those cases accord with the framework proposed in this paper.

Refusal to License

U.S. laws are clear in recognizing the unconditional "right to exclude others"; as was seen in the last section, this is less clear in Canada and in the European Union. While an innovator need not be a "guardian of the public interest," an exclusive licence of related patents where the licensee refuses to use or relicense them may be prohibited, even in the United States, if the licence creates a monopoly where a duopoly would exist in the no-licensing situation.[139]

Respecting a firm's right to the exclusive exploitation of its intellectual property is consistent with patent law and with principle P2 of the framework presented above. It is important to note that if this right were not protected and licensing were forced upon innovators, then the courts would be placed in the undesirable position of controlling prices. In other words, an innovator could set a price at a level high enough that it would not be acceptable to potential licensees. Hence, a "reasonable" price would have to be established.

There may be circumstances in which it is desirable to require the patentee to license its innovation – for example, in cases of abuse of a dominant position. Indeed, licensing has been used as a remedy under the misuse doctrine in the United States. A more difficult issue, taken up in McFetridge's paper in this volume, is whether compulsory licensing should be imposed simply because the innovation is "essential," even though no anticompetitive violation has occurred.

PRICE RESTRICTIONS

IN AFFIRMING THE DISTRICT COURT'S DECISION in *General Electric*,[140] the U.S. Supreme Court concluded that, because of its patent, General Electric (GE) should be allowed to include price restrictions in its licence to Westinghouse so as to achieve the same profits that it would obtain if it were to produce the product exclusively. The Court reasoned that since GE was not required to license, it would retain production rights for itself if price restrictions were prohibited. Since the licence, then, was deemed not to reduce competition relative to the no-licence situation, it was permitted.

Economic analysis provides support for the Court's concern that, in the absence of price restrictions, patentees might refuse to license their innovation to competitors. Katz and Shapiro show that this argument may be valid if the output of the licensee cannot be observed and the licensor must resort to fixed fees.[141] If the profits under licensing are less than the profits under exclusive production of the innovation, then the licensor will not have the incentive to license since competition would reduce profits, even though such a transfer is socially efficient. Resale price maintenance, output restrictions, or territorial restrictions might restore the incentives to license and permit the diffusion of the technology.

While the Court's ruling was consistent with the framework discussed above in recognizing the impact of price restrictions on the incentive to transfer the innovation, it obscured its decision by defining the set of allowable restrictions as those which are "reasonably within the reward which the patentee … is entitled to secure." It was not entirely clear what the Court meant by the "reasonable reward" – whether it referred to the expected return from past R&D effort or from exclusive exploitation of the patent. Turner argues that this rule is no more informative than a rule-of-reason standard, with little guidance and considerable confusion.[142] As we argued in justifying our principle P3, the Court should not engage in the former calculation. This confusion may explain the large number of subsequent decisions that have attempted to circumscribe the GE decision.[143]

More importantly, the Court's analysis was incomplete. While recognizing that GE may not have had the incentive to license without price restrictions, it failed to evaluate whether licensing with price restrictions was socially preferred to no licensing at all. In other words, a careful analysis of the benefits and costs of diffusion, as called for by principle P3, was not undertaken.[144] In the case in which the licensor and licensee compete in products other than the innovation, licensing with price restrictions on the innovation may not necessarily be better than no licensing. For example, if the licensee and the licensor are horizontal competitors in the absence of the licence, then under a licence-cum-price restriction the licensee will internalize the effect on the demand for the innovation of a reduction in the prices of its substitute products. Hence competition in other products in which the licensor and licensee compete may be dampened even though the price restriction is applied only to the innovation being transferred. According to principle P3 in the framework proposed above, if this restriction is necessary for the innovator to license, then these negative allocative effects should be weighed against the positive benefits of diffusion.[145]

In a later case, the Court took a stronger position on price restrictions in a situation that probably should have received a more tolerant treatment. In *Line Material*[146] two innovators with blocking patents were prevented from setting a resale price for the final good. The transfer of the blocking patents (an original patent and an improvement) was efficient, but such a transfer made the firms close competitors, necessitating some restriction, as in *General Electric*.[147] Such restrictions are socially efficient if the cross-licensed products are complements (for example, inputs in the production of a final product); resale-price maintenance would *lower* the price of the final good, relative to the price realized under separate production of the complementary inputs.[148] In this case, price restrictions in cross-licensing agreements should clearly be allowed. Output or territorial restrictions might be more acceptable to competition authorities, although the economic effects of these alternatives are not necessarily less harmful.[149]

Exclusivity in Contracts

Here, we present an overview of exclusive licensing arrangements – exclusive contracts, exclusive territories and exclusive dealing. An in-depth analysis of these arrangements and of other practices that mimic them is found in the Rey and Winter paper in this volume.

Exclusive Contracts

Under an exclusive contract, the licensor grants one or more exclusive licences (e.g., geographically separated), which restricts the right of the licensor to license others and possibly prevents it from practicing the technology itself. As noted earlier, there is a clear right to offer an exclusive licence, but not necessarily to offer it to *anyone*, and especially to a competitor in a concentrated market. If potential competition is eliminated by the transfer of an exclusive right, then this effectively represents a transfer of assets (the patent) from the licensor to the licensee, and merger standards should be applied.[150] Note that if IP were not involved, the agreement would be similar to a competitor's agreeing not to produce, which would be evaluated under a *per se* conspiracy standard.

If a firm is restricted from giving an exclusive licence, then it may vertically integrate with the potential licensee, which may be inefficient. In that case, the firm would be allowed under patent law to work the licence exclusively on its own. In other words, vertical integration is an alternative to exclusive licensing; if antitrust authorities intervene with an innovator's right to grant an exclusive licence, then the innovator may attempt to circumvent this rule through a reorganization of the firm. But a law that allows exclusivity when the assets reside with one firm but not when they are distributed between two separate firms would not seem to be a sound one.

Exclusive Territories

Under exclusive territories restrictions, licensees are restricted to certain areas where they are given exclusive rights to sell and/or produce the product. The benefits and costs of such exclusivity are well known.[151] Territorial restrictions that prevent the flow of parallel imports are generally tolerated domestically under competition law and internationally under patent law in Canada and the United States. This contrasts with the EU, where such segmentation is viewed as antithetical to market integration.[152]

While the European Court of Justice's decision in *Maize Seed*[153] was pivotal from an economic perspective, it did not go far enough. The Court's predominant concern was to ensure that private agreements do not compartmentalize the common market, a concern that is very different from the one based on economic efficiency in principle P3 of the framework discussed above.

Although the Court did allow some territorial protection in cases where the initial cost was high in order to induce investment in the product, it did not allow full and absolute territorial protection from imports of the product. In other words, the ruling allowed a licensee to be an exclusive producer in a country, but not an exclusive seller of the product. Unless transportation costs are high, this limited protection may not provide sufficient incentives for the potential licensee to carry the product, especially if large set-up costs of production are required or if free-riding by rival firms on advertising and other investments is easy.

In its rule-of-reason analysis, the Court failed to acknowledge the significant competition that existed in the industry; the fact that there were many other maize seed competitors was not a factor in the decision. This points to an important distinction between the EU approach towards vertical restraints and that followed in other jurisdictions: the goal of market integration biases competition policy against restrictions on intra-brand competition, even when there is significant competition between brands (inter-brand competition). Such a rule may not result in an efficient outcome.

The debate over the economics of exclusive territories is particularly interesting in an international context. There are two concerns with market segmentation: first, it may be a mechanism for facilitating a cartel among patentees;[154] second, there may be a concern that the division of markets facilitates a price discrimination scheme. While it is well known that price discrimination may be welfare-enhancing, in a global setting this result depends on whether a country is in the high-price or the low-price group, or on whether it is a net importer or exporter of technology.[155] However, the costs of allowing price discrimination on some high-priced items may be offset by the benefits of ensuring the transfer of low-price innovations to a particular country.[156] These trade-offs are discussed in depth in Anderson et al. in this volume.

Exclusive Dealing

Under exclusive dealing restrictions, the innovator promises the exclusive licensee not to transfer the innovation to the licensee's competitors; or, alternatively, the licensee agrees not to purchase its supplies from the licensor's competitors. In the first case, one might argue that the innovation should be available to all downstream firms so as not to harm competition, especially if IP is an essential good. However, a requirement of non-discriminatory licensing by a non-integrated licensor would conflict with the fact that, under patent law, a vertically integrated patentee (a licensor integrated with a licensee) has the right to exclusive use of the innovation. In other words, a rule that forces non-discriminatory licensing by a non-integrated firm but not be an integrated firm would depend on the distribution of assets. The rationale for such a policy is not clear,[157] and the policy may discriminate against relatively smaller innovators.

Tying and Extension of IPRs

Tie-ins require that another (patented or unpatented) product be purchased with the licensed product or technology. The U.S. law on ties-ins requires a showing of market power in the tying good, substantial commerce affected in the tied-good market, and distinct products. The question whether or not the first criterion is satisfied by a patent grant should now be clear: patents do not necessarily imply market power, as stated in principle P1 of the framework presented above.

Tying reduces transaction costs and many of the problems of uncertainty and contractual incompleteness that plague the exchange of new and relatively unknown technologies. For example, tying reduces the costs of monitoring to determine the use of the innovation; it also enables the licensor to measure the intensity at which the innovation is used so as to charge the appropriate royalty. Tying protects the innovator's reputation: when consumers have imperfect information and cannot identify the source of poor product performance (e.g., the product itself or repairs), suppliers of inputs may "free-ride" on the innovator's reputation by reducing the quality of the input. The innovator may therefore want to tie a new process to its servicing of the machine.

If the value of a patented process is unknown, tying encourages a licensee to accept the licence by allowing it to pay a lower price for the process but at the same time charging a royalty that depends on intensity of use. This is particularly important in the case of knowhow, where an innovator does not want to reveal too much information to the licensee. Alternatively, if the abilities of the licensees are unknown, tying allows a licensor to license several firms by setting a low price for the innovation and earning a high return from the successful firms through the tied product.[158]

The application of competition law should not be different for intellectual property in tying cases; as before, market power in the tying good and the proportion of the market that is tied up are important considerations. However, as noted above, many of the "benefits" of tying arise when new technology is concerned, thus generating uncertainty about the value of the innovation, monitoring costs, etc. Hence although the application of competition laws would be the same, the contracts receiving relatively tolerant treatment would include those relating to intellectual property.[159]

For example, in the *Hazeltine* case,[160] Hazeltine Research gave Automatic Radio Manufacturing Co. the right to use a bundle of 570 patents and 200 patent applications at a charge calculated as a percentage of Automatic's selling price – whether or not the patents were used – for a minimum payment of $10,000 per year. When Automatic refused to pay on the grounds that it had not used any of the patents in the bundle, Hazeltine sued to recover the minimum royalty. In its submission, Automatic claimed that the contractual restriction was a tie-in that based royalty payments on a percentage of sales on all the licensee's products, including non-patented ones, and therefore was an invalid extension of the patent.

The majority of the Court held in favour of Hazeltine, finding that this was not a *per se* misuse of the patents. The justices concluded that the royalties stipulated were not unreasonable, were the most convenient way of setting the business value of the privileges granted by the licensing agreement, and the agreement provided no unlawful extension of the area of the patent.

If one applies the framework developed above, it would appear that the majority decision in *Hazeltine* was correct. The determination of whether the decision was appropriate should be based on the usual antitrust concerns applied in non-IP cases – market power with respect to the tying good and the proportion of the market that is tied. However, some features of the IP, such as the high cost of metering the usage of the output that uses the innovation, may justify more tolerant treatment.

Since Hazeltine was not a manufacturer, it is more appropriate to compare the licence to an alternative pricing arrangement, such as a per-unit royalty on use, than to a no-licensing scenario: if competition is reduced compared to a less harmful agreement, then the offsetting pro-competitive effects should be considered. Although the majority did not engage in a direct consideration of other types of licensing arrangements in endorsing the agreement, it recognized that the latter generated cost savings since it was the "most convenient method of fixing the business value of the privileges granted by the licensing agreement."[161]

A second economic argument for allowing the tie that was not recognized by the Court parallels a result advanced in the optimal-taxation literature: a tax on total output is more efficient than a tax on intermediate inputs. A royalty is like a tax on the use of the innovation: if the royalty is placed on the patented input, the use of that input in production will be distorted; however, if the royalty applies to the output, the licensee will have the incentive to employ an efficient mix of inputs. Hence a royalty on total output may generate cost savings from efficient production.

Tying may be a contentious practice when after-markets exist, which is common for patented products in high-technology industries. For example, a manufacturer of computer hardware may distribute its computers to retailers who are willing to employ the manufacturer's operating system, sell its software, or purchase a maintenance contract from the manufacturer. Complications that arise from after-markets are examined in detail in the Church and Ware paper in this volume. The law and economics of tying, more generally, are discussed in detail in the Baxter and Kessler paper.

HORIZONTAL AGREEMENTS

IT IS UNLIKELY THAT HORIZONTAL AGREEMENTS WOULD BE ALLOWED in cases where horizontal competitors effectively combine their intellectual property assets and manage them jointly. If the goods are substitutes, then the joint assignment of the patents may result in higher prices for the two products than if they were managed separately.[162]

Eswaran provides an interesting framework for analyzing such a horizontal arrangement.[163] In a repeated-game framework in which firms confront each other over time, he argues that cross-licensing creates potential competition, which disciplines participants of the cross-licensing agreement to maintain the cartel price. The intuition is that cross-licensing (not involving the reciprocal use of each other's technologies) would exacerbate the consequences of a breakdown in that each firm would have the incentive to produce all the products,[164] thus ensuring a higher degree of cooperation. Moreover, the incentive to cheat on the cartel is lessened when firms are producing distinct goods rather than the full set of cross-licensed products.[165] In contrast to Priest,[166] who suggests that cross-licensing may not be harmful if other restrictions are not included in the contract, Eswaran argues that cross-licensing alone may be enough to support a collusive outcome and that restrictive clauses are redundant in that context. Therefore, he recommends that cross-licensing agreements be struck down when patents remain unused.

Eswaran applies his analysis to the *Hartford Empire* case,[167] in which the defendants were charged with conspiring and combining to monopolize and restrain commerce by acquiring patents that covered the manufacture of glass-making machinery and by excluding others from a fair opportunity to freely engage in commerce in such machinery and in the manufacture and distribution of glass products. More than 800 competing patents were involved, and all of the firms in the industry were licensing from a pool of patents that included field-of-use and output restrictions. The government sought a dissolution of the pool.

The U.S. Supreme Court found that by cooperative arrangements and binding agreements, the defendant corporations regulated and suppressed competition in the innovation and use of glassmaking machinery,[168] and employed their joint patent position to allocate fields of manufacture and to maintain prices of unpatented glassware. Despite this finding, the Court did not dissolve the pool. Having found that the continuation of certain activities would be beneficial to the glass industry, the Court instead prohibited some of the practices, especially pre-emptive patenting. In other words, the Court attempted to balance the pro-competitive aspects of the pool while eliminating its anti-competitive effects.

Eswaran would have taken a tougher stand than the Supreme Court: the Hartford pooling arrangement gave each member access to the others' technologies, which empowered the cartel to impose severe punishments on deviating members. Moreover, the division of fields discouraged cheating on the cartel relative to a situation in which all firms actually produced each others' products. Consequently, he argues, the anticompetitive effects of this arrangement most likely overwhelm any efficiency considerations, and the pool should therefore have been dissolved.

Eswaran's recommendation is consistent with the framework proposed above, in particular with Principle 3, in that he focuses on price effects in the product market rather than on the suppression of competition in innovation markets, which was a concern of the Court. However, in contrast to the usual argument that a reduction in innovation competition may result in a reduction in potential competition and in higher prices in the product market, Eswaran argues that the deleterious price effects in the product market are attributable to an increase, rather than a reduction, in potential competition brought about by parties to the agreement arming themselves with each other's innovations. In other words, prices in the product market may increase from such arrangements even if there is no reduction in innovation.

As the Court recognized, technologies may be exchanged, but not used, for non-anticompetitive reasons. For example, technologies may be exchanged in order to avoid costly infringement litigation, but not used because economies of scale make multiple production inefficient. More generally, horizontal arrangements that reduce transaction costs (as in *Broadcast Music*[169]) or litigation costs, or that allow for the combination of complementary inputs, should be evaluated under a rule-of-reason standard. The precise nature of this standard for joint ventures and other cooperative arrangements is examined more fully in Scotchmer's paper in this volume.

CONCLUSION

IN THIS PAPER, WE REVIEWED THE ECONOMICS of competition policy as it relates to intellectual property. We made several points. First, we recommended a policy that attempts to reconcile the fact that IP, as a public good, has an efficient *ex post* transfer price of zero with the fact that, without IPRs, *ex ante* investments would not be undertaken. We argued that competition policy should not be based on whether licensing generates too much or too little reward for the innovator's research efforts, but rather on the efficiency merits of the licensing practice, while respecting the basic exclusive rights provided by the patent grant.

Second, intellectual property differs from other property in its public good nature, which may imply a different application of competition law in some cases. For example, a price-fixing agreement between horizontal competitors would be *per se* illegal. In the case of IP licensing, while a price restriction between firms may dampen competition between the licensor and the licensee, the efficiency features of vertical restrictions (e.g., the elimination of free-riding) may mean that the restriction is not as deleterious as it would be in strictly horizontal contracts. Moreover, the benefits of diffusion may be sufficient to offset the negative effects. These considerations of both diffusion and the allocative effects of a mixed vertical/horizontal contract imply that competition policy should be more lenient towards restrictions between horizontal competitors than for non-IP goods. Such considerations may alter the evaluation of a practice, for example, from *per se* (in the case of a horizontal arrangement among competitors) to a rule-of-reason standard if the transfer of the technology is deemed sufficiently important.

In many cases, the application of the law may be the same as in non-patent cases – for example, for purely vertical arrangements – but certain criteria that are characteristic of innovations (such as uncertainty and specific investments) may justify the use of restrictive practices. Therefore, while the law may be the same, the percentage of cases involving IP that receive more lenient treatment will likely exceed that for non-IP cases. The usual efficiency arguments for vertical restrictions in contracts on unpatented products apply to IP,[170] as do the arguments against vertical restrictions that exclude firms with competing technologies from downstream markets (e.g., exclusive dealing) or that facilitate a cartel among competing patentees.

Just as competition law should not attempt to take on the mandate of patent policy in encouraging innovation, patent law should not attempt to rule on anticompetitive practices. In many of the cases on patent misuse in the United States,[171] contractual provisions were found illegal, although no analysis of market power or of the effect on competition was undertaken. Hovenkamp argues that allegations of IPR abuses should "be addressed under antitrust principles" rather than under "some other set of principles that are presumably to be found in patent policy, although they are not articulated in the *Patent Act.*"[172]

The division of tasks that we recommend in Principle 3 of our proposed framework may seem reminiscent of the historical conflict between patent and antitrust policy. In fact, the division of tasks that we propose differs from that precedent in an important way. Based on the fact that the two policies (should) strive to strike an efficient balance between dynamic and allocative efficiency considerations, this framework recognizes that patent rights promote, rather than hinder, competition. Consequently, in contrast to the old approach that undermined these rights by imposing constraints on contractual arrangements, this framework recommends that competition policy work with patent policy by providing adequate incentives for innovators to share their discoveries with others when this is efficient. In this sense, the division of tasks proposed here does not create tension between the two laws, but rather allocates complementary roles to patent and competition policy for striking the right balance between dynamic and allocative efficiencies.

NOTES

1   Louis Kaplow, "Extension of Monopoly Power through Leverage," *Columbia Law Review*, 85 (1985):515.

2   See W. Nordhaus, *Invention, Growth and Welfare: A Theoretical Treatment of Technological Change*, Cambridge: MIT Press, 1969. See also W. Bowman, *Patent and Antitrust Law: A Legal and Economic Appraisal* , Chicago: University of Chicago Press, 1973; W. Baxter, "Legal Restrictions on the Exploitation of the Patent Monopoly: An Economic Analysis," *Yale Law Journal*, 76 (1966): 267; Kaplow, "Extension of Monopoly Power"; R. Merges and R. Nelson, "On the Complex Economics of Patent Scope," *Columbia Law Review*, 90 (1990): 836; and G. Priest, "Cartels and Patent License Arrangements," *Journal of Law and Economics*, 20 (1977): 309, for further analyses of the patent/competition interface.

3   See R. Barro, "Economic Growth in Cross-Section of Countries," *Quarterly Journal of Economics*, 106(2) (May 1991): 407-444; and H. Demsetz, "How Many Cheers for Antitrust after 100 Years?" *Journal of Economic Inquiry*, April 1992, pp. 207-218.

4   Demsetz recognizes this trade-off in "Barriers to Entry," *American Economic Review*, 72 (1982): 47.

5   This view is stated clearly in a report of the Organisation for Economic Co-operation and Development (OECD) on *Competition Policy and Intellectual Property Rights* (Paris, 1989) and in *Atari Games Corp. v. Nintendo of America Inc.*, 897 F. 2d 1572.

6   Intellectual property rights can take the form of a patent, a copyright, a trade secret, or a trademark. Although the laws differ on the type of protection given, the economic issues regarding competition and incentives are similar.

7   The non-licensing abuse of a dominant position is the accumulation of patents (patent pyramiding) with the intention of excluding entry. For example, see *US v. El Dupont de Nemours and Company*, 351 US 377 (1956).

8   Other competition offences related to IPRs – for example, patent accumulation and violations concerning copyrights – are analyzed in other papers in this volume. See, for example, Rob Merges' paper on "killer portfolios" and Jeff Church and Roger Ware's paper on copyright protection.

9   Patent scope is defined as the range of products that are deemed to infringe the patent. The broader the patent, the more difficult it is for firms to "invent around" the patent, and the greater, therefore, will be the return earned by the patentee.

10 Nordhaus, *Invention, Growth and Welfare, supra*, note 2.

11 For example, see P. Tandon, "Optimal Patents with Compulsory Licensing," *Journal of Political Economy*, 90 (1982): 470; R. Gilbert and C. Shapiro, "Optimal Patent Length and Breadth," *Rand Journal of Economics*, 21 (1990): 106; P. Klemperer, "How Broad Should the Scope of Patent Be?" *Rand Journal of Economics*, 21 (1990): 113; N. Gallini, "Patent Policy and Costly Imitation," *Rand Journal of Economics*, 23 (1992): 52; J. Green and S. Scotchmer, "Novelty and Disclosure in Patent Law," *Rand Journal of Economics*, 21 (1990): 131.

12 See *supra*, note 11, Tandon, "Optimal Patents"; Gilbert and Shapiro, "Optimal Patent Length and Breadth."

13 Patent scope is defined here as the flow of profits that accrue to the innovator; more practically, it is the range of products that would infringe the patent.

14 Klemperer, "How Broad Should the Scope of Patent Be?" *supra*, note 11.

15 Gallini, *supra*, note 11.

16 In the models, price is the equilibrium outcome of the innovator and imitators competing in the market, given patent scope. This contrasts to the framework in Gilbert and Shapiro where price (or profit) is administered by the antitrust (or patent) authorities.

17 J. Green and S. Scotchmer, "On the Division of Profits in Sequential Innovation," *Rand Journal of Economics* (Spring 1995).

18 H. Chang, "Patent Scope, Antitrust Policy and Cumulative Innovation," *Rand Journal of Economics*, 26 (1995): 34-57.

19 A substantial literature on strategic incentives for licensing exists; see, for example, N. Gallini, "Deterrence through Market Sharing: A Strategic Incentive for Licensing," *American Economic Review*, 74 (1984): 931-41; K. Rockett, "Choosing the Competition and Patent Policy," *Rand Journal of Economics*, 21(1) (Spring 1990): 161-71; Eswaran, "Cross-Licensing of Competing Patents as a Facilitating Device," *Canadian Journal of Economics*, 27(3) (August 1994): 689-708. In most of these papers, licensing contracts are assumed to include only a royalty or a fixed fee, but no further restrictions that would be considered contentious under antitrust laws.

20 OECD, *Competition Policy and Intellectual Property Rights, supra*, note 5.

21 *United States vs. the Aluminum Company of America*, 148 F.2d 416 (2d Cir.1945).

22 U.S. Department of Justice and Federal Trade Commission, *Antitrust Guidelines for the Licensing of Intellectual Property* (1995). See also R. Gilbert and S. Sunshine, "Incorporating Dynamic Efficiency Concerns in Merger Analysis: The Use of Innovation Markets," *Antitrust Law Journal*, 63 (1995): 569-601.

23 More precisely, three markets have been identified in the *Guidelines* as being relevant: 1) product markets; 2) technology markets; and 3) innovation markets. The first two markets are conventional concepts that include, respectively, all substitute products and technologies that compete with each other.

24 The notion of an innovation market used in a recent proposed acquisition of General Motors' Allison Transmission Division by the German firm ZF of Friedrichshafen was challenged by the U. S. Department of Justice (DOJ) on the grounds that it would have resulted in a concentration of R&D assets that could have a significant impact on the future innovation in the market for heavy duty automatic transmissions. See "GM sees North American Profit in '94: US to Block Sales of Allison Unit," *Wall Street Journal*, Nov. 17, 1993.

25 For example, suppose that the coordination of patent and competition policy results in a rule that allows firms to include price restrictions in licensing contracts when large R&D expenditures are required. Then the task of the competition courts would be to determine *ex post* whether or not the *ex ante* incentives to innovate justify price restrictions. Such a rule, besides requiring expertise beyond that possessed by competition courts, would encourage firms to argue for contract restrictions on behalf of research, regardless of the innovation.

26 *Anticipating the 21st Century: Competition Policy in the New High-Tech, Global Marketplace*, Special Supplement, A Report by the Federal Trade Commission Staff, ch. 7, vol. 70, no. 1765, June 6, 1996.

27 A policy based on encouraging research may look very much like one based on encouraging diffusion in that both may require leniency so as to increase the patentee's profits from engaging in those activities.

28 *Anticipating the 21st Century*, p. S-72, *supra*, note 26.

29 The difference between the second and third approaches may appear to be one of semantics in that even potential competition analysis must evaluate effects from reduced competition in innovation. In fact, there is an important difference between these two approaches: under the potential-competition doctrine, antitrust authorities need only consider the impact on prices in the technology and product markets owing to reduced competition, rather than non-price effects (i.e., the level, speed, or diversity of R&D activity) evaluated under innovation market analysis.

30 See *supra*, note 26.

31 An alternative view of the competition policy treatment of IP is that after property rights are guaranteed under patent law (thus eliminating the public-good problem of R&D), IP becomes comparable to other assets; hence the same antitrust rules should apply to IP.

32 For further analysis of the interface between patent and competition policy in Canada, see S. Globerman and R. Schwindt, "Intellectual Property Rights: Anticompetitive Abuses and Competition Policy Antidotes," and R. D. Anderson, S. D. Khosla, and M. F. Ronayne, "Canadian Competition Law and Policy at the Centenary," both in *Canadian Competition Law and Policy at the Centenary*, edited by R. S. Khemani and W. T. Stanbury (Halifax, N.S.: The Institute for Research on Public Policy, 1991).

33   Under this doctrine, a contract will not be challenged if it is reasonable both as between the parties and with reference to the public interest, but it may be challenged even if no anticompetitive abuse has been identified. The doctrine has been held to be applicable to exclusive licensing arrangements, but they have usually survived scrutiny: see, for example, *Tank, Lining Corp. v. Dunlop Industrial Ltd.* (1982) 140 D.L.R. (3d) 659 (Ont.C.A.); *Barsch v. Avtex Airservices Ltd.* (1992) 107 A.L.R. 539, aff'd Fed. No. 5 and 9, unreported, August 27, 1993 (Fed. Ct.). For further discussion, see M. J. Trebilcock, *The Common Law of Restraint of Trade: A Legal and Economic Analysis*, Toronto: Carswell, 1986.

34   For a more complete discussion see Anderson et al., "Canadian Competition Law and Policy at the Centenary," *supra*, note 32.

35   There are no reported cases pertaining to these provisions.

36   See, for example, *Canada (Director of Investigation and Research) v. NutraSweet Co.* (1990) 32 C.P.R. (3d) 1 (Comp. Trib), discussed below.

37   A somewhat differently worded precursor to the current section 32 was introduced into anticombines legislation in 1910. Apparently, anticompetitive uses of patents were recognized very early in the evolution of competition policy. For more information on the specific forms of abuse, see section 32, *Competition Act*; see also Globerman and Schwindt, "Intellectual Property Rights," p. 463, *supra*, note 32.

38   Compulsory licensing may be invoked under both the *Patent Act* and the *Competition Act*.

39   In fact, it was not until 1967 that a case (*Union Carbide*) proceeded under the precursor to this section. Besides the *Union Carbide* cases – which did not go to trial – no other proceedings have occurred under section 32. See R. D. Anderson et al., "The Competition Policy Treatment of Intellectual Property Rights in Canada: Retrospect and Prospect," in *Canadian Competition Law and Policy at the Centenary*, edited by R. S. Khemani and W. T. Stanbury, Halifax, N.S.: The Institute for Research on Public Policy, 1991, p. 497.

40   *R. v. Union Carbide Canada Limited*, minutes of settlement in the Exchequer Court of Canada, December 9, 1969 and June 19, 1971, respectively. Also, *Annual Reports* of the Director of Investigation and Research for years ending March 31, 1970 and 1972.

41   *Canada (Director of Investigation and Research) v. NutraSweet Co.*

42   3 W.W.R. 11 [1984].

43   See, for example, *International Cone Co. Ltd. v. Consolidated Wafer Co.* (1926) 2 D.L.R. 1015 (Ex.C.R.).

44   *Bement v. National Harrow Co.* (1982) 186 US.S. 70.

45   Although not directly an IP case, *Canada (Director of Investigation and Research) v. Chrysler Canada Ltd.* (1989), 27 C.P.R. (3d) 1, aff'd (1991), 38 C.P.R. (3d) 25 (Fed.C.A.) – the first refusal-to-supply case to be reviewed by the new Competition Tribunal – had some IP features that indicate how future cases may be resolved. In this case, Chrysler stopped supplying auto parts to a Canadian distributor on terms more favourable than those available to distributors in the United States. In its decision, the Tribunal suggested that the existence of a trademark in particular, and of an IPR in general, does not necessarily imply the existence of a separate market.

46   Owners of trademarked goods appear to have the same protection against "grey goods" or parallel imports that bear a legitimate trademark, but that have not been authorized for importation by the trademark owner in Canada. See, for example, *Remington Rand Ltd. v. Transworld Metal Co. Ltd.* (1960) 32 C.P.R. 99; *Mattel Canada Inc. v. GTS*

Acquisitions and Nintendo of America Inc. (1989) 27 C.P.R. (3d) 358 (Federal Court, Trial Division); and *H.J. Heinz of Canada Ltd. v. Edan Food Sales* (1991) 35 C.P.R. (3d) (Federal Court, Trial Division).

47 For an offence to have occurred, it must be shown that (a) the firm is a major supplier of the product and (b) competition has been lessened substantially. There have been no exclusive-territory cases regarding intellectual property.

48 (1953) 13 Fox Pat.C.190 (Commr.)

49 *Canada (Director of Investigation and Research) v. NutraSweet Co.*

50 *Ibid.* The Director alleged that NutraSweet had engaged in several other practices, including customer meet-or-release and most-favoured nation clauses.

51 *Ibid.* This practice of removing a rebate from licensees that turned to other suppliers bears a resemblance to the practice of imposing a cost on licensees that used other suppliers in the *Microsoft* case.

52 It is important to note that an agreement that rationalizes output with efficiency results would benefit from the exemption for specialization agreements under section 86.

53 *Philco Products Ltd. v. Thermionics Ltd.* (1943) 3 D.L.R.

54 See, for example, *Philco Products Ltd.* et al. *v. Thermionics Ltd. et al.* (1943), 3 D.L.R., p. 455. For a detailed discussion of the case law on allegations of anticompetitive abuses as a defence in infringement cases, see Anderson et al., "Canadian Competition Law and Policy," *supra*, note 32.

55 Section 154 of the *Patent Code.* Article I, section 8 of the Constitution gives Congress the power to grant patent rights.

56 The most common abuse heard under this doctrine is the tying of a patented to an unpatented product, although other offenses have been cross-licensing, resale-price maintenance, non-competition clauses, and field-of-use restrictions.

57 For more information on this point, see Herbert Hovenkamp, *Federal Antitrust Policy: The Law of Competition and Its Practice*, St. Paul, Minn.: West Publishing, 1994, pp. 218-19.

58 35 U.S.C.A. § 271(d).

59 Section 3 pertains to tie-ins and exclusive dealing, while section 7 covers mergers and acquisitions.

60 Section 261 of the *Patent Act* states that "the patentee . . . may . . . grant and convey an exclusive right under application for patent or patents, to the whole or any specified part of the United States."

61 U.S. Department of Justice, Antitrust Division, *Antitrust Enforcement Guidelines for International Operations*, November 10, 1988. Although not law, the 1988 *Guidelines* do identify situations that are likely to arise in courts in the future and discuss how the DOJ will apply competition policy to IP.

62 U.S. Department of Justice and Federal Trade Commission, *Antitrust Guidelines for the Licensing of Intellectual Property.*

63 In the latter case, it will be important to show that no alternative, less restrictive measure could achieve the positive effects from the agreement.

64 Hovenkamp, *Federal Antitrust Policy*, pp. 218-19, *supra*, note 57.

65 *Motion Picture Patents Co. v. Universal Film Manufacturing Co.*, 243 US 502 (1916).

66 See, for example, *Morton Salt Co. v. G.S. Suppinger Co.*, 314 US 488 (1941); *B.B. Chemical v. Ellis*, 314 US 495 (1941); *Mercoid Corp. v. Mid-Continental Investment Co.*, 320 US 661 (1943); *Mercoid Corp. v. Minneapolis Honeywell Regulator Co.*, 320

US 680 (1943); *International Salt Co. v. United States*, 332 US 392 (1947); and *United States v. Loew's Inc.*, 371 U.S. 38 (1962).

67   *Dawson Chemical Co. v. Rohm and Haas Co.*, 448 US 176 (1980).

68   *Ibid*, pp. 221-22. It was also noted that the unpatented chemical had no alternative use and therefore producers of it would likely be found guilty of contributory infringement under section 271(c) of the *Patent Code*. There have been other instances in which ties were allowed between patented processes and unpatented components. In *Electric Pipeline Inc. v. Fluid Systems Inc.*, 1956 Trade Cases ¶68,300, 231 F. 2d 370, the tie was allowed since the patentee designed the system and components to meet customers' needs and because it guaranteed performance of the system.

69   *Jefferson Parish Hospital District No. 2 v. Hyde*, 466 US 176 (1984). In this case, a contract between a hospital and a anesthesiologist firm required that all services be performed by the firm. The respondent argued that this contract foreclosed the market (for this hospital). The Supreme Court reversed the Court of Appeal's decision that the contract was *per se* illegal and in violation of section 1 of the *Sherman Act*.

70   *Ibid.*, p. 37, note 7.

71   The recent *Guidelines* make this clear. Also, there is evidence that court decisions are beginning to follow this rule: in *Spectrum Sports v. McQuillan*, 113 S. Ct. 884, 890 (1993), the Court noted that "one cannot presume that a patent itself defines a relevant market."

72   *American Security Co. v. Shatterproof Glass Corp.*, 268 F. 2d 769 (3d Cir. 1959). It is important to note that this misuse charge can be avoided by offering a subset of the package at a different price or by lowering the royalty on the trade secret, after the patent expires. See, for example, *Western Electric Co. v. Stewart-Warner Corp.*, 631 F. 2d 333 (4th Cir. 1980); *Brulotte v. Thys Co.*, 379 US 29 (1964); and *Rocform Corp. v. Acitelli-Standard Concrete Wall*, 367 F. 2d 678 (6th Cir. 1966).

73   *Broadcast Music v. Columbia Broadcasting System Inc.*, 441 US 1, 99 S.Ct. 1551 (1979).

74   See, for example, *Automatic Radio Mfg. Co. v. Hazeltine Research Inc.*, 339 US 827 (1950); and *Miller Insituform, Inc.* et al. *v. Insituform of N. America et al.*, 830 F. 2d 60 6 (1987).

75   See, for example, *Beckman Instruments Inc. v. Technical Development Corp.*, 433 F. 2d 55 (7th Cir. 1970).

76   DOJ 1988 *Guidelines*, Case 10, p. 66.

77   This case is reviewed in more detail in the Rey and Winter paper in this volume.

78   *Transparent-Wrap Machine Corp. v. Stokes and Smith Co.*, 329 US 637 (1946).

79   Lenient treatment has been extended to non-exclusive grantbacks.

80   U.S. Department of Justice and Federal Trade Commission, *Antitrust Guidelines for the Licensing of Intellectual Property*, p. 23.

81   For examples of such cases, see *Hartford Empire Co.* et al. *v. United States*, 323 US 386 (1945); *SCM Corp. v. Xerox Corp.*, 564 F. 2d 1195 (2d Cir. 1981).

82   *Xerox Corp.*, 86 FTC 364 (1975).

83   Suspicious agreements between licensor and licensee are examined under the rule of reason. *Moraine Products v. ICJ America, Inc.*, 1976-1 T.C. 60,935 (C7 1976). See "The Competition Policy Treatment of Intellectual Property Licensing in the U.S. and Canada," Bureau of Competition Policy, March 1987, for an excellent discussion of the U.S. law in this area.

84   See, for example, *Blount Mfg. Co. v. Yale & Towne Mfg. Co.*, 166 Fed. 555 (C.C.Mass. 1909).

85   *United States v. General Electric Co.*, 272 US 476 (1926).

86   Although the result may not differ, the reasoning behind each type of award does.

87   *United States v. Univis Lens Co.*, 316 US 241 (1941).

88   See, for example, *Royal Indus. v. St. Regis Paper Co.*, 420 F.2d 449, 452 (9th Cir. 1969).

89   See, for example, *Newburgh Moire Co. v. Superior Moire Co.*, 237 F.2d 283, 293-4.

90   See, for example, *United States v. United States Gypsum Co.*, 333 US 364 (1947).

91   See, for example, *Barber-Colman Co., v. National Tool Co.*, 136 F.2d 339, 343-44 (6th Cir. 1943).

92   See, for example, *United States v. Line Material Co.*, 333 US 287 (1947).

93   Most notably, *Monsanto Co. v. Spray-Rite Service Corp.*, 465 US 752 (1984) and *Business Electronics Corp. v. Sharp Electronics Corp.* 485 U.S. 717 (1988) suggest that the courts are becoming more lenient towards resale-price maintenance in vertical cases. In contrast to price restrictions, output restrictions have been treated more leniently by the courts: see, for example, *Q-Tips Inc. v. Johnson and Johnson*, 109 F. Supp 657 (D.N.J. 1951).

94   In a sense, the restriction is on the product (rather than geographic) market. Field-of-use restrictions are legal in the United States – see *General Pictures*, 304 US 175 (1937), aff'd on rehearing 305 US 124 (1938) – as long as they are not used to extend the scope of the patent.

95   This is referred to as the "doctrine of the first sale" or the "exhaustion principle."

96   *Continental T.V. Inc. v. G.T.E. Sylvania, Inc.*, 443 U.S. 36 (1977).

97   For a comprehensive discussion of the balance between antitrust and patent remedies for restricting parallel imports of products embodying intellectual property, see R. D. Anderson, P. J. Hughes, S. D. Khosla, and M. F. Ronayne, "Intellectual Property Rights and International Market Segmentation: Implications of the Exhaustion Principle," working paper, Bureau of Competition Policy, Economics and International Affairs Branch, Hull (Quebec), October 1990. Where the competition approach fails, patentees may take recourse against infringing imports under section 337 of the U.S. *Tariff Act*. Trademark owners can receive some protection under section 42 of the *Lanham Trademark Act* or through the *Tariff Act* if the foreign and U.S. trademark owners are the same or are affiliated. Furthermore, the *Process Patent Amendments Act* of 1988 specifies that unauthorized imports of goods made by a process patent in the United States may constitute infringement.

98   *United States v. Westinghouse Electric Corp.*, 648 F2d 642 (1981). See, also, *Dunlop Co. Ltd. v. Kelsey-Hayes Co.*, 364 F Supp 1094 (1972), where the Court of Appeals upheld exclusive territories under section 261 of the *Patent Code*, 1973-2, Trade Cases, ¶74, 671.

99   See, for example, *U.S. v. Studiengesellschaft Kohle* (1981-2, Trade Cases, ¶64,394, 670 F2d 1122 (1981)).

100   For example, see the report, "Justice Department Files First Antitrust Suit Against Foreign Company Since 1992 Policy Change," 8858E, May 26, 1994, which describes a recent case where the DOJ alleged that a contract between S. C. Johnson and Bayer entrenched S. C. Johnson's dominance in a concentrated market.

101   See, for example, *Jefferson Parish Hospital Dist. No. 2 v. Hyde*, 466 US 2 (1984), although a patent was not at issue in this case.

102   *National Lockwasher Co. v. George K. Garrett Co.*, 137 F. 2d 255 (3rd cir. 1943).

103 See, for example, DOJ, "Microsoft Agrees to End Unfair Monopolistic Practices," 94-387, July 16, 1994.

104 See Priest, "Cartels and Patent License Arrangements," *supra*, note 2.

105 See, for example, *Standard Oil Co. v. United States*, 283 US 163 (1930) and *Hartford Empire Co. v. United States*, 323 US 386 (1945).

106 See example 8 in the *Guidelines*.

107 For example, *United States v. Automobile Manufacturers Association*, 307 F. Suppl, 617 (C.D. Cal 1969), modified sub nom. *United States v. Motor Vehicle Manufacturers Association*, 1982-83 Trade Case. (CCH) ¶65,088 (CD Cal 1982). The suppression of innovations was especially of concern since the agreement involved a large proportion of market participants.

108 For example, a pooling arrangement that would be acceptable to the DOJ is an arrangement such as that in *Broadcast Music, Inc. v. Columbia Broadcasting System, Inc.*, 441 U.S. 1 (1979), in which a blanket licence for copyrighted musical compositions reduced transaction costs.

109 Since the latter is closer to the objective of competition policy in the United States and Canada, many of the policies in the EU diverge dramatically from the policies in these jurisdictions. For a comprehensive review of competition treatment of intellectual property in the European Community, its member countries, and other jurisdictions, see OECD, *Competition Policy and Intellectual Property, supra,* note 5; and Richard Whish, *Competition Law*, third edition (London: Butterworths, 1993).

110 OECD, *Competition Policy*, p. 45, *supra*, note 5.

111 Commission Regulation No. 2349/84, 23 July 1984, OJ No. L.219/15, 16th August 1984 and OJ No. L 61, 4th March 1989.

112 In article 1(7) of the regulation, knowhow is defined as "a body of technical information that is secret, substantial and identified in any appropriate form." The distinction between patent and knowhow licences is emphasized in the EU legislation more so than in either the U.S. or Canadian legislation. Since knowhow is less public, a concern is that firms will use a knowhow licence to disguise a cartel. Consequently, the regulations require that the knowhow transferred be substantial.

113 Exempted practices are only bilateral; multilateral agreements (including knowhow pools, joint ventures, or reciprocal licensing agreements) fall outside these exemptions. The exempted practices include exclusive territories that do not preclude parallel imports, tie-ins for technical purposes, minimum royalty requirements, reciprocal non-exclusive grantbacks, and field-of-use restrictions. In contrast, the "black-listed" practices that are not exempted because they lack the benefits required by article 85(3) are no-challenge clauses, extension of the life of a patent, restrictions on markets or customers, royalties that do not reflect the use of the IP, quantity or price restrictions, unilateral grantback requirements, or practices that prevent parallel trade. The remaining practices are reviewed on a case-by-case basis and there is a 60-day period within which the Commission must make a decision or the practice is deemed exempted. The Commission provides an "escape clause" that enables it to withdraw the benefits of its exemption (for example, where competition is later found to be jeopardized).

114 Article 36 of the Treaty.

115 See, for example, *Vaessen/Morris*, OJ No L 19/32 (26th January 1979).

116 Article 2(1)(1) of patent regulation.

117 Article 3(9).

118 See, for example, in *AOIP/Beyrard*, OJ No. L 6/8 (13th January 1976); in licensing its patented electrical devices, Beyrard included improvement patents that extended the patent and required payment on expired patents or patents not used.

119 See, for example, *Raymond/Nagoya*, OJ L 143/39 (23rd June 1972) and *Kabelmetal/Luchaire*, OJ No. L 222/34 (22nd August 1975). A concern in the latter case was that the original licensor had the exclusive right to sublicense the improvements to others.

120 Article 2(1)(10) of the patent block exemption provides "an obligation on the parties to communicate to one another any experience gained in exploiting the licensed invention and to grant one another a licence in respect of inventions relating to improvements and new applications, provided that such communication or license is non-exclusive."

121 *Volvo/Weng*, Case 238/87, decided 5th October 1988.

122 As a result, it can be said that, in contrast to the United States (and, to some extent, Canada), a patentee has the exclusive right to "produce" the invention ("existence"), but it does not have the exclusive right to "use" the invention or products produced from it.

123 These conditions state that the knowhow must be "designed (a) to limit the licensee to supply its own needs, (b) to prohibit the licensee from constructing facilities for third parties, and (c) to provide a particular customer with a second source of supply"; see knowhow block exemptions, articles 3(7) and 4(2).

124 See, for example, *ENI/Montedison*, OJ No. L 5/13 (7th January 1987).

125 *Nungesser v. Commission* (hereafter *Maize Seed*), Case 258/78, 1982 E.C.R. 2015. This is the argument often used in U.S. cases – i.e., that a decrease in intra-brand competition may have the effect of increasing inter-brand competition.

126 *Boussois/Interpane*, OJ No. 13/204 (15th December 1986).

127 The provisions concerning territorial restrictions provide the starkest contrast between the policy of the European Union and those of the United States and Canada.

128 In contrast, field-of-use restrictions are exempted from article 85(1) under both patent and knowhow block exemptions.

129 The doctrine of exhaustion provides that once an innovator has placed its invention on the market, it cannot restrict the resale of that good. See, for example, *Centrafarm BV v. Sterling Drug Inc*, Case 15/74, 1974 E.C.R. 1147. The free movement of goods follows from articles 30 and 34 of the Treaty and from the Court of Justice's decisions on exhaustion. Negative clearances have been given for exclusive contracts when the parties to the contract were not restricted in their sales throughout the community. *Burroughs/Geha-Werke*, OJ L 13/53 (17 January 1972) and *Burroughs/Delplanque* OJ L 13/50 (17 January 1972).

130 *Nungesser v. Commission*, Case 258/78, 1982 E.C.R. 2015.

131 An open, exclusive licence does not completely limit the territory; in particular, parallel imports are not prevented. On the other hand, if it is an absolute exclusive licence, the licensee has complete exclusive rights in the territory and parallel importation is not allowed.

132 The defendant argued that the restrictions were necessary to encourage innovation because of local climate and soil conditions, that the product was fragile, or that inter-brand competition in maize seeds existed.

133 In this case, the goods are not considered to be "authorized" by the IPR holder.

134   See, for example, *Raymond-Nagoya*, in which the licensee was restricted to the Japanese and neighbouring markets for its licensed automobile parts.

135   See, for example, *Kabelmetal/Luchaire*. Note that field-of-use restrictions, which are analogous to territorial restrictions except that they are concerned with product rather than geographic space, are permitted under both block exemptions.

136   For example, Germany follows a case-by-case approach, prohibiting vertical restraints when market entry is restricted. Territorial restrictions are subject to sections 20 and 21 of the German *Act Against Restraints on Competition*. The territory of first sale by a manufacturing licensee can be specified under the patent right, and restrictions on foreign licences of German patent holders are allowed when the German market is not affected. Restrictions on German exports, however, are not permitted under the law. The U.K. approach towards vertical restraints is generally permissive.

137   For more information on this area, see Valentine Korah, *Patent Licensing and EEC Competition Rules Regulation 2349/84* (Oxford, U.K.: ESC Publishing Limited, 1985), p. 27. Korah defines a patent pool as the "bringing of patents together so that they may jointly be made available for use by all the parties, or licensed to outsiders for their joint benefit," whereas cross-licensing (or reciprocal exchange) involves "separate agreements" or "connected undertakings."

138   Patent block exemptions, article 5(1)(3) and 5(2). See, for example, *ENI/Montedison*, *supra*, note 124.

139   A refusal to license also becomes contentious when the innovator supplies the innovation to only one firm in the downstream market. Since this refusal is usually a condition of an exclusive contract, we examine a refusal to license in this context in the later section on exclusivity.

140   *United States v. General Electric Co, supra*, note 85.

141   This problem is analyzed in M. Katz and C. Shapiro, "How to License Intangible Property," *Quarterly Journal of Economics*, 101 (1986): 567.

142   D. Turner, "Basic Principles in Formulating Antitrust and Misuse Constraints on the Exploitation of Intellectual Property Rights," *Antitrust Law Journal*, 53(4),1984.

143   See the discussion on U.S. law in this paper.

144   In "Cartels and Patent License Arrangements," Priest argues that there may well have been a restraint of trade, but the government was ill-prepared and presented a sloppy case. If this really was a sham agreement, then it would fail the test set out in our economic framework and the Court should have granted the injunction.

145   In this example, there are no benefits from diffusion; for example, there are no diseconomies in production or product differentiation in good X that would make the production of that good by more than one firm socially desirable.

146   *United States v. Line Material Co, supra*, note 92.

147   In that case, the cross-licence agreement on blocking patents included price restrictions for each other and for sublicensees. The Court noted that such price restrictions violated the *Sherman Act* even when they may be "advantageous . . . to stimulate the broader use of patents."

148   This is attributed to the well-known principle that a monopolist of two complementary products sets lower prices than would be set by two separate duopolists of the products. See J. Tirole, *The Theory of Industrial Organization* (Cambridge, Mass.: MIT Press, 1990), ch. 4.

149   Although output and price restrictions may have a similar effect, the asymmetry of their treatment derives from the rights under the U.S. *Patent Code*, which stipulates

that a patentee can prevent the use or sale of its patented item (output restrictions) but does not stipulate the right to affect its value.

150   For example, see our earlier discussion of the U.S. case filed against S. C. Johnson and Bayer.

151   For example, see Tirole, *Theory of Industrial Organization*, ch. 4 and the references therein, *supra*, note 148.

152   That is, the EU is more concerned about reductions in intra-brand competition than are the other two jurisdictions. However, an increase in intra-brand competition may not imply an increase in competition overall, since competition that reduces the profit that can be earned from a new product reduces the incentive to develop competing brands or products.

153   *Nungesser v. Commission, supra*, note 125.

154   The use of exclusive territories to dampen competition between manufacturers is analyzed in P. Rey and J. Stiglitz, "The Role of Exclusive Territories in Producers' Competition," *Rand Journal of Economics*, 26(3), Autumn 1995.

155   Only 7 percent of patents granted in Canada were developed in Canada. This contrasts with between 20 and 50 percent in other major industrialized countries. R. Anderson et al. argue in "The Competition Policy Treatment of Intellectual Property Rights in Canada" (*supra*, note 39) that small countries should not necessarily adopt policies that are restrictive towards licensing agreements, noting that many such licences have efficiency-enhancing benefits. Restrictions on licensing contracts may reduce the incentive for innovators to transfer technologies to those countries.

156   Anderson et al. argue in "Intellectual Property Rights and International Market Segmentation " (*supra*, note 97) that the cost of higher prices is almost entirely offset by the benefits from ensuring the transfer of "low-price" products. They make the interesting observation that if exhaustion were implemented on a wide scale, IP laws would have to be harmonized since the lowest protection would become the realized protection, with competition from the country in which the patent expired flowing into the countries in which the patent has not expired. See also N. Gallini and A. Hollis, "A Contractual Approach to the Gray Market," working paper, University of Toronto, 1996.

157   One might recommend a tougher *ex ante* policy on the vertical integration of firms given that, *ex post*, patent law allows for more leniency of vertically merged firms.

158   The "leverage theory" says that tie-ins may enable an innovator to extend its market power into other markets, although this theory has generated considerable skepticism in the economics literature. For example, see Baxter, "Legal Restrictions on the Exploitation of the Patent Monopoly," and Hovencamp, *Federal Antitrust Policy* (*supra*, note 2 and note 57, respectively). Moreover, tie-ins may foreclose the tied market from competitors, requiring potential competitors to enter both levels.

159   The benefits and costs of tying apply to output royalties, except that output royalties may be a mechanism for foreclosing the market in which the innovation competes. A royalty on total output, whether or not the product is made using the licensed technology, increases the cost of using an alternative technology, as noted in the *Microsoft* case.

160   *Automatic Radio Mfg. Co. v. Hazeltine Research Inc, supra*, note 74.

161   *Ibid.*

162 This may be achieved by trading technologies that will not be used and charging a per unit royalty rate in order to raise the perceived marginal cost and therefore the price at which the firms compete.

163 Eswaran, "Cross-Licensing of Competing Patents," *supra*, note 19.

164 In other words, it is individually rational to produce from both technologies.

165 This is because, when the goods are imperfect substitutes, a given aggregate increase in a firm's output decreases the prices of the goods it produces by less if that increase is allocated between two goods than for one good.

166 Priest,"Cartels and Patent License Arrangements," *supra*, note 2.

167 *Hartford Empire Co. v. United States*, *supra*, note 81.

168 The classic case is the alleged conspiracy to retard the development of new technology in *United States v. Automobile Manufacturers Association*, which contended that the major automobile manufacturers engaged in a joint venture whose purpose was to retard investment in automobile pollution control equipment. The case ended in a consent judgment in which the automakers agreed to terminate their cooperative efforts without admitting that their prior conduct had violated the law.

169 *Broadcast Music, Inc. v. Columbia Broadcasting System, Inc.*, *supra*, note 73.

170 For example, see G. F. Mathewson and R. A. Winter, "The Economics of Vertical Restraints in Distribution," *New Developments in the Analysis of Market Structure*, edited by G. F. Mathewson and J. Stiglitz (Cambridge, Mass.: MIT Press, 1986); and Tirole, *Theory of Industrial Organization*, *supra*, note 148.

171 For example, the Court in *Morton Salt Co. v. G.S. Suppinger Co.* held that it was "unnecessary to decide whether [the patent owner] has violated the Clayton Act." In *B.I.C. Leisure v. Windsurfing Int'l Inc.* (1991) 761 F. Supp. 1032, the Court noted that while the misuse defence must show that competition in the relevant market is restrained, it also notes that "less evidence of anticompetitive effect . . . than in antitrust cases" may be needed.

172 In *Federal Antitrust Policy*, Hovenkamp observes that in *Lasercomb America, Inc. v. Reynolds*, (1991) 911 F. 2d 970, in which misuse was shown since the licensor insisted that the licensee refrain from developing competing software for 99 years, an antitrust violation was not at issue. He interprets this as a broader application for copyright defence than for patent defence. But since copyrights are easier to create than patents, the presumption of market power is weaker, and the possibility of anticompetitive behaviour is less likely. Canadian law does not revoke a patent if an abuse is found; the licence contract is struck down, but the misuse will not invalidate the patent right of the patent holder.

ACKNOWLEDGMENTS

THE AUTHORS THANK ARIANA BIRNBAUM AND ANINDYA SEN for their research assistance, as well as the Competition Bureau for research support. We are particularly grateful to Richard Gilbert and Robert Anderson for his insightful comments. The views expressed in this paper are those of the authors and not necessarily those of the Competition Bureau.

Comment

Richard Gilbert
Department of Economics
University of California, Berkeley

GALLINI AND TREBILCOCK PROVIDE a very useful and informed analysis of Canadian, U.S. and European Union (EU) competition law for transactions involving intellectual property. Canada and the United States are closer – both geographically and in jurisprudence – to each other than they are to the EU. The competition laws in Canada and the United States are both based on a philosophy of weighing economic costs and benefits. The European Union's laws are rather different. As the authors note, the EU is opposed to arrangements that may limit trade between the member states. Hence EU law discourages licensing restrictions such as exclusive territories.

There is another important aspect of EU law that differs from U.S. and Canadian law. Article 85 of the Treaty of Rome says that any contract or combination that adversely affects competition is illegal unless it is exempted. As a rough approximation, in the United States and in Canada, a licensing provision that adversely affects competition is legal until a court holds that it is illegal. In the EU, a provision that adversely affects competition is illegal unless permitted by the Commission through a formal exemption. The exemption can be an individual exemption for the provision, which is time-consuming and burdensome to obtain, or it can be a block exemption. A block exemption is a blanket exemption for a class of practices.

The U.S. Department of Justice released draft intellectual property (IP) guidelines at roughly the same time that the European Community (as it was then called) released its draft technology-transfer block exemption, which covered bilateral agreements involving patents and knowhow. There was much discussion about whether the IP guidelines and the technology-transfer block exemption converged on similar enforcement policies. In fact, the two documents could not converge because they are based on different legal principles.

For example, the IP guidelines could state that R&D joint ventures could harm competition, notwithstanding the fact that the U.S. antitrust agencies have not challenged an R&D joint venture for many years. The U.S. guidelines can describe conduct that could raise antitrust concerns while leaving the determination of the legality of any particular joint venture to a rule-of-reason analysis. In contrast, the EU must either issue a block exemption for R&D joint ventures or address each joint venture through the process of an individual exemption. Of course, the EU has considerable discretion to challenge conduct under article 85, and there are very few IP antitrust cases in the European

Union (or the United States). But the EU block exemption has to be quite specific in the description of permissible conduct.

I have dwelt on the U.S. IP guidelines and EU block exemption because I detect Canadian guidelines in their primordial state in the Gallini and Trebilcock paper. For that reason I have to go into "guideline mode" and be a bit picky, as is necessary for an administrative proceeding. (Recall when Sonny Bono asked his colleague in a Congressional committee why they had to be so legal. His colleague's response was to remind Sonny they were being legal because they make the laws.) I will focus on the four principles in the Gallini and Trebilcock paper that constitute a "framework for competition policy in IPRs."

The first principle is, "There should not be a presumption that an intellectual property right creates market power." This is correct economics and appropriate public policy. The IP community will appreciate a clear statement of this basic principle.

The second principle is, "The exclusive rights explicitly stated in the patent law should be respected by competition law." I suggest some clarification of the implications of this principle. The IP laws establish property rights for those who develop useful products or processes or creative expression. Competition law must respect these explicit rights. However, the antitrust principles that govern competitive conduct should be the same for IP as for other forms of property. The authors correctly note the need for competitive restraints in licensing arrangements. Similar arguments apply to restraints in other circumstances. Consider distribution arrangements. Both manufacturers and distributors may have to invest in assets that are specific to their relationship; for example, a service facility that is uniquely suited to a particular product. Vertical restraints may be necessary to protect these investments from free-riding and opportunistic behaviour. My concern is that this second principle should not imply that IP raises competition issues that are fundamentally different from those that apply to other forms of property. IP arrangements may justify more restraints more of the time, but other transactions may require them as well.

The third principle is, "Competition authorities should not base their policy on whether innovators have received a sufficient reward for their efforts, but should evaluate licensing contracts on their own merits." I take the authors' point to be that antitrust authorities do not determine the size, scope, or existence of the IP property right. In the United States, that is done by the Patent and Trademark Office and the Copyright Office, acting under the direction of Congress. The antitrust authorities govern only how the property rights may be used. The antitrust laws do not define the size or scope of a patent, but competition policies affect incentives for innovation by defining permissible restraints. Moreover, *ex ante* incentives for innovation can be a factor in the determination of economically efficient restraints. For example, the competitive effects of an arrangement that requires licensees to assign the licensor exclusive rights to new inventions may depend on the circumstances of competition in research and development. Thus *ex ante* innovation incentives may not be entirely separable from an analysis of the merits of a licensing arrangement.

The fourth principle is, "Licensing restrictions that do not reduce competition relative to a 'no licensing' situation should be allowed." The concept is close to what is in the U.S. IP guidelines, which state that "antitrust concerns may arise when a licensing arrangement harms competition among entities that would have been actual or likely potential competitors in a relevant market in the absence of the license." There is a subtle but important distinction between the "licensing arrangement" and a restriction in the licence. A restriction arguably could have adverse effects on competition even if the licence is pro-competitive. If you leave the statement as is, it invites fine-tuning of licensing arrangements – e.g., "You only licensed eight firms in the industry; why not all ten?"

The general issue addressed here is the conditions under which an antitrust authority may require a licensor to employ a less restrictive alternative. A simple benchmark is the state of competition without the licence. Unfortunately, that is not an entirely satisfactory benchmark. Consider Microsoft's licences for the use of its operating systems to computer manufacturers and retailers. The licence is beneficial relative to a "but-for" world with no licensing. Yet some aspect of the license may offend the antitrust laws – for example, by foreclosing competition from suppliers of competing operating systems. This could be analysed under the proposed framework by adopting an expansive view of the "but-for" world, which may include alternative licensing arrangements. However, that approach becomes rather arbitrary.

Restrictions in a licence need to be considered in the context of the entire licence. The U.S. IP guidelines address this concern in part by stating that "the Agencies will not engage in a search for a theoretically least restrictive alternative that is not realistic in the practical prospective business situation faced by the parties."

These are just some quibbles. This is a very nice paper. But a discussion of guidelines, even at this stage of development, puts you in the quibble business. Lawyers are detailed and precise in their thinking. You have to consider how any imprecision can be exploited by others and take that into account when you prepare your appropriately vague guidelines.

Donald G. McFetridge
Department of Economics
Carleton University

3

Intellectual Property, Technology Diffusion, and Growth in the Canadian Economy

INTRODUCTION

THE PURPOSE OF THIS PAPER IS TO EXAMINE SOME OF THE IMPLICATIONS of intellectual property rights for the diffusion of technological innovations and to discuss some aspects of the relationship between technology diffusion and economic growth. The paper describes the Canadian experience with compulsory patent licensing and discusses the implications of that experience for the use of compulsory licensing as a policy instrument in both developed and developing countries.

SOURCES OF ECONOMIC GROWTH

BROADLY DEFINED, THE CENTRAL ROLE OF INNOVATION is widely accepted as a source of growth in per capita income.[1] There is less agreement on the forms of economic organization most conducive to innovation. For example, there have been lengthy debates over the role of competitive markets or intellectual property rights in encouraging innovation.

The debate over the effect of competition on innovation and growth has taken place at several levels.[2] At an aggregate, impressionistic level, Porter (1990) finds a relationship between the intensity of competition in domestic markets and national competitive advantage. This leads him to advocate strong antitrust policies, even though the most successful countries in his study (Germany and Japan) do not have particularly strong antitrust policies (McFetridge, 1992).

At a more formal and disaggregated level, there is a considerable literature on innovative rivalry.[3] It is important to understand that, in this context, rivalry is a consequence of the expectation that the successful innovator will have some monopoly power. Absent the prospect of at least a limited monopoly – or, to paraphrase Schumpeter, if successful innovators were to be confronted with perfect and perfectly prompt competition from imitators – little innovative effort would be forthcoming.

If the innovator can anticipate some sort of exclusivity in the post-innovation phase, rivalry in the pre-innovation phase can be beneficial up to a point. This is an issue in the economics of the "second-best." In theory, a monopoly innovator who can appropriate the entire social benefit of its innovation will devote the appropriate amount of resources to that innovation.[4] Under these circumstances, rivalry is wasteful. If, however, the successful innovator cannot appropriate the entire social benefit of its innovation, a monopoly innovator will spend too little (relative to the ideal) on this innovation whereas rivalry might result in better and/or faster innovation. What is happening here is that the effect of one distortion (partially duplicative or redistributive rivalry) is offsetting the effect of another (incomplete appropriability of the benefits of innovation).

The extent of rivalry in innovation markets is determined in part by the strength of intellectual property rights. Other things being equal, the promise of a stronger right should attract more rivals. Indeed, the strength of the right could, in principle, be manipulated to attract the socially optimal number of rivals (Dasgupta and Stiglitz, 1980). This assumes that the knowledge base with which would-be innovators are working is common property. If, however, some of the knowledge required by would-be innovators is proprietary, stronger property rights in existing innovations could limit rivalry in ongoing or follow-on innovation.

The implication is that there are two aspects to the diffusion of innovation. One is the use of new knowledge, frequently in the form of new industrial technologies, by end-users. Some recent findings regarding the diffusion of new industrial technologies in Canada are discussed below.

The other aspect of diffusion is the use of new knowledge as an intermediate input by follow-on innovators. Here, patent law, particularly with respect to novelty requirements and patent breadth, is central. These issues are discussed by Acheson and McFetridge (1996) and in several papers in the present volume, and they are raised below in the context of the Canadian experience with compulsory licensing. Recent Canadian survey evidence on the use of patented technology as a base for follow-on innovations is also summarized.

DIFFUSION AND GROWTH

SURPRISINGLY LITTLE IS KNOWN ABOUT THE RELATIONSHIP between technology diffusion and economic growth. The existence of a statistical relationship between research and development (R&D) and total factor productivity is well established. This implies that R&D expenditures yield knowledge that is somehow put to use. Little or no attention is paid in this literature to the speed with which new knowledge is put to use.

Technology can either be diffused in disembodied form or be embodied in new vintages of equipment, materials or software. Users of new technologies may be the beneficiaries of spillovers to varying degrees. The speed of diffusion is likely to depend on whether a new technology is embodied or disembodied and on the extent to which it is appropriable, as well as on other characteristics (Griliches, 1991).

Other things being equal, if new knowledge is applied more quickly, its contribution is realized earlier. In a simple growth model, faster diffusion would result in a once-for-all increase in output. This increase would depend on the stock of new technology involved, on the rate of return to that new technology, and on the extent of the increase in the rate of diffusion. In an endogenous growth model in which there is some feedback from cumulative output or from the cumulative application of innovative effort, an increase in the speed of diffusion could also result in a sustained increase in the rate of growth of output.

Of course, the diffusion process itself is costly, and it is the net increase in output resulting from faster diffusion that should concern us. Faster is not necessarily better. The analysis should focus not so much on the rate of diffusion as on imperfections (market failures and government failures) in the diffusion process itself. The question is a familiar one: Are there diffusion externalities for which there are practical, remedial public policies? For the purposes of this paper, the question could be further refined to ask whether intellectual property law has played an important part in internalizing diffusion externalities and whether it could play a more productive role.

ECONOMIC THEORIES OF TECHNOLOGY DIFFUSION

THERE ARE SEVERAL ECONOMIC MODELS OF THE PROCESS of technology diffusion (Stoneman and Diederen, 1994). One is the contagion model, which proposes that the potential users of a technology learn about it passively by observing existing users. In this case, early adopters confer a benefit on later adopters in the form of a demonstration effect. In the presence of this positive demonstration-effect externality, the diffusion rate may be slower than is socially optimal.

A second alternative enables suppliers of technology to play an active role in the diffusion process through their pricing and advertising decisions. Suppliers may over- or under-advertise relative to the ideal. A firm with a monopoly on a new technology will tend to under-advertise. This result could be reversed if the respective characteristics of marginal and average customers differ, if persuasive rather than informative advertising is involved or if close substitutes are available at prices above marginal cost.

A third alternative is for potential adopters to play an active role in the diffusion process. Potential users may differ in their adoption costs. Those with lower adoption costs should be among the earlier adopters. If adoption costs are fixed in part with respect to the amount of technology adopted, larger users may be earlier adopters than smaller ones. This depends on the extent to which adoption experience is transferable and, if transferable, on the extent to which it is appropriable (see below). There may also be strategic factors at play. If the adoption of a new technology were to lead to a shift in market shares and oligopoly rents, the rate and incidence of adoption could be excessive as a consequence.

THE COMPLEMENTARITY OF INNOVATION AND DIFFUSION

TO UNDERSTAND THE ECONOMICS OF TECHNOLOGY DIFFUSION it is helpful to understand the relationship between innovation and diffusion. At one level, that relationship is obvious: without innovation, there would be nothing to diffuse. The relationship is more subtle than that, however, because innovation and diffusion are part of the same process. David (1993) has argued that access to the existing stock of technical information takes on increasing importance as innovation becomes more a matter of integrating and recombining existing scientific and technological findings. David emphasizes what he calls the "distribution power" of an economy, which, in this context, is simply the ability of innovative organizations to make use of the inventory of scientific and technological findings. It is partly a matter of awareness and partly a matter of negotiating terms of access when the knowledge involved is proprietary.

A recurring theme in the innovation literature is that innovation is frequently a joint process involving suppliers and potential customers (Rosenberg, 1982; Von Hippel, 1986; and McFetridge, 1993). Early studies emphasized feedbacks from users as a source of improvements in existing technologies. Recent studies have highlighted the importance of collaboration throughout the innovative process between suppliers and potential leading-edge users (Von Hippel, 1986; Midgely, Morrison and Roberts, 1992; and Carlsson and Jacobsson, 1994).

Others have argued that investing in innovation yields an ability to adopt outside technologies as a by-product. The joint-product nature of the return on R&D investment has been emphasized in empirical work by Cohen and Levinthal (1989). Similarly, Geroski, Machin and Van Reenen (1993) distinguish between the marginal rate of return on a specific innovation and the superior profitability, on average, of firms with a demonstrated ability to innovate. The latter could be attributable, in part, to a superior ability to make use of the knowledge of others. The implication of the argument that an investment in innovation also yields returns in the form of adoption capabilities is that this complementarity results in more of both. Innovation can promote diffusion, and *vice versa*.

THE SUBSTITUTABILITY OF INNOVATION AND DIFFUSION

WHILE INNOVATION AND DIFFUSION ARE COMPLEMENTARY in the sense that they are part of the same process, from another perspective they are substitutes. In order to provide an incentive to innovate, it may be necessary to charge a (marginal) price for the use of innovations that exceeds the (marginal) cost of disseminating them. This inhibits diffusion. Specifically, both end-users and follow-on innovators willing to pay the marginal cost would not be served. Thus there is a trade-off both between innovation and diffusion among end-users and between initial and follow-on innovation.

EMPIRICAL EVIDENCE ON DIFFUSION

DIFFUSION IN STUDIES OF RATES OF RETURN ON INNOVATION

A PARTIAL MEASURE OF THE CONTRIBUTION OF INNOVATIVE ACTIVITY to economic growth is the social rate of return on R&D, which is typically inferred from a statistical relationship between current and past R&D expenditures and total factor productivity (TFP). The vast majority of rate-of-return studies do not address the issue of diffusion at all. In some cases, that is because they do not have to. In pure cross-section studies, for example, the estimated rate of return on R&D is an equilibrium rate of return.

In time-series or pooled time-series/cross-section studies, there is a distinction between the impact and equilibrium effects of R&D on TFP. As a consequence, diffusion does or should matter, but this is seldom reflected in the specification of these models because they generally assume that an increase in the stock of R&D capital in one year exerts its full effect on TFP the following year.[5] Studies specified in rate-of-return form generally assume that an increase in the annual flow of R&D expenditures exerts its full effect on TFP the following year.[6]

The extent to which econometric studies of the relationship between R&D and TFP measure the social rate of return on R&D depends on the level of aggregation and on the extent to which they take "own" and outside R&D into account. Firm-level studies of own-R&D effects yield estimates of the private rate of return on R&D. Industry-level studies of own-R&D yield rate-of-return estimates that include intra-industry spillovers as well as the private rate of return. Griliches (1991) suggests that the respective diffusion patterns of private and spillover benefits are likely to differ. This implies that the lag structure of the relationship between either the stock or the flow of R&D and TFP should be allowed to vary between own and outside R&D with the level of aggregation. Again, the standard practice is to ignore potential differences in diffusion lags.[7]

The studies that do address the issue of diffusion lags take a number of different approaches. Some make use of estimates of diffusion lags found by others. For example Ulrich, Furtan and Schmitz (1986) assume, on the basis of earlier work by Evenson and others, that the first effects of R&D expenditures on malting barley are observed seven years after these expenditures are made.[8]

Other studies attempt to estimate the rate of diffusion simultaneously with the rate of return on R&D. Frequently, they take the approach of adopting the lag structure that maximizes the partial correlation between TFP and current and past R&D. This approach effectively assumes that the null hypothesis of a zero effect of R&D on TFP *should* be rejected and chooses the lag structure that does this most convincingly. That same approach has been adopted by a number of authors estimating the social rate of return on government agricultural R&D (Nagy and Furtan, 1984; Widmer, Fox and Brinkman, 1988; Harbasz, Fox and Brinkman, 1988; and Haque, Fox and Brinkman, 1989).

CHARACTERISTICS OF EARLY ADOPTERS OF INDUSTRIAL TECHNOLOGIES: RECENT CANADIAN EVIDENCE

ONE STRAND OF THE EMPIRICAL LITERATURE attempts to distinguish the characteristics of early adopters of specific new industrial technologies. This literature addresses the question whether earlier adopters have systematic adoption cost advantages over later ones. If, for example, there are indivisibilities in technology adoption, larger establishments will have a cost advantage over smaller ones. If adoption experience is transferable across establishments and at least partially appropriable, multi-establishment enterprises may have an adoption cost advantage over their single-establishment counterparts. If adoption experience is either not transferable or transferable but not appropriable, multi-establishment enterprises would not have an adoption cost advantage over single establishments.

The possibility that adoption experience is transferable and not fully appropriable suggests that there may be a diffusion externality. This would take the form of a demonstration effect and imply that later adopters should somehow compensate earlier adopters.

The empirical evidence regarding the existence of a demonstration-effect externality is ambiguous. There are a variety of empirical results, which are open to more than one interpretation. For example, a finding that, other things being equal, establishments owned by multi-establishment enterprises are not earlier adopters than establishments owned by single-establishment enterprises may imply that adoption experience:

- is not transferable;
- is transferable but not appropriable; or

- is transferable and appropriable, and can be purchased from outside specialists (such as consulting engineers).

In his study, McFetridge (1992, Tables 10-13) found that, other things being equal, the probability of using a given advanced manufacturing technology did not increase with multi-establishment scale. More recently, Baldwin and Diverty (1995, Table 3) have found that, other things being equal, the probability of an establishment using at least one of 22 advanced manufacturing technologies does not increase with multi-establishment scale. With respect to specific advanced manufacturing technologies, multi-establishment scale exerts a positive influence in only one instance – advanced communications and inspection technologies. This may, however, be more a matter of the applicability of the technologies than of the transferability of adoption experience.

Baldwin and Diverty (1995, Table 4) have also investigated the effect of multi-establishment scale on the number of advanced manufacturing technologies in use in a given establishment. They have found that the number of technologies is greater in establishments owned by larger enterprises. Other contributing factors include establishment growth, establishment scale, foreign ownership, and the fact that the establishment operates in an innovative industrial sector. The finding that establishments operating in innovative industries are more likely to be early adopters is consistent with the argument that the ability to innovate is also the ability to adopt.[9]

Baldwin, Gray and Johnson (1995) also uncover evidence pertaining to the inter-establishment transferability and appropriability of know-how. They find that, other things being equal, the probability that an establishment offers training to its employees does not increase with either establishment or domestic multi-establishment scale. The implication is either that training is not transferable or, if transferable, that it is not appropriable. If the latter were true, however, it would raise the question of why any training at all is provided.

INTELLECTUAL PROPERTY AND TECHNOLOGY DIFFUSION

POSSIBLE LINKAGES

AT THE MOST FUNDAMENTAL LEVEL, INTELLECTUAL PROPERTY RIGHTS promote diffusion by promoting innovation. If there is no innovation, there is nothing to diffuse. As is argued above, there are also complementarities between innovation and diffusion. In cases of user/supplier collaboration, innovation and diffusion occur together, at least for leading-edge users. Moreover, the knowledge accumulated through innovative activity can also be used to add value to the knowledge of others. At the same time, the capacity to innovate is also the capacity to make productive use of the knowledge of others. In encouraging innovation, intellectual property facilitates diffusion.

Intellectual property also influences the diffusion process itself. First, there is the disclosure requirement. In return for patent protection, a patentee must disclose his invention, and the disclosure must be sufficiently detailed to allow the invention to be reproduced. Using the patent, it may be possible to make non-infringing imitations and follow-on improvement inventions.[10]

The existence of a property right also facilitates market transactions in knowledge. If market exchange is to occur, rights must be defined and they must be enforceable.[11] The principal barrier to the sale of knowledge is that it must be disclosed to a potential buyer if it is to be evaluated but, once it has been disclosed, the buyer may not have any reason to pay for it. If the knowledge involved is protected by an intellectual property right, the buyer can be enjoined from using it until he has paid for it. Further protection against opportunism on the part of the buyer may take the form of field-of-use restrictions, "grantbacks," and best-effort clauses in licensing agreements. Protection against opportunism by the seller can take the form of contingent or running royalties, post-expiry royalties, and various forms of exclusivity.

Intellectual property rights or trade secrecy protection may also facilitate the transfer of tacit or uncodified knowledge. If, for example, the tacit knowledge involved is specific to the exploitation of a patent, the patent effectively protects that knowledge, which can be transferred under a patent licence. As for trade secrecy, it provides protection for tacit knowledge with broader uses.

The existence of exclusive rights may also inhibit diffusion. A familiar argument is that since the marginal cost of using existing knowledge is virtually zero, attempts by holders of intellectual property rights to extract positive prices for their inventions or creations result in a wasteful under-utilization of the latter. In this case, innovation and diffusion are substitutes. A stronger property right induces additional innovation but does so at the cost of restricting the diffusion of inframarginal innovations both to end-users and to follow-on innovators. The trade-off between innovation and diffusion among end-users lies at the heart of the Nordhaus (1969) optimal-patent-term model and its successors. More recently, the optimal-patent literature has focused on the trade-off between initial and follow-on innovation. This literature is discussed in Acheson and McFetridge (1996).

Of course, the efficient dissemination of knowledge requires only that the price to the *marginal* user be zero. Many pricing techniques allow the recoupment of the costs of innovative or creative activity from infra-marginal users. In this case, there is no tension between innovation and diffusion. In a neoclassical context, the trade-off remains only to the extent that price discrimination is costly or is otherwise ruled out.

The proponents of the evolutionary approach argue that the holders of intellectual property rights may simply not be aware of, or may not appreciate, all the possible uses of their innovations and will neither pursue them nor allow them to be pursued by others (Merges and Nelson, 1990). Under these circumstances, the ability of the holders of intellectual property rights to enjoin unauthorized use of their property, together with a refusal to license it, would inhibit both diffusion and follow-on innovation.

INTELLECTUAL PROPERTY AND THE
INTERNATIONAL DIFFUSION OF TECHNOLOGY

THE ROLE OF INTELLECTUAL PROPERTY in facilitating the international diffusion of technology has been the subject of considerable controversy. Much of the debate has centered around the question whether it is in the interest of individual countries, particularly developing countries, to maintain and enforce intellectual property rights. It has been argued that for countries that are essentially technology users, it is preferable to use the artistic creations and technological innovations of other countries without compensation – that is, to "free-ride."

It is argued in response that the recognition of intellectual property rights improves the access of using countries to the international pool of technology. One line of argument is that the maintenance of a national intellectual property system stimulates domestic innovation. This, in turn, serves to improve the ability of domestic firms to adapt and assimilate foreign technologies. There are two reasons for this. First, the capacity to innovate is also the capacity either to adopt or to imitate. The greater is the domestic innovative capability, the greater is the portion of the international technology pool that can profitably be applied domestically and the greater is the bargaining leverage of domestic importers (because they can credibly threaten to develop non-infringing imitations). Second, in the absence of domestic intellectual property protection, there may be no incentive to expend resources to adapt foreign technologies to domestic conditions.

A second line of argument is that technology simply will not be transferred to countries with weak or non-existent intellectual property regimes. There is some empirical evidence that this is the case (Primo Braga, 1990, p. 82; Mansfield, 1994). Mansfield (1994) finds that a significant fraction of U.S. firms are reluctant to transfer their newest and most effective technologies to affiliates or licensees in countries with weak intellectual property rights. Among the countries regarded as having the weakest property right regimes are India, Nigeria, Thailand, and Taiwan. Frischtak (1995, p. 208) concludes that, while there has been little or no relationship historically between the characteristics of national intellectual property rights regimes, on the one hand, and trade, technology transfer, and investment flows, on the other, this appears to be changing. Inadequate intellectual property protection is now cited as a serious disincentive to licensing.

This line of argument merits greater scrutiny. In cases where reverse engineering is possible or where the degree of disclosure in the patent is sufficient to allow imitation, foreign technology owners cannot control access to their technology, whether they transfer it abroad or not. The ability to deny access is limited to innovations that can only be exploited with additional know-how or other complementary assets. This know-how may be protected by trade secrecy or, in effect, by a patent if it is embedded in a patented invention. The transfer of the technology to countries with weak intellectual property protection could result in the disclosure and loss of this complementary know-how.[12]

It is important to distinguish between general and specific know-how. It may be difficult to deny access even to the most advanced technologies to a country with a high level of general know-how, much of it acquired through the education system. According to Nelson (1990, p. 77):

> . . . while access to technology is now relatively open, it is open only to those who pay the price in terms of making the major investments needed to absorb and master technology. In modern times these include, prominently, investment in education across a relatively broad front and, for a certain fraction of the population, relatively high levels of sophistication in applied sciences and engineering.

Countries with a significant general capacity for reverse engineering may be able to practice what Evenson (1990a) calls "drafting." Countries pursuing a drafting strategy may offer relatively weak intellectual property protection or none at all ("piracy"). According to Evenson (1990a, p. 352):

> . . . countries such as Korea have developed the capacity to copy and reverse engineer recently developed inventions from industrial countries. They are thus able to achieve technology that is [of] high value to them at low cost. An increase in investment upstream is quickly reflected in increased technology purchases (and pirating) and own R&D for firms in the draft.

Evenson argues that countries "in the draft" have no interest in strong intellectual property rights until they become significant technology exporters. The issue is somewhat more complex than that, however. It turns on both domestic and international factors. Three domestic factors must be considered: 1) the extent to which the requisite technologies allow reverse engineering; 2) the role of domestic intellectual property rights in providing an incentive to develop imitative and adaptive capabilities; and 3) the need for a specialized domestic innovative capability – for example, to develop medicines to treat indigenous diseases. If reverse engineering is technically feasible and if significant imitative, adaptive, and specialized innovative capabilities can be developed through the public innovation system, as Nelson suggests, Evenson may be correct. However, while the South Korean experience may support Evenson's argument, the Canadian experience (described below) does not.

There are also international considerations in the form of the threat of retaliation by countries whose innovations have been reverse-engineered. This may involve the imposition, threatened or real, of retaliatory duties on imports from reverse-engineering (drafting) countries. For example, the threat by the

United States to impose retaliatory duties on imports from South Korea is said to have been instrumental in inducing the latter to adopt stronger intellectual property laws.[13] Individual firms or groups of firms may also retaliate by refusing to invest in countries that do not protect their intellectual property. They might also promise to invest more in return for stronger intellectual property protection. The Canadian experience (discussed later on) with respect to pharmaceuticals is a case in point.

It is useful to consider the bargaining strategies available to firms that are dissatisfied with the degree of local protection of their intellectual property. They can deny access to technologies that cannot readily be reverse-engineered. They may also be able to deny, or at least impede, access to any complementary assets necessary to exploit their technologies.

Frischtak (1995) notes that the pursuit of a drafting strategy generally involves the provision of a differentiated bundle of intellectual property rights rather than no rights at all. This differentiated bundle may include "petty patents" and plant breeders' rights, as well as compulsory patent licensing, specified exclusions from patent eligibility, and the limitation of protection to either the product or the process.

INTELLECTUAL PROPERTY AND DIFFUSION: SOME EVIDENCE

PATENT DISCLOSURES AS A SOURCE OF TECHNOLOGICAL INFORMATION

THE PATENT SYSTEM IS INTENDED TO ENCOURAGE INVENTORS to publicize their inventions rather than keep them secret. The description of the invention in the patent application is intended to assist others in developing non-infringing applications and improvements. There have been questions, however, about whether patent disclosures are generally sufficient to allow replication of the invention involved. The evidence is that patent applications have not been one of the more important sources of technological information. Levin et al. (1987) found that patent disclosures rank sixth among seven potential sources of technical information they investigated. More important sources are independent R&D, reverse engineering, licensing, hiring employees of the inventing firm, and publications and trade fairs.[14]

There is survey evidence suggesting that the examination of patent applications is among the least important sources of information for Canadian high-technology firms (Industry, Science and Technology Canada, 1989) but is more important for medium- and low-technology firms. While this may reflect a difference in the industrial composition of these two groups, the reason may also be that for many high-technology firms, the pace of change is such that by the time a patent application is published, the technology described in it has been superseded.

For medium-technology firms, patent applications may be a potentially more fruitful source of information. This may also be true of firms in less developed countries. For example, Deolalikar and Evenson (1990) have found what they interpret as a disclosure effect of U.S. patenting on the patenting activity of Indian firms.

SOURCES OF INNOVATION IN GROWING SMALL AND MEDIUM-SIZED ENTERPRISES IN CANADA

BALDWIN (1994) SURVEYED 1,480 GROWING SMALL AND MEDIUM-SIZED enterprises (GSMEs) in Canada. He defined small and medium-sized enterprises (SMEs) in general as having fewer than 500 employees and less than $100 million in assets in 1984, and "growing" SMEs as firms that had experienced growth in employment, sales, and assets between 1984 and 1988.

The respondents to Baldwin's survey answered a lengthy questionnaire on the sources of their growth and on their growth strategies. A general conclusion reached by Baldwin is that:

- The respondents see managerial skills as the most important reason for their growth; they see service levels, flexibility, and quality as the most important sources of their competitive advantage.
- Innovative activity is much more pervasive than formal R&D among GSMEs.
- The ability to adopt new technologies is more important than an R&D capability as a source of growth for GSMEs.
- Technologies protected by intellectual property are not important sources of innovation for GSMEs.

As far as sources of innovation are concerned, the most highly ranked are, in decreasing order, customers, management, suppliers, marketing, and competitors. The least important sources on the list are Canadian and foreign patents, licences, and trademarks. This result holds for both product and process innovations, and it also holds if only the responses of the GSMEs for which each source of innovation is applicable are taken into account. In other words, the low ranking of patents as sources of innovation is not associated with their limited applicability. Even GSMEs that regard patents as a potential source of innovation rank them last in that respect (Baldwin, 1994, Table 3.4).

Baldwin also divides his sample into more successful and less successful firms on the basis of changes in market share. He finds that both groups rank Canadian and foreign patents last as sources for product and process innovations they make (Baldwin, 1994, Tables 3.10, 3.11). Respondents were asked to rank nine factors with respect to their importance as sources of growth. The GSMEs ranked management skills most highly as a source of growth. This is followed by skilled labour, marketing capability and access to markets. The ability to adopt technology was ranked seventh as a source of growth in all sectors although, in the manufacturing and business service sectors, there is little to choose between skilled labour, marketing capability, access to markets, cost of capital, access to capital, and technology adoption in terms of their absolute rankings. A formal R&D capability ranked eighth of nine factors as a source of growth (Baldwin, 1994, Table 1). For GSMEs as a group, the ability to adopt technology is considerably more important than the ability to perform R&D, but neither is among the more important sources of growth. For GSMEs in the manufacturing and business service sectors, technology adoption and R&D capabilities are also closer both to each other and to other sources of growth in their absolute rankings.

INTELLECTUAL PROPERTY AND DIFFUSION IN THE INNOVATION SURVEY

IN ANOTHER STUDY, BALDWIN (1995) REPORTS the intellectual property-related results of a 1993 survey of 1,595 large firms and 1,088 small firms with respect to their innovative activity. Some of these results have a bearing on the role of intellectual property in the technology diffusion process.

First, firms that had introduced major innovations were asked whether these innovations were supported in part under a transfer arrangement of some sort. The answers showed that 31 percent were supported by acquired technology and 20 percent by technology acquired under a licensing or transfer agreement; 6 percent involved the acquisition of the right to use specified patents, and 6.4 percent the right to use trade secrets or know-how. It is reasonable to conclude that 6 percent of the major innovations made by respondents to the survey were based on, or at least drew upon, externally acquired, patented technology.

SURVEY EVIDENCE ON INTELLECTUAL PROPERTY AND DIFFUSION: CONCLUSIONS

A NUMBER OF INFERENCES ARE SUGGESTED by recent Canadian survey evidence. First, patent disclosures are generally not an important source of technological information. Second, for growing small and medium-sized enterprises, access to technology is not high on the list of sources of growth and patented technology accounts for a relatively small portion of technology acquired for purposes of subsequent innovation. Third, a relatively small proportion of major technological innovations in Canada are based on externally acquired, patented technology. Note, however, that this does not necessarily imply that patented technologies are not important or potentially important as a source of follow-on innovation in some industries or lines of business.

COMPULSORY LICENSING IN CANADA

THERE ARE PROVISIONS FOR THE COMPULSORY LICENSING OF PATENTS in the *Patent Act* and of integrated circuit topographies, copyright, trademarks, and patents in the *Competition Act*. The following discussion focuses on this aspect in each act.

The *Patent Act* provides for compulsory licensing in the event of patent abuse, which has historically been interpreted as a failure by the patent holder either to "work" (i.e., exploit) the patent locally or to allow others to do so. Until 1993, the *Patent Act* also provided for compulsory licences to manufacture patented food products and to manufacture or import patented medicines. The *Competition Act* provides for the compulsory licensing of patents that have been used in some anticompetitive fashion.

COMPULSORY LICENCES FOR LOCAL WORKING

CANADIAN PATENT LAW PROVIDES FOR COMPULSORY LICENCES in cases of patent abuse. Patent abuse is deemed, in sections 65 (c) to (f) of the *Patent Act*, to have occurred under the following circumstances:[15]

- if the demand for the patented article in Canada is not being met to an adequate extent and on reasonable terms;
- if, by reason of the refusal of the patentee to grant a licence or licences on reasonable terms, the trade or industry of Canada, the trade of any person or class of persons trading in Canada, or the establishment of any new trade or industry in Canada is prejudiced and it is in the public interest that a licence or licences should be granted;
- if a trade or industry in Canada or any person or class of persons engaged therein is unfairly prejudiced by the conditions attached by the patentee to the purchase, hire, licence, or use of the patented article or to the using or working of the patented process; or
- if it is shown that the existence of the patent, being a patent for an invention relating to a process involving the use of materials not protected by the patent or for an invention relating to a substance produced by such a process, has been utilized by the patentee so as unfairly to prejudice in Canada the manufacture, use, or sale of any materials.

Prior to their repeal in 1993, patent abuse was also deemed to have occurred under sections 65(a) and (b):

- if the patented invention, being one capable of being worked within Canada, is not being worked within Canada on a commercial scale, and no satisfactory reason can be given for that non-working; or

- if the working of the invention within Canada on a commercial scale is being prevented or hindered by the importation from abroad of the patented article by the patentee or persons claiming under him, by persons directly or indirectly purchasing from him, or by other persons against whom the patentee is not taking or has not taken any proceedings for infringement.

There have been relatively few applications for compulsory licences under section 65 (or its predecessor, section 67). The Economic Council of Canada (1971, p. 68) reported that between 1935 and 1970 there had been 53 applications for licences under this section. Of these, 11 had resulted in licences being granted, 9 had been refused, 32 had been withdrawn or abandoned, and one was pending.

Since 1970 there have been 43 applications for compulsory licences under section 65, the last such application having been filed in June 1989. Of those 43 applications, 6 have resulted in compulsory licences, 6 have been refused, 25 have been withdrawn or deemed abandoned, and 6 are outstanding.[16] All licences granted have been non-exclusive. With respect to the 25 cases that have been withdrawn or deemed abandoned, the Canadian Intellectual Property Office (CIPO) was informed that the parties had reached a "voluntary" agreement in four cases.

The last compulsory licence issued under section 65 (or section 67) was in 1984. With respect to the six compulsory licences that have been issued, the form of patent abuse found in four cases was a failure to work it in Canada on a sufficient scale.[17] This form of abuse was eliminated from the *Patent Act* pursuant to the implementation of the North American Free Trade Agreement (NAFTA) in 1993.

COMPULSORY LICENCES FOR LOCAL WORKING: MOTIVATION AND IMPLICATIONS

IN TERMS OF EITHER THE NUMBER OF APPLICATIONS or the number of licences granted, compulsory licensing under section 65 has had almost no impact on the use of patented technologies in Canada. This may be because a licence is of little value in itself without the associated know-how. The amount of information disclosed in the patent may not be sufficient to enable it to be worked commercially; and unless the licence is exclusive, the patentee has little or no incentive to provide the requisite know-how. In this case, compulsory licences provide access rather than additional knowledge, as noted in the *Working Paper on Patent Law Reform* (Consumer and Corporate Affairs, 1976, pp. 105-6):

Such provisions are more likely to be of relevance only to an experienced applicant who is anxious to adopt the new technology and has the capability and initiative to do so on his own without cooperation from the patentee. Compulsory licences provide access to inventions but are not an effective vehicle for full technology transfer.

The apparent lack of interest in compulsory licences for local working may also imply that patentees are seldom misinformed about the commercial prospects for local working.[18] If they are not working the patent in Canada, it is probably not profitable for a licensee to work it either.

An alternate view is that the actual number of applications for licences substantially understates the influence of this section of the Act. Section 65 strengthens the hand of potential users in dealing with the patentee. When threatened with an infringement suit, a user can file or threaten to file an application for a compulsory licence on the grounds of patent abuse.[19] According to CIPO officials, many of the applications filed under section 65 are apparently in response to allegations of infringement by the patentee. The parties generally settle, but settlements may be more favourable to users than they would be if there were no compulsory licensing provisions. The threat of applying for a compulsory licence may benefit many more domestic licensees as well as result in more extensive licensing.

That this may result in private benefits to domestic licensees is evident. The question is whether this "surplus" is increased in addition to being redistributed. Although section 65(2)(c) allows for it, compulsory licences have generally not been sought on the grounds that the technology is not available in Canada on reasonable terms.[20] Thus it would seem that Canadians already have the benefit of the patented technology both as disclosed in the patent and as embodied as goods and services sold in Canada.

Additional surplus resulting from local working might take the form of additional domestic spillover benefits derived either from the local commercial exploitation of the patent or from local follow-on innovation that builds on the patented technology. Spillover benefits may take the form of transferable learning by employees or suppliers of the licensee, or of consumer benefits resulting from follow-on innovations. These local spillover benefits need not come at the expense of the countries in which the patentee would otherwise have worked the patent.[21]

It was the view of the Economic Council of Canada (1971, p. 91) that domestic working was essential for technology diffusion:

> All patents should normally become eligible for an automatic non-exclusive licence to manufacture in Canada five years after the application of the patent . . . One purpose of this recommendation is to give Canadian producers who believe themselves capable of working a Canadian patent and competing effectively with it in the market, while paying a reasonable, incentive-maintaining royalty to the patentee, the opportunity to do so. This would add to the effective dissemination of technology in Canadian industry because it would encourage the working of a wider range of patents in Canada.

The authors of the *Working Paper on Patent Law Reform* took a similar view. They explicitly rejected mercantilist and naive Keynesian rationales for local working. Instead, they saw local working as a means of learning (Consumer and Corporate Affairs Canada, 1976, pp. 102-3): "By encouraging local working of inventions (preferably under license to Canadian enterprises), Canadian industry will have an opportunity through increased exposure and experience with new technology to develop its technological capabilities."

While compulsory licences for local working may have been intended as a means of promoting domestic industrial learning by doing, they were likely to have been most useful in instances where the potential local licensee was already in possession of sufficient learning (know-how) to undertake either commercial exploitation or follow-on innovation, or where little know-how beyond the patent disclosure itself was required. That is, the situations in which compulsory licences were most effective were precisely those in which the *initial* learning benefits to the local licensee would have been the smallest. Nevertheless, compulsory licensing may have facilitated *subsequent* spillover learning both from local commercial exploitation and from follow-on innovation.

COMPULSORY LICENSING OF INVENTIONS FOR THE PREPARATION OF FOODS AND MEDICINES

UNTIL 1987, PATENT PROTECTION OF FOODS AND MEDICINES IN CANADA took the form of a patent on the specific *process* that produced them. This concept of product protection by process protection was taken from the British *Patent Act* of 1919. Britain had apparently adopted the approach of protecting the underlying process rather than the product in order to weaken the patent position of German chemical producers in the British market. The idea was to allow product imitations as long as they made use of a process that differed from that of the patentee. While this policy apparently contributed to the development of the British chemical industry, its main effect in Canada was to induce the inventor of a new chemical entity to take out a patent on each of the possible processes by which it could be produced. The result was the same as would have been achieved with a product patent, although a great deal more costly.

Between 1923 and 1993, Canadian patent legislation provided for compulsory licences to manufacture foods produced with a patented process. This provision was embodied in section 41(3) and most recently section 39(3) of the *Patent Act*.

Between 1923 and 1969, section 41(3) also provided for compulsory licences to manufacture medicines produced with patented processes. Between 1969 and 1993, section 41(4) and subsequently 39(4) provided for compulsory licences to manufacture *or import* medicines produced with patented processes.

Between 1935 and 1969, there were 49 applications for licences to manufacture either foods or medicines. Of these, 22 were granted, 23 were withdrawn, and 4 were refused (Economic Council of Canada, 1971, p. 70). Most of these applications involved medicines, and a number of them were the subject of protracted litigation.

Since 1969 there have been 12 applications under section 41(3) or section 39(3) for licences to manufacture foods produced with a patented process. Licences have been granted in four cases, two for animal feed, and two for aspartame. The last licence granted was in 1989. In 1993, the provision for compulsory licences to manufacture food was repealed pursuant to the implementation of the NAFTA.

Between 1969 and 1992 there were 1,030 applications for compulsory licences, under section 41(4) and subsequently section 39(4), to import or manufacture medicines produced under patented processes. Licences were granted in 613 cases. Details are presented in Table 1.

TABLE 1

LICENCE APPLICATIONS AND GRANTS UNDER SECTIONS 41(4) AND 39(4) OF THE PATENT ACT, 1969-92

	Applications Filed	Licenses Granted
1969	45	3
1970	31	52
1971	20	24
1972	16	21
1973	19	19
1974	26	19
1975	24	17
1976	22	26
1977	28	33
1978	25	16
1979	23	19
1980	37	9
1981	18	15
1982	2	11
1983	43	13
1984	77	7
1985	132	54
1986	22	62
1987	26	68
1988	14	33
1989	14	26
1990	26	10
1991	53	20
1992	292	36

Source: Canadian Intellectual Property Office, unofficial tabulation.

CANADIAN EXPERIENCE WITH COMPULSORY LICENCES TO IMPORT PATENTED MEDICINES

THE POLICY OF AWARDING COMPULSORY LICENCES to import patented medicines was extremely controversial. The relevant sections of the *Patent Act* were amended in 1987 and then repealed in 1993 (retroactively to 1991).

Events during the period 1969-83 were examined in detail by the Commission of Inquiry on the Pharmaceutical Industry (Eastman Commission), which reported in 1985. The Eastman Commission found that compulsory licensing reduced the cost to consumers of the drugs so licensed by $211 million in 1983 and concluded that compulsory licensing was "an effective component of an appropriate patent policy for the pharmaceutical industry" (p. xix). The Commission also concluded, however, that the 4 percent royalty rate paid by compulsory licensees was insufficient to compensate patentees for their R&D expenditures and that patentees should be granted "a short period of market exclusivity" of four years between the receipt of regulatory approval to market a new drug (Notice of Compliance) and the entry of compulsory licensees.

The Commission recommended that compulsory licensees pay a 14 percent royalty rate. This was intended to compensate patentees for the 10 percent worldwide average R&D/sales ratio in the pharmaceutical industry plus promotional expenditures amounting to 4 percent of sales. These licence fees were to be paid into a fund from which patentees would draw according to a formula based on their Canadian R&D intensity and on the sales of their drugs by compulsory licensees. Under the Commission's approach, patentees could "earn" higher royalties by locating more of their R&D in Canada.[22] The marginal incentive to relocate R&D in Canada was potentially significant. It would have been equivalent to the prevailing R&D tax credit for a patentee with 6 percent of its sales under compulsory licence.

Compulsory licensing led to the development of a domestic generic-drug industry of sorts. Fine chemicals were largely imported from infringing sources. The existence of generic alternatives, together with formularies and substitution rules, reduced drug costs for consumers. Generic-drug pricing was oligopolistic, and generic-drug prices in Canada tended to be above prices of equivalent off-patent drugs in the United States.[23] In some cases, the benefits of generic alternatives were captured by pharmacists (Anis, 1989, ch. II).

Patentees also responded strategically to the expectation of being subject to compulsory licensing. For example, Corvari (1991) found that compulsory licensing reduced the ratio of informative advertising (e.g., in medical journals) to persuasive advertising.

The 1987 amendments to the *Patent Act* were embodied in Bill C-22. Insofar as compulsory licensing was concerned, this legislation was in the Canadian tradition of regulatory taxation and cross-subsidization (McFetridge and Lall, 1991). It had the following provisions:

- Patentees were guaranteed 10 years' protection (market exclusivity) against the exercise of compulsory licences to import.
- Patentees were guaranteed seven years' protection against the exercise of compulsory licences to manufacture in Canada.
- Patented medicines developed in Canada were eligible for protection from compulsory licensing entirely (section 41.16).
- The prices of patented medicines were to be regulated by a new Patented Medicines Prices Review Board. The Board was also mandated to report annually on the Canadian R&D expenditures of manufacturers of patented pharmaceuticals.

The Pharmaceutical Manufacturers Association of Canada (PMAC), the industry association representing the patentees, also undertook to raise its Canadian R&D/sales ratio to 8 percent by 1991 and to the worldwide level of roughly 10 percent by 1996. The PMAC had largely fulfilled this commitment by 1992 when the Canadian R&D/sales ratio of its members reached 9.8 percent (see Table 2). As Table 3 indicates, some of the multinationals increased their Canadian R&D by a large percentage. It has also been noted, however, that with a few exceptions – Merck Frosst and Connaught being the most prominent – these expenditures constitute a very small fraction of parent R&D and that they remain below the minimum efficient scale for in-house R&D in this industry.[24]

With Notices of Compliance (signifying the regulatory approval of a drug) being granted after an average of 7 years, the market exclusivity guaranteed in Bill C-22 implied a patent term of approximately 17 years in the case of

TABLE 2

R&D EXPENDITURES IN THE CANADIAN PHARMACEUTICAL INDUSTRY, 1988-95

	R&D Expenditures as a Percentage of Sales: Patentees	R&D Expenditures as a Percentage of Sales: PMAC Members	Basic Research as a Percentage of Current R&D Expenditures
1988	6.1	6.5	19.1
1989	8.2	8.1	23.4
1990	9.3	9.2	27.2
1991	9.7	9.6	26.5
1992	9.9	9.8	26.4
1993	10.6	10.7	25.3
1994	11.3	11.6	21.9
1995	11.8	12.5	22.2

Source: Patented Medicines Prices Review Board (1996), pp. 24-25.

TABLE 3

CANADIAN R&D EXPENDITURES OF MULTINATIONAL PHARMACEUTICAL
COMPANIES, 1986-94
C$ MILLIONS

Companies	1986 R&D	1988 R&D	1990 R&D (Rank)	1992 R&D (Rank)	1994 R&D (Rank)
Glaxo Canada Ltd.	1.3	6.9	19.0 (37)	27.8 (29)	33.0 (27)
Astra Pharma Inc.	2.4	3.7	7.9 (71)	12.8 (61)	20.8 (47)
Miles Canada Inc.	1.3	3.1	9.9 (59)	13.4 (56)	20.3 (50)
Ciba-Geigy Canada Ltd.	6.7	9.4	14.0 (44)	18.7 (44)	18.0 (55)
Sandoz Canada Inc.	2.5[a]	5.5	8.3 (68)	12.0 (64)	15.7 (64)

Note: Ranking is determined by the firm's position among the top 100 industrial R&D spenders in Canada.

a   1987.

Sources: *Financial Post*, Special Report on Research and Development, 1986 and 1988; *The Globe and Mail*, Report on Business, R&D Top 100, 1990 and 1992; *The Globe and Mail*, Report on Business, R&D Top 50, 1994, Research Money, June 1995.

compulsory licences to import and 14 years in the case of compulsory licences to manufacture. While they opposed this legislation fiercely, the generic-drug producers continued to seek licences both to import and to manufacture domestically. Being allowed to manufacture domestically under compulsory licence roughly 14 years from the date of application in Canada, these producers were also in a position to export these medicines to the United States as they became off-patent in that country. Corresponding U.S. patents typically expire two years prior to the expiry of the Canadian patent.

Although the provisions for limited compulsory licensing were to remain in place for 10 years before being reviewed, the government introduced further amendments to the *Patent Act* in 1992; known as Bill C-91, they were proclaimed law in 1993. They eliminated compulsory licensing retroactively to December 1991, ostensibly in order to conform to the draft Trade-related Intellectual Property Rights (TRIPs) agreement of December 1991 and to bring

Canada into line with other developed countries, none of which were engaging in compulsory licensing of medicines.[25] The government also saw the presence of a strong property right as a means of attracting R&D investment. In his deposition to the Senate Standing Committee on Banking, Trade and Finance (Canada, Senate, 28:124; 21/1/93), the Minister of Industry and Science testified that:

> . . . the pharmaceutical industry is in the process of restructuring globally. It has reoriented its operations to serve global markets more efficiently and selects the most competitive business environment it can find for new facilities . . . . The degree of patent protection provided for innovations is the most critical factor. With our current system of compulsory licensing we could not hope to attract these investments.

The government argued that the elimination of compulsory licensing added only three years to the patent protection already provided under Bill C-22. The estimated additional cost to consumers was $129 million over five years.[26] Provincial governments and consumer groups disputed this figure, citing much higher estimates of consumer losses.

The PMAC was joined in its support of Bill C-91 by the university medical and pharmaceutical research community and by several small, Canadian-based, innovative pharmaceutical companies (Allelix, Biochem Pharma, and Quadra Logic) as well as by a long-time Canadian producer of fine chemicals (Raylo). Some of these firms were involved in relationships with multinationals (Quadra Logic with Cyanamid, Biochem Pharma with Glaxo). They maintained that strong domestic patent protection was essential to enable them to raise capital and form alliances. Without strong patents, they argued, discoveries made in Canadian universities would continue their "long tradition" of being exploited elsewhere.

Industrial opposition to Bill C-91 came from the generic-drug producers, the largest of these being Apotex and Novopharm, and from fine-chemical producers operating as compulsory licensees (Delmar, Torcan, Canlac, Apotex Fermentation). The fine-chemical producers had invested in facilities to manufacture patented drugs under compulsory licence in Canada for sale in Canada as well as in the United States and other countries, as the corresponding patents in those countries expired. They were concerned about their loss of "first mover" advantages in U.S. and other foreign generic-drug markets, about what they regarded as the premature repeal of the regime set out under Bill C-22, and about the retroactivity of the legislation. The government pointed to the flood of licence applications (see Table 1) and argued that without retroactivity the effects of compulsory licensing would continue for 10 or more years.

Apotex argued that the government was terminating compulsory licensing just as the regime was about to bear fruit in the form of an innovative domestic drug industry. The scenario, according to Apotex, was that the profits derived from compulsory licences to import were used to finance entry into

TABLE 4

TOP 10 R&D SPENDERS AMONG PHARMACEUTICAL COMPANIES
IN CANADA, 1994

Companies	C$ Millions
Merck Frosst Canada Inc.	103.5
Connaught Laboratories Ltd.	79.0
Apotex Inc.	46.7
Wyeth Ayerst Canada Inc.	35.3
Glaxo Canada Ltd.	33.0
Marion Merrell Dow (Canada) Inc.	31.8
Hoffman LaRoche Ltd.	24.5
Novopharm Ltd.	23.6
Biomira Inc.	23.1
Astra Pharma Inc.	20.8

Source: *The Globe and Mail*, Report on Business, R&D Top 50, Research Money, June 1995.

fine-chemical production and that the experience gained in that area was beginning to be applied to the development and manufacture of new drugs for domestic and foreign markets.[27] Apotex is now the third-largest R&D spender in the Canadian pharmaceutical industry (see Table 4).

As a scenario for a technology diffusion policy, this has some flaws. Almost 20 years of compulsory licensing had elapsed by the time the generic-drug industry moved into fine-chemical production. This movement occurred *after* Bill C-22 reduced the profitability of compulsory licences to import. While some generic-drug companies had progressed towards new-drug development, their achievements were limited both in absolute terms and relative to the small innovative (non-generic) Canadian companies.

THE IMPACT OF COMPULSORY LICENCES TO
IMPORT PATENTED MEDICINES ON INNOVATION AND DIFFUSION

ALTHOUGH ATTEMPTS WERE MADE TO CAST THE DEBATE about both Bills C-22 and C-91 in terms of technological innovation and diffusion, compulsory licensing under section 41(4) and its successor section 39(4) was essentially concerned with the prices paid by end-users (consumers) of patented medicines or by their agents (provincial governments). The protagonists in the debate advanced two competing innovation scenarios, neither of which is compelling although both make eminent sense as political bargains. The generic-drug producers argued that the continuation of compulsory licensing was required to provide them with the cash flow necessary to complete their belated transformation into innovative (R&D-performing and patenting) firms. The patentees argued that the repeal of compulsory licensing was necessary to provide an incentive to locate a larger proportion of their worldwide innovative (R&D) activities in Canada.

The Eastman Commission's cursory comparison of the respective R&D intensities of the pharmaceutical industries in Canada and in other small developed countries implies that, over the first 15 years of its existence, compulsory licensing neither augmented nor diminished Canadian innovative capabilities. Others argue that significant opportunities for the development of an innovative domestic pharmaceutical industry were lost. While the profits of compulsory licensees might have found their way back into new-drug development in Canada, there was no particular reason for them to do so, as pointed by G. Terzakian, president of Raylo Chemicals, in a letter to the Senate Standing Committee on Banking, Trade and Commerce (Canada, Senate, 28:36; 21/1/93):

> When compulsory licensing was introduced, the intention was to help establish a pharmaceutical manufacturing and R&D base in Canada. This in turn would provide employment and reduce drug costs. This sequence of events has not occurred. Over the years the major generic pharmaceutical firms in Canada obtained compulsory licences to offer relatively new products at lower cost by importing them from the cheapest source available world-wide. Rather than create a pharmaceutical manufacturing industry in Canada, they encouraged foreign companies in countries where pirating of patent protection is allowed, to provide them with low-cost products. This proved to be an extremely profitable endeavour for the Canadian generic firms. But it did nothing to encourage the manufacture of these drugs in Canada. In fact, it had the seriously detrimental effect of reducing both such manufacture as well as R&D.

The generic-drug industry, having until that time confined its activities largely to importing active ingredients from countries with no patent protection, began its halting transformation towards innovation and domestic fine-chemical production after Bill C-22 had reduced the profitability of compulsory licences to import and, indeed, had cast the long-term future of compulsory licensing into question. While one company, Apotex, has become a relatively large R&D spender, plans for fine-chemical production depend on the continued ability of Canadian compulsory licensees to be up and running and enter new markets for generic drugs in the United States before U.S.-based producers could get started. Thus the planned evolution of the generic-drug industry towards fine-chemical production owed less to the accumulation of knowledge under compulsory licensing than to a government-guaranteed headstart over foreign generic-drug producers.

Whether the growth in the Canadian R&D expenditures of multinational pharmaceutical companies after Bill C-22 was a direct consequence of the stronger domestic patent regime or merely the fulfilment of a political bargain is debatable. This goes, again, to the issue of whether compulsory licensing had made a Canadian location more vulnerable to technology leakage or reduced the opportunities for local collaboration, and whether Bills C-22 and C-91 remedied this situation. These questions do not appear to have been confronted directly.[28]

Additional Canadian evidence on this issue would be useful. This might take the form of time-series analysis of either Canadian pharmaceutical R&D as a proportion of worldwide R&D or pharmaceutical patents granted to Canadian resident inventors as a proportion of worldwide pharmaceutical patents both before and during compulsory licensing.

Insofar as the international evidence is concerned, studies of the locational determinants of pharmaceutical R&D (Taggart, 1991) find that it is attracted to countries with good pools of scientific personnel and expeditious drug approval processes. It is not clear whether international differences in drug price regulation influence the locational decision. Beyond this, the industry has considerable flexibility to respond to international differences in "political climate" and thus to reward favourable political decisions by host governments and punish unfavourable ones.

The experiences of countries that have changed the amount of patent protection they offer to pharmaceuticals may also be instructive. For example, pharmaceuticals effectively became eligible for patent protection in Italy in 1978 after nearly 40 years of ineligibility. The consequences of this switch in regimes are investigated by Scherer and Weisburst (1995), who find that pharmaceutical R&D spending in Italy did not increase relative to six other developed countries after 1978. They also find that the number of U.S. pharmaceutical patents granted to both Italian firms and Italian affiliates of multinationals increased relative to six other developed countries after 1978. They interpret this as an increase in the propensity to patent rather than as a shift in emphasis from imitative to innovative R&D. They conclude that the availability of domestic patent protection neither increased aggregate pharmaceutical R&D nor made it less imitative.[29]

The consequences of the shift in patent regimes in Italy are also investigated by Challu (1995). He concludes that patent protection served to reduce, rather than increase, the number of new drugs invented in Italy. Using his data on new drugs invented in Italy, one finds that there is an upward trend in new-drug inventions during the period 1966-77 and a downward trend during the period 1978-90, and that the difference is statistically significant.[30] Scherer and Weisburst (1995) note, however, that the invention of new drugs in Italy after 1978 may also have been inhibited by the stringent price controls imposed on the industry at that time.

Correa (1995) surveys anecdotal evidence from a number of countries that changed their intellectual property regimes as applied to pharmaceuticals. He concludes that the elimination of product and process patents on pharmaceuticals in both Brazil and Turkey did not discourage foreign direct investment in the pharmaceutical industries of those countries and that the absence of product patent protection in Argentina did not deter foreign direct investment in that country's pharmaceutical industry. Correa also cites evidence suggesting that the existence of patent protection in Nigeria has not resulted in investment in the pharmaceutical industry in that country.

In an earlier study, Scherer (1977) surveyed the existing evidence on the relationship between the strength of national intellectual property rights and national innovative activity. Much of the evidence involved pharmaceuticals. Scherer concluded that there was "no clear link" between the strength of intellectual property protection and the number of new drugs introduced per dollar of gross domestic product (p. 39).[31] He also cited evidence that new drugs were more frequently introduced in Britain before the United States during the period 1962-74, even though there was compulsory licensing in Britain but not in the United States (p. 42). Scherer noted, however, that the United States introduced more stringent drug-testing regulations during this period, and that this may have had a confounding effect.

While much of the available evidence is dated and leaves something to be desired in terms of experimental design, it does imply that, absent the political bargain to this effect, the limitation and ultimate elimination of compulsory licensing in Canada would not likely have increased the amount of pharmaceutical R&D undertaken in this country. Further evidence as to whether multinationals were responding to an increase in the strength of local property rights or fulfilling a political bargain may be available soon. Being precluded by the NAFTA and the TRIPs agreement from returning to compulsory licensing, the government now has little in the way of sanctions with which to threaten multinationals who return to their earlier practices.[32] However, multinationals may be reluctant to bear further reallocation costs even though there is no particular advantage to a Canadian location.

COMPULSORY LICENSING UNDER SECTION 32 OF THE COMPETITION ACT

THE COMPULSORY LICENSING OF PATENTS, COPYRIGHTS, and registered integrated circuit topographies may also be ordered by the Federal Court of Canada under section 32 of the *Competition Act* if the Court finds that one of those protected rights has been used to unduly restrict competition. The statute also provides for other remedies, including voiding a licence or other agreement pertaining to the use of intellectual property, enjoining the execution of a licence or other agreement, revoking a patent, and expunging a trademark or an integrated circuit topography.

Under section 32, licensing arrangements that are found to lessen competition unduly can be declared void or their execution can be enjoined in whole or in part. No cases brought under section 32 have been reported, but two cases brought under earlier legislation have been settled.[33] These cases, both of which involved Union Carbide, illustrate the problems that competition policy can pose for efficient licensing. The Union Carbide cases involved two sets of patents – the extrusion patents and the printing patents. With regard to the printing patents, the licensing patents at issue were: royalty rates that decreased as volume increased, field-of-use restrictions, no-challenge clauses, and post-expiry restrictions on licensees. The practices at issue with respect to the licensing of the extrusion patents were the imposition of higher royalties on licensees not purchasing resin from the patentee or his nominee, and post-expiry restrictions on licensees.

The apparent concerns of the Director of Investigation (who, as head of the Bureau of Competition Policy, was responsible for the enforcement of the *Competition Act*) in these cases had to do with discrimination against low-volume Canadian licensees, the limitation of export opportunities for Canadian licensees, and the resin-tying arrangement. These concerns are in the Canadian tradition of preoccupations over the terms of local access to foreign technologies. All the licensing practices listed by the Director are potentially surplus-increasing from a global perspective.[34]

The Canadian approach stands in marked contrast to that of the United States. In that country, compulsory licensing has frequently been employed as a remedy for the anticompetitive use of intellectual property. Anticompetitive actions have generally involved some form of cross-licensing of competing patents, of tying, or of post-expiry restrictions. Failure to work or license an invention or creation is not an anticompetitive act in the United States, where no obligation exists either to do either (United States, Department of Justice and Federal Trade Commission, 1995, §2.2). In Canada, compulsory licensing has been used either to induce local working or to reduce the effective term of the Canadian patent (see above). It has yet to be used as a remedy for anticompetitive acts involving intellectual property.

Recently, concerns have been raised in the United States that the refusal to license a patent may be anticompetitive when it allows the patentee to block follow-on research. If follow-on research is impossible without the invention, then the patentee's refusal to license cannot reduce competition below the level that would have prevailed if the patentee had not made the invention in the first place, and his or her actions therefore cannot be anticompetitive. If follow-on research is possible without the patentee's contribution yet the patentee is able to block it, this may be anticompetitive behaviour and compulsory licensing could be a remedy.

A refusal to license those involved in follow-on research may be anticompetitive if the initial patent is overly broad. Some argue that this is true in general. If that is the case, the remedy lies with the intellectual property authorities rather than the competition or antitrust agencies. Patents may be overly broad only in certain instances where the patent examiners have erred. Compulsory licensing could be used in those instances to rectify mistakes made in granting the original patent.

Barton (1995) argues that the U.S. Patent and Trademark Office has erred both in granting excessively broad patents and in failing to apply the utility criterion in developing technological fields such has biotechnology. This has the potential of allowing a patentee to control an entire field of research (such as research on schizophrenia) even though his or her invention did not enable it. This could be remedied either by compulsory licensing or by treating refusal to license under these circumstances as an abuse of dominance. One form of compulsory licensing especially well suited to cases of sequential improvements is an improvement patent.

The *Magill* decision of the European Court of Justice illustrates the problems involved in using competition law to force patents or other intellectual property to be worked or made available on more favourable terms to follow-on innovators. In *Magill*, the European Court of Justice ordered the owners of three sets of copyrighted television listings to license their listings at a reasonable royalty rate to a weekly TV guide. The Court reasoned that the refusal of the broadcasters to license their listings prevented the production of a new product and was therefore an abuse of dominance. However, this would appear to be misguided in that no weekly guide would have been possible had the individual television listings not been produced in the first place. The refusal to license the intellectual property right does not reduce competition below what it would be if the initial innovation (the television listings) had not been made. Thus the Court may have taken a myopic rather than a life-cycle view of the innovative process.

Taken as it stands, this decision implies that in Europe an intellectual property owner may be obliged to license intellectual property at least when it is deemed to be an essential input. This moves European competition law closer to the historic Canadian approach under sections 67 and 65 of the *Patent Act*. If the Canadian experience is any guide, the impact of this on patentees will be minimal where know-how is also required. It may have a greater impact in the area of copyright and in the case of patents where know-how is not required.

ALTERNATIVES TO COMPULSORY LICENSING

THERE ARE A NUMBER OF WAYS OF FACILITATING local working or local follow-on inventive activity without resorting to compulsory licensing.[35] Some are consistent with the TRIPs and NAFTA agreements, while others are not.

Options that are no longer available include the termination of patent rights and split-term patents. The Canadian *Patent Act* of 1869 initially provided for the automatic forfeiture of the patentee's rights if the invention involved was not worked in Canada within two years. This was subsequently replaced by the compulsory licensing provisions described above. The Economic Council of Canada (1971) suggested that non-exclusive compulsory licences to manufacture in Canada be available as a matter of right after five years from the date of application for the Canadian patent. This would have avoided the cumbersome adjudication associated with applications for compulsory licences. The *Working Paper on Patent Law Reform* (Consumer and Corporate Affairs, 1976) proposed a two-tier system under which continued patent protection would be contingent on local working. It was argued that this was preferred to a non-exclusive compulsory licence in that it gave the patentee an incentive to transfer know-how to the Canadian licensee.

A number of other possible measures are consistent with international treaties. One possibility is a widened research-use exemption. A highly qualified right now exists in this area (Eisenberg, 1989).[36] On the basis of cases decided in the United States, a research-use defence does not appear to be available when the defendant's research is motivated by a commercial purpose (p. 1023) Eisenberg also suggests that it is reasonable to infer that the potential research exemption may be broader than this:

> The timing of the disclosure requirement suggests that there are limits to the patent holder's exclusive rights even during the patent term. If the public had absolutely no right to use the disclosure without the patent holder's consent until after the patent expired, it would make little sense to require that the disclosure be made freely available to the public at the outset of the patent term. The fact that the patent statute so plainly facilitates unauthorized use of the invention while the patent is in effect suggests that some such uses are to be permitted. (p. 1022)

Other possibilities include process protection for products, weaker novelty requirements, and petty or utility patents. Product protection through process protection allows a product to be imitated so long as the process involved is different. This can be frustrated by a patentee who patents all possible processes. Petty patents continue to exist in some countries (Evenson, 1990*b*). They are for minor improvements or adaptations. This is equivalent to a weaker novelty requirement. The virtues of weaker novelty requirements have been extolled by Scotchmer and Green (1990) and Merges and Nelson (1990), and they may be greater yet when viewed from the perspective of a developing or drafting country.

Several aspects of the Japanese system lead to what might be termed "compulsory voluntary licensing." Ordover (1991) cites a number of features that favour imitators (McFetridge and English, 1990). First, the Japanese system requires disclosure of the invention when a patent application is filed rather than when the patent is granted.[37] Second, under the Japanese system a patent can be contested at the time of application rather than when it is granted. This increases the pressure on potential patentees to enter into licensing arrangements. Third, Japan has relatively weak novelty requirements. Follow-on inventors may be able to reverse-engineer an invention during its application period, improve it slightly, and apply for an improvement patent. This may block the original invention, thus forcing the originating patentee into a cross-licensing arrangement. Similar provisions could be used by drafting countries wishing to maintain the appearance of a strong intellectual property regime.

Conclusion

Diffusion and Growth

The joint contribution of innovation and diffusion to economic growth is universally acknowledged, but little is known about the marginal contribution of the rate of diffusion. Empirically, attention is focused on innovative effort, to the virtual exclusion of concerns regarding diffusion. Faster or more complete diffusion may increase per capita income and/or the rate of growth, but such an outcome is not automatic. Existing rates of diffusion could be either too fast or too slow. Existing government programs may be compensating for a diffusion externality or they may be crowding out internalizing market institutions.

Intellectual Property and Diffusion

Intellectual property is generally regarded as providing an incentive to engage in innovative or creative endeavour. Innovation and diffusion are complementary in many respects. To this extent at least, intellectual property encourages diffusion. But the role of intellectual property goes beyond this: it facilitates disclosure and provides a basis for market transactions in knowledge.

Intellectual property regimes have evolved over time and have varied from country to country. What regime might be in the global interest is a matter of debate, and national interests may well differ from the global interest. While some make the argument that strong intellectual property rights are in the interest of all countries at all stages in their development, that proposition is difficult to accept. On the other hand, it seems likely that the adoption of successively stronger regimes will be part of the growth process.

Compulsory Licensing and Technology Diffusion

For many years it was accepted wisdom in Canada that Canadians could only benefit from new technologies if they were worked in Canada. Over the past 15 years, the emphasis has shifted to attracting R&D. The rationale is the same: local working and local R&D provide on-the-job experience benefits that complement the knowledge disseminated by educational institutions. If some of this learning is transferable domestically, local working or local R&D may be efficient, but the benefits involved will not be reflected in the terms a potential local licensee is able to offer. A compulsory licence is a potential solution (at the patentee's expense) but not, in the Canadian experience, a very good solution.

Absent international political repercussions, compulsory licensing would appear to be ideal for a country that is following a drafting strategy because it needs access rather than know-how. South Korea is usually presented as an example, but Canada apparently does not qualify: Canada sought learning in addition to access and may have obtained neither.

In the case of the pharmaceutical industry, Canada has considered three policies and tried two. One is compulsory licensing, which weakened the formal property right. The second, suggested by the Eastman Commission, began with a weak property right, and the patentee could then strengthen that right (that is, derive greater royalty income from it) by locating more R&D in Canada. The third policy is to have a strong patent right – an approach that was adopted in 1993 (retroactively to 1991).

Compulsory licensing of patented medicines has always had much more to do with the price of medicines to end-users than with technology diffusion. The direct consequences of the changes in patent regimes for the diffusion of technology have, in any case, been minimal. The Eastman Commission was of the view that compulsory licensing did not further reduce the already limited local R&D of the multinationals. At the same time, compulsory licensing itself did virtually nothing to create an innovative domestic drug or fine-chemical manufacturing industry. There was some growth in the R&D expenditures of domestic generic-drug firms and some new entry into fine-chemical production after Bill C-22 (1987). While this may have been a natural outgrowth of compulsory licensing, it was more likely part of the political effort by the generic-drug industry to retain its remaining privileges under compulsory licensing. Similarly, while the growth in the Canadian R&D activities of the multinationals after 1987 may have been a natural consequence of the stronger Canadian patent right, it was more likely part of the political bargain that eliminated compulsory licensing. Since a return to the old policy is ruled out, this bargain will become increasingly difficult for the government to enforce. In this event, local R&D spending by multinationals will have reached its high watermark and is likely to begin a slow decline.

COMPETITION VERSUS LOCAL WORKING

CANADIAN PATENT POLICY HAS HISTORICALLY BEEN PREOCCUPIED with local working while generally ignoring conventional concerns regarding the anticompetitive use of patents. This places Canadian policy squarely at odds with the approach taken in the United States. Canadian accession to the NAFTA and the TRIPs agreements has resulted in amendments to the *Patent Act* that have reduced the potential for conflict, but Canada retains the capacity to order the licensing of patents when the products involved are not available on reasonable terms in Canada or when the lack of a licence is prejudicial to a Canadian industry. While licences have apparently never been granted for these reasons, the possibility that they could be granted remains. This possibility would appear to be remote at present, but developments such as the *Magill* decision in the European Court of Justice could raise concerns about future Canadian interpretation of both section 65 of the *Patent Act* and section 32 of the *Competition Act*.

Problems could also arise if Canadian patent policy were to place greater emphasis on competition. The provisions of the *Competition Act* regarding horizontal arrangements are very poorly suited to dealing with patent pools and similar arrangements.[38] The adjudication of tying and package licensing and market restriction issues by the Competition Tribunal could be equally unsatisfactory.[39]

NOTES

1   For overviews, see Jorgenson (1994) and OECD (1992).

2   There is a vast but inconclusive statistical literature on the relationship between national characteristics and policies, on the one hand, and national growth rates, on the other. On the lack of statistical robustness of these relationships, see Levine and Renelt (1992) and Levine and Zervos (1993).

3   This literature is summarized in Gilbert and Sunshine (1995).

4   Evolutionary theorists would dispute that a monopoly innovator has the information required to pursue the ideal or socially optimal research strategy; see Merges and Nelson (1990).

5   Mairesse and Sassenou (1991, p. 24) argue that the creation of a stock of R&D from current and past R&D expenditures allows for a diffusion lag "in principle." This is correct if the value of past R&D expenditures declines only because they are superseded by subsequent R&D expenditures. In this case, the decay rate of past R&D expenditures is equal to the rate of diffusion of the results of current R&D expenditures and diffusion rates are effectively embodied in R&D stock measures. While decay and diffusion rates could be equal in the aggregate, where past R&D can only be superseded by subsequent R&D, this need not be the case at the industry level or below. R&D at the industry level can be superseded by current or past R&D in other industries.

6   For example, Hall and Mairesse (1995) estimate the following rate-of-return model:

$$TFP_{it} = a + b \, (R/Q)_{it-1}$$

where R/Q is the R&D to sales ratio. They interpret their estimate of parameter b as the rate of return on R&D.

7   For example, Coe and Helpman (1995) estimate the following model:

$$\ln TFP_{it} = \ln a_i + b \ln SD_{it} + c \ln SF_{it}$$

where SD and SF are foreign and domestic R&D stocks, respectively, and the subscripts refer to country i and year t. While the authors do not address the issue of diffusion lags directly, they do investigate the consequences of assuming a faster decay rate when constructing their R&D stock measures. This is equivalent to assuming a faster diffusion lag if past R&D decays because it is superseded by subsequent R&D. With two

R&D stocks, this equivalence is unlikely. In any event, the authors find that their elasticity estimates are sensitive to the decay rate assumed (1995, p. 884).

8   Ulrich, Furtan and Schmitz (1986, pp. 112-13) also assume that in the absence of an annual "maintenance expenditure" R&D is subject to decay. This raises the interesting question whether their assumptions about decay are consistent with their assumptions about diffusion. The authors' assumptions imply that malting barley R&D is subject to supersession by *other* agricultural and non-agricultural R&D.

9   Baldwin and Diverty (1995, Table 4) also find that establishments owned by enterprises engaged in R&D use more advanced manufacturing technologies. This is consistent with the proposition that innovation and adoption are joint products of R&D.

10   Caballero and Jaffe (1993) use patent citations as a measure of the extent to which the current generation of patentees have learned from their predecessors. The fact that an existing patent is cited in a patent application need not imply, however, that the applicant actually drew upon the knowledge disclosed in the cited patent.

11   The importance of the patent right in providing a framework for technological cooperation was emphasized in testimony before the Senate Standing Committee on Banking, Trade and Commerce by Graham Strachan, chief executive of Allelix Biopharmaceuticals Inc. of Toronto:

> One of the most important assets for attracting partners is a strong and defensible patent position. Patents define the invention. They allow the rights to be licensed and they allow value to be judged and assessed. . ... Strategic alliances are critical to the success of the Canadian-based biopharmaceuticals industry and proper competitive patent protection is essential for attracting and forming such partnerships. (Canada, Senate, 25:156-57; 18:1:93)

In his paper in this volume, Merges discusses the various ways in which intellectual property facilitates market and "quasi market" (or quasi internal) exchange.

12   In earlier work, Mansfield concluded that technology transfer abroad did not increase the probability of foreign reverse engineering or accelerate its timing. Host country benefits from foreign direct investment take the form of demonstration effects rather than reverse engineering effects. Host countries also benefit from increased opportunities for collaboration between foreign affiliates and local customers and suppliers. This interaction generally does not come at the expense of home country collaboration; see McFetridge (1994) and the references therein.

13   See McFetridge and English (1990) and the references therein. In his comments on an earlier version of this paper, F. M. Scherer stated that it was the threat of U.S. trade action rather than internal factors that was decisive in South Korea's decision to strengthen its intellectual property rights.

14   It is arguable that information would not be obtainable via licence agreements if there were no patent protection.

15   Sections 65(a) and 65(b) were incompatible with Article 28 of the TRIPs Agreement and with the NAFTA. They were repealed under the NAFTA *Implementation Act* of 1993.

16   These are licences that have not been formally withdrawn and not been officially deemed abandoned. According to Peter Davies of the Canadian Intellectual Property Office, the probability that these applications will result in licences being awarded is remote.

17   The type of abuse in the other two cases is not stated in the summary statistics.

18   This would contradict one of the assumptions of the evolutionary approach, which holds that patentees are generally ill-informed regarding the commercial prospects for technologies under their control and, for this reason, advocates that the ability of patentees to restrict the application of their technologies be subject to severe limitations; see Merges and Nelson (1990).

19   This would be in addition to the patent *misuse* defence to an action for infringement or to recover unpaid royalties. The misuse defence renders a patent unenforceable until the misuse has ceased. Misuse generally involves an attempt to extend the duration or scope of a patent. Examples of misuse found by the courts in the United States include post-expiry royalties or tying arrangements; see Weinschel (1995, pp. 10-11).

20   CIPO summary tables show two instances in which applicants for compulsory licences alleged abuse under section 65(2)(c). Requests for licences under that section were rejected by the Commissioner of Patents in both instances.

21   For example, there may be demonstration effects from local working; see McFetridge (1994). Compulsory licensing also increases the bargaining power of follow-on innovators at the expense of pioneering innovators. This may or may not increase the aggregate amount of innovation; see Scotchmer (1991) and Acheson and McFetridge (1996). Whether compulsory licences granted by Canada under section 65 of the *Patent Act* can be construed as an attempt to optimize the incentives for pioneering and follow-on innovation from a global perspective is another question entirely.

22   Under the Commission's proposal, the ith patentee's royalty income I_i would be:

$$I_i = \{[(CR/CS)_i + 0.04]SCL_i\}\{[(WR/WS) + 0.04]/[(\Sigma\, CR_i / \Sigma\, CS_i) + 0.04]\}$$

where CR_i and CS_i are Canadian R&D and sales of the ith patentee, SCL_i is the sales of the ith patentee under compulsory licence, the summations are over all patentees in Canada (i.e., the Canadian industry), and WR and WS are worldwide R&D and sales for the pharmaceutical industry. Given that Canadian industry R&D intensity was roughly 5 percent and worldwide R&D intensity was roughly 10 percent, a \$1 increase in Canadian R&D spending would earn a patentee with 10 percent of its sales under compulsory licence an additional 16 cents in royalty income.

23   See, for example, the testimony of Dr. Bellini of Biochem Pharma before the Senate Standing Committee on Banking, Trade and Finance (Canada, Senate, 27:74-5; 20/1/93) and the letter of Dr. Terzakian of Raylo Chemicals to the Committee (28:36-7; 21/1/93).

24   Using worldwide pharmaceutical R&D spending data from *Scrip: World Pharmaceutical News* (August 4, 1995), 1994 Canadian R&D expenditures as a percentage of worldwide expenditures can be calculated for selected multinationals. These percentages are as follows: Glaxo, 1.3; Hoffman LaRoche, 1.0; Merck, 6.1; Pfizer, 0.7; Sandoz, 1.2; Ciba, 1.4; Eli Lilly, 1.7. In his testimony before the Senate standing Committee on Banking, Trade and Commerce, Dr. Michael Spino of Apotex commented that Merck was one of a few multinationals with the "critical mass" for in-house research in Canada (Canada, Senate, 28:30; 21/1/93).

25   In testimony before the Senate Standing Committee on Banking, Trade and Commerce, Michael Wilson, the Minister of Industry and Science explained the government's reasoning as follows:

> Since 1987 when C-22 was passed, the international community has moved significantly in the direction of stronger patent protection. Canada, the only developed nation with compulsory licensing in medicines was becoming more and more iso-

lated on this issue. We were rapidly becoming less attractive for investment in pharmaceuticals than our trading partners. (Canada, Senate, 28:123; 21/1/93)

26   Testimony of Michael Wilson, Proceedings of the Standing Senate Committee on Banking, Trade and Commerce (Canada, Senate, 28:126, 21/1/93).

27   Testimony of Dr. Michael Spino before the Senate Standing Committee on Banking, Trade and Commerce (Canada, Senate, 28:25; 21/1/93). This argument was also made by Jack Kay, president of the Canadian Drug Manufacturers Association (the association of generic-drug producers):

> It is important not to lose track of the fact that, under compulsory licensing, what the government envisioned back in 1969 was that the generic industry would grow and mature from being copy-cats to being innovators. We are now at that stage where the two major companies, Novapharm and Apotex, are undertaking innovative research. We have new products which are under development for the treatment of cancer and AIDS but we require continued cash flow which was guaranteed to us under Bill C-22, which stated that there would be no negative change until 1996, to bring these products to fruition. (27:112; 20/1/93)

28   The Eastman Commission was of the opinion that compulsory licensing had not affected the research intensity of the Canadian pharmaceutical industry. At approximately 5 percent, it was in line with its counterparts in other small developed countries. The government's view was apparently that innovative activity had fallen well short of its potential and was becoming increasingly unattractive.

29   While aggregate pharmaceutical R&D in Italy did not increase, the proportion accounted for by Italian affiliates of multinationals could have increased. To the extent that they could no longer copy medicines protected by patents in other countries, Italian pharmaceutical firms must also have become less imitative.

30   Drug inventions are taken from Challu (1995, Table 5). The sample is confined to the 12-year period after which drug inventions became patentable and the 12-year period immediately preceding this. The estimated regression equation is:

$$NEWDR = 1.59 + 10.86\ DPAT + 0.45\ TIME - 0.90\ DPAT \times TIME$$
$$\qquad (1.22)\quad (3.04)\qquad\quad (2.53)\qquad\qquad (3.58)$$

where $NEWDR$ = number of new drugs invented in Italy; $DPAT$ = dummy variable equal to 1 in 1978 and after; and $TIME$ = time trend, beginning at 0 in 1966. t statistics are in brackets below the coefficient estimates; R^2 = 0.39.

31   The countries with the highest new-drug/gross-domestic-product (GDP) ratios during the period 1940-75 – Switzerland and Denmark – protected only processes during that period. The United States and Belgium, which protected both products and processes, ranked third and fourth. Italy, which protected nothing, ranked thirteenth. Canada, which protected processes only and which had compulsory licensing for the last six years of the sample period, ranked fifteenth (p. 38). This type of comparison ignores possible trends within the sample period and does not take into account factors other than intellectual property protection. Nevertheless, Scherer's findings raise the intriguing possibility that protecting new drug as a product as well as protecting the process by which it is made adds little to the incentive for innovation in pharmaceuticals.

32   Bill C-91 is scheduled for review in 1997. The manufacturers of patented pharmaceu-
      ticals are lobbying for a further extension of their periods of exclusivity. R&D decisions
      may be influenced by this lobbying effort; see Bourette (1996).

33   For a historical survey of the treatment of intellectual property under competition
      legislation in Canada, see Anderson, Khosla and Ronayne (1991).

34   The competitive impact of post-expiry royalties would depend on whether the patentee
      and licensees would be competing after the expiry of the patent.

35   Compulsory licensing may have other roles to play. Employed in conjunction with an
      extended patent term, it can be a means of offering a given incentive to invent at a lower
      cost in terms of the deadweight loss from restricted use; see, for example, Tandon (1982).

36   Section 55.2 (6) of the *Patent Act Amendment Act, 1992*, R.S. c .2, 1993 confirms a sim-
      ilar exception to the patentee's exclusive rights in Canadian law for acts done privately
      and on a non-commercial scale or for a non-commercial purpose or for experiments
      relating solely to the subject matter of the patent.

37   The Canadian Intellectual Property Office now publishes applications 18 months after
      they have been filed. This is, on average, 18 months before the patent is granted.

38   There are no provisions under section 45 for rule-of-reason consideration of agree-
      ments that result in a substantial reduction of competition. Given the historic
      Canadian concern with access, Canadian courts would probably not take a life-cycle
      approach and ask whether an innovative sequence would have occurred in the
      absence of anticipated restrictions on competition; see McFetridge (1995).

39   Section 77 is concerned solely with the access of new competitors to the market. It is
      unlikely that the Competition Tribunal will take the effect of market restrictions on
      either static total surplus or on innovation into account in section 77 cases.

BIBLIOGRAPHY

Acheson, Keith and D. G. McFetridge. "Intellectual Property and Endogenous Growth," in
    The Implications of Knowledge-based Growth for Micro-Economic Policies. Edited by Peter
    Howitt. Calgary: University of Calgary Press, 1996, pp. 187-235.
Anderson, R. D., S. D. Khosla and M. F. Ronayne. "The Competition Policy Treatment of
    Intellectual Property Rights in Canada: Retrospect and Prospect," in *Canadian
    Competition Law and Policy at the Centenary*. Edited by R. S. Khemani and
    W. T. Stanbury. Halifax: Institute for Research on Public Policy, 1991, pp. 497-538.
Anis, Aslam H. "Essays on the Effects of Government Policy on Firm and Industry
    Behaviour." Unpublished Ph.D. thesis, Carleton University, Ottawa, 1989.
Arrow, K. "Economic Welfare and the Allocation of Resources for Invention," in *The Rate
    and Direction of Inventive Activity*. Edited by R. Nelson. Princeton, N. J.: Princeton
    University Press, 1962, pp. 609-25.
Baldwin, John R. *Strategies for Success: A Profile of Growing Small and Medium-Sized
    Enterprises (GSMEs) in Canada*. Cat. No. 61-523. Ottawa: Statistics Canada, 1994.
——. "Innovation and Intellectual Property: Findings from the Innovation Survey." Micro-
    Economics Analysis Division, Ottawa: Statistics Canada, 1995 (mimeo).
Baldwin, John R. and Brent Diverty. "Advanced Technology Use in Manufacturing
    Establishments: What Influences Incidence and Intensity Decisions." Micro-economics
    Analysis Division, Ottawa: Statistics Canada, 1995 (mimeo).

Baldwin, John R., Tara Gray and Joanne Johnson. "Technology Use, Training and Plant-Specific Knowledge in Manufacturing Establishments." Mimeo. Ottawa: Statistics Canada, Micro-economics Analysis Division, 1995.

Barton, John H. "Patent Breadth and Antitrust: A Rethinking." Paper presented to the Federal Trade Commission hearings on "Global and Innovation-based Competition," November 27, 1995.

Bourette, Susan. "Pharmaceuticals Need Strong Patent Protection: Study." *The Globe and Mail*, Report on Business (March 20, 1996): B-4.

Caballero, R. and A. Jaffe. "How High Are the Giant's Shoulders: An Empirical Assessment of Knowledge Spillovers and Creative Destruction in a Model of Economic Growth." *NBER Macroeconomics Annual, 1993*, Cambridge, Mass.: National Bureau of Economic Research, 1993, pp. 13-74.

Canada, Senate. Standing Committee on Banking, Trade and Commerce. *Proceedings*, Third Session, Thirty-fourth Parliament, 1991-92-93.

Carlsson, Bo and Staffan Jacobsson. "Technological Diffusion Systems and Economic Policy: The Diffusion of Factory Automation in Sweden." *Research Policy*, 23 (1994): 235-48.

Challu, Pablo M. "Effects of Monopolistic Patenting of Medicine in Italy since 1978." *International Journal of Technology Management*, 10 (1995): 237-51.

Coe, D. and E. Helpman. "International R&D Spillovers." *European Economic Review*, 39 (May 1995): 859-87.

Cohen, W. M. and D. A. Levinthal. "Innovation and Learning: The Two Faces of R&D." *The Economic Journal*, 99 (1989): 569-96.

Commission of Inquiry on the Pharmaceutical Industry. *Report of the Commission of Inquiry on the Pharmaceutical Industry*. Ottawa: Supply and Services Canada, 1985.

Consumer and Corporate Affairs Canada. *Working Paper on Patent Law Reform*. Ottawa, 1976.

Correa, Carlos M. "Intellectual Property Rights and Foreign Direct Investment." *International Journal of Technology Management*, 10 (1995): 173-99.

Corvari, Ronald J. "Strategic Advertising Behaviour and Public Policy in the Canadian Pharmaceutical Industry." Unpublished Ph.D. thesis, Carleton University, Ottawa, 1991.

Dasgupta, Partha and Joseph Stiglitz. "Uncertainty, Industrial Structure and the Speed of R&D." *Bell Journal of Economics*, 11 (June 1980): 1-28.

David, P. "Knowledge, Property and the System Dynamics of Technological Change." *Proceedings of the World Bank Annual Conference on Development Economics 1992*. Washington: The World Bank, 1993, pp. 215-48.

Deolalikar, Anil and Robert E. Evenson. "Private Inventive Activity in Indian Manufacturing: Its Extent and Determinants," in *Science and Technology: Lessons for Development Policy*. Edited by Robert E. Evenson and Gustav Ranis. Boulder, Colo.: Westview Press, 1990, pp. 233-53.

Economic Council of Canada. *Report on Intellectual Property*. Ottawa, 1971.

Eisenberg, Rebecca S. "Patents and the Progress of Science: Exclusive Rights and Experimental Use." *The University of Chicago Law Review*, 56 (1989): 1017-86.

Evenson, Robert E. "Survey of Empirical Studies," in *Strengthening Protection of Intellectual Property in Developing Countries: A Survey of the Literature*. Edited by Wolfgang E. Siebeck. Discussion Paper No. 112. Washington: The World Bank, 1990a.

——. "Intellectual Property Rights, R&D, Inventions, Technology Purchase and Piracy in Economic Development: An International Comparative Study," in *Science and*

Technology: Lessons for Development Policy. Edited by Robert E. Evenson and Gustav Ranis. Boulder, Colo.: Westview Press, 1990*b*, pp. 325-55.

Fox, G., A. Haque and G. Brinkman. "Product Market Distortions and the Returns to Federal Laying Hen Research in Canada: Reply and Further Results." *Canadian Journal of Agricultural Economics,* 38 (July 1990): 351-56.

Frischtak, Claudio, R. "Harmonization versus Differentiation in International Property Rights Regimes." *International Journal of Technology Management,* 10 (1995): 200-13.

Geroski, Paul, Steve Machin and John Van Reenen. "The Profitability of Innovating Firms." *Rand Journal of Economics,* 24 (Summer 1993): 198-211.

Gilbert, Richard J. and Steven C. Sunshine. "Incorporating Dynamic Efficiency Concerns in Merger Analysis: The Use of Innovation Markets." *Antitrust Law Journal,* 63 (Winter 1995): 569-601.

Griliches, Z. *The Search for R&D Spillovers.* Working Paper No. 3768. Cambridge, Mass.: National Bureau of Economic Research, 1991.

Hall, Bronwyn H. and Jacques Mairesse. "Exploring the Relationship Between R&D and Productivity in French Manufacturing Firms." *Journal of Econometrics,* 65 (1995): 263-93.

Haque, A., G. Fox and G. Brinkman. "Product Market Distortions and the Returns to Federal Laying Hen Research in Canada." *Canadian Journal of Agricultural Economics,* 37 (March 1989): 29-46.

Harbasz, C., G. Fox and G. Brinkman. "A Comparison of ex post and ex ante Measures of Producers Surplus in Estimating the Returns to Canadian Federal Sheep Research" *Canadian Journal of Agricultural Economics,* 36 (November 1988): 489-500.

Industry, Science and Technology Canada. "Appendices for the Survey of Intellectual Property Rights in Canada: Final Report." Ottawa, 1989 (mimeo).

Jorgenson, Dale W. "Investment and Economic Growth." Simon Kuznets Lectures. Yale University, New Haven, Conn., November 1994, pp. 9-11.

Levin, R., et al.. "Appropriating the Returns from Industrial Research and Development," in *Brookings Papers on Economic Activity,* 3. Edited by M. Baily and C. Winston. Washington: The Brookings Institution, 1987, pp. 783-820.

Levine, D. and D. Renelt. "A Sensitivity Analysis of Cross-Country Growth Regressions." *American Economic Review,* 82 (1992): 942-63.

Levine, D. and S. Zervos. "What Have We Learned About Cross-Country Growth Regressions?" *American Economic Review,* 83 (May 1993): 426-30.

Mairesse, J. and M. Sassenou. "R&D and Productivity: A Survey of Econometric Studies at the Firm Level," *STI Review,* 8 (April 1991): 9-44.

Mansfield, Edwin. *Intellectual Property Protection, Foreign Direct Investment and Technology Transfer.* Discussion Paper 19. Washington: International Finance Corporation, 1994.

McFetridge, D. "Globalization and Competition Policy," in *Productivity Growth and Canada's International Competitiveness.* Edited by T. J. Courchene and D. D. Purvis. Kingston: John Deutsch Institute, 1992, pp. 133-80.

——. "The Canadian System of Industrial Innovation," in *National Innovation Systems.* Edited by R. Nelson. Oxford, U.K.: Oxford University Press, 1993, pp. 299-323.

——. "Canadian Foreign Direct Investment, R&D and Technology Transfer," in *Canadian Based Multinationals.* Edited by S. Globerman. Calgary: University of Calgary Press, 1994, pp. 151-78.

——. "Competition Policy and Cooperative Innovation." Paper presented at a conference on "Competitive Industrial Development: The Role of Cooperation in the Technology Sector," University of Toronto Law School, Toronto, May 19, 1995.

McFetridge, D. and H. English. "Intellectual Property and the GATT Negotiations: Some Areas for Discussion," in *Pacific Initiatives in Global Trade*. Edited by H. English. Halifax: Institute for Research on Public Policy, 1990, pp. 159-72.

McFetridge, D. and A. Lall. "Is There a Theory of Deregulation?" in *Breaking the Shackles: Deregulating Canadian Industry*. Edited by W. Block and G. Lermer. Vancouver: Fraser Institute, 1991, pp. 7-28.

Merges, Robert P. and Richard R. Nelson. "On the Complex Economics of Patent Scope." *Columbia Law Review*, 90 (1990): 839-916.

Midgely, David F., Pamela D. Morrison and John H. Roberts. "The Effect of Network Structure in Industrial Diffusion Processes." *Research Policy*, 21 (1992): 533-52.

Nagy, J. G. and N. H. Furtan. "Economic Cost and Returns from Crop Development Research: The Case of Rapeseed Breeding in Canada." *Canadian Journal of Agricultural Economics* (1984): 1-14.

Nelson, Richard R. "On Technological Capabilities and Their Acquisition," in *Science and Technology: Lessons for Development Policy*. Edited by Robert E. Evenson and Gustav Ranis. Boulder, Colo.: Westview Press, 1990, pp. 71-80.

Nordhaus, W. *Invention, Growth and Welfare*. Cambridge, Mass.: MIT Press, 1969.

OECD, *Technology and the Economy: The Key Relationships*. Paris: Organisation for Economic and Co-operation Development, 1992.

Ordover, Janusz A. "A Patent System for Both Diffusion and Exclusion." *Economic Perspectives*, 5 (1991): 43-60.

Pakes, Ariel and Mark Schankerman. "The Rate of Obsolescence of Patents, Research Gestation Lags and the Private Rate of Return to Research Resources," in *R&D, Patents and Productivity*. Edited by Zvi Griliches. Chicago: University of Chicago Press, 1984, pp. 73-88.

Patented Medicines Prices Review Board. *Eighth Annual Report*. Ottawa, 1996.

Porter, Michael E. *The Competitive Advantage of Nations*. New York: MacMillan, 1990.

Primo Braga, Carlos. "The Developing Country Case for and against Intellectual Property Protection," in *Strengthening Protection of Intellectual Property in Developing Countries: A Survey of the Literature*. Edited by Wolfgang E. Siebeck. Discussion Paper No. 112. Washington: World Bank, 1990.

Rosenberg, N. *Inside the Black Box: Technology and Economics*. New York: Cambridge University Press, 1982.

Scherer, F. M. *The Economic Effects of Compulsory Patent Licensing*. New York: New York University Graduate School for Business Administration, 1977.

Scherer, F. M. and Sandy Weisburst. "Economic Effects of Strengthening Pharmaceutical Patent Protection in Italy." *International Review of Industrial Property and Copyright Law*, 6 (1995): 1009-24.

Scotchmer, Suzanne. "Standing on the Shoulders of Giants." *Economic Perspectives*, 5 (1991): 29-41.

Scotchmer, Suzanne and Jerry Green. "Novelty and Disclosure in Patent Law." *Rand Journal of Economics*, 21 (1990): 131-46.

Stoneman, P. and P. Diederen. "Technology Diffusion and Public Policy." *Economic Journal*, 104 (July 1994): 918-30.

Taggart, J. "Determinants of Foreign R&D Locations in the Chemical Industry." *R&D Management*, 21 (1991): 221-40.

Tandon, P. "Optimal Patents with Compulsory Licensing." *Journal of Political Economy*, 90 (1982): 470-86.

Ulrich, A., H. Furtan and A. Schmitz. "Public and Private Returns from Joint Venture Research: An Example from Agriculture." *Quarterly Journal of Economics*, 101 (February 1986): 103-29.

United States Department of Justice and the Federal Trade Commission. *Antitrust Guidelines for the Licensing of Intellectual Property*. Washington, 1995.

Von Hippel, Eric. "Lead Users: A Source of Novel Product Concepts." *Management Science*, 32 (1986): 791-805.

Weinschel, Alan J. "The United States Perspective on the Intellectual Property/Antitrust Interface." Paper presented at the Canadian Bar Association 1995 Annual Competition Law Conference, 1995.

Widmer, L., G. Fox and G. Brinkman. "The Rate of Return to Agricultural Research in a Small Country: The Case of Beef Cattle Research in Canada." *Canadian Journal of Agricultural Economics*, 36 (March 1988): 23-35.

Comment

F. M. Scherer
John F. Kennedy School of Government
Harvard University

I BELIEVE MY ROLE HERE IS TO DISSENT, so I shall do so as vigorously as possible in these brief comments.

One thing I have noticed, *inter alia* in Don McFetridge's paper, is that there seems to be some pejorative attached to the expression "free-rider." I do not know why that should be. It is, to be sure, better than being called a pirate. But I believe the Canada Court of Exchequer got it essentially right in *Merck and Company vs Sherman and Ulster Ltd.*: "It would. . . be unrealistic to think that the returns from the Canadian market have any important bearing on whether research on an international scale will go on or not."

In my new textbook, comprising a series of case studies, I try to do some analysis of what the effect would be if all of the less developed countries (LDCs) around the world, which thus far have not granted drug patents, actually began giving such patents. Without the LDCs, the equilibrium is about 42 or so new chemical entities per year. The best estimate I can make is that you would have roughly 50 new chemical entities per year in total by bringing the Third World into the drug-patenting realm. Third World nations are not moving in that direction, as Don suggested, because they think it is a good thing to have strong patent rights internally. They are doing it either because the United States has threatened them with section 301 sanctions or because they have to go along with the Uruguay Round Agreements.

In this comment, I will give some examples of compulsory licensing and its actual effects. Consider compulsory licensing in the pharmaceutical industry. We do not yet have the results of a natural experiment for Canada, but we have a very nice natural experiment that my student, Sandy Weisburst, has examined in some detail (Scherer and Weisburst, 1995).

In 1978, the Italian Supreme Court said it was unconstitutional for Italy to deny drug product patents. At that time, Italy had the leading generic-drug industry in the world. It exported generic drugs all over the world, including to Canada and the United States, for sale as generics because there were no Italian product patents. In 1978, Italy had to start granting drug product patents. What happened?

One way of measuring the effects is to observe what happened to the number of drug patents taken out in the United States. You have to go back to the United States because there were no product patents in Italy before 1978. Drug patents applied for by Italian firms in the United States rose, beginning around about 1978, much more rapidly than U.S. drug patents overall.

How about R&D on pharmaceuticals in Italy? Before 1978, world R&D spending on pharmaceuticals grew more rapidly than in Italy. Afterwards, worldwide R&D in the drug industry continued to grow more rapidly than that of the Italian drug industry.

If R&D is going up more slowly in Italy than in the universe, but patenting is going up more rapidly, what is happening? The answer is that the propensity to patent is changing. As R&D expenditures explode, the universe's patents per billion dollars of R&D fall. But Italian firms, now that they can take out Italian patents, are hiring patent attorneys, and they are obtaining patents in the United States also. Moreover, after the change, you find more multinationals buying Italian firms.

After the 1978 change in patent law, what happened to the number of new chemical entities? The series introduced from Italy is very erratic, but a moving average reveals the contrary of the expected hypothesis: Italy introduces fewer, not more, new chemical entities.

As I said, Italy had the leading generic-drug industry in the world at the time. What happens to Italy's balance of trade on pharmaceutical products? The dotted line in Figure 1 shows exports equal to imports. Italy had a positive balance of trade before its Supreme Court required a patent policy change. Afterwards, one sees a precipitous drop in Italy's balance of trade. The reason is that as the Italian firms lost their ability to be early developers of generic drugs, they were no longer the leading generic-drug exporter to the rest of the world that does not have drug patents. India took over that role. Meanwhile, the multinational drug companies no longer had to produce in Italy in order to sell drugs in Italy, therefore, they were exporting more to Italy from other locations.

The moral of this story is that a change in legislation did not lead, at least thus far, to the development of a viable Italian new-drug developing industry.

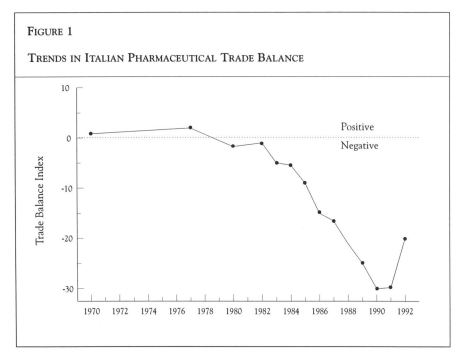

FIGURE 1

TRENDS IN ITALIAN PHARMACEUTICAL TRADE BALANCE

There may be other reasons that confounded this conclusion that time con-straints force me to overlook.

The United States has had more experience with compulsory licensing than any other nation in the world. Under antitrust decrees, we have licensed literally tens of thousands of patents. Table 1 presents a brief summary of the companies that had major compulsory licensing decrees, affecting at least 20 percent of their product line sales. I performed a statistical analysis to deter-mine the effects of compulsory licensing on their R&D expenditures. The most important question I explored was whether compulsory licensing destroys or inhibits incentives to invest in research and development. This is a question I first tackled as a student at the Harvard Business School in 1957-58. The IBM decree and the AT&T decree of 1956 had been issued. The *Wall Street Journal* said that those government interventions were going to put an end to innova-tion by such companies. We talked to about 40 companies and did a statistical analysis on 70 or so. The only thing we found was that compulsory licensing had reduced the propensity to patent marginal inventions.

What about the R&D incentive? When data on individual company R&D became available in 1976 for the first time, I went back to this question (Scherer, 1977). I took significant compulsory licensing decrees and linked dummy variables, indicating varying degrees of compulsory licensing severity, to R&D expenditures. I asked how the R&D/sales ratio in 1975 varied, control-ling for industry and size of the company with a past, significant compulsory

TABLE 1

SAMPLE COMPANIES WITH COMPULSORY LICENSING DECREES OF APPRECIABLE SCOPE

Company	Number of ML Cases	Fields or Products Affected	Major Impact	Future Patents?	Last Year Affected
Airco	1	Carbon dioxide products	No	Yes	1962
American Air Filter	1	Air filters	No	No	1946
American Can	1	Can closing machinery	Yes	Yes	1955
American Cyanamid	1	Aureomycin	No	No	1967
American Motors	1	Pollution control devices	No	Yes	1975
A. T. & T.	1	Telephone equipment and components	Yes	Yes	1975
Ball Brothers	1	Glass bottle making machinery	No	No	1947
Bausch & Lomb	1	Opthalmic goods	Yes	Yes	1958
Bendix	3	Aircraft instruments, air brakes, hydraulic brakes	Yes	Yes	1958
Bristol-Myers	1	Ampicillin case pending	No	Yes	1975
Carrier Corp.	2	Air conditioning equipment, cooling coils	Yes	No	1945
Chrysler	1	Pollution control devices	No	Yes	1975
Cincinnati Milacron	1	Milling machines	No	No	1954
Corning Glass Works	3	Light bulbs, flat glass, glass containers	Yes	No	1947
A.B. Dick	1	Duplicating machines	Yes	Yes	1958
DuPont	2	Titanium pigments; nylon and other chemicals	Yes	No	1952
Eastman Kodak	2	Motion picture film; Kodachrome	Yes	No	1954
Emhart (Hartford-Empire)	1	Glass bottle making machinery	Yes	Yes	1975
Exxon	1	Synthetic rubber	No	No	1942
Ford Motor Co.	1	Pollution control devices	No	Yes	1975
General Cable	1	Fluid-filled cables	No	No	1948
General Electric	6	Incand. lamps, light bulbs, fluid-filled cables, switches, fluor. lamps, elec. equipment	Yes	Yes	1958
General Motors	2	Busses, pollution control devices	No	Yes	1975
Hughes Tool	1	Oil well equipment	No	No	1958
IBM	1	Tabulating machines and tab cards	Yes	Yes	1961
Kearney & Trecker	1	Milling machines	No	No	1954
Merck	1	Drug patents of German affiliate	No	No	1945
Minnesota Mining	2	Abrasives, Scotch and magnetic tape	Yes	Yes	1974
NCR	1	Cash registers	No	No	1947
NL Industries	1	Titanium pigments	Yes	Yes	1950
Owens-Corning	1	Fiberglass	Yes	Yes	1954
Owens Illinois	3	Glass bottles and closings, bottle machinery	Yes	No	1947
Pfizer	1	Tetracycline	No	No	1967
Phelps-Dodge	1	Fluid-filled cables	No	No	1948
Pitney-Bowes	1	Postage meters	Yes	Yes	1964
PPG Industries	1	Flat glass	Yes	Yes	1953
RCA	1	Television	Yes	Yes	1968
Robertshaw Controls	1	Temperature controls	No	Yes	1962
Rohm & Haas	1	Plexiglass and related acrylics	Yes	No	1948
Singer	1	Sewing machines	No	No	1964
Syntex	1	Synthetic steroids	Yes	No	1958
U.S. Gypsum	1	Gypsum board	Yes	No	1951
Westinghouse Elec.	4	Incand. lamps, switches, fluor. lamps, elec. equipment	Yes	Yes	1954
Xerox	1	Copying machines	Yes	Yes	1975

Source: Scherer (1977), pp. 70-71.

licensing decree. The standard hypothesis would be that R&D in the companies subjected to compulsory licensing fell. To the contrary, I found a statistically significant elevation of compulsory licensing decree companies' R&D relative to companies of comparable size without decrees. I also checked the impact on market structure and found that there was no discernable impact on market structure attributable to compulsory licensing.

These results are consistent with those from many other surveys – e.g., Taylor and Silberston (1973); Levin et al. (1987); and Cohen, Nelson and Walsh (1996). As many other surveys show, for large, well-established corporations, patents are not, in general, very important to the research and development investment decision. There may be exceptions, however; some exceptions were already identified in our 1958 book: for small, start-up firms, or for larger firms that are getting started in a wholly new technology, a very different story may emerge. There, in many cases, patent protection really is important.

Let me give you one further example. Figure 2 shows the distribution of gains on 670 high-tech venture portfolio investments. On the horizontal axis, I have a measure of the returns on the investment. That is to say, the largest block covers those investments which yielded 10 times or more their initial stake. On the right-hand side, we have those which were essentially losers.

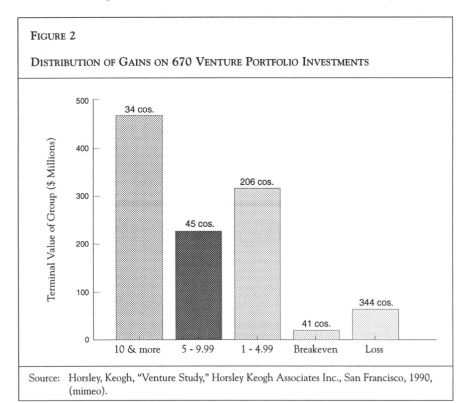

FIGURE 2

DISTRIBUTION OF GAINS ON 670 VENTURE PORTFOLIO INVESTMENTS

Source: Horsley, Keogh, "Venture Study," Horsley Keogh Associates Inc., San Francisco, 1990, (mimeo).

This figure illustrates that high-technology start-ups are an extremely risky type of lottery. Thirty-four start-up companies – 5 percent of the sample – earned 41 percent of all the returns on investment. This is a very risky, very skewed distribution over which, among other things, it is very difficult to hedge against risk by forming portfolios. For situations like this, patent protection is important to attract investments. So with these kinds of companies, one needs to be very careful. But for most large, well-established companies, I do not think one really needs to fear doing some social engineering with the competition policy laws.

BIBLIOGRAPHY

Cohen, Wesley M., Richard R. Nelson and John Walsh. "Appropriability Conditions and Why Firms Patent and Why They Do Not in the American Manufacturing Sector." Paper presented at a Conference on the Economics and Econometrics of Innovation, Strasbourg, France, June 3-5, 1996.

Levin, Richard C. et al. "Appropriating the Returns from Industrial Research and Development," in *Brookings Papers on Economic Activity*, 6, Edited by M. Baily and C. Winston. Washington: The Brookings Institution, 1987, pp. 783-832.

Scherer, F. M. *The Economic Effects of Compulsory Patent Licensing*. Monograph Series in Finance and Economics. New York: New York University, 1977, pp. 67-78.

Scherer F . M. and Sandy Weisburst, "Economic Effects of Strengthening Pharmaceutical Patent Protection in Italy," in *International Review of Industrial Property and Copyright Law*, 6 (1995): 1009-24.

Taylor C. T. and Z. A. Silberston, *The Economic Impact of the Patent System*. Cambridge: Cambridge University Press, 1973.

Robert P. Merges
School of Law
University of California, Berkeley

Antitrust Review of Patent Acquisitions: Property Rights, Firm Boundaries, and Organization

INTRODUCTION

THE ACQUISITION OF PATENTS, by assignment or long-term exclusive license, is recognized as a potential technique for amassing monopoly power. This paper summarizes the history of antitrust treatment of patent acquisitions under U.S. law, comments on the industrial milieu that gave rise to the classic acquisition cases, and speculates that under contemporary conditions the dominance of the large, vertically integrated R&D firm is giving way to more diverse organizational forms. The emergence of organizational forms such as strategic partnering and joint ventures is changing the industrial landscape. One result is that large, all-encompassing firms that are vertically integrated into R&D are less common. This makes it less likely that "killer patent portfolios," of the type made famous in the *United Shoe* case, will dominate whole industries. On the other hand, certain patent-acquisition practices that have not been widely employed until now are opening the way for new types of anticompetitive behavior. For example, some firms now acquire third-party patents that are then resubmitted to the Patent Office and broadened to cover competitors' products. This practice raises serious patent policy questions and highlights the need to adapt antitrust doctrine to new patent-acquisition practices.

THE SHERMAN ACT

ALTHOUGH SECTION 2 OF THE SHERMAN ACT by its terms prohibits three distinct offences – (1) monopolization, (2) attempts to monopolize, and (3) combination or conspiracy to monopolize – in practice they are usually merged into the generic offence of "monopolization." The offence is made out when a firm is shown to have the requisite intent to achieve or maintain monopoly power in a relevant market. A defendant need not have actually *achieved* monopolization; "a dangerous probability" that it could have been achieved is enough. Unlike section 1 of the *Sherman Act*, which requires at least two separate entities to contract or combine to unreasonably restrain trade, a single firm acting alone can be found to violate section 2. Section 2 outlaws the acquisition of monopoly power, in other words the power to fix prices or exclude or restrict competition in a relevant market. Relevant markets are determined with reference to the substitutability (i.e., the cross-elasticity of demand) of other products or services.

PATENT ACQUISITIONS: THE LEGACY OF UNITED SHOE

THERE IS A GROWING AWARENESS THAT MAPPING from a patent onto a product space is less than perfect, and that patents often cover only a single component or feature of a product. Indeed, this is implicit in many of the older cases, where the presence of large patent portfolios is the harm complained of. No one would have thought in *United Shoe* to complain of a single patent as the reason why the defendant firm dominated the entire shoe industry, for example. Although the simple presence of a patent is sometimes said to confer monopoly power, it is now usually understood that this is not necessarily so.

At the same time, it is important to understand that the mere accumulation of patents, no matter how many, is not itself a violation of the *Sherman Act*. This rule, and the corollary that acquisitions to intentionally monopolize an industry are actionable under the *Sherman Act*, are the important lessons of *United Shoe*. Because the case laid down the basic rules on patent acquisitions, and because it emerged out of an era of large, vertically integrated R&D operations, it is worthwhile to review it in some detail.

The case began when the U.S. Department of Justice brought an action against the United Shoe Machinery Corporation in 1935. The complaint alleged various antitrust violations stemming from mergers, leasing practices, and patent accumulations. On the latter score, the complaint pointed out that United Shoe completely dominated the market for shoe production equipment, in part through its more than 2,000 shoe machinery patents. It was thought that by dint of this huge patent portfolio, no new entry in the field was feasible. Hence, the thinking went, the patents represented a *de facto* impenetrable barrier to entry and thus a *per se* violation of the antitrust laws.

One problem with the government's case became evident right away: only about 5 percent of the total of 2,000 patents had been acquired from outsiders. The vast majority of the patents – over 95 percent – flowed from in-house R&D efforts. And, on closer inspection, the court-appointed master Carl Kaysen (whose report in the case is a classic of the empirical industrial organization literature),[1] found that many of the patents were acquired by United Shoe to protect itself from infringement suits, to keep certain avenues of development open, and to settle patent controversies. The Court found no violation of the

Sherman Act, apart from United Shoe's leasing practices; Judge Wyzanski even stated that its position in the industry was the result of "superior skill, foresight and industry."[2]

Even so, the Court issued a clear warning regarding United's practice of wholesale patent acquisitions: "most of these purposes could have been served by non-exclusive licenses. Taking the further step of acquiring the patents . . . buttressed United's market power. In some instances . . . the acquisitions made it less likely that United would have competition."[3] From this statement, as mild as it may look, many inferred some chilling consequences. It was one of the first discussions of the acquisition of patents outside a conspiracy or cartel context.[4] And it was the first time a court had hinted that the judiciary would review the nature and consequences of single-firm patent acquisitions in the course of antitrust analysis. Indeed, subsequent courts picked up on the theme. Several cases culminated in a finding of antitrust liability, in part due to patent-acquisition practices deemed anticompetitive under section 2.[5]

Contemporary Application: SCM *v.* Xerox

An important case from the 1980s ratified and updated the lessons of *United Shoe*. In this case, SCM Corporation claimed that Xerox had monopolized the convenience (plain paper) office-copier market and had unlawfully excluded SCM from the market.[6] Among other things, SCM alleged that Xerox had acquired patents that it refused to license and that allowed it to dominate xerography technology. In particular, SCM charged that monopolization began with Xerox's licenses from the Battelle Memorial Institute (Battelle), a non-profit, tax-exempt research institute that held all xerography patents stemming from the pioneering work of Chester Carlson. Under an important 1956 agreement, Xerox paid Battelle 55,000 shares of Xerox stock and a promise to sponsor $25,000 worth of research a year, in exchange for title to four pioneering xerography patents held by Battelle. The license also granted exclusive rights to all remaining Battelle-held patents, any future xerography patents, and associated know-how.

This 1956 agreement formed the foundation of SCM's 1969 exclusion claim. At the time of the agreement, Xerox had experienced commercial success in two applications of xerography and was deriving 40 percent of its profits from xerography. However, none of these products were convenience office copiers, the product market SCM claimed was monopolized by Xerox. Xerox defended on the grounds that, in essence, the Battelle patents were merely supplementary, and that it possessed sufficient technology in 1955 to manufacture an automatic plain-paper copier. Nevertheless, it was not until the introduction of its 914 model in 1960 that Xerox actually began to manufacture its first convenience copier. From 1960 through 1970, Xerox was able to dominate the plain-paper copier industry.

SCM's exclusion claim, filed in 1969, was premised on the contention that in 1969 Xerox had violated section 2 of the *Sherman Act* by willfully acquiring monopoly power in the plain-paper copier market. SCM also argued that Xerox's conduct, particularly its refusal to license the plain-paper patents, continued to exclude SCM from the relevant market.

After a jury had found antitrust liability, its verdict was rejected by the District Court judge hearing the case. On appeal, the Second Circuit Court concurred with the trial judge, refusing to find a *Sherman Act* violation in Xerox's actions. Most important for our purposes, the Court distinguished the Xerox patent acquisitions from those criticized (in dictum) in *United Shoe*. The difference in the Xerox case was there was no market power *at the time of the acquisition.* Since the patents were acquired four years before the production of the first plain-paper copier, the Court stated that "the patent system would be seriously undermined, however, were the threat of potential antitrust liability to attach upon the acquisition of a patent at a time prior to the existence of the relevant market and, even more disconcerting, at a time prior to the commercialization of the patented art."[7] The Court also stated that, in determining the legality of the acquisition of patents under section 2, "the focus should be upon the market power that will be conferred by the patents in relation to the market position then occupied by the acquiring party."[8]

In rejecting SCM's claim that Xerox's refusal to license patents amounted to an ongoing act of monopolization, the Court reasoned that "such conduct is expressly permitted by the patent laws." "A patent holder," the Court continued, "is permitted to maintain his patent monopoly through conduct permissible under the patent laws."[9] Consequently, when a patent owner lawfully acquires one or more patents covering technology over which the patent holder eventually holds monopoly power, no antitrust violation is made out. And of course it then follows that maintaining this monopoly by refusing to license one or more of the patents is also not actionable under the antitrust laws.

While announcing the important principle that patent acquisitions are to be judged with regard to market conditions at the time of the acquisition – an eminently reasonable approach under most circumstances – the Xerox holding is limited in some important respects. Most patents are acquired as part of an ongoing R&D effort, and rarely will all acquisitions be in place before a product is on the market. The industrial R&D process is much more fluid in most cases; research and marketing are not so cleanly demarcated. Thus patents will often be acquired after market conditions (including, in some cases, the achievement of market dominance by the acquiring firm) have become established. Under these circumstances the holding in *Xerox* gives no comfort to the acquiring firm. If market dominance is already in place, patent acquisitions may well form at least part of a Sherman section 2 case. Indeed, commentators continue to emphasize the importance of patent-acquisition patterns as an earmark of monopoly power.[10]

Patent Acquisitions Coupled With
Other Anticompetitive Behaviour

A particularly clear example of patent acquisitions that form part of a larger anticompetitive scheme comes from the case of *United States v. Hartford-Empire Co.*[11] The investigation culminating in this case grew out of the activities of the defendant, Hartford, which was at the center of a series of mergers and multi-firm agreements in the glass bottle industry. The ultimate effect of the concentrated and coordinated industry structure was an industry divided neatly along geographic and product lines. One key element in the arrangement involved patents. As part of the cartel arrangement, Hartford had succeeded in tying up virtually the entire glass container industry by purchasing and internally developing all of the important patents relating to the processes and machines. Hartford continually pressed its dominance in the glass container market by ardent patent enforcement against competitors and multiple cross-licenses, each laden with field-of-use and other restrictions.[12] In holding that there were violations of sections 1 and 2 of the *Sherman Act*, the District Court explicitly mentioned the efficacy of the patent arrangements in guaranteeing that the anticompetitive industry structure would continue well into the future.

This holding emphasizes – albeit unintentionally – an aspect of patent policy that has become acutely clear in recent years. Beginning with the writings of economists and lawyers concerned with incorporating some sense of dynamics into antitrust analysis, manifested most clearly in the work of economist Richard Gilbert, and up to the recent Department of Justice "Guidelines on Technology Licensing," a growing body of work argues that patent control can crucially affect market conditions and hence the ultimate development of technology in an industry. Gilbert's "innovation markets" analysis states the issue most clearly. As cases such as *Hartford-Empire* emphasize, these issues have not been lost on the courts in the past. The lesson for contemporary policymaking is that no less than before, antitrust enforcement must take account of dynamic effects that could in future flow from the combination of patent control and other variables. In particular, when employed in conjunction with current practices such as territorial or product-market division, patent control may crucially affect tomorrow's industry structure and competitive environment. This suggests at the very least that remedies in antitrust enforcement activities should – as they have in the past – continue to take account of the dynamic impact of patent control. It also suggests (more speculatively, at least) that where current practices involving possibly anticompetitive behavior are linked with patent coordination and control, the overall impact on future industry structure and innovation must be thought through very carefully.[13]

INDUSTRIAL STRUCTURE AND THE "KILLER PATENT PORTFOLIO"

UNITED SHOE, DESPITE ITS DOCTRINAL IMPORTANCE, emerged from a different era in economic history. Large-scale vertical integration in many industries was the order of the day then; it appears to be less so now. And, more important, regardless of overall patterns of industrial concentration, it is clear that one key aspect of firm operations is increasingly less vertically integrated than in the past: R&D.

Although no single indicator measures the intensity of R&D concentration or integration, the overall pattern is convincing. Consider first the hand-wringing that almost always accompanies the annual release of U.S. Patent Office data on the 10 largest patentees for the previous year. Typically in the past 10 years a Japanese firm has headed the list, and between 6 and 9 of the top 10 firms have been Japanese. Many decry this trend as a sure sign that R&D leadership is inevitably slipping away to Tokyo. While this is not the place to address the topic of the overall balance of R&D leadership, it is fairly plain that the angst in this case is misplaced.

What is happening is not a slippage of R&D leadership, but a radical change in the firm-level distribution of R&D activity. For while R&D at GE and Corning Glass may be slipping, joint ventures between GE and other firms and Corning and other firms are receiving numerous important patents. At the same time, small start-up companies, often headed by former employees of big firms such as these, are also receiving important patents. Many of these are then licensed back to the big firm. Alternatively, the innovative technology is embodied in products sold as inputs to the big firm. Through these and myriad other organizational mechanisms, formerly concentrated R&D efforts are being dispersed across an industry. This phenomenon has been called many things: outsourcing, downsizing, and strategic partnering, to name a few. The economic truth behind the buzzwords is the growing "dis-integration" of industrial R&D in many sectors of the modern economy. And, it must be noted, intellectual property rights are playing a key role in the process. Venture capital is tightly linked to early-stage intellectual property positioning, as all venture capitalists will attest. The increased facility of start-up venture financing, to which patents surely contribute, is a key reason why R&D can be dis-integrated in the modern economy.

With this dis-integration, the era of the "killer patent portfolio" is slipping away, as complex organizational forms replace the simple, vertically integrated R&D model of the past. Intellectual property rights – particularly patents – are playing a crucial role in this process. To understand their role, and to lay the basis for our argument that patent acquisitions must be handled very carefully in antitrust enforcement actions, we need to consider how stronger property rights lead to greater organizational diversity.

Intellectual Property Rights and the Organization of Production

ONE OF THE FIRST INDICATIONS OF THE CHANGING LANDSCAPE of industrial R&D is the large increase in the volume and sophistication of commercial transactions that have an intellectual property component. Why has intellectual property become the subject of an increasing volume of transactions? Why are so many firms exchanging intellectual property rights now? The answer, as we will see, revolves at least partly around the growing diversity in the organization of R&D and hence an increase in what might loosely be termed "patent-acquisition activities."

There are essentially three interrelated reasons for the growth in intellectual property commercial transactions. First, there is more intellectual property than there used to be, and it is worth more because it is more readily enforced by the courts. The United States Congress and, to a lesser extent, the state legislatures, are creating more intellectual property each year, and where the United States leads in this area other countries tend to follow. Second, the growth in intellectual property has increased awareness in the business community of the intellectual property aspects of traditional transactions. Now there is often an intellectual property dimension to transactions that in the past were conducted without mention of these rights. Third, and perhaps most interesting, intellectual property rights make more feasible the organizational structures that are increasingly being used to produce goods and services. Since these organizations are at least partially based on contracts, they provide a growing source of commercial transactions that necessarily include an intellectual property component.

Intellectual property rights appear to enhance and, in some cases, enable these contract-based organizations, which run the gamut from consulting arrangements to outsourcing agreements in which firms purchase components they formerly manufactured themselves, to joint ventures and franchising arrangements.[14] In general, intellectual property rights make such transactions less risky and hence more frequently feasible, because they make it easier for the licensor – often the supplier of a productive input – to police the activities of the licensee. The strong policy favoring injunctions is one example of how licensors can use intellectual property rights to police licensees' activities. Another example is courts' strict adherence to the field-of-use limitations contained in many licensing agreements. In these and other ways intellectual property rights give the input supplier greater control over the activities of the licensee, which makes the external production of inputs and the concomitant transfer by contract more feasible. To put it another way, intellectual property rights reduce the licensee's opportunistic possibilities and thereby lower transaction costs.

While it is important not to overstate the significance of intellectual property rights in the emergence of these new organizational forms, it is also important to point out some likely causal links, all of which turn on the potential for tighter contractual control, at lower cost, that comes with property rights. The most obvious illustration of how property rights confer tight control is the example alluded to above, the availability of quick injunctions in the event of a breach. Since injunctions are much more easily obtained in intellectual property infringement cases than in run-of-the-mill commercial contract disputes,[15] the inclusion of intellectual property in a commercial arrangement gives the owner of that property right much more leverage with which to police the licensee's behavior. It follows that, at the margin at least, the availability of intellectual property will make a supplier more likely to rely on contracts, as opposed to integration or some other transactional form. In this way property rights, including intellectual property rights, contribute to the growth of contract-based exchange.

Note that it is difficult to argue that contract terms can substitute fully for the enhanced control conferred by the strong injunction policy of intellectual property law. It is well established, for example, that courts do not necessarily enforce contractual provisions stipulating to specific performance or other injunctive remedies.[16] In addition, even if an enforceable contractual provision to this effect were assumed, such a clause would be expensive to draft and negotiate,[17] and someone would have to establish its enforceability. As I have argued elsewhere, these are precisely the kinds of costs that "off-the-rack" intellectual property rights serve to lower or eliminate.[18]

Intellectual Property Rights and the "Propertization" of Labour: The Parable of the Fish

A simple but increasingly common relationship that shows how important intellectual property rights have become in structuring R&D is the consulting agreement. Because the consultant can control the use and dissemination of her work product by contract, she has an incentive to enter into a consulting agreement rather than an outright employment agreement. This partly explains why employees find it feasible to become consultants.

A consultant can generally only sell a given unit of labour once, and can sell it only to a single firm. Intellectual property in effect "propertizes" her labour, making it possible to sell the same unit of output multiple times to multiple firms.[19] Of course, for this to work the consultant must produce something that intellectual property law protects, and she must retain ownership of her work product, typically by contract. If we assume ownership of a protected work, however, intellectual property rights allow her to transform her efforts from a one-time service into a multiple-use commodity. This conversion of services into an asset that the producer can trade many times of course enhances the potential economic returns from such work.

The old parable of the fish illustrates well how reusable techniques and information can pose a public-goods problem and how intellectual property law solves that problem. In the parable, a fisherman is instructing a neophyte in the essence of his trade. "Catch fish for people," he says, "and you will make a fine living. But teach someone to fish, and you will starve." Intellectual property introduces a third possibility: teach multiple people to fish, but prohibit them from retransferring the fishing techniques and even limit the uses of the techniques with contracts. Under this scenario, the fisherman supplies a product, but that product is fishing techniques instead of fish. By limiting the licensee's ability to retransfer the techniques, the fisherman eliminates the downside of transferring techniques instead of goods. In addition, when a buyer is in a better position to invest in boats and fish processing equipment, the sale of techniques will increase efficiency all around. Instead of forcing the fishing expert to invest in these assets to ensure a return on his or her know-how, the expert can sever that know-how and sell it to those who already possess these assets. In a world in which fishing techniques are subject to a property right, firms that buy their own fishing fleets and hire fishing consultants may turn out to be more profitable than those that stick to the old production arrangement. In this respect, intellectual property rights can be seen as a mechanism for lowering the costs of a certain type of exchange and thereby facilitating a finer division of intellectual labour.

When property rights are poorly specified in the law, however, experts should invest in their own assets. As David Teece has illustrated so clearly,[20] firms often invest in co-specific assets as a way of capturing returns from research and development expenses.[21] In other words, when the R&D performer is not in the best position to produce these co-specific assets, strengthening intellectual property rights can increase efficiency by making it possible to disaggregate production of R&D from production of these co-specific assets. It appears that this is just what is occurring in, for example, the biotechnology industry. Pharmaceutical firms continue to invest in scale-up, marketing, and distribution assets, while dedicated biotechnology companies and academic researchers perform much of the actual R&D. The results of the R&D, owned by the dedicated biotechnology company, are accessed contractually by the pharmaceutical firm.

Returning to the fishing example, one can view the property right in fishing techniques as a substitute for fishing services. The property right in the techniques allows the owner of the right to transfer the techniques themselves, as opposed to fish or fishing services. In one sense the essence of the transaction has not really changed: the fisherman is still selling an input into the firm's production process. But the property right in techniques, together with whatever business strategy the owner of the right employs to exploit it, enhances the profitability of a business based on the licensing of techniques, which in turn makes it more likely that the relevant industry structure will include at least some firms that specialize in the sale of techniques. If so, the property right in fishing techniques and the firms that come to specialize in the sale of such techniques enhance the production potential of the industry. Thus the property right – or rather, the transaction it enables – may actually create value in some cases. This is a specific example of the Stiglerian view of increasing specialization as a general result of economic growth.[22]

In addition, once intellectual property rights are introduced into a transactional setting, they open up the possibility for another type of exchange altogether. In some cases, the property right is actually the motivating force behind the transaction. Just as the property right in fishing techniques creates a market for those techniques *qua* techniques, intellectual property rights create the possibility for certain transactions that would not otherwise be feasible. These transactions, in the aggregate, comprise new markets. In this sense, the introduction of intellectual property rights, in some cases at least, offers the potential to affect the organization of production in industries that commonly employ techniques and know-how. Ideally, these rights can even make existing commerce more efficient by increasing the viability of firms that specialize in the creation of techniques.

Of course, simply creating property rights does not guarantee such benign effects. If other factors – especially the transaction costs of integrating intangible inputs such as techniques into the production process – militate against the success of such specialized firms, property rights alone will not make them viable.[23] Williamson, for example, argues:

> At least occasionally, vertical integration backward into research is the most attractive way to overcome the dilemma posed when high-risk programs are to be performed: the sponsoring firm (agency) assumes the risk itself and assigns the task to an internal research group. It essentially writes a cost-plus contract for internal development. That this does not have the debilitating incentive consequences that often result when similar contracts are given to outside developers is attributable to differences in the incentive and compliance machinery: managers are employees, rather than "inside contractors" . . . and thus are unable to appropriate individual profit streams; also the internal compliance machinery to which the firm (agency) has access is vastly superior to and more delicately conceived than the policing machinery that prevails between organizations. Internal organization thus arises in part because of its superior properties in moral hazard respects.[24]

Furthermore, if property rights create more transaction costs than they eliminate (i.e., if the gains from specialization are outweighed by the increased transaction costs of more arm's-length exchange), they will soon become associated with extortion and rent-seeking rather than with enhanced production possibilities. Note, of course, that transaction costs are present even in vertically integrated production; only if they are much higher than the gains from specialization will that specialization appear too costly.[25] These are detailed empirical questions that are best answered in the context of individual industries.

My principal aim is to spell out a theoretical relationship between the structure of property rights and the volume of arm's-length contracting.

But property rights do make feasible some experiments in specialization, as well as other organizational innovations. As recent economic history suggests, some of these experiments work. As long as this continues to happen, and as long as intellectual property rights are part of the experimental mix, firms will continue to generate new types of intellectual-property-related transactions and the organizational forms that grow out of them.

Quasi-integration, Dis-integration, and Reintegration

THE FISHING TECHNIQUES EXAMPLE ALSO ILLUSTRATES other forms of economic production. One of these has come to be called "quasi-integration." This is production that is midway between complete integration and total dis-integration. The classic case of complete integration is the manufacturer of automobiles that owns the supply of all of its inputs: everything from iron mines to rubber plantations to a work force entirely composed of full-time employees. The Ford Company of the Model-T era comes to mind.[26] The traditional rationale for this extensive integration is that managerial control over the entire production process is more efficient than the alternative of acquiring each input through a market transaction. Firms such as GE and DuPont were early pioneers in the movement to apply the logic of vertical integration to R&D, assembling huge teams of dedicated researchers and similarly large patent portfolios.

An example of complete dis-integration is harder to imagine, but consider the production of birthday cakes in a town in which there are only small specialty stores and there is no bakery. In such a town, one who wishes to make a cake will have to get eggs and milk and butter from the dairy store, wheat and sugar from the grocery store, candles from the hardware store, and perhaps other ingredients from other specialty stores. Then the baker of the cakes will sell them in a market transaction to those retail stores that wish to resell them. This is what is meant by dis-integrated production: each input into the final product, as well as the final product itself, must be purchased through an arm's-length market transaction.

Now consider an example of quasi-integration. Imagine a firm in the software industry that is composed strictly of independent consultants, none of whom are employees, working on leased computers and hired by clients on a contract basis to produce specified types of computer programs for a specified fee. This firm assembles its components strictly by contract, on a limited-purpose, limited-time basis. In one sense the firm is nothing but a collection of contracts organized around a specific task. Note that despite the contracted-in nature of the inputs, the ongoing nature of the task necessitates some management . This management is what differentiates quasi-integration from dis-integration. In truly dis-integrated production the transactions are discrete spot-market contracts;

in quasi-integrated production the consultants assemble the inputs by contract, but they combine the inputs into an ongoing production process. The consultants perform the contracts over a period of time, rather than instantaneously in a spot-market transfer. In the lexicon of contracting, quasi-integration involves relational, rather than one-shot, discrete contracts.

With this as background, we return to the story of the fishing consultant. One can easily imagine a two-pronged agreement between the fishing consultant and the firm. The consultant agrees to: (1) teach members of the firm how to fish, and (2) transfer her property right in fishing techniques to the firm. In exchange, imagine that the fishing consultant receives a portion of her compensation in the form of equity issued by the other party. This is an example of quasi-integration. It is certainly not an example of integration: the fishing consultant contracts with the firm rather than becoming an employee. It is not really an example of dis-integration either; though the input supplied by the consultant is transferred via contract, the consultant helps implement the technique and disseminate it throughout the firm over time, and the equity compensation gives the consultant an ongoing interest in the activities of the firm.

Thus intellectual property rights can enhance market transfers, not only by propertizing labour, but also by facilitating quasi-integration.[27] In the fishing example, this took the form of joining the property right with a service component. To the extent that the intellectual property right makes the transaction more feasible, it contributes to the desirability of the quasi-integrated organizational form.

Intellectual property rights can also facilitate complete dis-integration. Take as an example the organization of production in the music industry. A firm that sells musical recordings need not employ the musicians or the composer, and the artist herself can arrange for the actual production of the music as she sees fit. Artists license their rights to musical compositions and recordings, and they usually transfer the license and the master tapes to the sales firm. Because a large record label will have entered into such transactions with hundreds of musicians, almost none of whom are employees, the production of music can be described as dis-integrated production.

The dis-integrated nature of music production requires the integration of a large number of musical properties in order to assemble a formidable music portfolio.[28] Although to some extent the same logic that leads firms in other industries to integrate vertically is present here, this approach rarely involves actually hiring creators as employees. There seems to be broad agreement that the nature of creative work is incompatible with employee status. What the firm integrates, then, is property rights, rather than the actual services of the creators. These transactions would be much more expensive without some way of easily dividing up the output of a creator into discrete assets – in other words, without formal intellectual property rights.

In an alternative organizational form, holders of intellectual property rights covering certain works license those rights to a central institution, which then typically issues blanket licenses. The right holders remain independent, however. The best example of this is in the market for music performance rights, in which the American Society of Authors, Composers and Publishers and rival organizations play this integrating role. The key here is that these institutions serve to integrate a large pool of properties, while allowing musicians to remain independent of the firms that package and disseminate music on a large scale.

A CASE STUDY IN QUASI-INTEGRATION: JOINT VENTURES

JOINT VENTURES ARE INCREASINGLY POPULAR,[29] and they proliferate as firms recognize their advantages. These include (1) compensating for in-house weaknesses or technological gaps, (2) filling out product lines and portfolios, (3) positioning the firm to enter lucrative new markets, and, most important, (4) reducing the costs, risks, and time required to develop new products and process technologies.[30] Indeed, David Teece has written that contractual governance structures such as joint ventures may come to displace the "managerial capitalism" of the large, integrated firm that Alfred Chandler argues lay at the heart of economic growth in the twentieth century. Teece says:

> [Today's] challenges are somewhat different, and the organizational forms suited to each may vary to some degree, and may also differ from those that were effective in the [era studied by Chandler, i.e., the late nineteenth to the mid-twentieth centuries] . . . Perhaps it is because classical economies of scale and the unit price advantages can be accessed contractually in today's markets. Flexible specialization and contracting may today yield greater advantages than economies of scale and scope generated internally.[31]

Whatever the motivations behind the growth in joint ventures and despite their potential problems,[32] I am interested in the role of intellectual property rights in facilitating their formation. I believe the same factors are at work in the growth of a wide range of increasingly common organizational forms,[33] and that many common legal disputes grow out of transactions connected to these organizations.

The literature directed at joint venture organizers features helpful pointers about the use of intellectual property. To begin with, it emphasizes the importance of contractual restrictions on the venture's use of technology licensed in from the partners. For example, one book aimed at managers states that :

> [Joint venturers] can use exclusive licensing provisions, right-of-first-refusal provisions, non-competition agreements, and other contractual provisions to protect knowledge from disseminating to unauthorized third parties . . . .

[T]echnology licenses that are based on control of patents often provide that certain information cannot be passed on or used in another application (or for another purpose) without the owner's explicit permission.[34]

Intellectual property rights are more than just another issue the joint venture agreement must deal with. Seen more broadly, these rights facilitate the very formation of the venture itself, because they codify discrete quantities of technology that the partners license into the venture, making it easier to keep track of which partner contributed to the technology. They also help the partners manage the output of the venture. First, these rights represent real assets that the partners can allocate if they wind up the venture. This undoubtedly saves a good deal of time and energy because the parties need not, at the time of dissolution, specify in detail all the research results produced by the venture during its life. Second, these rights organize relations between the venture and its "parents" by providing a discrete asset that the venture can license or assign. Again, this saves the costs of specifying exactly what technology the venture has created and exactly what rights the venture will have. The venture's intellectual property rights cover the technology, and they define the limits of the venture's rights with respect to its technology. The venture would have to specify all of this at length by contract in the absence of these rights.

In light of this it is not surprising that the empirical data, though sketchy, suggest that intellectual property rights play a significant role in many joint ventures. The legal practitioner literature,[35] the quasi-armchair data,[36] and reports of litigated cases[37] confirm the importance of intellectual property in joint ventures, especially those with an R&D component.

To some extent, the growth of a distinct field that handles complex commercial transactions with an intellectual property component goes some way toward expanding the trend. The dissemination of know-how in a new legal field is a crucial step in advancing promising techniques and establishing the field's legitimacy, just as it is in newly emerging scientific and engineering disciplines. We know now that lawyers – especially commercial lawyers – truly are "transaction cost engineers," as Professor Ronald Gilson so aptly put it.

PATENT ACQUISITIONS, ORGANIZATIONAL FORMS, AND INTELLECTUAL PROPERTY THEORY

TRADITIONAL ECONOMIC MODELS MAKE TWO CRUCIAL ASSUMPTIONS relevant to a discussion of patent acquisitions. First, they assume that actors exchange intellectual property rights only in pure, unbundled forms. This ignores an important issue: because it is difficult to trace the source of an idea, value it, and determine a cutoff point beyond which an agreement will not require compensation for a benefit, the market for ideas and the intellectual property rights that cover them is most troublesome. This may well explain why outright assignment of patents so seldom allows the assignor to appropriate much of the patent's "value added." It also explains why licensors so often join intellectual property rights to some tangible product, or at least to know-how or other transferable assets of the licensor. These additional components may make it easier to value the package of benefits that the licensor is bestowing.

The second major problem with conventional intellectual property theory is that it makes what can be termed the "one-to-one mapping error." That is, it assumes for the most part that a single intellectual property right covers a single commercial product that occupies a distinct market in the economic sense. This is almost always an inaccurate assumption. In fact, the typical commercial product is covered by many patents, not just one. This is quite obvious in the case of complex, multicomponent products. It is no less true of products that are seemingly more discrete, such as individual microprocessors or pharmaceutical products. Patents cover not only the basic concept in these cases – a microprocessor design or chemical entity – but also numerous ancillary features: improvements (e.g., modified circuits or chemical structures), process technologies used in manufacturing, and associated components (pin or board configurations, or dosage forms or drug delivery systems). It is also important to note in this regard that with the growth of intellectual property this trend will only intensify. More components will be covered by more patents. And therefore the one-to-one mapping assumption will become even less accurate.

There are two implications of all this: rights are difficult to transfer by themselves; and when they are transferred they very seldom bestow power in a distinct economic market. This means that now that we are for the most part beyond the era of the "killer patent portfolio," patent acquisitions take on different forms. Antitrust policy must be sensitive to this. For example, an exclusive patent license accompanying the sale of an input may well have the same economic effect as an outright assignment. Under traditional case law such as *United Shoe*, however, the license and sale might not even be considered an acquisition at all. After all, the two firms still appear to be independent, and the patent is held (nominally) by the licensor, who also sells the input. But the economic effect is much more like a straight acquisition. Hence there is a need to expand the meaning of patent "acquisitions", in light of current practices evolving against a background of greater organizational complexity.

It must be observed that although patent acquisitions take on many forms, they have very different effects in a world where patents are more common and organizational diversity is flourishing. More patent acquisitions may be necessary under these circumstances, both because they help structure the complex transactions that cross firm boundaries, and because they are made necessary by the growth in the sheer volume of extant patents. To restrict them in an era when firms rely on complex transactional strategies to carry out their business model successfully would be very deleterious. After all, as Lewis Kaplow noted some years ago, firms consider both the bundle of property rights themselves *and* the transactional rules that accompany them when evaluating the incentive effect of the patent system. We should not forget this valuable insight in a rush to prevent the possible amassing of monopoly power through patent acquisitions.

THE NEW THREATS

WHILE IT IS STILL POSSIBLE THAT KILLER PATENT PORTFOLIOS will be assembled in the future, for the reasons outlined above it is less likely now than in the *United Shoe* era. However, a new breed of patent acquisitions poses difficult challenges for antitrust doctrine. Some of these practices, singly or in combination, may present opportunities to update the antitrust doctrines used to police patent acquisitions.

"STRATEGIC" PATENT ACQUISITIONS BY RIVALS

A DIFFICULT PROBLEM IS PRESENTED WHERE A FIRM BUYS UP PATENTS solely to slow down the competitors. It is not a requirement of U.S. patent law that a patent be "worked" in order to remain valid. This, together with the fact that a patent can of course be assigned freely, means that the acquisition of patents for "blocking" purposes is perfectly permissible under U.S. law.

While technically permissible, this practice is completely at odds with the underlying theory of the patent system (especially if adopted on a large scale). The inventions at issue in such cases would never really be implemented; in fact, the object of these patent acquisitions is to take a working technology out of circulation! If the acquiring party successfully acquires and asserts a patent that covers a rival's product, the result will be an injunction in favor of the patent-holding party. This has the effect of shutting down the only entity actually practicing the technology. Of course, if the acquiror who asserts the patent has a competitive product, she may well continue to sell a perfectly viable substitute for the technology covered by the acquired patent.

One way to address this issue is to revive a consideration long neglected under U.S. patent law. In some older cases, injunctions were sometimes denied where the plaintiff in an infringement suit was not actually practicing the patent at issue, on the basis that the objective of patent law is to put advanced technology in the hands of consumers. If the infringer was doing so, but the patentee was not (and, crucially, appeared to have no plans to), the courts sometimes opted against an injunction during the litigation stage. In some extreme cases they even continued this arrangement after trial, resulting, in effect, in a form of compulsory license that would stay in effect until the patentee himself implemented his own technology. It might make sense under current conditions to revive the practice of at least considering this issue, given the mischief that can follow from the assertion of unworked patents. I have argued for a similar result where blocking patents produce the same sort of "holdup" problems with negative externalities for the consuming public.[38]

Recently there has been a twist on the practice of acquiring patents strictly for blocking purposes. Some cases have revealed that firms are acquiring a third party's patent, filing a re-examination or re-issue request in the Patent Office, and "re-engineering" the patent to block a competitor's product. In *Hewlett-Packard v. Bausch & Lomb, Inc.*,[39] for example, Bausch & Lomb purchased a third-party patent "admittedly for the [sole] purpose of gaining leverage in negotiations . . . with HP."[40] Bausch and Lomb found the need to redraft one claim of the patent, however, to insure that it covered HP's products. This they did by using false affidavits regarding the initial intent behind the original claim language. While the courts caught on to the deceptive affidavits in this case,[41] they expressly noted that the general practice of acquiring a patent and filing a re-issue request to cover competitive products was permissible because it was not expressly proscribed by the statute.

The problem caused by this practice stems from the lack of notice to the potential defendant against whom the re-examined patent might be asserted. It is one thing to stand accused of infringing a patent that from the outset covered one's commercial products; it is another thing to be accused of infringing a patent whose claims were re-engineered expressly for the purpose of patent litigation. There is no way to know what claim language the patent office will issue in a re-issue until the final decision is made; this is when the defendant sees the newly re-issued patent for the first time.

Patent law, by its terms, contains no restriction on this type of activity. It thus falls to antitrust doctrine to police the anticompetitive effects of such practices. I would argue for a doctrine that at the very least considers these patent acquisitions suspect, and in appropriate cases denies injunctions for the reasons outlined earlier. To put it more forcefully, it ought to be possible to mount a Sherman section 1 challenge to the practice. This would have the salutary effect of shifting the procedural balance. Instead of merely giving the patent litigation defendant a defence, it would give her an affirmative counterclaim. Moreover, it would give her the basis to argue for treble damages – not generally available to a patent infringement defendant in the usual case. Where the acquisition and/or re-issuance of a third party would give the acquiring party market power solely through the exclusionary effect on the defendant's commercially marketed products, antitrust inquiry is warranted.

Conclusion

THE ERA OF THE KILLER PATENT PORTFOLIO IS LARGELY GONE, to be replaced by an economic landscape of more diverse organizational forms and the dis-integration and dispersion of R&D-intensive activities. At the same time, new patent-acquisition strategies have emerged that bear watching from an antitrust perspective, because of their anticompetitive potential. Thus patent-acquisition doctrine has not become extinct; it is merely in need of some evolutionary adaptation.

NOTES

1   See Carl Kaysen, *United States v. United Shoe Machinery Corporation: An Economic Analysis of An Antitrust Case*, 1956.
2   110 F. Supp. 295, 344 (D.Mass. 1953), aff'd *per curiam*, 347 U.S. 521 (1954) (quoting from *United States v. Aluminum Co. of Am.*, 148 F.2d 416, 430 (2d Cir. 1945)).
3   110 F. Supp. 295, 333 (D. Mass. 1953), aff'd *per curiam*, 347 U.S. 521 (1954).
4   See *United States v. Parker Rust-Proof Co.*, 61 F. Supp. 805 (E.D. Mich. 1945) (exclusive license to existing and future patents, trade secrets, and trademarks acquired by dominant firm).
5   See, for example, *Dollac Corp. v. Margon Corp.*, 164 F. Supp. 41 (D.N.J. 1958), aff'd on other grounds, 275 F.2d 202 (3d Cir. 1960); *Western Geophysical Co. of Am. v. Bolt Assoc., Inc.*, 305 F. Supp. 1248 (D. Conn. 1969) (exclusive license to key technology acquired by a dominant firm); *Chandler v. Stern Dental Laboratory Co.*, 335 F. Supp. 580 (S.D. Tex. 1971) (allegation that defendant used exclusive license to conspire to monopolize by suppressing sales of patent product and promoting sales of other products).
6   *SCM Corp. v. Xerox Corp.*, 645 F.2d 1195, 1205 (2d Cir. 1981). But, see *Image Technical Services, Inc. v. Eastman Kodak Co.*, 1997-2 CCH Trade Cases ¶71,908 (9b Cir. 1997) (finding intellectual property rights a pretext for anticompetitive behavior).
7   645 F.2d 1195, 1206 (2d Cir. 1981), cert. denied, 455 U.S. 1016 (1982).
8   *Id.*, p. 1208.
9   645 F.2d, p. 1204.
10 See Raymond Klitzke, "Patent Accumulation and Pooling Offer Additional Opportunities for the Monopolist to Maintain Its Competitive Position," *Marquette Law Review*. While accumulated and licensed patents do not in themselves constitute an earmark of antitrust violation, it is a key factor in finding a violation.
11 46 F. Supp. 541 (N.D. Ohio 1942), modified, 323 U.S. 386 (1945), remanded, 65 F. Supp. 271 (N.D. Ohio 1946).
12 *Id.* Restrictions of this kind are not only of historical interest. See, for example, *General Talking Pictures Corp. v. Western Elec. Co.*, 305 U.S. 124 (1938). See also Stephen J. Davidson, "Selected Legal and Practical Considerations Concerning 'Scope of Use' Provisions," *Computer Law*, October 1993, p. 1. Davidson argues that:

> . . . such restrictions [i.e., tight field-of-use limitations] (or the lack of express authorization for a particular use) may be used by the licensor in an effort to extract excessive license or renewal fees after the licensee has become reliant on the software in its business. Claims of default and termination based on such restrictions or lack of express authorization, or based on ambiguity over what uses are permitted, can threaten the licensee's very ability to continue in business. The courts are all over the place on these issues, and the opinions in those cases that have been decided in the past few years suggest that the decisions were based more on the

courts' gut level sense of justice than any uniform rules of law. . . . The ability of software licensors to terminate or threaten termination of their licenses or support agreements based upon alleged default by unauthorized use is a very real threat to licensees who are reliant upon the software for continuation of their day-to-day business operations. (*Id.* p. 1, 5.)

13 See P. Areeda and D. Turner, *Antitrust Law*, ¶ 819, (1994). Professors Areeda and Turner argue that placing limitations on the patent rights of an acquiring party depends upon the extent of power it already possesses in the relevant market into which the patented products enter.

14 On the latter, see James A. Brickley and Frederick H. Dark, "The Choice of Organizational Form: The Case of Franchising," *Journal of Financial Economics*, 18 (1987): 401, 403-07, ; Gillian K. Hadfield, "Problematic Relations: Franchising and the Law of Incomplete Contracts," *Stanford Law Review*, 42 (1990): 927. The franchise relationship carries with it the possibility of mutual opportunism.

15 On injunctions in intellectual property cases, see Robert P. Merges, "Of Coase, Property Rights, and Intellectual Property," *Columbia Law Review*, 94 (1994): 2655. On the availability of injunctions in commercial transaction cases, see Scott E. Masten, "A Legal Basis for the Firm," in *The Nature of the Firm*, edited by Oliver E. Williamson and Sidney G. Winter, 1993, pp. 195, 205 ("[S]pecific performance is infrequently applied in commercial settings . . .").

16 See Alan Schwartz, "The Myth That Promisees Prefer Supracompensatory Remedies: An Analysis of Contracting for Damage Measures," *Yale Law Journal*, 100 (1990): 369.

17 See Masten, *supra*, note 15, p. 207, (pointing out the advantages of relying on standard common law principles in the area of employment law, as opposed to replicating them in services contracts, which "would . . . require reviewing and repeating the entire case law in each contract, obviously forfeiting a substantial economy").

18 See Merges, *supra*, note 15, pp. 2664-73.

19 Commentators at least since Locke have asserted that everyone owns his or her labour; in Locke's case, this was an outgrowth of his starting point that everyone owns his or her own body. John Locke, *Two Treatises of Government*, pp. 328-29, (1690), Peter Laslett (ed.), 1960. But when these commentators refer to a property right in one's labour, they are talking about the right to bargain for a wage before engaging in work – in essence, the right not to be a slave. By contrast, I am referring to the conversion of labour into a tradeable asset or property right. "Assetization" might be a more appropriate term for what I have in mind; but since this sounds even worse than "propertization" I will stick with the latter. On a related phenomenon, see Tamar Frankel, *Securitization: Structured Financing, Financial Assets Pools, and Asset-Backed Securities*, 1991.

20 See David J. Teece, "Profiting from Technological Innovation: Implications for Integration, Collaboration, Licensing and Public Policy," *Research Policy*, 15 (1986): 285, 294 .

21 This of course implicates issues of patent misuse, which govern tie-ins. See Louis Kaplow, "The Patent-Antitrust Intersection: A Reappraisal", *Harvard Law Review*, 97 (1984): 1813 ; Byron A. Bilicki, "Note," "Standard Antitrust Analysis and the Doctrine of Patent Misuse: A Unification Under the Rule of Reason," *University of Pittsburg Law Review*, 46 (1984): 209 ; Mark A. Lemley, "Comment," "The Economic Irrationality of the Patent Misuse Doctrine," *California Law Review*, 78 (1990): 1599.

But see Kenneth J. Burchfiel, "Patent Misuse and Antitrust Reform: 'Blessed Be the Tie?'," *Harvard Journal of Law and Technology*, 4 (1991): 1 (defending patent misuse on the basis that the antitrust standard is difficult and expensive); Robert P. Merges, "Reflections on Current Legislation Affecting Patent Misuse," *Journal of the Patent and Trademark Office Society*, 70 (1988): 793 (defending a separate doctrine of patent misuse). See, for example, *Senza-Gel Corp. v. Seiffhart*, 803 F.2d 661, 665 and n.5 (Fed. Cir. 1986) (finding patent misuse in a tie-in situation); cf. *USM Corp. v. SPS Technologies, Inc.*, 694 F.2d 505, 511 (7th Cir. 1982) (Posner, J.) (concluding that there is an increasing convergence of patent-misuse analysis with standard antitrust analysis), cert. denied, 462 U.S. 1107 (1983); Thomas M. S. Hemnes, "Restraints on Alienation, Equitable Servitudes, and the Feudal Nature of Computer Software Licensing", *Denver University Law Review*, 71 (1988): 577-79.

22 The economist George Stigler is associated with the view that economic growth inevitably brings with it an increase in firm specialization, even with regards to research and development. This suggests the inevitability of specialized production of fishing techniques. See Oliver E. Williamson, *Markets and Hierarchies: Analysis and Antitrust Implications*, New York: Free Press, 1975, pp. 197-205, (discussing Stigler's views on the organization of research activities, especially the tendency to specialize). Note that business historian Alfred Chandler has argued that firm specialization and economic growth are codetermined, and thus to some extent specialization causes growth. See Alfred D. Chandler, Jr., *The Visible Hand*, Cambridge, Mass.: Belknap Press, 1977, pp. 15-36.

23 Of course, intellectual property rights also increase the bargaining leverage of the licensor, which is one reason the legal system must carefully consider the extension of these rights into new product markets. See Robert P. Merges, "Intellectual Property Rights and Bargaining Breakdown: The Case of Improvement Inventions and Blocking Patents," *Tennessee Law Review*, 62 (1994): 75.

24 See Oliver Williamson, *Markets and Hierarchies*, *supra*, note 22, chapter entitled "Market Structure in Relation to Technical and Organizational Innovation," pp.-203-4.

25 See Harold Demsetz , "The Theory of the Firm Revisited," in *Ownership, Control and the Firm*, p. 144 (discussing the presence of transaction costs inside firms).

26 See Alfred D. Chandler, Jr., *Scale and Scope: The Dynamics of Industrial Capitalism*, Cambridge, Mass.: Belknap Press, 1990, p. 208.

27 This is somewhat analogous to the Japanese *keiretsu*. For a description, see Ronald J. Gilson and Mark J. Roe, "Understanding the Japanese Keiretsu: Overlaps Between Corporate Governance and Industrial Organization," *Yale Law Journal*, 102 (1993): 871, 882-95.

28 For example, Warner/Chappell, a large music publishing company, is said to hold over 700,000 copyrights to musical compositions. David Sinacore-Guinn, *Collective Administration of Copyrights and Neighboring Rights: International Practices, Procedures, and Organizations*, Boston, Toronto: Little Brown and Company, 1993, p. 198.

29 See Kathryn Rudie Harrigan, *Managing for Joint Venture Success*, 1986; Jeremy Main, "The Winning Organization," *Fortune*, September 26, 1988, pp. 50, 52 ("Kathryn Harrigan, a Columbia University business professor, says the number of such ventures [joint ventures, partnerships, or other agreements] began to pick up in the early 1980s, from a growth rate of some 6% a year to around 22%. She looks for much faster growth in the next few years."); John P. Karalis, *International Joint Ventures* § 1.1, 1992.

30   Committee on Japan, National Research Council, *U.S.-Japan Strategic Alliances in the Semiconductor Industry: Technology Transfer, Competition, and Public Policy* 17, 1992; see, also, Morton I. Kamien et al., "Research Joint Ventures and R&D Cartels," *American Economic Review*, 82 (1992): 1293 (describing a formal model of research joint ventures).

31   David J. Teece, "The Dynamics of Industrial Capitalism: Perspectives on Alfred Chandler's Scale and Scope," *Journal of Economic Literature*, 31 (1993) :199, 216-18, (citation omitted).

32   See, for example, Jennifer F. Reinganum, "The Timing of Innovation: Research, Development, and Diffusion," in *Handbook of Industrial Organization*, edited by Richard Schmalensee and Robert D. Willig, 1989, pp. 849, 851 (summarizing models of research joint ventures, and concluding that a "robust" finding is that "firms who are not members of the research joint venture are left worse off as a result of innovation").

33   For more on the growing diversity of organizational forms in U.S. industries, see Michael L. Gerlach and James R. Lincoln, "The Organization of Business Networks in the United States and Japan," in *Networks and Organizations*, edited by Nitin Nohria and Robert G. Eccles, 1992, pp. 491, 495-96.

> [N]etwork forms appear to be proliferating as corporate downsizing and streamlining, often in response to competitive challenges from Japan and Europe, have encouraged joint ventures, subcontracting, industry consortia such as Sematech, and other cooperative arrangements among firms. Finally, new manufacturing technologies and production systems have led to stronger bonds and closer working relationships between manufacturers and subcontractors. *Id.*

34   Harrigan, *supra*, note 29, p. 148.

35   See, for example, Karalis, *supra*, note 29, § 2.25, pp. 64, 67-68:

> If a joint venture engages primarily in research and development, its output will be primarily technology. This technology may include patentable inventions, copyrightable works or trade secrets. In addition to creating its own technology, the joint venture may improve upon technology transferred to it by one or more of its shareholders. It may also acquire, and improve upon, technology created by others. Rights in this technology are acquired by license agreement. . . . *Id.* (footnotes omitted);

See, also, John P. Sinnott, "Selection Strategy for Foreign Patent Application Filing," in *Global Intellectual Property Series 1992: Practical Strategies*, Patent Practicing Law Institute, 1992. Sinnott adds some interesting points:

> The character of the patent portfolio, moreover, should reflect the foreign business format that is likely to be chosen. Illustratively, the number and character of the patents in a license portfolio could be significantly different from the patents in a joint venture portfolio. A joint venture portfolio probably would be much more extensive and be weighted more toward process patent rights than the patents required for a less complicated product patent license program. Certainly, the United States concern that wants to enter, let us say, a joint venture in some country will be in a superior bargaining position if a large and relevant portfolio of patents can be presented to the prospective foreign business associate and to the host government's financial authorities who so frequently have the power to authorize royalty payments. *Id.* pp. 29-30.

36   See, for example, Mark Casson, *The Firm and the Market: Studies on Multinational Enterprise and the Scope of the Firm,* 1987, pp. 137- 41 (describing the example of Pilkington's patented glass technology, which has been diffused internationally by means of joint ventures).

37   In a recent search I found more than 10 cases involving joint ventures and intellectual property since 1980. See, for example, *Hockerson-Halberstadt, Inc. v. Nike, Inc.,* 779 F. Supp. 49 (E.D. La. 1991) (refusing to dismiss suit, despite defendant's argument that plaintiff had not formed its joint venture when defendant's acts of infringement occurred, because the inventors who assigned all their intellectual property to the joint venture specified that it was to have the right to sue for past infringements).

38   Robert P. Merges, "Intellectual Property Rights and Bargaining Breakdown: The Case of Improvement Inventions and Blocking Patents," *Tennessee Law Review,* 62 (1994): 75. One corollary is that manufacturers sometimes consider licensors whose primary business is the issuance of pure or naked licenses as marginal contributors to the advancement of an industry, and sometimes even as mere extortionists. See Edmund L. Andrews, "Inventor Wins Hot Wheels Case," *New York Times,* 11 November 1989, p. 35 (describing lawsuit by prolific inventor Jerome Lemelson, who is widely known for asserting broad but vague patents against entire industries). The notion of taking the unworked status of a patent into account thus extends further than the context discussed here.

39   882 F.2d 1556 (Fed. Cir. 1989).

40   *Id.*

41   See Robert P. Merges, *Patent Law and Policy* 838 *et seq.,* 1992, (discussing the "inequitable conduct" aspect of the case).

Comment

Neil Campbell
McMillan Binch

THE POINTS ROBERT MERGES MAKES WITH RESPECT to patent acquisitions probably apply to a wider spectrum of intellectual property rights. There is a typology of competition problems in this area. The "killer portfolio" is only one of the concerns that competition law must be prepared to address. Merges highlights the potential for tactical or strategic acquisitions to be used as part of a broader pattern of activities that may buttress the exercise of market power. The points he makes are a very useful starting point from which to deal with these issues in the context of other types of intellectual property as well.

There is some very important theoretical material in the paper. First, intellectual property rights facilitate organizational diversity and efficient transacting in a variety of ways. I agree with the theoretical relationship, and I think it is implicit in the paper that the patent system is presumed to have exogenously determined the right amount of intellectual property rights. But, the implication of the theory is that the ideal degree of intellectual property rights protection should vary in accordance with the efficiencies arising from the expanded scope for contractual and organizational arrangements. I think an interesting empirical question has been left unresolved: How important a role has the strengthening of patent protection, at least in the United States, played in developing a range of other organizational forms?

The second important theoretical point Merges makes, which I also agree with, is that the increase in intellectual property rights also creates more opportunities for tactical or strategic misuse. Those opportunities for misuse are important in determining how much protection for intellectual property rights is desirable. I think the potential for misuse is probably not limited to patent or other intellectual property rights acquisitions; it applies to a number of other areas. The focus on acquisitions may therefore be unnecessarily narrow for the strong theoretical core of the paper.

How significant the misuses are is another empirical question that needs to be addressed. One could try to assess how far the misuses outweigh the efficiency benefits of having greater scope for contractual arrangements and organization forms. But there is also another important policy question: To what extent is the acquisition versus other misuses the problem we want to focus on? I believe that, given the narrowness with which product markets are often defined, the market power problem can arise well short of a "killer" portfolio of 2,000 patents. So while I accept the generalization that the killer portfolio is being replaced by other, more selective and targeted misuses that are becoming more problematic, it would be desirable to deal with both in a competition law regime. I would not overplay the shift, since I do not think it carries many policy implications. Ultimately, competition law should be able to deal with both of these problems.

The difference between product markets and "innovation markets" has a bearing on this. In the area of patent acquisitions, the focus must be on product markets; the innovation market concept is not very helpful in what we would want a competition law regime to accomplish. In these situations, the innovation has already occurred and the patent already exists. Whether it is the killer portfolio, the selective blocking, the suppression or the buttressing, the concern is the misuse of patents in such a way as to allow somebody to leverage market power in a product market. If this is correct, then the traditional competition law framework should be adequate. It may not be necessary to do very much other than to heighten awareness among competition enforcement agencies that there are situations where the competition laws could usefully be brought to bear in a selective way when there is a particular kind of abuse.

To what extent is the present Canadian competition law and policy framework adequate for tackling the types of abuses Merges enumerates? Section 32 of the *Competition Act* allows a court to make specific remedial orders when intellectual rights are used in a manner which lessens competition unduly. In addition, we could use our merger law, the abuse of dominance provision or the conspiracy offence, all of which have some potential for addressing the types of situations he describes. Thus it does not appear that Canada needs new law in this area.

Part II
Contractual Practices and
Organizational Arrangements

William F. Baxter   &   Daniel P. Kessler
Law School   School of Business
Stanford University   Stanford University

The Law and Economics of Tying Arrangements: Lessons for the Competition Policy Treatment of Intellectual Property

INTRODUCTION

A TYING ARRANGEMENT EXISTS WHEN A PRODUCER SELLS ONE PRODUCT, the tying product, only to those who also buy from that producer a second product, the tied product. Examples of tying include the sale of motion picture projectors on the condition that the projector only be used to project the seller's own movies,[1] the leasing of canning machinery on the condition that the lessor also buy salt tablets to be used in its operation,[2] and the sale of replacement parts for copying machines by the manufacturer on the condition that the buyer purchase repair services.[3] As these cases indicate, tying arrangements arise frequently in markets involving intellectual property.

American antitrust jurisprudence first encountered tying arrangements in the context of patent infringement. The early law treated tying with hostility, describing it as "hardly serv[ing] any purpose beyond the suppression of competition."[4] The hostility was rooted in the fear that tying would infringe on the rights both of competitors to "free access to the market for the tied product"[5] and buyers to "free choice between competing products."[6] In an era in which the antitrust laws were enforced in order to prevent the aggregation of "economic power," these were harsh condemnations indeed. For these reasons, tying was held illegal *per se* under section 1 of the *Sherman Act*, section 3 of the *Clayton Act*, and section 5 of *the Federal Trade Commission Act*, prohibiting arrangements without regard to the circumstances or economic effects of the particular restraint.

The *per se* prohibition against tying arrangements, however, presented operational and theoretical problems. On a practical level, the prohibition on tying arrangements could infringe on a wide variety of ordinary, inoffensive transactions. Tying doctrine, read broadly, could prohibit the tying of tires to the purchase of a car, the tying of trousers to the purchase of a jacket, and the tying of shoelaces to the purchase of shoes. Indeed, private plaintiffs succeeded in classifying ordinary business arrangements as illegal ties in several cases, including an automobile sold with a factory-installed radio[7] and a product sold with delivery.[8]

In theoretical terms, the *per se* evaluation of tying failed to acknowledge that simple economic models suggest that tying either improves or does not alter social welfare. These models generally proceed along the following lines. Assume that consumers value a monopolized good, the tying good, at v_m, which is produced at marginal cost c_m. The tied good is produced competitively at marginal cost c, where c is less than consumers' valuation of the tied good. The monopolist could require the consumer to purchase the tied good with the tying good, but if it did, it could not charge more than $v_m + c$. If the monopolist did charge more than $v_m + c$, the consumer would not purchase the package of the tied and tying goods and would instead purchase only the tied product on the competitive market for its marginal cost. Thus the monopolist can do no better than earn profits of $v_m - c_m$; in short, there is only one monopoly profit that can be extracted, so tying cannot enhance monopoly power.

Moreover, the traditional analysis advances several welfare-enhancing motivations for tying, such as economies of scope, protection of goodwill, and risk-sharing.[9] A manufacturer of photocopiers might require users of the machine to obtain repair services or supplies from it in order to ensure the successful operation of the machine and to avoid customer dissatisfaction. Alternatively, if the tying product has uncertain value to customers, as in the case of an innovation, then charging less for the innovation and tying it to a good whose demand is correlated with the revealed value of the innovation can insure customers against the possibility of an imprudent purchase.[10]

In response to overreaching in practice and the increasing importance of economics to antitrust law, American courts have become increasingly reluctant to impose *per se* antitrust liability for tying claims, both in general and in intellectual property cases. Despite this judicial reform of tying doctrine, though, the *per se* label for tying cases has remained. Thus American tying law has evolved in a confusing and often internally contradictory way. On the one hand, courts have begun to conduct rule-of-reason-like analyses, weighing the existence of market power and the possibility of foreclosure against the pro-competitive effects of the several legitimate business justifications for tying. On the other hand, the hallmark of a *per se* prohibition is that it "avoids the necessity for an incredibly complicated and prolonged economic investigation . . . in an effort to determine . . . whether a particular restraint has been unreasonable."[11] At least four Supreme Court justices have recognized the shortcomings of existing tying doctrine, writing in the recent *Jefferson Parish* case that "tying doctrine incurs the costs of a rule-of-reason approach without achieving its benefits: the doctrine calls for the extensive and time consuming economic

analysis characteristic of the rule of reason, but then may be interpreted to prohibit arrangements that economic analysis would show to be beneficial."[12]

Canadian law, in contrast, has evaluated tying arrangements in a more
consistent way, under the rule of reason.[13] Canadian courts have been reluctant
to prohibit tying under the common-law doctrine barring unreasonable
restraints of trade. And, the formulation of section 31.4 of the *Combines
Investigation Act* (now section 77 of the *Competition Act*) only prohibits tying
when the practice has one or more specified exclusionary effects that lessen or
are likely to lessen competition substantially.

The purpose of this paper is to provide a unified positive and normative
evaluation of the law and economics concerning tying arrangements, using
examples involving intellectual property. The first section reviews recent
research in industrial organization. It concludes that the traditional analysis
– that there is only one monopoly profit that can be extracted, so tying cannot
enhance monopoly power – is incomplete. As several scholars have observed,
tying can affect welfare adversely on both the demand and the supply sides.[14]
Some conditions under which various economic models predict that tying will
be socially harmful or socially beneficial are elaborated.

The second section outlines the current state of American legal doctrine.
It begins with the source of the black-letter law behind the *per se* rule, the early
patent infringement cases. Then, it discusses the judicially created mitigations
that have proliferated in recent years. The third section presents suggestions for
tying and intellectual property law reform, including the development of a
"structured rule of reason" that builds on the Canadian approach.

THE ECONOMICS OF TYING ARRANGEMENTS: RESEARCH IN INDUSTRIAL ORGANIZATION

TRADITIONAL ECONOMIC ANALYSES OF TYING CONCLUDE that it is at worst
inoffensive and frequently socially constructive. However, recent research
that relaxes the assumptions underlying the traditional model has shown that
the welfare implications of tying are ambiguous, particularly in markets for
intellectual property. The most fundamental source of this ambiguity is the
trade-off between the benefits from dynamic incentives for investment in innovation and the distortions from static monopoly. To induce parties to invest in
the production of intellectual property, governments create monopoly rights
to the profits from inventions and discoveries. These incentives to invent,
however, necessarily create inefficiency. Once the invention exists, its use is
non-rival; from a social perspective, the invention should be available to all.
Tying, or any potential distortion, can either enhance or reduce social welfare,
given the distortion that results from government-created monopoly rights that
are needed to induce innovation.

For the purposes of exposition, assume that two markets exist: first, a market in which intellectual property with government-created monopoly rights is sold or rented by inventors to manufacturers, and second, a competitive market in which final output incorporating the intellectual property is produced and sold to consumers. We consider the impact of tying and bundling intellectual property in two sections. First, we will examine the effects of tying on welfare through its influence on the demand for intellectual property. We consider the welfare implications of price discrimination in intermediate-goods markets achieved through tying and bundling, and the welfare implications of tying due to the vertical externality between the owner of intellectual property and producers. Second, we will examine the effects of tying on welfare through its influence on the supply of intellectual property and related inputs to production. In this section we emphasize three competing welfare effects of tying: a) as a commitment device, b) in the foreclosure of tied product markets, and c) in providing dynamic incentives for innovation.

Demand-Side Effects of Tying

The most common extension of the traditional analysis allows consumers to have unobserved heterogeneous valuations for the tying product. If they do, then it may not be profitable for the monopolist-owner of intellectual property to sell the property unbundled at a uniform price; the monopolist may choose to second-degree price-discriminate. Variation from simple pricing rules can take two forms: the bundling of several intellectual properties, and the tying of intellectual property to another intermediate good.

Examples of price discrimination through the bundling of intellectual property have been discussed in the law and economics literature for more than 30 years. A famous example of bundling is discussed by Stigler,[15] who describes the then-common practice of block-booking movies.[16] Following Stigler, suppose there are two theaters, A and B, which purchase the rights to show two movies and sell the final good of an evening out. A is willing to pay $9,000 for film 1, $3,000 for film 2, and $12,000 for the package; B is willing to pay $10,000 for film 1, $2,000 for film 2, and $12,000 for the package. There are no interaction effects in the display of the films; the sum of the valuations of each film is equal to the valuation of the bundle. For simplicity, assume that the costs of operating the theaters, except for movie rights, are zero.

If the monopoly owner of the movies rents each film individually, profit maximization requires that it rent film 1 for $9,000 and film 2 for $2,000, for a total profit of $22,000. But if it rents only the bundled package, it can charge $12,000 for the package, have both theaters remain as customers, and earn a total of $24,000; bundling increases profits.

This example illustrates three important points about bundling. First, it is most effective when each consumer's valuations across goods are negatively correlated.[17] In the example, theater A's willingness to pay for film 1 is less than theater B's, but theater A's willingness to pay for film 2 is greater than theater B's. Second, bundling facilitates price discrimination by homogenizing demand curves. If valuations are unobservable to the monopolist, then the monopolist cannot necessarily price discriminate among heterogeneous consumers. However, if bundling allows the monopolist to charge high-valuation consumers more than low-valuation consumers by averaging across products, then it renders the unobservability of heterogeneity irrelevant.

Third, bundling is welfare-neutral, if consumers' purchasing patterns are invariant to the existence of the bundle. In general, the welfare effects of bundling involve a trade-off. Welfare gains from price discrimination through bundling arise out of the propensity of bundling to make available products to those who, because of monopoly output restrictions, would not have otherwise bought. Two types of welfare losses from this price discrimination can arise: losses from selling to customers with valuations lower than the marginal cost of production (for the purpose of achieving more complete rent extraction), and losses from reductions in total output.[18] Since intellectual property is non-rival, the first type of welfare loss is unlikely to be important. Thus, in terms of a simple heuristic, price discrimination from bundling intellectual property is likely to be welfare-improving if it expands the base of customers using the property, and welfare-reducing if it contracts the customer base.

The effects of price discrimination due to tying are analyzed in a similar fashion. Tying can be used to facilitate price discrimination if higher consumption of the tied good signals higher valuations for the tying good and the seller of the tying good can prevent arbitrage in the tied good. The tied good, in effect, meters use of the intellectual property. The monopolist charges less than the monopoly price for the tying product, but more than the competitive price for the tied product. In this way, tying results in high-valuation customers paying more and low-valuation customers paying less, relative to the uniform-pricing case.[19]

However, price discrimination from tying has ambiguous welfare effects, as does price discrimination from bundling. Tying reduces welfare by reducing consumption of the tied good; it increases welfare by increasing consumption of the tying good. Thus, price discrimination from tying necessarily reduces welfare if it does not expand the market for the tying good; on the other hand, price discrimination is likely to increase welfare if distortions from reductions in the consumption of the tied good are smaller than the gains from expansions of the market for the tying good.

Tying is also used to address vertical externalities between monopolist inventors and final-goods manufacturers. These externalities can take many forms; we consider two here. To begin with, consider the application of the service-externality/retailer moral-hazard model to markets for intellectual property.[20] Suppose that manufacturers combine intellectual property with competitively produced inputs to create an end product of variable quality. Consumers have preferences over both the quantity of the end product and its quality. Increasing quality requires costly actions by manufacturers, but inventors and manufacturers cannot completely specify contractually all the actions that manufacturers must take. Without any vertical control by the inventor, the manufacturer will choose to take less of the costly action than would be taken by an integrated manufacturer-inventor.

Tying can enable the inventor to control the uncontractible actions or "service level" that manufacturers take. If use of the tied good is correlated with the unobservable actions that control quality, then tying use of the complementary good to the intellectual property can align the manufacturer's incentive with the inventor's. From the perspective of social welfare, however, this may or may not be favorable. In general, monopolist-inventors may desire either socially too much or too little quality. Monopolists want the manufacturer to supply quality according to the marginal consumer's valuation, but the optimal level of quality is based on the average consumer's valuation. Thus vertical control by the inventor of the manufacturer through tying can result in socially excessive quality if the marginal consumer desires more quality than average; tying can result in socially insufficient quality if the marginal consumer desires less quality than average. However, if the dispersion of preferences over quality in the population is small, then welfare losses from quality distortions due to tying are likely to be smaller than welfare gains from aligning the manufacturer's incentives with the inventor's.

The "input substitution" problem provides another example of how tying can enhance inventors' profits but have an ambiguous effect on welfare in the presence of vertical externalities.[21] Suppose that manufacturers combine intellectual property with a competitively produced input in variable proportions, such that the input and the intellectual property are substitutes. Then tying the competitive input to the intellectual property will, in general, be privately optimal for inventors but have two competing welfare effects. The tie will generally result in a decrease in final output, but it will also correct the "downstream" manufacturers' underutilization of the intellectual property in their production process – a problem that would exist without the tie due to inventors' monopoly markup.

SUPPLY-SIDE EFFECTS OF TYING

THIS SECTION DISCUSSES THREE SUPPLY-SIDE EFFECTS OF TYING: provision of a commitment device, facilitation of foreclosure of tied product markets, and encouragement of the production of intellectual property. In contrast to demand-side effects, which focus on the uses of intellectual property, supply-side effects focus on the production of intellectual property and related intermediate inputs.

First, tying can enable inventors to commit credibly to manage their intellectual property rights in a socially constructive manner. If manufacturers must incur sunk costs in order to use a piece of intellectual property, then optimal contracts between inventors and manufacturers may involve a commitment from inventors to take costly actions to maintain the value of the intellectual property. An output-based royalty payment acts as just such a commitment: it is a bond that penalizes the inventor's sale of clone ideas and provides the incentive to protect against plagiarists.[22] If inventors enhance the value of the intellectual property after licensing or selling it to manufacturers, then royalty payments to them rise; if they fail to do so, then royalty payments fall. Tying the purchase of a "metering" product to the intellectual property can therefore improve welfare by reducing inventors' moral hazard.

In contrast, tying can have an adverse impact on social welfare if it is used as a tool to foreclose other markets.[23] Foreclosure of tied markets with intellectual property is a profitable strategy if there is a cost-advantage to producing and the tie represents a strategic commitment to selling the tied good.[24] This can be accomplished, for example, by the inventor building a factory that combines the intellectual property with a complementary tied good and only offering the intellectual property to the manufacturer in its embodied form. In these cases, if the tied good is produced with economies of scale, then the inventor can use the intellectual property to obtain early sales in the tied-product market. If these sales later provide a persistent cost advantage (arising, for instance, out of decreasing costs due to learning-by-doing), and competitive producers of the tied product understand this, then no one will enter the market for the tied good, and the inventor will be able to establish a monopoly in that market as well.

Central to showing that leverage through tying injures social welfare, however, are two key assumptions. First, there must be a cost advantage to be obtained from early entry, and second, it must be persistent. If the tied product is produced with constant returns to scale, or cost advantages due to pre-emptive production are easy to obtain or short lived, then the inventor will not have the ability to "leverage" its original monopoly into the tied product market. Second, the tie must represent a strategic commitment to produce the tied product. Thus ties that are neither immediately profitable due to demand-side effects nor dependent on investments whose costs can not be recouped, are insufficient to establish commitment and, therefore, leverage. Without commitment, potential competitors will not be dissuaded from entering the tied-good market. The firm establishing the tie could not credibly threaten to remain in the tied-good market until it obtained a cost advantage.

Even under these assumptions, the impact of leverage and the consequent exclusion of competition in the tied-good market on social welfare is indeterminate. One reason for this is that under increasing returns to scale, the exclusion of firms does not necessarily reduce welfare. Indeed, foreclosure from tying may actually increase consumers' surplus.

Perhaps the most fundamental observation about the impact of tying on the supply of intellectual property further complicates the welfare analysis.

Even if tying increases static deadweight losses, it may be dynamically optimal if it increases inventor profits, thereby inducing more innovation. At the heart of the trade-off between dynamic gains and static losses are two types of questions. First, does existing intellectual property law provide incentives for individuals to undertake the optimal level of innovation? If it does not, then enabling inventors to earn higher profits through tying may be globally welfare-improving, even if it is locally welfare-reducing. On the other hand, if existing intellectual property protection does in fact result in too little innovation, a substantial literature suggests that higher profits for inventors may not correct the problem.[25] To the extent that innovation is a race to obtain a discovery first, then inventors may choose R&D technologies that are more socially risky than optimal. This is not surprising: if a race for a patent is a winner-take-all game, private payoffs depend on being first, even though being a close second may be almost as good from a social standpoint. Thus increasing the size of the reward for a successful innovation may only induce inventors to choose riskier paths in order to beat their rivals. The increase in the price would, in this instance, be dissipated by business stealing rather than going toward increasing innovation.

AMERICAN ANTITRUST LAW GOVERNING TYING ARRANGEMENTS

THE DEVELOPMENT OF THE PER SE RULE

DISAPPROVAL OF TYING ARRANGEMENTS UNDER THE ANTITRUST LAWS began in the realm of intellectual property. Judges first encountered ties in the course of evaluating patent infringement claims. In the typical early case, inventors of a patented machine would license their inventions under the condition that it be used only with unpatented supplies, purchased from them. Until 1917, the antitrust laws were not raised in these tying cases; courts routinely enforced licensing agreements on the grounds that "Congress alone has the power to determine what restraint" should be imposed on "the ingenuity of patentees in devising ways in which to reap the benefits of their discoveries."[26]

This changed with the *Motion Picture Patents* case.[27] In 1909, all the established manufacturers of motion-picture cameras and projectors joined with motion-picture producers to form the Motion Picture Patents Company (MPPC). A private antitrust claim arose because the newly created MPPC licensed the Universal Film Manufacturing Company to manufacture projectors for sale to theaters on the condition that the projectors would be used solely to project films made by MPPC's licensees. Possibly because of a wide range of questionable behavior,[28] the Supreme Court refused to allow the patentee to "extend the scope of its patent monopoly by restricting the use of it to materials necessary in its operation, but which are not part of the patented invention."[29]

This reasoning was bolstered by the passage of section 3 of the *Clayton Act* in 1914, which identified tying as a matter of particular antitrust concern.[30]

The *per se* prohibition of tying developed after this. In cases similar to *Motion Picture Patents*, ties between salt tablets and canning machines[31] and between shoe leather and shoe manufacturing machines[32] were judged to be illegal "extensions" of patent monopolies under section 3 of the *Clayton Act*. And in 1958 the Supreme Court extended this reasoning to the *Sherman Act*, creating modern tying doctrine. In *Northern Pacific Railway Co. v. United States*, the Court explicitly stated that section 1 of the *Sherman Act* prohibited Northern Pacific from requiring purchasers or lessors of land along its rights-of-way to ship commodities produced on that land over its rails. Any tie in which the seller "has sufficient economic power . . . to appreciably restrain free competition in the market for the tied product," where an appreciable restraint was defined to be one in which a "not insubstantial" volume of interstate commerce is affected,[33] was declared to be illegal *per se*.

Black-letter law, then, requires that a *per se* tying claim have four elements.[34] First, the tying and tied products must be two distinct products. Second, the two products must be tied together. Third, as part of the "sufficient economic power" requirement, the seller must have economic power in the market for the tying product. Fourth, for a "not insubstantial" volume of interstate commerce to be affected, the absolute dollar volume of trade in the tied product must be non-trivial.

In *Northern Pacific* and other cases in the following decade, the black-letter *per se* rule against tying was liberally interpreted and vigorously enforced. The requirement of "sufficient economic power" in the tying product market, a potentially powerful brake on the proliferation of tying doctrine, remained virtually non-binding. In *Northern Pacific*, the Court explicitly stated that tying cases seldom require "a full-scale factual inquiry into the scope of the relevant market for the tying product and into the corollary problem of the seller's percentage share in that market."[35] Indeed, *Northern Pacific* began a chapter of tying jurisprudence that suggested that economic power could be presumed from the "uniqueness" of the tying product; in dicta, the Court explained that intellectual property protected by patent or copyright would have "a distinctiveness sufficient [to imply] anticompetitive consequences."[36]

The Court converted this dicta into law in the *Loew's* and *Fortner Enterprises* cases. In *United States v. Loew's, Inc.*, the Court found that the seller of a copyrighted motion picture would be presumed to have sufficient economic power to have employed an illegal tie.[37] The notion that product uniqueness alone could imply power was extended to markets for a relatively homogeneous product, credit, in *Fortner Enterprises v. United States Steel Corp.* In that case, Fortner alleged that competition for prefabricated houses (the tied product) was restrained by U.S. Steel's abuse of power over credit (the tying product). Justice Black presented the majority's view that "the economic power over the tying product can be sufficient even though the power falls far short of dominance and even though the power exists only with respect to some of the buyers in the market," and reversed summary judgment for U.S. Steel on the grounds that the jury could infer power from the defendant's "unique" credit terms.[38]

RETREAT FROM THE PER SE RULE

MITIGATION OF THE STRICT PER SE RULE began shortly after it was established, in both Supreme Court and lower court decisions. Areeda argues that this mitigation has taken several forms: requiring plaintiffs to show tying-product market power; allowing defendants to offer a legitimate business justification defence; requiring plaintiffs to provide evidence that the tying and tied products are distinct; and requiring plaintiffs to show that the defendant could foreclose competition in the tied product.[39] We discuss each of these forms of mitigation in turn.

At the highest level, the Supreme Court gave bite to the "sufficient economic power" element, starting with its rehearing of the *Fortner Enterprises* case.[40] After remand, the plaintiff, Fortner, prevailed in the lower courts, which held that U.S. Steel had sufficient economic power in the tying-product market: credit. U.S. Steel appealed and the Court reversed, signaling a retreat from its earlier decision to allow the inference of economic power. It wrote that sufficient economic power required proof that "the seller has the power, within the market for the tying product, to raise prices . . . or to require purchasers to accept burdensome terms that could not be exacted in a completely competitive market."[41]

The teeth in the sufficient economic power element have persisted in later Supreme Court and lower court decisions, as Areeda, Elhauge, and Hovenkamp have observed.[42] *Jefferson Parish Hospital District No. 2 v. Hyde*, 466 U.S. 2, 26-29 n. 7-8 (1984), for example, confirmed that tying is *per se* illegal only when significant power in the market for the tying product is shown: a hospital's 30 percent market share did not trigger the *per se* rule against tying, notwithstanding the presence of market imperfections that further reduced competition. The Court's recent refusal to grant summary judgment to a defendant accused of tying competitively produced photocopiers to brand-specific repair parts in *Eastman Kodak v. Image Technical Services*, 112 S.Ct. 2072, 2089 n. 29 (1992) may also be consistent with a strong economic power requirement, because the record in that case did not reject the hypothesis that informational imperfections may have given Kodak significant market power in the combined markets for photocopiers and the repair parts demanded over the life of the machine, despite the competitive market for photocopiers alone. Most lower courts have followed this lead and compelled plaintiffs to define a relevant market and show substantial market power, using a 30 percent market share as a rough benchmark for the minimum amount of market power necessary to give rise to a *per se* illegal tying claim.[43]

Defendants have also been allowed to offer the affirmative defence that there was a legitimate business justification for the tie. Early cases allowed a limited business justification defence. In *United States v. Jerrold Electronics Corp.*, 187 F. Supp. 545 (E.D. Pa. 1960), aff'd per curiam, 365 U.S. 567 (1961), in which the defendant bundled together the components of community antenna television systems and installation service, the Supreme Court affirmed the lower court's finding that Jerrold's policy of full-system sales was justified by the "launching of a new business with a highly uncertain future," although the defence was held to have lost its legitimacy as the industry developed. Even through the *Loew's* and *Fortner Enterprises'* expansions of the *per se* prohibition of tying, business justification defences such as cost savings were considered doctrinally permissible.[44]

And even when a legitimate business justification defence has not been allowed explicitly, it has been allowed through the easing of the two-product requirement. The business justification defence has been held to play a role in determining whether the tied and tying products are distinct, because the classification of two items as a single product for the purposes of the antitrust laws should depend on the procompetitive virtues of selling the two items together.[45] Indeed, in the *Anderson Foreign Motors* case, the Court wrote that it would take into account the "business justification for the product combination" in its consideration of this issue.

The legitimate business justification defence was expanded and clarified by *Jefferson Parish*. In that case, the majority affirmed the rationale outlined by *Jerrold Electronics*[46] and acknowledged another business justification defence, buyer preferences, writing that "buyers often find package sales attractive; a seller's decision to offer such packages can merely be an attempt to compete effectively − conduct that is entirely consistent with the *Sherman Act*."[47] Following *Jefferson Parish*, the Court wrote in dicta in *NCAA v. Board of Regents* that "tying may have procompetitive justifications that make it inappropriate to condemn without considerable market analysis,"[48] and observed in *Eastman Kodak* that "anticompetitive effects of Kodak's behavior [may be] outweighed by its procompetitive effects."[49] Lower courts, too, have consistently considered business justifications, approving ties for all of the reasons cited by the Supreme Court plus others, such as improved product quality or increased product value.[50]

Jefferson Parish also contained language that has been interpreted by lower courts to require a showing of at least a possibility of anticompetitive foreclosure in the tied product market, moving tying law further from its *per se* roots. Some circuits have interpreted *Jefferson Parish* as requiring a likelihood of anticompetitive effects: the Fifth Circuit, for example, has held that "an illegal tie may be shown by proof that the tying firm 'exert[s] sufficient control over the tying market . . . to have a likely anticompetitive effect on the tied market."[51] The First Circuit has imposed a potentially higher hurdle, "proof of anticompetitive effects in the market for the tied product."[52] The Seventh Circuit has interpreted the anticompetitive effects requirement even more strictly, writing that

One of the threshold criteria that a plaintiff must satisfy under both the *per se* and rule of reason analyses in order to show that such an extension of the seller's market power may pose a threat of economic harm and unlawful restraint of trade is that there is *a substantial danger that the tying seller will acquire market power in the tied product market.*[53]

The development of American tying law concerning intellectual property reflects the progression of general tying law. Indeed, *per se* disapproval of tying arrangements under the antitrust laws began in the realm of intellectual property. Some lower courts are still taking a strict stance against tying involving intellectual property.[54] However, other lower courts have integrated their treatment of tying in intellectual property cases into current tying jurisprudence:[55] *per se* treatment with rule-of-reason-like exceptions.

CONCLUSION

OVER TIME, THE LAW AND ECONOMICS OF TYING have come closer together. Beginning with patent infringement cases, early American law treated tying with considerable hostility, holding tying to be *per se* illegal: it interfered with the rights of buyers and competitors to "unrestrained" trade. In stark contrast, early economic theory suggested that it did not reduce social welfare; in simple economic models, it had only welfare-enhancing motivations.

On the other hand, recent economic research that relaxes the assumptions used in the early models has shown that the welfare implications of tying are ambiguous, particularly in markets for intellectual property. And current American law has moved away from a strict *per se* treatment of tying in several dimensions. Plaintiffs are increasingly required to show market power in the tying-product market or the possibility of foreclosure in the tied-product market; defendants are increasingly allowed to present business justifications as an affirmative defence.

The *per se* label, however, has remained part of American tying law. As the U.S. Supreme Court observed in *Jefferson Parish*, this conflict between the label and the law burdens tying doctrine with the costs of extensive analysis required by the rule of reason, while depriving it of the full benefits arising out of the rule's flexibility.

Canadian tying law has taken a different route. Tying has received rule-of-reason treatment by statute and under Canadian common law. Moreover, section 77 of the *Competition Act* structures the rule-of-reason inquiry by prohibiting tying when the practice "is likely to a) impede entry into or expansion of a firm in the market, b) impede introduction of a product into or an expansion of sales of a product in the market, or c) have any other exclusionary effect in the market."

The welfare indeterminacy of tying calls for just such an approach: rule-of-reason treatment, where the inquiry is structured using the results of economic models. This "structured rule-of-reason" approach might retain a full-fledged rule-of-reason analysis for arrangements with truly indeterminate or adverse welfare implications, but it might reduce the scope of inquiry if the arrangement is unlikely to be socially harmful.

Research in industrial organization, particularly involving markets for intellectual property, can illuminate the development of antitrust policy that promotes competition but preserves incentives. For example, if tying or bundling intellectual property is used to facilitate price discrimination, it reduces welfare if it does not expand the market for the tying good. On the other hand, if it does expand the market, then it can increase welfare. Also, models that predict that the leverage of monopoly power over an intellectual property right can be extended into a tied-product market require that a cost advantage be obtained in producing the tied good and that the tie represents a strategic commitment to selling it. Finally, any antitrust treatment of tying in the realm of intellectual property should recognize that even if tying increases static deadweight losses, it may be dynamically optimal if it induces inventors who would otherwise innovate too little from a social perspective to increase their output.

NOTES

1   *Motion Picture Patents Co. v. Universal Film Manufacturing Co.*, 243 U.S. 502 (1917).

2   *International Salt Co. v. United States*, 332 U.S. 392 (1947).

3   *Eastman Kodak Co. v. Image Technical Services*, 112 S.Ct 2072 (1992).

4   *Standard Oil Co. (Cal.) v. United States*, 337 U.S. 293, 305-6 (1949).

5   *Northern Pacific Railway Co. v. United States*, 356 U.S. 1 (1959).

6   *Id.*

7   *Automatic Radio Mfg. Co. v. Ford Motor Co.*, 390 F.2d 113 (1st Cir.), cert. denied, 391 U.S. 914 (1968).

8   *Anderson Foreign Motors v. New England Toyota Distributors*, 475 F. Supp. 972 (D.Mass. 1979).

9   See, for example, M. Whinston, "Tying, Foreclosure, and Exclusion," *American Economic Review*, 80 (1990): 837 and W. Baxter and D. Kessler, "Toward a Consistent Theory of the Welfare Analysis of Agreements," *Stanford Law Review*, 47 (1995): 615, for a discussion.

10 See, for example, J. Lunn, "Tie-in Sales and the Diffusion of New Technology," *Journal of Institutional and Theoretical Economics*, 146 (1990): 249, for a review and example.

11 *Northern Pacific*, *supra*, note 5, p. 5.

12 *Jefferson Parish Hospital District No. 2 v. Hyde*, 466 U.S. 2 (1984).

13   R. Anderson and S. Khosla, "Recent Developments in the Competition Policy Treatment of Tied Selling in the U.S. and Canada," *Canadian Competition Policy Record*, 6 (1985): 1.

14   See, for example, L. Kaplow, "Extension of Monopoly Power Through Leverage," *Columbia Law Review*, 85 (1985): 515.

15   G. Stigler, "A Note on Block Booking," *Supreme Court Review*, 1963; see also M. Burstein, "A Theory of Full-Line Forcing," *Northwestern University Law Review*, 55 (1960): 62.

16   Block-booking movies was declared illegal by the Supreme Court in *United States v. Loew's*, 371 U.S. 38, 45 (1962).

17   See, for example, H. Varian, "Price Discrimination," in *Handbook of Industrial Organization*, New York, chapter 10, 1989.

18   See, for example, W. Adams and J. Yellen, "Commodity Bundling and the Burden of Monopoly," *Quarterly Journal of Economics*, 90 (1976): 475, and R. Schmalensee, "Gaussian Demand and Commodity Bundling," *Journal of Business*, 57:S211 (1984).

19   See, for example, J. Tirole, *The Theory of Industrial Organization*, 1988, Sec. 3.3.1.5. Tying can also facilitate price discrimination in other settings. F. Mathewson and R. Winter show (in "Tying as a Response to Demand Uncertainty," Working Paper, University of Toronto [1996]) that tying can be both profitable for a monopolist using two-part pricing, and welfare improving when the demands for the tied and tying goods are stochastic and positively correlated. In their model, tying can be profitable because it offers the monopolist an opportunity to extract increased rents from intensive users; it can be welfare improving because it leads to greater reliance on variable prices to collect rents and to a corresponding drop in the fixed fee such that a larger set of consumers purchases.

20   See, for example, Tirole, *supra*, note 19, Sec. 4.2.2.

21   See F. Warren-Boulton, "Vertical Control with Variable Proportions," *Journal of Political Economy*, 82, 2 (1974): 783

22   See C. Hall, "Renting Ideas," *Journal of Business*, 64 (1991): 21.

23   Courts and researchers have expressed concern that ties can be used to "extend the life" of a patent or other intellectual property grant beyond its statutory period. A typical "extension of patent life" consists of a "hybrid license" that ties a patent license to a license to use a related trade secret not protected by patent, where the trade-secret license extends beyond the life of the patent. The fact that the trade-secret license is for a longer term than the patent cannot, by itself, provide the inventor with returns equivalent to those from a longer patent. Consider the simple economic model in the introduction. If consumers value the use of the patent at v_m per year, and the patent's life is k years, then the total consumers' surplus from the use of the patent is equal to $C = \sum_k v_m/ (1 + r)^i$. The manufacturer cannot extract surplus after the kth year, because the patent would be public information. Neither tying a competitively produced good to the monopoly intellectual property nor collecting the surplus over a period of more than k years changes this analysis.

However, "patent life extensions" can affect profits and social welfare if they fall into one or more of the industrial organization theories regarding tying discussed in this essay. For example, patent/trade-secret ties can affect welfare if they foreclose competition in the market for processes related to use of the patent. Or, as pointed out by Mathewson and Winter using the *NutraSweet* case (see the discussion in note 19 above), "patent life extensions" can affect welfare if they serve as a price-discrimination tool.

24 This discussion follows Whinston, *supra*, note 9.

25 See Tirole, *supra*, note 19, section 10.2.2.1.

26 *Henry v. A.B. Dick Co.*, 224 U.S. 1 (1912). See also *Tubular Rivet and Stud Co. v. O'Brien*, 93 Fed. 200 (D.Mass. 1898).

27 *Motion Picture Patents Co. v. Universal Film Manufacturing Co.*, 243 U.S. 502 (1917).

28 In fact, the MPPC sought to use its control over cameras and projectors to control the production, distribution, and exhibition of motion pictures. It was involved in continuous antitrust litigation and was dissolved in 1918, after losing both the private action discussed above and a suit by the government.

29 *Id.* p. 517.

30 See, for example, the discussion of the report of the House of Representatives on section 3 of the *Clayton Act*, discussed in P. Areeda, E. Elhauge, and H. Hovenkamp, *Antitrust Laws*, secs. 1700d and 1701b.

31 *International Salt Co. v. United States*, 332 U.S. 392 (1947).

32 *United Shoe Machinery Corp. v. United States*, 258 U.S. 451 (1922).

33 356 U.S. 1 (1958), p. 6.

34 See, for example, Areeda, *supra*, note 30, Sec. 1702. It is important to note that tying claims that do not meet the conditions for *per se* illegality may be illegal under a general rule-of-reason prohibition against unreasonable restraints of trade, as in *Jefferson Parish Hospital District No. 2 v. Hyde*, 466 U.S. 2, 18-25, or in *Fortner Enterprises v. United States Steel Corp.*, 394 U.S. 495, 497-500 (1969).

35 356 U.S. 1, 45 n. 4.

36 *Id.* p. 46.

37 371 U.S. 38 (1962). See also *Siegel v. Chicken Delight, Inc.*, 448 F.2d 43 (9th Cir. 1971), cert. denied, 405 U.S. 955 (1972) for an extension of this presumption to trademarked products.

38 394 U.S. 495, 502-03, 506 (1969).

39 See Areeda, Sec. 1701c2, *supra*, note 30. Areeda has also argued that courts have increasingly restricted plaintiffs' ability to show injury due to tying.

40 *United States Steel v. Fortner Enterprises*, 429 U.S. 610 (1977).

41 *Id.* p. 620.

42 See Areeda, *supra*, note 30, Secs. 1733e-f and 1739h2-h4.

43 See, for example, *Breaux Bros. Farms v. Teche Sugar Co.*, 21 F.3d 83, 87 (5th. Cir 1994), citing *Grappone, Inc. v. Subaru of New England, Inc.*, 858 F.2d 792, 797 (1st. Cir 1988) and *Will v. Comprehensive Accounting Corp.*, 776 F.2d 665, 672 (7th. Cir. 1985) cert. denied, 475 U.S. 1129 (1986).

44 See, for example, *Loew's*, 371 U.S. pp. 54-55.

45 See, for example, *Johnson v. Nationwide Industries*, 715 F.2d. 1233, 1236-7 (7th. Cir. 1983) and *Hirsh v. Martindale-Hubble*, 674 F.2d 1343, 1347-8 (9th. Cir. 1982). For a discussion, see T. Baker, "The Supreme Court and the per se Tying Rule: Cutting the Gordian Knot," *Virginia Law Review*, 66 (1980): 1235, and Areeda, *supra*, note 30, Secs. 1741b and 1760c2.

46 466 U.S. 24 n. 39.

47 466 U.S. 12 n. 25.

48 468 U.S. 85, 104 n. 26 (1984).

49 112 S.Ct. p. 2092.

50   See, for example, *Principe v. McDonald's Corp.*, 631 F.2d 303, 308-310 (4th. Cir. 1980), *Johnson v. Nationwide Industries*, 715 F.2d 1233 (7th. Cir. 1983), and *Hirsh v. Martindale-Hubble*, 674 F.2d 1343, 1348 (9th. Cir. 1982), discussed in Areeda, *supra*, note 30, Sec. 1760c1.

51   *Roy B. Taylor Sales, Inc. v. Hollymatic Corp.*, 28 F.3d 1379, 1382 (5th. Cir. 1994) and *Breaux Brother Farms v. Teche Sugar Co.*, 21 F.3d 83, 86 (5th. Cir. 1994), citing *Jefferson Parish*, 466 U.S. pp. 15-18, 26-29.

52   *Wells Real Estate v. Greater Lowell Board of Realtors*, 850 F.2d. 803, 815 (1st. Cir. 1987), cert. denied, 488 U.S. 955 (1988).

53   *A.O. Smith Corp v. Lewis, Overbeck, and Furman*, 979 F.2d. 546, 549 (7th. Cir. 1992), citing *Sandburg Village Condominium Association No. 1 v. First Condo Development Co.*, 758 F.2d. 203 (7th. Cir. 1985).

54   See, for example, *Lasercomb America v. Reynolds*, 911 F.2d 970, 973 (4th. Cir. 1990).

55   See, for a discussion, Areeda, *supra*, note 30, Sec. 1781d2.

ACKNOWLEDGMENTS

WE WOULD LIKE TO THANK Rob Anderson, Einer Elhauge, Nancy Gallini, Nancy Horsman, and Michael Smart for their assistance and comments. The views expressed here are not necessarily theirs or those of the Director of Investigation and Research, the Department of Industry Canada or the Government of Canada.

Comment

Ralph A. Winter
Department of Economics
University of Toronto

IN MY DISCUSSION OF THIS EXCELLENT CONTRIBUTION, I will briefly review some of the possible incentives for tying. In particular, I will address the issue of whether tying can serve to leverage monopoly power from one market to another. The idea that a monopoly can leverage its monopoly power into another market is one of the most contentious ideas in antitrust economics, often eliciting nods from most practitioners in the audience and furrowed brows from economists.

William Baxter and Daniel Kessler address the question of leveraging monopoly power in a basic model. The model is the simplest one that is able to capture the Chicago argument that monopoly profits can be collected only once and that tying cannot therefore be used to collect monopoly profits in a second market. The model is effective in countering the common belief that a monopolist has the power and incentive to coerce buyers into a contract they do not want, in this case a contract that requires them to purchase a second good at a higher-than-competitive price. But I shall argue that the model is too simple to offer a complete understanding of the concept of leveraging monopoly power. Under some market conditions, consumers will voluntarily enter contracts that effectively provide their supplier with a monopoly in a second market or, in the context of innovation, a monopoly in a market that lasts beyond the patent period.

I begin by reviewing Baxter and Kessler's (Chicago) argument on leverage when consumers are homogenous, clarifying what the argument must depend upon. I introduce heterogeneous consumers into the model, which allows a review of the price discrimination motives for tying. Finally, I describe the sense in which tying can serve to extend or leverage monopoly power.

The simplest model described has a monopoly in one market and perfect competition in a second. Consumers buy only one unit of the good and all attach a value of B to this one unit. In this model, the monopolist can do no better than to sell the product for a price of B. This extracts the entire surplus from the transaction. Tying does not generate additional surplus and cannot generate additional profits. The monopolist can extract the entire profit – which equals the entire surplus – only once.

The point is correct as stated if consumers are all identical and each purchases a single unit. An alternative model, which I think is in the minds of some participants in the debate about whether leverage is possible, adds to the most basic model the assumption that consumers purchase multiple units of the monopolized good and have a (common) downward sloping demand curve for the good. In this case, the monopolist can do better than simply charging a simple monopoly price in its own market. Constraining consumers to purchase from it a second good (at a high price) would increase the monopoly profits, because even the profit-maximizing monopoly price leaves some surplus on the table. Consumers would accept a tying contract that generated additional profits for the monopolist, because the contract would leave them with a higher surplus than would forgoing the monopolist's product altogether. Recognizing this, the monopolist knows that tying dominates simply selling one good at the optimal uniform price. The contract that the monopolist and the (homogenous) consumers will agree to will include Ramsey prices for the two goods, if the possible prices must be uniform. Any other uniform prices leave gains to improvement for both consumers and the monopolist.

The logical problem with this extended model, however, is that whenever tying is feasible, so is two-part pricing. Two-part pricing, in which total surplus is maximized through variable prices set at marginal costs, dominates tying. Thus when consumers are homogenous, the correct response to the argument that tying can serve to leverage monopoly power from one market to another is not "monopoly profits can be collected only once," but rather "two-part pricing can collect all of the surplus from a transaction and therefore dominates tying." Allowing consumers to be heterogeneous leads us into price discrimination, or surplus extraction as explanations of tying. There are two roles that tying can play in price discrimination. One is very familiar and exemplified by the IBM case of computers (more precisely, adding machines) and cards. Tying the variable input, cards, to the purchase of a computer serves to extract a higher price from more intensive users, who are precisely the users who are willing to pay a higher price. The second role is less familiar. In this story there are two variable inputs that are (possibly) independent in any consumer's demand, but the demands for the two inputs are correlated across consumers. The assumption corresponds to the *Standard Stations* case, where *Standard Stations* and other gasoline providers tied the sale of gasoline to automobile accessories such as tires and batteries in their contracts with gasoline stations.[1]

A seller with monopoly power over only one good (gasoline) could use the strategy of charging a fixed fee and a higher-than-cost variable price. This strategy, which economists call the "Disneyland strategy" following Walter Oi's famous article, allows the monopolist to extract a higher price from more intensive demanders.[2] The mark-up on the variable input is like a tax on quantity, and is profitable because the quantity demanded is a signal of the willingness to pay. If the seller is allowed to tie two goods that are correlated in demand, however, it will exploit this strategy to collect a tax, or mark-up, on both goods. Spreading the distortion from a tax across two goods is always more efficient than taxing a single good; greater surplus is created and the monopolist can capture at least some of this additional surplus. In the case where the demands are perfectly correlated, the two-variable prices are again Ramsey prices. Examining the impact of tying in this kind of scenario is somewhat difficult, because the problem turns out to be non-concave, but in a forthcoming article with Frank Mathewson, I show that allowing tying expands the set of consumers that transact in the market.[3] Tying in this context is never Pareto inferior and can be Pareto superior.

The two kinds of price discrimination incentives are combined in some cases. The 1989 *Digital Electronics Company* matter in Canada, settled by an undertaking prior to any legal action, concerned DEC's strategy of tying their software updates to the servicing of hardware for their computers. This is like the IBM case in that consumers buy one large item, a computer, and purchase variable inputs in quantities that reflect their intensity of use. The difference in this case is that there are two variable inputs: software updates and servicing. The two variable inputs could be tied together because DEC found it more profitable to "tax" the variable purchases of two inputs rather than only one. Efficient or multiproduct pricing involves mark-ups on all variable inputs. (An alternative hypothesis for this case is clear: if consumers cannot identify whether the source of any problems with computing lies in the software versus the hardware, then allowing independent service providers would lead to a distortional externality. The costs in loss of reputation of any cutback in quality by either DEC or the service providers would be shared among the firms. This externality is internalized under tying.)

I have discussed the price discrimination motivations for tying that followed from introducing heterogeneity into the demand side of the simplest models of tying. I will conclude by returning to the issue that I started with: whether tying can be used to leverage monopoly power from one market to another. To bring the discussion into an intellectual property context, I will discuss leverage through tying in the case of a contractual extension of a patent period.

In the simplest patent model, a monopolist prices a good at the monopoly price up to some time T, when the monopoly ends. Then consumers purchase at prices determined by the postpatent market structure. Suppose the monopolist and the buyers enter into longer-term contracts. The insistence on long-term contracts by a seller (with liquidated damages or some penalty for exit by the buyer) is, logically, an example of tying, because the buyer must purchase the future requirements of a good as a condition of purchasing the current requirements. The future good is tied to the current good.

Two hypotheses or theories can explain a patent extension case. (The *NutraSweet* case in Canada involved allegations of patent extension.) One is the price discrimination story. If consumers are heterogeneous, the monopolist cannot extract all available rents through a two-part pricing scheme. Charging a fixed fee and higher-than-marginal cost prices for both the current good and the future good will dominate. This is simply the price discrimination theory that I have described above, with the current good and the future good as the two products. This theory could apply in the case where the postpatent market structure is perfectly competitive. Tying (patent extension) here serves to extend the monopoly power for longer than the patent itself provides for, yet the effect is not anticompetitive. Patent extension as price discrimination can increase total surplus and even result in a Pareto superior allocation.

The second hypothesis that can explain patent extension is that the extension is the result of the monopolist insisting, to the consumers' collective detriment, on long-term contracts as a means of extending its period of protection against competition. Suppose that the market structure that will follow the patent is only imperfectly competitive: a duopoly. Suppose further that the duopolist's decision to enter depends, endogenously, on how many buyers it would attract if it did enter. Then each buyer may be willing to sign a long-term contract for only a small concession in price – a small "bribe" to protect the incumbent against competition – simply because all other buyers are entering the contract and the impact of the single buyer's decision on future market structure is negligible. Buyers' decisions to enter long-term supply contracts with the monopolist are distorted by the externality that each such decision imposes on all other buyers. The patent protection is extended by contract to the detriment of the buyers entering the contracts.[4]

Moreover, a second externality distorts the monopolist's and buyers' incentives to enter a long-term contract, given the endogenous entry decision of the potential entrant in the future, as Aghion and Boulton point out in their well-known 1987 article.[5] The entrant is made worse off by the current market participants' decision to enter a long-term contract with liquidated damages, because to enter the market in the future the entrant must offer a lower price to attract the buyer away from the incumbent.

Both of the externalities act to allow the incumbent to extend, or leverage, its current monopoly power from the current market for its patented product to the future in a way that is socially inefficient, possibly to the detriment of all buyers as well as the future entrant. This explanation of tying as an instrument for leverage applies to the specific context of contracting in the presence of patents. The theory does not apply directly to the more common discussion of leverage from one product market to another (currently existing) product market, because it depends on the assumed contracting dynamics – specifically, the inability of the potential competitors in the second market to offer current contract offers to buyers. However, if the dynamics of the second market are important in the sense that the product in this market is being developed or costs are decreasing over time, then the argument would apply.

The resolution of the leverage issue, then, is that tying can be used as an instrument for leveraging monopoly power from one market into another, but the argument for leverage in a particular context must rely upon externalities among buyers or externalities on future entrants into the second market. An explanation for leverage cannot start by assuming that a monopolist has the power and incentive to impose on buyers a contract that they do not want. It must explain why the seller and each individual buyer would find it in their interests to enter contracts that collectively result in a second monopoly.

Finally, in terms of policy, this is a resolution with a paradox. When the market structure of the secondary market is perfectly competitive, the distortional externalities that I have discussed are not present. In the patent extension case, for example, the future alternatives for each buyer are given by the competitive price in the future, independent of the contracts entered into by any buyers. In this case, the price discrimination hypothesis must be presumed. Tying should not be presumed to reduced social welfare even if competition in the secondary market is pre-empted completely. Only when the secondary market is imperfectly competitive are there distortional externalities that give rise to the possibility of leveraging monopoly power. Thus the pre-emption of competition through tying is more likely to be problematic the less intense the competition being pre-empted. The pre-emption of some competition is worse than the pre-emption of perfect competition.

NOTES

1   *Standard Oil Co. of California v. United States.*
2   Oi, Walter Y, "A Disneyland Dilemma: Two-Part Tariffs for a Mickey Mouse Monopoly," *Quarterly Journal of Economics*, 85 (1971): 77-90.
3   Mathewson, Frank and R. A. Winter, "Tying as a Response to Demand Uncertainty," *Rand Journal of Economics*, in press, 1997.
4   This type of argument is developed nicely in Ilya Segal and Michael Whinston, "Naked Exclusion and Buyer Coordination," Harvard Institute of Economic Research Working Paper, September 1996.
5   Aghion, Phillipe and Patrick Boulton, "Contracts as a Barrier to Entry," *American Economic Review*, 77 (1987): 388-401.

Patrick Rey   &   Ralph A. Winter   6
Institut d'économie industrielle   Department of Economics
University of Toulouse   University of Toronto

Exclusivity Restrictions and Intellectual Property

INTRODUCTION

THE OBJECTIVE

THE ECONOMIC EXCHANGE OF PRIVATE GOODS involves inherent exclusivity. If I provide you with a product you require, other sellers are foreclosed from providing the same product to you at the same price. If I have a limited supply of a product for sale, your purchase of the product excludes other buyers from purchasing the same units. Our relationship may even be one in which I supply only to you, and you purchase a particular product only from me.

Exclusivity restrictions are contractual restrictions that go beyond the exclusivity inherent in exchange. In a contract between a buyer and a seller, these restrictions may be placed on either party. The buyer may purchase the product or the rights to a technology under the restriction that it can resell only in a specified market or country, or that it can adopt the technology only for specified uses and, in turn, have the right to be the only reseller in that market. An exclusive-supply restriction prevents the seller from supplying a specified product to any other purchaser. An exclusive-dealing contract prevents the buyer from purchasing the product of any competing supplier.

The objective of this paper is to analyze exclusivity restrictions in contracts for the exchange of rights to the use of intellectual property, i.e., licensing contracts. The intellectual property rights (IPRs) exchanged in these contracts can be legally established and protected by patents, copyright, or trade-secret law.[1] Patents can protect, for a limited time, the rights to ideas that satisfy the criteria of novelty, non-obviousness, and usefulness. Copyright protects the expression of an idea, it does not protect against the independent creation or expression of the idea by others. Trade secrets or know-how refer to information that has value because of its secrecy. Trade-secret law has no fixed term. Like copyright law, trade-secret law does not protect against the threat of independent creation. Some familiar examples of all three types of intellectual property rights are: a new production process or product would be patented; a book or computer software would be copyrighted, and types of information related to production or marketing would be protected by trade-secret law.

In contracts for exchange of intellectual property – licensing contracts – we can identify four main types of exclusivity restrictions.

Exclusive licensing – This is an exclusive right by the licensee to use the licensor's innovation or to sell products embodying the innovation. It is a restriction on the licensor against selling this right to any other party. An inventor or laboratory, for example, may retain ownership of patent rights to produce a new product, but sell an exclusive license for the worldwide production rights to a firm that has assets specific to producing it. Where the potential market for the product is divided into different regions or countries because trade among the regions is barred – either by design, through exclusive territories, or inherently because of trade barriers or high transportation costs – then the IPR owner faces a choice between exclusive and non-exclusive licensing within each autonomous territory.[2]

Pavel Belogour, a Northeastern University economics student, registered a patent on shock absorbers for in-line skates in early 1996. As of April 1996, Belogour was fielding inquiries from a number of manufacturers and faced the choice of a) selling the patent outright, b) licensing exclusive worldwide rights to the design to a single firm, or c) licensing the rights non-exclusively to a number of different manufacturers.

Exclusive territories – Alternatively, Belogour could license separate rights to the sale of shock absorbers in Canada, the United States, and Europe. Where a market can be divided into geographical territories such as countries, each territory may be assigned exclusively to one licensee. These contracts involve not a single restriction, but bilateral restrictions or an exchange of rights: the licensee is given the exclusive right to its own territory, but gives up the right to sell elsewhere. This exclusivity restriction has two main variants: first, open-territory exclusivity, which is the contractual right to be the sole licensee located in the territory, e.g., the only domestic licensor (but without protection against competition by imports from other territories), and second, complete or closed-territory exclusivity, which is the right to the complete exclusive rights to any use within the territory.

Under exhaustion law the sale of an article embodying IPR exhausts the right of an IPR owner to restrict the conditions of use and resale (see Anderson et al., "Intellectual Property Rights and International Market Segmentation in the North American Free Trade Area" in this volume). Where this rule applies, such as in Europe, open-territory exclusivity is feasible but closed territories are not.

Exclusive grant-backs – Under these restrictions, the licensor of a technology receives the exclusive patents on all improvements to a technology that the licensee discovers in implementing or adapting the technology to new uses.[3] Exclusive grant-backs are distinguished from exclusive licensing by the fact that they are assigned to future innovations-improvements to a technology that are not yet discovered at the time of contracting.[4]

Exclusive dealing – Exclusive dealing prevents the licensee from adopting substitute technologies. It parallels exclusive-dealing restrictions in the distribution of products – outside the context of intellectual property – under which a retailer cannot carry the competing brands.

Exclusivity restrictions represent one end of a spectrum of restrictions that link the terms of a contract to the terms of other contracts entered into by one of the contractual parties. They simply preclude entry into specific other contracts; for example, an exclusive licensing contract disallows any contract between the licensor and another licensee of the intellectual property. Other types of restrictions are less categorical, but can in some market circumstances have the effect of an exclusive contract. An obvious example is a contract in which the exclusivity restriction is not a constraint but an option, attached to more generous licensing terms, that the licensee has the right to select. The following are some other forms of contracts on this spectrum.

Requirements tying – This is a restriction that ties the right to buy one good to the obligation to buy all the requirements of a second good from the same buyer. That is, the seller in a tying contract gains the exclusive right to provide the second good.[5]

Most-favoured-client clause – This clause guarantees that a buyer receive the lowest price of any offered by the seller over the period of the contract. The initial price is lowered to match any price reductions offered by the seller to other purchasers.

Meeting-competition clause – This is a guarantee by the seller that it will meet any price offered to the buyer by competing sellers.[6]

Output-royalty contract – This scheme specifies that the payment made by the licensee to the licensor be on the basis of the total units of a product sold by the licensee, whether or not these units incorporated the technology or product offered by the licensor.[7] The resale of competing products is not prohibited as in an exclusive-dealing contract, but it is implicitly taxed at the same rate as the purchase (or sale) of the contractual product.

Non-linear pricing contract – This includes minimum quantities or discounts such as sliding royalties. Suppose a seller were simply prohibited from setting contracts that explicitly or indirectly excluded rivals. In some cases, the seller could simply forecast the quantity demanded by each buyer and require that this amount be purchased as a condition of the contract.[8] On the other side of the market, the buyer of an input can, in some cases, exclude rivals by simply purchasing all the available supply of a critical input.

Each of these restrictions plays a variety of contractual roles in different market settings. In some, the restriction may have the effect of exclusivity. In tying contracts, exclusivity is explicit. A most-favoured-client clause or a meeting-competition clause may deter potential competitors on one side of the market or the other from entering the market, and in that sense result in *de facto* exclusivity. An output royalty, once established, reduces to zero the cost to the licensee of substituting away from competitors' inputs toward the licensor's product in the output produced. This reduces the incentive to purchase substitute inputs, possibly to the extent of leaving the output-royalty setter as an exclusive supplier of the input.

While our discussion focuses on the four explicit forms of exclusivity in licensing contracts (exclusive licensing, exclusive territories, exclusive grant-backs, and exclusive dealing), we outline the potential of the restrictions both as exclusionary and as efficiency-enhancing instruments.

THE FRAMEWORK

The Goals

Our goals in analyzing the economics of exclusivity restrictions are a) to delineate the market conditions, structures, and strategic circumstances under which the various forms of exclusivity are used in licensing contracts (the positive issue), b) to identify which of these uses tend to be socially desirable and which are undesirable (the normative issue), and c) to describe the evidence that tends to distinguish the desirable from the undesirable uses.

In competition policy analysis, the positive and normative analyses must be tightly linked, in the sense that a policy on the legality of a restriction under particular market circumstances must be consistent with a theory of why the restriction is observed. This point is simple, but not always followed. For example, the view that territorial exclusivity should be prohibited because it reduces competition or lessens international trade, and that competition or free trade is a goal in itself, has had some influence on the law of exclusivity in licensing contracts. The approach we favour is to ask first why the exclusivity is observed. Is it naked market division by competing firms masquerading as a vertical arrangement? Or does it represent the decision by an innovator to partition its exclusive and universal right to the patent into territorial exclusive rights?

Then we attempt to identify the efficiency effects implied by the explanation. This involves, for the vertical explanations of territorial exclusivity, identifying possible consistencies in or conflicts between the patent holder's desire for competition among licensees and the social desirability of that competition.

The Normative Criteria

Policy or normative analysis requires a set of normative criteria. We adopt the standard criterion – economic efficiency or the sum of profits plus consumers' surplus. There are three classes of relevant markets or activities that can be affected by the law on restrictions in licensing contracts and in which efficiency effects must therefore be assessed: product markets, technology diffusion through licensing (or imitation), and innovation.

A licence contract or package of contracts may yield efficiencies such as lower costs or an increase in output in product markets. It generally represents the diffusion of technology, and it may affect the incentives for R&D. The importance of these must be weighed against the possible suppression of output in each of the three activities.

The basic goal of maximizing economic efficiency merits clarification on three points. First, competition law should take as a constraint the property right of exclusivity that is provided by patent or other IPR protection. To take a simple example, suppose a patent provides a firm with exclusive rights to the sale of a product, but other firms have assets that are more complementary to the production and sale of the product. A decision by the patent holder to offer an exclusive licence does not create additional exclusivity or monopoly power; the exclusive licence represents simply the transfer, to another firm, of the exclusive right to the sale of the product. A law that required compulsory, non-exclusive licensing might enhance competition in the product market, but it would violate the constraint that the patent rights of exclusivity be respected.

To consider a more controversial example that we will return to, suppose the patent confers exclusive rights to the product in a market consisting of two distinct geographical areas, A and B. Suppose further that two separate firms are best placed to produce and sell the good in each of these territories. The patent holder, with the right to sell exclusively in these two areas might want to split this right into two parts – the right to sell exclusively in A and the right to sell exclusively in B – and license each part separately. Splitting the intellectual property right in this way does not create additional market power beyond that conferred by the property right. A law such as the exhaustion principle that prohibited exclusive territories would violate the constraint to respect the right of exclusivity in the original intellectual property right. Under some conditions, however, the prohibition of closed-territory distribution might increase product competition at the expense of reduced incentive for innovation. If this is the case, the interests of an economic community or trading block may dictate a policy against closed-territory distribution when this policy is counter to global welfare. (We discuss this possibility in the section entitled "Other Contractual Restrictions.")

Second, competition law should not incorporate the need for additional incentives for innovation beyond those provided by the systems of intellectual property rights. For example, competition authorities should not accept, as a defence for monopolizing a particular market, the inadequacy of the incentive to innovate provided by patent law in that market.

An implication of these two points is that the impact of practices on incentives for innovation enters competition policy asymmetrically. On the one hand, a licensing practice is considered anticompetitive if it suppresses the incentive for innovation. A merger among most of the R&D-intensive firms in an industry that had the result of suppressing the race toward superior technology would be considered anticompetitive, for example. On the other hand, the positive incentive for innovation that can result from increased concentration and profits in a product market does not enter the assessment of competition policy. This positive effect is not balanced against the efficiency costs of increased product-market prices.

In short, we assume that a) the goal of competition policy is to maximize welfare, presuming that patent law and other forms of legal protection of intellectual property rights are the appropriate instruments for achieving the right incentives for innovation, and b) that these incentives can be met without the additional protection that would be provided by a tolerance toward concentration or monopolization in particular industries. It is not up to competition authorities to fine-tune the intellectual property right protection offered by patent law and related instruments.

In an international context the assumed goal of maximizing efficiency is the sum of welfare across countries. Of course, the objective of competition policy in each country is to improve the welfare of its own citizens. The conflict between national and international efficiency arises in the design of competition policy on territorial exclusivity. If exclusive licensing across countries is serving as an instrument for price discrimination in a particular good, then in general there is no efficiency in prohibiting the practice. But the country in which prices are highest will benefit from a prohibition on complete territorial exclusivity in this case.

A less obvious conflict is suggested by the following example. Suppose a country or economic community with a common competition law prohibits closed-territory exclusivity internally. This may, in some circumstances, increase the competition in the product markets within the community, depending on the amount of innovation and the rate at which new products are introduced. This increase in competition comes at the expense of weakening the property right of exclusivity conferred by the IPR, as we have explained above, and therefore weakening the incentives for innovation. But because an economic community or country has only a share of the world market, however, it will bear only a share of the costs of reduced innovation. The competition policy that is optimal for national or community interests may be different from the policy that is optimal globally.

THE ECONOMICS OF EXCLUSIVITY RESTRICTIONS

A GENERAL PRINCIPLE: COMPARISON OF THE HORIZONTAL AND VERTICAL EFFECTS OF A RESTRICTION

BEFORE EXAMINING THE PRIVATE AND SOCIAL INCENTIVES for the various types of exclusivity, we set out a general principle that will be the common basis for our assessment of all of the restrictions. This is the distinction between the horizontal and vertical effects of contractual restrictions. Contracts that coordinate activities among horizontal competitors in a market, in the sense of reducing competition among them, are horizontal. For example, contracts that facilitate price-fixing have horizontal effects in product markets. Contracts that pool exclusive rights to license among dominant firms may prevent entry by other firms, which is another horizontal effect.

In contrast, the coordination of the incentives of a downstream licensee with the interests of an upstream producer or licensor is a vertical effect. The strict categorization of contracts into horizontal and vertical agreements is simplistic in reality, but agreements tend to be dominated by either horizontal or vertical effects and motives.

Outside the context of intellectual property, the horizontal effects of contracts are normally identified with collusion or cooperation among competitors in a product market, or barriers to entry into a product market. In intellectual property, horizontal effects can be measured across the three markets or activities: the product market in which a good using a technology is sold; the market for the rights to the use of a technological innovation, i.e., technology diffusion; and innovation or R&D that leads to the discovery of new technologies and products.

Suppose, for example, that firms possessing most or all of the assets specific to innovation in a particular class of products or processes were to pool their patents, assign them to a jointly owned corporation, and sign exclusive licensing contracts with the corporation for the use of the innovation. (That is, the licensing contracts excluded firms outside the cartel.) This arrangement would have horizontal effects in the diffusion of the technology, as the use of the technology is restricted to firms in the cartel. If, in addition, the firms signed exclusive grant-back clauses that assigned the rights to any improvements or related technology to the joint venture, the incentives for innovation would be affected by the joint ownership of any new technology – a horizontal effect in innovation.[9] Horizontal product-market effects would result if the technology in the production of goods in a market had no close substitutes and the goods had few close substitutes.

The guiding principle of assessing contractual restrictions in intellectual property, just as in conventional product markets, is that restrictions that are motivated by horizontal effects tend to be inefficient, and contracts with vertical effects, for example, those that are designed to coordinate the incentives of a licensor and licensees, tend to be efficient. Agreements that reduce competition in a product market will lead to prices that are higher and further away from marginal costs. This represents a loss of profits plus consumer surplus, or an inefficiency.

Horizontal effects in diffusion and in the product-market are higher costs and prices in the final product market and, perhaps, inferior products. Contracts with horizontal effects in the diffusion of technology will primarily be those that exclude some firms from using patented technology. The inefficiencies involved are the higher cost that the excluded firms must pay and the effects of reduced competition in the product market.

The impact of increased concentration on innovation is, in theory, more ambiguous than the impact on either of the other two activities. Suppose that concentration increases as a result of the merger of two competitors in this sector. The merger will have two principal effects on the incentive to innovate. First, before the merger a horizontal externality between the two firms affects the degree of innovative activity: an increase by either firm reduces the expected profits of the other firm by reducing its prospects of having the leading technology. This externality causes the duopolists' competitive level of innovation to be higher than the level that would maximize joint profits. The internalization of this competitive externality in the merger means that innovation should decrease with the merger.[10]

The second effect, offsetting the first, is that when either duopolist discovers a new technology, it will capture the entire profit from it if the competing firm can either imitate the new technology by inventing around it or if the competing firm benefits technologically in the development of the next generation of the product or process. The internalization of this effect means that with monopoly there is a tendency toward increased innovation. A positive effect of monopoly on R&D activity also follows from the fact that monopoly profits generate greater internal capital, and for R&D, internal capital is a cheaper source of capital than external capital. These sources of positive externalities in innovation between the two firms imply a tendency for innovation to increase with mergers. On balance, economic theory offers no categorical predictions on the net effect.

Empirical work on the impact of concentration on R&D activity has not produced unambiguous answers either, as Gilbert and Sunshine (1995a) discuss. But there is some empirical support for the view that, on balance, competition enhances innovation. Scherer (1984) finds that at high concentration levels there is a negative correlation between concentration and expenditures on R&D, although Levin et al. (1985) finds that cross-industry differences may account for some or all of Scherer's finding. In a large series of case studies,

Porter (1990) argues that a competitive industry environment has a strong and positive effect on innovation.

Rapp (1995) argues that the lack of theoretical or empirical support for the position that concentration reduces R&D means that this threat of increased concentration in the "innovation market" should not be a major factor in antitrust enforcement. Gilbert and Sunshine's persuasive response is that innovation-market analysis "provides a useful tool to reach certain anticompetitive transactions that may not be reached by the traditional tools" (1995, p. 82). The importance of increased concentration in innovation activity in antitrust cases depends on the particular facts of the case.

The effect of prohibiting a class of restrictions in licensing contracts that are driven purely by vertical or efficiency considerations is a loss of surplus. The costs of diffusing the technology through licensing are greater. Firms respond by licensing less, and the result is not only more costly but less technology diffusion. The lower returns from licensing in turn reduce the incentive to patent. Instead of patenting, firms will tend to keep new discoveries secret and reduce R&D spending.

The effects of the decrease in competition are potentially more severe in diffusion and innovation than in product markets. Less competition in product markets leads to higher prices, but high prices are mainly a transfer from buyers to sellers; the impact on welfare of high prices from reduced competition is largely a second-order effect. Higher costs or inferior products as a result of suppressing competition in diffusion or innovation are not a transfer, but a loss of efficiency on every unit sold in a market. In industries where patent licensing is most important, the pace of innovation is a much more important indicator of social welfare than prices are.

EXCLUSIVE LICENSING

AN EXCLUSIVE LICENCE IS THE ASSIGNMENT OF EXCLUSIVE RIGHTS to the use of a technology for a period of time to a single party by the owner of the technology. It differs from outright sale of the patent in that the licensor retains ownership rights – the rights to the patent for the period after the licensing contract has expired and before the patent has expired. We distinguish exclusive licensing from territorial exclusivity, which is treated next, by using the former to describe the case where there is only one definable market area for the patent, or where there are separate markets and the barriers to trade between them are complete. The IPR owner has no scope for dividing the market (further) into territories, but considers whether to issue an exclusive licence for each market.

Consider, therefore, a licensor with an innovation that can potentially be used in a single market. Why would the licensor choose to license exclusively to a single firm? The licensor will choose this option when it is preferred to the following alternatives: a) direct production and sale of the good embodying the innovation rather than licensing to another party, b) sale of the patent out-right, and c) non-exclusive licensing. We first evaluate this choice when it is driven by contractual efficiency or vertical incentives.

Vertical Incentives

Exclusive Licensing Versus Direct Production

The choice of exclusive licensing over developing the innovation and produc-ing a final product in-house is the Coasian choice of a market transaction over vertical integration. If the innovator does not own the assets complementary to production of the intellectual property, it is generally more efficient to license the intellectual property rights to someone who does. The joint ownership of the rights to the use of complementary assets is necessary for production effi-ciency. The purchase or lease by the innovator of the complementary assets is an alternative that would achieve joint ownership of complementary assets, but is easily ruled out as inefficient in many cases.[11]

Exclusive Licensing Versus Sale of the Patent

Why would the innovator not simply sell the patent to the developer of the innovation, rather than license the exclusive rights to the use of the patented idea? The sale of a patent transfers all rights to the intellectual property; exclu-sive licensing is distinguished from outright sale in that it leaves the ownership rights to the property, after the licensing contract period with the innovator. A royalty contract leaves the innovator with the rights to a share of the profits from the use of the property. Outright sale is, in fact, a common solution. But exclusive licensing will still be chosen over the sale of the patent in some cases, for two reasons. First, asset markets in general and intellectual property markets in particular are subject to asymmetries of information about the value of the assets. The owner of an innovation typically has more information about the future value of the innovation than the prospective purchaser of the rights to the innovation. In markets where sellers (current owners) are better informed about the assets' values than buyers (prospective owners), the contracts that emerge in the market leave the sellers with some residual claim on the profits earned by the buyers or on the value of the asset (Gallini and Wright, 1990).[12] The residual claim on intellectual property is retained through a royalty on buyers' profits, revenue or sales, and through the residual ownership rights. Contracts that leave some share of returns with sellers emerge under asymmet-ric information, because they signal the value of the asset: a high-quality seller is more willing to rely on royalty contracts (i.e., more willing to sacrifice a larg-er drop in a fixed licensing fee for a given royalty) because this seller anticipates a high level of royalty revenues.

The second reason that the innovator would retain ownership rights is an incentive effect. The innovator may own or expect to own some assets that may be complementary to the innovation in some future uses. An innovator in the process of discovering related technologies, in particular, may prefer to retain ownership in order to license the technologies in a package. Retaining ownership rights could elicit more efficient innovation in related technologies (efficient, that is, in maximizing the combined profits of the innovator and licensee) since the new discoveries would affect the value of the existing innovation.

Exclusive Versus Non-exclusive Licensing

The most important comparison among the alternatives listed is between exclusive and non-exclusive licensing. Given that an innovator has decided upon licensing, why would an exclusivity restriction be struck?

One answer that explains many aspects of licensing contracts is that exclusivity is necessary to protect the returns on specific investment by the licensee against hold-up. Specific investments are expenditures by the licensee on assets that have value only in connection with the use of the innovation.[13] Hold-up potentially occurs in the entry of either a second licensee, through a subsequent licensing contract, or the innovator itself after the specific investment has been sunk by the original licensee. Unless the original licensee's return on investment is protected by exclusivity, the incentive to invest is dampened or eliminated. The investment is distorted because of the non-appropriability or positive externality on the subsequent entrant's profits that an additional dollar of investment involves. The investment in a distribution system, advertising, and quality to build up brand name capital for a product will be compromised if the licensee-investor who incurs the expense of the investment captures only a share of the benefits. (The positive externality will be captured by the owner of the patent, who can sell the right to entry into a profitable market.) Exclusivity restrictions in licensing contracts can be an efficient contractual guarantee against hold-up.

Where protection against hold-up is the explanation for exclusivity, efficiency is enhanced, even in the product market, taking as given the extent of innovation. Without exclusivity, the product might not be developed at all, and at the very least the investment in product-specific assets such as the distribution system and the product brand name would be diminished.

This prediction does not hold, however, if the following situation is the explanation for exclusivity. Suppose that no additional investment in product-specific assets is needed beyond the assets already owned by potential licensees (to set aside the explanation of exclusivity as protection against hold-up). Suppose that if two licensees were to compete in this market, the products offered would be very similar and the competition therefore very intense, but that a single licensee would earn monopoly profits. Finally, and critically, suppose that the patent holder had to collect payment through a fixed fee rather than a royalty.

In this case, the sale of an exclusive licence would generate revenues equal to the monopoly profits, and the sale of two non-exclusive licences would generate revenues equal to the sum of duopoly profits. With little product differentiation between the licensees, the revenues are greater and an exclusivity restriction is therefore profitable.

The explanation assumes that variable royalties are not feasible. If a linear royalty were feasible, then in theory it could be set sufficiently high, adding to the marginal cost of each licensee, to elicit the price that maximized the profits of all participants. Fixed fees could then allocate the shares of this collective profit. But it is enough for the explanation that there be some efficiency cost or disadvantage to raising variable royalty rates. There are three possible disadvantages to using royalties. The first is the significant cost of monitoring the output (or use of licensed input) by licensees; the second is the "variable proportions distortion," i.e., an attempt to tax the quantity of input used by licensees would lead them to substitute inefficiently toward other inputs;[14] and the third is that if the patent holder retained the residual claim, the licensee would have less incentive to invest in product-specific assets or sales effort. All of these factors will inhibit the use of the royalty rate to counter the effect of excess competition among the licensees. Exclusivity would be the superior instrument.

Under this theory, efficiency in the product market would be enhanced by prohibiting exclusivity if the patent holder's next best alternative were non-exclusive licensing. But this would violate the constraint that competition law should respect the right conferred by intellectual property laws. The patent holder has the right to exclusive use of its intellectual property; an exclusive licence merely transfers this right to an agent with a comparative advantage in its use.

When exclusive licensing is chosen for these vertical or contractual reasons, then it is socially efficient in that it facilitates the allocation of an asset to the use that is of highest value (that is, of highest private and, in the absence of additional economic distortions, social value). When exclusivity restrictions are prohibited, then where an innovator is deterred from licensing at all, the diffusion of the innovation is inhibited. Where specific investment by the licensee is inhibited by the prohibition of exclusivity protection, or where the innovator is forced into the inefficient choice of vertical integration, the allocation of resources in the product market will be inefficient. The exclusive legal right to intellectual property is granted to the innovator by a patent or other intellectual property protection. Exclusive licensing represents the transfer of this right to another party who attaches higher value to it because this party owns assets that are complementary to it.

Horizontal Incentives

Exclusivity restrictions may, in fact, be part of an inefficient horizontal scheme. In the simplest case, the licensor and the licensee compete in the same product market. The sale of an exclusive licence for a product that is a close substitute for the licensee's product may simply represent the sale of the rights to a monopoly in a product market. Duopolists can always strike a mutually profitable contract in which one sells the other the exclusive rights to a market. This follows from the fact that monopoly profits exceed the sum of duopoly profits when products are close substitutes. Similarly, duopolists or oligopolists may assign exclusive licensing rights to a third party to exploit the market, with the result that the market is monopolized. Where the gains from the transfer of exclusive rights to a technology can be identified as the sale of the rights to monopolize a market, the restriction is inefficient.

Exclusivity is also a critical component of patent pools, which are horizontal agreements to share the rights to exploit future innovations. We do not consider patent pools in this report, but discuss briefly their vertical counterpart, grant-backs, below.

EXCLUSIVE TERRITORIES

EXCLUSIVE TERRITORY RESTRICTIONS IN LICENSING AGREEMENTS take two forms. Open-territory restrictions guarantee that the licensee will be the only licensed firm in a specified territory. They do not protect against competition from licensees outside the territory. In an international licensing context, for example, an open-territory restriction is a guarantee that no other domestic firm will be licensed; it does not protect against imports from other licensees. Full, or closed-territory restrictions offer licensees complete, exclusive right to customers within a territory.

A government policy or legal principle that allows open-territory exclusivity but prohibits closed-territory exclusivity is the exhaustion principle. Exhaustion is the removal of the rights of IPR owners to control parallel imports of legitimately manufactured foreign versions of their products (Anderson et al., 1990). At present, the doctrine does not apply to the movement of goods across most borders, but it does apply within the European Community and to internal trade in the United States. (For a detailed analysis of the exhaustion principal, see Anderson et al., "Intellectual Property Rights and International Market Segmentation in the North American Free Trade Area," in this volume.)

The patent holder has exclusive right to the sale of a product or use of a process in each country where the patent is valid. Dividing its market into exclusive territories does not create new exclusivity rights or monopoly power, it simply divides the existing right. It would be wrong, therefore, to argue for prohibiting territorial restrictions simply on the grounds that they, by their very nature, prevent competition. We must consider the private incentives that could lead to territorial restrictions, and which of them are consistent with social efficiency.

Vertical Incentives for Closed-Territory Restrictions

In the following, we discuss the incentives for closed territories and the adequacy (or even advantages) of open-territory exclusivity. There are several possible incentives for the stronger of the two exclusive-territory restrictions, closed-territory distribution.

1. Protection against hold-up: Where a licensee must make a substantial investment in specific assets such as developing the reputation of a product through high-quality service and advertising, exclusivity restrictions may be necessary to ensure that the licensee receives the whole return to this investment. Free-riding or positive externalities can occur from not only the establishment of a future licensee in the country or territory to which the licensee has been assigned but also from imports from other countries.

   The positive externality may be reciprocated. In a potential market consisting of two equal-sized countries, for example, if each licensee exports to the country of the other licensee, then expenditures on such things as domestic advertising and service quality will increase both domestic demand and exports by the other licensee. This reciprocity does not, however, negate the inefficiency resulting from the externality: each licensee will under-invest in promoting the product because it does not receive the full return on the investment. Closed territories prevent this externality. To protect the return on specific investments, it may be enough to offer domestic exclusivity. If the inherent barriers to trade (such as the transportation costs of economy-wide trade barriers) are low, however, the advantage of having a location in the market being served as opposed to a foreign location will be inadequate.

2. A simple incentive for dividing up a downstream market with exclusive restrictions is that, in a world economy with low trade barriers, competition among licensees may drive down the profits that licensees could earn from the innovation and, therefore, the fees that an IPR owner could earn from licensing. This explanation parallels the second explanation we offered for the choice of exclusive licensing over non-exclusive licensing, where a patent holder faces particular transaction costs in relying on variable royalties for collecting rents.

   Suppose that licensees do not need to make specific investments (in order to set aside incentive 1), that licence contracts can be sold only with fixed fees, and that royalties are impossible because of the costs of monitoring downstream quantities or revenues. Then a licensor selling the rights to single licensees in each of two contingent countries can a) sell to each country the right to be a (differentiated) duopolist in an international market by means of licensing contracts without complete exclusivity or b) sell to each the right to be a monopolist in half of an international market. Monopoly profits in a market (or the sum of monopoly profits in two halves of a market) generally exceed the sum of duopoly profits, meaning that exclusivity is the most profitable option.

3. Vertical territorial division may be necessary to eliminate incentive distortions among licensees in setting product quality, price, product service, and product differentiation in other forms that arise from competition among the licensees. If the only decision licensees had to make were which price to set and whether variable royalties were feasible, the variable royalty could be used as an instrument to offset the profit-destroying impact of low prices.[15] Licensees do more than set prices, however. They spend resources on developing local markets and on product service, for example. As the economic literature on contracts in product distribution shows, vertical restraints are necessary in this case to maximize profits (see Rey and Tirole, 1986; Mathewson and Winter, 1986). Variable royalty alone is almost never sufficient to elicit the exact collective-profit-maximizing choices of prices and other downstream decisions. Here distortions in downstream decisions are caused by differences between the mix of instruments (such as price and product quality) that is most effective for promoting product competition and the mix that is most effective for promoting competition among licensees selling the same product. Vertical territorial restrictions can emerge as an instrument that resolves the incentive distortions among licensees and the licensor by simply assigning the entire ownership of a market territory to each licensee.

4. Price discrimination: If the demand elasticities of a product in two countries or regions are very different, the overall profits from licensing are maximized if the two countries can be established as separate countries and different prices charged in each. Total profits are maximized by charging a higher price in the market with the more inelastic demand. This incentive is more important, perhaps, for field-of-use restrictions in licensing contracts that restrict the field in which a licensee may use an innovation (and typically give the licensee exclusive rights to that field in a given territory).

Horizontal Incentives for Closed-Territory Restrictions

1. The simplest horizontal incentive for exclusive territorial restrictions in a licensing contract is the "sham" agreement. Suppose that an otherwise competitive group of firms can sign a contract with the holder of a patent that has a trivial technical value in the production of the

market good. If the contract calls for territorial exclusivity, the contract is very valuable to the firms because it divides the market.

2. A less obvious incentive for territorial division among licensees is to dampen competition between two licensed products – a horizontal effect at the upstream level of production. Rey and Stiglitz (1995) show, in the context of distribution, that exclusive territories can reduce interbrand competition by altering the perceived demand curve that each producer faces. The reduction in demand elasticity induces an increase in the equilibrium price and producers' profits. It is rational for individual producers to use exclusive territories in their model if they can commit themselves not to secretly renegotiate payment schemes to dealers (royalty schemes in the context of licensing). The double mark-up effect on retail prices, which causes a loss in total profits in a single distribution system considered in isolation, increases profits in the context of a strategic game between producers where they can publicly commit to payment schemes with downstream agents before competing on price. In effect, vertical territorial restrictions allow each manufacturer to commit itself to a less aggressive stance ("reaction function") in price competition.

3. Another possible horizontal incentive for territorial division, again at the level of product competition or competition among different licensed products, is that dividing the market for each product may facilitate collusion. Suppose two licensors are attempting to collude on prices. It may be difficult or impossible to collude on the royalty rates charged in licence contracts because these contracts are infrequent, idiosyncratic, and negotiated bilaterally.[16] The final prices set by licensees may therefore be the focus of the collusive agreement. This agreement is more easily monitored if licensees sell in only one territory rather than competing across territories, especially internationally, where licensees' costs of exporting to other countries fluctuate with exchange rates. The noise in final prices due to exchange-rate movements and the flow of parallel imports across borders could frustrate attempts to coordinate the prices charged in each country without the facilitating device of territorial restrictions.

Incentives for Choosing Closed-Territory Over Open-Territory Restrictions

Would a patent holder ever choose open territories over closed territories? If one extends the argument of Fargeix and Perloff (1989), there is a private advantage to open territories. Fargeix and Perloff consider the situation of a manufacturer selling to two countries, each with one dealer, and note that the familiar double mark-up problem may lead the two dealers to charge a price that is higher than the privately efficient price. The problem is a vertical externality: in setting the price, the dealer does not consider the profits flowing upstream as a result of the wholesale mark-up. Gray markets or competition between the two dealers for each market may mitigate or resolve the problem: if the domestic firm's cost advantage in the domestic market is t dollars per unit of a good sold, then the price that either dealer can charge domestically cannot exceed the production cost plus t. Any higher price would be subject to undercutting by the foreign firm. The constraint on downstream prices can increase the total profits of all participants in the distribution system by negating the double mark-up problem. This argument now requires that licensing contracts contain a royalty, rather than just a fixed fee. (A royalty contract is subject to vertical externalities, as downstream licensees do not consider the upstream royalty flowing to the licensor.) The consequence is that the price of the product, or of any product using the innovation, is too high. For licensing contracts with variable royalties, open-territory exclusivity may be preferred to closed-territory exclusivity.

Policy Implications

The policy of allowing open-territory exclusivity is non-controversial. Therefore, we consider the issue of whether closed-territory distribution should be allowed and, internationally, whether the policy of exhaustion is appropriate. If a licensor's rights to control the production and distribution of a product are exhausted with the sale of the product, parallel imports cannot be controlled and closed-territory distribution is thus prohibited.

It is clear that where the use of territorial-exclusivity restrictions is driven by any of the three horizontal incentives, welfare is higher when the use is prohibited. Where this is the case, however, a non-interventionist policy cannot be supported. Patents do not give the right to suppress competition among different patented products. The potential inefficiency of territorial restrictions is most obvious in the case of sham agreements, where the agreement serves no purpose except as a vehicle for dividing markets.

Two final policy questions to be discussed are first, can any of what we have termed the vertical incentives for territorial restrictions justify intervention on efficiency grounds, and second, how, in practice, can the presumptively efficient uses of the restrictions be distinguished from the inefficient uses.

Where exclusive-territory restrictions serve to support specific investment by licensees, efficiency arguments support the legality of the contracts. Where the restrictions serve simply to maximize profits by suppressing competition among licensees (incentive 2), the efficiency of product market competition and technology diffusion (i.e., leaving aside innovation incentives) may or may not dictate a policy of non-intervention. If incentive 2 is operative and exclusive

territories are prohibited, then the diffusion of the technology may be less efficient. There will be less incentive to license to a firm in Canada, for example,
because the prospective increase in North American competition will lower the
fee that a U.S. licensee would willingly pay. On the other hand, if a product is
licensed in Canada and the United States, competition in the product market
would be higher with open- than with closed-territory distribution.

To reach a policy prescription on this point it is enough to invoke the
principle discussed in our introduction (under "The Normative Criteria"):
competition policy should respect the right of a patent holder to exclusively
exploit its innovation in all the markets where its patent is valid. A patent
holder does not create additional monopoly power by dividing up its potential
market and selling each section to a different firm. The patent holder would be
allowed under the law to use its innovation exclusively in each country or territory. A competition policy that allows vertical territorial division is simply
allowing the transfer of this right to a firm that is better equipped to use the
right efficiently. Allowing the patent holder to use territorial division is simply
to respect the rights that are conferred by patent law.

It is important to note, however, the possible conflict under this theory
of closed-territory distribution between the interests of an economic community, trading block or country deciding on the legality of the practice within
its borders, on the one hand, and the global interest, on the other. With the
prohibition of closed territories, the community may consider the benefits of
increased product market competition to be higher than the costs of reduced
incentives to innovate. The benefits of increased innovation that accrue to
consumers in other countries might be ignored. The conflict between an individual country's incentives to protect intellectual property rights and the global
interest is well known, as a single country can free-ride on the protection
offered by other countries. That the same conflict can arise in the context of
the policy of exhaustion has not been widely appreciated.

Along the spectrum between obvious sham agreements and genuinely
efficient uses of vertical restraints, however, are cases that are difficult to cate-
gorize. In their well-known casebook, Easterbrook and Posner (1981) cite Priest
(1977), who argues that the tip-off as to whether a case of market division is
horizontal or vertical is whether the rents from the licensed activity go to the
licensee or to the patent holder:

> A licence that provides only a trivial royalty but specified fixed prices or
> quantity limitations is likely to conceal a cartel. A licence requiring royal-
> ty rebates should be treated similarly. In both cases the patent holder has
> no plausible argument that the arrangement maximizes his own return.
> Arrangements of this sort cannot be justified as serving the coordination
> function of the patent system either. If the patent holder is intent on
> developing the invention's prospects, even at the expense of current
> income the licence should provide for technology or patent grant-backs
> for the patentee's exclusive benefit. If these grant-backs are omitted from

the license, or if all licensees are given a right to use improvements without additional royalty, then the lack of monetary return to the patentee in the licence arrangement becomes highly suspicious (Easterbrook and Posner, 1981, p. 277).

Under our analysis, this test is correct. If royalty payments, fixed or variable, are very small, then the value of a licensing contract is not in the right to use an innovation. The value must then be in the restraints themselves. The significance of the innovation can also be determined in some cases by direct observation or expert assessment.

One cannot, however, infer from the absence of variable royalty payments in a licensing contract that the restraints should be prohibited, when the fixed fees are substantial. The output of the licensee may be difficult to monitor. Profit-sharing with the licensor as the result of a royalty may reduce the licensee's incentive to conduct product development and sales activities. And a contract with a small royalty or none at all, in which nearly the entire profits are retained by the licensee, may select the highest quality licensees. If any of these factors are important, the restrictions in the licensing contract, such as territorial division, may reflect an attempt by the licensor to maximize the value of its licenses, without any horizontal coordination at the licensor or product level.

Easterbrook and Posner (1981, p. 277) point to another test of whether an agreement is efficient or a cartel: the impact on the price of a competing product. If the price of the competing product increases, one should presume that the agreement is horizontal. This test assumes that the prices of the product are strategic complements. If three firms are Bertrand competitors (competing in price), then a collusive agreement between two of them will raise the equilibrium price charged by the third. The reaction curves of Bertrand competitors are upward-sloping, meaning that the reaction of the third firm to the price increases of the colluding firm is to raise its own price.

If the firms are Cournot competitors (competing in quantity), however, then the effect of an agreement between two firms on the equilibrium price charged by a third firm is ambiguous. The two colluding firms will reduce their quantities, causing the outside firm's quantity to increase, as the reaction curves of Cournot competitors in quantity are downward-sloping. The reduction in the colluding firms' quantity leads to an increase in the market-clearing price of the outside firm's product, but the reaction of this firm in increasing its own quantity leads to an offsetting decrease in this price.

A better test would be the effect of an agreement on the quantities sold by a competing firm. The impact of an agreement on a competing firm's output is positive if the agreement is collusive and negative if the agreement reduces costs – whether the market is characterized by (differentiated) Bertrand or by Cournot competition. Of course, this test would require that all extraneous influences on quantities sold be controlled for, which limits the usefulness of the test.

A related test that has been applied extensively in the area of horizontal mergers is the following: Do competitors' stock market prices rise or fall with the agreement? An increase in competing firms' stock market values outside an agreement signals a collusive effect; a decrease signals a cost reduction. These tests could distinguish a vertical agreement from an agreement with strong horizontal effects.

The economics of field-of-use restrictions are similar to the economics of the exclusive territories. Price discrimination may be a stronger motive where the licensor has kept a class of customers or business to itself. Alternatively, the licensor may simply have assets that are complementary to only one class of business, which leads to the decision to licence out the other. (An example of a field-of-use restriction described in the U.S. *Intellectual Property Guidelines for the Licensing of Intellectual Property* is the licensing of a software package for sales of data processing to medical group practices but not hospitals.)

Exclusive Grant-Backs

GRANT-BACK CLAUSES IN LICENSING CONTRACTS require the licensee to grant the patent holder the rights to any future innovations related to the licensed innovation, including improvements in the innovation or additional inventions related to the applicability of the innovation to particular uses.

An efficiency explanation of grant-backs is that they can guarantee the common ownership of a group of patents on complementary processes or products. The transaction costs of the future development of innovations are lower if these innovations can be licensed from a single licensor. As in any market, the joint ownership of the rights to license complementary products or processes leads to lower prices for these licenses. Furthermore, the coordination of additional improvements and their diffusion among licensees is enhanced if the ownership of the rights to the improvement is centralized.

A horizontal and inefficient incentive for grant-backs is that they may increase concentration in the innovation market. Two firms that are engaged in an intensive race for innovation that is dissipating profits have an incentive to establish a licensing contract that gives the rights to current and future innovation to one of them (the licensor). Providing that the two firms collectively have a large share of the innovation market, that is, a large share of the assets specific to innovation in a class of products, the result will be the suppression of the licensee's incentives to innovate. The effect is that of a merger in the market for innovation.

The position of the parties before the licensing agreement can provide important evidence to distinguish efficient from inefficient exclusive grant-backs. If they are both competing in the innovation market, the grant-back contract may serve the purpose of lessening competition in innovation. If the licensees were not competing against the licensor in innovation, the grant-back contract is likely to be efficient.[17]

EXCLUSIVE DEALING

Definition and Example

We use the term exclusive dealing to refer to the restriction on the licensee that it not deal with the licensor of a competing product. An example of this restriction is the U.S. case *National Lockwasher Co. v. George K. Garret Co.*[18] In this case, the patentee of a type of lockwasher stipulated in several standard-form contracts with manufacturing licensees that the licensee not produce competing lockwashers. In this case, an attempt to enforce the patent against infringement was unsuccessful, because the Court found the patent invalid under the patent misuse doctrine. It found that the price involved the use of "the lawful monopoly granted by the patent as a means of suppressing the manufacture and sale of competing unpatented articles."

Vertical Incentives

In the context of product distribution, exclusive dealing can be an efficient way of ensuring that other manufacturers do not free-ride on a producer's investment in its product (Marvel, 1982). Exclusive agency may be efficient in the life insurance or automobile markets because without the restriction, customers attracted to an agent by the advertising of one seller may end up purchasing the product offered by another seller at the same agency. Any expenditure by the seller to improve the product offered by the licensee is also subject to free-riding in the case of a common agent. The free-riding, which would lead to underinvestment in the promotion of products, disappears when each agent represents only a single seller.

In licensing contracts, the analogous incentive would be provided by the risk of free-riding on know-how provided by the licensor as part of the contract. The provision of know-how appears to be the one dimension of the licensor's expenditure that is vulnerable to free-riding.

Another incentive for exclusive dealing is that it can encourage development of relationship-specific technology by both parties. The licensee is encouraged to devote its investment expenditure toward more specific capital simply because it is contractually constrained against exploiting general capital (at least within the contractual term). The licensor will invest more in specific capital, knowing that the absence of other suppliers to the licensee in the future reduces the threat of the licensee leaving the relationship (modifying the licensee's "threat point"). This reduces the likelihood that the return to the investment in specific capital will be held up. Put simply, commitment by one party to a bilateral contract (in this case, by agreeing to exclusivity restrictions) makes the specific investment by the other party to the contract more secure.

The U.S. *Guidelines* on antitrust and intellectual property recognize the potential efficiency benefit of exclusive dealing, which is that it encourages specific investment.

Horizontal Incentives

The argument concerning the inefficient use of exclusive-dealing restrictions is simple, but contentious. It is that a producer (or licensor) with a monopoly in a product market can prevent the entry of a competitor by using the exclusive-dealing restrictions on each buyer. The Chicago school's response to this argument is that a buyer (or licensee) will not accept such a contractual restriction unless the transaction price is reduced to compensate the buyer for the cost of the restriction. It pays the buyer and the seller in any transaction to strike a contract that maximizes their combined net benefit (Bork, 1978).

Aghion and Boulton (1987) offer an effective response. They do not deal with exclusivity restrictions explicitly, but because in their model buyers purchase one unit or none, the analysis can be applied to exclusive dealing (see also Rasmussen et al., 1991). Their response is that the Chicago school's analysis assumes that the benefits from exclusive contracting are internalized by the contractual parties. In fact, there are two kinds of externalities. First, a potential entrant into the market is harmed by an exclusive-dealing restriction, since it reduces its likelihood of entry or reduces the profitability of successful entry (by the requirement that a lower price be offered to attract buyers into dropping the incumbent's product entirely). Second, and more important, in a market with many buyers, the decision by each buyer to enter into an exclusive-dealing contract imposes a cost on other buyers by reducing the chance of successful entry by another firm.[19] The upshot of these externalities is that a seller can bribe a buyer into entering an exclusive contract with only a small price reduction. The total cost to the buyers' side of the market can be much larger than the total bribe that must be paid to buyers to accept the restriction. Therefore, exclusivity can be an inefficient choice.

The necessary condition for this theory is that the licensor have a large share of the product market, or at least that it have a significant advantage over other differentiated licensors in the competition for a significant number of buyers.

OTHER CONTRACTUAL RESTRICTIONS

EXCLUSIVITY RESTRICTIONS, WHEN THEY ARE ANTICOMPETITIVE, have the effect of directly excluding firms from one or the other side of the market. Other contractual restrictions create a link between the contract in question and other contracts entered into by one party to the contract, but the link is not so extreme as to prohibit the other contracts. The effect of these other restrictions can be the same as exclusivity. That is, they can lead to the same market outcome as an exclusivity restriction. We do not consider in detail the incentives for each of these restrictions, but outline the sense in which such contracts involve exclusivity in at least some market circumstances. Where the equivalence holds, we indicate the extent to which the policy analysis of the exclusivity restrictions extends to these other instruments.

EXCLUSIVITY AS AN OPTION

IN SOME CONTRACTS, EXCLUSIVITY IS NOT A RESTRICTION but an option that a buyer or licensee can choose in return for more favourable royalty terms. In the case where the exclusivity option is chosen, the economics of the contract are the same as those we have outlined. The option form of the contract, as in any contract offer by a seller, is a response to asymmetric information on the part of the buyer about the costs and benefits of the contract terms, the market conditions or the inherent value of the product sold (Riordan, 1984; Mas-Colell et al., 1995).

TYING

THERE ARE TWO TYPES OF TYING RESTRICTIONS: bundling (for example, the bundling of patents in licensing contracts), and requirements tying. In the latter, which is most relevant here, the buyer's right to buy one product is tied to the obligation to buy all requirements of a second product exclusively from the same seller. (For an analysis of tying, see Baxter and Kessler, "The Law and Economics of Tying Arrangements: Lessons for the Competition Policy Treatment of Intellectual Property," in this volume.)

MOST-FAVOURED-CLIENT CLAUSE

A MOST-FAVOURED-NATION CLAUSE (MFC) guarantees that a buyer receive the lowest price of any offered by the seller over the period of the contract. The initial price is lowered to match any price reductions offered by the seller to other purchasers.

The following example illustrates the potential exclusionary effect of an MFC. Suppose an exclusive licence to sell a product in an area is worth $100, and being one of the sellers of the product in the market is worth $40. Selling a licence to a producer in this market for $90, with an MFC agreement, will preclude the entry of the second producer: the second producer would pay at most $40, but selling to the second producer at this price would require a refund of $50 to the first seller. The sale to the second producer will not take place, and the first contract is identical (payoff-equivalent) to a contract with exclusivity and a price of $90.

Why would this type of contract be entered into? It could be a response to a prohibition of exclusive licensing (but in intellectual property, exclusive licenses are not illegal). Or it could offer the benefits of exclusivity such as protecting the investor in specific assets against hold-up and more flexibility. Suppose that the profits in the market are uncertain because it is not known whether the product will be a success. The MFC will protect the first seller against entry if profits (demand) are low (in which case entry would preclude a normal realized rate of return to investment). But if the product is very successful, the MFC will not prevent entry – and this is as it should be, because in the case of successful entry the *ex post* efficient number of sellers is (probably) larger and adequate returns on investment assured, even with the additional seller.

The role played by MFC clauses in this setting, when licensing fees are fixed, is the same as the role played by exclusivity. In other settings, MFC can protect sellers against the risk that their competitors will face lower marginal costs. (The profits in highly competitive industries are sensitive to differences in marginal costs.) Suppose licensing fees are variable royalties and it is known that there will be additional licensees in the market (so there is no exclusivity effect). The initial licensees face the risk that later licensees will pay lower royalties and therefore be able to undercut them. If the licensing fees contain a fixed fee as well, the licensor could share in the profits from undercutting the initial licensees in a joint hold-up of the initial licensees' quasi-rents.

Distinguishing the MFC's efficient and exclusionary roles can be difficult, since for either role the practice is more likely the larger or more efficient the seller is relative to other sellers. In a recent case in Canada, outside the intellectual property context, contractual links such as MFC were forbidden together with exclusionary restrictions.[20]

MEETING-COMPETITION CLAUSE

A MEETING-COMPETITION CLAUSE (MCC) IS A GUARANTEE by the seller that it will meet any price offered to the buyer by competing sellers. The practice has been analyzed as a facilitating device for cartels; price chiseling by one cartel member will be automatically met with a meeting-competition clause. Knowing this, cartel members are discouraged from cheating. In product markets or licensing contracts, a monopolist incumbent could also pre-empt underpricing by a new entrant by using an MCC to automatically match it. The outcome can be equivalent to an exclusive-dealing restriction. There is a parallel here with the collective action problem among buyers that is associated with the inefficiency of exclusive dealing: each buyer would like the MCC because of the chance that entry will be successful, but the MCC can make buyers collectively worse off because it reduces the probability of successful entry.

OUTPUT ROYALTY

THIS SCHEME SPECIFIES THAT THE PAYMENT MADE BY THE LICENSEE to the licensor be determined on the basis of the total units of a product sold by the licensee, whether or not these units incorporated the technology or product offered by the licensor. Resales of competing products are not prohibited as in the exclusive-dealing contract, but they are implicitly taxed at the same tax or royalty rate as the input in the contract.

An example of the practice is the *Hazeltine* case, in which the holder of patents for a particular component of radios licensed the use of the component in exchange for a royalty calculated on the basis of the total number of radios produced, whether or not they incorporated the particular component. A more recent case within the intellectual property area is the *Microsoft* matter, which was resolved in a consent decree between Microsoft and the U.S. Department of Justice. Among other practices, Microsoft had been charging a royalty to producers of personal computers on the basis of the total number of computers sold rather than just for those computers sold with the operating system software provided by Microsoft.

The practice appears similar to an exclusivity restriction on buyers in that the purchase of substitute products, which, while not prohibited (or taxed at an infinite rate) as under exclusivity contracts, is nonetheless taxed. In an assessment of the efficiency of output royalties, there are at least two opposing considerations. On the one hand, taxing rivals' output is a simple and direct form of raising their costs. In the simplest of oligopoly models, prices rise when each firm is allowed to tax its rivals' sales. On the other, charging a royalty based on all inputs (or on output) has the effect of spreading out the distortion inherent in a price-cost mark-up over many goods. The seller faces the constraint that buyers can purchase elsewhere whether an input price or an output royalty is charged. Under a royalty contract, the buyer faces a zero opportunity cost of switching to the seller's input, but when the input is intellectual property, this is precisely the cost that the buyer should be facing in input mix decisions. In "The Use of Output Royalties by Input Suppliers" (in progress), we examine how these forces play out under different market conditions.

THE LEGAL TREATMENT OF EXCLUSIVITY RESTRICTIONS IN THE UNITED STATES, THE EUROPEAN COMMUNITY, AND CANADA

IN THIS SECTION OF THE REPORT WE COMPARE THE LEGAL TREATMENT of exclusivity restrictions in licensing contracts in the United States and the European Community. We discuss the sections of the *Competition Act* that apply or could apply to these restrictions in Canada and the Competition Tribunal's interpretation of these sections in a recent case.

THE UNITED STATES

THE U.S. PATENT ACT SPECIFICALLY ALLOWS FOR EXCLUSIVE LICENCES.[21] Nothing in the antitrust laws forbids exclusive licensing. A licensor is not obliged to create competition among its licensees and territorial exclusivity is not prohibited.

The April 1995 U.S. *Antitrust Guidelines for the Licensing of Intellectual Property* clarify the Department of Justice's and the Federal Trade Commission's approach to licensing practices. (For a discussion of the *Guidelines*, see the introduction to this volume by Anderson and Gallini.)[22] These *Guidelines* set out the basic principles that are behind the agencies' approach. Among these principles are the following: "the same antitrust principles apply to intellectual property as apply to other forms of property, with appropriate recognition of the distinguishing characteristics of intellectual property"; "antitrust enforcement should not unnecessarily interfere with the licensing of intellectual property rights"; and "the existence of an intellectual property right does not, by itself, give rise to a presumption of market power."[23]

With respect to exclusivity restrictions, the *Guidelines* specifically recognize that field-of-use clauses, territorial exclusivity, and other forms of exclusivity may serve procompetitive ends by allowing efficient use of property:

> These various forms of exclusivity can be used to give a licensee an incentive to invest in the commercialization and distribution of products embodying the licensed intellectual property and to develop additional applications for the licensed property. The restrictions may do so, for example, by protecting the licensee against free-riding on the licensee's investment by other licensees or by the licensor. They may also increase the licensor's incentive to license, for example, by protecting the licensor from competition in the licensor's own technology in a market niche that it prefers to keep to itself. These benefits of licensing restrictions apply to patent, copyright, and trade secret licenses, and to know-how agreements.[24]

With respect to the potential detrimental effect of exclusivity restrictions, or licensing contractual restrictions in general, the following are some key points made in the *Guidelines*.

1. The lessening of competition is considered from the perspectives of innovation by the licensor, the licensor's competitors, and the licensees; foreclosure of licensees from access to competing technologies; and the facilitation of price-fixing or market division in product markets. These are the dimensions of innovation markets, technology markets, and goods markets that we discussed in the section entitled "The Economics of Exclusivity Restrictions." The goods markets reflect the use of the product technology; the technology market reflects the diffusion of the technology.

2. The benchmark against which the impact of any licensing restrictions is measured is their effect on competition among likely competitors in the absence of the licenses, as opposed to the absence of the licensing restrictions.

3. The *Guidelines* introduced an (arguably) new concept, the "innovation market." referring to those firms that own assets specific to innovation in a common class of technologies or products. This is not a market in the sense that an economist would use the term (a set of transactions in which a product is exchanged). But it is a useful label to attach to the innovating firms, because it allows the criterion of the significance of market share to be used to assess the risk of anticompetitive effects.

4. An important consideration is whether the licensor and licensees' relationship is vertical or horizontal. To the extent that they would have been competitors in the absence of the arrangement, their relationship is horizontal. In a consideration of the potential anticompetitive effects on prices, technology diffusion or R&D, the focus is on arrangements among parties in a horizontal relationship. The potential anticompetitive effect depends on how concentrated the three classes of markets are, the share each of the parties has of those markets, and the barriers to entry into those markets. A vertical licensing arrangement may harm competition if, for example, it facilitates horizontal coordination of prices or output among entities in a market.

5. The framework for evaluating licensing restraints in most cases is the rule of reason, although not in restraints such as naked price-fixing, which are by their "nature and necessary effect so plainly anticompetitive" as to be treated as unlawful *per se* (p. 2).

6. Exclusivity restrictions on the licensor (e.g., exclusive licensing or exclusive territories) are of concern only if the licensees, or the licensee and the licensor, have a horizontal relationship.

7. Grant-backs and the acquisition of intellectual property rights are examples of exclusive arrangements that may give rise to concern.

8. Exclusive dealing is in general to be evaluated under the rule of reason. The agency will consider the extent to which exclusive dealing a) promotes the exploitation and development of the licensor's technology by, for example, encouraging investment in and development of specific technology, and b) anticompetitively forecloses the development of competing technologies. In this evaluation, the agency will examine the degree of foreclosure, the duration of the exclusive-dealing contract,

and the market conditions – including concentration, ease of entry, and market elasticities.

9. In evaluating the potential anticompetitive risk of grant-backs, the agency will consider mainly the technology and innovation markets. The potential efficiencies of grant-backs are recognized.

10. The *Guidelines* offer an antitrust "safety zone" in that the agencies will not challenge a restraint in an IPR licensing arrangement if a) the restraint is not *facially* anticompetitive, and b) the licensee and licensor collectively account for no more than 20 percent of each relevant market that is affected significantly by the restraint. This is generally applied to goods markets. With respect to technology and innovation markets, the agencies will not challenge a restraint that may affect competition if it is not facially anticompetitive and there are four or more independent technologies or innovators in addition to the technologies controlled by the parties to the arrangement.

THE EUROPEAN COMMUNITY[25]

EXCLUSIVE LICENSING AND TERRITORIAL EXCLUSIVITY have received substantial attention in the European Community (EC), because of the view that territorial restraints conflict with the goal of integrating the markets of the EC countries. The Federal Trade Commission's policy toward territorial restrictions is "aimed at preserving the free movement of goods within the Community balanced against the need to give firms sufficient incentives to invest in a given territory" (OECD, 1989, p. 61). The protection in the law of parallel imports (e.g., the imports into one member state of a product produced under licence in another state), is contained in the legal decision in the articles of the Treaty of Rome relating to movement of goods between EC member states.

Articles 30 and 34 of the Treaty of Rome provide for the free movement of goods, and the decisions of the Court of Justice establish the exhaustion doctrine. This doctrine was established for patented goods in *Centraforam BV v. Sterling Drug Inc.*:

> In relation to patents, the specific subject matter of the industrial property is the guarantee that the patentee, to reward the creative effort of the inventor, has the exclusive right to use an invention with a view to manufacturing industrial products and putting them into circulation for the first time, either directly or by the grant of licenses to third-parties, as well as the right to oppose infringements.

> An obstacle to the free movement of goods may arise out of the existence, within a national legislation concerning industrial and commercial property, of provisions laying down that a patentee's right is not exhausted

when the product protected by the patent is marketed in another Member State, with the result that the patentee can prevent importation of the product into his own Member State when it has been marketed in another State.

Whereas an obstacle to the free movement of goods of this kind may be justified on the ground of protection of industrial property where such protection is invoked against a product coming from a Member State where it is not patentable and has been manufactured by third parties without the consent of the patentee and in cases where there exist patents, the original proprietors of which are legally and economically independent, a derogation from the principle of the free movement of goods is not, however, justified where the product has been put onto the market in a legal manner, by the patentee himself or with his consent, in the Member State from which it has been imported, in particular in the case of a proprietor of parallel patents.[26]

In short, EC law allows open-territory exclusivity in most cases, but it does not allow closed territories.

The EC law on grant-backs is also more restrictive than the U.S. law. Non-exclusive grant-backs are allowed under the "Block Exemptions to the Treaty of Rome for Patents and for Know-How." These exemptions are removed for patent licensing agreements that oblige a licensee to "assign wholly or in part" improvements or new applications to the licensor and for any know-how grant-backs under which the licensee is not free to license its improvements to others, provided it does not divulge still-secret licensor know-how, among other conditions. Roughly, non-exclusive grant-backs are allowed in most cases, and exclusive grant-backs are prohibited.

CANADA

A NUMBER OF SECTIONS OF CANADA'S *COMPETITION ACT* could be applied to various exclusivity restrictions in intellectual property licensing contracts.[27] Section 32 provides for application by the Attorney-General for remedial measures with respect to the abuse of patents, copyrights, trademarks or registered industrial designs. The practices in question have to have had "undue" anticompetitive effects under this section, and the remedial measures taken must not violate Canada's international obligations with respect to the protection of intellectual property. Section 32 has not been applied in any recent cases. As section 29 of the *Combines Investigation Act*, however, it was pertinent to negotiated settlements with Union Carbide of Canada regarding its licensing agreements.[28]

The Union Carbide matter focused on restrictive provisions in the licensing agreement for use of the company's patented processes and machines for extracting polyethylene film from resin and treating this film for printing. The exclusionary or potentially exclusionary restrictions included sliding-scale royalties, field-of-use restrictions, grant-back provisions, and provisions restricting the type of film that licensees were allowed to treat using the patented process.

Section 77 deals specifically with the practices of tied selling, exclusive dealing, and territorial market restriction. The section provides a remedy of prohibition where these practices are engaged in "by a major supplier of a product in a market, or . . . is widespread in a market, [and] is likely to (a) impede entry into or expansion of a firm in the market, (b) impede introduction of a product . . . or expansion of sales of a product, or (c) have any other exclusionary effect in the market, with the result that competition is or is likely to be lessened substantially."[29]

These are reviewable practices rather than *per se* offences, and remedial action can be applied for where the practices have resulted or are likely to result in a substantial lessening of competition, among other conditions. A recent matter addressed under the tied-selling provision was that of the Digital Equipment of Canada (DEC).[30] DEC tied the sale of updates for its copyrighted operating system software to hardware servicing on its equipment. The director's position was that DEC's practices represented the leveraging or extension of market power derived from IP rights on software into the servicing market, which impeded entry and expansion of third-party service providers into that market. This matter was resolved by an undertaking in October 1992 in which DEC agreed to drop the tying restriction.

This case raises two economic questions: Why did DEC find it profitable to tie software to servicing? What are the efficiency implications? There are two plausible explanations for the practice. First, the inability of buyers to distinguish between software and hardware faults would lead to an externality that would distort the incentives to provide high-quality servicing, and increased quality would benefit DEC's as well as the service provider's reputations. An externality such as this is internalized through vertical integration or tying. Second, there was perhaps a correlation among buyers between a) the value that they placed on the software, and b) the intensity with which the system was used and, therefore, the quantity of servicing required. Under this condition, tying, together with marking up the price of servicing over cost, allows a greater share of the surplus to be extracted from high-value users – a standard price-discrimination explanation of tying. Neither of these explanations supports prohibiting the practice on the criterion of efficiency.

Sections 78 and 79 of the *Competition Act* are important in terms of their potential application to anticompetitive abuse of intellectual property rights. These sections provide a case-by-case review of restrictive trade practices engaged in by dominant firms. Section 78 provides a non-exhaustive list of practices that may be considered anticompetitive, and section 79 allows the Competition Tribunal wide discretion in invoking remedies on application by the Director. The list includes "requiring or inducing a supplier to sell only or primarily to certain customers, or to refrain from selling to a competitor, with the object of preventing a competitor's entry into, or expansion in, a market" where the practice has or is likely to have "the effect of preventing or lessening competition substantially in a market."[31]

Section 79, subsection (5) exempts any act "engaged in pursuant only to the exercise of any right or enjoyment of any interest derived under the *Copyright Act, Industrial Design Act, Patent Act, Trademarks Act* or any other Act of Parliament pertaining to intellectual or industrial property." As the Director has explained, however, "This exception does not provide a blanket exemption for intellectual property holders from the application of the abuse provisions. The wording of the exception suggests that the provisions remain applicable to practices which are shown to constitute *abuses* of intellectual property rights (as opposed to the mere exercise of such rights)."

The first decision by the Competition Tribunal under the abuse of dominance provisions, *NutraSweet*, dealt with a number of exclusivity provisions related to intellectual property rights.[32] NutraSweet had a Canadian patent on the artificial sweetener, aspartame, which expired in 1987. The central allegation of the director in this case, filed in 1989, was that the NutraSweet Company had extended its market power beyond the life of the patent by using anticompetitive, exclusionary practices. These practices included the combination of an allowance offered to buyers (primarily diet soft-drink manufacturers) to encourage them to display the NutraSweet logo with a requirement that customers displaying this logo use exclusively the NutraSweet brand, aspartame. This, the tribunal concluded, created an "all or nothing" choice for buyers. The restraint appears to have been effectively an inducement to exclusive purchasing for buyers. Other clauses that the director alleged were exclusionary included meeting-competition, or "meet-or-release" clauses, which gave NutraSweet the option to meet any lower price offered to buyers, and most-favoured-client clauses, which provided each buyer with the guarantee that its price would be the lowest price paid by any customer.[33]

NutraSweet was a U.S. company whose U.S. patent did not expire until 1992. (NutraSweet's European patents had expired at the time of the case.) Canada accounted for about 5 percent of worldwide sales of aspartame. The diet soft-drink manufacturers were the main buyers (85 percent) of aspartame in Canada, with Coke and Pepsi being by far the largest purchasers. NutraSweet's only rival was Holland Sweetener Company, a joint venture between two large companies including Tosoh of Japan. Marketing in Canada was conducted by Tosoh Canada.

Economic theory offers at least two potential models of the competitive impact of exclusive purchasing requirements in a case like NutraSweet. One theory that sees exclusivity restrictions as anticompetitive follows the logic of Aghion and Boulton (1987) (discussed in the section entitled "Other Contractual Restrictions"). In a monopolized market where it is probable that another firm will enter in the future, for example, where another firm is attempting to gain entry into the market, each buyer has an incentive to accept a relatively small "bribe" to enter an exclusive-dealing contract with the incumbent. This is in spite of the fact that accepting such a contract makes it more difficult for the new firm to enter and deters it from investing in productive capacity, thereby reducing the likelihood of a more competitive market structure in the future.

The same argument holds for meet-or-release clauses, which could deter entry by committing the incumbent to counter attempted entries that use underpricing. Most-favoured-client clauses have, in combination with the meet-or-release clauses, a subtle entry-deterring effect. An attempt by a prospective entrant to get a toe-hold in the market by underpricing the incumbent in a contract with one buyer will lead to lower prices at all buyers, as the incumbent responds to the entrant's lower price (communicated to the incumbent by the buyer through the buyer's meet-or-release obligation). The entrant's potential toe-holds all disappear as it attempts to secure one of them. For these clauses, as for basic exclusivity contracts, buyers may sign contracts that deter entry or reduce its likelihood, even when they are collectively better off refusing them.

Two externalities account for this collective action problem. The buyer does not incorporate into its decisions any costs of entry barriers or future delay in entry that accrue to the entrant. More importantly, while the buyer is harmed by a reduced chance of entry when it signs an exclusive contract, it bears only a small part of the cost of the contract's influence on the market structure of the future. It does not take into account the cost of suppressed competition to the other buyers in the market. The suppression of competition through exclusive dealing, in this theory, works through the failure of buyers to internalize the social effects of their decisions to accept contracts.

This theory requires two conditions: first, that the potential entrant not be a viable alternative for buyers in the market at the time of the contract with the incumbent, and second, that the size of the market segment using exclusivity restrictions (in this case, Canada) be large relative to the entire market for the product (the world). These two conditions underlie the central theme that buyers' decisions (to accept exclusive-dealing contracts) are distorted because buyers collectively determine the likelihood of future entry, but each individual buyer bears only a small fraction of the cost of reduced likelihood of entry when it enters an exclusive-dealing contract. In addition, the larger the number of buyers the greater their collective action problem.

None of these conditions is valid in the NutraSweet case. Canada had only 5 percent of the world market of aspartame. Actions taken by Canadian buyers had therefore almost no impact on the investment of prospective entrants in capacity in the future, contrary to the anticompetitive theory that we have outlined. Nor was Tosoh, NutraSweet's rival, merely a prospective future entrant. Tosoh was producing aspartame in 1989. While it had total capacity at its one plant of only 500 tonnes, compared with a total quantity sold worldwide of 7,500 tonnes, the U.S. market remained monopolized under the NutraSweet patent. Tosoh's capacity was much larger than the entire Canadian market, meaning that it would be able, and presumably willing, to supply the entire Canadian market at a price equal to the price of aspartame in Europe.

The other theory of the anticompetitiveness of NutraSweet's contracts is that the meeting-competition clauses and the most-favoured-client clauses discourage Tosoh from even making offers to buyers in the Canadian aspartame market. The meeting-competition clause would automatically provide the incumbent with the opportunity to meet its price offers, leaving Tosoh without accepted offers. And Tosoh would foresee that any attempt to gain a toe-hold entry by making an offer to a particular buyer would be met – through a combination of meeting-competition and most-favoured-client clauses – with price drops not only for that buyer, but also for all other buyers.

This theory might hold some explanatory power in an economy where the cost of putting offers together or organizing entry into a geographical area is very large, and where buyers are somehow incapable of soliciting bids from the entrant. But these characteristics do not hold for aspartame, and the theory is rejected by the fact that the large buyers, Coke and Pepsi, did approach Tosoh for competitive bids. Also, as the tribunal noted, the meet-or-release and most-favoured-client clauses were in the contracts at the behest of the buyers.

An alternative theory for exclusivity in this case is that NutraSweet was able to offer each buyer an exclusivity and price package that was more attractive than the best package that Tosoh could offer. When Coke and Pepsi approached Tosoh to solicit bids, Tosoh's response was that it was unprepared to supply the buyer's entire requirements.

In this theory, the decision by NutraSweet to effectively impose an exclusive-dealing restriction changes the nature of the competition from competition within the market to competition for the market (Mathewson and Winter, 1987; McAfee and Schwartz ,1994). A manufacturer can, if its market position is dominant enough, impose exclusive dealing and raise its price above the level that it would set in the market duopoly game without exclusive dealing. In this case, exclusive dealing would be anticompetitive according to this theory. But in some circumstances, the dominant firm will offer exclusive-dealing contracts even if it has to lower its price to induce buyers to accept. In the famous *Standard Fashions* case, Standard Fashions dropped its price by 50 percent to induce buyers to accept the exclusive-dealing restriction. Increasing the market share to 100 percent may more than compensate the dominant firm for the price drop necessary to induce buyers to accept the restriction.

In this case, potential competition replaces actual competition as the force that disciplines prices in the market. As the theory of contestability emphasizes, prices may be effectively disciplined by potential competition, even when the market appears to be monopolized. The measure of competitiveness in a market is not the market structure alone, but whether potential entrants stand ready to supply firms in the market.[34]

The question then becomes whether Tosoh's position as a potential entrant was strong enough to have a downward influence on prices in the market. In its decision, the tribunal states "We agree with Tosoh's view that it was being used by Coke and Pepsi to obtain a better price from NSC and that there was little chance that either of them was seriously considering giving all of its Canadian business to Tosoh." (p. 83)

The description of a potential entrant as being used by buyers to obtain a better price is a description of potential competition at work.

But how significant was the power of this potential competition in disciplining prices in the market? This answer is suggested by the second major allegation by the director (dismissed by the tribunal) that NutraSweet's prices were too low to be competitive. Pricing below acquisition cost is a potentially anticompetitive practice under section 78 of the *Competition Act*.

A predatory pricing theory of NutraSweet's pricing and contract practices would require that NutraSweet set prices below cost in 1989 in the expectation that the resulting exclusion from the Canadian market would so deter Tosoh from investing in world capacity that future prices would rise in Canada. The fact that Canada only has a 5 percent share of the world market, among other factors, makes this difficult even to contemplate.

Conclusion: Implications for Canadian Policy

WE HAVE REVIEWED THE ECONOMIC AND LEGAL TREATMENT of exclusivity restrictions in licensing contracts in three jurisdictions. We conclude here with a discussion of the implications for Canadian policy on these contractual restrictions. Our focus is on exclusive territorial restrictions, for two reasons. First, as a policy issue the restriction of exclusive licensing is tied closely to this class of restrictions. Second, exclusive dealing has attracted less attention in case law and policy.

There is a striking difference between the legal treatment of exclusivity restrictions in licensing contracts in North America and the EC. Closed territories are prohibited in the EC, on the basis that they run afoul of Treaty of Rome guarantees of free flow of goods between EC member states. There are no legal barriers to national territorial restrictions in North America. While open-territory exclusivity is generally permitted in the EC, a licensor cannot offer an exclusive licensee in a member state protection against imports from another licensee.

In the light of the economic analysis of exclusive territories, where along the spectrum between the EC and U.S. legal treatment of territorial restrictions should Canadian policy be positioned? We base our policy analysis on the assumption that competition policy should maximize economic efficiency, but it should take as a constraint a recognition of the rights granted by patent law and other legal protection of intellectual property. We assessed the efficiency implications of six possible private incentives for territorial exclusivity against this criterion.

The simplest incentive for territorial exclusivity applies in the case where a licensor is constrained by the market and information to use fixed fees to collect royalties. Here, to the extent that competition would be intense among licensees, territorial division of the market for its product among N licensees will be more profitable because each licensee is worth $1/N$ of monopoly profits. Without exclusivity, each licence is worth $1/N$ of the total profits from the more competitive market.

This incentive may offer a rationale for exclusivity as guaranteeing an efficient diffusion of technology. A prohibition would discourage extensive technology diffusion, by means of a greater number of geographically specialized licensees. The constraint that competition policy should recognize the rights conferred by patent law is also operative. A patent gives a licensor the exclusive right to a product in all the territories where the patent is valid. Territorial restraints are simply the division of this right before it is transferred to individuals better positioned to exploit it. This suggests a policy closer to U.S. than EC law. Subsection (5) of section 79 of the *Competition Act* incorporates the constraint that patent rights be respected more explicitly than even the U.S. competition law does, although the *NutraSweet* decision suggests that this subsection may not be a significant exemption. The second vertical incentive for territorial exclusivity and for the closely related exclusive licensing and field-of-use restraints is to protect specific investment against hold-up. This explanation favours laissez-faire treatment of these restraints purely on efficiency grounds.

To the extent that these motivations explain vertical territorial restraints, the prohibition of these restraints will harm the efficiency of goods markets, the diffusion of technology and, since profitable exploitation of innovations is constrained, the incentives for innovation. Our normative framework allows no room for the consideration that horizontal competition among licensees – for example, the free flow of a product among EC member states – is a goal in itself, independent of the efficiency consequences.

Exclusivity is not always explained as a purely vertical phenomenon, however. Where territorial division is simply a disguise for market division among licensees that had a horizontal relationship before the licensing agreement, it should be prohibited. Where two or more licensors use vertical territorial division as a facilitating device to coordinate prices or outputs among their products, the restraint is also inefficient and should be disallowed. In terms of the Canadian *Competition Act*, we would expect that this prohibition would be invoked under section 45 dealing with conspiracy. A section 79 application would not be necessary.

A more subtle horizontal effect of vertical territorial division is the dampening of competition among licensors who commit publicly to licensing contracts. Where two or more licensors of closely substitutable products are observed to announce the terms of their licensing contracts or communicate the terms of their licence contracts and commit to these contracts, competition authorities should have the legal mandate to disallow the contracts.

NOTES

1   We do not consider trademark law in this paper.

2   That is, the decision on exclusivity versus non-exclusivity is taken once distinct geographical markets have been determined.

3   Non-exclusive grant-backs, in which the licensor receives the rights – but not the exclusive rights – to the technology improvement are an alternative.

4   Exclusive grant-backs were the central issue in *Transparent-Wrap Machine Corp. v. Stokes and Smith Co.*, 329 U.S. 637 (1946).

5   For example, in the Digital Equipment of Canada (DEC) matter, DEC tied the sale of its copyrighted operating software to hardware servicing on its equipment. (Director of Investigation and Research, Bureau of Competition Policy, Annual Report for the year ending March 31, 1993, p. 14.)

6   Both most-favoured-client clauses and meeting-competition clauses were issues in *Canada (Director of Investigation and Research) v. The NutraSweet Co.* (1990), 32 C.P.R. (3d) 1. This case is discussed in the section of this paper entitled "The Legal Treatment of Exclusivity Restrictions in the United States, the European Community, and Canada").

7   Before the recent *Microsoft* consent decree, Microsoft required a royalty on each unit shipped by downstream personal computer manufacturers, rather than on the number of units of MS-DOS shipped.

8   The exclusionary effect of a minimum quantity restriction was an issue in the *Microsoft* matter.

9   As discussed in the section of this paper entitled "The Legal Treatment of Exclusivity Restrictions in the United States, the European Community, and Canada," the recent U.S. Department of Justice *Antitrust Guidelines for the Licensing of Intellectual Property* refer to innovation as a "market." Indeed, this is seen as an innovation in antitrust enforcement (see Hay, 1995; Rapp, 1995; Hoerner, 1995; and Gilbert and Sunshine, 1995b). Innovation is not a market in the sense that economists use that term – a set of transactions in which a particular good is exchanged – but the terminology is common to both senses of the word.

10   This dampening effect of monopolization on innovative activity can also be expressed by comparing the incentives for innovation under the two extreme market structures, monopoly and competition. Kenneth Arrow (1962) noted that a monopolist's incentive to innovate is provided only by the increase in profits in moving from an old to a new technology, whereas in the competitive market the gain to a "drastic" innovation (one that allows monopolization due to the superiority of the product or process) is full monopoly profit.

11   If all assets were easily transferable, then the joint assets could be owned efficiently by the innovator or the owner of complementary assets; the two means of achieving joint ownership would be equally efficient. The equivalence can be broken by wealth constraints (a small inventor of a new car engine component cannot buy General Motors) or by the recognition that some kinds of assets, such as human capital, are inalienable. The economic theory of asset ownership is developed by Grossman and Hart (1986) and Hart and Moore (1990).

12   In markets where splitting residual claims is not practical, such as the used car market, the result of asymmetrical information is that the market transactions will shrink or disappear altogether (Akerlof, 1970).

13　More precisely, the degree of specificity of the asset to a use or relationship is measured by the proportion that the asset's value is greater in that use than in the next best use.

14　The substitution is inefficient with respect to the collective profits of the licensor and the licensee, because the input mix should ideally be based on opportunity costs. The royalty is not an opportunity cost.

15　The royalty would be set at a level where the horizontal competitive externality between licensees exactly offset the vertical externality associated with the double mark-up effect, and full profits would be realized without territorial exclusivity.

16　Note the contrast between the assumptions necessary for this incentive for territorial restrictions, the collusion-facilitating effect, and the assumptions necessary for the previous horizontal motivation, the Rey-Stiglitz effect. The assumption under the collusion-facilitating effect is that the royalty terms in the license contract cannot be monitored by cartel members; in the Rey-Stiglitz theory, the contract must be observed and committed to.

17　Exclusive cross-licensing and patent pooling by amalgamating exclusive rights to related technologies are not considered in this chapter.

18　*National Lockwasher Co. v. George K. Garret Co.*, 137 F.2d 255 (*3rd dir.* 1943). This case is discussed in OECD, 1989, p. 69.

19　The probability of successful entry by another firm increases with the number of buyers, free from any exclusive dealing contracts with the incumbent.

20　*Director of Research and Investigation (Canada) v. Dun and Bradstreet.*

21　USC section 261.

22　Department of Justice and Federal Trade Commission Issue Joint *Antitrust Guidelines for the Licensing of Intellectual Property*, April 6, 1995.

23　*Guidelines*, p. 2.

24　*Guidelines*, p. 5.

25　This section relies heavily on the excellent summary found in OECD, *Competition Policy and Intellectual Property Rights*, 1989.

26　*Centraforam BV v. Sterling Drug Inc.*, Case 15/74, 1974 E.C.R. 1147, at 1162-63. Quoted in OECD, 1989.

27　A recent discussion of the Canadian law can be found in George N. Addy (Director of Investigation and Research in Canada), "Competition Policy and Intellectual Property Rights: Complementary Framework Policies for a Dynamic Market Economy." Notes for an Address to the XXXVIth World Congress of the AIPPI, Bureau of Competition Policy, June 19, 1995.

28　Director of Investigation and Research, *Annual Report for the Year Ended March 31, 1968*, p. 42, *Annual Report . . . 1970*, pp. 54-56, and *Annual Report . . . 1972*, pp. 29-30.

29　*Competition Act* (R.S.C. 1985, Chap. C-34, Amended 1988), section 77 (2).

30　Director of Investigation and Research, *Annual Report for the Year Ended March 31, 1993*, p. 14.

31　*Competition Act*, section 78 (h).

32　*Canada (Director of Investigation and Research) v. The NutraSweet Co.* (1990), 32 C.P.R. (3d) 1.

33　In addition, the Director alleged that NutraSweet had been selling below its acquisition cost, one of the potentially anticompetitive practices listed in section 78. The tribunal found, however, that NutraSweet had not engaged in below-cost predatory pricing.

34 Tosoh is reported in the evidence of the case as being unprepared to supply the entire requirements of the large buyers, but this presumably means that it was unwilling to supply the requirements at a price that the buyers would willingly pay.

BIBLIOGRAPHY

Aghion, Philippe and Patrick Boulton. "Contracts as a Barrier to Entry." *American Economic Review*, 77, 3 (June 1987): 388-401.

Akerlof, George A. "The Market for 'Lemons': Qualitative Uncertainty and the Market Mechanism." *Quarterly Journal of Economics*, 84 (1970): 488-500.

Anderson, R. D. et al. "Intellectual Property Rights and International Market Segmentation: Implications of the Exhaustion Principle." Working Paper, Bureau of Competition Policy (October 1990).

Arrow, Kenneth. "Economic Welfare and the Allocation of Resources to Invention." *The Rate and Direction of Inventive Activity.* National Bureau of Economic Research, 1962, pp. 609-20.

Bork, Robert H. *The Antitrust Paradox.* New York: Basic Books, 1978.

Brandenburger, Adam M. and Barry J. Nalebuff. "The Right Game: Use Game Theory to Shape Strategy." *Harvard Business Review* (July-August 1995): 57-73.

Easterbrook, Frank H. and Richard A. Posner. *Antitrust.* American Casebook Series, 2nd ed., Chicago: West Publishing, 1981.

Fargeix, Michael and Jeffrey Perloff. "The Effects of Tariffs in Markets with Vertical Restraints." *Journal of International Economics*, 26 (February 1989): 99-117.

Gallini, Nancy and Brian Wright. "Technology Transfer under Asymmetric Information." *Rand Journal of Economics* (Spring 1990): 147-60.

Gilbert, Richard J. and Steven C. Sunshine. "Incorporating Dynamic Efficiency Concerns into Merger Analysis: The Use of Innovation Markets." *Antitrust Law Journal*, 63 (1995a): 569.

———. "The Use of Innovation Markets: A Reply to Hay, Rapp, and Hoerner." *Antitrust Law Journal*, 64, 1 (Fall 1995b): 75-82.

Grossman, Sanford and Oliver Hart. "The Costs and Benefits of Ownership: A Theory of Vertical and Lateral Integration." *Journal of Political Economy*, 94 (1986): 691-719.

Hart, Oliver and John Moore. "Property Rights and the Nature of the Firm." *Journal of Political Economy*, 48 (December 1990): 1119-58.

Hay, George A. "Innovations in Antitrust Enforcement." *Antitrust Law Journal*, 64, 1 (Fall 1995): 7-18.

Hoerner, Robert J. "Innovation Markets: New Wine in Old Bottles?." *Antitrust Law Journal*, 64, 1 (Fall 1995): 49-75.

Levin, Richard C. et al. "R&D Appropriability, Opportunity, and Market Structure: New Evidence on Some Schumpeterian Hypotheses." *American Economic Review*, 75, 2 (May 1985): 20-25.

Marvel, Howard P. "Exclusive Dealing." *Journal of Law and Economics*, 25 (1982): 1-25.

Mas-Colell, Andreu, Michael Whinston and Jerry Green. *Microeconomic Theory.* Oxford University Press, 1995.

Mathewson, G. F. and R. A. Winter. "The Competitive Effects of Exclusive Dealing: Comment." *American Economic Review*, 77, 5 (December 1987): 1057-62.

——."The Law and Economics of Vertical Restraints," in *The Law and Economics of Competition Policy*. Edited by G. F. Mathewson and M. J. Trebilcock. Vancouver: Fraser Institute, 1986.

McAfee, Preston and Marius Schwartz. "Opportunism in Multilateral Vertical Contracting: Non-discrimination, Exclusivity, and Uniformity." *American Economic Review*, 84, 1 (March 1994): 210-30.

Organization for Economic Co-operation and Development. *Competition Policy and Intellectual Property Rights*. Paris: OECD, 1989.

Porter, Michael. *The Competitive Advantage of Nations*. Cambridge: Harvard University Press, 1990.

Posner, Richard A. *Antitrust Law: An Economic Perspective*. Chicago: University of Chicago Press, 1976.

Priest, George. "Cartels and Patent Licence Arrangements." *Journal of Law and Economics*, 309 (1977): 326-30.

Rapp, Richard T. "The Misapplication of the Innovation Market Approach to Merger Analysis." *Antitrust Law Journal*, 64, 1 (Fall 1995): 19-49.

Rasmussen, Eric, Mark Ramseyer and John S. Wiley, Jr. "Naked Exclusion." *American Economic Review*, 81, 5 (December 1991): 1137-45.

Rey, Patrick and Joseph E. Stiglitz. "The Role of Exclusive Territories in Producers' Competition." *Rand Journal of Economics*, 26, 3 (Autumn 1995): 431-51.

Rey, Patrick and Jean Tirole (1986). "Vertical Restraints from a Principal-Agent Viewpoint," in *Marketing Channels: Relationships and Performance*. Edited by L. Pelligrini and S. Reddy. Lexington (Mass.): Lexington Books, 1986, pp. 3-30.

Riordan, Michael. "Uncertainty, Asymmetric Information and Bilateral Contracts." *Review of Economic Studies*, 51 (January 1984): pp. 83-93.

Scherer, F. M. *Innovation and Growth: Schumpeterian Perspectives*. Cambridge: MIT Press, 1984.

Schwartz, Marius. "The Competitive Effects of Vertical Agreements: Comment." *American Economic Review*, 72 (December 1987): 1063-68.

Comment

Marius Schwartz
U.S. Council of Economic Advisers and
Georgetown University

THE TREATMENT OF BOTH EXCLUSIVITY RESTRICTIONS AND R&D and intellectual property in the economics literature is complex and riddled with ambiguities. Treating both theses areas in one paper, as the authors do, therefore is bound to raise difficult issues. Nevertheless, the paper makes some useful contributions. Rey and Winter have nicely outlined the different types of exclusive practices: direct exclusivity restrictions and indirect practices that do not require explicit exclusivity, but may have the same effect. An example of the latter is certain most-favoured-customer clauses (that commit a firm to match an entrant's price, a commitment which may deter entry). The authors also describe the various motivations for exclusivity practices effectively; and here I agree with the principle that, at least as a first pass, to predict welfare effects it is necessary to understand motivations and whether the parties are in a vertical or horizontal relationship or whether, as Baxter and Kessler put it in their paper ("The Law and Economics of Tying Arrangements: Lessons for the Competition Policy Treatment of Intellectual Property,"), they supply complements or substitutes – a more general distinction that captures the essence of "horizontal" versus "vertical."

I would like to comment on three areas. The first is the use of exclusivity to prevent opportunism by the licenser, the second is the interface between competition policy and incentives to innovate, and the third is the NutraSweet case or, more generally, exclusivity and foreclosure.

I think in some ways Rey and Winter understate the importance of exclusivity in preventing opportunism by the licenser against a licensee (or franchisee). They make the point, for example, that most-favoured-client (MFC) clauses – which say that if I give a lower royalty to somebody else, then you're eligible for that same discount – are a powerful way to prevent opportunism, i.e., to prevent the licenser from bringing in a second licensee once the first has made specific investments. But Preston McAfee and I have shown (*American Economic Review*, 1994) that the argument that MFC clauses can prevent opportunism works when the contract is a linear price or a royalty, but does not work when it is more complicated, for example, a two-part tariff.

To see this, suppose the optimal downstream market structure is to have two licensees. Suppose they are symmetric, but they are differentiated in their products, which is why two are required for efficiency. The profit-maximising contract specifies a two-part tariff where the output royalty is positive, because you want to nudge up the marginal cost of the downstream firms in order to correct for the fact that, otherwise, competition downstream results in product prices that are below what an integrated two-product monopolist would choose. So the royalty is positive (above the licenser's marginal cost, which is assumed for simplicity to be zero).

This profit maximizing arrangement can be sustainable only if it is immune to opportunism. But the licenser might, after having licensed one firm and collected a fixed fee, want to turn to a second one and say: "Look, ignoring the first firm, the best bilateral deal for us is for me to cut my royalty to you to zero (my marginal cost). In exchange for this lower royalty, I will charge you a higher fixed fee." That is the nature of the opportunistic deviation.

The question is: Can you prevent this kind of opportunism by telling the first licensee that you are going to have an MFC? It depends on what is meant by MFC. If it means that the first firm is entitled to trade in its contract for any additional contract that is offered to another firm later, which I think is a reasonable interpretation, then the MFC does not solve the opportunism problem. This is because once the second licensee accepts a contract with a lower royalty and a higher fixed fee that makes the first licensee just indifferent to accepting the deviation offer, it is not going to pay the first licensee to pay this higher fixed fee in exchange for the same lower cost reduction. The reason is that a reduction in marginal costs for the licensee is less valuable to it once it faces a competitor that already has lower costs.

This ties in with the point that to prevent opportunism, you might really need to commit yourself to an exclusive territory or some kind of explicit exclusivity, or charge a two-part tariff at the outset that only one firm will accept. You may not be able to solve the problem simply with multiple firms coupled with an MFC.

The second area I want to comment on is the relationship between competition policy and innovation incentives. There is inherent tension between the static competition policy approach and intellectual property that is designed to increase innovation; and I think the point that should be constantly stressed is that competition policy should respect, at least to some extent, the intellectual property constraints.

For example, why would competition authorities want to prevent a licenser from awarding exclusive territories – closed-territory exclusivity, which the European Union sometimes prevents (at least within the Community when territories coincide with state boundaries) – when, in fact, the licenser has the option of simply licensing itself as the exclusive seller in these two jurisdictions? Why the inconsistent treatment? Since that exclusivity right has been granted under intellectual property, why tinker with it under antitrust policy?

This inconsistent treatment extends beyond intellectual property, of course. In vertical relationships, restraints not allowed through contract often are allowed through integration. This is a perennial stumbling block in the thinking about vertical relations. Do you want to push firms into something that achieves the same harm (e.g., integration), but is perhaps less efficient?

The third point is that the distinction between intellectual property and other property should not be exaggerated, because antitrust law recognizes the importance of incentives to encourage investments in all property, not just in intellectual property. We must remember that incentives are, for investments of all sorts, important to antitrust, and not just as antitrust pertains to intellectual property. But, given the importance of incentives, what do we do about the antitrust essential-facility doctrine in intellectual property cases? How high a threshold do we want to set before we invoke the essential-facility doctrine and argue that a facility that is created through intellectual property really does cross the line and requires an antitrust intervention?

Still in the area of competition policy and innovation incentives, the authors take the perspective, which I find intuitively appealing, that there ought to be a division of labour between competition policy and intellectual property policy. In other words, we should use intellectual property to provide the right incentives, and then worry about competitive problems through antitrust, and we should use antitrust to refine the incentives. As I have already sensed some disagreement with that proposition from other papers in the volume, my initial unease may have been somewhat justified. I think I still believe it, but I am less sure. In particular, the following argument may justify some shared jurisdiction as opposed to strict division: The intellectual property system is pretty rigid; 17-year-long patents apply in all industries, which is unlikely to be optimal. The antitrust authorities, by nature of their responsibilities, perform case-specific investigations, which provide them with some specific information. Does it not make sense to take advantage of that specific information to make some refinements in the degree of protection of profit awarded to IPR holders?

The last point on this broad topic is that I found confusing the use of the word "asymmetry" to describe the treatment of innovation incentives in competition policy. The authors state that if an anticompetitive merger or practice reduces innovation incentives, it should be opposed. But if an anticompetitive practice increases innovation incentives, it should not be allowed as a defence. I do not find this to be asymmetric. What the authors are saying is: "We should establish the right innovation incentives through intellectual property policy, conditional on competition policy succeeding in doing its job of maintaining competition." Therefore, given this division of labour, anything that is anticompetitive should be opposed on competition grounds regardless of whether it decreases innovation incentives or increases them. Thus there is no "asymmetry" of treatment.

On a somewhat different note, I think people worry a little bit too much about the incentives to innovate and not enough about the efficiency with which innovation takes place. What we really care about is not the quantity of R&D investment, but the quality. If firms merge, and that reduces the incentives to conduct R&D (as the U.S. *Guidelines* say because the race externality is internalized) but R&D is coordinated so that one subsidiary now pursues approach A and another subsidiary pursues approach B, the actual effect could easily be greater innovation output for less R&D investment. I think Rey and Winter probably make this point, but it should be stressed a little bit more.

Turning to the third and last area, I would like to make one comment regarding the exclusive deal in the *NutraSweet* case. The authors make an analogy with contestability and they say that there could be a situation where competition within the market is efficiently changed to potential competition for the market. With potential competition for the market, the big buyers do better because they get the low prices, albeit with one supplier instead of two.

But we normally do not care about big buyers: implicit in most antitrust is that the big buyers can take care of themselves. They can shop around; they can threaten to integrate. What we care about is small buyers. In the *NutraSweet* case there were two big buyers, Coke and Pepsi, but there might have been small buyers too: small producers of soft drinks. I would worry about a situation where a big buyer cut an exclusivity deal with one producer of aspartame (such as NutraSweet). Even if these two firms are better off, if the effect was to deny business to a second aspartame entrant and deprive small buyers of actual competition (because of economies of scale in the production process), I would worry about the deal. Incidentally, I think that the economists who pushed contestability were advancing it as a cure for exploitative monopoly power against small buyers, not against big buyers, so to use the term contestability in the *NutraSweet* context, where the buyers were Coke and Pepsi, is not in the spirit of traditional "contestability."

Suzanne Scotchmer
Department of Economics, and
Graduate School of Public Policy
University of California, Berkeley

R&D Joint Ventures and Other Cooperative Arrangements

INTRODUCTION

Antitrust policy and intellectual property rights apparently seek different ends. On the one hand, the patent system gives incentives for R&D precisely by granting monopoly power, and strategic alliances should permit the effective exercise of that power. On the other hand, the mission of the antitrust authorities is to curb market power. Anderson et al. (1991) point out that in the early part of this century the prevailing wisdom was that these two bodies of law conflict, but more recently economists and lawyers have come to view patents and patent enforcement as procompetitive.

In the United States mergers, including research joint ventures (RJVs), are scrutinized under the *Sherman Act* and the *Clayton Act*, as interpreted in the *Merger Guidelines* of 1992, and in the 1995 Federal Trade Commission and Department of Justice *Antitrust Guidelines for the Licensing of Intellectual Property* (hereafter "*Guidelines*"). In Canada, mergers are scrutinized under the *Competition Act*, as interpreted under the 1991 *Merger Enforcement Guidelines*, and a 1995 discussion paper issued by the Director of Investigation and Research called "Strategic Alliances under the *Competition Act.*" The 1995 U.S. Guidelines have recognized the special status of R&D by establishing the concept of "innovation markets."

Both U.S. and Canadian antitrust doctrine are more suspicious of horizontal mergers than of vertical mergers. For horizontal mergers, the test of monopolization is typically market share, subject to certain defences and safe harbours. To apply the legal principles regarding mergers to RJVs, one needs a notion of the "market." In the case of R&D, there are at least two possible definitions: the product market where patent holders will sell their products, and the R&D arena where firms compete for patents. Hoerner (1995) raises the question of whether U.S. antitrust law applies to the latter, since there is no "commerce" in innovation. However, the U.S. Guidelines implicitly dismiss this concern by defining an "innovation market." The Canadian Guidelines do not make an explicit distinction between product markets and innovation markets, but apply the test of whether the venture "unduly lessens or prevents competition" to both.

There are two stages at which firms involved in R&D can form alliances. We will use the term "RJV" for alliances that are formed before the firms have invested in R&D and received patents, and "licensing" for alliances made after patents have issued. Other authors in this volume examine which contractual practices are legal *ex post*. We will ask why it is useful to permit cooperation at the *ex ante* stage. We shall also attempt to illuminate the potential abuses of lenient antitrust treatment in innovation markets and how antitrust law and the *Guidelines* should be and have been applied to recent proposed mergers.

A question that is implicit in this paper is whether the *Guidelines* are too prohibitive or too lax. If too prohibitive, they might prohibit alliances that would improve efficiency, for example, by avoiding the duplication of R&D expenditures. If too lax, they might facilitate collusion in product markets or retard innovation. Influential papers by Ordover and Willig (1985) and Jorde and Teece (1989; 1990) argued before the new guidelines were issued that cooperation among researchers should be treated leniently and that RJVs should have a "safe harbour," provided the cooperation does not extend directly to product markets. The *Guidelines* did not embrace this view wholeheartedly, but rather devised the notions of "innovation markets" and "technology markets," so antitrust doctrine can be applied directly to the R&D context without creating a special exemption. This view is well articulated by Gilbert and Sunshine (1995).

The first section summarizes the basic antitrust treatment of horizontal mergers, focusing on how both sets of guidelines apply to RJVs. The next section contains some stylized examples showing how the opportunities for *ex ante* contracting under the *Guidelines* can enhance or obstruct efficiency, and it discusses why *ex post* licensing would not suffice. The content of this section echoes Hay (1995). The third section discusses vertical mergers in the R&D context, and the fourth section concludes with a short discussion of the interaction between patent law and antitrust treatment. In the Appendix, we illustrate these arguments with examples taken from the economics literature. Throughout we allude to the treatment of these issues in the economics literature.

RESEARCH JOINT VENTURES AS
HORIZONTAL MERGERS IN INNOVATION MARKETS

ASIDE FROM *PER SE* VIOLATIONS OF ANTITRUST LAW that do not typically concern RJVs, a showing that a merger or business practice is anticompetitive typically involves showing market power in a defined market. A large part of antitrust law is devoted to defining markets and market power. Particularly relevant to innovation markets is the fact that potential competitors – firms that could enter the market with small fixed costs in a short period of time – are counted for antitrust purposes as part of the market (see Rapp, 1995, p. 39).

The most stylized notion of an innovation market – certainly the one that has received the most attention from economists – is probably a patent race. Assuming that the effect of an RJV is to replace a patent race, we must understand what would happen in a patent race. Our discussion is in two parts: innovation markets for product patents and innovation markets for patents on production technologies, which we stylize as cost-reducing innovations. The reason for separating these cases is that there is an interaction between RJVs and licensing in the case of cost-reducing innovations that is not an issue with product patents.

INNOVATION MARKETS FOR PRODUCT PATENTS

THE ANTITRUST AUTHORITIES SHOULD (and could under the *Guidelines*) treat the following two stylized cases differently.

- Patents in the product market are broad, so that all firms in the patent race (potential RJV members) pursue a single patent, which covers the whole product market.
- Patents in the product market are relatively narrow, so that all firms in the patent race (potential RJV members) would receive different patents, and the patents would be mutually non-infringing, but serve the same market.

For example, the firms could be pursuing a single vaccine or they could be pursuing slightly different vaccines that are all patentable and non-infringing.

The first situation is what is usually meant by a "patent race," and it has been well studied (see Reinganum, 1989, for a survey). The literature makes three somewhat conflicting observations about the efficiency of races compared with investment by a single firm: a) they inefficiently cause firms to duplicate each other's investments, b) they cause firms to diversify their research strategies, and c) they efficiently cause firms to accelerate innovation. If the duplication argument is right, then a joint venture would unambiguously increase social welfare, since it would reduce wasteful duplication. If the second observation is right, then the RJV may reduce the diversity of approaches and also the probability of success, which may be inefficient. If the third observation is right, then a joint venture will decrease social welfare (but increase joint profit) by reducing R&D spending and delaying the invention.

All three arguments conclude that R&D spending will be reduced by cooperation among firms that would otherwise race. However, in the first case the reduction is efficient, whereas in the second and third cases it might not be. The *Guidelines* and the economics literature (see Gilbert and Sunshine, 1995) stress the second and third arguments, with the implication that reducing R&D spending is inefficient.

Whether or not reductions in spending engineered by an RJV are efficient, the firms will argue to the antitrust authorities that eliminating the patent race increases profits and eliminates cost duplication and should thus be permitted. In order to evaluate this argument, the antitrust authorities must decide whether the R&D technology is more like example 1 (high fixed costs) or example 4 (high variable costs) in the Appendix. And of course this must be done before R&D has occurred, so there is no direct evidence about the cost structure of doing R&D. Examples 1 and 4 illustrate the first and third effects of RJVs – that they can efficiently eliminate duplication and that they can inefficiently delay innovation. For a discussion of the second effect (a reduction in diversity of research strategies), We refer the reader to Wright (1983), who compares "patents, contracts and prizes" as methods to encourage or discourage entry of firms with different research strategies. Later papers with a similar approach include Dasgupta and Maskin (1987), Bhattacharya and Mookherjee (1986), and Allen (1991). While these papers recognize that diversity in approach is efficient, they mostly do not address the question of how such diversity is affected by cooperation.

A final inefficiency of patent races (Minehart and Scotchmer, 1995), is that information might be suppressed (leading to inefficient investment decisions) if firms must share their information only by observing each other's investment decisions (see examples 3 and 4). For example, in a patent race, each firm might invest simply because it sees other firms investing and infer (perhaps erroneously) that, according to the information possessed by other firms, the investment is likely to pay off. Symmetrically, a firm might abstain from investing, even though its own information is propitious, simply because other firms are not investing and the firm therefore infers (perhaps erroneously) that the other firms' information is less propitious. Incorrect information can be reinforced in equilibrium in such a way that the investment outcome is the wrong one. RJVs can remedy this problem by giving firms incentive to share their information.

A common kind of RJV is an agreement that falls short of complete merger, in which the firms assign their research facilities to a jointly owned subsidiary, and the subsidiary owns any resulting patents. The patents are then licensed back to the parent firms. With no restrictions on royalties, such an arrangement has the same outcome in the product market as the simple merger discussed above; the subsidiary should license back at a royalty that supports the monopoly price. On the other hand, if royalties are prohibited, the resulting competition could be severe enough so that firms would prefer a patent race to the RJV, and the benefits of the RJV would not be realized. Even so, in some cases the efficiencies of the RJV might outweigh the ex post competitive effects. Economic studies that focus on this circumstance include d'Aspremont and Jacquemin (1989), Kamien et al. (1992), and Suzumura (1992). However, these analyses rely heavily on particular types of interaction in the product market, where profit is assumed to be protected by oligopoly pricing even without royalties.

RJVs have efficiency effects that can either efficiently reduce duplication or inefficiently delay innovation. Both types of efficiency effects are attenuated if there are potential entrants to the innovation market. The fact that there is a patent race means that R&D in the innovation market is relatively profitable. For example, if the patent is profitable enough so that two firms would race for it, each with a 50 percent probability of winning, then it is reasonable to think that a third firm will enter the race if the first two merge their interests into a single firm. The R&D costs saved by a merger of the first two firms will be re-introduced by entry of the third. Thus, to the extent that the purpose of RJVs is to reduce duplicated spending, potential competition obstructs this purpose. But to the extent that RJVs inefficiently retard innovation, potential competition can limit the damage. The possibility of entry into the innovation market means that the antitrust authorities need not be so vigilant, since any impact of cooperation, positive or negative, will be muted.

We now turn to the second type of product innovation, one where the patents in the product market are narrow so that, absent a joint venture, the researchers would likely pursue mutually non-infringing technologies. But then the hazard of an RJV is entirely different; namely, it might facilitate collusion *ex ante* that would be illegal *ex post*. The RJV might prefer to have only one patented product in the market, or at least to price the competing products as a joint monopolist, both of which options would clearly lessen competition. Such an RJV would presumably not be allowed.

Gilbert and Sunshine (1995) and Hoerner (1995) describe several merger actions by the Federal Trade Commission (FTC) and the Department of Justice (DOJ) where the firms would otherwise have pursued competing, mutually non-infringing technologies. For example, when Roche Holding Ltd. wanted to acquire Genentech[1] the acquisition was denied, partly on grounds that the two companies were independently developing therapies for AIDS/HIV. In U.S. vs. GM and ZF,[2] the DOJ prohibited the acquisition because even though the two firms (selling automatic transmissions) served geographically different product markets, the DOJ was worried that the merger would reduce innovation. Boston Scientific Corp.'s proposed acquisition of Cardiovascular Imaging Systems and SCIMED[3] was challenged by the FTC on grounds that the acquisition would lessen competition in the development of intravascular ultrasound catheters and related products. Although SCIMED was not already in any of the related markets, the FTC argued that it was a likely entrant in the near future. The consent decree involved a licence to a fourth company.

In these cases and others described by Hoerner (1995), the antitrust authorities speculated about what would happen if the RJV did not form. It is difficult to have confidence in speculations (Harris and Jorde, 1984, argue strongly that the antitrust authorities should ground their findings in observations and not speculations), and one could imagine how the speculative negotiations would end up favouring the firms.

As in the first case, potential competition mitigates the hazard because with entry the RJV cannot avoid a patent race. If the RJV pursued only one patentable technology in a market where patent law permits several, then potential competitors would step in to replace the competitors who have joined the RJV.

In summary, there are three speculative conclusions that could sensibly satisfy the antitrust authorities that mergers in innovation markets do not lessen competition:

1. Entry into the innovation market is sufficiently easy that the RJV could not successfully reduce the number of patents issued in a given market.
2. Patent protection in the product market is sufficiently broad that competing patents will not issue in any case.
3. The potential RJV members are pursuing similar enough research methods toward a single technology so that reducing R&D does not reduce the probability of success or delay the invention.

However, if the antitrust authorities are in the realm of speculation, they should notice that if conclusion 1 holds, then the firms will not find much benefit in forming an RJV. And conclusion 2 should be tempered by the realization that the intensity of R&D might be inefficiently reduced.

In the Appendix, we illustrate these arguments using examples from the economics literature. In each example, we comment on whether an RJV would be efficient or inefficient and how the efficiency effect could (or not) be predicted in advance. The first four examples show efficiency effects of RJVs in avoiding duplication, delegating effort to the least-cost firms, and facilitating the transfer of information. The fifth example is a standard model in economic theory that leads to the conclusion that RJVs can delay innovation and are therefore inefficient. One purpose of laying out the examples is to illustrate that the duplication argument is most defensible when firms must bear large fixed costs to enter the innovation market, whereas the retarding innovation argument is relevant when the variable costs are most important, since they are most affected by racing. It seems to us that the variable-cost argument, illustrated in example 5, is overemphasized in the economics literature.

Innovation Markets for Cost-Cutting Innovations

There is another type of innovation market – for cost-reducing innovations – where the benefits of *ex ante* contracting in avoiding duplicated costs may not be realized because it is difficult to fine-tune licensing restrictions. Suppose that competitors in a product market can make an R&D investment that cuts the unit cost of production. Efficiency would require that one firm bear the R&D

cost and license the cost reduction to other firms, who then compete. This outcome is difficult to achieve, whether or not RJVs are permitted.

Consider first what happens with *ex post* licensing and no RJV. Suppose, as is efficient, that only one firm invests, while the others know they can license. If the innovator licenses without royalties, then it reduces its own profit. Clearly a better scheme is to license with a royalty equal to the cost reduction. The non-innovating firms will accept such a licence *ex post*, but are no better off than they are without an innovation. The innovator has no incentive to share the profit from the cost reduction *ex post*, even though it has an incentive to diffuse it. Instead, it will prefer to license in such a way (high royalties) that the product price is high and it collects all the profit surplus from the licencees. Consequently, it is more profitable to be the licenser (innovator) than the licensee, and this discrepancy in profit will lead to a patent race, even though R&D costs are duplicated.

An RJV is not a very effective remedy for this problem, mainly because there are no natural restrictions on licensing to govern how the RJV should license to its members. First, if the RJV cannot license to its members with royalties, then *ex post* competition among the members may erode profit so much that they would not form the RJV. Second, if royalties are unrestricted, the RJV can support the monopoly price, which could be even higher than the market price before the cost reduction. Such an outcome is not consistent with the objectives of merger policy, but to proscribe it, the antitrust authorities must either prohibit royalties entirely (the case already discussed) or try to regulate them. Regulating royalties is very different from proscribing certain practices, and in any case, it is not clear what the right regulation would be. One possibility is that the royalty could equal the reduction in the unit costs of production, which would maintain the previous market price for the duration of the patent. But aside from practical enforcement difficulties, such a royalty might not cover the cost of R&D, even when the cost-reducing technology is socially efficient. (These ideas are developed in example 5 in the Appendix)

Cost-cutting innovations are discussed by Gallini (1984), who points to licensing as an *ex post* incentive to avoid duplication; Gallini and Winter (1985), who discuss the incentives to undertake such innovations (without focusing on antitrust remedies); and d'Aspremont and Jacquemin (1988), Kamien et al. (1992), and Suzumura et al. (1992), who discuss firms' incentives to share proprietary knowledge (without focusing on licensing).

It seems that the *Guidelines* do not give clear guidance as to what royalty a cost-reducing RJV can charge. And it is not clear what rule should be suggested. A royalty equal to the cost reduction might appear appropriate since it would achieve the purpose of encouraging an RJV instead of a patent race, and would also accord with the principle that RJVs should not facilitate collusion *ex ante* that would be prohibited *ex post*.

But this is not the best rule. Suppose the reduction in production costs for the life of the patent is less than the R&D cost. The cost-reducing innovation might still be efficient, since the value of the innovation lasts even beyond its patent life. However, an RJV (or firm) would not invest unless the members could charge a higher *ex post* price than the previous price. Such a price could only be achieved with a royalty larger than the cost reduction.

RESEARCH JOINT VENTURES AS
VERTICAL MERGERS: SEQUENTIAL INNOVATION

THE ANTITRUST TREATMENT OF VERTICAL RELATIONSHIPS is, in general, more lenient than that of horizontal relationships. Mergers between vertically related firms, where one firm produces an input to another firm's product, typically do not lessen competition in product markets. On the positive side, they may overcome some inefficiencies, such as those due to bargaining and double markups.

A similar intuition applies in the R&D context. There are two natural interpretations of "vertical relationship." The first is that one innovation is a foundation for the next, as when the first is "basic research" and the next is an "application." The second is that the second innovation is an improved version of the first. We treat these two problems separately, as they raise different issues.

Economists have studied the area of basic and applied research extensively, with the objective of determining how patents should be structured to ensure that the basic innovators receive enough profit to cover their costs, given that most of the profit is due to later applications owned by other firms. From an antitrust perspective, this is an easy case. There are important advantages to permitting *ex ante* merger, and there is little potential for abuse (as illustrated in example 6).

The vehicle by which profit is transferred from applications of basic research to the owner of the basic patent is licensing. But a potential problem of licensing *ex post* is that fees are negotiated after all costs have been sunk. Since the fees will therefore not reflect the two patent holders' respective R&D costs, there is no reason to think that each patent holder's costs will be covered by the licence agreement that is negotiated *ex post*. In particular, if the R&D cost of the application is relatively high, then the second innovator might be stymied from investing if it thinks that the licence fee negotiated *ex post* will not leave enough revenue to cover the sunk R&D costs.

Ex ante agreements can remedy this problem. As long as the commercial value of the application is greater than its incremental R&D cost, the two firms could reach some agreement before sinking the incremental R&D costs such that both firms profit. *Ex ante* and *ex post* licensing are not redundant contracting tools, since the *ex ante* agreement can promote research that would otherwise not take place.

The second interpretation, in which the second product is an improved version or some other variant of the first, is more difficult, at least when the first patent is narrow so that the second product does not infringe. The products of the two firms would compete in the market *ex post*. Such competition would be lessened or eliminated if the firms merged *ex ante*. Prohibiting the merger would therefore be consistent with the *Guidelines* and the principle, articulated in the conclusion, that *ex ante* mergers should not facilitate practices that would be prohibited *ex post*. However, the argument against merger loses its force if, absent the merger, the second firm would not innovate. In that case, the competition that *would* follow the second innovation becomes irrelevant, since no second innovation would follow. Since the firms might make the latter argument whether or not it is true, the antitrust authorities are again in the position of having to assess what would happen absent the RJV (i.e., to speculate).

If the second product infringes, the antitrust treatment is more straightforward. Whether or not there is an *ex ante* RJV, the two firms' pricing policies will be linked through a licensing agreement, presumably with royalties. Merging their interests *ex ante* in an RJV will not change the product prices, unless there were *ex post* restrictions on the licensing agreement that were not imposed *ex ante*. Letting the firms merge *ex ante* has the same efficiency advantage as in the case of basic and applied research, namely, without the RJV, the second inventor might fear an *ex post* "hold-up" for high licensing fees, and would therefore not invest.

A recent case that illustrates these ideas is Glaxo,[4] in which Glaxo proposed to acquire Wellcome. Glaxo was the sole seller of a migraine remedy that was administered by injection. The product would be improved if it could be administered differently, and Wellcome was working on a non-injectable version (as was Glaxo). The consent decree required that the Wellcome R&D assets be sold, unless it could be demonstrated that the firms were not potential competitors.

The antitrust treatment assumed that without the merger, Wellcome might achieve the non-injectable product. If that product did not infringe Glaxo's patent on the injectable version, then the apparent intent of patent law would be that they should compete in the market. An *ex post* licence to merge the two firms would not be permitted, and this proscription should not be overcome by an *ex ante* merger. The rationale for the antitrust treatment is obvious.

However the prospect of competition between the first and second products might be severe enough that, absent the joint venture, Wellcome would not invest in the improved product. In that case the *ex ante* alliance would not lessen competition, since the product would either not be invented or it would be invented by Glaxo. While this line of reasoning is sensible, one could imagine the antitrust authorities would be sceptical, since the firms would make such an argument whether or not it was true. As in the cases above, the effectiveness of antitrust policy is limited by the inevitability of speculative counterfactual arguments.

Conclusion

We HAVE ARGUED THAT IN INNOVATION MARKETS, horizontal and vertical mergers (RJVs) serve purposes that cannot be served by *ex post* licensing. Licensing serves the purpose of diffusing new technologies, as can RJVs. But RJVs serve the additional purpose of reducing inefficiencies in R&D investment, which is why scholars such as Ordover and Willig (1985) and Jorde and Teece (1990) have argued that they should be permitted. But RJVs can also be used to facilitate practices that would be prohibited *ex post*, such as consolidating ownership of patents that serve a single market. And they can inefficiently reduce R&D spending.

A difficulty of applying antitrust guidelines to RJVs is that the absence of anticompetitive effects can only be justified with hypothetical counterfactuals, usually involving some notion that R&D investment, absent the joint venture, would be inefficient or would not occur at all, or that entry into the innovation market is frictionless. Hypotheticals such as entry are relevant to product markets as well as innovation markets, but merger analysis in product markets mostly relies on existing market shares as a guide. There is no clear analogy for innovation markets.

A sensible-sounding and easy-to-articulate principle for the antitrust treatment of *ex ante* alliances is that they should be permitted except when they a) facilitate practices *ex ante* that would be prohibited *ex post* by restrictions on licensing or b) inefficiently reduce R&D spending. The first proscription is sensible, because it seems to balance the efficiency concerns that make RJVs desirable with a concern for the fact that they can be abused. The second proscription is delicate, because an RJV can reduce R&D spending in ways that can be efficient or inefficient.

Applying the principle to the example where the potential members of the RJV would otherwise pursue mutually non-infringing patents in the same market, we notice that the RJV monopolizes the market just as it would be monopolized if all the patents were licensed to a single firm *ex post*. Since the latter would be prohibited the former should also be prohibited, and that is efficient.

However, consider the case of potential product improvements where there would be no investment without an RJV. Suppose the firms would invest if they could form an RJV that would license *ex post* at a royalty that avoids *ex post* competition. Such an RJV would not lessen competition, but would it violate the principle? One could argue that *ex post* there would be no competition (absent the RJV) since there would be no innovation, hence licensing restrictions are irrelevant. However, the firms could make such an argument whether or not the improved product would actually be stymied without a joint venture. The antitrust authorities are therefore in the difficult position of distinguishing when it is true.

The arguments in this paper seem to agree with the principle articulated by Gallini and Trebilcock (1995), that antitrust treatment should not concern itself with incentives to innovate (which is the proper domain of intellectual property law), but should ensure that monopoly power is not extended beyond the intended boundaries of patents. For example, *ex ante* mergers should be allowed if *ex post* infringement and licensing would create monopoly power in any case.

However, Gallini and Trebilcock's principle seems ambiguous in the case where an innovation, such as a product improvement, would not be made absent the joint venture. An argument that might be consistent with the Gallini/Trebilcock principle is that if Congress had intended such an improvement to be made, then either it would be infringing, so that neither *ex post* licensing nor *ex ante* merger would violate antitrust laws, or patents would last longer, so that the improved product would be profitable even with *ex post* competition. Since Congress made no such provisions, one should logically conclude that it did not intend such improvements to occur, hence the *ex ante* merger should be prohibited.

But one could also interpret Gallini and Trebilcock's principle as silent in this case. Since there is no lessening of competition due to the merger, antitrust law simply does not apply. (See Trebilcock's comment on this paper for his interpretation of these principles.)

The second reason to proscribe RJVs, namely, if they inefficiently reduce R&D investment, arises when there is a discrepancy between what is efficient for the firms and what is efficient for society. As long as the firms' and society's interests coincide (as when the RJV reduces duplication of research efforts), then RJVs are socially beneficial. They should be allowed, provided they do not facilitate collusion in the product market. But the firms' interests and society's interests may diverge in the optimum amount of R&D spending; for example, when the RJV would reduce the variance in research approaches or delay innovation. In that case, RJVs would be inefficient.

The difficulty in applying antitrust law to RJVs is that the antitrust authorities must concern themselves with two competing sets of arguments: collusion in the product market that goes beyond the intent of patent law, and also the rate of spending in the innovation market. Mergers of R&D firms have implications for both.

Even if one agrees with the principle that antitrust treatment should not concern itself with incentives to innovate except by respecting patent rights, the same simple rule cannot be applied in reverse. That is, a sensible patent policy must take into account the antitrust treatment of R&D firms. Consider, for example, the rule governing whether RJVs can form to avoid duplication in patent races. If such RJVs are disallowed, then duplication of R&D costs in patent races can only be reduced by reducing the value of the patent, for example, by shortening it or making it narrower. A problem with the patent solution, which does not afflict the RJV solution, is that the same patent life and breadth apply to all innovations. By reducing the value of patents, innovation in other markets might be eliminated entirely. This problem can be avoided with the RJV solution, since RJVs are industry specific.

APPENDIX

EXAMPLE 1

RJVs avoid cost duplication.

Suppose that a patent has value v and costs c. Then if $1/2\, v > c$, each of two competitive firms would invest, assuming that each one receives the patent with probability $1/2$. This is inefficient. If they formed a joint venture instead, they would agree to bear the cost c only once, and share the profit $v - c$ such that each firm receives at least $1/2\, v - c$. Such a joint venture unambiguously improves social welfare, since the same monopoly distortions due to the patent arise in any case, and the R&D cost is reduced. The RJV achieves the much-touted efficiency effects without increasing monopoly power, since only one firm will own the patent *ex post* in any case.

The only reason this RJV might be in jeopardy under the *Guidelines* is that it reduces R&D spending. Of course in this instance (as opposed to Example 5 below), the reduction is efficient.

Patent races also fail to coordinate research efficiently when firms have different research costs. Suppose the expected R&D costs of firms A and B are $c_a < c_b$. Efficiency requires that only firm A invest. The efficient patent life would just cover the costs c_a. But without some coordinating mechanism, the private information on costs cannot be made public. Neither firm knows which has lower costs, and even if they did, the patent might be valuable enough to inspire them both to invest.

A more complicated version of this problem is discussed by Gandal and Scotchmer (1993), who show in a certain context that the first-best delegation of research effort could be implemented with budget balance, incentive constraints, and individual rationality if either research costs or effort levels were unobservable, but not if both were unobservable. The following example illustrates these points in a much simpler case.

EXAMPLE 2

RJVs can remedy the problem that patent races do not necessarily delegate effort to the low-cost firms.

Suppose that the value of a patent is 1 and each firm's cost of achieving it is distributed uniformly on [0,1]. Each of the two firms, ($i = 1, 2$), observes its own cost, c_i, but not the other firm's cost. If both firms invest in R&D then each receives the patent with probability $1/2$, so that if both invest, firm 1's expected profit is $1/2 - c_1$. However, with probability $1/2$, $c_2 > 1/2$, and firm 1 is the only firm that invests. Its profit is $1 - c_1$. We shall assume that if both firms' costs are higher than $1/2$, then only one firm invests in equilibrium, and each firm has probability $1/2$ of being the first to declare whether it will invest. Thus the expected profit of firm 1 in a patent race as a function of its own cost c_1 is $\Pi(c_1) = 3/4 - c_1$ if $c_1 < 1/2$, and $\Pi(c_1) = 1/2 (1 - c_1) + 1/2 (1 - c_1)^2$ if $1/2 < c_1 < 3/2 - \sqrt{3}/2$, and 0 otherwise. Firm 2's profit function is symmetric. This equilibrium is inefficient for two reasons: a) both firms might invest, and b) even if only one firm invests (in particular when both have a cost higher than $1/2$), the high-cost firm might invest instead of the low-cost firm.

A joint venture can mitigate these inefficiencies. To take a simple contracting mechanism that achieves efficiency, suppose the firms agree to state their respective costs, delegate research effort to the firm that states the lowest cost, and share both the proceeds and the cost of the innovation equally. Misrepresenting costs can only hurt a firm, so each firm will state its costs honestly. The expected profit of each firm is $1/2 - 1/4 c_i (2 - c_i)$, since for firm i the expected cost is half of $c_i(1 - c_i) + \int_0^{c_i} c\, dc$ and the distribution of c is uniform. However, we notice that the expected profit is not less than in a patent race for all c_i (e.g., if $c_i = 0$). A problem faced by the RJV is that it must find a contracting mechanism that both induces firms to report their costs accurately (otherwise the RJV cannot delegate to the least-cost firm) and ensures that the profit is distributed such that neither firm prefers the patent race. This is not always possible. Although the RJV might be able to achieve full efficiency, low-cost firms can often do better than the patent race.

EXAMPLE 3

If firms disagree about the profitability of an investment, their differing information may be shared incompletely in a patent race and investment may, therefore, be inefficient. An RJV may be a remedy.

A much more subtle problem with R&D is that firms may have different expectations about its profitability, and there may be no objective basis for predicting success. "Optimists" may invest, although they would be dissuaded if they knew that according to the information of other firms they should be "pessimists." RJVs can address this problem. The following example is from Minehart and Scotchmer (1995).

Suppose there are two firms, and with probability $1/2$ each firm observes the true state of the world, $\omega \in \{B, G\}$, where the state G indicates that investment in a project would be profitable. With probability $1/2$ each firm observes an uninformative signal. Thus each firm has a signal $\sigma^i \in \{B, G, U\}$, $i = 1, 2$, where U means "uninformed." Each firm has probability $1/2$ of observing the true state or observing the signal U and remaining uninformed.

Suppose that the expected value of investing in a project is only positive if the posterior probability that $\omega = G$ is at least $\bar{p} = 3/7$. Will firms take efficient investment decisions when they observe only their own signals and the other firm's action? One can check that the following is an equilibrium: Firm 1(symmetrically firm 2) invests unless $\sigma^1 = B$ or unless $\sigma^1 = U$ and firm 2 does not invest. If $\sigma^1 = B$, then firm 1 knows that $\omega = B$, so investment is unprofitable. If firm 2 does not invest, then firm 1 knows that firm 2's signal is not G. If firm 1's signal is U, firm 1's posterior belief that $\omega = G$ is then $1/3$, which is less than $\bar{p}$.

The equilibrium can be inefficient. If both firms have signal U, an observer who could observe both signals would hold the posterior belief that $\omega = G$ with probability $1/2$, which would elicit investment. However, while it is an equilibrium for both firms to invest, it is also an equilibrium for neither firm to invest. If neither invests, each firm's posterior belief in $\omega = G$ is $1/3$, which makes investment seem unprofitable. The latter is an inefficient outcome that could be remedied if the two firms could share their information explicitly in a joint venture rather than implicitly by observing each other's investment behaviours.

EXAMPLE 4

Rivalry can undermine the decentralized sharing of information even further.

Example 3 did not have rivalry effects in the sense that either firm was willing to invest if its posterior belief in $\omega = G$ was at least $3/7$, irrespective of whether the other firm invests. Suppose, however, that $\bar{p}$ (the posterior probability that $\omega = G$) must be at least $4/5$ if the other firm invests. Such an assumption might reflect the fact that each firm receives the patent with probability $1/2$, and for two firms to invest, the expected value of the patent must be even larger.

Then the equilibrium strategies identified in Example 3 are still an equilibrium, but when the signals are (U,U), there is only one equilibrium action, namely, where neither firm invests. The equilibrium where both firms invest vanishes.

Of course it is not efficient that both firms invest; the best equilibrium would be an asymmetric equilibrium in which one firm invests. Without rivalry effects this cannot happen (Minehart and Scotchmer, 1995), but it is possible when there are rivalry effects. However, in this example it cannot happen, and underinvestment is an inevitable consequence of decentralization. Suppose to the contrary that firm 1's strategy is to invest if and only if $\sigma^1 = G$, and firm 2's strategy is to invest if and only if $\sigma^2 \in \{G, U\}$. Then at the signals (U,U), firm 1 will not invest, and firm 2 has posterior probability $1/3$ that $\omega = G$, which is too small to elicit investment.

EXAMPLE 5

RJVs can inefficiently reduce rates of R&D spending. Patent lives can be shortened if RJVs are prohibited.

Suppose there are two firms in a patent race, they invest at rates x_1, x_2 respectively, and their respective profit functions are $g^i(x_1, x_2, v) - c^i(x_1, x_2)$. The function g^i represents the firm's expected profit, which increases with its own rate of investment and with the patent value v, and decreases with the other firm's rate of investment, which lowers the probability that firm i receives the patent. The expected cost c^i decreases with the other firm's rate of investment because on average the patent race terminates sooner. A Nash equilibrium, say x_1^*, x_2^*, satisfies $\partial/\partial x_i\, g^i(x_1^*, x_2^*, v) - c^i(x_1^*, x_2^*) = 0$ for each i. If the firms form a joint venture in which they cooperate in choosing rates of investment, the rates of investment must maximize $\Pi^J(x_1, x_2, v) \equiv g^1(x_1, x_2, v) + g^2(x_1, x_2, v) - c^1(x_1, x_2) - c^2(x_1, x_2)$. Evaluated at the Nash equilibrium, we see that $\partial/\partial x_1\, \Pi(x_1^*, x_2^*, v) < 0$ if the externality imposed by firm 1 on firm 2 is negative $(\partial/\partial x_1\, g^2(x_1^*, x_2^*, v) - c^2(x_1^*, x_2^*) < 0)$, and $\partial/\partial x_1\, \Pi(x_1^*, x_2^*, v) < 0$ if the externality imposed by firm 1 on firm 2 is positive, as discussed by Kamien et al. (1992). One would expect the externality to be negative if the patent race involves pure rivalry: a higher rate of investment by the competitor reduces the probability of winning the patent. One would expect the externality to be positive if, for example, the new technology is a cost reduction that can be partly appropriated by the competitor *ex post*, even if the patentholder seeks to prevent it.

Assuming that the profit functions are strictly concave, it follows that a joint venture will reduce the rate of investment if the externality is negative and increase it if the externality is positive. Whether reducing investment is a good thing depends on whether, absent the joint venture, the rate of investment would be higher or lower than the optimum rate. In the case of pure rivalry (negative externalities), the rate of investment can be too high, and in the case of positive externalities, it can be too low. It seems clear that in the case of positive externalities joint ventures should be permitted (Kamien et al., 1992).

However, in the case of pure rivalry, the conclusion is less clear. Suppose that the patent life can be adjusted according to whether joint ventures will form or a patent race will occur. A longer patent life will be required to elicit specified rates of investment if the firms form a joint venture than if they race. A longer patent life is socially costly because it prolongs monopoly distortions. Thus the better policy would be to curtail the patent life and prohibit joint ventures from restraining competition in R&D.

In this example, the RJV can either increase or decrease the rate of investment, but will decrease it in the usual case of a patent race. The decrease will delay innovation, an outcome the patent authorities might want to avoid.

EXAMPLE 6

RJVs can achieve cost-cutting innovations.

Suppose two firms, $i = 1, 2$, are competitors in an oligopoly. An investment in R&D will reduce the marginal cost of production. Suppose the firms' per-period profits are given by functions π^1 and π^2 of their marginal costs mc_1, mc_2. Special cases of these profit functions would be those that arise in Bertrand competition or in Cournot competition. Each profit function should be non-decreasing in the other firm's marginal cost and decreasing in its own marginal cost. A cost-cutting innovation will benefit the innovating firm, hurt its competitor, and benefit consumers through a price reduction.

We now compare three scenarios: 1) the cost-cutting innovation is licensed *ex post* so that the competitor also uses the new technology but pays royalties to the innovator; 2) the two firms form a joint venture before investing in the cost reduction so that they become one firm and collude *ex post* in the product market; and 3) the two firms form a joint venture to invest jointly in the cost reduction and then compete in the product market with or without royalties.

1. **Ex post licensing with royalties** – The outcome of licensing *ex post* depends on whether the licenser can make a lump sum payment to the licensee in return for very high royalties. If so, then the two firms will achieve the monopoly product price, and the licenser will share the high profit through the lump sum price. The licenser will give just enough profit to the licensee to induce the licensee to license rather than compete using the old technology. If no such lump sum payments are permitted, then (under mild conditions) the best licensing offer is a royalty equal to the cost reduction. In both cases the licensee will be kept to exactly the same profit as without the new technology, and all the surplus profit will accrue to the innovator. Consequently, it is better to be the innovator/licenser than the licensee, and the profit-sharing available with *ex post* licensing will not avoid a patent race. This problem can be remedied with an RJV.

2. **Collusive research joint venture** – Now suppose that the firms form an RJV and jointly own the cost-reducing innovation. Their best use of the patent is to charge themselves (the RJV members) a high enough royalty to support the monopoly price and then redistribute the profits. Even though the monopoly price might be lower than would be the case without the cost-reducing innovation (depending on the amount of cost reduction), this is an outcome that would presumably make the antitrust authorities shudder. Assuming that the authorities would find monopoly pricing anticompetitive, what restriction should they impose on royalties? The natural option is to restrict

the royalty to the cost reduction. This is a good rule, provided the additional profit they earn from the cost-reducing innovation is greater than the R&D cost. Otherwise the RJV will not form, even if there is some royalty at which the cost-reducing innovation would increase the profit of all firms and still reduce the product price. Then the potential social and private gains from innovation are lost.

3. **Non-collusive research joint venture** – If the RJV is permitted to form but prevented from charging royalties to its members, the benefits of the RJV are seriously reduced. The firms may prefer to race for a proprietary innovation – which can then be licensed instead of reducing the costs of R&D through a joint venture – than having to compete in the product market without royalties. It is not obvious which of these two outcomes is socially more efficient.

EXAMPLE 7

Vertical relationships in R&D

Suppose the private consumer value of a basic invention (e.g., a bio-engineering technique) is zero and its cost is c_1. Suppose the social value of an application (drug) will be s per period if it is sold competitively (at the efficient marginal-cost price) and it can be achieved at cost c_2. Its maximum incremental social value is therefore $s/r - c_2$. We shall assume that if the product is sold by a monopolist patentholder, its market profit is $\pi(s) < s$ per unit time.

If the basic invention costs c_1, the social value of the first product is $-c_1 + \max\{0, s/r - D(s, T) - c_2)\}$, where $D(\bullet)$ is the summed and discounted deadweight loss when the product is sold by a monopolist for a patent life T. The second-generation product is facilitated by the first product, and its expected surplus, $\max\{0, s/r - D(s, T) - c_2)\}$, must therefore be counted as part of the value of the first product. Otherwise the first product will be deemed to have no value. To have sufficient incentive to invest, the first innovator must collect some of the profit from second-generation products.

A social planner who could cover the costs with lump-sum taxation would have the first firm invest if $-c_1 + \max\{0, (s/r - c_2)\} > 0$, and then let the product be supplied competitively. However, if the revenue is collected through monopoly protection, as is inevitable with patent protection, the costs of the joint innovations can only be covered if T is at least large enough so that $[\Pi(s, T) - (c_1 + c_2)] \geq 0$, where $\Pi(s, T) = \int_0^T \pi(s) e^{-rt}dt$.

Suppose first that *ex ante* contracts are prohibited entirely. After the second product has been invented, the two patentholders will hold blocking patents on it and will have to reach an *ex post* licensing agreement in order to bring it to market. On the basis of symmetry, it is reasonable to assume they will share the bargaining surplus equally. Since the costs c_1 and c_2 are sunk, the bargaining surplus is $\Pi(s, T)$, so if the innovation is made, innovator i receives $1/2\Pi(s, T) - c_i$, $i = 1, 2$. Due to the *ex post* "hold-up" problem there may not be investment in the application, even if it adds a positive amount $\Pi(s, T) - c_2 > 0$ to joint profit. This is not only inefficient, it is also preventable with *ex ante* contracting.

With an *ex ante* agreement (before sinking c_2), the second investment will be made whenever it adds to joint profit, namely when $(\Pi(s, T) - c_2 \geq 0$, which is a weaker criterion than the one that applies when deals can only be struck ex post, namely $1/2\Pi(s, T) - c_2 \geq 0$. Thus RJVs can overcome a problem that may arise when only *ex post* licensing is available, namely, the *ex post* holdup problem, which could undermine the second firm's incentive to invest. (This example is taken from Green and Scotchmer, 1995.)

NOTES

1 Roche Holding Ltd., 113 FTC 1086 (1990).
2 *United States v. General Motors Corp. and ZF Friedrishshafen*, A.G., Civ. No. 93-530, filed 1993, DOG Case 4027.
3 Complaint of the FTC, Docket C-3573, File 951-0002, ordered entered 1995, 60 Fed. Reg. 32,323.
4 FTC File 951-0002, 60 Fed. Reg. 1,948 (March 9,1995).

ACKNOWLEDGMENTS

WE THANK NANCY GALLINI AND RICHARD GILBERT for useful remarks, and Preston Moore for supplying useful material. None of them is responsible for any misguided opinions or misrepresentations of the law that might appear in this paper.

BIBLIOGRAPHY

Addy, George N. "Competition Policy and Intellectual Property Rights: Complementary Framework Policies for a Dynamic Market Economy." Address to the 36th World Congress of the AIPPI, Montreal, 1995a.
——. "Strategic Alliances under the Competition Act." Bureau of Competition Policy, Industry Canada, 1995b.
Allen, Beth. "Choosing R & D Projects, An Informational Approach." *American Economic Review Papers and Proceedings*, 81, 2 (1991): 257-61.
American Bar Association Antitrust Section. "The 1992 Horizontal Merger Guidelines: Commentary and Text." 1992.

Anderson, Robert D., S., Dev Khosla and Mark F. Ronayne. "The Competition Policy Treatment of Intellectual Property Rights in Canada: Retrospect and Prospect," in *Canadian Competition Law and Policy at the Centenary*. Edited by R. S. Khemani and W. T. Stanbury. Halifax: Institute for Research on Public Policy, 1991, pp. 497-538.

Besen, Stanley M., Sheila N. Kirby and Steven C. Salop. "An Economic Analysis of Copyright Collectives." *Virginia Law Review*, 78, (1991): 383-411.

Bhattacharya, Sudipto and Dilip Mookherjee. "Portfolio Choice in Research and Development." *Rand Journal of Economics*, 17 (1986): 594-605.

Bhattacharya, Sudipto, Jacob Glazer and David E. M. Sappington. "Licensing and the Sharing of Knowledge in Research Joint Ventures." *Journal of Economic Theory*, 56, (1992): 43-69.

Choi, Jay P. "Dynamic R& D Competition under 'Hazard Rate' Uncertainty." *Rand Journal of Economics*, 22, 4 (1991): 596-610.

Dahdough, Thomas N. and James F. Mongoven. "The Shape of Things to Come: Innovation Market Analysis in Merger Cases." *Antitrust Law Journal*, 64 (1996): 405-41.

Dasgupta, P. and E. Maskin. "The Simple Economics of Research Portfolios." *Economic Journal*, 97 (1987): 581-95.

Gallini, Nancy T. "A Strategic Reason to License." *American Economic Review*, 1984.

——. "Patent Policy and Costly Imitation." *Rand Journal of Economics*, 23, 1 (1992): 52-63.

Gallini, Nancy T. and M. Trebilcock. "Intellectual Property Rights and Competition Policy: A Framework for the Analysis of Economic and Legal Issues," in *Competition Policy and Intellectual Property Rights in the Knowledge-Based Economy*. Edited by Robert D. Anderson and Nancy T. Gallini. The Industry Canada Research Series. Calgary: University of Calgary Press, 1998, pp. 17-64.

Gallini, Nancy T. and Ralph Winter. "Licensing in the Theory of Innovation." *Rand Journal of Economics*, 16 (1985): 237-53.

Gandal, Neil and Suzanne Scotchmer. "Coordinating Research through Research Joint Ventures." *Journal of Public Economics*, 51 (1993): 173-93.

Gilbert, Richard J. and Gilbert C. Sunshine. "Incorporating Dynamic Efficiency Concerns in Merger Analysis: The Use of Innovation Markets." *Antitrust Law Journal*, 63, (1995): 569-602.

Green, Jerry and Suzanne Scotchmer. "On the Division of Profit in Sequential Innovation." *Rand Journal of Economics*, 26 (1995): 20-33.

Harris, Robert G. and Thomas M. Jorde. "Antitrust Market Definition: An Integrated Approach." *California Law Review*, 72 (1984): 1-67.

Hoerner, Robert J. "Innovation Markets: New Wine in Old Bottles?" *Antitrust Law Journal*, 64 (1995): 49-82.

Jorde, Thomas M. and David J. Teece. "Innovation and Co-operation: Implications for Competition and Antitrust." *Journal of Economics Perspectives*, 4 (1990): 75.

—— . "Innovation, Co-operation and Antitrust." *High Technology Law Journal*, 4 (1989): 1.

Katz, Michael. "An Analysis of Cooperative Research and Development." *Rand Journal of Economics*, 17, 4 (1986): 527-43.

Katz, Michael and Janusz Ordover. "R & D. Co-operation and Competition," in *Brookings Papers on Economic Activity*. Edited by Martin Neil Baily and Clifford Winston, 1989, pp. 137-204.

Klemperer, Paul. "On the Optimal Length and Breadth of Patent Protection." *Rand Journal of Economics*, forthcoming.

Loury, Glenn C. "Market Structure and Innovation." *Quarterly Journal of Economics*, XCIII, 3, (1979): 395-410.

Matutes, Carmen, Catherine Rockett and Pierre Regibeau. "Optimal Patent Design and Diffusion of Innovations." Mimeo, Universitat Autnoma de Barcelona and Northwestern University, 1991.

Merges, Robert P. and Richard R. Nelson. "On the Complex Economics of Patent Scope." *Columbia Law Review*, 90, 4 (1990): 839-916.

Minehart, D. and S. Scotchmer. "*Ex Post* Regret and the Decentralized Sharing of Information." Working Paper 95-58, Industrial Studies Program, Department of Economics, Boston University, 1995.

Nordhaus, William. *Invention, Growth and Welfare.* Cambridge: MIT Press, 1969.

Ordover, Janusz A. and Robert D. Willig. "Antitrust for High-Technology Industries: Assessing Research Joint Ventures and Mergers." *Journal of Law and Economics*, 28, (1985): 312.

Rapp, Richard T. "The Misapplication of the Innovation Market Approach to Merger Analysis." *Antitrust Law Journal*, 64 (1995): 19-47.

Reinganum, Jennifer. "The Timing of Innovation: Research, Development, and Diffusion," in *Handbook of Industrial Organization.* Edited by R. Schmalensee and R. Willig. New York: North Holland, vol. 1, chapter 14, 1989.

Schmitz, James A., Jr. "On the Breadth of Patent Protection." Mimeograph, SUNY-Stonybrook, 1989.

Scotchmer, Suzanne. "Standing on the Shoulders of Giants: Cumulative Research and the Patent Law." *Journal of Economic Perspectives,* Winter 1991.

——."Protecting Early Innovators: Should Second Generation Products Be Patentable?" *Rand Journal of Economics*, 27 (1996): 322-31.

Scotchmer, Suzanne and Jerry Green. "Novelty and Disclosure in Patent Law." *Rand Journal of Economics*, 21, 1 (Spring (1990): 131-46.

Spence, A. M. "Cost Reduction, Competition and Industry Performance." *Econometrica, 52* (1984): 101-21.

U.S. Department of Justice and Federal Trade Commission. *Horizontal Merger Guidelines*, 1992.

Wright, Brian. "The Economics of Invention Incentives: Patents, Prizes and Research Contracts." *American Economic Review*, 73 (1983): 691-707.

Comment

Michael J. Trebilcock
Faculty of Law
University of Toronto

SCOTCHMER MAKES AN IMPORTANT DISTINCTION between research joint ventures (RJVs) and *ex post* licensing: RJVs involve cooperation *ex ante* in making R&D investment, while licensing occurs *ex post* the commitment of R&D investment. She shows that efficiencies realizable with RJVs may not be possible through licensing (diffusion); hence the two stages of cooperation may be complements rather than substitutes.

The author argues in her conclusion that her paper can be read as supporting the view of Gallini and myself that antitrust treatment in innovation markets should not pay attention to incentives for R&D, but should rather assume that patent policy provides the appropriate incentives and concern itself with constraining attempts to engross additional market power. However, in my view, Scotchmer's analysis in fact diverges in important respects from ours and would have antitrust policy concern itself directly with questions of appropriate incentives to innovate in many contexts.

This failure to disengage antitrust policy objectives from intellectual property policy objectives raises serious concerns over bounded institutional competence and justiciability. In order to effect a major institutional division of labour, I would argue that antitrust policy *cannot* adopt a *total welfare* perspective on intellectual property issues, because this will necessarily implicate (*inter alia*) issues of socially optimal innovation policy. Thus, a more partial perspective is imperative that focuses primarily on consumer welfare effects in product or output markets (not innovation markets) and primarily on price effects of RJVs relative to non-RJV scenarios in these markets. Evidence of offsetting productive efficiency gains from RJVs in various settings might be treated as completely irrelevant (except insofar as they are reflected in relatively short-run price effects) or, a less extreme option, might be made the subject of a demanding burden of proof that is borne by the parties to any such arrangements in demonstrating net total welfare gains from such arrangements, even if in the product market in question there are net consumer welfare losses (by analogy with the efficiencies defence in Canadian merger law). In other words, in order to render institutionally tractable the complex theoretical constructs and indeterminacies surrounding the competitive implications of various arrangements or practices relating to intellectual property rights, some rough rules of thumb (decision-rules) involving appropriate evidentiary presumptions and burdens of proof are necessary in order to reduce public and private transaction costs and to enhance predictability (and thus reduce risk), albeit unavoidably offset by an error cost factor.

In beginning to think about how to formulate these decision rules, I review the four major classes of RJVs analysed by Scotchmer in her paper.

Broad Product Patents Coterminous With Product Market

IN THE CASE OF PATENTS IN THE PRODUCT MARKET that are broad so that all firms in the patent race pursue a single patent that covers the whole product market, the literature suggests that patent races may cause duplication of effort (which is inefficient), but that patent races may increase R&D spending (which may be efficient). How should antitrust authorities view an RJV in this context that delegates investments in R&D to the least-cost firm and shares costs and revenues?

Scotchmer, in contrast to Gallini and me, would have the antitrust authorities try to sort out whether duplication costs dominate faster rates of innovation, or vice versa. While on a total welfare or even consumer welfare test, this may be appropriate, it directly implicates antitrust authorities in the question of optimal investments in innovation. In our approach we would be content to compare the RJV scenario with the racing scenario and ask whether there has been a substantial lessening of competition in the *output* market (not the innovation market), focusing principally on prices rather than the pace of innovation. The answer seems clearly no – in any scenario there will only ever be one patented product (entailing significant market power).

MULTIPLE NARROW PATENTS IN THE PRODUCT MARKET

IN THE CASE OF PATENTS IN THE PRODUCT MARKET that are relatively narrow so that each firm in the patent race is pursuing a different patent, with resulting patents that would be mutually non-infringing but serve the same market (i.e., are substitutes), Scotchmer argues that RJVs should be permitted in some cases, for example, where they a) avoid duplication costs, b) delegate efforts to least-cost firms, and c) facilitate the transfer of information about expected costs or profitability, and not in others, such as where RJVs inefficiently lessen R&D spending and delay inventions and where they reduce the number of substitutes serving a single market. She acknowledges that while these distinctions may be clear in theory, they are difficult to make in practice. Again, I think the source of the problem is that the distinctions directly implicate antitrust authorities in evaluating optimal levels of investment in innovation.

Suppose six pharmaceutical companies are working on different drugs or vaccines for headaches, depression, or AIDS. These are mutually non-infringing; that is, they are six different treatments for the same condition. By forming an RJV, assuming barriers to entry by other companies are high, the six firms can concentrate their efforts on developing only one such product, sharing the reduced costs and the enhanced monopoly profits.

Here we have the classic Williamsonian trade-off between consumer welfare losses and productive efficiency gains (consumer welfare versus total welfare). In my view, at least in Canada, we should do as we do with mergers and view the consumer welfare losses from the RJV, in other words, enhanced monopoly prices, as presumptively anticompetitive and cast a heavy burden of proof on the members of the RJV to show substantial offsetting productive efficiency gains. Or one could take a more extreme view and do as U.S. and EU competition authorities seem to do in the case of mergers, and, at least formally, ignore the efficiency gains altogether, focusing only on the price effects of the RJV relative to the non-RJV scenario.

RJVs That Reduce Unit Production Costs

SCOTCHMER THEN ADDRESSES ANOTHER SCENARIO where competitors in a product market can make an R&D investment that reduces the unit costs of production. She argues that efficiency would require that one firm bear the R&D costs and license the cost reduction to other firms, which then compete with each other in their output markets. She concludes that this outcome is difficult to achieve whether or not RJVs are permitted, mostly because it is difficult to calibrate the royalty rates so as simultaneously to induce the investment in the cost-reducing innovation and to induce licensees to adopt the innovation. In the absence of a mutually profitable licensing arrangement, all firms will invest in R&D to realize the cost-reducing innovation, thus inefficiently duplicating R&D costs. Again, I am concerned that this framework of analysis requires antitrust authorities to evaluate alternative arrangements for achieving optimal rates of innovation at least cost.

In the above case, I certainly would not require competitors to enter into a RJV *ex ante* or commit themselves *ex ante* to license the cost-cutting innovation to all members of the RJV. Would I prohibit such an arrangement? Again, I would focus on the output or product market. If the RJV does not increase product prices or reduce output (in the relatively short run) relative to the non-RJV scenario, I would see nothing objectionable in a process-licensing arrangement among competitors (much as in the GE-Westinghouse case discussed by Gallini and me in our paper). We would ask whether the RJV produces a less desirable competitive outcome in the product or output market, in *terms of prices*, than does the non-RJV scenario. In other words, I would focus on product markets, not innovation markets (the conceptual utility of which I am sceptical), and mostly on prices, not rates or costs of innovation, if the competition issues in contexts such as this are to be rendered tractable and justiciable. Scotchmer rightly emphasizes that this analysis entails speculative counterfactuals, but these do not seem to me to be any more speculative than the counterfactuals involved in any *ex ante* merger review and certainly less speculative than if all kinds of alternative rates and costs of innovation scenarios are viewed as germane to the analysis.

Vertical RJVs

THE FINAL SCENARIO DISCUSSED BY SCOTCHMER is vertical RJVs involving complementary innovations, such as basic and applied research. In this case, if R&D investments in the application are relatively high, the second innovator may be deterred from investing if it thinks that the ex post negotiated licence fee will not leave it enough revenue to cover the prior sunk R&D costs. *Ex ante* agreements may resolve this problem. This case is clearly unproblematic. However, Scotchmer posits a case where the first product has commercial value in its own right, and the second product is merely an improved version of the first. In this case, the second product could not have been invented without the first, but the two products are potential competitors in the product market. Suppose that the two firms form an RJV to develop and market the second (improved) product (while abandoning the first). Scotchmer worries that antitrust authorities would be hostile to such an arrangement, presumably because the improved product is no longer competing with the initial product. But this case seems straightforward in the framework Gallini and I propose. Does the RJV scenario substantially reduce competition in the output market relative to the non-RJV scenario? If the holder of the patent for the basic or initial product chooses not to license, that right is inherent in the intellectual property rights. Thus if the patent holder chooses to licence and abandon the first product, this arrangement is not less competitive than the non-RJV scenario and indeed ensures that consumers have access to the superior product.

If, on the other hand, the improvement is non-infringing and does not require licensing, then an RJV should be viewed as purely horizontal, which is conceptually the same case as multiple holders or potential holders of narrow patents in the same product market (Scotchmer's Scenario B). It should be viewed as objectionable despite the fact that the RJV may save on R&D costs, subject arguably to a demanding reverse onus of proof of offsetting productive efficiency gains that would be compared to the size of the dead-weight losses associated with any likely adverse price effects.

In short, transposing the complex and often indeterminate analytics on intellectual property rights and competition to an institutional adjudicative forum raises major challenges in terms of bounded institutional competence, transaction costs, and justiciability. Framing decision-rules that yield determinate outcomes in most cases, while generating an acceptable level of error costs, will not be easy. However, assuming that decisions will be made by economic virtuosos with a full information set rather than individuals of average competence, conscientiousness and foresight would be an exercise in unwarranted and costly romanticism.

Jeffrey Church   &   Roger Ware
Department of Economics   Department of Economics
University of Calgary   Queen's University

8

Network Industries, Intellectual Property Rights and Competition Policy

INTRODUCTION

IN THIS PAPER WE CONSIDER THE INTERACTION OF COMPETITION POLICY and intellectual property rights in the context of industries where the existence of network externalities means that questions of standardization and compatibility are important. Industries where concerns regarding standardization and compatibility are prominent include consumer electronics, information processing, and telecommunications.

Questions regarding standardization and compatibility in these industries are important because of the fundamental nature of the products: they are components of systems. The products supplied in these industries are of little value in and of themselves; in order to be of value they must typically be part of a system. There are two different kinds of systems where compatibility is important. In the first, the system consists of similar products linked together in a network. In the second, the system consists of differentiated, complementary products.

The classic example of a network system is a telephone exchange. Two other examples are facsimile machines, or more accurately their communication standards, and the Internet. The network need not be cables in the ground, it may consist of individuals who adopt a similar word-processing program and derive benefits from being able to swap files with others. For a network system, the value of joining the network increases with the number of others who are also connected to compatible networks. The size of the network is usually referred to as its installed base.

When a system consists of complementary products, consumption services are produced when two or more compatible products interact and form a system. In many such cases, the value of one component (the "hardware") depends on the variety of compatible complementary components ("software").[1] Examples abound in consumer electronics: televisions and programming, compact disc players and compact discs, video game systems and video games, FM radios and FM radio stations, video-cassette recorders and prerecorded programming. This "hardware-software" paradigm is not restricted to consumer electronics, and the hardware need not literally be hardware. In computers, the hardware good is an operating system and the relevant software goods are the applications. Other examples are credit cards (hardware) and the stores that accept them (software); natural gas powered vehicles (hardware) and natural gas filling stations (software); ATM cards (hardware) and ATM teller machines (software). In all of these cases the value of the hardware depends on the availability of differentiated software. Increases in the variety of differentiated software increase the value of hardware.

Systems that consist of a hardware unit and differentiated software can usefully be regarded as "virtual networks," and the properties of these systems are, under certain circumstances, similar to those of network systems (see Katz and Shapiro 1985, 1994; Farrell and Saloner, 1985; Church and Gandal, 1993). In particular, they share the important characteristic that under certain circumstances, the value of a component system will also depend on the total number of consumers who adopt compatible systems. If the production of software is characterized by increasing returns to scale and free entry, then increases in sales of hardware (adoption by others of the same hardware) benefits existing users by increasing demand for, and hence supply of, software. The more users there are who adopt a common hardware standard, the better off they will all be due to lower software prices and more software varieties (see Church and Gandal, 1993, 1995). The positive relationship between adopters and the size of a network is known as a network effect.

An important implication follows from the positive relationship between the value of network benefits and the size of the network: the existence of a network externality. The externality arises because when individuals consider joining a network, they will consider only their private benefits and costs. However, there is a positive external effect on others on the network associated with adoption: the value of the network to them has increased since the size of the network has expanded.

The existence of network effects means that the adoption decision by consumers will depend on the existing size of a network (its installed base) and consumers' expectations regarding the growth of the network. Consumers, after all, will recognize that the value of joining the network depends on not only its present size, but its future size. The relationship is complicated, since the size of the installed base is likely, at least in part, to determine future growth. A larger installed base today makes the network more attractive to join tomorrow. Moreover, the expectation of a larger installed base tomorrow increases the size of the installed base today. These positive feedback effects are the primary reason why the behaviour of industries characterized by network externalities is fundamentally different from that of other industries. It also suggests that these industries will be characterized by unique competition policy and intellectual property rights issues. Moreover as we shall see, the interaction and potential for conflict between intellectual property rights and competition policy is likely to be greater in network industries. Indeed, competition policy may play a very important, socially beneficial role in *compressing* or *attenuating* the scope of intellectual property rights in network industries.

The basis for our argument is very simple: network externalities plus strong intellectual property protection *potentially* equals sustained market dominance. This suggests a role for competition policy, and in particular that antitrust enforcement can be used to limit intellectual property rights in network industries. In many instances, the extent of protection in network industries is undesirable and unintended because the existing types of intellectual property rights are ill-suited for network industries. This should be neither controversial nor surprising: intellectual property rights are, after all, an extraordinarily blunt instrument, providing the same degree of protection across all industries and all products. In these circumstances it is readily apparent that some *ex post* fine-tuning of the strength of intellectual property rights could be socially desirable.

Intellectual property rights are a creation of the state designed to overcome the incentive problems for the creation of knowledge that follow from the fact that knowledge is a public good. Optimally, the extent of intellectual property rights is determined by trading off *ex ante* incentives for investment in research and development against the social cost of *ex post* inefficient production associated with market power. However, in network industries, network externalities and intellectual property protection interact to limit the number of competing systems and can result in standardization, that is, monopolization.

We begin the paper with an overview of competition in network industries. In the next section we argue that the installed base of a de facto standard provides its sponsor with the ability to raise prices and exclude entry, that is, the installed base creates market power in an antitrust market. We will argue that this has implications for the design of intellectual property rights: the analysis in the fourth section strongly suggests that the current regime could result in the overprotection of intellectual property in network industries. We illustrate this in the fifth section with a case study of the U.S. experience in protecting computer software. We interpret the retreat from copyright protection for software, both in terms of limits imposed by the misuse and fair use doctrines and in terms of what is copyrightable, as a recognition by the U.S. courts that copyright protection, designed to protect literary works, is inappropriate for software.

We consider the role for antitrust enforcement in the sixth section. In particular, we focus on two situations: a) where system sponsors restrict access to their installed base, either through intellectual property rights in an interface or the installed base itself, for instance, copyright protection of software, and b) where system sponsors initially introduce open systems and encourage third-party supply of complementary products, but then manipulate standards or product specifications to render third-party complementary products incompatible, unnecessary, or inferior and in the process monopolize the supply of complementary products. In both instances, we argue that enlightened antitrust enforcement can be welfare improving. Not only are the incentives provided by existing intellectual property rights inefficiently large, but the *ex post* behaviour of the dominant firm is inefficient, and the appropriate antitrust remedy involves limiting the extent of protection for their intellectual property.

COMPETITION IN NETWORK INDUSTRIES

WE HAVE OBSERVED THAT THE DISTINGUISHING FEATURE of systems markets is network effects. The benefit that consumers realize from joining a network depends on the number of other consumers who also join the same (or a compatible) network. In the case of direct network externalities, this arises because the "quality" of the network depends directly on the number of subscribers. In the case of indirect network externalities, an increase in the number of subscribers lowers the price of compatible software and increases the variety of software available.

As a result, the expectations of consumers regarding the future size of a network will be paramount in their adoption decision, and their expectations are likely to be positively correlated with the existing installed base. This has a number of implications for competition in network markets.[2]

Chicken or egg? – There is the potential for severe coordination problems if joining a network involves making a sunk investment. If the network does not grow, then consumers will be stranded and the expected benefits associated with the sunk investment and membership on the network will not be realized. This makes consumers reluctant to join new networks. They would be willing to join a new network if they knew that others were also willing to join, but because no one is presently on the network they do not believe that others are willing to join, so they do not. If the externality is indirect, consumers would be willing to buy hardware if software was available, but software suppliers are reluctant to supply software until consumers demonstrate that a market exists by buying hardware. Moreover, at a different level, a hardware firm might not introduce a new technology if it does not think that complementary software will be supplied. Complementary software will only be introduced if the hardware is introduced and consumers adopt it.

Standardization – Network markets are highly susceptible to "tipping," or standardization. This means that the result of competition between competing, incompatible technologies is that one becomes the de facto standard. *De facto* standardization means that all consumers adopt the same technology. If one system or technology can establish an initial edge in the size of its installed base, then this can serve as an effective (and correct) signal to consumers that other consumers will also adopt this system. Establishing a small initial advantage leads to the creation of a very large sustained advantage, which results in exclusive adoption. If all consumers believe that video rental outlets will only have video cassettes available in the VHS format for rental (or initially just more variety available in VHS format), they will only buy VHS video cassette recorders. Their expectation is self-fulfilling, since their purchase decision means that only VHS format tapes will be available (or more and more video stores reduce their library of Beta tapes or specialize in VHS). Firms that recognize that they are competing in a market with network externalities against rivals with incompatible technologies can be expected to compete very aggressively to establish an initial installed-base advantage. De facto standardization is more likely to occur the stronger network effects are relative to the extent of consumer heterogeneity. If consumers have sufficiently heterogeneous preferences, then the advantage of a closer match between the preferences of some consumers can exceed the advantage from a larger network, and multiple, incompatible, differentiated networks can coexist.

Multiple equilibria – Given the preceding two observations, it is easy to see that, depending on the expectations of consumers, network markets are likely to have multiple equilibria. For instance, if there are two competing technologies (A and B), this means that both could be viable, there could be de facto standardization on network A or on network B, or neither technology is adopted.

Lock-in – The chicken and egg coordination problem described above is complicated by lock-in. There are two aspects to lock-in. The first is the need to duplicate sunk investments in order to switch networks. The costs of adopting a technology, to the extent that they are sunk and the networks are incompatible, imposes switching costs on consumers who switch to *another network*. The second is that to the extent that the installed base of the second network is not currently as large nor likely to be as large as the incumbent network in the future, the benefit from joining it is less. Lock-in means that a proprietary sponsor of a technology has an incentive not to grow its network, but to exploit its locked-in installed base. Promises by a firm to expand its network by charging low prices or providing lots of inexpensive software in the future are not necessarily credible: that is, fulfilling such a promise may not be in the firm's best interests if its installed base is large enough.

BATTLES FOR STANDARDS, COMPATIBILITY, AND ADOPTION

COMPETITION IN NETWORK INDUSTRIES is fundamentally about standard-setting and compatibility. It is also about choosing the ground on which to compete: whether to agree on a standard, even one more advantageous to one's rival than oneself, so that the battleground can be the traditional one of product competition within a standard; or to fight for the victorious standard, so that if you win, there will be no product competition to worry about, at least not if your products have strong protection through intellectual property laws.[3] The literature on network externalities distinguishes between three different situations. These are a) battles between incompatible standards; b) battles over compatibility; and c) standard-setting by voluntary agreement.

In a battle of standards, two or more incompatible systems compete against each other. There are many obvious examples: VHS versus Beta, Visa versus American Express, Macintosh versus Windows versus OS/2, and Nintendo versus Sega. In standards battles, the competitive efforts of firms will be directed towards increasing their present installed base and manipulating the expectations of consumers regarding the future size of the installed base. The incentives for these kinds of behaviour exist precisely because a firm has intellectual property rights in its technology and is trying to maximize their value. Sponsors can often partially internalize the network externality by charging early adopters (who provide benefits to later adopters) low prices.

A battle over compatibility arises when the technology of one firm has become the de facto standard (perhaps by triumphing in a battle of standards) so that all, or almost all, consumers have adopted its products. The battle is now over the issue of compatibility. Can the dominant firm maintain incompatibility between its products and those of its competitors? Rather than compete with a different technology, competitors will find it more profitable to compete against the incumbent by offering compatible technologies. The monopolist supplier of the standard will only remain a monopolist if it can restrict access by its competitors to its installed base. That is, the monopolist supplier will have an incentive to keep its system *closed*. This can be viewed as a firm trying to maintain the value of its property rights in its sponsored network.

Standard-setting by agreement occurs when multiple firms have developed or are in the process of developing incompatible new technologies and these firms perceive that none of their technologies is likely to win a standards battle. Moreover, it may also be the case that in the event of competition between new, incompatible technologies, not only does neither win the standards battle, but neither technology even survives. This arises because the diversity of incompatible technologies and approaches may mean that the expectations of consumers are *fragmented*. The competition between standards makes it difficult for consumers to correctly select the technology that will remain viable. As a result, they are reluctant to make the necessary sunk investments and they stay with their old technology. One way for firms introducing a new generation of technology to avoid this fragmentation is to agree to a standard. This can be done either through national or industry standard-setting bodies, or less formally when firms simply agree to a common standard. In both cases, the standard is usually realized by cross-licensing of technology. The game here is for the competing firms to agree to a common standard in order to assure adoption by consumers. One view of such a standard-setting process is that firms voluntarily renounce or reduce the extent of their intellectual property protection in order to ensure successful adoption (see Farrell, 1989).

Battles for Standards

In a battle for standards, firms undertake strategies to convince customers that the size of their installed base will dominate those of their rivals. They can do this either by directly affecting the expectations of consumers or, by investing in their installed base, they try to exploit the link between expectations and the size of the current installed base. Of course the extent to which they are willing to invest in increasing the size of the network depends on their ability to capture the benefits from doing so, which in turn depends on being able to restrict access to their network by competing suppliers.

A crucial distinction between indirect and direct network externalities is the nature of the installed base. If the externality is direct, the installed base equals the number of consumers who purchase the technology. The relevant installed base in a hardware-software setting, when the network externality is indirect, is not the number of consumers who have adopted compatible hardware, but rather the variety of software. Of course the size of the installed base of software will depend on the number of consumers who adopt compatible hardware. However, in the case of indirect network externalities, hardware firms can create an installed base by either directly supplying software titles or inducing supply from independent software firms.

There are several strategies firms can take to influence consumers' expectations regarding network size.

Penetration pricing – This is strategic pricing to increase sales early in the life cycle of the product in order to build up the installed base (see Farrell and Saloner, 1986b; Katz and Shapiro, 1986a). Firms strategically lower their price, perhaps below marginal cost, in order to convince consumers to join the network. In computer software, the product is often given away. A recent spectacular example of this was Netscape's free distribution of its web browser. This raises interesting questions about predation, since a firm need only price like this until it has established a sufficient installed base that the market is tipped towards its standard and its rivals are forced to exit. Moreover, in order to do this it need not price below marginal cost, just strategically lower its price to induce customers to join its network and not that of its rivals. Thereafter it can raise its prices without fear of entry, precisely because of the size of its installed base. The larger installed base tomorrow means that consumers will pay more to join. Thus future consumers benefit when consumers today adopt a technology and increase the size of its installed base. This is just another way of saying that network effects give rise to network externalities. The use of penetration pricing is a way for a firm to (partially) internalize the externality and transfer (through lower prices) some of the benefit to consumers today. Penetration pricing is thus similar to a plan to tax consumers in the future in order to subsidize adoption decisions today.

Insurance – Firms can lower the risk to consumers of joining the wrong network by providing insurance against being stranded, i.e., not benefiting from the sunk investment required to join the network. This can be done through sophisticated pricing contracts where the ultimate price paid depends on the size of the network (see Dybvig and Spatt, 1993; or Thum, 1994). Alternatively, firms can supply the required hardware to join on short-term leases (Katz and Shapiro, 1994, p. 103). Both of these reduce the risk to consumers that they will be locked in, and make it easy to change networks.

Second-sourcing – Firms can license their products in order to create competition (see Farrell and Gallini, 1988; Shepard, 1987). This is a means to commit to low prices now and in the future, both of which serve to increase the size of the installed base now. IBM's introduction of the PC and Matsushita's licensing of the VHS standard are the classic examples. Moreover, firms can have aggressive licensing schemes that promote the creation of complementary software. Philips and SONY pursued such a strategy when they introduced the compact disc (see Grindley, 1995, p. 117).

Advertising and marketing – Promotional efforts will be aimed at manipulating the expectations of consumers. Visa emphasizes in its commercials that its credit card is accepted at more places than American Express. American Express responds by including in its monthly bill a list of businesses that have recently started accepting its card. Katz and Shapiro report that WordPerfect recently sued Microsoft over its advertising, which claimed that Microsoft Word was the world's most popular word processor (Katz and Shapiro, 1994, p. 107).

Hostage – A firm can also commit to grow its network and not exploit its installed base by making valuable assets hostages (Katz and Shapiro, 1994, p. 104). For instance, a firm's reputation for not exploiting its installed base may be very valuable if it produces multiple products or introduces new generations of technology. Alternatively, it may invest in large sunk expenditures that it can only hope to recover by promoting future growth in the installed base. Investments in plant capacity, for instance, might serve as a signal of private information to consumers that the firm really does expect substantial growth in the size of the network. The huge amounts paid for broadband spectrum by firms interested in offering second generation personal communications services is an excellent example.[4]

Investments in complementary components (software) – In component systems, the relevant installed base is complementary software or components. Hardware firms can make strategic investments to increase the supply of components.[5] For instance, both Nintendo and Sega produce many of the most popular video games for their systems, and Microsoft supplies a wide array of application programs (Word, Excel, etc.) for use with its Windows operating system.

In hardware/software industries, what typically influences adoption decisions by consumers is the relative number of software titles available. Consequently, hardware firms can increase the relative size of their installed base not only by increasing the software available for their system but also by reducing the variety of software available for competing systems. Nintendo was able to maintain incompatibility between video games provided for its system and competing video game systems by using a lock-out system. This consisted of a "master" chip in the game console and a "slave" chip in the game cartridges. The slave chip in the cartridges contained the 10NES computer program. The signal generated by the 10NES program instructed the master chip to unlock the game console and allow the game cartridge to access the console. The slave and master chips were patented and the 10NES program copyrighted. Third-party developers who wanted to supply software for Nintendo systems had to obtain game cartridges from Nintendo. In return for a supply of game cartridges, developers agreed not to make their games available for other video game systems.[6]

Microsoft had similar restrictive covenants with independent software developers writing application software for Windows 95.[7] The recent merger between Silicon Graphics and Alias was challenged by the U.S. Federal Trade Commission (FTC) over concerns regarding the possibility that other workstation manufacturers would be competitively disadvantaged if Alias' software products were only compatible with Silicon Graphics hardware.[8]

Product preannouncements or vaporware – A firm preannounces its product by informing consumers about the future availability of its products (see Farrell and Saloner, 1986b). The idea is to convince consumers to wait for the release of your product rather than buy now from a competitor. If effective, this limits the growth of the competitor's installed base. Microsoft did this when its early rival in DOS operating systems came to the market with a significantly better product than MS-DOS. Within a month of the release of DR-DOS 5.0, Microsoft announced the imminent arrival of its MS-DOS 5.0, which matched the features of DR-DOS 5.0. The new version of MS-DOS was not commercially available until a year after the release of DR-DOS (see Baseman, Warren-Boulton, and Woroch, 1995, p. 272). One of the allegations by the U.S. Department of Justice in its monopolization antitrust suit against IBM was that IBM announced its intention to enter segments of the market where there was actual or potential competition, even though it knew that it was unlikely to enter these segments within the time frame announced.[9]

Strategic behaviour by a sponsor of its installed base is only contemplated because the winning firm has property rights in the network and thus finds it profitable to attempt to internalize the network externality. If the network were non-proprietary, then firms would have significantly less incentive to make investments in increasing the size of their installed base. As a result, the coordination problems inherent in network industries may mean that no technology is successfully adopted. On the other hand, the formal analysis of these kinds of strategies indicates that they can promote, but do not necessarily result in, inefficient standardization or standardization on the wrong technology.

Inefficient standardization means that welfare would be greater if more than one network was available. This is possible because there is typically a trade-off between standardization and variety. Standardization is valued since if all consumers adopt the same technology, the benefit from the network external- ity is maximized. On the other hand, this means a reduction in product variety, and to the extent that variety is valued, entails real costs. The social value of a greater variety of networks in the short run is that it makes possible a closer match between the qualities of products and the tastes of consumers. The ten- dency in the theoretical literature is for the equilibrium to be characterized by insufficient standardization or too much variety (see Farrell and Saloner, 1986a; Chou and Shy, 1990; Church and Gandal, 1992a and 1996b). However, in a world of uncertainty there is an additional advantage of multiple networks in the long run: they have an "option" value in the sense that standardization on tech- nology A may preclude a subsequent change to technology B if technology B in fact turns out to be superior. The relative experience of selecting a standard for high-definition television (HDTV) in the United states and Japan is illus- trative (see Katz and Shapiro, 1994, p. 106; see also Farrell and Shapiro, 1992b, on HDTV). The all-digital standard adopted in the United States is viewed to be superior to the hybrid analogue/digital standard chosen by the Japanese.

The possibility of lock-in to an inefficient standard arises due to the exis- tence of an installed base for the established technology. A large installed base provides an incumbent technology with an advantage over new technologies. Despite the technical superiority of a new technology, consumers might be reluctant to adopt it if they believe that it is unlikely to eventually have an installed base *comparable* with the existing technology. Consumers are unlikely to bear the costs and risk of adopting a new technology if they believe that others will not also adopt it (see Farrell and Saloner, 1985 and 1986b). Coordination problems among consumers mean that a switch in standards might not occur even if total surplus would ultimately be greater with a change in standards. A bias towards existing products with an installed base is called *excess inertia.*

This possibility is sensitive to the expectations of consumers. If expecta- tions are less fragmented, then there is more likely to be *insufficient friction* (see Katz and Shapiro, 1986a, 1992 and 1994). Insufficient friction arises when a change to a new technology is socially inefficient. This can arise when the new technology is, *ceteris paribus,* better than the old technology and the present generation of consumers adopt it. This can be inefficient since the present generation of consumers do not take into account that they are stranding pre- vious generations of consumers: the welfare of consumers on the old standard is harmed since the size of their network is no longer increasing. The work of Katz and Shapiro suggests that strategic behaviour by sponsored networks with cost advantages in the future limits the ability of existing sponsored technologies to engage in penetration pricing and internalize the network externality. This is because such behaviour limits the ability of the old technology to charge high prices to future consumers. As a result, a profit maximizing sponsor of the old technology cannot afford to compete as aggressively for more consumers today. Moreover, a new sponsored technology is able to replace a socially preferred, unsponsored standard because it is able, unlike its unsponsored rival, to engage in penetration pricing (see Katz and Shapiro, 1986a and 1992). Both of these factors contribute to insufficient friction as one incompatible technology replaces another.

Battles for Compatibility

Firms that are suppliers of technologies that have become de facto standards need to maintain a closed system in order to preserve their monopoly. Often the installed base of an incumbent is a sufficient barrier to entry to exclude entrants whose products are incompatible. For instance, firms producing new audio technologies that are not compatible with the existing installed software base are likely to have difficulties getting their technologies adopted unless they offer significant advantages over the existing technology.[10] Of course, the question of compatibility is not exogenous. Either by design or exercise of property rights, incumbent firms may be able to block compatibility.[11] Furthermore, suppliers of complementary products will be deterred unless their products are also compatible with the system of the network sponsor. For instance, manufacturers of IBM plug-peripherals were forced to exit when they were unable to maintain compatibility, and Atari was not able to supply video games for Nintendo video game controllers until it broke Nintendo's lock-out code.

Firms with large installed bases are unlikely to have socially adequate incentives to attain compatibility with rivals (see Katz and Shapiro, 1985 and 1992, for formal demonstrations of this proposition). While compatibility would increase the size of the network and the social benefits from the network externality, it is likely to decrease the profits of the incumbent firm. Competition between networks depends on the relative size of the installed base. A relatively large proprietary installed base usually means that the incumbent is relatively unrestrained by competition. Compatibility equalizes the installed bases of the entrant and the incumbent and changes the nature of the competition between the firms. Compatibility eliminates the installed base advantage and thus the monopoly of the incumbent. Dominant firms often attempt to frustrate and disrupt compatibility using the strategies described below.

Refusal to deal – There are two types of refusal cases. In the first, dominant firms refuse access to new entrants, and by exercising their property rights they can exclude entrants from the network, that is, enforce incompatibility.

This has been the case for press pools, automated bank machine (ABM) networks, credit cards, and telephone networks. The second kind of refusal occurs when the dominant firm asserts its intellectual property rights and refuses to license. For instance, Apple historically refused to license its operating system and vigilantly enforced its copyright to prevent entry by clone manufacturers.[12]

There is a subtle but important difference between these two cases, which highlights one of the differences associated with intellectual property, and which we will discuss below. Incompatibility in the refusal to deal cases is attained by the dominant firm simply denying access to its network. This is relatively easy to do when the network is physical, for example, a telephone or an ABM network. However, the refusal-to-license cases are more subtle, since the compatibility or interconnection is not with a physical network *per se* but is attained if the entrant's hardware is compatible with the incumbent's installed base of software. In these circumstances, well-defined intellectual property rights over software will be necessary to exclude entrants from access to the installed base since entrants will be able to interconnect technically, if not legally, by building adaptors or copying software.

Predatory product innovation – Firms can try and introduce incompatibility by making frequent and unannounced changes in product standards. Again, it is useful to distinguish between cases where changes in product standards make competitors incompatible and those where they make complementary products supplied by third parties incompatible.

An example of changing product standards that disadvantaged a competitor occurred when Microsoft introduced Windows 3.1 (this example is from Baseman, Warren-Boulton, and Woroch, 1995, p. 277-278). Microsoft did not license to the manufacturer of DR-DOS a beta version to test for compatibility. If you started Windows 3.1 on a machine that was not running MS-DOS, you apparently got a false error message! Microsoft also warned developers who were designing application software to take advantage of the Windows 3.1 graphical user interface and users running Windows that they might encounter problems with a lack of compatibility and interoperability unless they used MS-DOS. Moreover, Microsoft apparently refused to make any effort to ensure that Windows 3.1 was compatible with competing operating systems. Baseman, Warren-Boulton, and Woroch report that concerns over incompatibility between DR-DOS and Windows resulted in "significant declines in DR-DOS retail sales" (Baseman, Warren-Boulton, and Woroch; 1995, p. 278). The introduction of Windows helped to further disenfranchise DR-DOS from the IBM-PC compatible network.

In the cases involving IBM peripherals, IBM redesigned its computer systems to exclude competing plug-compatible peripherals.[13] In the late 1960s and early 1970s, a number of firms had figured out how to make plug-compatible peripherals (e.g., disk drives and tape drives) to work with IBM mainframe computers. These products were plug-compatible because it was possible to unplug the IBM peripheral and plug in the competitor's peripheral with no loss of function. In response to a significant loss of its market share for disk drives, IBM introduced a new disk controller that had a different interface with the central processing unit (CPU). This effectively made existing third-party disk drives incompatible with IBM CPUs. Moreover, IBM introduced a technological tie. Consumers had the option of renting an integrated unit that included both the new disk controllers and the CPU. The rental price of the new disk controller was 40-60 percent less when it was included in an integrated unit. Inclusion of the disk controller with the CPU made it impossible to plug in the disk drives and controllers of competing peripherals (see Brock, 1989, for details of the IBM peripheral cases).

NETWORK INDUSTRIES, INTELLECTUAL PROPERTY RIGHTS, AND MARKET POWER

THE PURPOSE OF GRANTING INTELLECTUAL PROPERTY RIGHTS is to create a degree of monopoly protection for innovators. The standard analysis underlying this is that innovations are a form of public good in that once they are created, it is socially desirable to disseminate them widely at marginal cost. Such low-cost dissemination would destroy the incentive to innovate, because it robs the innovator of any prospect of profit. If the innovator's property right can be protected, assuring some monopoly profit, then the incentive to innovate is stronger, but dissemination will be inefficiently small because monopoly prices would deter some users whose benefit exceeded dissemination costs. The traditional role of intellectual property rights is to optimize the trade-off between these benefits and costs, by creating enough but not too much protection for the innovator's property right.

Antitrust policy also concerns itself with market power, but with finding remedies for its creation and abuse. Market power in and of itself is usually not illegal, but under section 2 of the *Sherman Act* in the United States and sections 78 and 79 of the *Competition Act* in Canada (the abuse of dominance provisions), abuse of market power is illegal. Intellectual property rights by definition assign exclusive rights of use and thus appear to create monopolies. Given the potential of intellectual property rights to create market power, competition policy and intellectual property rights may act in opposition to one another, one acting to create monopoly rights and the other to destroy them.

However, in most industries this conflict is illusory. The Second Circuit Court in the United States observed that "When the patented product is merely one of many products that actively compete on the market, few problems arise between the property rights of a patent owner and the antitrust laws [citations omitted]."[14] The conflict disappears because in most instances the protection afforded by intellectual property rights, while granting exclusive use, does not usually result in the creation of market power in a well-defined antitrust market.[15] The courts in the United States have observed that when a "patented product is so successful that it evolves into its own economic market . . . or succeeds in engulfing a large section of a preexisting product market, the patent and antitrust laws necessarily clash."[16]

The Collision between Intellectual Property Rights and Antitrust in Network Industries

Intellectual property rights and network externalities reinforce each other, not just to help create de facto industry standards, but also to create market power. Standardization means that the protected technology has not only engulfed the market: it has become the market, and intellectual property protection can effectively exclude others from entering and producing compatible products. If the installed base of the protected technology is large enough and network effects are important enough, then the protected standard will be an antitrust market: the sponsor will have market power. Consumers will not substitute away from the de facto standard when its supplier raises its price. Those who are already on the network will be locked in by their sunk investments. Existing consumers are likely to stay and new consumers to still choose the incumbent's technology, even if it is priced above competitive levels, because of the advantages it offers due to its larger network.

This installed base is also a significant entry barrier. In order to compete with the existing technology, entrants will have to overcome the product quality advantage that the incumbent's installed base provides. If network effects are very important, it may not be enough to simply offer a superior product at a low price. Instead, it may be necessary for the entrant to convince consumers that its product will replace the existing technology as the standard and thus provide comparable network benefits. These requirements significantly increase the fixed and sunk costs of entry, and as a result pose a significant barrier to entry for firms producing incompatible products.

In the Microsoft investigation, the U.S. Department of Justice determined that a significant barrier to entry for a new incompatible operating system was the necessity to sponsor an installed base of applications comparable to that available for MS-DOS and Windows.[17] In the *Southam* merger case in Canada,[18] the Director of Investigations challenged the acquisition of the *North Shore News* and the *Real Estate Weekly*, since Southam was already the publisher of the two daily newspapers in Vancouver. The Competition Tribunal accepted that network effects created barriers to entry into the market for real estate advertising. Network effects arise because the greater the number of advertisements, the greater the readership, the more effective the advertising, and thus the greater the number of advertisers. The success of a new entrant will depend on the number of advertisers it can attract. In competition with the installed base (the number of advertisers of the existing papers), the new entrant may have difficulty selling advertising space, independent of how favourable its rates are, if advertisers do not believe that others will also advertise.[19]

If the presence of a large installed base deters entry of incompatible technologies, then the existence and enforcement of property rights can play a key role in deterring entry of compatible technologies marketed by competing firms. Denying a competitor access to a network has in a number of cases led to successful monopolization cases, typically under the essential facilities doctrine, and to court-ordered access.[20]

Access to the installed base or network, however, may not require direct physical access, which can be easily rebuffed through a simple refusal to interconnect. This is typically the case when the externality is indirect, but may also apply to cases where the externality is direct but interconnection is not physical. Instead the existence and vigilant enforcement of intellectual property rights may deter entry. Intellectual property rights can deter entry under several circumstances:

1. Intellectual property protects the standard from being copied and produced by others. For instance, in the case of an operating system, copyright protects the literal copying of the code. Firms would infringe copyright protection if they were to make and market an exact copy of another firm's copyrighted operating system. In the case of an operating system, a competing product that is not an exact copy may run into compatibility problems.

2. Intellectual property protects interfaces, thus excluding both complementary products and hardware units that do not incorporate the protection from being part of the network. An example is the lockout systems used by both Nintendo and Sega for their video games. These systems precluded non-sanctioned suppliers of video games from being played on Nintendo or Sega game consoles. At the same time, it also made it difficult for Nintendo games to be used on other game system consoles. A more subtle example is copyright protection of the "look and feel" of a software interface as in the *Lotus v. Paperback*[21] and *Apple v. Microsoft*[22] cases. For instance, in the *Lotus* case, competing suppliers of spreadsheets are potentially excluded due to the cost to consumers of switching if they do not have the same menu hierarchy and run Lotus macros[23].

3. Intellectual property rights in complementary products may also preclude entry of other systems. Refusing to make software available in formats that work with other systems and enjoining others from copying software can have the effect of denying access to an installed base of software for a competing technology. Concerns over precisely this type of behaviour have been prominent in the regulation of cable

television in the United States and related antitrust cases.[24] *Magill* is a landmark case in the European Community involving refusals to license weekly television listings. TV guides have the property that the more channels they list, the more valuable they are to consumers (this case is discussed in detail in "Refusals to License," below).

THE IMPLICATIONS OF NETWORK EXTERNALITIES FOR THE DESIGN OF INTELLECTUAL PROPERTY RIGHTS

EVEN IF THE BALANCING ACT BETWEEN INTELLECTUAL PROPERTY RIGHTS and competition policy were successfully resolved for conventional industries, the preceding discussion has created a *prima facie* case for the view that the same balance will not work well in industries where network externalities are important.[25]

First, where network externalities are present, a given price increase will involve greater deadweight costs than in the conventional case. In the case of direct network externalities, if the monopolist raises the price of access, then some consumers will no longer purchase access, creating the usual deadweight loss. In addition, however, the benefits of those remaining on the network are also reduced, since the magnitude of the benefits from the network externality is reduced. In indirect networks, a hardware price increase not only deters some consumers who would have purchased hardware, but by reducing demand for complementary software, it reduces the variety and increases the price of complementary network products.[26]

Second, since network industries are "tippy," an initial head start provided by intellectual property protection can become permanent. A firm that is able to establish a standard first, before rivals enter, is likely to keep the advantage for a long time. The installed base of users built up during the honeymoon period provides a powerful motive for future users to stick with the innovator, particularly if the latter is able to restrict compatibility with its standard.

Third, network effects may also expand the horizontal scope of patent or copyright protection. Even if a new product is as equally functional as the existing, patent-protected one, users may be reluctant to buy the new product, because they value compatibility with the installed base of existing users and files. Thus, the effective scope of the patent might cover a whole market, even if the ostensible scope covers only a narrowly defined product. The *Lotus v. Borland* case – where Borland found it necessary to offer "Lotus compatibility" for their Quattro Pro spreadsheet, prompting Lotus to sue for copyright infringement – is an example of this issue.

Fourth, the dynamic innovation framework is usually critical in network industries, since they are invariably research intensive, technologically progressive industries. If the process of innovation entails successive generations of innovations building upon each other, then network effects can provide a first-mover advantage, bolstered by intellectual property rights, which may well inhibit subsequent innovation. Moreover, the incentives to the winner of an innovation race may be inefficiently large when the winner can feel confident that product market competition from runners-up will be minimal.[27]

Fifth, intellectual property rights for interfaces can provide significant rewards for essentially no social benefit when the choice of the interface is essentially arbitrary and, *ex ante*, there are numerous alternatives that are all essentially equivalent. *Ex post* de facto standardization, however, means that intellectual property rights provide considerable protection and market power for the chosen interface.

Finally, overly strong intellectual property protection can retard industry-wide, cooperative standards setting.[28] As a result, firms whose technology is well protected are either less willing to allow their technology to be part of a common standard or require a greater reward from participating in the common standard. Moreover, to the extent that their technology is protected by patents or copyright, firms have more to gain if their technology is incorporated in the standard.

In summary, network externalities create a bias toward monopoly in the standard monopoly-incentives trade-off on which intellectual property rights policy is based. Monopoly prices are more costly, and monopolies are less likely to be replaced quickly through the workings of competition. All of this provides a case for weakening the scope of intellectual property rights for products where network effects are important. First, less of such protection is desirable; and second, any given "amount" of protection is likely to result in greater long-run market power.

These special properties of network industries have implications for the appropriate type of intellectual property protection. The arguments amount to a case for weaker intellectual property protection in network industries, because of the tendency for dominant standards to develop and be exploited. We now want to review how the current instruments of protection measure up against this conclusion.

It has become common place among legal scholars to claim that patents confer more market power than copyright.[29] If so, a simple prescription would be to allocate copyright protection in network industries and patent protection elsewhere in the economy. The early denial of patent eligibility for software combined with the CONTU (National Commission on New Technological Uses of Copyrighted Works) initiative, are in fact consistent with this prescription.

However, the conclusion that patents confer more market power than copyrights is at best only partially true, and is dangerously misleading when applied to network industries. For any given product, the creator would in most cases prefer patent protection to copyright. A patent has a broader scope: it protects not only the unique form of expression created by the inventor, but also other forms that embody the inventor's idea. Also, a copyrighted invention can be legally recreated, provided no copying occurs, which is not true of a patented invention. Finally, the longer life of a copyright is economically redundant in most cases: most new products have exhausted their ability to earn supracompetitive returns before the end of a patent term, which puts the two forms of protection on an equal footing as far as the effective duration of protection.

Rather than looking at the *ex post* market power conferred on a given innovation, a more appropriate question is what form of intellectual property right will give the right kind of protection *ex ante* to a particular industry. And, "the right kind of protection" must be judged in terms of the length, scope, and the overall effect on efficient innovation and competitive market structure. In network industries, judged in these terms, copyright protection does particularly badly. Copyright protection rewards idiosyncratic expression, but eschews the useful and the functional. Recall that patents can protect the application of an idea, but copyright can protect only its expression. In network industries, it is often the precise expression that confers market power. Where there is a de facto standard or interface, either with a vertically related product or with consumers themselves, then compatibility with that standard may be vital for entry and competition in the market. Thus, both in *Nintendo*, and in *Lotus v. Borland*, copyright protection (would have) conferred a disproportionate degree of market power. By contrast, such interfaces would often fail to meet the *new, useful, and non-obvious* test for patent protection.

Finally, because there is no "novelty" requirement, the process of incremental development can be handicapped by a morass of copyrights with little useful purpose. Thus, perversely, copyright protection is likely to be stronger than patent protection in network industries, especially where it is directed at products where the gains from protection are minimal and the costs substantial.

It has been argued that this perversity inherent in copyright can be rescued by the *merger doctrine* (see Warren-Boulton, Baseman, and Woroch, 1995*a* and 1995*b*). The merger doctrine in copyright law exempts from copyright protection those creations that are deemed to be the unique expression of an idea. Its proponents argue that it will be applied precisely in the cases where there are interfaces and de facto standards. There does not seem to be much jurisprudence to support this contention, however. Indeed, a more likely interpretation is that before an interface exists, it could be expressed in many forms, perhaps an infinite number. So the actual, arbitrary expression of an interface is anything but the unique expression of an idea (a connector plug could be round or square or any other shape, for example, as long as the two halves are reverse images of each other).[30]

We argued above that network industries probably deserve weaker intellectual property protection than non-network industries. Since copyright protection has been very much at the forefront of U.S. jurisprudence, the tendency of recent court decisions to draw back the applicable areas of copyright in computer software is a change in direction we and other commentators believe is appropriate. A more ambitious task is to assess whether the increasing role played by patents will work well or whether a new *hybrid* form of protection should be considered, at least for the software industry, since it would be very difficult to create a network property right with broad applications. Proposals for hybrid protection typically suggest automatic anticloning protection plus compulsory licensing of the innovation to other developers after a relatively short period.[31] In the next section we use a case study of computer software in the United States to illustrate that existing types of intellectual property rights are ill-suited for network industries. In particular, we show the difficulties of creating an appropriate balance between *ex post* efficiency and *ex ante* incentives using conventional forms of intellectual property rights.

THE ROLE OF INTELLECTUAL PROPERTY RIGHTS IN A CRITICAL NETWORK INDUSTRY: A CASE STUDY OF COMPUTER SOFTWARE

THE COMPUTER INDUSTRY IS A GOOD EXAMPLE of a dynamic industry with complex network attributes and a major impact on the economy as a whole. The computer industry is usually divided into hardware and software: hardware refers to the physical components, including the computer's central processor and input-output devices. Software refers to the programs that are executed by the computer, which can consist of applications that are further developed by users with their own files, like word processing or spreadsheet software, or dedicated applications like games or programs that destroy viruses. The network effects are both direct and indirect. The direct effects stem from the value to computer users in exchanging files: examples are accounting firms that exchange spreadsheet files with clients and benefit greatly the more clients use the same (or at least file compatible) software; writers and academics who want to ship papers and articles to each other over the Internet in the same file format; and high school students who want to be able to take their computer games to a friend's house and operate them on the friend's machine. The indirect network externalities arise because the larger are the number of users of a given hardware system, the larger will be the market for software, and hence the more software varieties will be available at a lower price.

Intellectual property protection plays an important role in the computer industry. In the hardware industry it is the conventional one of encouraging innovation. Software, because it consists fundamentally of code, or language, appears at first sight to be analogous to a literary medium, and hence amenable to the forms and objectives of copyright protection. In particular, it is important to protect against literal copying or *cloning* of code. However, a deeper analysis indicates that for many cases, the distinction between hardware and software can be spurious: a piece of computer hardware runs a program of electronic instructions just as does a program that runs on that hardware. In both cases, the element of novelty is in the list of instructions itself, and not whether it is hardwired or encoded and stored on a disk.

Moreover, software has a functional purpose. This means that difficulties are going to arise over the extent of permissible non-literal copying, namely, what is expression and what is function. Protection against non-literal copying that is too broad will result in unintended protection of function.

COPYRIGHT AND TRADE SECRET PROTECTION FOR COMPUTER SOFTWARE

IN THE EARLY DAYS OF SOFTWARE, it was thought that trade secret law provided protection.[32] Trade secret law protects technology that companies attempt to keep secret. An infringement of a trade secret requires some element of "breach of trust." Simple observation by a rival (e.g., through an unrestricted licensing agreement) or even reverse engineering of a software product has not been considered a violation of trade secrets by the courts (see Gilburne and Johnston, 1982, note 127, pp. 233-37). It was argued that since object code is unreadable by humans, the secret could remain intact even after the software had been distributed. In addition, to further emphasize the point that these secrets were not sold or provided to others, lawyers for software companies created the shrinkwrap license concept: software was being licensed rather than sold to customers. The license contained provisions that required customers to keep the software confidential.[33] The effectiveness of trade secret protection is limited by the difficulty of monitoring. Given that there is no registration of trade secrets, enforcement through an infringement suit can be costly and unrewarding. Moreover, within a few years of a new software program being marketed, the requirement of secrecy by the plaintiff may be increasingly hard to sustain.

The development of extensive copyright protection for computer programs and software began in 1978 with the CONTU report, which recommended that "full copyright protection" be extended to all forms of computer software. The U.S. Congress implemented these recommendations in amendments to federal copyright law enacted in 1980. The scope of copyright protection for computer programs has evolved dramatically in the courts in the nearly 20 years since CONTU. We will discuss these developments in some detail.

We begin by describing some of the basic features of copyright protection. First, neither registration nor examination is usually required for a copyright to be established; thus, there is no monitoring or scrutiny of copyright until there is a court challenge. Second, copyright protection extends for a much longer period than other forms of protection, including patents. Under both the 1976 U.S. *Copyright Act* and the Canadian *Copyright Act*, protection extends for the owner's lifetime plus 50 years (75 years for entities). Third, there is no requirement that a creation be *non-obvious*, or useful, or that it should represent a significant discrete step in the state of the art. In fact, the more useful a copyrighted product is, the weaker its degree of protection may be.

What is striking about the recent U.S. jurisprudence on software copyright cases is that the courts have struggled steadily to mold an unwieldy instrument in the service of economic efficiency, in some cases stretching the legal boundaries of copyright protection as well as making creative interpretations of the law. We will first describe the early case law on software copyright, which set a broad standard of protection, and then discuss the areas in which the courts have drawn back the scope of protection. In each case we will respond to an issue that has particular consequences for network industries.

The Path to *Whelan* and the High-Water Mark of Copyright Protection for Software

From the beginning, the courts have struggled with the problem of the literal expression of a piece of software, which is presumably its code, versus the intended effect, which is the functions a user is able to perform and the appearance of these functions on a computer monitor. Just as a book can be effectively copied by changing a few words, a software program can be copied by writing a few lines of code differently. Unlike the case of books, two computer programs can appear identical to the user, even though some of the code may be different. Despite these difficulties, the courts affirmed the copyrightability of source code, object code, microcode, applications programs, and operating systems. In each case, courts found the literal elements of computer programs copyrightable only over vigorous opposition. By the mid-1980s the courts had reached a consensus that computer programs themselves were "literary works" that could not be literally copied, and that on-screen outputs of a program were "audiovisual works" that could not be literally copied.

The courts then turned to non-literal infringement. Copyright law was developed originally to counteract the unauthorized printing of books. Much of the poor fit with computer software that has been debated in the law and economics literature stems from the literary origins of copyright law. The problem that has arisen continually has to do with the relationship between idea and expression, the latter being protected while the former is not. Computer programs, unlike literary works, are utilitarian and functional, and small changes in expression are trivial and incidental to the utilitarian purpose. Courts must therefore identify and protect the incidental material, while leaving the functional aspects of the program free to be duplicated (unless they are protected under some other medium, for example, through patents). Most courts have drawn in some way from the seminal application of copyright law to a functional product, the hundred-year-old case of *Baker v. Selden*.[34] Selden had created a method of double-entry accounting and published books of tables for users to follow the method. The Supreme Court held that while the book was copyrightable expression, the idea behind the accounting method was not.

The high-water mark for the scope of copyright protection for software was *Whelan*[35] in 1986, in which the Third Circuit set back the cause of economic efficiency by protecting nearly all elements of a computer program against non-literal infringement. The case concerned a custom software program for dental record keeping. The client developed a substantially similar program of their own, which they began marketing, leading to the suit. The Court adopted a very broad notion of the "idea" behind the software: namely, the efficient management of a dental laboratory. Given that the purpose of the program was the idea, all the details of the program to implement the idea, such as its logical structure, sequence, and organization, became protected expression.

An application of the ruling in *Whelan* that was important for a later case was *Lotus v. Paperback*.[36] Paperback began to market an essentially identical version of the Lotus 1-2-3 spreadsheet program, with some lines of code changed. The Court found in favour of Lotus, citing the *Whelan* case.

Altai: The Courts Begin to Retreat From Copyright Protection for Functional Aspects of Software

The *Altai*[37] case in 1992 was a landmark in the evolution of copyright protection of computer software. The Court in *Altai* devised a procedure that has become known as "abstraction-filtration-comparison." In very basic terms, the idea is that the court must first analyse the program into its abstract logical structure, and then "filter" out unpredictable idea components at each level of the hierarchy of abstraction, starting from basic code and moving up to subroutines, software modules, and so on. Very significantly, the Court also identified other factors deemed to be unpredictable. First, elements of the program dictated by efficiency were considered unpredictable, because they effectively merge idea and expression.[38] Second, the Court removed from protection elements of the program that were standard or dictated by external factors.

Once the unpredictable elements had been filtered out, what remains is "a core of protectable expression."[39] *Altai* is generally interpreted as narrowing considerably the scope of copyright protection. In the *Altai* case itself, the Second Circuit affirmed that the program in dispute "effectively contained no protectable expression whatsoever."[40] The approach devised by the *Altai* Court has obtained widespread acceptance and has been cited by courts in Canadian cases.[41]

Although *Altai* created a consensus framework for the courts to work with, before long problems with abstraction-filtration-comparison began to surface. An obvious problem is the immense technical demands placed on judges to understand the construction of software programs at a very advanced level. Even to a sophisticated observer, the abstraction-filtration-comparison process may not in fact lead to a unique conclusion for any given piece of software. The

Lotus v. Borland[42] case uncovered another problem with *Altai*: its approach of paring down to a base of copyrightable material obscures the problem of whether some software elements should be copyrightable at all. Borland included an option of the Lotus 1-2-3 menu hierarchy in its Quattro Pro spreadsheet, without using any of Lotus's code to create it. Lotus sued for copyright infringement. The District Court found for Lotus, concluding that since it was possible to "generate literally millions of satisfactory menu trees" and command hierarchies, the menu hierarchy in Lotus was arbitrary expression and thus subject to protection.[43] The First Circuit reversed, holding that the Lotus menu structure was a "method of operation" which, under section 102(b) of the *Copyright Act*, cannot be protected since it is functional. The case was appealed to the U.S. Supreme Court, but in January 1996 the Court deadlocked, so the decision of the First Circuit stands. It has been argued that copyright simply does not extend to the "certain results" (a phrase from the *Copyright Act*) of a computer program. In other words, what a program does, rather than the code itself, is not protected (Karjala and Menell, 1995). Hence, any functional aspect of the program is certainly not protected.

In *Apple v. Microsoft*,[44] at issue was the graphical user interface Apple had developed for its Lisa and Macintosh computers. Apple charged that Microsoft's Windows program infringed on Apple's copyrights, mainly for the "look and feel" of the program to the user (the use of screen icons, etc.). The many suits of this campaign were complicated by the existence of licensing arrangements between the two parties. By the end of the series of suits, the courts had found that virtually no elements of Apple's graphical user interface were held to be protectable. In its reasons the Court argued that the exclusionary criteria of merger, functionality, and originality effectively excluded the graphical interface from protection.

Reverse Engineering Does Not Infringe Copyright

Some system sponsors have attempted to use copyright protection to restrict access to interfaces. Specifically, they have embedded interface information required for compatibility or interoperability in software programs that are (validly) protected by copyright. The sponsors then claim infringement when the interface information is uncovered through reverse engineering or decompilation of the copyrighted software program. Software must be reverse engineered into human-readable object code because it is distributed only in machine-readable source code. In the *Nintendo*[45] and *Sega*[46] cases, holders of valid copyrights alleged that the process of reverse engineering produces "a human-readable adaption of the object code and a virtual reproduction of the original source-code version of the program" (McMannis, 1993, p. 44) and thus constitutes infringement.

Nintendo and Sega attempted to lock out unauthorized video games, produced by independent game suppliers, using property rights on the interface between game cartridges (software) and game consoles (hardware). Atari (Nintendo) and Accolade (Sega), aspiring video-game manufacturers, engaged in reverse engineering in order to derive the source code of the lock-out programs. Nintendo and Sega both were successful at the district level in winning copyright infringement claims. However, these judgments were both reversed on appeal, the Courts holding that reverse engineering in these instances was fair use under section 107 of the *Copyright Act*, and thus any copying of the source code in the process did not constitute infringement. The *Nintendo* and *Sega* cases established that reverse engineering that was necessary to achieve compatibility is fair use.[47] The Court in *Nintendo* observed that "An author cannot acquire patent-like protection by putting an idea, process, or method of operation in an unintelligible format and asserting copyright infringement against those who try to understand that idea, process, or method of operation."[48] Intermediate copying necessary to understand unprotected functional elements is fair use, since it is for the purpose of research. This was reaffirmed in *DSC Communications Corp. v. DGI Technologies Inc.*,[49] where a District Court found that reverse engineering of firmware in a microprocessor in order to design a competing compatible microprocessor was fair use.[50]

Applying an Antitrust Standard to Copyright Protection: The Misuse Doctrine

The misuse doctrine, developed first in patent law and more recently in copyright cases, is interesting for our main thesis that antitrust interventions should be used to *fine tune* the role of intellectual property rights in network industries. In a partial sense, this is how misuse operates. A defendant in an infringement suit can claim that the holder of the intellectual property right is misusing the property right if they are engaging in conduct that violates an antitrust standard of lessening competition. The most common forms of such misuse are tying arrangements and refusals to license. If the court finds in favour of the defendant, the property right is usually suspended until the plaintiff ceases the misuse.

The doctrine was first established with patents in the case of *Morton Salt*.[51] Morton Salt held a patent to a device for inserting salt into canned food. However, the company tied the sale of this device to the purchase of salt tablets. The U.S. Supreme Court not only dismissed an infringement suit, but broadly chastised the plaintiff for misusing the property right granted to it in the interests of public policy.

The first major application of misuse to copyright did not occur until 1990. Although not yet endorsed by the Supreme Court, the Fourth Circuit's decision in *Lasercomb America Inc. v. Reynolds*[52] effectively opened the gates for a flood of misuse defences in copyright infringement cases. Lasercomb held copyrights to CAD/CAM software in steel die making. In its license agreements, Lasercomb required that licensees refrain from developing competing software for a period of 99 years. Holiday Steel first made unauthorized copies of the Lasercomb software, then developed and marketed its own almost identical software program. Lasercomb sued for infringement, leading to the misuse defence. In its ruling for the defence, the Court found that "a misuse of copyright defence is inherent in the law of copyright just as a misuse of patent defence is inherent in patent law."[53]

A valid question arising in misuse cases is what standard the court should apply in judging misuse. Since the property right was conferred to grant a degree of market power, however small, it cannot be sufficient for an infringement defendant to claim that the plaintiff has market power. Although the U.S. courts have not been altogether clear on this point, two schools of thought may be identified.[54] The traditional approach takes a punitive attitude to any apparently restrictive licensing arrangements operated by the intellectual property right holder. The second approach is to judge a finding of misuse by the criteria of the antitrust statutes. In logic it is perhaps difficult (especially to economists) to see what other approach might be taken. As Judge Poser put it, "If misuse claims are not tested by conventional antitrust principles, by what principle shall they be tested? Our law is not rich in alternative concepts of monopolistic abuse; and it is rather late in the day to try to develop one."[55] The 1988 U.S. *Patent Misuse Reform Act* encoded, for patents at least, the use of an antitrust standard in judging misuse cases.

A logical inconsistency lies at the heart of the misuse doctrine that has implications for its application to network industries, and particularly to software (Paredes, 1994, develops this idea in detail). The holder of the intellectual property right is penalized for an abuse of market power, associated, but not necessarily coinciding, with the intellectual property right itself. But the remedy, even based on an antitrust evaluation, is not to correct the abuse of market power directly, but to "take back" the intellectual property right, if only temporarily. If the latter has been legitimately awarded, then a misallocation of resources will result: a policy instrument is being applied to the wrong target. The best illustration of this inconsistency occurs in tying cases, which form a substantial proportion of the misuse defences in computer software. From late 1990 to 1994 six copyright misuse cases were heard involving tie-in licensing arrangements.[56] *PRC Realty Systems* illustrates the point. The plaintiff designed a software package to download real estate listings from a national database. The package was licensed to the defendant, NAR, who also agreed to use their "best efforts" to persuade member realtors to purchase printed books of listings from PRC. The Fourth Circuit accepted misuse by PRC of its copyright, in that the "best efforts" provision constituted a tie with an unprotected market. As a result the Court suspended PRC's copyright until it ceased its tied licensing provisions.

The logical approach to the finding of an antitrust violation is to correct it directly, not to nullify a perfectly valid copyright in order to achieve a distinct antitrust objective. In the case of a tie to a copyrighted product, the court should simply outlaw the tie, with appropriate damages, rather than take back the copyright, when its existence may have served a useful purpose in fostering the innovation. Thus, misuse should not be allowed as a defence in an infringement case with tying: rather, the defendant should be encouraged to countersue on antitrust grounds.

In some cases the patent or copyright is itself the instrument of market power (i.e., there is no anticompetitive tying arrangement), and here the application of the misuse doctrine using the antitrust standard is also appropriate. A good example is *Data General v. Grumman*[57] (reviewed in detail in "Predatory Product Innovation," below). Data General held an undisputed copyright of a diagnostic program, but refused to license it to a small service company, Grumman. Though Grumman's claim that the refusal to license amounted to monopolization under section 2 of the *Sherman Act* was unsuccessful, the Court was willing to consider that it could have been.

SOFTWARE PATENTS TO THE RESCUE?

THE MOST IMPORTANT NEW DEVELOPMENT in intellectual property protection for computer software is the broad acceptance of patent protection. Patent protection was not thought to be available for software until recently. U.S. court decisions ruled that patent protection could not be applied to mental processes,[58] scientific principles,[59] laws of nature,[60] or mathematical algorithms.[61] The Supreme Court in *Gottschalk v. Benson*[62] ruled that a computer program was a mathematical algorithm and therefore not protected.

While some earlier cases had suggested that software was patentable under certain limited conditions,[63] two recent landmark cases, *Alappat*[64] and *Beauregard*,[65] have completely redefined the possibilities for patenting software. The crux of *Alappat* centred on whether software by itself could be considered a "machine" and therefore eligible for patent protection. Alappat invented a rasterising routine that could be embodied either in software or hardwired into a computer. The U.S. Patent and Trademark Office (USPTO) granted a patent for the latter embodiment but not the former. From scientific and economic points of view this is clearly absurd: both media carry out the function of the invention efficiently and are functionally identical. If one is patentable, then so is the other. The Court of Appeals for the Federal Circuit reversed the USPTO's earlier decision and affirmed patents for all forms of the invention.

The *Alappat* Court developed a two-step procedure for evaluating patent claims in software. The first step is to classify the claim as to whether it is directed to a "process," "machine," "manufacture," or "composition of matter."

The second step is to identify whether the claimed subject matter is useful or provides utility.

In *Beauregard*, the USPTO once again permitted a patent for a program running on a computer. However, IBM also filed an application to patent the same program when stored on a disk. IBM's motives had to do with the difficulty of suing for infringement when only the running program is patented. IBM claimed that the software on a disk was an "article of manufacture," which was an allowed category. The USPTO rejected this claim, citing the "printed matter" exception.[66] However, in the face of considerable industry support for IBM, the USPTO dropped their opposition to IBM's appeal (Laurenson, 1995, p. 816). The Court of Appeals for the Federal Circuit subsequently issued a precedential order requiring that the USPTO accept that the printed matter exception does not apply to the storage of general purpose software on a computer storage medium. Clearly, the printed matter of a computer program is *functional*.

In light of *Beauregard, Alappat,* and other similar cases, the USPTO was forced in June of 1995 to propose new guidelines for patenting software. The new USPTO *Guidelines for the Patentability of Computer Related Inventions* codified the two-step test set forth in *Alappat*. In the first stage the claim is classified as to whether it is statutory or not, in other words, whether it is "process," "machine," "manufacture," or "composition of matter." In the second step, the claim is assessed to see if it is a non-statutory product (information or a natural phenomena) or a non-statutory process (manipulates abstract ideas or solves a purely mathematical problem).

The consensus is that software is now patentable. In theory, at least, there is now a nice complementarity between patent and copyright protection for software. Title 35 of the *Patent Act* appears to provide protection for the method of operation of a computer program. Copyrights, which, under section 102(b) of the *Copyright Act*, explicitly exclude the protection of the method of operation will protect the expression of that method of operation. As Lemley (1995) argues persuasively, it is not just that the courts have been overprotecting software with copyrights for some time, but also that they have been granting protection to the ideas inherent in software programs, contrary to the spirit of the *Copyright Act*, because no other form of protection was available. As Lemley argues, "Much of what has been considered the copyrightable 'structure, sequence and organization' of a computer program will become a mere incident to the patentable idea of the program or of one of its potentially patentable subroutines" (Lemley, 1995, pp. 26-27).

The open question concerning patents for software is, will they provide an appropriate form of protection? First, critics have suggested that too many substitute avenues exist for any given set of results in computer software, so that once a general method is known, patents will not adequately protect the innovator. The opposing concern is that if the USPTO awards patents for *any* method of achieving a given result, then protection will be too broad and will slow subsequent innovation (see the discussion of this issue in Samuelson, Davis, Kapor, and Reichman, 1994).

Second, a key feature of patents is that applications are scrutinized by the respective patent offices in the United States and in Canada, to see if the new invention meets the criteria that it is *new, useful, and non-obvious*. One objection that has been raised to extensive patenting of software is the difficulty of evaluating prior art. That is, in order to meet the requirements of being new, useful, and non-obvious, the patent examiner must have a clear sense of what has gone before and what new contribution the current application makes. The problem is there is a two-decade gap in patent records, corresponding to the period in which software patents were not awarded.

In providing comments on the proposed (now adopted) USPTO Guidelines, the staff of the Federal Trade Commission (FTC) expressed concern that reducing the subject matter test placed more emphasis on the novelty and non-obviousness tests to identify software deserving a patent. The staff noted that there are difficulties in identifying prior art due to incomplete information on what existing art is, primarily because a historic reliance on copyright and trade secrets means that information has not been accumulated.[67] A good example of the difficulties is the *Compton's* case, where a patent was granted covering all multimedia CD-ROM applications, then reviewed and withdrawn.[68]

Third, critics of an increased role for patents in protecting software have emphasized primarily that software innovations are incremental: that is, they build in small steps on the body of innovation that has gone before. The goals of the patent system emphasize, by contrast, granting monopoly property rights only to innovations that represent substantial improvements over the prior art. The result may be a bad match with, for example, important but small innovations going unprotected (and thus less likely to be created).

Finally, the staff of the FTC have expressed concern that overbroad patenting of software may inhibit innovation.[69] This is a "second order" argument about patenting. The usual model, of course, suggests that greater protection will increase the incentives for innovation because of the monopoly rents created by the patent property right. But if each innovation builds on the work of prior innovations, the more expensive and less widely available are those prior innovations, then *ceteris paribus*, the more costly and difficult to achieve will be the current generation of innovations (see Scotchmer, 1991).

ANTITRUST ISSUES RAISED BY INTELLECTUAL PROPERTY RIGHTS IN NETWORK INDUSTRIES

IN THIS SECTION WE CONSIDER THE ROLE THAT ANTITRUST CAN PLAY in recalibrating intellectual property rights in network industries. We argue that in certain instances, antitrust can be a practical second-best remedy to the problem of inappropriately strong intellectual property rights. In fact, given the political-economy difficulties associated with the creation of new forms of intellectual property protection for network industries, the use of antitrust to engage in *ex post* fine-tuning may in fact be second-best optimal. By fine tuning, we mean that antitrust can be used to adjust the balance between incentives for innovation and efficient diffusion. In this section, we will identify types of behaviour engaged in by the holders of intellectual property rights that are potentially *ex post* inefficient. Given the tendency identified above for intellectual property protection to be excessive in network industries, we argue that antitrust enforcement can be an institutional response to improve efficiency *ex post*. This means that antitrust can be used to circumscribe the scope of intellectual property rights, by imposing obligations on holders of intellectual property right or imposing constraints on the exercise of intellectual property rights or both. In essence, our argument is that antitrust authorities should be *less* concerned with the potential impact of antitrust enforcement on incentives for innovation in network industries than they might be in other industries.

We consider two different situations where the otherwise legitimate exercise of intellectual property rights raise antitrust concerns in network industries. The first involves using intellectual property rights to prevent access by competitors to an installed base of a dominant technology. The second involves using intellectual property rights to exclude suppliers of complementary products.

ACCESS AND INTELLECTUAL PROPERTY RIGHTS

THE FIRST SET OF CIRCUMSTANCES where antitrust has a legitimate role to play in curtailing intellectual property rights arises when a firm uses its intellectual property rights to restrict or eliminate access by rival suppliers to their installed base. Variants of these cases have shown up in three different forms: a) refusal to license (both installed bases and interface standards), b) vertical merger and foreclosure, and c) horizontal merger. We consider each in turn.

Refusal to License

Abusive behaviour on the part of a dominant firm to exclude competitors and reduce intrasystem competition by using intellectual property rights to curtail or deny access to its installed base can take two forms. The firm can either refuse to license its complementary products or it can refuse to license its interface, which allows rival firms access to its network. The refusal to license is enforced by vigilant enforcement of intellectual property rights in either the complementary goods or the interface. Representative cases involving refusals to license complementary products and copyright infringement include *Magill* and numerous cases involving telephone directories.[70] *Lotus v. Borland* is a leading case where a firm with proprietary rights in an interface exerted those rights to deny entry by a competitor.[71]

Refusal to License a Complementary Product

Magill involved the licensing of weekly television listings in Ireland and Northern Ireland. Prior to entry by Magill, the four broadcasters had reserved for themselves the right to publish comprehensive weekly listings of their program schedule. The program listings of the broadcasters enjoyed copyright protection as literary works and compilations under both Irish and British copyright legislation. The BBC and RTE[72] each published weekly listings for their two channels, while the weekly listings for the two independent British channels were licensed on an exclusive basis to the *TV Times*. As a result, consumers interested in knowing the weekly schedules for the six available television channels in advance were forced to purchase *three* different TV guides. The four broadcasters made their weekly listings available to third parties, but reproduction rights were only granted under very restrictive licenses that limited the extent of duplication.[73] Initially *Magill TV Guide* followed the licensing terms and produced a guide containing weekend listings and highlights of the upcoming week. Subsequently it began publishing comprehensive weekly listings for all four broadcasters. While the Irish High Court upheld an injunction on copyright violation, the European Commission found that the refusal to license amounted to abuse of dominant position and ordered the four broadcasters to make their listings available to third parties on nondiscriminatory terms. Subsequent appeals to the EC Court of First Instance (CFI) and the European Court of Justice affirmed the European Commission's ruling.

The listings for each broadcaster can be interpreted as a complementary product. By refusing to license, the four broadcasters were restricting access to their complementary product. The new entrant (Magill) was attempting to produce a hardware product (its TV guide) that was compatible with the complementary products supplied for its three competitors. The European Commission and the CFI held that the refusal to license copyrighted material was abusive and that in such circumstances if mandatory licensing was the only means of redress, it was an appropriate remedy. The broadcasters' dominant position followed from the fact that they were the only suppliers of the information (raw materials) required to produce a TV guide. Their refusal to license was abusive because it a) eliminated the emergence of a new and useful product – comprehensive weekly listings, and b) maintained their monopoly in weekly listings. The lesson of the *Magill* decisions is that refusal by a dominant firm to license intellectual property rights can constitute abuse of dominant position and such an antitrust violation in the EC can result in compulsory licensing.[74]

Similar issues have arisen involving copyright and monopolization in the market for telephone directories in Canada and the United States. In the United States, the courts have denied that telephone directories are copyrightable. In Canada, the onus on the telephone companies to provide listing information has been determined in the regulatory arena.

Feist attempted to enter the market for telephone directories in northwest Kansas by licensing white page listings from the incumbent, Rural Telephone. When the two companies were unable to reach an agreement, Feist entered by simply copying Rural's listings. Rural sued Feist for copyright infringement; Feist responded by bringing suit against Rural for illegal monopolization under section 2 of the *Sherman Act*. The copyright infringement suit reached the Supreme Court of the United States.[75] Both the District and Appeals Courts held that Feist had infringed Rural's copyright. However, the Supreme Court reversed, holding that facts are not copyrightable and neither is a collection of facts. Compilations are copyrightable, provided there is some minimal level of originality or creativity. The Court determined that the presentation of the listings in the white pages was insufficiently creative and original to merit copyright protection.[76] Similarly, in *Bellsouth Advertising & Publishing Corp. v. Donnelly Information Publishing Inc.*,[77] the Court held that Bellsouth's yellow pages, though clearly compilations, were not copyrightable on two counts: a) the organization was insufficiently original since their organization and format were similar to other yellow page directories, and b) since the number of alternative means to organize yellow page listings is limited, the merger doctrine applies.[78]

At the same time, Feist was successful at the district level court in showing that Rural's refusal to deal amounted to illegal monopolization.[79] The District Court based its determination on Rural Telephone's monopoly power in the market for yellow page advertising and the anticompetitive intent of the refusal to deal. Rural was ordered to license its white page listings to Feist at a *reasonable rate*.

Feist alleged that without comprehensive white page listings, yellow page advertisers would be reluctant to place ads in Feist's directory. Incomplete white page listings would limit the usefulness of Feist's directories to consumers, and as a result, consumers would prefer Rural's complete directories. Since consumers would prefer to access a single directory, advertisers would prefer Rural's directory and not Feist's. In network terms, the number of listings can be viewed as the installed base of complementary products. Rural, by refusing to license, excluded Feist from its installed base.

Rural's conviction was overturned on appeal.[80] The Appeal Court held that there was insufficient evidence on the record to establish that Rural's refusal to license harmed competition.[81] Feist did not provide any empirical evidence that Rural's refusal to license had limited the attractiveness of its directories to either consumers or advertisers. Of course, since Feist had copied Rural's listing, its directories were in fact complete, and it is not surprising that the evidence the Court sought was not forthcoming. The Court needed to consider the counterfactual of what would have happened if Feist's listings had in fact been incomplete. More importantly, the Court did acknowledge that under a rule of reason, a monopolist could run into antitrust difficulties if it refused to license copyrighted materials.

In Canada, the issue of the availability of telephone listings in machine-readable form has been addressed in the regulatory arena. The CRTC initially determined that Bell Canada had to make only its non-residential listings available, and then only in their entirety.[82] The CRTC ruled that privacy considerations mitigated against the release of residential listings, and that geographic unbundling of the non-residential listings could infringe Bell's copyright.

It soon became apparent that the terms and conditions of the tariff established were significant entry barriers. After a request to review and vary its original positions, in Telecom Decision 95-3 the CRTC substantially reversed its earlier stance. Along with ordering rate reductions, the CRTC ordered Bell Canada and other telephone companies under its jurisdiction to make both their residential and non-residential listings available in machine-readable form at the level of the local exchange. The telephone companies agreed to unbundle, but did not give up their copyright. However, the CRTC also instituted a deletion mechanism. Residential subscribers could phone a 1-800 number and opt out of having their listing provided to any third parties such as telemarketers and independent directories, though their listing is still included in the directory of the telephone companies. When an appeal to the CRTC by the independent publishers of directories was unsuccessful, they successfully appealed to the Federal government.[83]

Intellectual Property Protection of Interfaces

In *Lotus v. Borland*, Lotus brought a copyright infringement suit against Borland for including an emulation mode and key reader when it introduced its Quattro Pro spreadsheet. The emulation mode replaced Quattro Pro's hierarchy of menu commands with that of Lotus 1-2-3. The key reader allowed Quattro Pro users to run macros written for Lotus 1-2-3. The inclusion of the emulation mode, the key reader, and the ability to read Lotus 1-2-3 files ensured compatibility between Quattro Pro and the Lotus 1-2-3 network.[84] Borland did not copy any of the code comprising Lotus 1-2-3, just the words and menu command hierarchy.

The District Court accepted that the menu and command hierarchy in Lotus 1-2-3 was copyrightable expression. It did so on the basis that "it is possible to generate literally millions of satisfactory menu trees by varying the menu commands employed."[85] Borland appealed, and the First Circuit ruled that since the menu of commands was in fact a "method of operation," it was not copyrightable. Lotus appealed to the Supreme Court. The Supreme Court split evenly when one justice recused himself, thus the First Circuit's decision stands.[86]

Economics of Refusals to Deal

In the examples considered above, it is clear that the extent of intellectual property protection required recalibration by antitrust enforcement or other means. In both the *Magill* and *Lotus* cases, intellectual property rights had the effect of preventing new entrants from entering the market with differentiated products that were arguably of higher quality. The use of intellectual property rights to block access to the incumbent's installed base not only involves static welfare losses by preventing competition, it also reduces competition in innovation markets by reducing incentives for entrants to innovate and produce differentiated but compatible products. The *Lotus* case is an excellent example of intellectual property rights interacting with network externalities to create a de facto standard and considerable market power, despite the fact that the interface is essentially arbitrary and numerous equivalent alternatives existed *ex ante*. Similarly, in both the directory cases and *Magill*, little or no innovation expense and effort was required to produce the complementary products.

The use of intellectual property rights to restrict access to an installed base by an incumbent can be inefficient *ex post* (see the formal analysis of Katz and Shapiro, 1992; Farrell and Saloner, 1992). Katz and Shapiro demonstrate in a simplified model that when an entrant can only enter profitably if its lower cost (but homogenous) product is compatible, then an incumbent with strong property rights will reduce welfare by blocking entry. Antitrust enforcement to ensure compatibility can be welfare improving.

Farrell and Saloner consider the incentives of a dominant firm to affect the cost of compatibility between it and a rival technology with a smaller installed base. They show that the dominant firm has an incentive to increase the cost of compatibility. Costs of compatibility can be raised through product design and specifications, diligent intellectual property rights enforcement or changing product specifications. Moreover, increases in the cost of compatibility can reduce welfare when they contribute to excessive intersystem or network competition that reduces the extent to which the benefits from network externalities are realized.

In essence, our argument is that there are instances where access to the installed base of an incumbent is an "essential facility." Without access to the installed base, entry by competing suppliers is not feasible. The leading essential facility case is *MCI Communications Corp. v. AT&T*.[87] As set forth in *MCI*, the essential facility doctrine consists of four elements: a) control by a monopolist of a facility or resource serving the monopolist's market, b) the inability of an entrant to practically or reasonably duplicate the facility, c) the denial of the use of the facility to a competitor or entrant, and d) the feasibility of providing access to entrants.[88]

The antitrust remedy for mandating access to an installed base would typically impose the burden of compulsory licensing on the incumbent. The usual requirement is that intellectual property be available on a non-discriminatory basis at reasonable royalty rates. The downside to this approach is that it essentially involves regulation of the terms and conditions of access to the installed base. This may severely strain the resources and expertise of both the courts and antitrust authorities. However, the observation that compulsory licensing entails non-zero costs is not equivalent to showing that those costs exceed the benefits of compulsory licensing. Compulsory licensing as a remedy under the U.S. antitrust laws is an open issue.[89] The U.S. IP *Guidelines* note that there is no general obligation to license intellectual property, but then qualifies this by observing that market power is "relevant to the ability of an intellectual property owner to harm competition through unreasonable conduct in connection with such property."[90]

Horizontal Merger

The Borland/Ashton-Tate merger consent decree is an interesting example of using antitrust to reduce the extent of intellectual property rights.[91] In 1991 the U.S. Department of Justice allowed Borland International's acquisition of Ashton-Tate to proceed, subject to a consent decree that imposed limits on the extent of the merged firm's property rights by requiring it not to bring infringement suits under certain conditions. At the time of the merger, the two leading products in the market for relational database management system software (RDBMS) compatible with DOS-based computers were Borland's Paradox and Ashton-Tate's dBASE. The market share of the two products was on the order of 60 percent. The U. S. Department of Justice allowed the merger to proceed, under the condition that Borland refrain "from initiating or making any claim or counterclaim that asserts claims of copyright infringement in the command names, menu items, menu command hierarchies, command languages, programming languages and file structures used in and recognized by dBASE."[92]

At the time of the merger, Ashton-Tate had threatened to file or had filed copyright infringement suits against so-called "xBASE clones." These firms produced RDBMS software that was compatible with the dBASE standard: dBASE users could switch to these firms' products without having to forgo use of complementary products compatible with the dBASE standard (compatible tools, trained users, and customized programming to manage and create databases based on the dBASE programming language). The U.S. Department of Justice believed that continued copyright infringement suits would hamper the ability of the clone manufacturers to prevent Borland from raising prices for Paradox and dBASE after the merger. Presumably if the copyright infringement suits were successful, the merger would have led to a virtual monopoly in the RDBMS market. Consumer lock-in and network effects associated with the dBASE standard posed significant entry barriers for a different standard. As part of the consent decree, Borland also agreed to swiftly resolve Ashton-Tate's infringement suit against Fox in a manner consistent with the decree.[93] By lowering barriers to entry to intrasystem competition, the consent decree leads to the potential for an increase in efficiency *ex post*.

Vertical Merger and Foreclosure

Competition between competing systems depends on the relative sizes of their installed bases. Consequently, firms have an incentive to increase the size of their installed base and reduce the size of their rival's installed base. Initiatives of this kind are most often seen when network effects are indirect, since it is relatively much easier for firms to manipulate their installed bases when they are complementary products. Potential antitrust liability has arisen in cases where firms have foreclosed access of rival hardware products to software. In these situations, software is typically available or potentially available to all systems but is foreclosed through vertical merger (or its equivalents such as exclusive licensing arrangements). Hardware firms have acquired software suppliers and as a consequence "open" installed bases of software that were available for all hardware technologies become "closed" and compatible with only the technology of the acquiring hardware firm. Five recent antitrust cases in the United States have featured concerns over the effect of vertical merger or integration between hardware and software firms. These are *Nintendo*, *Primestar*, *TCI*, *Microsoft*, and *Silicon Graphics*.[94]

In *Nintendo*, Atari Games claimed copyright misuse as a defence on infringement claims over the 10NES lock-out program code. Atari alleged that terms of the licence agreements between Nintendo and third-party game developers that prohibited the game developer from adapting or offering any game, or its derivative developed for Nintendo, for another home video game or computer system, contributed to a violation of section 2 of the *Sherman Act* and copyright misuse.

The U.S. Department of Justice alleged that the terms of the partnership agreement in *Primestar* were designed to restrain competition in the market for multichannel subscription television. Primestar was a joint venture among subsidiaries of seven of the major cable television companies (so-called multiple systems operators or MSOs) and a subsidiary of General Electric. The General Electric subsidiary operated the only available *medium-power* direct broadcast satellite (DBS). Furthermore, many of the MSOs were either major suppliers or had substantial ownership interests in suppliers of national programming services; that is, cable channels like Home Box Office and CNN. The U.S. Department of Justice alleged that the terms of the Primestar agreement were designed to restrict the access of high-powered DBS suppliers of multichannel subscription television to programming services controlled by the MSOs. The small dish size and low installation costs of high-power DBS make it a viable alternative to cable in urban areas. The case was settled by a consent decree, four aspects of which are germane.

1. Cable systems controlled by the MSOs were prohibited from entering into or renewing agreements that gave them exclusive distribution rights to any existing specified national cable channel, any existing regional sports channel, or any new regional sports channel.

2. The MSOs were prohibited from enforcing any existing contracts that restricted the ability of a programming service provider to supply a competing DBS system.

3. The MSOs were prohibited from entering into agreements – either with other MSOs or programming suppliers – that would restrict access to programming by competitors of the MSOs. In particular, two types of agreements were prohibited. Enjoined were agreements between a cable channel or programming service controlled by the MSOs and another programming service wherein the two programming services agree to the terms and conditions with which they will deal with distributors of programming. An example would be an agreement not to supply a competing DBS provider. Also prohibited are agreements between two MSOs that restricted the terms and conditions under which they would purchase independent programming. An example would be an agreement between two MSOs not to purchase independent programming if it is also provided to a competing distributor.

4. Terms of the partnership agreement that prevented partners from offering their programming on either an exclusive basis or on more favourable terms to other distributors were abrogated.

In addition, as a result of antitrust complaints initiated at the state level, the MSOs were required to supply programming in which they had an ownership interest to other distributors.

When the U. S. Department of Justice filed suit challenging the acquisition of Liberty Media Corporation by Tele-Communications Inc. (TCI), it was the first challenge of a vertical merger under section 7 of the *Clayton Act* in more than a decade.[95] TCI, the largest MSO in the United States, and Liberty, another large MSO, both had numerous programming interests. One of the provisions of the pending consent decree requires TCI and Liberty to supply their video programming on a non-discriminatory basis to other competing multichannel television providers.

One of the terms of the *Microsoft* consent decree requires that nondisclosure agreements between Microsoft and independent software developers have a maximum duration of a year and that the terms of these agreements cannot restrict the developer from supplying application software for competing operating systems, provided that the developer does not disclose proprietary information. The U.S. Department of Justice had alleged that the nondisclosure agreements Microsoft sought from independent software vendors in return for information that would allow them to provide programs compatible with Windows 95 were anticompetitive because they restricted the ability of independent software firms to provide software for competing operating systems.

The U.S. Federal Trade Commission (FTC) reached a consent decree (which was recently approved) with Silicon Graphics Inc. (SGI). This consent decree allowed SGI to acquire two of the three leading graphic entertainment software companies. Prior to the merger, the products of the two companies (Alias Research Inc. and Wavefront Technology Inc.) were compatible only with SGI workstations. Alias, however, had been negotiating with other workstation manufacturers to port its products to their workstations. One of the provisions of the consent agreement is that SGI enter into a porting agreement with another significant workstation manufacturer for Alias's two major software titles.

Church and Gandal (1996a) examine the strategic or market power rationale for, and efficiency effects of, this class of vertical merger and foreclosure. They demonstrate that it can be a profit-maximizing strategy for a hardware firm to profitably merge with software suppliers and restrict the supply of software to competing systems. This strategic rationale for merger and foreclosure is profitable when it increases the market power of the firm in the market for hardware. If hardware is sufficiently homogenous, it can be an effective monopolization strategy. Moreover, when foreclosure occurs for strategic reasons, it is always inefficient. Associated with foreclosure is a welfare-reducing decrease in software variety for those consumers who purchase the foreclosed system. Other consumers consume a less preferred hardware system in order to maintain access to a larger installed base of software.

Strategic foreclosure is profitable because of the differential in the installed base of software varieties available to the two competing systems. This increases the demand for the hardware of the foreclosing system and reduces demand for the foreclosed hardware. The market-share effects of foreclosure depend on the extent to which hardware is differentiated. The less differentiated the hardware, the greater the relative importance of software, and hence the greater the market share increase from foreclosure. Moreover, the demand effect may make the foreclosing technology sufficiently more attractive to consumers that the foreclosing firm can raise the price of its hardware. Integration and foreclosure is a "fat-cat" strategy in the terminology of Fudenberg and Tirole (1984): the strategic effect is to make the pricing behaviour of the foreclosing firm less aggressive. However, the direct effect of foreclosure is exclusionary: the smaller relative installed base of the foreclosed firm reduces its demand.

The profitability of foreclosure depends on the trade-off between lost software profits (from not supplying the competing system) and increased hardware profits (from the increase in demand). Foreclosure is always profitable and results in monopolization when the extent of product differentiation is insignificant. In this case the foreclosing firm does not forgo any software profits (since no consumers purchase the competing system), hardware market share doubles, and the price of hardware increases. Similarly, even if foreclosure does not result in monopolization, it can be profitable if the relative increase in software varieties increases both the market share and price of the foreclosing firm's hardware.[96]

INTELLECTUAL PROPERTY RIGHTS AND EXCLUSION OF COMPLEMENTARY PRODUCTS

A SECOND SET OF CASES INVOLVES EXCLUSION BY THE SYSTEM sponsor of competing providers of complementary products. These cases are unusual in that our analysis of network competition suggests that system sponsors should find it to their advantage to encourage competition and plentiful supply of complementary products. However, there are two sets of circumstances where a system sponsor may find it profitable to exclude third-party suppliers of complementary products. Both arise when intersystem competition is no longer important, that is, when a) the system is dominant or a de facto standard, or b) the system is no longer competitive in the market for systems. Third-party suppliers of complementary products can typically be excluded by tying, or system sponsors can monopolize the markets for complementary products by engaging in predatory product innovation.

Tying

The sponsor of a standard can exclude suppliers of complementary products by tying supply of its proprietary standard to supply of complementary goods. This can be done by a) contractual terms where the tying arrangement is explicit; b) *de facto* bundling where the proprietary standard is not available as a separate product; or c) a technological tie (this is a special case of item b).

A representative case involving bundling is *Digidyne*.[97] In *Digidyne*, access to the installed base of software was controlled by licensing of the operating system. Data General manufactured the NOVA minicomputer system, which consisted of its central processing unit (CPU) and its proprietary operating system, RDOS. It refused to license its operating system for use on any other CPU including those made by Digidyne, which emulated Data General's CPU. The Court accepted the argument that the refusal to license amounted to tying the sale of Data General's hardware to its operating system.[98] The Court determined that a market for RDOS operating systems existed on the basis of lock-in, and that due to copyright protection, Data General had market power.[99] Because of sunk investments in training and application software, consumers were locked in to the RDOS standard and, via the effective tie, to Data General's hardware. Had Data General been willing to license its operating system, rival hardware manufacturers would have been able to compete effectively, even where consumers were locked in to software. Of considerable interest was that by 1979, 93 percent of Data General's CPU sales were to locked-in customers. The *Nintendo* and *Sega* cases are examples of technological tying (see "Reverse Engineering Does Not Infringe Copyright,"above, for a discussion of these cases). Both of these firms used a lock-out technology, which created compatibility problems for the video games of unauthorized suppliers.[100]

Predatory Product Innovation

Predatory product innovation involves changing the design attributes or interfaces in the system to make third-party complementary components incompatible. This type of innovation is a mechanism to create a technological tie by excluding existing suppliers of complementary products. It is useful to distinguish between two different sets of circumstances under which predatory product innovation occurs. The first corresponds to the two leading cases: the IBM peripheral cases and *Berkey*.[101] These cases correspond to efforts by a sponsor who introduces a closed system to keep it closed. The second set of circumstances corresponds to more recent cases such as *Silicon Graphics* and *Microsoft*.[102] In these cases, a system sponsor introduces an open system and then closes out producers of complementary products.

The *Berkey* case arose out of the introduction by Kodak of its 110 photographic system, which consisted of a new colour print film and the Pocket Instamatic Camera. Kodak was the dominant producer of film: its market share was over 80 percent. Berkey was a competing photofinisher and camera manufacturer. It alleged that Kodak's introduction of its new film without advance notice to its rivals was a violation of section 2 of the *Sherman Act* (monopolization). Without advance notice, competing camera manufacturers, photofinishers, and photofinishing equipment manufacturers were disadvantaged because the new system was backwards incompatible: the new film did not work in old cameras and was not compatible with the existing photofinishing technology. This gave Kodak a competitive advantage in the markets for photofinishing and cameras. To the extent that the new film was destined to become a standard, introducing a backwards incompatible technology without advance notice delayed the entry of competition into photofinishing and cameras and, at least temporarily, reserved the market for complementary products to Kodak. Of course we might expect that Kodak would prefer many suppliers of complementary products to help establish its new standard. However, perhaps due to its superior characteristics and Kodak's sponsorship, Kodak deemed it profit maximizing to preclude such second-sourcing. Kodak's conviction at the District Court level was overturned on appeal. The Court ruled that Kodak did not have an obligation to predisclose its design standards prior to their introduction. The innovation in *Berkey* corresponds to the introduction of an entirely new network or standard. It disenfranchised both the complementary goods of Kodak and those supplied by competitors. In addition, purchasers of the new film are not able, *when it is introduced*, to source either of the two complementary goods, cameras or photofinishing, from secondary sources.

System sponsors encounter the following dilemma (Saloner, 1990). On the one hand, in order for consumers to maximize the benefits from network externalities, hardware and software should be compatible. The problem with compatibility, however, is that it results in a system with standardized interfaces. Standardized interfaces provide entrants with an opportunity to provide compatible products and thus introduces competition.

Saloner observes that this is exactly what happened when IBM introduced System 360 in the 1960s. System 360 was designed so that across the different CPUs in the product line, hardware peripherals and software were compatible. As a result, competing manufacturers of plug peripherals were able to enter. IBM's competitive response was to lower prices, move to long-term leases, and change interfaces, which resulted in the exit, after incurring heavy losses, of 15 of the 17 peripheral manufacturers.[103] On the issue of product redesign, the Courts held that as long as the changes in product design were beneficial to consumers, then they were not anticompetitive.[104] The *Transamerica* Court did find that IBM's redesign of some of its System 370 CPU did unreasonably restrict competition, because it involved a degradation in performance and appeared to have been done only to exclude competing peripherals.[105] A similar complaint against IBM by the European Commission resulted in a very different resolution. IBM agreed to an undertaking whereby it would supply interface and network architecture documents to competing suppliers of peripherals, and it further agreed to publish changes in specifications in advance.[106]

More recently, concern about anticompetitive standards manipulation were raised in both the *SGI* and *Microsoft* cases. An element of the SGI consent decree[107] is that SGI commits to maintain an open standard, publish the application program interfaces for its operating systems and computers, and offer non-discriminatory programs to encourage the development of third-party software.[108] The FTC was concerned that the acquisition of Wavefront and Alias provides SGI with an incentive to discriminate against independent providers of competing software, thereby foreclosing them from the market or raising their costs. Since SGI provided substantial aid to independent software producers before the merger, the FTC ordered it to essentially maintain its pre-merger practices after the merger.

A number of allegations were made concerning standard manipulation in the *Microsoft* case. However, while these allegations were apparently part of the U.S. Federal Trade Commission's investigation, they were not part of the settlement reached with the Department of Justice.[109] In particular, it was alleged that Microsoft withheld information regarding system updates from competing application software developers in order to give its designers a competitive head start (see Blair and Esquibel, 1995, p. 260; Hanna, 1994, p. 439). Furthermore, it appears that Microsoft also did not fully release all of the application programming interface, reserving some undocumented system calls to itself. This allowed it to write superior application software (see Baseman, Boulton-Warren, and Woroch, 1995, p. 277; Hanna, 1994, p. 439).

In addition, Microsoft has steadily engaged in "creeping monopolization" by including additional features in each new generation of its operating systems. This bundling of features reduces or eliminates the demand for stand-alone application software that performs the same function and is independently supplied. One report notes that the inclusion in its operating system of dozens of functions, from back-up utilities to e-mail software, has resulted in the bankruptcy of many once-profitable independent companies.[110]

More recently, Microsoft included access to its computer online service in its operating system upgrade, Windows 95. The U.S. Department of Justice was sufficiently concerned about the competitive implications in the market for online services of this bundling that it threatened to hold up or block the release of Windows 95.[111] Moreover, installing Windows 95 and accessing the Microsoft Network can disable access to other online providers.[112] Most recently, providers of server software on the World Wide Web have asked the Department of Justice to investigate Microsoft after it began bundling its web server software with its Windows NT operating system.[113] Microsoft has announced plans to include its browser software in its next updates of both Windows 95 and Windows NT, leading one commentator to conclude that there will then likely be no need for a separate stand-alone browser.[114]

A recent case that has aspects of both a refusal to deal and predatory product innovation is *Data General Corp. v. Grumman Systems Support Corp.*[115] The behaviour at issue was a monopolist's right to unilaterally refuse to license intellectual property. While it could be interpreted as a refusal-to-license case, it is probably better understood as an example where technological change is used to exclude third-party suppliers of complementary products.

Data General had a 5 percent share of the market for minicomputers, but it had a 90 percent share of the aftermarket in service for its computers. The leading third-party maintainer (TPM), Grumman, had a 3 percent market share. The case arose out of Grumman's acquisition, duplication, and use of a diagnostic program proprietary to Data General. The District Court found that Grumman had infringed on Data General's copyright and awarded almost $27.5 million in damages. Grumman subsequently appealed on the basis that the District Court had not fully considered its defence and counter claim that Data General's refusal to license the diagnostic program amounted to monopolization. The Appeals Court affirmed.

Following the Supreme Court's formalization in *Grinnell*, monopolization requires that a) Data General have monopoly power in a market and b) engaged in exclusionary conduct to maintain its monopoly power.[116] Data

General and Grumman both agreed that the market for service was a legitimate antitrust market, and it appeared that Data General's 90 percent share, evidence of substantial barriers to entry, and supracompetitive service pricing indicated monopoly power. The monopolization claim depended on a determination of whether Data General's refusal to license was exclusionary.

However, in making that determination, the Court noted that amendments to the patent laws in 1988 provided an antitrust exemption for refusals to license patents. The relevant amendment provides that a patent owner does not engage in misuse or illegal extension by refusing to license.[117] Moreover, this finding is consistent with prevailing case law.[118]

The Court found, however, that the same sort of legislated exemption for copyright did not exist in the *Copyright Act*. The Supreme Court in *Kodak* noted that "It is true that as a general matter a firm can refuse to deal with its competitors. But such a right is not absolute; it exists only if there are legitimate competitive reasons for the refusal."[119] The *Data General* Court was willing to presume that refusals to license copyrighted material to competitors is a valid business justification, but refused to endorse Data General's position that such a refusal could never be exclusionary, that is, invalid. The Court subsequently ruled, however, that Grumman did not present sufficient evidence to rebut this presumption and avoid summary judgment.

Of considerable interest here, however, was the change in Data General's policies towards TPMs as the market for system sales diminished. The Court noted that there were three phases to the relationship between Data General and the TPMs. Initially, Data General viewed entry by TPMs with suspicion and hostility. However, as Data General apparently realized that second-sourcing of maintenance provided it with a means to make a commitment to its customers of low prices and a variety of service options, it adopted very liberal policies towards TPMs. It provided training for TPMs, sold parts to them, did repair work for them, and provided them with diagnostic tools. The third phase corresponds with a decline in sales of systems in the primary market. Data General adopted policies that attempted to limit the effectiveness of the TPMs. It ceased providing repair services for TPMs, selling parts directly to them, providing them access to its training programs, and licensing its diagnostic software.

The key distinction between these cases and that of *Berkey* and the peripheral cases is that in these cases the system sponsor begins with an *open* system that allows second-sourcing or third-party provision of complementary products. In some cases second-sourcing is, in fact, actively encouraged as the system sponsor recognizes that it is a means to commit to low prices and a wide variety of complementary products and thus provides a competitive advantage in the market for the system or hardware good. However, once the standard is established or sales of the system-good in the primary market are of lessor importance, the system sponsor manipulates standards or product specifications to render third-party complementary products incompatible, unnecessary, or inferior. In doing so, the system sponsor *closes* up its system and monopolizes the supply of complementary products.

Economic Analysis of Tying

While the courts in the United States have generally adopted a restrictive stance against tying,[120] the economics of tying are not nearly as straightforward. In the case of complementary products, while it is clear that tying can be a particularly effective exclusionary device – especially in the case of systems-goods – the welfare implications are not necessarily negative. Moreover, if a perfect price squeeze is possible, then if tying is observed, it must be to enhance efficiency and not to extend monopoly power (see Ordover, Sykes, and Willig, 1985).

Following Ordover, Sykes, and Willig, suppose that a system consists of two components, A and B, and that neither provides any stand-alone consumption benefits. Component A is produced only by firm 1 (perhaps because of intellectual property rights) and its marginal cost is c_A. There is free entry into the production of component B and its marginal cost is c_B. Consumers' willingness to pay for a system is v. The maximum profit per consumer is $v - (c_A + c_B)$. The monopolist can extract this by setting its price equal to $v - c_B$. This leaves consumers just willing to purchase and suppliers just willing to supply component B at price c_B. There is no market power rationale for the monopolist of component A to enter production of component B and tie sales of B to sales of A. If the monopolist charged p_A for component A, then the maximum it could charge for component B if it was tied is $v - p_A$ and its profits per consumer will still be $v - (c_A + c_B)$.

If the B components are differentiated but a system still consists only of one A and one B component, a monopolist supplier of A would *reduce* its profits if it tied consumption of A to its B component (this result is due to Whinston, 1990). Suppose that B is supplied by firm 1 and a rival (firm 2). Then some consumers will prefer the system AB_2, and if B is tied to A, these consumers may opt not to purchase a system and as a result do not purchase A. On the other hand, not tying A to B_1 allows the monopolist to raise the price of A and sell to all consumers, thereby increasing its profits. It can raise its price for A since it need not convince consumers who prefer AB_2 to purchase AB_1. Alternatively, not tying A to B allows the monopolist to extract surplus created by both B_1 and B_2 by raising the price of A, just as it did when B was homogenous.

There are, however, two situations where firms do have a market power motivation to tie. These are to price discriminate and to foreclose system competition.

Price Discrimination

Suppose that consumption of a homogenous component B is elastic and that there are two different types of consumers: "high" and "low" types (this discussion follows Tirole, 1988). The high types demand more of component B than the low types for any price of B (p_B). *Ex ante* the monopolist cannot identify an individual's type. If there are n_h high types and n_l low types, then the total number of consumers is $n_h + n_l = n$. Suppose that consumption of A alone provides no benefit: then the monopolist of A essentially sells access to the benefits provided by consuming component B. If component B is competitively supplied at marginal cost c_B, then the monopolist has two choices. It can sell component A for $CS_l(c_B)$ where $CS_l(c_B)$ is the consumer surplus or benefit that the low types realize from optimally consuming component B when its price is c_B. The monopolist's profits would then be $nCS_l(c_B)$. On the other hand, it could raise the price of A to $CS_h(c_B)$ and earn profits of $n_h CS_h(c_B)$. Raising the price of A to $CS_h(c_B)$ means that only the high types will purchase a system and thus component A. The monopolist, however, can do better if it ties.

Tying allows the monopolist to price-discriminate between the high and low types based on their intensity of use for component B. Tying is a mechanism to meter consumption: sales of the complementary product B indicate the intensity of use and if intensity of use reflects benefits, it can be used to price discriminate, that is, extract more surplus from those who realize substantial benefit. By tying consumption of A to B, the monopolist in A is able to monopolize B. It will then maximize its profits by raising the price of B above marginal cost to p^*_B and setting $p_A = CS_l(p^*_B)$. Raising the price of B above its marginal cost requires the monopolist to lower its price for A or demand by the low types will go to zero. At the margin, the profits from the sale of B to the low types equals the decrease in profits from the reduction in the price of A to the low types. Since the profit from the sale of B is greater to the high types, as they, by definition, demand more, and the decrease in the price for the high types is the same as for the low types, profits must increase. Of course, in order to keep the price of B above c_B, the monopolist must exclude consumers from purchasing B from alternative suppliers. This requires the monopolist to tie B to A. The incentive to price-discriminate provides an economic explanation for why a monopolist supplier of a standard would tie the standard to complementary products. Excluding suppliers of complementary products permits them to raise the price of complementary products and extract more surplus from consumers. Alternatively, not excluding competing producers of complementary products means that the system sponsor will be forced to increase the price of the protected standard. Saloner observes that the price of IBM's operating system for its System 370 has risen steadily since the introduction of competition in hardware and peripherals (Saloner, 1990, p. 151).

The welfare effects of such a tie are ambiguous. If the monopolist was serving both groups prior to tying, welfare is reduced since the price of B is raised above its marginal cost. On the other hand, if the monopolist was only serving the high types prior to the tie, then the tie increases welfare since the low types are now served.

Greenstein (1990) extends this analysis to consider the incentives for, and effects of, changing interfaces to render components supplied by competing suppliers incompatible. If imitation of a new design interface is not instantaneous, then a monopolist supplier of a component in which the interface is embedded has an incentive to periodically redesign the interface. This effectively disenfranchises existing competing suppliers of components and provides the monopolist with a monopoly in the supply of components, while competitors play catch-up and engage in reverse engineering to re-establish compatibility. During this time the monopolist is unconstrained by competition for components and can increase its profits by engaging in price discrimination. As competitive entry retards its ability to price discriminate, the monopolist will once again have an incentive to redesign its interfaces. Such design modifications are obviously socially wasteful, both in terms of the monopolist's expenditures and its competitor's expenditures to reverse engineer the new design.[121] These expenditures to eliminate and restore compatibility make it more likely that the price discrimination allowed by incompatibility is socially inefficient.

Greenstein also observes that the incentive for the monopolist to redesign its system depends on the importance of backwards compatibility. Maintaining compatibility with an installed base of complementary products mitigates the incentives of the firm to redesign its interfaces. However, this means that system redesigns require some minimal degree of technological improvement to induce consumers to switch from one standard to another. This, of course, makes it difficult to disentangle legitimate and anticompetitive interface changes.[122] Saloner suggests that since compatibility is often obtained not by producing identical products but simply products that are compatible, the system sponsor can change standards/interfaces such that its complementary products remain compatible but those of its competitors do not (1990, p. 142). This means that consumers will have, at the margin, an additional incentive to stick with components produced by the system sponsor. Moreover, it also reduces the effective constraint of maintaining backwards compatibility.

Foreclosure

Tying can also be an effective means to eliminate competition in the market for systems (our analysis here follows Whinston, 1990). Suppose that the ability of a system sponsor to raise the price of its protected hardware is constrained by the existence of a competing, albeit inferior, system. This means that the firm is not able to execute fully a price squeeze, since if it tries to raise the price of its hardware, consumers can substitute to alternative hardware if compatible software is available. This means that though consumers would prefer to assemble systems AB_1 or AB_2, if the price firm 1 charges for A is too high, they will switch to a competitive supplier for component A. Suppose, however, that firm 1 ties sales of its A component to its proprietary component, B_1. Then, in the pricing game between B_1 and B_2, firm 1 has an additional incentive to price B_1 aggressively: acquiring more market share for B_1 increases sales of its A component. Thus tying is a "top-dog" strategy in the terminology of Fudenberg and

Tirole (1984). If there are fixed costs associated with the production of component B, then the increase in price competition for component B and loss of market share to firm 1 might induce the rival producer of component B to exit the market. As a result, of course, the alternative producer of the A component is also forced to exit. It is quite possible that this monopolization strategy of the systems market is profitable. The welfare implications of this exclusionary tying are, however, ambiguous. On the one hand, welfare is increased because of the fixed costs savings and consumption by all consumers of the preferred A component. On the other hand, welfare is reduced since some consumers are now forced to purchase B_1 instead of B_2.

Predatory Product Innovation and Monopolization of Complementary Products

As we outlined above, the situation we have in mind here is when a system sponsor engages in secondary sourcing to commit to competition and variety in complementary goods market, but then subsequently engages in product redesign or strategic standard manipulation to disenfranchise existing third-party suppliers and monopolize complementary product markets.

Our discussion here is closely related to the recent debate over market power in aftermarkets.[123] The *Kodak* decision by the U.S. Supreme Court and a number of related cases has raised the prominence of the issue of aftermarkets.[124] Aftermarkets exist when there is an intertemporal pattern to consumers' purchases. Typically, consumers initially purchase a hardware good and then subsequently purchase software, maintenance, upgrades, and so on. The initial purchase is in the primary market; subsequent purchases are in the aftermarket. Aftermarket issues arise due to incompatibilities between systems and intellectual property rights that the manufacturer of the primary good has over some aftermarket products, which prohibit entry. This gives it *proprietary aftermarkets*.

In the *Kodak* case, the primary markets were those for micrographic and copying equipment. The aftermarkets were service and parts for Kodak micrographic and copying equipment. Image Technical Services and other independent service organizations (ISOs) brought suit against Kodak when it refused to supply them with parts. The ISOs charged that Kodak was illegally tying parts (the tying good) with its service (the tied good), and in doing so was monopolizing the service aftermarket. Kodak was granted summary judgment by the District Court, on the basis that Kodak's lack of market power in the equipment market *necessarily* precludes a finding of market power in the market for parts and thus one of the requirements to find a *per se* illegal tie was not met. Kodak argued that consumers compared costs of purchasing different systems using "life-cycle pricing." This means that they compared the total costs of owning and operating a system when they made their purchase decision in the primary market. Thus there is only one market, the market for systems, and if Kodak tried to raise the price of its aftermarket products, competition in the primary market would force it to lower its price or lose sales in the equipment market to its rivals. As a result, it argued, it does not exercise market power in aftermarkets. On appeal the summary judgment was overturned and the reversal upheld by the Supreme Court. The Supreme Court concluded that it was a matter of fact, not law, whether competition in the primary market eliminates market power in aftermarkets, and thus had to be determined on a case-by-case basis. This followed from the Supreme Court's observations that "significant information and switching costs" might break the link between the primary and aftermarkets alleged by Kodak. Kodak was found guilty on remand to District Court of monopolizing the service markets for its high-volume photocopiers and micrographic equipment. The ISOs were awarded $23.9 million in damages.[125]

Following Kattan (1993), the question of the importance of aftermarkets for antitrust can be divided into two separate issues. The first is, are aftermarkets antitrust markets? The second is, even if they are, does competition in the primary market constrain the exercise of market power in proprietary aftermarkets of the system sponsor?

The extent to which consumers are locked in to the primary product determines the degree to which the aftermarket is in fact a market for antitrust purposes. If consumers do not face significant switching costs, then in response to price increases in aftermarkets, they can substitute to other systems of primary products. However, if they are locked in, then monopoly suppliers in aftermarkets will have market power, and the extent of that power will depend on the extent of lock-in. The extent of lock-in depends on the costs associated with switching to a different primary product or system. As we argued above, there are two elements to these costs: a) the need to make sunk investments similar to those already made in the old primary product, and b) the potential loss of network benefits. The more important network benefits, the more likely it is that aftermarkets for a primary product are an antitrust market. Not only in systems markets, but also in aftermarkets, the existence of strong network effects means that the brand of a firm can define a market.

The question of the existence of market power in aftermarkets and the potential mitigating influence of competition in the primary market is germane to our discussion of predatory product innovation. Suppose that there are two hardware firms with constant and equal marginal cost C and that competition in the market for hardware is over price, that is, Bertrand. Consumers assemble systems that consist of a single unit of hardware and many varieties of software. Their demand for software variety is elastic, and their willingness to pay for hardware depends on the benefit or consumer surplus from consuming software. Let the cost of a representative variety of software be c. Then, after a consumer has purchased a unit of hardware, the situation is as in Figure 1, where the inverse demand curve for software variety is denoted $P(Q)$.

If the market for software is monopolized by the system sponsor (the hardware firm), then it will set a price of P^m for software and earn monopoly profits

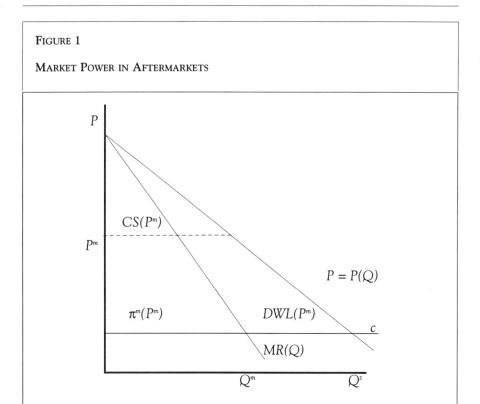

FIGURE 1

MARKET POWER IN AFTERMARKETS

of $\pi^m(P^m)$, and the consumer will realize consumer surplus of $CS(P^m)$. Anticipating monopoly supply in software, $CS(P^m)$ is the maximum a consumer will pay for hardware. The equilibrium price of hardware is $P^H = C - \pi^m(P^m)$. The hardware firms will bid for the right to be the monopolist in the aftermarket, and in doing so will dissipate all of the profit. Notice that there is market power in the aftermarket and that there is a welfare loss of $DWL(P^m)$, even though the hardware firms do not earn monopoly profits.

Suppose now that by second-sourcing, hardware firm A (but not hardware firm B) could commit to the competitive price of software, c. Consumers of system A would then consume Q^s software varieties and realize surplus of $CS(P^m)$ $+ \pi(P^m) + DWL(P^m)$. Hardware firm A would monopolize the systems market by charging $P^A = DWL(P^m) + C - \epsilon$, where ϵ is negligible. At this price, it offers consumers greater surplus than the maximum hardware firm B can and still break even.[126] If both hardware firms are able to second-source to ensure competition in the aftermarket, then the equilibrium hardware price will be $P^H = C$ and consumer surplus will be $CS(P^m) + \pi(P^m) + DWL(P^m) - C$. This is obviously the socially efficient outcome.

The ability to commit to a competitive outcome in aftermarkets is both socially and privately optimal *ex ante*. However, once the system is the de facto standard or, alternatively, system (hardware) sales are small, then the system sponsor has an incentive to monopolize the aftermarket and earn monopoly profits. The extent of $\pi(P^m)$ that it can capture will depend on the competitive alternatives available to consumers and the extent of their lock-in. If the system is a de facto standard, then consumers cannot switch to another system as prices in the aftermarket increase, and the system sponsor will be able to capture all of $\pi(P^m)$. On the other hand, if there is another system (with second-sourcing in its aftermarket) then the firm will only be able to capture $min[C, \pi(P^m)]$. In any event, this results in a quantity distortion and welfare reduction in the aftermarket. Antitrust enforcement could play a role in mitigating this welfare loss by placing a restraint on the ability of firms to eliminate second-sourcing, typically by changing standards.

In these circumstances antitrust enforcement and scrutiny can be seen as a supplementary measure to overcome what is at heart an incomplete contracting problem.[127] *Ex ante*, both consumers and firms would agree to antitrust enforcement to constrain the behaviour of the firm.[128]

While our analysis has focused on the *ex post* efficiency effects in the aftermarket, there are also potentially important effects on incentives for innovation. The potential to be excluded by predatory product innovation reduces the incentives for complementary product suppliers to engage in research and development and developing new applications (see Menell, 1987, pp. 1361-62). Moreover, if there are economies of scale in R&D, then closed systems reduce the extent of the market and thus the incentives for R&D if it is not system specific: complementary product producers can provide similar components for multiple systems (see Menell, 1987, p. 1344).

NOTES

1   The assumption that the value of hardware is increasing in the variety of compatible software distinguishes the analysis here from the "mix and match" literature on compatibility. In Matutes and Regibeau (1988) and Economides (1988) systems are formed by combining complementary products in fixed proportions.

2   The seminal contributions on network externalities are a series of papers by Farrell and Saloner (1985, 1986a, 1986b) and Katz and Shapiro (1985, 1986a). Katz and Shapiro (1994) and Besen and Farrell (1994) are excellent surveys on the economics of network industries. In what follows we draw liberally on all of these papers. See also Gilbert (1992).

3   This point is the focus of Besen and Farrell (1994).

4   "Wireless Auction Raises a Record $10.2-billion," *The Globe and Mail*, 7 May 1996, B11.

5   See Church and Gandal (1992, 1996a and 1996b) for an analysis of strategic investment in software by hardware firms.

6   See *Atari Games Corp. v. Nintendo of America*, 975 F.2d 832 (Fed. Cir. 1992), McManis (1993, p. 45) and Hanna (1994, p. 407-408).

7   *United States v. Microsoft Corp.*, 56 F.3d 1448 (D.C. Circuit 1995).

8   See FTC News Release, "FTC Settlement Would Preserve Competition on Price and Innovation for Entertainment Graphics Software and Hardware," June 9, 1995 and Silicon Graphics, Inc.: Proposed Consent Agreement, 60 Federal Register 35032 (July 5, 1995).

9   For a list of the allegations in the Department of Justice's monopolization suit against IBM see *United States v. International Business Machine Corp.*, 1975 CCH Trade Cases ¶60104.

10 Compare the experience of the compact disc with later digital technologies (digital audio tape, digital compact cassette, and the mini disc).

11 The costs of making a technology backwards compatible will depend on the design decisions of the incumbent.

12 See *Apple Computer v. Franklin Computer Corp.*, 714 F.2d 1240 (3rd Cir. 1983).

13 The four significant cases were: *Telex v. International Business Machines Corporation*, 510 F.2d 894 (10th Cir. 1975); *California Computer Products. v. International Business Machines Corporation*, 613 F.2d 727 (9th Cir. 1979); *Memorex Corp. v. International Business Machines Corporation*, 636 F.2d 1188 (9th Cir. 1980), cert. denied, 452 U.S. 972 (1981); *Transamerica Computer Co., Inc. v. International Business Machines Corporation*, 698 F.2d 1377 (9th Cir. 1983).

14 *Atari Games Corp. and Tengen Inc. v. Nintendo of America, Inc, and Nintendo Co., Ltd.*, 1990-1 CCH Trade Cases ¶68946.

15 Traditionally, courts in the United States have tended to presume the existence of market power from patent or copyright protection. See, for example, *United States v. Loew's, Inc.* 371 U.S. 38 (1962) where market power is presumed from copyright protection and *International Salt Co. v. United States*, 332 U.S. (392) 1947, where it is presumed from patent protection. In *Jefferson Parish Hospital District No. 2 v. Hyde*, 466 U.S. 2 (1984) at 16 the U.S. Supreme Court observed in dictum that "if the government has granted the seller a patent or similar monopoly over a product, it is fair to presume that the inability to buy the product elsewhere gives the seller market power." The U.S. Department of Justice and the Federal Trade Commission's *Antitrust Guidelines for the Licensing of Intellectual Property* (1995), hereafter the IP *Guidelines*, do not automatically equate intellectual property rights protection with market power, noting that "there will often be sufficient actual or potential close substitutes" that will prevent the exercise of market power (§2.2). The IP *Guidelines* observe (at footnote 10) that the matter has not been resolved by the courts.

16 *SCM Corp. v. Xerox Corp.*, 645 F.2d 1195 (2nd Cir. 1981) at 1203.

17 See *United States v. Microsoft Corp.*, Proposed Final Judgement and Competitive Impact Statement, 59 Federal Register, 42845 (August 19, 1994).

18 *Canada (Director of Investigation & Research) v. Southam Inc. et al.* (1992) 43 Canadian Patent Reporter (3d) 161 (C.T).

19 See Ross (1993) for discussion of entry barriers in the *Southam* and other decisions by the Tribunal. The Tribunal described the network effects as a coordination problem for advertisers.

20 Well-known examples are *Associated Press v. United States*, 326 U.S. 1 (1945), and *MCI Communications Co. v. AT&T*, 708 F.2d 1081 (7th Cir.), *cert denied*, 464 U.S. 891 (1983).

21 *Lotus Dev. Corp. v. Paperback Software Int'l.*, 740 F Supp 37 (D Mass 1990).

22 *Apple Computer, Inc. v. Microsoft Corp.*, 709 F. Supp. 925 (N.D. Cal. 1989) (Apple I); *Apple Computer, Inc. v. Microsoft Corp.*, 717 F. Supp. 1428 (N.D. Cal. 1989) (Apple II); *Apple Computer, Inc. v. Microsoft Corp.*, 759 F. Supp. 1444 (N.D. Cal. 1991) (Apple III); *Apple Computer, Inc. v. Microsoft Corp.*, 779 F. Supp. 133 (N.D. Cal. 1991) (Apple IV); *Apple Computer, Inc. v. Microsoft Corp.*, 799 F. Supp. 1006 (N.D. Cal. 1992) (Apple V); *Apple Computer, Inc. v. Microsoft Corp.*, 821 F. Supp. 616 (N.D. Cal. 1993) (Apple VI); *Apple Computer, Inc. v. Microsoft Corp.*, 35 F.3d 1435 (9th Cir. 1994) (Apple VII).

23 A macro is a sequence of commands, incorporated in a simple program.

24 *The Cable Television Consumer Protection and Competition Act*, Pub. L. No. 102-385, 106 Stat. 1460 (1992) contains a number of provisions intended to prevent restrictions on access or availability to programming. See also the related discussion of the *Primestar* case below in the section "Vertical Merger and Foreclosure."

25 The following discussion draws freely on two excellent papers by Joseph Farrell (1989, 1995).

26 See Farrell and Shapiro (1992b) for a simulation exercise, which attempts to illustrate the magnitude of this welfare cost of monopoly in the presence of network effects.

27 For a formal analysis that installed base advantages contribute to inefficient patent racing see Kristiansen (1995).

28 Both Farrell (1989) and Menell (1987) consider the effects that intellectual property protection have voluntary standard setting.

29 See, for example, Paredes (1994, pp. 305-308), Stack (1993, p. 335) and *Saturday Evening Post Co. v. Rumbleseat Press*, Inc., 816 F.2d 1191 (7th Cir. 1987).

30 This point is forcefully made by Samuelson (1995). She observes the merger doctrine may not be of much practical use when applied to de facto standards and interfaces.

31 See for example the papers which comprise the symposium on new forms of intellectual property rights "Symposium: Toward a Third Intellectual Property Paradigm," *Columbia Law Review*, 94 (1994): 2307.

32 Good discussions of the role played by trade secrets in computer software can be found in Menell (1987, pp. 1351-53) and Lemley (1995, p. 3).

33 Courts have largely upheld this position and continue to do so. *Data General Corp. v. Digital Computer Controls, Inc.*, 297 A2d 433, 436 (Del. Ch. 1971) (program with 500 copies sold still qualifies as a trade secret), aff'd, 297 A.2d 437 (Del. 1972). More recent case are *Data General Corp. v. Grumman Systems Support Corp.*, 825 F. Supp. 340, 354-55 (D. Mass. 1993); *Management Science of Am. v. Cyborg Systems, Inc.*, 1977-1 CCH Trade Cases ¶61472.

34 *Baker v. Selden*, 101 U.S. 99 (1879).

35 *Whelan Associates Inc. v. Jaslow Dental Laboratory Inc.*, 797 F.2d 1222 (3d Cir. 1986).

36 *Lotus Dev. Corp. v. Paperback Software Int'l.*, 740 F. Supp. 37 (D Mass 1990).

37 *Computer Assocs. Int'l, Inc. v. Altai, Inc.*, 982 F.2d 693 (2d Cir. 1992).

38 This is a point that highlights a concern of economists about the application of copyright law: the more utilitarian is the element of the program, the less it is protected. Patent law, of course, takes the opposite approach.

39   *Altai*, 982 F.2d at 710.

40   *Computer Associates Int'l v. Altai, Inc.*, 982 F.2d 693, 714 (2d Cir. 1992).

41   *Delrina Corp. v. Triolet Sys.*, 9 B.L.R. 2d 140 (Ont. Ct. Just. 1993); *Matrox Elect. Sys. v. Gaudreau*, 1993 R.J.Q. 2449, 2457-58 (Mont. Ct. Just. July 28, 1993).

42   *Lotus Dev. Corp. v. Borland Int'l*, 49 F.3d 807 (1st Cir. 1995).

43   *Lotus Dev. Corp. v. Borland Int'l*, 49 F.3d 807 (1st Cir. 1995) at 810-811.

44   See *supra*, note 22.

45   *Atari Games Corp. v. Nintendo of America*, 975 F.2d 832 (Fed. Cir. 1992).

46   *Sega Enterprises v. Accolade, Inc.*, 977 F.2d 1510 (9th Cir. 1992).

47   See McManis (1993) for an extensive discussion of fair use in the context of reverse engineering. McManis suggests that the use of a lock-out device to eliminate competition may well be misuse of copyright (p. 28). Forrester (1992) and McManis (1993) contain discussions regarding the legality of reverse engineering in the European Community and the European Community Directive on the Legal Protection of Computer Programs, Council Directive 91/250 14 May 1991 O.J. (L122/42). Forrester's discussion of the "acrimonious" debate surrounding the legality of reverse engineering in the European Community is informative. The Directive provides that reverse engineering necessary to achieve interoperability does not infringe copyright.

48   *Atari Games Corp. v. Nintendo of America*, 1992-2 CCH Trade Cases, ¶69,969.

49   DC North Texas 3-94-CV-1047-X 9/1/95. See BNA *Patent, Trademark, & Copyright Journal*, 50 (October 12, 1995): 682.

50   Firmware is software fixed into a semiconductor.

51   *Morton Salt Co. v. Suppiger* 314 U.S. 488 (1942).

52   *Lasercomb America, Inc. v. Reynolds* 911 F.2d 970 (4th Cir. 1990).

53   *Lasercomb America, Inc. v. Reynolds* 911 F.2d at 973.

54   See Paredes (1994) and Hanna (1994) for discussion of misuse standards in patent and copyright infringement cases.

55   *USM Corp. v. SPS Technologies, Inc.*, 694 F.2d 505 (7th Cir. 1982) at 511, *cert. denied*, 482 U.S. 1107 (1983).

56   *Service & Training, Inc. v. Data General Corp.*, 963 F.2d 680 (4th Cir. 1992); *PRC Realty Sys. v. National Ass'n of Realtors*, 972 F.2d 341 (4th Cir. 1992); *Advanced Computer Serv. of Mich., Inc. v. MAI Sys. Corp.*, 845 F. Supp. 356 (E.D. Va. 1994); *Electronic Data Sys. Corp. v. Computer Associates Int'l, Inc.*, 802 F. Supp. 1463 (N.D. Tex. 1992); *Microsoft Corp. v. BEC Computer Co.*, 818 F. Supp. 1313 (C.D. Cal. 1992); *Sega Enter. Ltd. v. Accolade, Inc.*, 785 F. Supp. 1392 (N.D. Cal. 1992), rev'd on other grounds, 977 F.2d 1510 (9th Cir. 1992).

57   *Data General Corp. v. Grumman Systems Support Corp.*, 36 F.3d 1147 (1st Cir. 1994).

58   *In re Shao Wen Yuan*, 188 F.2d 377 (C.C.P.A. 1951).

59   *O'Reilly v. Morse*, 56 U.S. (15 How.) 61 (1854).

60   *Eibel Process Co. v. Minnesota & Ont. Paper Co.*, 261 U.S. 45 (1923).

61   *Mackay Radio & Tel. Co. v. Radio Corp. of America*, 306 U.S. 86 (1939).

62   *Gottschalk v. Benson*, 409 U.S. 63 (1972).

63   *Diamond v. Diehr*, 450 U.S. 175 (1981).

64   *In re Alappat*, 33 F.3d 1526.

65   *In re Beauregard*, 35 USPQ 2d 1383 (Fed. Cir. 1995).

66   The printed matter exception holds that an article, consisting of printed matter stored or printed on a substrate, is non-patentable when the novelty of the article resides in

the printed matter, and whose purpose is informative, not functional. See Laurenson (1995, p. 817).

67 Comment of the Staff of the Federal Trade Commission, Docket No. 9505 31 44-5144-01 (September 26, 1995).

68 A discussion of this case can be found in Yoches (1995). Compton's has appealed the decision.

69 Comment of the Staff of the Federal Trade Commission, Docket No. 9505 31 44-5144-01 (September 26, 1995).

70 *Radio Telefis Eirann (RTE) & Anor v. Commission of the European Communities*, 1995 CCH CEC ¶400 and for directory cases, see for example, *BellSouth Advertising & Publishing Corp. v. Donnelly Information Publishing Inc.*, 719 F. Supp. 1551 (S.D. Fla. 1988), affirmed 933 F.2d 952 (11th Cir. 1991), vacated and new trial ordered 1992-2 CCH Trade Cases ¶70,058, reversed 999 F.2d 1436 (11th Cir. 1993); *Rural Telephone Service Co. v. Feist Publications, Inc.* 957 F.2d 765 (10th Cir.), cert. denied, 113 S. Ct. 490 (1992); *Great Western Directories, Inc. v. Southwestern Bell Telephone Co.*, et al., 1995-2 Trade Cases ¶71,123; CRTC Telecom Decision 95-3 March 8, 1995 *Provision of Directory Database Information and Real-Time Access to Directory Assistance Databases.*

71 *Lotus Dev. Corp. v. Borland International, Inc.*, 799 F. Supp. 203 (D.Mass. 1992) reversed 49 F.3d 807 (1st Cir. 1995). Two other leading cases concerning interface information and specifications are *Nintendo* and *Sega*, considered in "Reverse Engineering Does Not Infringe Copyright," above.

72 RTE has a statutory monopoly for both radio and television broadcasting *originating* in Ireland.

73 In particular, licensees could only reproduce daily or weekend listings and highlights of the week's schedule.

74 For further discussion of this case and its important implications for the relationship between intellectual property rights and competition policy in the European Community see Tritell and Metaxas-Maranghidis (1995) and Forrester (1992).

75 *Feist Publications, Inc. v. Rural Telephone Service Co.*, 111 S. Ct. 1282 (1991).

76 See *BNA Patent, Trademark, & Copyright Journal*, 41 (1991): 443-44 for a summary of this case.

77 999 F.2d 1436 (11th Cir. 1993).

78 For a summary and discussion of the case see *BNA Patent, Trademark, & Copyright Journal* 46 (1993): 421. The merger doctrine provides that when the expression of an idea is unique, expression merges with idea, and thus the expression is no longer protected by copyright.

79 *Rural Tel. Serv. Co. v. Feist Publications, Inc.*, 1990-1 CCH Trade Cases ¶69,022.

80 *Rural Telephone Service Co., Inc. v. Feist Publications, Inc.*, 1992-1 CCH Trade Cases ¶69,724.

81 The Court applied a two-part test to determine whether a monopolist's refusal to deal with a competitor is a section 2 violation: (i) evidence of antitrust injury or anti-competitive effect; (ii) given evidence of harm to competition, is there a legitimate business or, read broadly, an efficiency justification for the refusal to deal.

82 See CRTC Telecom Decisions 90-12 and 92-1. Bell is the largest telephone company in Canada, providing local and long distance service in Ontario and Quebec. The CRTC is the Canadian Radio-Television and Telecommunications Commission.

83 In Telecom Decision 95-14 the CRTC declined to revise the deletion mechanism to be competitively neutral. On 26 June 1996 the Federal Government ordered that all

publishers of directories have equal access to listings. See "Manley Announces Changes to Rules on White Page Directories," Industry Canada News Release 7411.e 26 June 1996; Scott Feschuk, "Ottawa Allows White-Page Competition," *The Globe and Mail*, 27 June 1996, p. B1.

84   This network is composed of Lotus 1-2-3 users and their files as well as compatible complementary products such as macros, software enhancements, consulting and training services, etc. It thus is characterized by both direct and indirect network externalities.

85   *Lotus Dev. Corp. v. Borland International, Inc.*, 799 F. Supp. 203, 217 (D.Mass. 1992).

86   *Lotus Development Corporation v. Borland International, Inc.*, Supreme Court of the United States 94-2003(January 16, 1996).

87   *MCI Communications Corp. v. AT&T*, 708 F.2d (7th Cir. 1983) *cert. denied* 464 U.S. 891 (1983).

88   See Areeda (1990) for a discussion of the doctrine. Farrell (1995) has also suggested that the essential facilities doctrine can play a role in redressing inefficiently strong intellectual property right protection in network industries.

89   For extended discussions see Kobak (1996) and Rosen (1994). We revisit American jurisprudence regarding compulsory licensing *infra* at text accompanying note 116. Forrester (1992) suggests that when there is an anticompetitive effect when a domi-nant firm refuses to license intellectual property rights, withholds access to interface specifications, and more specifically, refuses to license intellectual property that firm is potentially liable under the abuse of dominant position provisions in the Treaty of Rome (section 86) in the European Community.

90   IP *Guidelines*, section 2.2.

91   *U.S. v. Borland International, Inc., and Ashton-Tate Corp.*, 1992-1 CCH Trade Cases ¶69,774.

92   §IV.A of the Consent Decree *U.S. v. Borland International, Inc.*, 1992-1 CCH Trade Cases ¶69,774.

93   See §IV.C of the Consent Decree *U.S. v. Borland International, Inc.* Fox was the largest of the xBASE clone manufacturers.

94   *Atari Games Corp. and Tengen, Inc. v. Nintendo of America Inc. and Nintendo Co., Ltd.*, 1992-2 CCH Trade Cases ¶69,969; *United States v. Primestar Partners, L.P. et al.*, Proposed Final Judgement and Consent Decree 58 Federal Register 60672 (November 17, 1993); *United States v. Tele-Communications, Inc.*, Proposed Final Judgement and Consent Decree 59 Federal Register 24723 (May 12, 1994); *United States v. Microsoft*, 1995-1 CCH Trade Cases ¶70,928; Silicon Graphics, Inc.: Proposed Consent Agreement, 60 Federal Register 35032 (July 5, 1995).

95   "Cable TV Operator, Programmer Resolve Division Concerns over Vertical Merger," *Antitrust and Trade Regulation Reporter*, 66 (May 5, 1994): 512-13.

96   Church and Gandal consider a sequential game in which there are two producers of differentiated hardware and two producers of software. The game specification allows for the possibility of retaliation by the foreclosed firm: it can integrate with the remaining independent software firm in response to foreclosure. For integration and foreclosure to be profitable it must be the case that retaliation is not profitable. Retaliation might not be profitable because it involves internalizing a pricing exter-nality between hardware and software. An integrated firm has an incentive to lower the price of its hardware in order to sell more software in the aftermarket. Bidding for consumers in the hardware market makes retaliation unprofitable. Thus retaliation by

integrating and foreclosing is less profitable than not retaliating because retaliation does not restore the *ex ante* situation.

97   *Digidyne Corp. v. Data General.* 734 F.2d 1336 (9th Cir. 1984), *cert. denied*, 473 U.S. 908 (1985).

98   Moreover, licensees were also required to purchase minimum amounts of peripheral hardware or pay program license charges.

99   In this respect, this decision was an important precursor to *Eastman Kodak Co. v. Image Technical Services, Inc.*, 112 S. Ct. 2072 (1992).

100   *Atari Games Corp. v. Nintendo of America*, 975 F.2d 832 (Fed. Cir. 1992) and *Sega Enterprises v. Accolade, Inc.*, 977 F.2d 1510 (9th Cir. 1992).

101   See the discussion of the peripheral cases in Brock (1989) and *Berkey Photo, Inc. v. Eastman Kodak Co.*, 603 F.2d 263 (2d Cir. 1979), cert. denied, 444 U.S. 1093 (1980).

102   See *supra* at note 94 for case cites.

103   See Brock (1989) and *Transamerica Computer Co., Inc. v. International Business Machines Corporation*, 698 F.2d 1377 (9th Cir. 1983) at 1381.

104   See Brock (1989, p. 178) and Von Kalinowski 3 *Antitrust and Trade Regulation Reporter* §21.04[2].

105   *Transamerica Computer Co., Inc. v. International Business Machines Corporation*, 698 F.2d 1377 (9th Cir. 1983) at 1383. Similarly in *Northeastern Tel. Co. v. AT&T Co.*, 651 F.2d 76 (2nd Cir 1981) cert. denied, 455 U.S. 973 (1983) an affiliate of AT&T was found guilty of predatory conduct when it overdesigned equipment required on the Bell System that was incompatible with a small manufacturer of telephone equipment.

106   For the text of the undertaking see "Undertaking Given By IBM," *Bulletin of the European Community*, 10 (1984):96-103.

107   See *supra* at note 94.

108   See *supra* at note 94 §IV.A and §IV.B.

109   See Blair and Esquibel (1995, p. 260) and Baseman, Warren-Boulton, and Woroch (1995, p. 301). They were, however, fundamental to the *Memorandum of Amici Curiae in Opposition to Proposed Final Judgement* (January 10, 1995) and Judge Sporkin's finding that the proposed consent decree was not in the public interest. See Lopatka and Page (1995) for further details.

110   Christopher Anderson, "The Software Industry," *The Economist*, 25 May 1996, p. 58.

111   See Amy Cortese and Kathy Rebello, "Windows 95," *Business Week*, 10 July 1995, p. 94-104, and Kathy Rebello, Peter Burrows and Mark Lewyn, "Oh Microsoft, Poor Microsoft," *Business Week*, 26 June 1995, p. 38.

112   Christopher Anderson, "The Software Industry," *The Economist*, 25 May 1996, p. 58.

113   "U.S. Asked to Probe Microsoft's Proposal for Free Software," *Wall Street Journal*, 20 February 1996, p. A4.

114   Stephen Wildstrom, "Browsers: The Race Heats Up," *Business Week*, 1 July 1996, p. 18.

115   *Data General Corp. v. Grumman Systems Support Corp.* 36 F.3d 1147 (1st Cir. 1994).

116   *U.S. v. Grinnell Corp.*, 1966 CCH Trade Case ¶71,789.

117   35 U.S.C. §271(d) (1988).

118   See, for instance, SCM *v. Xerox*, 645 F.2d 1195 (2nd Cir. 1981).

119   *Eastman Kodak Co. v. Image Technical Services, Inc., et al.*, 1992-1 CCH Trade Cases ¶69,839 at footnote 32.

120   The Courts in the U.S. have generally held that a tie is *per se* illegal if the following four conditions are met: (i) there are two separate products; (ii) the existence of a tie

is demonstrated; (iii) the firm has market power in the tying good; and (iv) a substantial amount of commerce is affected. This formulation is set out by the U.S. Supreme Court in *Jefferson Parish Hospital District No. 2 et al. v. Hyde*, 466 U.S. 2 (1984) at 15-18.

121 Greenstein also notes the incentive that the monopolist has to make reverse engineering difficult.

122 Ordover and Willig (1981) suggest that an action is predatory only if its profitability is contingent on the exit of rival firms. They apply this general standard of predatory behaviour to innovations in system markets.

123 See Kattan (1993), Shapiro and Teece (1994), Borenstein, MacKie-Mason, and Netz (1995), and Shapiro (1995) for discussions about the existence of market power in aftermarkets. For an insightful discussion of market power in aftermarkets, which predates the current controversy, see Saloner (1990).

124 See *Eastman Kodak Co. v. Image Technical Services, Inc.*, 112 S. Ct. 2072 (1992). Other aftermarket cases include *Data General Corp. v. Grumman Systems Support Corp.*, 36 F.3d 1147 (1st Cir. 1994); *Virtual Maintenance Inc. v. Prime Computer Inc.*, 957 F.2d 1318 (6th Cir. 1992); *Service & Training, Inc. v. Data General Corp.*, 963 F.2d 680 (4th Cir. 1992); *Digidyne Corp. v. Data General Corp.*, 734 F.2d 1336 (9th Cir. 1984), *cert. denied*, 473 U.S. 908 (1985).

125 See *BNA Antitrust and Trade Regulation Reporter*, 69 (October 19, 1995): 440-41.

126 The maximum B can offer is by setting $P^B = C - \pi^m(P^m)$, which gives consumer surplus of $CS(P^m) + \pi(P^m) - C$. At price P^A system A gives consumer surplus of $CS(P^m) + \pi(P^m) + DWL(P^m) - P^A$. Equating the two and solving for P^A is the profit maximizing price for firm A.

127 Note that the incentive to exploit or hold-up the installed base is not easily solved by firms developing a reputation not to act opportunistically. Consider a model where demand in the aftermarket by a consumer every period is given by $P(Q)$ and consumers arrive sequentially, one per period, and live forever. Then provided firms have a discount factor less than one so that future profits are not valued the same as current profits, the size of the installed base will eventually become so large that the firm will have an incentive to exploit its installed base and forgo new system sales. If profitable, it can lower its price of hardware for new customers in order to mitigate the effect in its primary market of an increase in price in its aftermarket. See the discussion in Borenstein, MacKie-Mason, and Netz (1995) and Shapiro (1995).

128 Borenstein, MacKie-Mason, and Netz (1995, p. 473-74) provide a detailed explanation for why private contracting is not likely to be an adequate solution to this hold-up problem.

ACKNOWLEDGMENTS

WE ARE GRATEFUL FOR HELPFUL COMMENTS from Rob Anderson, Brian Rivard, Mark Lemley, Murray Hamley, and participants in the Authors' Symposium. Jeffrey Church wishes to acknowledge the gracious hospitality of the Canadian Competition Bureau during the period when much of this paper was written.

BIBLIOGRAPHY

Ahern, P. J. "Refusals to Deal After *Aspen*." *Antitrust Law Journal*, 63 (1994): 153-83.

Areeda, P. "Essential Facilities: An Epithet in Need of Limiting Principles." *Antitrust Law Journal*, 58 (1990): 841-53.

Baseman, K., F. Warren-Boulton, and G. Woroch. "Microsoft Plays Hardball: The Use of Exclusionary Pricing and Technical Incompatibility to Maintain Monopoly Power in Markets for Operating System Software." *Antitrust Bulletin*, 40 (1995): 265-315.

Besen, S. and J. Farrell. "Choosing How to Compete: Strategies and Tactics in Standardization." *Journal of Economic Perspectives*, 8 (1994): 117-31.

Blair, R. and A. Esquibel. "The *Microsoft* Muddle: A Caveat." *The Antitrust Bulletin*, 40 (1995): 257-64.

Borenstein, S., J. MacKie-Mason, and J. Netz. "Antitrust Policy in Aftermarkets." *Antitrust Law Journal*, 63 (1995): 455-82.

Brandenburger, A. and B. Nalebuff. "The Right Game: Use Game Theory to Shape Strategy." *Harvard Business Review*, July-August 1995, pp. 57-71.

Brock, G. "Dominant Firm Response to Competitive Challenge: Peripheral Equipment Manufacturers' Suits Against IBM," in *The Antitrust Revolution* (1st ed.). Edited by J. Kwoka, Jr. and L. White. Glenview, Illinois: Scott, Foresman and Company, 1989.

Chou, C. and O. Shy. "Network Effects without Network Externalities." *International Journal of Industrial Organization*, 8 (1990): 259-70.

Church, J. and N. Gandal. "Network Effects, Software Provision and Standardization." *Journal of Industrial Economics*, 40 (1992a): 85-104.

——."Integration, Complementary Products and Variety." *Journal of Economics and Management Strategy*, 1 (1992b): 651-75.

——."Complementary Network Externalities and Technological Adoption." *International Journal of Industrial Organization*, 11 (1993): 239-60.

——.*Do Indirect Network Effects Lead to Inefficiencies?* Mimeo, University of Calgary, 1995.

——.*Systems Competition, Vertical Merger, and Foreclosure.* Working Paper 6-96, Sackler Institute, Tel-Aviv University, 1996a.

——."Strategic Entry Deterrence: Complementary Products as Installed Base." *European Journal of Political Economy*, 12 (1996b): 331-54.

Dybvig, P. and C. Spatt. "Adoption Externalities as Public Goods." *Journal of Public Economics*, 20 (1983): 231-47.

Economides, N. "Desirability of Compatibility in the Absence of Network Externalities." *American Economic Review*, 79 (1988): 1165-81.

Farrell, J. "Standardization and Intellectual Property." *Jurimetrics Journal*, 30 (1989): 35-50.

——."Arguments for Weaker Intellectual Property Protection in Network Industries." *Standard View*, 3 (1995): 46-49.

Farrell, J. and N. Gallini. "Second-Sourcing as a Commitment: Monopoly Incentives to Attract Competition." *Quarterly Journal of Economics*, 103 (1988): 673-94.

Farrell, J. and G. Saloner. "Standardization, Compatibility, and Innovation." *Rand Journal of Economics*, 16 (1985): 70-83.

——."Standardization and Variety." *Economic Letters*, 20 (1986a): 71-74.

——."Installed Base and Compatibility: Innovation, Product Preannouncements, and Predation." *American Economic Review*, 76 (1986b): 940-55.

———."Converters, Compatibility, and Control of Interfaces." *Journal of Industrial Economics*, 40 (1992): 9-35.

Farrell, J. and C. Shapiro. "Standard Setting in High Definition Television." *Brookings Papers on Economic Activity: Microeconomics*, 1 (1992).

Fisher, F. M., J. J. McGowan, and J. E. Greenwood. *Folded, Spindled, and Mutilated: Economic Analysis and U.S. v. IBM*. Cambridge, Mass: MIT Press, 1983.

Forrester, I. S. "Software Licensing in the Light of Current EC Competition Law Considerations." *European Competition Law Review* ,13 (1992): 5-20.

Fudenberg, D. and J.Tirole. "The Fat-Cat Effect, the Puppy-Dog Ploy, and the Lean and Hungry Look." *American Economic Review*, 74 (1984): 361-66.

Gilbert, R. "Symposium on Compatibility: Incentives and Market Structure." *Journal of Industrial Economics*, 40 (1992): 1-8.

Gilburne, M. and R. Johnston. "Trade Secret Protection for Software Generally and in the Mass Market." *Computer Law Journal*, 3 (1982): 211-72.

Glazer, K. L. and A. B. J. Lipsky. "Unilateral Refusals to Deal Under section 2 of the *Sherman Act*." *Antitrust Law Journal*, 63 (1995): 749-800.

Greenstein, S. "Creating Economic Advantage by Setting Compatibility Standards: Can 'Physical Tie-Ins' Extend Monopoly Power?" *Economics of Innovation and New Technology*, 1 (1990): 63-83.

Grindley, P. *Standards, Strategy, and Policy*. Oxford: Oxford University Press, 1995.

Hanna, R. "Misusing Antitrust: The Search for Functional Copyright Misuse Standards." *Stanford Law Review*, 46 (1994): 401-48.

Karjala, D. S. and P. S. Menell. "Applying Fundamental Copyright Principles to *Lotus Development Corp. v. Borland International, Inc.*" *High Technology Law Journal*, 10 (1995): 177-92.

Kattan, J. "Antitrust Analysis of Technology Joint Ventures: Allocative Efficiency and the Rewards of Innovation." *Antitrust Law Journal*, 61 (1993): 937-76.

Katz, M. and C. Shapiro. "Network Externalities, Competition, and Compatibility." *American Economic Review*, 75 (1985): 424-40.

———. "Technology Adoption in the Presence of Network Externalities." *Journal of Political Economy*, 94 (1986a): 822-41.

———. "Product Compatibility Choice in a Market with Technological Progress." *Oxford Economic Papers*, NS 38 Supplement, 1986b, pp. 146-65.

———. "Product Introduction with Network Externalities." *Journal of Industrial Economics*, 40 (1992): 55-84.

———. "System Competition and Network Effects." *Journal of Economic Perspectives*, 8 (1994): 93-115.

Koback, J. B., Jr. "Running the Gauntlet: Antitrust and Intellectual Property Rights." *Antitrust Law Journal*, 64 (1996): 341-66.

Kristiansen, E. G. *R&D in the Presence of Network Externalities: Timing and Compatibility*. Mimeo, Institute of Economics, Norwegian School of Economics and Business Administration, 1995.

Laurenson, R. "Computer Software 'Article of Manufacture' Patents." *Journal of the Patent and Trademark Office Society*, 77 (1995): 811-24.

Lemley, M. A. "Convergence in the Law of Software Copyright." *High Technology Law Journal*, 10 (1995): 1-34.

Lopatka, J. E. and W. H. Page. "Microsoft, Monopolization and Network Externalities: Some Uses and Abuses of Economic Theory in Antitrust Decision Making." *The Antitrust Bulletin*, 40 (1995): 317-71.

Matutes, C. and P. Regibeau. "Mix and Match: Product Compatibility without Network Externalities." *Rand Journal of Economics*, 19 (1988): 221-34.

McManis, C. "Intellectual Property Protection and Reverse Engineering of Computer Programs in the United States and the European Community." *High Technology Law Journal*, 8 (1993): 25-99.

Menell, P. "Tailoring Legal Protection for Computer Software." *Stanford Law Review*, 39 (1987): 1329-37.

Morgan, M. "Canadian Copyright and Computer Software: Back to the Future?" *Canadian Intellectual Property Review*, 12 (1995): 161-204.

Ordover, J., A. Sykes, and R. Willig. "Nonprice Anticompetitive Behaviour by Dominant Firms toward Producers of Complementary Products." In *Antitrust and Regulation: Essays in Memory of John J. McGowan*. Edited by F. Fisher. Cambridge, Mass.: MIT Press, 1985.

Ordover, J. A. and R. D. Willig. "An Economic Definition of Predation: Pricing and Product Innovation." *Yale Law Journal*, 91 (1981): 8-53.

Paredes, T. "Copyright Misuse and Tying: Will Courts Stop Misusing Misuse?" *High Technology Law Journal*, 9 (1994): 271-336.

Rosen, N. "Intellectual Property and the Antitrust Pendulum: Recent Developments at the Interface Between the Antitrust and Intellectual Property Laws." *Antitrust Law Journal*, 62 (1994): 669-94.

Ross, T. W. "Sunk Costs as a Barrier to Entry in Merger Cases." *University of British Columbia Law Review*, 27 (1993): 75-92.

Saloner, G. "Economic Issues in Computer Interface Standardization." *Economics of Innovation and New Technologies*, 1 (1990): 135-56.

Samuelson, P. "An Entirely New Legal Regime Is Needed." *The Computer Lawyer*, 12 (1995): 11-17.

Samuelson, P., R. Davis, M. D. Kapor, and J. H. Reichman. "A Manifesto Concerning the Legal Protection of Computer Programs." *Columbia Law Review*, 94 (1994): 2308-431.

Scotchmer, S. "Standing on the Shoulders of Giants." *Journal of Economic Perspectives*, 5 (1991): 29-41

Shapiro, C. "Aftermarkets and Consumer Welfare: Making Sense of *Kodak*." *Antitrust Law Journal*, 63 (1995): 483-511.

Shapiro, C. and D. Teece. "Systems Competition and Aftermarkets: An Economic Analysis of *Kodak*." *Antitrust Bulletin*, 39 (1994): 135-62.

Shepard, A. "Licensing to Enhance Demand for New Technologies." *Rand Journal of Economics*, 18 (1987): 360-68.

Stack, S. J. "Recent and Impending Developments in Copyright and Antitrust." *Antitrust Law Journal*, 61 (1993): 331-45.

Stewart, D. "Patenting of Software-Proposed Guidelines and the Magic Dividing Line that Disappeared." *Journal of the Patent and Trademark Office Society*, 77 (1995): 681-98.

Thum, M. "Network Externalities, Technological Progress, and the Competition of Market Contracts." *International Journal of Industrial Organization*, 12 (1994): 269-89.

Tirole, J. *The Theory of Industrial Organization*. Cambridge, Mass.: MIT Press, 1988.

Tritell, R. and G. Metaxas-Maranghidis. "Intellectual Property Rights versus Antitrust: Lessons from *Magill*." *Journal of Proprietary Rights*, 7 (1995): 2-3.

Warren-Boulton, F., K. Baseman, and G. Woroch. "Copyright Protection of Software Can Make Economic Sense." *The Computer Lawyer*, 12 (1995a): 18-28.

——. *The Economics of Intellectual Property Protection for Software: The Proper Role for Copyright.* Mimeo, University of California, Berkeley, 1995b.

Whinston, M. "Tying, Foreclosure, and Exclusion." *American Economic Review*, 80 (1990): 837-59.

Yoches, E. R. "The Compton's Reexamination – A Sign of the Times." *The Computer Lawyer*, 12 (1995): 14-18.

Comment

Joseph Farrell
Federal Communications Commission, and
University of California, Berkeley

L ET ME START WITH THE DISCLAIMER THAT THESE ARE MY OPINIONS and they may not coincide with those of the Federal Communications Commission or any commissioners.

The general topic of Jeffrey Church and Roger Ware's paper is the relationship between network effects and intellectual property, a topic that I also have worked on. But today, instead of talking about the *interactions* between network effects and intellectual property, I would like to suggest that there is a very close *analogy* between the two.

I will begin with the familiar question: Why is this good different from every other good? The traditional answer is that intellectual property, unlike other goods, is technologically non-rival (it is like a cold: I can give it to you and I still have it myself), but excludable (if I choose not to give it to you, then provided the technology and the law support me in this, you will not have it). So it is not like national defence, where it is unfeasible for one person to have it and not another.

But these characteristics do not make intellectual property unique. Plenty of other goods are technologically non-rival but excludable. For instance, network externalities are technologically non-rival in the sense that if we achieve compatibility, we interconnect and share the network externalities. As a matter of fact, it is better than non-rival: when we share, we both have more. The same is true of economies of scale. If we share production, then we both have more scale, and so we both get more economies of scale. Similarly, with economies of density, if we share whatever it is that has economies of density, then we are both more efficient. And network externalities and economies of density and scale are also excludable.

To illustrate how some of these concepts apply to the telecommunications world where I spend most of my time these days, consider two networks: first, a relatively large one with nine subscribers, three to a switch, and three switches; and second, a relatively small network with a mere three subscribers and one switch. You will notice two points about this:

- Given a somewhat random distribution of the three small network subscribers in the area, the loops or lines that the small network has to provide the connectors to the switch are longer than the average loop supplied by the large network. There is an economy of density: if you have more subscribers in a given area, then because of the fixed cost involved in setting up switches and the shorter loops, you will have a lower average cost.

- Absent interconnection, the three subscribers on the small network can only talk to each other, and the nine subscribers on the big network can also only talk to each other. Absent interconnection, therefore, both the economies of density and the network externalities are not only excludable, but excluded.

It does not have to be that way. Just as with intellectual property, it is a policy choice whether exclusion is permitted as a competitive tool. Sharing network externalities and economies of density does not diminish them. It is not like pizza. It is like information, like intellectual property. In fact it is better, because not only does sharing not diminish them, it actually increases them.

However, it does diminish the competitive advantage that the dominant carrier gets from not sharing, if (as in often the case) the inefficiency hits the smaller carrier much harder. Therefore, if permitted, it is a natural competitive tool, to either implement or threaten exclusion.

The question then becomes: In what circumstances should exclusion be a legitimate competitive tool? For intellectual property there are special rules for when exclusion is appropriate and when it is not. Just to take a very naive statement of that, for a patentable innovation with no cumulative complications, it is regarded as appropriate for the first 17 years and inappropriate thereafter.

What about the other technologically non-rival but excludable efficiencies that I mentioned? Well, with network externalities we do not really have a general policy indicating in which circumstances it is a legitimate competitive tool to exclude. It is similar with economies of density or of scale.

We have special rules for intellectual property, and they are fairly well developed and well studied. In contrast, for other non-rival excludable goods, we do not have a well-developed set of rules that say when exclusion is legitimate as a competitive tool and when it's not.

In February the *Telecommunications Act* passed. My interpretation of the *Telecommunications Act's* interconnection provisions is they state that exclusion is inappropriate as a competitive tool in some aspects of the telephone industry. I do not think this suggests that exclusion from technologically non-rival but excludable economies is inappropriate everywhere or always. As a matter of fact, the analogy with intellectual property makes it clear that this would be an unwise suggestion. Similarly, ubiquitous sharing of economies of scale would lead to a very different kind of economy. But I think the *Telecommunications Act* does say it is appropriate for some aspects of telecommunications now. This seems to me a pretty reasonable view: it has been far more than 17 years since Alexander Graham Bell, so the *ex ante* incentive effects may have somewhat dissipated.

Not only is exclusion declared inappropriate as a competitive tool in telecom, but so – much harder and more complex to enforce – is any implied threat of exclusion. What do I mean by an "implied threat of exclusion"? Well, it amounts to an issue of how negotiations are conducted. It is important to be aware that issues of interconnection in telecommunications are not usually phrased the way they are in the computer industry.

In the computer industry, it appears to be common for firms to decide: "No, we're not going to be compatible with x." In telecommunications, that appears to be rare. Instead, the question is almost universally phrased as: "Yes, we will interconnect with x, but on the following terms." So it has changed from being a yes-no decision (such as Jeffrey Church and Roger Ware discuss, and as I have discussed elsewhere) into a pricing decision.

That makes it much more complicated to intervene, because if a competing carrier is using the incumbent's facilities – as it does under interconnection and especially unbundling – there is some real cost to the incumbent. The incumbent should not necessarily have to provide interconnection at a zero price. But then the question becomes: What will be the price?

The papers in this volume ask what role antitrust or intellectual property policy should play in these relationships. I have to ask: Where are the regulators in that discussion? It seems to me that some regulation is often going to be involved in those prices, because if the threat of refusing to interconnect is not a legitimate competitive tool, then completely unstructured negotiations with a default outcome of no interconnection will also not lead to the right results.

If you believe that, then regulators must intervene at least to provide a backdrop to the negotiations. Some people will tell you that the New Zealand experience represents a situation where the regulators decided to stay out, and these interconnection negotiations are conducted purely in the shadow of antitrust law or competition law. My understanding is that this is not quite right, since there was a statement that if things did not go well, regulators would step in.

This discussion is one view of what U.S. policymakers are trying to do with this interconnection proceeding. By declaring that exclusion is not a legitimate competitive tool, and by implementing a number of other rules and regulations about how the relationships between incumbents and entrants should be governed, we are trying to turn this potentially natural monopoly industry into an unnatural monopoly industry. Then having done that, we hope that we can stand back and watch successful entry and workable competition take place, creating a natural non-monopoly.

Part III
Broader Policy Issues and
Comparative Perspectives

Derek Ireland
Office of Consumer Affairs
Industry Canada[1]

9

Competition Policy, Intellectual Property and the Consumer

INTRODUCTION

PURPOSE AND APPROACH

THE PURPOSE OF THIS PAPER is to bring a consumer perspective to the debate on the interactions between competition policy and intellectual property and to set out the issues and possible agenda for future research and policy formulation. It is hoped that by adding to, and illuminating the consumer perspective on, an already complex topic, the paper will help to inform the work of competition policy and intellectual property practitioners, consumer advocates, and other members of the policy community in the years ahead.

Competition policy, intellectual property rights, and the consumer interest raise a number of complex issues and policy interactions and frictions. This brief paper can only touch the surface of a complicated set of questions that, in our view, will bedevil policymakers, innovators/creators, producers of goods and services, marketers, and consumers and their representatives for the foreseeable future.

The paper is based on a literature review and on the integration of past and current work of the author and other analysts over the last decade, including:

- work by Consumer and Corporate Affairs Canada about six years ago, which summarized the Price Waterhouse survey on the use of intellectual property rights by Canadian businesses, and the department's policy development work for the negotiations of trade-related intellectual property (TRIP) agreements within the Uruguay Round, together with more recent work of the Corporate Governance Branch of Industry Canada, which builds on and extends this previous analysis;

- work by the author and many others over the past half-decade on the interactions between competition policy and other policy fields, including intellectual property, innovation, and industrial and trade policies;

- work by the Office of Consumer Affairs (OCA) and its predecessors, the Competition Bureau, Industry Canada's Corporate Governance Branch, the Organisation for Economic Co-operation and Development (OECD), and other groups on the links between competition policy, intellectual property, and the consumer interest;

- OCA/federal government surveys on biotechnology, intellectual property, and the consumer conducted by Optima, CROP Environics, and others (this work is ongoing and includes focus group research on environmental and agricultural issues and biotech applications conducted in the first half of 1996 when this paper was being completed, and the current OCA research program on "Biotechnology, the Consumer and the Canadian Marketplace"); and

- recent work by the OCA on innovative, framework-based approaches to consumer law and policy, and on the market for, and economics of, information, with particular emphasis on the implications of the Internet and other aspects of the information highway for markets, competition, and consumer behaviour.

The author also benefited from a review of many of the draft papers being prepared under the Competition Bureau/University of Toronto work program.

The rest of this paper is structured as follows. The next section provides an overview of the extent to which competition policy and intellectual property rights serve the consumer interest. Some of the difficulties that arise in attempts to integrate the consumer perspective into the competition policy/intellectual property debate are then examined. Consumer values are changing rapidly, providing a moving target for policymakers, and they differ greatly, depending on the consumer's age, socio-economic status, geographic location, and attitudes towards the threats and opportunities posed by the new strategic technologies. The complexity of the consumer perspective argues for a new sensitivity and new approaches to identifying consumer concerns and for ensuring that their richness is fully addressed in the formulation of public policy.

The final section sets out some thoughts on the public policy and research agendas for the future. Three appendices conclude the paper – one on the background and analytical framework for this paper; one on the issues and policy frictions raised by the information economy; and one on some of the intellectual property issues that could raise consumer concerns over the short to medium term.

HIGHLIGHTS

GIVEN THE DECLINING IMPORTANCE OF THE CONSUMER MOVEMENT and the decreasing attention given to consumer issues in recent years, why is it important to bring a consumer perspective to the study of the relationship between intellectual property (IP) and competition policy? One reason is that the consumer interest is underlined in the purpose clause of the *Competition Act* and is prominent in many aspects of IP law – for example, in the concept of "passing -off" under trademark law. A second reason is that, while the consumer constituency often appears diffused and even disorganized, when galvanized it has the potential to bring about significant political and economic change in a way that is not possible for the better-organized but smaller constituencies surrounding competition and IP laws.

The central thesis of this paper is that consumers, in making their purchasing decisions, are concerned with more than matters of price, quality, and choice – the traditional purview of competition policy. Consumers are also applying social, political, "lifestyle," and other broader concerns to their purchasing decisions. This development is posing new challenges to both private sector marketers and government policymakers, including those concerned with competition policy and intellectual property. As described in Appendix A, these challenges involve an interesting mix:

- externalities, such as information and other market failures addressed in the economic literature and, to some degree, in current competition law and IP policy; and

- broader non-economic criteria – fairness, ethics, natural justice, distributive justice, and paternalism – that normally do not come under the purview of competition law and IP but continue to raise concerns for policymakers in the provinces, at the federal level, and increasingly in international fora (as underlined by the growing interest in the environment, human rights, and labour rights in international trade negotiations).

With its focus on competitive markets, consumer welfare, product choice, and total economic efficiency, competition policy generally serves the consumer well. Canadian consumers are also generally well served by effective intellectual property laws and enforcement, which result in part from the efforts of Canadian governments to balance stakeholder interests in framing IP law and policy. However, frictions can arise between competition and IP policy, on the one hand, and the consumer perspective, on the other. These frictions may result from the fact that competition law focuses on total efficiency while intellectual property law is concerned with the innovation process and the claims of inventors and creators, leaving consumers and their representatives limited opportunities and resources to influence those laws, compared with the much greater resources and contacts of the business and creative communities in Canada. Moreover, as the scope of competition and IP issues becomes global, international responses are required from the consumer movement, but its experience with international strategic alliances has been limited until now.

Interactions between the two policy fields and the consumer interest are further complicated by the diversity of the consumer perspective. Compared to the typical consumer of 30 years ago, his/her counterpart today is, on average, better educated and better informed, more self-reliant, and more value-conscious; has a more international perspective; and is less willing to accept without question the claims of government, industry, and other so-called "elites." At the same time, the differences across consumer groups may be just as important as the norm, reflecting a greater recognition of the "vulnerable consumer" with limited literacy and life skills, the rising gaps in income and consumer purchasing power, and regional, rural/urban, and demographic differences (linked in part to immigrant populations).

Consumer attitudes also vary with respect to the risks and rewards of new technologies. For example, biotechnology can provide important benefits to industry, the consumer, and the total economy. However, survey and focus-group research conducted by the federal government and others indicate that, while there is some public awareness, the technology and its implications are not well understood by the general public. The issues involved here include:

- the labelling of new, genetically altered foods;
- the quality and credibility of public information;
- the extent to which regulatory processes are understood, have the full confidence of the buying public, and are able to address ethical and other broader considerations;
- the ethical concerns raised by the patenting of life forms; and
- questions about who benefits, who pays, and who carries the risks.

Compared to biotechnology, the new information technologies raise a different but still challenging set of issues related to the protection of copyright, personal privacy, consumer fraud, and the potential for abuses of market power. However, in both cases there is a need to better understand the effects of these enabling technologies – as well as the marketplace and ethical issues they raise – on market behaviour, structure, and outcomes.

This brings us to the future research and policy agenda. The work of the Office of Consumer Affairs and others underlines the importance of social science research, focus-group analysis, and longitudinal and other survey methods to better identify the consumer perspective in all its complexity, diversity, and perversity. This is needed to support both corporate strategy and government policy formulation, in particular with respect to the new technologies. At the same time, the social science research should be complemented by more theoretical research that will give appropriate attention to the consumer perspective

and feedback to producers and marketers by applying models of industrial organization, game theory, and endogenous growth theory, for example.

The text suggests as well that the competition authorities need to explore
more flexible and sensitive analytical techniques and interpretations of the
consumer perspective and of dynamic versus static efficiencies. This could
involve modifying for antitrust purposes the advances in benefit/cost analysis
being developed and applied by the World Bank, among others. As well, both
competition and IP authorities need to consider how to expand the opportunities available to consumers and their representatives to influence administrative
priorities and policy formulation. For their part, consumer associations and
other non-governmental organizations (NGOs) require better-researched and
articulated policy advocacy, and more effective alliances with other groups,
including the private sector.

All of this will be taking place in a world where the partitions of the past
between science, commerce, the economy, and ethics are coming down. The
debate between these different worlds is being joined in the marketplace as well
as in domestic policy development and in international fora, and it will set the
broader context for competition policy, intellectual property rights, and the
consumer perspective in the years ahead.

COMPETITION POLICY, INTELLECTUAL PROPERTY AND THE CONSUMER INTEREST

BUILDING AN UNDERSTANDING OF THE LINKS and potential tensions between
the three sets of laws should start from the recognition that competition,
intellectual property, and consumer laws share common origins in fair-trade
practices and marketplace framework laws. The tasks of promoting the consumer
interest and protecting the consumer when markets fail to do so are fundamental
not only to consumer protection laws; they are also relevant to various aspects
of intellectual property statutes (e.g., the passing-off of trademarks, the fair use
of copyrights) and of competition law (e.g., rules regarding misleading advertising and other questionable marketing practices).

There are also important overlaps between the three sets of laws.
Prohibitions against misleading advertising and misrepresentation can
be found in both competition and consumer laws in Canada and elsewhere,
and the two sets of laws are administered by the same agency in some jurisdictions. Prohibitions against the abuse of intellectual property are found in
many competition statutes, and provisions on unfair and anticompetitive trade
practices are found in IP conventions under the World Trade Organization
(WTO) and the North American Free Trade Agreement (NAFTA). Given
their common origins and purposes and the overlaps among them, the boundaries
between competition, intellectual property, and consumer laws are to some
extent artificial.

COMPETITION POLICY AND THE CONSUMER

FOR OBVIOUS REASONS, WITH ITS FOCUS ON COMPETITIVE MARKETS, consumer welfare, and economic efficiency, competition policy (including competition law) serves the consumer interest well in many and perhaps most circumstances.[2] The link with the consumer interest is perhaps most direct with respect to the marketing practices provisions of Canada's *Competition Act*, which are designed to provide a level playing field for businesses in the areas of advertising, warranties, referral, selling, and other promotional practices, while at the same time protecting consumers from misleading advertising and other forms of deceptive marketing practices. Many of the other sections of the *Competition Act* and the competition statutes of other jurisdictions – including the sections concerned with conspiracies, abuses of dominant position, and merger review – are largely concerned, both in law and in practice, with the provision of competitive prices and product choices to consumers and other users.

Lower prices and greater consumer choice are also the major guiding principles in the many representations made by the Competition Bureau's Director of Investigation and Research over the years to regulatory boards and tribunals in the areas of transportation, telecommunications and the information highway, electrical and other energy matters, financial services, and international trade.[3] As well, for many years, the Bureau has worked closely with other branches and divisions within Industry Canada and with other federal departments and agencies, as well as with provincial governments and non-government groups, to ensure that their policies promote competitive markets, economic efficiency, and the interests of consumers and other marketplace participants. In short, enhancing consumer welfare is central to competition law, enforcement practice, and competition policy advocacy in Canada and elsewhere.

However, given the total efficiency approach underlying the Canadian law,[4] there is at least the possibility that the Bureau will not challenge such business practices as mergers, dominant positions, research and development (R&D) joint ventures, territorial restrictions, and related vertical arrangements[5] if they provide significant efficiency gains to producers and to the economy as a whole, even though they may decrease consumer welfare. As well, competition policy may be prepared to accept a longer patent term, a broader patent scope, and more restrictive licensing practices and vertical arrangements than would consumers on the basis of a strict consumer-welfare test.

At the same time, the potential conflict between competition law and the consumer perspective could operate in the opposite direction. Consumers may be prepared to accept a merger, a strategic alliance, a licensing agreement, or an abuse of dominance or intellectual property that could lead to losses in consumer welfare and total economic efficiency in the short run but might result in major breakthroughs in new products and technologies[6] in the long run.

For purposes of consistency, transparency, and credibility, competition enforcement agencies have traditionally been forced to apply similar competition and efficiency tests and comparable discount rates to future benefits and costs, as well as to all market participants – large and small businesses, individual inventors, the final consumer – across all of their enforcement cases. However, the efficiency and related tests and discount rates applied by consumers and other stakeholders can vary greatly depending on the enforcement case, the public policy issue, media attention, the public mood, and the distributional, fairness, and equity concerns raised by the enforcement matter.

In short, under certain circumstances, consumers may be prepared to accept a more relaxed and favourable trade-off between, on the one hand, near-term, static efficiency losses (and the generation of short-term monopoly rents), and on the other, dynamic efficiency gains, than has traditionally been allowed under competition law, in order to achieve a broader public policy purpose with respect to human rights, the environment, medical science, and technological advancement more generally. This brings in the broader socio-economic criteria discussed in Appendix A. For similar reasons, consumers and the general public may be prepared to accept a longer patent term and broader patent scope in instances where these attributes could lead to a major medical or other scientific breakthrough.

In a broader sense, there are potential frictions between the fundamental principles of competition law and practice and the changing consumer interest (as described later in this paper and in Appendix A). The purpose clause of the *Competition Act* encompasses a number of other principles that go beyond the promotion of economic efficiency and the flexibility and adaptability of the Canadian economy, and the provision to consumers of competitive prices and product choices. The *Competition Act* is also intended to make room for expanded opportunities for Canadian participation in world markets while at the same time recognizing the role of foreign competition in Canada; and to ensure that small and medium-sized enterprises have an equitable opportunity to participate in the Canadian economy.

These additional principles are not necessarily inconsistent with economic efficiency, competitive markets, and the consumer interest,[7] but there may be at least the theoretical possibility for conflicts and trade-offs that would run counter to the consumer interest.[8] It is also worth noting that calculations of consumer surplus as a welfare measure at times do not address such considerations as product safety, consumer information, protection of personal information, consumer redress, or some of the other concerns that are becoming part of the consumer's increasingly complex utility function.

Perhaps most important, competition agencies must look at the consumer interest, and measure consumer welfare in the aggregate. They lack the information and mandate to take advantage of the richness and diversity of the consumer perspective (a topic that is addressed later on in this paper) in order to give different weights to different classes of consumer. It could be argued, for example, that competition and other authorities should give more credence to consumers who feel particularly strongly about a specific issue such as the patenting of life forms, environmental protection, or the concentrations of corporate power and family wealth in Canada. However, competition agencies would not feel comfortable in making value judgments in those areas.[9] Accordingly, such complexities are generally the purview of other policy fields, including intellectual property rights, tax law, lobbying legislation, and consumer protection policy and law.

There are other reasons, of a more legalistic and administrative nature, why consumers and their representatives may, from time to time, doubt that they are being well served by Canadian competition law and institutions. There has been an ongoing debate about whether consumers benefit sufficiently from the so-called criminal or penal provisions of the *Competition Act* in view of the high burden of proof that is required in order to obtain a conviction in matters of conspiracies, bid-rigging, unfair marketing practices, and retail price maintenance.

This concern was addressed in part through the 1986 amendments to the act, which established the Competition Tribunal to address certain cases such as mergers, abuses of dominant position, refusals to deal, and other non-price vertical restraints, following civil or administrative law practices. The 1986 amendments were based on the view that, by changing these issues into reviewable matters, compliance with the act and consumer welfare would be advanced because of the greater probability of conviction than under the penal provisions. Based on the success of the reviewable provisions over the past decade, the Competition Bureau is now assessing the potential to expand these provisions to include marketing practices that do not encompass an element of criminal fraud.

Certain competition policy practitioners and commentators have argued that, except for naked price-fixing and market-sharing agreements, strategic alliances and other horizontal arrangements that hold the potential of generating significant efficiency gains that could offset any losses in consumer welfare should be considered as reviewable matters requiring a total-efficiency test.[10] This possibility, however, is not being considered in the round of amendments currently being discussed by the Competition Bureau and by the government.

This leads to a second problem from a consumer perspective: whereas the penal provisions of the *Competition Act* provide for the right of private action,[11] the Bureau's Director of Investigation and Research holds a monopoly on taking reviewable cases to the Competition Tribunal. Input from consumers and their representatives is limited to complaints and submissions to the Director and his staff, and to their capacity to gain standing on specific cases being considered by the Tribunal – a capacity, incidentally, that businesses, their trade associations, and their legal counsel would like to see highly restricted. As well, at the present time, penalties under the reviewable provisions are limited to cease-and-desist orders, divestitures, and other non-financial remedies. Therefore, even if a consumer group had an opportunity to take a reviewable matter before the Competition Tribunal, it is far from obvious that there would be an incentive to do so.

Given the growing application of class action suits and contingency fees in Canada, removing the Director's monopoly on reviewable cases and including in the act administrative fines and other financial penalties for reviewable matters, could offer important opportunities for consumer groups to promote consumer interests and obtain Tribunal judgments that would help to finance their future activities on behalf of competition and the consumer. These possible options were raised in the Competition Bureau's 1995 discussion paper and subsequent consultations on amendments, but were not included in the amendments package subsequently placed before Parliament.

The final problem faced by consumers and their representatives in influencing the direction and enforcement of the *Competition Act* lies outside the realm of competition law and institutions in Canada. It is a problem related to the weakness of the Canadian consumer movement and to the lack of consensus and understanding across the movement regarding the importance of competitive markets and of effective enforcement of competition law to promoting consumer welfare.

INTELLECTUAL PROPERTY AND THE CONSUMER

RESEARCH CONDUCTED BY CONSUMER AND CORPORATE AFFAIRS CANADA some years ago[12] – and then by Industry Canada, Statistics Canada,[13] and others – has underlined the importance of intellectual property rights (IPRs) to industry performance, business operations, cultural development, technology transfer, Canada's two-way trade, and the achievement of a broader range of public policy objectives. Not surprisingly, IPR utilization and intellectual property interests vary significantly according to the sector and to the size of the company. Larger Canadian firms employing advanced technologies with significant R&D budgets and major export sales use IPRs extensively. However, it was found that intellectual property rights are also important to many smaller Canadian companies that use less advanced technologies and mainly serve the Canadian market.

The research and consultations that took place at the same time also indicated that because Canada is a net importer of goods that embody IPRs, Canadian companies are concerned about both excessive and inadequate IP standards and enforcement. More specifically, many groups expressed concerns with the potentially inhibiting effects of excessive IP protection worldwide on research and education in Canada. Small businesses, consumer organizations, and other non-government groups with limited resources also expressed concerns about the high cost of IP litigation. In short, views on intellectual property vary across business groups and sectors, and there may be room for alliances on IP issues between certain segments of the business community and NGOs, including consumer groups.

Traditionally, Canadian governments have attempted to strike an appropriate balance between the rights and obligations of creators, users, industry, and consumers in developing, modernizing, and implementing IP statutes. As well, compared to competition law, IP law and policy may be better positioned to address innovation, technology, and dynamic efficiency factors, which are difficult to measure in a competition case but can be so important to certain classes of consumers and to overall consumer welfare in the long run.

As well, consumers and their representatives may have reason to be concerned with the potential for monopoly profits that is associated with the circumscribed property rights granted under IP statutes. In recent years, these consumer concerns have been embodied in changes to the compulsory licensing provisions of the *Patent Act* that were designed to bring the patent protection provided in Canada to name-brand pharmaceutical manufacturers into line with international norms and with Canada's international trade and IP obligations.

Moreover, it can be argued that, since the Reagan era, the interests of creators, producers, the larger international corporations, and the American entertainment industry have tended to dominate the intellectual property debate in most countries of the Group of 7 Industrialized Nations (the G-7, including Canada) and at international fora, including the General Agreement on Tariffs and Trade (GATT) and its successor, the WTO, as well as NAFTA and the World Intellectual Property Organization (WIPO). However, this trend should be viewed in a broader context that includes such developments as the globalization of markets; freer international trade; the emergence of consumer sovereignty on an international scale; and the growing recognition of the importance of innovation, technology diffusion, and strategic information and knowledge to jobs, growth, consumer welfare, and our overall economic well-being.

Generally speaking, research has shown that, with some important exceptions,[14] intellectual property rights have limited but positive effects on markets and economic performance:

- Intellectual property covers only portions of production processes and final products, and generally provides limited market exclusivity because substitutes are readily available and competitors are in a position to produce and market competing products through reverse engineering.

- IPRs have limited effects on product prices, consumer choices, and market competition.

- The information disclosure inherent in the IP bargain is important to technology diffusion.

- Consumers generally have been well served by the new technologies, products, services, creations, and ideas – as well as by technology transfer and diffusion, public disclosure of information and more accurate consumer information, and lower consumer search costs – made possible, in part, by effective IPR regimes.

In addition, whereas consumers are generally treated as a single group in consumer-welfare and total-efficiency calculations under competition law,[15] IP policies and laws have the potential to be sensitive to the needs and interests of, and to the strength of views held by, different groups of consumers. It can be argued that when balancing the interests of different stakeholders, IP policy-makers will find it easier to give greater weight to creators and producers who speak with a single voice than to consumer groups that hold divergent views and speak with many voices. And this may be true for many IP issues, as it is for other public policy issues. In reality, however, the views of consumer, religious, and other social and public-interest groups continue to be given important weight by Canada's intellectual property and other regulatory and policy authorities with respect to biotechnology, the patenting of life forms, the review of Canada's *Patent Act* (Bill C-91) that is to take place in 1997, and the labelling of genetically engineered products.

Nonetheless, despite some successes in individual cases, the consumer movement in Canada generally lacks the financial and technical strength and the broad consensus across issues needed to play a major and effective role in the formulation and implementation of IP policy and law. While consumer groups are generally consulted and are members of important consultative committees, the consumer voice can often be muted by lack of resources, expertise, and consistency. And yet, as IP issues touch on the very essence of our economic and social well-being, the consumer/citizen perspective becomes all the more important to the formulation of appropriate IP policy, law, institutions, and consultative bodies so as to effectively balance stakeholder interests and to bring us together as Canadians rather than divide us on the basis of narrow economic interests.

The IP issues that could be sources of debate and conflict with the consumer perspective in the coming years are listed in Appendix C,[16] along with a discussion of the reasons for these possible frictions. Many of these issues are being addressed in other papers as part of this work program and therefore, with a few exceptions, will not be addressed in detail here. However, the partial listing provided in Appendix C clearly underlines the need for the consumer movement to be better organized in order to promote the consumer interest across a broader range of intellectual property issues.

This could also have an international dimension. Canada's freedom of action is constrained by our international obligations under the TRIPs/WTO agreements, NAFTA, and WIPO. Initiatives to make IPRs more sensitive to consumer interests may require alliances between Canadian consumer groups and their counterparts in other countries and at the international level. International consumer alliances could well be needed in the future in order to counteract the strength of the international/stateless corporation and of the international business lobby that is now emerging, often around issues of intellectual property, competition policy, and innovation.[17] The Canadian consumer movement, like business and IP associations and competition law enforcement agencies, will need to respond to the forces of globalization and freer international trade by forging new alliances with consumer groups in other countries and at the international level, and with other non-government groups in and outside Canada that have similar concerns on particular cross-border policy issues.

THE COMPLEXITY AND DIVERSITY OF THE CONSUMER PERSPECTIVE

THIS SECTION WILL ATTEMPT TO SET OUT THE CONSUMER PERSPECTIVE in all of its complexity, diversity, and perversity – the last as perceived at times by business groups, government, and other stakeholders. First, we will attempt to provide a picture of the typical Canadian consumer – a picture that has changed greatly in recent years.[18] Second, we will return to a theme stressed throughout this piece – that consumers cannot be viewed as a single entity but rather as a very diverse set of marketplace participants with important differences that are determined by a range of social, demographic, and attitudinal characteristics. Finally, we will share with the reader the results of some research conducted by the Office of Consumer Affairs in collaboration with other parts of Industry Canada and other federal departments, on consumer attitudes towards biotechnology. Not only are these results important in themselves but they may shed light on consumer attitudes and fears regarding other advanced technologies, including information technologies, which are addressed in Appendix B.

A PROFILE OF THE TYPICAL CANADIAN CONSUMER[19]

ONE PROBLEM BEING FACED by producers, marketers, and government policymakers is that the consumer, like the economy itself, is in transition. Consumer attitudes and expectations regarding government and industry and their own role in the marketplace are changing and will likely continue to change for the foreseeable future. One possible profile of the "typical" Canadian consumer (see Box 1) may be helpful as a point of reference for assessing differences among Canadians as consumers.

The reader should be cautioned however, that this profile is only a generalized one and provides only a snapshot taken at a single point in time. For government, industry, marketers, consumer groups, and other NGOs, the typical Canadian consumer is an elusive moving target, with many subtleties and contradictions.

BOX 1

THE CHANGING CANADIAN CONSUMER

- In general, consumers are better educated, better informed, more demanding, more self-reliant, and less confident that government can defend their interests – an attitude consistent with the greater independence and accountability encouraged by businesses that have become high-performance workplaces.

- Consumers are more price- and value-conscious, have less loyalty to major brands, and are more risk-averse – the result of low income growth during the 1990s, higher consumer debt, less job security, lower transfers from government, and concerns about future pensions. As well, larger consumer debt makes the typical consumer more sensitive, economically and politically, to small shifts in interest rates and bank service charges.

- "Voluntary" simplicity is the fashion: many (but by no means all) consumers have adopted a simpler lifestyle, with less work and consumption, less interest in material goods and in "keeping up with the Joneses," and more time for leisure and family – a matter of choice for some and the consequence of reduced income for others.

- Consumers are more prepared to delay major purchases since for many families these involve replacement rather than a first acquisition.

- Demographically, the consumer base is changing: consumers are getting older and living longer, have more time for product search, and are demanding the very best, as the number who are in retirement or semi-retirement grows.

- Consumers have a reduced attachment and loyalty to a single employer and industry; with layoffs, early retirement, job and career changes, and high staff turnover, we are more likely to respond to events in our role as consumers than as workers/producers.

- With international travel and products and cross-border advertising, a new type of consumer emerges – the demanding international consumer, corresponding to the international corporation.

THE INCREASING DIFFERENCES FROM THE "TYPICAL CONSUMER"

BOX 1 PRESENTS A QUITE FAVORABLE PICTURE OF THE DEMANDING, well-informed consumer who increasingly has the tools and time to pursue his/her self-interest in the marketplace. However, as usual, averages and the "typical" cover up important differences and exceptions. For example, there remain many consumers who are vulnerable and have only limited literacy and other life skills. As well, the number of families with both spouses working or with only one parent is growing; these families lack the time to collate consumer information, find the best buy, and participate effectively in the modern, increasingly complex marketplace. These differences from the "typical" consumer cut across a wide range of social, economic, demographic, and technological categories.

Gaps in wages, in per capita and household incomes, and in consumer purchasing power are beginning to widen in Canada. The process may have begun later here than in the United States, but it could accelerate over the next few years in response to such factors as further cutbacks in government expenditures on the social safety net, increases in government user fees, continuing high unemployment, job insecurity, structural changes in the economy and the labour force, and the apparent trend for technological change to favour those who are better educated and more highly skilled. Thus growing differences in incomes and purchasing power are related in part to the divergences among us with respect to education, skills, employment opportunities, job security, and consumer debt loads – and these divergences appear to be widening.

Income gaps are also linked to the changing age profile of Canadians. One possible approach to understanding the impact of this development on consumer trends is to group Canadians into three age categories:

1. The older "baby boomers," who have made most of their major household purchases and have more time for product search and analyzing consumer information, may be reluctant to make major purchases because of uncertainty about jobs and about their future pension from government, private employers, etc. In any case, they will need to spread their pension income and net assets over a greater number of years because they are living longer.

2. The "middle-boomers" are about halfway through their careers – families with two people working full time and little time for product search and analyzing consumer information; or families with only one worker, struggling to keep their heads above water (the spouse may have time for product search and information, but not the money to spend). This group also includes the many alternative families of today, which may have characteristics of each. The middle-boomers are "the meat in the sandwich," sharing some of the concerns of the older boomers about pensions and job security, and looking over their shoulders at the frustrated younger baby-boomers and post-baby-boomers[20] who may be gaining on them.

3. The younger baby-boomers and post-boomers, many of whom are making a late start in their careers (or see little opportunity for advancement in their current jobs) and therefore are delaying their household formation, families, lifetime commitments, and house and major household purchases.

There is growing evidence that the quite modest income gains that Canadians have enjoyed over the past decade or so have largely accrued to older members of the population.[21] The real wages and family incomes of younger Canadians appear to have fallen quite significantly over the recent past. Growing wage and income gaps between younger and older generations appear to be related in part to the dominance of the baby-boomers in our demographic structure and to their profound effects on labour markets and opportunities for career advancement.

To the extent that household incomes remain stagnant on average, changing consumption patterns for the foreseeable future may be determined more by demographic changes than by economic trends. In work conducted for OCA by Strategic Projections,[22] the major growth markets projected in the future on the basis of demographic change were compared to changes in market opportunities if future consumer spending patterns are assumed to be in line with the significant income changes of the last few decades (see Box 2). It is clear that consumer markets changing in line with demographic trends would look quite different from markets dominated by strong household income growth, consistent with postwar trends.

Consumer attitudes and spending patterns are also likely to be different, depending on where Canadians live and where they were born and/or grew up. To date, we have seen only anecdotal evidence on potential differences in consumer attitudes and behaviour between people who were born in Canada and recent immigrants (from Hong Kong and other Asian sources, for example). However, one study concerning Vancouver's Chinese community suggests that these differences could be quite marked.[23] One issue that needs investigating is whether recent immigrants would look to government for consumer protection

---

Box 2

Two Consumer Market Scenarios

If the population continues to age and household incomes are held constant, the high-growth consumer spending categories over the next 20 years will be:

Owned vacation homes, gifts and contributions, prescribed medicines, other health care goods, eyeglasses, motels, property taxes, hair-grooming services, bottled gas, lottery tickets, lawn and garden equipment, homeowners' insurance, medical and pharmaceutical products, newspapers, inter-city transportation, women's hair, and winter-weight coats.

If the population age profile does not change and household incomes continue to grow as in the past, high-growth consumer spending categories over the next 20 years will be:

Office machines and equipment, recreation equipment rentals, mutual funds, pension funds, tour operators, mortgage loan interest, televisions and video equipment, cable and pay TV, lotteries, trucks and vans, child care, radios and sound systems, stoves, ranges and microwave ovens, motor vehicle rentals, paid lodging, credit unions, films and photo supplies, other health care, musical instruments.

Marketers' sales and profits could vary quite significantly, depending on whether demographic or income trends dominate Canada's future consumer spending patterns.

---

or would depend more on families and friends and on their cultural links and organizations.

New Canadians could bring quite different perspectives on the respective roles of government, industry, and the individual in disciplining the market-place – perspectives that could become important to policy debates, particularly in metropolitan centres such as Vancouver, Toronto, and Montreal, where recent immigrants tend to be concentrated. One would also expect to see differences between Canadians living in larger centres and those who live in smaller communities and rural areas. These differences could reflect lifestyle and occupational factors, as well as gaps in income and employment opportunities. These are all matters that require further research.

As a result of survey work done by CROP Environics over the past several years, we have quite detailed data showing that, in this dimension as well, citizens of Quebec are "distinct" in that they bring quite different attitudes to their market transactions, compared to consumers in the rest of Canada. Relative to their counterparts elsewhere, Quebec consumers are a little more insecure and therefore prudent, are more likely to be "hedonistic" and therefore take pleasure from consumption, and are more likely to adopt attitudes and lifestyles involving deconsumption and voluntary simplicity.[24]

The CROP Environics data also enable us to segment Canadian consumers in terms of their broad attitudes towards the risks, benefits, and acceptance of new technologies. The firm's 1995 survey shows that perhaps fewer than 1 in 10 Canadians are eager to embrace the goods and services provided by the new technologies, while about 50 percent or so bring varying degrees of enthusiasm to purchases of high-technology goods and services. At the other end of the spectrum, about 1 in 10 Canadians continue to resist and distrust technology, while the remaining 30 percent display varying degrees of reluctance to become full participants in the high-tech market and economy.

In tracking technology attitudes and ownership since 1992, CROP Environics uncovered both a growing enthusiasm for the possibilities offered by technology and growing anxieties about the potential for its misuse. The lesson for marketers and government policy is that, when launching new products and new technology policies, they should be sensitive to the major differences among Canadians regarding their faith in, familiarity with, and utilization of, technology and that products and policies geared only towards technology enthusiasts could find a very narrow audience.[25]

Finally, and perhaps paradoxically, differences in consumer views and behaviour may also reflect the successful efforts of manufacturers and marketers in differentiating their products, segmenting markets, and promoting profitable market niches for themselves. As consumers, we are encouraged to express ourselves, our status, and our lifestyles through our consumer spending. If, at the end of the day, consumers are more difficult to satisfy and can no longer be treated as a homogeneous group, suppliers should congratulate themselves on their marketing success, and governments and others will need to accept the resulting diversity.

These differences in consumer perspectives and attitudes will need to be addressed in formulating competition and IP policy and law in the years ahead. They will also influence the broader public policy context within which consumer and business framework law and policy are formulated and implemented in Canada.

THE SPECIAL CONSUMER ISSUES RAISED BY BIOTECHNOLOGY[26]

THE POTENTIAL FOR TENSIONS BETWEEN INTELLECTUAL PROPERTY and consumer interests is becoming a reality today with respect to biotechnology, the patenting of life forms, and the possible negative reaction of consumers to genetically altered food products entering the marketplace.[27] With the successful development of genetic-engineering techniques in the 1970s, research on applications has been accelerating in a wide range of fields, such as health, agriculture, the environment, fisheries, mining, and forestry. The key difference from traditional methods is that it is now possible to implant traits from one species into entirely different species (e.g., animal genes into plants).

The potential benefits from biotechnology go beyond questions of industrial application and competitiveness. Biotechnology clearly offers the potential for enhancing the quality of life through new medicines, increased product choice for consumers, and new ways of addressing environmental problems. Most of the current biotechnology activity in Canada, which has enjoyed strong growth in recent years, is focused on health care. As well, there are examples of "green technologies," including the use of naturally occurring bacteria and fungi to decrease the harmful effects of chemicals and oil spills, and to clean up toxic wastes. Moreover, the jobs associated with biotechnology development and applications are knowledge-intensive and have a high value-added component.[28]

While such applications can bring major economic and social benefits, the process and implications are not well understood by the public, nor integrated with their values. This lack of understanding may inhibit consumers from accepting the new technologies.[29] Genetically engineered food products are now beginning to enter the marketplace, and the issues for consumers are safety, information, and choice. The regulatory processes are already in place to address the safety issues, but broader questions remain regarding whether:

- adequate studies are undertaken to ensure that all the potential implications are fully assessed both in the short term and over time before products are approved; and

- regulatory processes explicitly take into account values and ethical considerations, and the costs and benefits for society as a whole, associated with the introduction of particular biotechnology-based products.

Critics have also raised broader ethical concerns related to the "ownership" of life.[30] The major concern is that patents on life forms could increase the "commodification" of, and diminish respect for, all life. However, such concerns appear to be less evident with regard to patents on lower life forms (e.g., bacteria) than to more sophisticated life forms (e.g., farm animals and human body parts). Some believe, as well, that it is unethical to put genetic resources under private control through patent monopolies. Accordingly, IPR issues continue to be a source of contention raised by the UN Convention on Biodiversity.

Concerns have also been raised about the amount of information available to consumers to enable them to exercise informed choice. In particular, the question of choice has been raised in the context of whether the new genetically engineered products (e.g., novel foods) should be identified as such.

Views are divided among industry, consumer groups, and government about the desirability and feasibility of labelling genetically engineered products. Industry has adopted the view that mandatory labelling is needed only to identify health, safety, or nutritional concerns or differences, not to identify the process by which the foods were derived (i.e., through genetic engineering). Some consumer groups, however, are insisting on the right to choice, implying that the products must somehow be distinguished from traditional products. In addition to the labelling issue *per se*, there is clearly a need for education and information on the potential benefits and implications of genetically engineered products. Policy work is needed, therefore, on the advantages and drawbacks of various techniques (labelling, symbols, advertising and other forms of marketing, more general information, etc.) to provide consumers with the information they need to make their own choices about biotechnology and related products, and on the respective roles that industry, government, consumer groups, and other NGOs can play in providing that information.

In this regard, Agriculture and Agri-food Canada (AAFC) is currently working to develop guidelines for the labelling of novel foods. Some genetically engineered products are now entering the marketplace with no labelling or identification. In order to respond to these consumer information and other concerns, a federal working group, which includes the Office of Consumer Affairs, is now directing a multi-year program of in-depth social science research through omnibus surveys by Optima and CROP Environics and through focus groups and follow-up economic and policy analysis. Not only are the results of this work, which began in March 1986, illuminating for biotechnology but they may also provide some insights for other enabling technologies now being supported by the federal government under Technology Partnerships Canada and other policy and program initiatives.

The Optima study, *Understanding the Consumer Interest in the New Biotechnology Industry*, suggested that markets could be divided into three categories of descending consumer acceptance. Health care biotechnology (or "biotech") products were thought to be the most readily acceptable by the Canadian public, followed by those products which provide clear benefits to the consumer, such as more flavour, better nutrition of food products, etc. The least favoured products were those which provide few advantages to the consumer but offer potentially significant benefits to the producer, such as longer shelf life, less damage through handling of food products, and so on (see Box 3). For example, the use of the hormone supplement rBST[31] would raise milk production and therefore would likely improve dairy farm revenues and profits. However, dairy production in Canada is under supply management, with no competition between producers and no capacity to separate milk with the hormone supplement from the regular milk supply without supplement. As a consequence, consumers would likely be forced to accept some milk with hormone supplement and would not expect to enjoy any of the benefits of higher productivity through lower prices.[32] Consumers have made it clear in the surveys that they have no interest in accepting all of the risk and receiving little or no benefit.[33]

The latest CROP survey identified two quite distinct groups of consumers as defined by their interpretation of the opportunities and threats posed by biotechnology. The pessimists saw biotechnology as a threat to their personal autonomy, while the optimists saw it as an avenue for personal advancement. For the former group, biotech products threaten basic values of personal security and autonomy.

Box 3

CONSUMER INTEREST AND BIOTECHNOLOGY

According to the November 1994 Industry Canada survey conducted by Optima:

- 57 percent of respondents agreed that patents on animals developed through biotechnology are acceptable if these animals are used to develop cures for diseases;
- 53 percent of respondents agreed that patents on plants developed through biotechnology are acceptable if these plants are used to increase crop yield;
- 35 percent of respondents agreed that patents on animals developed through biotechnology are acceptable for developing animals with less fat.

The survey and other work also underlined that the public expects government to take the lead role in several areas, including: safety, ethics, and the provision of information about biotech products and processes. At the same time, many consumers view the current testing and review systems of government and industry with considerable scepticism, calling for multi-stakeholder review processes, with input from NGOs.

Table 1 shows the percentages of consumers who would very likely buy different types of food products. As expected, the most acceptable product conveys some advantage to the consumer – i.e., better taste – and the least desirable only benefits the producer – i.e., faster-growing fish. The implication for marketers is that products that provide little benefit to the consumer will be a tougher sell; it may therefore be better to focus R&D and product development on goods that offer more tangible benefits to the consumer. For policymakers and regulators, the implication is that consumers will want to minimize their health and safety risks on products that provide few readily apparent advantages to them (e.g., rBST). While these nuances of consumer acceptance and risk will be important to specific competition enforcement cases and to the broader development of competition and IP policies, they probably hold greater implications for policies and regulations related to health, safety, packaging, and labelling.

One surprising aspect of the CROP survey results is the clustering of socio-cultural factors that distinguish those very likely to buy these products from all other Canadians. The group most likely to buy was dominated by men below the

TABLE 1

CONSUMER PREFERENCES REGARDING BIO-ENGINEERED PRODUCTS
PERCENTAGES

Bio-engineered products	Very likely to buy	Somewhat likely to buy	Total of both
Tomatoes that have been altered for longer shelf life and better taste	12	31	43
Fruits and vegetables that have been genetically altered to be more resistant to insects	9	33	42
Pork that has been given hormone supplements to produce a leaner meat	5	22	27
Milk that is similar to human milk, easier to digest, and which comes from genetically altered cows	4	14	18
Milk from cows that have been given hormone supplements (somatotrophine) to increase their milk production	3	14	17
Salmon that has been genetically altered to grow faster	3	14	17

Source: CROP Environics, *3SC Monitor 1995: Canada's Monitor of Social Change* (Montreal, 1996).

age of 35 who enjoy relatively high socio-economic status, as determined by schooling, income, and similar factors. These consumers are outwardly directed and their motivations for buying are pride (obtained by being first to try a superior product) and their desire to have new experiences.

Those not likely to buy biotechnology products fell into two major groups: 1) those for whom security and stability is paramount in their lives; and 2) those seeking autonomy and personal fulfilment. To the extent that these two groups continue to be important, the markets for some biotechnology products could be quite limited.

The implications of these results for government policy also need to be explored in greater depth. As noted above, labelling is an important issue. Regulations that require the labelling of biotechnology products would provide those insecure consumers with the details they need about exactly what has been changed in these new products. Labelling would also provide autonomy-seeking consumers with choices about whether to buy or not. At the same time, labelling can be costly and perhaps ultimately ineffective once the number of products on the market that involve some kind of biotechnology application becomes larger. To repeat, more work is needed on the costs and benefits of mandatory labelling, compared to other ways of providing consumers with the information they need to make their own marketplace choices.

While the United States appears to have moved ahead of Canada in biotechnology patenting and development, reactions and progress in Europe are broadly similar to the Canadian experience to date. According to Consumers International, an organization of consumer groups from different countries, studies conducted in Europe between 1991 and 1993 found that half the respondents believed that biotechnology could improve their lives over the next 20 years. Support for biotechnology varied considerably, depending on the type of application and the perceived risk associated with it; and genetic engineering drew a more negative response than other biotechnologies.

To summarize, consumers have some superficial awareness of biotechnology, but true knowledge is limited. For example, consumers generally lack the knowledge to differentiate between traditional biotechnology applications and new genetic-engineering applications. As well, more is known about food applications and less is known about health care and environmental outcomes that could generate much greater benefits for our quality of life and economic and social well-being.

Because of this lack of knowledge, many consumers tend to weigh the benefits only slightly ahead of the risks, and the more risk-averse among us tend to magnify the risks and are therefore highly influenced by negative media and other reports. And because consumers are wary of this generally unknown technology, many of them want maximum protection through government regulation and maximum control over their own purchasing decisions. This results in pressures for mandatory labelling of all biotechnology products.

As a result of these information asymmetries and of the apparent mistrust of government, industry, and science (see Appendix C), significant differences are emerging between consumer groups, industry, and government regulators. Industry and government fear that mandatory labelling would be costly, inefficient, and intrusive – and, in fact, would result in "re-regulating" everyday products that may or may not contain some biotechnology element. From a public-interest perspective, there may also be a danger that mandatory labelling would give a false sense of comfort; that it could be used by sellers to fragment markets, reduce competition, and raise prices; and that it would reduce public pressure on the real issue – the need for government regulators and industry to ensure that products are safe and perform as advertised, with minimum unintended side effects.

CONCLUDING COMMENTS AND THE RESEARCH AGENDA FOR THE FUTURE

MANY, BUT NOT ALL, ELEMENTS OF THE CONSUMER PERSPECTIVE with respect to competition policy and enforcement can be addressed in the following ways:

- A broader, more flexible, and more sensitive approach by competition authorities to the determination of what constitutes consumer welfare and production efficiency gains; this approach would go beyond calculations of static efficiencies in order to capture the dynamic, long-term effects and opportunities, both negative and positive, of a business practice on consumers overall, on different classes of intermediate users and final consumers, on producers, and on the economy as a whole.[34]

- The opening-up of avenues for consumers and their representatives to influence the priorities and work of competition agencies and IP authorities and to take class actions and other cases, supported perhaps by contingency fees and the potential for relatively generous financial awards, to the courts, tribunals, and other adjudicative bodies.

Compared to competition law, the authorities responsible for intellectual property policies and laws arguably are in a better position to address consumer perspectives in all their diversity and complexity. This, in fact, is being done with respect to biotechnology and the patenting of life forms. In a broader sense, the formulation of IP law in Canada is cognizant of the fact that this country is a net importer of technology and intellectual property, and that the social consensus around the importance of high levels of IP protection is somewhat less prominent in Canada than in our major trading partners, particularly the United States.

At the same time, when the stakes for creators and producers are very high (as occurs whenever the *Patent Act* is reopened for amendment), IP authorities and legislatures understandably give greater attention to well-funded, highly expert industry and IP associations who at times[35] speak with a single voice than to poorly funded consumer groups who bring a diversity of opinions to the table and do not have the time and money for expert analyses and submissions.

Accordingly, in their consumer advocacy work with respect to both competition and IP policy, consumer associations and other public-interest groups are responsible for bringing to the policy formulation process responsible, well-researched positions based on a good understanding of the issues and constraints, and on a coherent view of the marketplace, consumer interests, and citizen perspectives.

The above points out the need for the development, outside the bounds of competition and IP policy, of mechanisms for effectively bringing the consumer perspective into the debates on competition policy, IPRs, innovation policy, and other public policy issues. This, to some degree, is the role of Industry Canada's Office of Consumer Affairs, but with its staff of 25 and limited financial resources, the Office cannot do it alone. Therefore, OCA is actively seeking partnerships, alliances, and research joint-ventures on these and related consumer issues, both within and outside government.

The research and policy agendas for the future could also include the following topics:

- Continuing efforts are needed to ensure that the consumer perspective and the results from the social science research now being conducted are fully addressed in, and incorporated into, the national biotechnology strategy and the 1997 Review of the *Patent Act* (Bill C-91).

- Similar research – including omnibus and panel surveys, focus groups, behavioural and statistical modelling, etc. – is needed to determine the implications of the Internet/World Wide Web and of other parts of the information highway for market structure and transactions, corporate strategy, consumer behaviour, and the interactions/frictions between competition policy, intellectual property rights, and the consumer interest.

- Consumer, competition, intellectual property, and marketplace perspectives should play an important role in the preparation of Industry Canada's Sustainable Development Strategy (to be completed over the next year or so) in future changes to the *Canadian Environmental Protection Act*, in the modernization of other environmental statutes in Canada, and in the evaluation of major projects and policy changes with important consequences for the environment.

- The consumer movement needs tools and resources to contribute to, and intervene effectively on, the complex issues associated with competition policy, intellectual property, and the consumer. This requires effective alliances between consumer groups and other associations and NGOs, and greater success by the consumer movement in expanding its membership base and non-government revenues, and in raising its visibility, effectiveness, and credibility, both within and outside government. These efforts, in turn, need broad-based financial and technical support from all government departments, federal and provincial, that have consumer interests and responsibilities and would benefit from the advice and expertise of a strong consumer movement in Canada.

This policy analysis should be supported by theoretical research that gives greater attention to the consumer perspective and to consumer feedback to producers/marketers – for example, with respect to the development, application, and interpretation of models of industrial organization and game theory, and of endogenous-growth theory.

As noted at the outset, this paper only touches on the complex nexus of issues raised by competition, intellectual property, and the consumer. These questions also raise broader concerns regarding the links, and the need for integration, between scientific, commercial, economic, and ethical values. At one time, these values were developed in separate worlds, but the partitions of the past are no longer water-tight. The debate between these different worlds is now being joined in the marketplace as well as in other fora.

The world of science is currently influencing the profits available to producers and the surplus provided to consumers. In addition, as stressed throughout the paper, consumers are increasingly bringing their ethical values to the marketplace. Consistent with this, under the endogenous-growth models – which, in the author's view, better capture current market realities than the traditional linear models – scientific endeavour, research and development, and the commercialization of the resulting creations and inventions are driven by market signals, user/consumer preferences, and broader societal norms regarding science, ethics, and the economy. In short, the partitions that shielded the scientific and R&D worlds from outside influences are coming down as science and innovation become fundamental to the information- and knowledge-based economy.

All of us will need to further our joint exploration of innovative ways to integrate these diverse values into the decisions made by government, scientists, producers, consumers, and citizens, and to ensure that decisions on science, research and development, intellectual property, and other framework rules are disciplined by both the commercial needs and the broader ethical values of Canadian society.

We will also need to explore the respective roles of government, industry, and non-government organizations in this regard. Our research to date underlines the fact that, compared to other marketplace issues, Canadians

– as consumers, citizens, and voters – expect government to continue to play a leading role in the integration of scientific, commercial, economic, and ethical values in the development of intellectual property, biotechnology, consumer labelling, and related policies and framework rules.[36] At the same time, when industry and government interests appear to be closely aligned, consumers/voters are more comfortable if third parties, such as consumer groups or other NGOs, are also at the table.

These questions take us well beyond the theme of this conference and publication, but they will help to set the broader context for both competition policy and intellectual property rights in the years ahead.

APPENDIX A: ANALYTICAL FRAMEWORK

THE BROADER SOCIO-ECONOMIC
CRITERIA OF THE MODERN CONSUMER

THERE IS GROWING EVIDENCE FROM SURVEY AND FOCUS-GROUP RESEARCH done by the Office of Consumer Affairs and other sources that when consumers make their purchasing decisions, they bring more than price, quality, and choice questions – the traditional purview of competition policy and law – to the marketplace. The data suggest that consumers are also applying social, political, lifestyle, and other broad socio-economic criteria in deciding what, where, and when to purchase (see Box A-1).

Companies that successfully address these broader criteria can expect to enjoy higher consumer acceptance, sales, and market share in domestic markets and to be better positioned to export their products and technologies to other highly industrialized countries where similar concerns are influencing consumer decisions. And obviously, companies and industries – in particular those involved in the information- and knowledge-based economy, where IP rights, competitive markets, and easy market entry are essential to innovation, industry success, and national competitiveness[37] – ignore these broader criteria at their peril.[38]

Similarly, public policies that effectively address these broader concerns of consumer citizens will achieve greater public acceptance, political support, and legitimacy and will help to bring Canadians together as scientists, creators, producers, workers, and consumers. On the other hand, ignoring these social concerns in formulating policy will lead to tensions among different socio-economic groups and will fracture the social consensus so important to implementing policy, law, and regulation in the Canadian federal democracy.

It is argued in the main body of the text that, from the point of view of consumer welfare and total economic efficiency, competition policy in Canada can only partially address these broader socio-economic notions of health, safety, fairness, and so on. The same can be said of intellectual property policy, with

---

BOX A-1

BROADER SOCIO-ECONOMIC CRITERIA BEING USED BY CONSUMERS

Privacy and security of information: key issues emphasized in discussions on the information highway, telemarketing, and financial sector reform.

Access for all who want and need basic network services: banking, telephone, cable/satellite television, and perhaps, in the future, computer access to the information highway.

Political concerns: for example, past boycotts of South African products and California grapes, and the recent boycott of French wines and other French products in response to nuclear testing.

Notions of fair treatment: arguably the strongly negative consumer reaction to Rogers Cablevision's "negative option marketing" strategy in early 1995 to introduce new TV channels and Canadian content went beyond matters of quality, content, packaging, and price to a sense that consumers were being treated badly by a federally regulated monopoly in a privileged market position provided largely by a state entitlement.

The quality and timeliness of the consumer information: this can be related to the economic question of transaction costs but can go beyond this question to notions of consumer annoyance with a supplier who is caught (or is perceived to be) trying to mislead, misrepresent, misinform, or ignore the information and related needs of the consumer (as in the Rogers case above).

Concerns with information asymmetries between buyers and sellers, heightened by the major differences among Canadians in computer literacy and access to the information highway and the Internet.

Growing recognition that a significant percentage of Canadian consumers are functionally illiterate and therefore **lack the basic skills** to be full and effective marketplace participants.

Lifestyle: the major focus of advertising and promotion of many leisure and luxury goods – e.g., beer, wine, cosmetics, luxury cars.

Perceptions of risk and the sharing of health, safety, and other risks between producers and consumers, particularly when key product features are hidden, as seen in the consumer opposition to the introduction of rBST (recombinant Bovine Somatotrophine) into the Canadian milk supply (recall the thalidomide disaster of 30 years ago and more recent cases, such as breast implants and the current "mad cow" disease in the United Kingdom). It is increasingly apparent that consumers and the media in these instances are no longer prepared to fully accept the word of government, industry, and the scientific community regarding the "scientific evidence" that a certain product or technology is absolutely safe.

The environment: danger of consumer boycotts in Europe because of consumer perceptions of the sustainability of Canadian forestry practices, and the growing scepticism of consumers with advertising claims that a certain product or technology is environmentally friendly.

Broader social, ethical, and moral values: for example, public concerns regarding the patenting of life forms and the introduction of rBST, which go beyond economic parameters to capture our basic values and sense of right and wrong.

its focus on the innovation process and the provision of a limited monopoly right to inventors and creators.

At the same time, some of the criteria described in Box A-1 are undoubtedly met in part by competition policy and intellectual property rights. In many markets, strong competition is the best guarantee of virtually universal access. Information asymmetries and the transaction costs that arise from the provision and use of consumer information are addressed (directly or indirectly) under the abuse-of-dominance, vertical-restraint, and other provisions of many competition laws, and under the misleading-advertising provisions of the *Competition Act*.[39]

Intellectual property authorities in all of the major industrialized countries are wrestling with the ethical and moral issues raised by the patenting of life forms and genetic engineering. Moreover, the positive and negative externalities associated with the environment and the new information technologies are being addressed by competition and IP authorities in many countries; one issue being addressed by both is shopping on the Internet, which is raising copyright concerns for IP policy as well as market-power and misleading-advertising concerns for competition policy.

At the same time, many of these notions of market failure, fairness, and natural justice are beyond the purview of competition and IP policy and have traditionally come under other policy fields, including consumer protection. For whatever reason, governments and the people who elect them in modern industrialized societies have not fully trusted in markets and selective interventions under competition, intellectual property, and other business framework laws to address these broader socio-economic concerns.

Accordingly, the view advanced throughout the paper is that these notions, which go beyond economic-efficiency criteria, do need to be addressed in developing other public policies in the areas of biotechnology, innovation, the information highway, privacy law, product safety policy and law, technical standards, and consumer information law and policy. All of these require a balanced approach that cuts across the interests of creators, users, workers, and consumers to ensure that national policies bring us together as Canadians.

In particular, successfully addressing these consumer perspectives is important to the development of public trust in market operations, institutions, and outcomes. It is the author's view that in a modern economy fairness and efficiency are two sides of the same coin in building stronger markets and greater public trust in market institutions and outcomes. Market participants who enter transactions with fears that they will not be treated fairly by others will incur higher-than-necessary product search and transaction costs, will conduct strategic "game playing" and "rent-seeking" to protect their interests, and will often not participate fully in the market economy – only reluctantly and out of necessity. These fairness concerns result in higher costs and less efficient market outcomes for all.

These issues may also be important to the kinds of marketing, investment, technology, export, and related advice that Industry Canada provides to companies that produce high-technology products (and that employ more advanced technologies), which are protected under patent, copyright, trademark, and/or trade secrecy law. Consumer confidence in the marketplace is of paramount importance to creating economic prosperity and opportunity in the information- and knowledge-based economy of the future.

The Policy Legacy of Consumer Protection Law

The analytical framework for this paper is also provided, in part, by the policy legacy of consumer protection law in Canada and other industrialized countries, and by the reforms that may be needed in light of a variety of factors:

- the globalization of markets;

- freer international trade;

- regulatory reform and the modernization of many business framework laws, such as the *Competition Act* and the *Patent Act*;

- greater competition and product choice in most consumer markets;

- the information-technology revolution;

- the growth of the service and small-business sectors;

- constitutional developments in Canada and new obligations under the Agreement on Internal Trade, the WTO, and NAFTA;

- the dramatic growth in cross-border consumer transactions and distance selling, which is expected to accelerate in the near term as shopping on the Internet increases; and

- consumer perceptions of both the benefits and risks and hidden hazards of the new technologies – e.g., biotechnology, information technologies, and environmental technologies.

This is the subject of a recent paper prepared for the Office of Consumer Affairs and presented to the Roundtable on Consumer Policy and Law, held at the University of Toronto in June 1996.[40] In this paper, the authors explore the market failures, externalities, and other socio-economic concerns that have traditionally been the foundation for consumer protection, and evaluate these concerns in relation to the dramatic changes that have taken place over the past 30 years in markets, technology, government, and the law. According to the authors, the policy legacy for consumer protection includes several forms of market failure.

- Monopoly and oligopoly power in markets, which from the point of view of consumer protection translated into concerns with inequalities in bargaining power, where consumers had few options except to purchase from and contract on terms set by large and powerful manufacturers and retailers.

- Negative externalities arising from transactions where the parties, even when acting voluntarily and with full information, ignore the costs imposed on involuntary third parties. Consumer protection concerns in this category have included product safety hazards for children, motor-vehicle safety standards, personal privacy and protection of personal information, health concerns (e.g., from smoking for smokers and non-smokers alike), and environmental externalities.

- Major information asymmetries between manufacturers/vendors, on the one hand, and customers/consumers, on the other, which provided the single most important rationale for consumer protection in the past. The authors argue that virtually all transactions involve certain information asymmetries; the challenge is to determine the types of products, technologies, and transactions where the asymmetry is so grave that some kind of public policy response is needed. These responses may be particularly needed in the areas of health and safety, especially when hazards are hidden and are embodied in unfamiliar high-technology products and so-called "credence" goods.

- Other forms of transaction cost – apart from information costs – that affect consumers in their marketplace dealings, such as the costs of effectively pursuing complaints and acquiring consumer redress.

- Provision of public goods (such as consumer education and more general consumer and market information), which because of their non-rivalrous and non-excludable character are likely to be sub-optimally supplied by private economic agents; and the collective action (free-rider) problems that consumers face as a large, diffuse, and unorganized political constituency.

- Controversial, non-economic rationales for government intervention in the marketplace, such as distributive justice and paternalism – e.g., consumer transactions involving minors and the effects of advertising on children. The authors argue that in liberal societies with workably competitive markets, non-economic justifications for policy interventions on behalf of the consumer should be approached with considerable caution.

The authors conclude that, because of freer international trade, of greater competition and product choice in markets, and of the other changes in the external environment listed earlier in this appendix, many aspects of this policy legacy are less important now than they were 30 years ago. At the same time, the fundamental principles of consumer protection remain the same, and thus many of these considerations in altered form will remain important in future efforts to modernize consumer policies and laws in Canada and elsewhere.

APPENDIX B: THE CONSUMER AND THE INFORMATION ECONOMY

COMPETITION POLICY, INTELLECTUAL PROPERTY RIGHTS, and the consumer perspective come together in evaluating the importance of consumer information and acceptance to the success of biological, environmental, infor-mation, and other enabling technologies.

As stated earlier, biotechnology and genetic engineering will not achieve their full potential to improve our health and economic well-being if con-sumers believe they are being misled about the true nature of genetically altered products or are being forced to accept too much of the risk in return for too little of the benefit. Similarly, "green" products and other products and tech-nologies that are reputed to promote environmental goals will not be accepted by the marketplace if consumers do not believe the claims of marketers regarding the environmentally friendly nature of their product offerings. The information highway will not achieve its full potential for producers, marketers, or con-sumers if consumers and other purchasers come to believe that their personal data are not properly protected and that the highway is largely a source of false claims, electronic-commerce scams, and misleading and confusing information that takes too much time for them to collate, verify, and apply. Arguably, the success of Technology Partnerships Canada and the other innovation initia-tives of governments and business depends as much on consumer acceptance of the resulting products and technologies as on the effective use by industry of government financial and technical support.

The Office of Consumer Affairs and its partners in other parts of Industry Canada, in other government departments, and outside government will be wrestling with these complex issues for a long time. However, the work to date on specific issues and the Office's research on information markets and eco-nomics suggest a few insights and possible lessons learned that could be of assis-tance in future policy development.

Some of these were provided by the Roundtable on the Market for Information held by the Office of Consumer Affairs on March 29, 1996. This gathering brought together 25 academics and policymakers from throughout Canada, plus one key speaker from the United States. Among other questions, the Roundtable provided an opportunity to evaluate the implications of the Internet and other aspects of the information highway for consumer confidence, participation, and transactions in the electronic marketplace. In many respects, shopping on the Internet was used as a metaphor and illustration of future opportunities and risks.

It was noted that shopping on the Internet is still quite limited, and that the World Wide Web, while growing dramatically in terms of use, users, and Web sites, is still largely employed for browsing, entertainment, education, academic research, and other kinds of non-commercial "surfing." Consumer shopping on the Web is expected to advance rapidly in the years ahead (from a currently very small base), but it is not known at this time if electronic marketing and shopping will come to play a major role in comparison to traditional forms of advertising, marketing, and purchasing. As noted later on, the Web is not for every purchaser, vendor, and transaction.

The Web is raising concerns with respect to:

- intellectual property protection, particularly copyright infringement;
- competition policy and the potential for increasing dominance in the distribution and retail sectors and for major brand names to become even more powerful;
- misleading advertising, misrepresentation, and electronic fraud;[41] and
- privacy and the protection of personal data.

However, the general view of the Roundtable's participants was that electronic shopping should, on balance, advance competition, consumer welfare, small business opportunity, and marketplace efficiency.

One of the conclusions from the Roundtable was that more Canadian research is needed on the implications of the Internet and electronic shopping for markets, consumers, producers, and current framework rules, *before* consideration is given to whether new, stronger, and/or special rules are needed to address the unique challenges posed by the Internet, the information highway, and shopping on the Web. Once improvements are made in various areas – such as privacy, transparency, simplification, interjurisdictional matters, enforcement cooperation on cross-border transactions,[42] and understanding of the market power implications of intellectual property rights when these are provided to network industries – the current framework rules covering both traditional and electronic transactions may well prove to be quite adequate. Accordingly, it may be possible to limit the major changes to improving administration and enforcement through such means as greater scope for private actions, class action suits, and contingency fees; alternative dispute resolution; multi-stakeholder involvement in voluntary codes of practice and other forms of self-regulation and industry self-management; higher penalties and the granting of awards to consumer and other public-interest groups; and other avenues that would better enable consumers and smaller firms, working alone or in concert, to protect themselves and pursue their self-interest.

This conclusion is based on two perspectives that gained support as the Roundtable went on:

1. As noted above, there is no evidence or consensus that electronic transactions will come to dominate the marketplace of the future. It is not obviously in the public interest to develop special rules to cover a small portion of the total consumer market when the market mischief is not markedly different from traditional transactions; in other words, a scam is a scam, whether through telemarketing, electronic marketing, direct sale, or retail purchase.

2. The greater competition and marketplace efficiency made possible by the Internet/information highway should solve many and perhaps most market problems, with honest traders competing effectively with and forcing out fraudulent vendors and other vendors who do not properly protect copyright and the personal data of their customers. These efficiency gains were identified as resulting from such factors as lower search and evaluation costs for consumers; the interactions between purchasers and vendors (which, among other benefits, allow for an improved match between a vendor's offerings and a given customer's needs); the global reach that provides opportunities for smaller vendors to aggregate and make a profit on sales from diverse geographic locations (the death of distance and of locational economics); the ability of vendors to change their prices and product offerings virtually daily; and the price arbitrage that results from the above.

The Internet and other parts of the information highway are clearly instruments of individual empowerment. One concern, therefore, is that new framework rules or overzealous enforcement of existing copyright or other rules will prevent the information highway from achieving its full potential to facilitate information sharing, joint research and policy development, and effective strategic alliances across consumer and other public-interest groups in different parts of Canada and in the global economy. At the same time, in an era of government downsizing, regulatory reform, and self-reliance, empowerment also requires that individuals, families, companies, and NGOs accept greater responsibility for their own actions and for protecting themselves from the new forms of threat and mischief made possible by the electronic marketplace.

The current thinking is that the Internet and other parts of the information highway should, on balance, support the consumer interest by providing better and cheaper information. However, recent research by Sunil Gupta and others suggests that the Internet will affect some producers and consumers more than others. For the time being, consumers on the Internet will be concentrated among better educated, higher-income people who are younger, who are more often male than female, who are computer-literate, and who have the time to search the Net for the rapidly expanding number of product offerings now available on the system. At the same time, it is noted that the Internet is now becoming a mainstream medium that appeals to people other than the technology enthusiasts of the early months. These later users tend to be both more demanding and less computer-sophisticated than the early "surfers."

Gupta goes on to argue that because of the lower costs of searching and evaluation, the Internet will be the preferred instrument for seeking product-related information when:

- manufacturers are more knowledgeable than retailers;
- purchases occur less often but have a high price to justify some search and evaluation effort;
- local sellers are not available; and
- prices vary greatly depending on the distributor's location or identity.

The Internet could also be used for complex, customized products that can be experienced and evaluated electronically, and it could also be the preferred medium for seeking information on products that are purchased frequently but are constantly changing (computer software, for example).[43]

For all of these reasons, we need to know more about the actual market, competition, and consumer effects of the Internet and the information highway before considering new and tougher rules developed especially for these emerging technologies. Given the unknowns discussed above and the rapid changes occurring in these technologies, special rules developed now are just as likely to have negative as positive consequences.

The information highway and information-based economy also raise broader questions for consumer research, advocacy, and education. It is important to assess the consumer perspective and involve the consumers and their representatives very early in the development of new products and services based on new, unfamiliar technologies. Early involvement of the consumer and his/her concerns paid major dividends in the successful launch of electronic funds transfer in Canada,[44] and we believe that similar benefits will result from the current social science research on biotechnology and the consumer.

In supporting the introduction and commercialization of new technologies, governments, like marketers, need to conduct in-depth social science research – including omnibus and panel surveys, focus groups, and behavioural modelling and forecasting – in order to explore and understand the diversity of consumer opinion, to identify the depth and strength of consumer concerns on both the economic and non-economic dimensions, and to fully understand the dangers and risks as perceived by different groups of consumers.[45] Consumer feedback should be used to develop and implement cost-effective consumer information and education programs that address with sensitivity consumer concerns about and perceptions of the new technologies.

As markets and products become increasingly more complex, differentiated, and segmented, and as the new technologies contain hidden features that can unsettle consumers, consumer education and information are more and more important. This process must begin at the primary and secondary school levels. The provinces will need to take the lead by placing greater emphasis on this often ignored aspect of the education process; however, the federal government can provide important analytical, curriculum, and technological support through programs such as SchoolNet[46] and the Consumer Connection product being developed by OCA and its partners on the Industry Canada information system, Strategis.

Other government measures should be implemented to complement and make more effective the growing availability of less formal mechanisms for consumer education and information. As noted above, the Internet and other aspects of the information highway are expected to become important vehicles for providing consumers with the information they need to spend their dollars wisely. At present, the Internet can be a source of confusing and conflicting consumer information and product claims, but the expectation is that Internet intermediaries will emerge who, for a small price, will assist the consumer through this maze of information to find what he/she wants.

Government-operated consumer information systems can be used to support this process. As noted above, over the next year, the Office of Consumer Affairs, with its partners in both the public and the private sector, will be placing on Industry Canada's Strategis system information for consumers designed to help them to increase their knowledge of Canadian consumer laws and policies, seek redress, and better understand the implications of broader economic and policy developments for consumer spending and attitudes. At the same time, the Office and others will be testing on the system the conferencing capabilities of the Consumer Research Information Network, which is designed to enable consumer groups and others in all parts of the country to come together electronically to conduct joint research, policy analysis, and consumer advocacy. The Roundtable expressed strong interest in using this electronic conferencing capability to conduct future research on the market for information.

In addition, as more Canadians work in what is coming to be called the high-performance workplace,[47] where employees are encouraged to be independent, critical, and self-assertive, employees will bring these new "show me" attitudes into their households and consumer spending decisions, thus accentuating the emergence of the demanding, well-informed consumer discussed earlier.

To summarize, the application to the Internet and the information highway of copyright and other IP laws, misleading-advertising and misrepresentation statutes, and other framework laws will be challenging us for a long time. One view that is beginning to emerge is that government enforcement of these laws will be impossible and that the problems must be addressed through family decisions, individual responsibility, and perhaps private actions. As well, there are related concerns that the inappropriate and overzealous application of IP, competition, consumer protection, and other laws developed for the traditional marketplace, where face-to-face transactions were the norm, will impede the realization of the full potential of the Internet/information highway and other forms of electronic commerce to enhance market efficiency, consumer confidence, and participation in the free market, as well as the ability of the information highway to bring Canadians together in the pursuit of common public policy goals.

This returns us to the main theme of this paper – intellectual property, competition law, and the consumer in the information-based economy.

APPENDIX C: POSSIBLE SOURCES OF DEBATE AND FRICTION BETWEEN INTELLECTUAL PROPERTY RIGHTS AND THE CONSUMER PERSPECTIVE

POSSIBLE SOURCES OF FRICTION between intellectual property and the consumer perspective in the next few years include the following:

- The potential for consumer representation, more effective and less costly redress, and the use of alternative dispute resolution when intellectual property rights come into conflict with the consumer interest.

- The 1997 review by a Parliamentary Committee of Bill C-91, with particular emphasis on pharmaceutical prices and related health issues, reflecting the competing goals of affordable drugs versus adequate rewards for the development of new medicines.[48]

- Biotechnology, the patenting of life forms, and the provision of labelling and other consumer information for genetically altered products; the patenting of life forms and genetic engineering raise several issues:

  - competition concerns – the danger that "first-movers" in securing a patent and commercializing the resulting product or technology will enjoy a lasting competitive advantage that could be seen as an abuse of dominant position and of intellectual property;
  - issues of product safety and consumer information and choice – the extent to which consumers should be warned, through labelling or other information, that a particular product has been genetically altered;
  - moral concerns – about whether investors, producers, and marketers should be able to profit from the patenting of living matter; and,
  - environmental issues – the danger that the patenting and commercialization of life forms and genetic material will, over time, place greater stress on biological diversity, which is already in decline.

- Parallel imports, grey marketing, and the application of the "exhaustion principle" within the NAFTA area. The author finds persuasive many of the procompetitive arguments for allowing some forms of international market segmentation and thus placing some restrictions on parallel imports and grey marketing. At the same time, these arguments need to be better explained to lay people, who at times are perplexed to find that competition agencies and academics are supporting these types of market segmentation and trade restriction under a free-trade regime like NAFTA.

- The Phase II copyright amendments (tabled in Parliament in the spring of 1996), which, among other matters, address neighbouring rights aimed at providing royalties to producers and performers of sound recordings; a levy on recordable, blank audio media, such as cassettes and tapes, to remunerate creators for private copying of their musical works; greater protection to exclusive distributors of books in the Canadian market; and exceptions from copyright laws for groups such as non-profit educational institutions, libraries, archives, and museums, as well as people with perceptual disabilities.

- The application of copyright and other marketplace laws to the Internet and other aspects of the information highway. As noted in Appendix B, it may be very difficult to enforce various forms of protection – national copyright and other IP laws; consumer protection statutes; privacy laws; codes of practice; other types of voluntary standards; competition and securities laws; etc. – in the case of distance selling and other electronic transactions on the Internet:

  - when the buyer and seller reside in different countries;
  - when the one may not even know where the other resides and cannot even confirm his/her identity; and
  - where messages, advertisements, offers to buy and sell, and other information flows could be going through a large number of countries with neither party to the transaction knowing which countries have been unwitting intermediaries in facilitating the deal. "Buyer, creator and vendor beware" may be the only answers, but beware of what, who, and from where?

- Treatment under competition law of licensing, cross-licensing, research joint ventures, and other business arrangements that could lead to the abuse of intellectual property rights and of dominant positions in the market.

- The appropriate length of patent term, and whether – and under what conditions – increasing private returns through stronger IP protection (and perhaps more permissive competition law treatment of intellectual property) translate as well into increasing social returns and consumer welfare. These returns depend in part on the extent of technology spillovers and diffusion and on whether spillovers and diffusion ultimately provide benefits to the consumer in terms of lower prices, improved product quality, new products, and greater choice.

• The growing cost of new inventions and securing regulatory approvals that are in place to protect the consumer. It can be argued that strong IPRs (and permissive competition policies) are needed for inventors to recoup the costs and delays of regulatory approvals. Without strong IP protection, some new products would never be made available to the consuming public. However, striking the right balance between consumer, producer, and broader societal interests is not easy. For example, research by the Office of Consumer Affairs suggests that, for biotechnology and related products, the consuming public may not be prepared to lower health and safety standards and accept greater risk in order to secure lower prices and greater product choice.

• The danger that demands for even higher levels of IP protection by well-organized business lobbies in other jurisdictions will lead to pressures to match those new levels in Canada – either because of new obligations under international trade agreements or because of more informal pressures to ensure the competitiveness of, and a level playing field for, Canadian exporters – at the expense of IP users, smaller businesses, and the final consumer.

There are essentially five reasons why intellectual property rights can raise concerns for consumers and their representatives.

• **Information asymmetries** – Consumers and consumer groups may not be fully familiar with the new economic literature of the past 25 years, which suggests that consumer-welfare and total-efficiency gains can be realized by using IPRs to differentiate products, establish exclusive territories, prevent parallel imports, and stimulate R&D and innovation, for example. Many non-business NGOs and members of the general public may be more familiar with previous perspectives, which stressed the competitive harm that could arise from granting a limited monopoly right under IP law, rather than with the more permissive "rule-of-reason" approach to IPRs now used in competition and other public policies.

• **Growing mistrust of government, industry, and other so-called elites** – These information asymmetries are being exacerbated by the general public's apparently growing mistrust of government, industry, the scientific and academic communities, labour unions, and other key stakeholders. According to some commentators, the questioning by Canadians of their elites is underlined by the failure of the

Charlottetown Accord, which was supported by virtually all high-profile groups in Canada.

- **Legitimate concerns about too-strong IPRs** – Particularly when combined with network externalities, commercially important technical standards, and/or cross-border mergers, strategic alliances, and other corporate arrangements, IPRs can lead to abuses of dominant position and to monopoly and oligopoly positions in markets.

- **Income and wealth transfers** – There are legitimate concerns that, under certain circumstances, higher IP standards and stronger enforcement might, for example, lead to efficiency gains for producers but at the expense of consumer welfare. This is probably one of the sources of tension between consumer groups and the pharmaceutical, chemical, and entertainment industries, which advocate stronger IPRs to support R&D, innovation, and the creative process.

- **Broader ethical, moral, fairness and distributional concerns** – Some members of the general public argue that competition policy, with its emphasis on total efficiency, and IP policy, with its focus on innovation, are poorly equipped to address such questions as genetics, reproductive technologies, and the patenting of life forms.

The central message from these issues is that technological change, the globalization of markets, and the changing concerns of consumer citizens are requiring that IP and competition policy practitioners take better account of the richness and diversity of the consumer perspective in developing policy, enforcing their laws, and addressing the interactions between intellectual property rights and competition.

NOTES

1   This paper, written with contributions from Terry Leung, Bernard Keating, Anne Pigeon, and Hubert Laferrière, presents the views of the author and does not represent the opinions and policy positions of the Office of Consumer Affairs or of Industry Canada.

2   This section draws heavily from J. Shore, Consumer Policy Framework Secretariat, *Competition Policy and the Consumer Interest* (1991). See as well, George N. Addy, "An Evolving Consumer Protection Framework for the Contemporary Marketplace," remarks of the Director of Investigation and Research to the 5th International Conference on Consumer Law, Osgoode Hall, Toronto,May 25, 1995. Speaking on behalf of the Minister, Addy stressed that the protection of the consumer interest is an important part of the Minister of Industry's responsibilities. He indicated that once the appropriate legislative changes have been made, the union of the Competition Bureau with the consumer protection responsibilities of the Consumer Products

Branch will provide important benefits by establishing a modern framework approach that brings together in one place the tools that all kinds of consumers need to participate effectively in the marketplace. Addy noted as well that many of the jurisdictions have seen the benefits from combining competition and consumer protection activities within a single organization.

See also a recent draft report that is circulating in mimeo form, Robert H. Lande, "A Unified Theory of Consumer Sovereignty: Antitrust and Consumer Protection Law Combined," University of Baltimore School of Law, June 1996. In this document, Professor Lande compares and contrasts the two areas of law and argues that they ultimately support one another as the two components of an overarching unity – consumer sovereignty. Antitrust is intended to ensure that markets provide consumers with a competitive range of options to choose from, undiminished by price fixing, anticompetitive mergers, or other restraints to trade. Consumer protection is then intended to ensure that consumers can choose effectively among these options without being impeded by deception or the withholding of important information.

3   See, for example, the Director's submission on the information highway: G. Addy, "Notes for Remarks to the Advisory Council on the Information Highway", 1994.

4   To varying degrees, total efficiency is the guiding principle in most other modern competition statutes. For example, the total efficiency approach is employed in the *Antitrust Guidelines for the Licensing of Intellectual Property*, issued on April 6, 1995 by the U.S. Department of Justice and the Federal Trade Commission.

5   For example, contractual arrangements that pass the total-efficiency test by reducing the free-rider problem and allowing distributors and retailers to benefit from their marketing and other investments, may be viewed less positively by consumers who, as a result, enjoy less product choice and no longer have access to parallel imports at lower prices (under circumstances where consumers fully recognize that these "grey-market" goods may provide less consumer information, no warranties, and fewer other add-ons).

6   For example, a new environmental technology, a major advance in computer technology that would make the information highway accessible to all, a cure for cancer, a great new computer game or other home entertainment.

7   For example, Michael Porter and many others argue that international competitiveness must be based on strong rivalry, efficient domestic markets, demanding and well-informed consumers, and strong enforcement of antitrust and other framework laws. Without efficient markets, rivalry, and demanding consumers at home, national industries cannot and will not develop the products, technologies, skills, and expertise necessary to successfully compete abroad. See, for example, Michael E. Porter, *The Comparative Advantage of Nations*, The Free Press, 1990.

8   It could be argued that policy conflicts can also operate in the opposite direction. Consumer policies and laws that benefit one group of (perhaps well-organized) consumers at the expense of other consumers, or that impose costly, "command-and-control" regulatory regimes on other marketplace participants in the name of product safety, consumer information, personal privacy, or broader social goals, could potentially have a negative impact on economic efficiency, domestic competition, international competitiveness, and in the long run the broader consumer interest. Similar to intellectual property and competition law, consumer policy and law also require balance based on the careful weighing of stakeholder interests, including the perspectives of different groups of consumers.

9   It should be noted that the World Bank and other international agencies have developed techniques for incorporating such value judgments into their benefit/cost models and evaluations of projects. This is done by giving different weights to the benefits and costs accruing to different economic actors, based (for example) on socio-economic status and public policy objectives. See, for example, Heng-Kang Sang, *Project Evaluation: Techniques and Practices for Developing Countries*, New York: Wilson Press, 1988.

10   Regarding the first proposal, see: Bureau of Competition Policy, "Discussion Paper: *Competition Act* Amendments," June 1995. Regarding the potential for most horizontal arrangements to be treated as a reviewable matter, see Thomas W. Ross, "Proposals for a New Canadian Competition Law on Conspiracy," *The Antitrust Bulletin*, Winter 1991.

11   A right which, admittedly, has been used rarely.

12   See, for example, Consumer and Corporate Affairs Canada, *Intellectual Property and Canada's Commercial Interests*,1990; and *Global Rivalry and Intellectual Property*, edited by Murray G. Smith, The Institute for Research on Public Policy, 1990.

13   John R. Baldwin, "The Use of Intellectual Property Rights by Canadian Manufacturing Firms: Findings from the Innovation Survey," Statistics Canada, Micro-Economics Analysis Division, draft, March 1996. This study underlines the strong links between intellectual property usage and the innovativeness of an industry, particularly with respect to such industries as chemicals, pharmaceuticals, refined petroleum, and electrical products and machinery.

14   These include the important role of patents in the pharmaceuticals and chemicals industries and the importance of copyright law to the entertainment and computer software industries. In addition, a second paper in this volume has argued that IPRs can also be very important to network industries. IP protection in these industries can result in substantial market power, in large part because industries with network effects are prone to standardization. See Jeffrey Church and Roger Ware, "Network Industries, Intellectual Property Rights, and Competition Policy," in this volume, chapter 8, pp. 227-86.

15   The rest of this paragraph provides a quite favourable picture of the ability of intellectual property to address diverse stakeholder views. The other side of the coin is that, compared to competition policy with its total efficiency paradigm within a well established social benefit/cost framework, the analysis of IP issues can be somewhat less rigorous and, therefore, in greater danger of being heavily influenced by specific industry interests, the creative community, or other special interest groups.

16   A number of these consumer perspectives are taken from an informal issues paper by Ross Duncan and Hubert Laferrière, "Intellectual Property and the Consumer Interest: Issues in Canadian IP Law from the Consumer Perspective," Industry Canada, Consumer Policy Branch, March 1993.

17   For example, business associations in the United States, Europe, and Japan formed a highly effective alliance in the second half of the 1980s to support higher levels of intellectual property protection and stronger IP enforcement under the GATT TRIP agreement. This kind of international business lobby alliance was seen as unprecedented at that time, but we can readily see similar international business lobbies emerging around these same issues or other international business concerns in the future.

18   For example, in a recent presentation to Industry Canada, Alain Giguère of CROP Inc. in Montreal stressed that the deep recession of the early 1990s marked a dramatic change in Canadian consumer attitudes towards greater caution and self-reliance,

less loyalty to brand names, greater emphasis on price and quality, and less emphasis on status (and "keeping up with the Joneses"). In short, hard economic times have brought Canada closer than ever before to the model of the demanding, well-informed consumer that Porter and others believe is essential to competitive advantage in international markets. If you can sell to the Canadian consumer in his/her current funk, you can probably sell anywhere.

Political commentators have captured the same change in mood among the Canadian electorate. This, for example, is the central thesis of a recent book by Peter C. Newman, *The Canadian Revolution, 1985-1995: From Deference to Defiance*, Toronto: Viking Penguin, 1995. Newman argues that over the past decade Canadians have undergone a dramatic upheaval and lost faith in their touchstone institutions in government, the military, business, labour, academia, the church, and other parts of Canadian society. Over this period, the Canadian trait of deference to authority was replaced by a new mood of defiance. Newman also examines the growing differences among Canadians. On page 77, he argues that "in a country which once prided itself on being classless, two distinct Canadian classes emerged: the first was the thin crust of computer literate, superbly educated, mentally flexible young men and women who could master the radical workplace changes of the electronic society; the second, the road kill on the information highway."

19 The profile in Box 1 is drawn from a number of sources, including the background studies for the Consumer Policy Framework Project of Consumer and Corporate Affairs of the early 1990s, the work of Michael Porter at roughly the same time – in particular his Canadian study, *Canada at the Crossroads*, 1991, and most recently David K. Foot, *Boom, Bust and Echo: How to Profit from the Coming Demographic Shift* Toronto: Macfarlane, Walter & Ross, 1996.

20 Called at times the X-Generation or Youth Group, typically between 18 and 30 years of age.

21 See, for example, Judith Maxwell, "Social Dimensions of Economic Growth," Eric J. Hanson Memorial Lecture, University of Alberta, January 25, 1995. On page 6, Maxwell noted that real earnings of 25-30-year-olds with full-time jobs have fallen 20 percent relative to those of mature workers since 1974. In Canada, the growing wage gaps are between young and mature workers, whereas in the United States, the growing divergence is between high-skill and low-skill workers.

Preliminary evidence suggests that divergences in wages and household income may have displayed even sharper growth over the past few years, in response to cutbacks in government spending and a slow recovery from a deep recession. These growing income gaps are taking place during a period when disposable income per capita and household incomes on average declined in real terms while consumer/household indebtedness as a percentage of income rose quite markedly. One consequence of these negative trends is a remarkable rise in the number of consumer bankruptcies since the recession supposedly came to an end in the early 1990s.

22 Tom McCormack, President, Strategic Projections, "Household and Household Spending Trends," presented to the Office of Consumer Affairs, Industry Canada February 29, 1996.

23 For example, the September 12-18 edition of Business in Vancouver reported that the Toronto-based firm Nielsen SRG Company had released the first comprehensive survey of the spending habits of the Vancouver Chinese community, which has an adult population of about 200,000; 53 percent of this population has been in Canada less

than five years. The survey indicated that compared to other Canadians, the Chinese community spends more heavily on restaurant meals, pays cash for cars, and travels away from home a great deal.

24 See CROP Environics, *3SC Monitor 1995: Canada's Monitor of Social Change* Montreal, 1996, chapter 6.

25 Ibid., chapter 7.

26 Biotechnology is the use of living organisms, or parts or products thereof, to produce goods and services. Biotechnology encompasses traditional techniques such as the use of yeast – a living organism – to make beer, bread, and wine; and breeding techniques designed to produce better-tasting, more-nutritious fruits and vegetables, special varieties of flowers, or animals that produce leaner meat. Biotechnology also encompasses newer techniques, such as genetic engineering or recombinant DNA (deoxyribonucleic acid) techniques, which involve the transfer of specific genetic information from one organism to another. Most of the controversy is associated with this new area of biotechnology, but because of confusion regarding the terms, the controversy can spill over into traditional techniques that have been with us for a long time.

27 This subsection draws heavily from a speech by Terry C. Leung, a senior OCA officer (now retired), "Biotechnology: A Government Perspective," remarks to the Food Biotechnology Communications Network Forum on Consumer Information and Labelling, Montreal, December 6, 1995.

28 The industrial distribution of North American biotechnology firms is as follows: health-related biotechnology, 42 percent; diagnostic, 26 percent; agricultural, 15 percent; chemicals, environmental, and services, 9 percent; and other suppliers, 8 percent. The North American food biotechnology market is growing rapidly. Estimates by Ernst and Young indicate that the total market has grown by 76 percent each year, from C$2.3 billion in 1990 to C$9.3 billion in 1994. Food biotechnology companies are located mainly in Ontario, Quebec, and British Columbia, which account for roughly three quarters of the 121 biotechnology companies in Canada. The North American industry is dominated by smaller companies with fewer than 50 employees.

29 While public awareness of certain biotechnology products and applications is on the rise, there remains a very limited number of products on the market for which consumers can express either support or opposition. Therefore, future demand must be measured by intent to purchase and hypothetical support for biotechnology products rather than by actual consumer purchase behaviour. This provides complications for both marketers and government policymakers.

It has also led to some questions regarding the validity of the survey results discussed in the text. According to some critics in government and industry, because few consumers have direct experience with these products and technologies, the survey questions are hypothetical and the responses are based on perceptions and, therefore, are of dubious value. There is clearly some truth to this. However, government and industry also need to be aware that perceptions can be as important as reality to our decisions as consumers and voters. To cite an example from the health and safety field, it is in reality more dangerous to drive ourselves to a destination than to fly, but many of us believe the opposite. The explanation seems to be that, in driving, consumers have control, whereas we lose control as passengers in an aircraft. This element of "control" appears to be important in addressing perceptions of risk.

30 Recent controversy in Canada and elsewhere has revolved around the patenting of the so-called Harvard genetic (or onco-) mouse. This mouse received a patent from

the U.S. Patent Office over eight years ago, but the Commissioner of Patents in Canada rejected the patent application for the Harvard onco-mouse on technical grounds in a decision made on August 4, 1995. The applicants have now appealed this decision to the Federal Court, but a final decision on this matter could take a number of years. For many, this decision and the resulting appeal underline the need for the federal government to develop a comprehensive policy on the patenting of higher life forms that balances legal, economic, and ethical considerations. At the present time, while Canada does not allow patents on higher life forms, patent protection can be obtained for most other categories of biotechnological innovation, including unicellular inventions.

31 This is a hormone supplement – generally called recombinant Bovine Somatotrophine (rBST) or in the United States, recombinant Bovine Growth Hormone (rBGH) – that is given to cows to increase their milk production. Commentators have suggested that it is both ironic and unfortunate that one of the earliest biotechnology products put forward by industry for regulatory approval involved a basic foodstuff consumed in particular by children, where supply management apparently prevents the consumer from enjoying any of the benefits. Our understanding is that this product, while it has received regulatory approval in the United States, has yet to find a ready market in that country. Biotechnology and its proponents in industry and government might have been better served if media and public attention had been focused on a different product with a more favourable public profile, fewer market constraints, and a more equal distribution of the benefits and risks between industry and the consumer.

32 The Competition Bureau for decades has been putting forward proposals designed to inject more competition and efficiency into the Canada farm supply-management system; the Macdonald Commission of a decade ago, and the Canadian Porter study of five years ago proposed similar changes. To date, these proposals for change have had no evident effect. As well, U.S. challenges under NAFTA to the very high tariffs now in place on dairy, poultry, and other products protected by supply management – the result of the tarification process adopted in the Uruguay Round Agreement – have, at the time of writing (summer 1996), had no success.

33 Recent research on the effects of risk and ambiguity on consumer choices have indicated that it is the degree of risk, not just the existence of risk, which influences consumer choices. The studies note that there are five characteristics of risk that impinge on consumers' estimation of risks and benefits:

- voluntary risks – whether consumers voluntarily accept risks or not;
- dread – do consumers dread the outcome of the risk?
- control – whether consumers control the level or amount of risks;
- ambiguity – whether the risks are identifiable and quantifiable; and,
- severity – how dangerous are the outcomes?

These five characteristics suggest that improved communications of the risks are needed. For example, the strongly negative reaction of consumers to the mad-cow disease disaster in the United Kingdom reflects in part anger towards the authorities when new information is made public after the fact.

34 It is recognized that, taken too far, this approach may be in conflict with the traditional economic-efficiency paradigm of competition law in Canada and elsewhere. We are not arguing that consumer protection should become an integral part of

competition law. These are different, albeit highly related, policy fields with different mandates, policy legacies, and constituencies. Rather, this is to argue for less mechanical and more in-depth analyses of the consumer perspective and of static and dynamic efficiencies within the context of the consumer-welfare and total-efficiency paradigms now employed by competition authorities. As well, while consumer welfare versus total efficiency continues to be debated in competition policy circles – see, for example, Donald McFetridge, "The Prospects for the Efficiency Defense," *Canadian Business Law Journal*, April 1996 – the approach suggested here could be encompassed within either a consumer-welfare or total-efficiency paradigm.

As noted earlier, the World Bank and other groups are extending the traditional benefit/cost models to take greater account of uncertainties, dynamic efficiencies, and distributional effects. To cite one hypothetical example of how a more sensitive approach could be applied, a proposed merger of two brand-name pharmaceutical companies could lead to higher prices in the short to medium term, but in the long run (over the next 10 years) it could increase the probability of discovering the AIDS (acquired immune deficiency syndrome) vaccine from (say) 20 to 50 percent. Traditional calculations and comparisons of the consumer-welfare losses against the expected value of the dynamic efficiency gains – with equal weights being given to the impacts on all stakeholders – could result in the merger being challenged by an antitrust agency. However, the merger might not be challenged if sufficient weight were given to the potential long-term benefits to be provided to AIDS victims. At the very least, this alternative approach could be the subject of sensitivity testing by the agency or of adjudication by a court or tribunal.

Another hypothetical example provided by the discussant to this paper involved an anticompetitive merger of two tobacco companies. He argued that allowing the merger would raise cigarette prices and thus discourage consumption of this product, which in turn would provide important health, social, and economic benefits. This example does point out the dangers of taking a broader approach too far. However, the present author's response to this example is that the competition agency should challenge the merger on anticompetitive grounds and that government should use more effective ways to raise cigarette prices (e.g., through higher taxes) and discourage cigarette smoking (e.g., through public awareness programs on the negative effects of smoking on health and the resulting costs to Canada's health care system). In fact, these essentially are the instruments used by Canadian governments over the last number of years.

As well, competition law and consumer protection agencies could benefit from conducting joint research and sharing experiences. The synergies between the two fields of law and policy perhaps could be better exploited by having the two come under the same agency, as in Australia and the United States (with the Federal Trade Commission). Now that the Consumer Products Directorate is under the administrative responsibility of the Competition Bureau's Director of Investigation and Research, the Canadian competition authorities may wish to investigate the Australian and FTC experience and lessons learned from this perspective.

35 But not always, as seen in the sharp differences between the brand-name and generic drug manufacturers over compulsory licensing under the *Patent Act*. These differences provide latitude for informal or formal alliances between consumer groups and the generic drug manufacturers in Canada, for example.

36 See, for example, Optima Consultants, "Understanding the Consumer Interest in the New Biotechnology Industry, (Ottawa, November 1994. As noted on page 31, a major

objective of the study was to obtain information about attitudes towards the expected role of government with respect to biotechnology. Most respondents placed a high value on government roles in the areas of safety and information – in particular, on protecting the safety of biotech workers, determining the safety of biotech products, enforcing regulations on activities in biotech, consulting the public on the regulation of biotech products and uses, and conducting a public information campaign on biotechnology.

37　This is a central theme of the recent OECD report, *Technology, Productivity and Job Creation*, Paris: OECD, 1996. These issues are also being explored by Industry Canada's Corporate Governance Branch in its work on a "Canadian intellectual property policy in a global, knowledge-based economy." This work stresses the strategic economic importance of intellectual property rights to consumer and producer welfare and to the international competitiveness of workers, firms, and nations as knowledge becomes the most important resource in the global economy. Using endogenous-growth theory as a frame of reference, the new economics of IPRs consider not only the firm but, as well, the national economy within a global trading system. Endogenous-growth theory suggests that IP policies not only should address the effects of IPRs on trade, investment, and innovation, but also should better understand the implications of knowledge spillovers both within a national economy and across borders.

38　It may seem self-evident that companies and industries that ignore these broader concerns of their customers will lose market share and could ultimately disappear. However, recent experience suggests that Canadian firms and industries have varied considerably in their capacity to respond to these broader issues, leading to major public policy concerns and initiatives to maintain markets, jobs, communities, and lifestyles. For example, it could be argued that the Canadian forestry and wild-fur industries were slow to respond to threatened and actual European consumer boycotts. As well, until recently, the chemicals, petroleum, pulp and paper, and other industries may have been slow to appreciate the implications of environmental concerns for their bottom lines. In fairness, these issues represented new territory for a number of these industries, and their commercial implications may not have been clear until later. Nonetheless, in each case some kind of public policy intervention appeared to be needed, arguably to advance the public interest and to "protect the industry from itself" in attempting to preserve markets, jobs, communities, and/or lifestyles. Accordingly, at times governments are under pressure from the media, the general public, and even the industry itself to address the negative externalities from the failure of industry to respond to these new market forces. These government efforts, in turn, run the danger of diverting scarce resources from other public policy objectives and can lead to second-best solutions for markets, consumers, and the total economy – solutions that can become entrenched because of the rents accruing to certain stakeholders.

39　In this regard, Canada is different from many other jurisdictions where misleading advertising and other marketing practices fall under consumer protection laws. Included among these other jurisdictions are some Canadian provinces.

40　See G. Hadfield, R. Howse, and M. Trebilcock, "Rethinking Consumer Protection Policy," a paper presented at the Roundtable on Consumer Policy, University of Toronto, June 20, 1996.

41　Two types of electronic mischief made possible by the Internet are the activities of "hit and run" electronic scammers who are able to make their fraudulent claims and promote their low-quality or hazardous products one day, and then close down their Web site the next day and show up again later at a new site, leaving virtually no paper trail; and the potential for fraudulent vendors to forge the Web sites of honest sellers.

42   For some areas of framework law, these improvements would take the form of fine-tuning; however, for consumer law – which is a shared responsibility between the federal and provincial governments – these improvements may require more fundamental changes to consumer law and administration in Canada, probably under the auspices of the Consumer Measures Committee of the Internal Trade Agreement. Enforcement cooperation and harmonization of cost-of-credit rules across Canadian jurisdictions are two of the current projects of this Committee that would be consistent with the concerns raised during the Roundtable. In complementary research, OCA is exploring the feasibility of more framework- and principles-based approaches to consumer law in Canada – approaches that philosophically would be closer to those employed in competition law and in the other framework laws administered by Industry Canada.

43   See, for example Sunil Gupta, Director, HERMES Project, University of Michigan Business School, "The World Wide Web as a Source of Commercial Information and Vendor Evaluation," a paper presented to the OCA Roundtable, March 29, 1996.

44   Over the past six years, consumer representatives have worked closely with the financial institutions and others to develop a highly successful electronic funds transfer (EFT) system in Canada to meet the needs of both industry and consumers. In 1990, the Consumers Association of Canada first got involved in this issue by undertaking an analysis of consumer-related issues, publishing articles, and securing consumer feedback. Soon after, a working group of government, consumer, and industry representatives was formed, which led to the development in 1992 of a Voluntary Code of Practice endorsed by the federal government, all provincial governments, the industry groups, and most consumer groups. Canada's system of national electronic funds transfer is reportedly superior to many operating in other industrialized countries, reflecting:

- the development of a user-friendly system that meets consumer needs in terms of privacy, redress, and other concerns;
- increased dialogue between industry and consumers, along with enhanced trust and respect; and
- recognition by Canadian financial institutions that addressing consumer interests in the planning of new consumer-oriented systems can be of mutual benefit.

45   User feedback and consumer acceptance play an important role in the new endogenous-growth models where science and technology, research and development, and innovation are market- and customer-driven (and, therefore, endogenously determined), rather than exogenous to the economic system as in the traditional growth models. See, for example, "Science and Technology: Perspectives for Public Policy," Occasional Paper Number 9, Industry Canada (July 1995). In chapter 5, Professor McFetridge compares the linear and feedback models of innovation and the policy implications of each. He stresses that the feedback model focuses on the cumulative and interdependent nature of the innovative process.

These issues are further explored in *The Implications of Knowledge-based Growth for Micro-economic Policies*, edited by Peter Howitt, Calgary: University of Calgary Press, 1996. On page 3, it is noted, with respect to the endogenous-growth model, that the

46   SchoolNet, which is Internet-based, is a cooperative initiative of the provincial, territorial, and federal governments, the academic community, and industry announced by the federal government in August 1993. Its objective is to enhance educational opportunities and achievements in elementary and secondary schools across Canada by electronically linking them and by making national and international education resources available to Canadian teachers and students. Industry Canada has committed $1.6 million to the project over a four-year period starting in 1994-95.

47   The high-performance workplace is characterized by a customer focus, commitment, continuous improvement, job enrichment, autonomous work groups, participative decision making, employee empowerment, employee-centred workplace policies, worker/management cooperation, innovative compensation plans, continuous learning, a commitment to training, and external partnerships.

48   In a study published in February 1996 by the Patented Medicines Prices Review Board, it was reported that the prices of 86 percent of the top-selling patented drugs either stayed the same or declined in 1994. The study also found that since the Board was created in 1987, price increases for patented drugs have been below the rate of inflation and that Canadian prices for patented drugs are decreasing when compared to prices in other industrialized countries. In fact, in 1994 Canadian prices, on average, were below the median international prices for the first time. Price levels for patented drugs in Canada in 1994 ranked below those in the United States, Switzerland, and Germany, and were above those in the United Kingdom, Sweden, France, and Italy.

increasing returns, externalities, and imperfect competition found in the innovation process provide a rationale for government intervention. However, this should not be taken too far. Aggregate models that posit market failure do not make reasonable allowances for government failure.

Comment

Dennis A. Yao
Wharton School
University of Pennsylvania

DEREK IRELAND GAVE US QUITE AN AMBITIOUS AND EXPLORATORY AGENDA to consider. For my discussion, I will address only a small portion of the paper. My comments are largely focused on the organizational and political-analysis aspects, and less so on the economic aspects.

In my comments, I would like to think about how one can take some of the consumer issues raised in Derek's paper and put them into a competition agenda. I have questions and not many answers, although you can probably tell what my answers will be from the questions.

The first question is, What is the problem? Derek mentions a number of concerns that consumers may have, and I think some of them, with respect to the competition agencies, stem from a concern that the efficiency goal is not being handled quite right. Perhaps we do not have the dynamic/static trade-off right.

Another set of problems has to do with whether the objectives of competitive agencies are too narrowly defined. Implicit in Professor Trebilcock's comment – "we may not want to adopt a total welfare approach to thinking about what the competition agency should do" – is the notion that competition agencies do not typically address a full range of social objectives. The consumer perspective might, for example, introduce distributional issues; while part of welfare, such issues are also very far from what the competition agencies are good at handling.

So there are these two potential sets of problems. The first concerns the current way of dealing with efficiency problems; the second suggests that some objectives may be missing.

Because we have already devoted much time in this conference to the former, I will focus on the latter problem. First, I wonder about the significance of this problem. Markets will likely handle most of the non-distributional concerns that the consumer has with respect to issues concerning biotechnology, the information superhighway, and the like. Where the market fails, might consumer concerns, for example, be handled outside the competition agency by other governmental institutions? Other government agencies deal with, for example, labelling issues, information provision, or maybe even the development of the infrastructure through which an emerging market like electronic commerce could be developed quickly. It is not obvious that the competition agency should get involved in those areas. If these avenues do not work, then there may be a political failure, which at least raises a legitimate question as to whether existing organizations – e.g., the Competition Bureau – could be used to remedy such problems.

I think that at this stage, with respect to Derek's research agenda, we do not have a lot of answers about whether the problems can be successfully addressed outside the competition agency. I suppose we could say we need more study. A practising lawyer might not want me to engage in hypotheticals given a dearth of facts, but as an academic, I can say: "Yes, but what if we did think there were residual problems? How might we think about them in the context of a competition agenda?"

As an aside, the U.S. Federal Trade Commission (FTC) is concerned with both competition and consumer protection. Both missions are intended to ensure that the markets work efficiently. For example, antitrust makes sure that the playing field is level; consumer protection ensures the consumers are informed so they can make good choices within the market. If conditions are set so that markets work, one could argue that these two objectives should work well together.

Having said that, at the FTC there is a consumer protection group and there is an antitrust group, and neither necessarily knows what the other is doing. That is not an ideal state of affairs, yet it is unsurprising, given the press of urgent matters that the FTC faces.

Returning to the question of whether a competition agency should have a broader set of objectives, consider the following example: suppose that two tobacco companies wish to merge. After the conventional analysis is performed, the view is reached that prices are going to increase in the tobacco industry. So, according to conventional merger analysis, the merger should be stopped. Right? Well, maybe not. This is the kind of example where two goals would have to be balanced if competition authorities were to consider goals in addition to a protecting competition goal.

I have two concerns here: Can the competition agency handle these kinds of issues effectively or efficiently? And what are some of the costs and risks of dealing with nonefficiency objectives? I will explore briefly the kind of problem a competition agency might have in dealing with the broader agenda than the one with which it normally deals.

Including non-economic criteria as part of the agency's decision making would be a very big step. At the policy level, say, if one is formulating guidelines, it may not be so hard to state; but on a case-by-case level, it would be very difficult, indeed virtually impossible, to implement consistently.

The staff in the agencies understand how markets work. They know how to use efficiency-oriented principles. Generally, they do a great job. But do they understand how to think about broader social goals? It is difficult enough to deal with dynamic efficiency without having to assess non-economic criteria as well. The further away the competition agency moves from efficiency, the less it can rely on reasonably well-established economic principles.

Perhaps bringing a competition agency to solve some of these non-economic issues would be like putting a football player in as the 10th player on a baseball team. You could respond, of course, What about Deion Sanders? Well, maybe the Canadian Competition Bureau has a Deion Sanders. But it is likely to be poor public policy to depend on the existence of a brilliant (or incredibly arrogant) decision-maker.

What are some of the costs and risks associated with, say, expanding the agenda of a competition agency? One risk is that this gives the agency more discretion. Generally, such agencies consist of unelected, appointed people, and it is not clear how much policy discretion they should be given. More discretion also means more inconsistency. It will be easier for a decision-maker, because he/she has so many different goals to balance, to justify a possibly arbitrary decision. This is a real problem for business in terms of being able to predict what is going to happen. Moreover, consumers (voters) are going to wonder why the agency is doing what it is doing, and the agency itself may lose some credibility as a result.

Another problem within an agency that makes trade-offs among difficult-to-compare goals is that it may reduce the importance and weight of economic analysis and increase the importance and weight given to persuasive statements about how one should weigh, for example, health concerns versus economic concerns.

Finally, I think a potentially large problem would be that when a broad range of goals are put on an agency's menu, this opens the agency to more political pressure. It is very nice when Senator Thurmond calls up and says, "I have 500 voters who are going to lose their jobs in South Carolina as a result of your action, please think about it carefully," and the agency can respond, "Yes, sir, we understand, but the goal of our agency is to make sure that competition is maintained." With a single goal (or a narrow set of goals), competition authorities will have an anchor and a compass for deciding or even resisting pressures from the outside. The compass is harder to use if the objectives are mixed. People can come in and push you around a little bit more.

In conclusion, I am sympathetic to the concerns raised by Derek, especially since I have worked on the consumer protection side. However, I am not convinced that competition policy is the right instrument for handling these problems.

Willard K. Tom   &   Joshua A. Newberg[1]
Bureau of Competition   Federal Trade Commission, and
Federal Trade Commission   University of Texas, Austin

10

U.S. Enforcement Approaches to the Antitrust-Intellectual Property Interface

> Since patents are privileges restrictive of a free economy, the rights which Congress has attached to them must be strictly construed . . . .[2]

> The intellectual property laws and the antitrust laws share the common purpose of promoting innovation and enhancing consumer welfare. The intellectual property laws provide incentives for innovation and its dissemination and commercialization by establishing enforceable property rights for the creators of new and useful products, more efficient processes, and original works of expression. . . . The antitrust laws promote innovation and consumer welfare by prohibiting certain actions that may harm competition with respect to either existing ways or new ways of serving consumers.[3]

IN THE HALF CENTURY SPANNED BY THE EPIGRAPH, the relationship between antitrust and intellectual property (IP) has undergone substantial, well-documented changes.[4] Less thoroughly explored are the doctrinal and institutional settings in which these changes occurred and their practical implications for enforcement decisions with respect to particular cases. These subjects are the task of the present paper. In the pages that follow, we review the relationship between competition law and intellectual property licensing restraints in U.S. antitrust enforcement policy. Our primary purpose is to provide a framework for understanding the *1995 Antitrust Guidelines for the Licensing of Intellectual Property*, issued jointly by the U.S. Department of Justice and the Federal Trade Commission (FTC) last year.[5]

The paper is divided into five sections. First, we introduce the core principles that have defined the way in which the relationship between intellectual property and antitrust was understood in three periods: 1) the early years after passage of the *Sherman Act*, 2) the period – especially the latter part of the period – from 1912 to the mid-1970s, and 3) the modern period, as represented by the 1995 *Guidelines*. Second, we look at some of the cases and policy statements in that middle period and compare how they were viewed then with how they would be analyzed under the *Guidelines*. We devote the third section to a discussion of how the two approaches fit into the pattern of other contemporaneous doctrines found in antitrust and in intellectual property law. In the fourth section we describe the costs and benefits of the two approaches. In the fifth section, we examine some of the more interesting specific issues dealt with in the *Guidelines* and in enforcement actions brought by the Department of Justice and the FTC in recent years.

BACKGROUND AND CORE PRINCIPLES

THE EARLY YEARS

IN THE FIRST 50 YEARS AFTER THE ENACTMENT OF THE *SHERMAN ACT* in 1890, antitrust was no match for intellectual property in the perceived conflict between the two bodies of law. When faced with competition law challenges to the exercise of intellectual property rights, courts tended to resolve disputes by deferring to the prerogatives of the intellectual property holder.[6] This deference was substantially based on an understanding that intellectual property rights constitute private property with regard to which the owner is entitled to nearly unfettered discretion.[7] The IP holders' discretion extended, for the most part, to licensing restraints which, when infrequently challenged, typically fell within the expansive protections of the late 19th- and early 20th-century doctrine of "freedom of contract."[8]

THE PATENT-ANTITRUST "CONFLICT" AND THE "SEPARATE SPHERES" MODEL

BEGINNING WITH THE *BATHTUB* CASE OF 1912[9] and the *Motion Picture Patents* Case of 1917,[10] the Supreme Court expressly recognized that intellectual property rights are subject to the "general law,"[11] including the "positive prohibitions" of the *Sherman Act*.[12] For most of the period from then until the mid 1970s, there was a perceived tension between the two bodies of law.[13] This tension manifested itself in two related legal constructs. The first was the presumption that the ownership of intellectual property confers upon the IP holder a monopoly. The second was the understanding of antitrust and intellectual property as rigidly separate spheres of law.

The Presumption of Monopoly

The predominant understanding of the relationship between antitrust and intellectual property during much of the middle period was that intellectual property confers a monopoly upon its owner.[14] The IP monopoly is not merely tolerated. As the Supreme Court declared, in a patent/antitrust case early in this period, "[t]he very object of the [patent] laws is monopoly."[15] From this simple and intuitively appealing perspective, intellectual property forms the monopoly law mirror image to the *Sherman Act* antimonopoly law. "The patent law," the Court explained in the *Motion Picture Patents* case, "protects . . . [the patentee] in the monopoly of that which he has invented and has described in the claims of his patent."[16]

Antitrust and Intellectual Property as Separate Spheres

To be sure, the monopoly was a distinctly limited and qualified one.[17] But it was not limited in the modern sense in which we now view a patent as lacking market power if it is constrained by the availability of substitutes.[18] Instead, it was limited in a formalistic sense[19] by the metes and bounds of the patent grant.[20] Within the scope of the patent conferred by Congress, the right of the patent holder was almost absolute.[21] One step over the line demarcated by the patent grant, however, and the patent holder was subjected to potential antitrust liability,[22] to loss of enforceability of the patent through the doctrine of patent misuse,[23] or to both. As one might expect under this type of legal regime, the courts devoted considerable energy to deciding precisely what conduct was within the scope of the patent grant[24] and what conduct overstepped the boundaries.[25]

THE GUIDELINES WORLD

THE "SEPARATE SPHERES" MODEL WAS SUBSTANTIALLY ERODED in the 1970's by a number of scholars[26] whose work profoundly influenced the perspective of the 1995 IP *Guidelines*[27] and its predecessor, the 1988 International *Guidelines*.[28] The work of those scholars, particularly that of Professor Bowman, constituted a direct attack on the most fundamental premise of the "separate spheres" world: that antitrust and intellectual property were in tension. Bowman begins the first chapter of his book on patents and antitrust as follows:

> Antitrust law and patent law are frequently viewed as standing in diametric opposition. How can there be compatibility between antitrust law, which promotes competition, and patent law, which promotes monopoly? In terms of the economic goals sought, the supposed opposition between these laws is lacking. Both antitrust law and patent law have a common central economic goal: *to maximize wealth by producing what consumers want at the lowest cost.*[29]

This insight was reflected (with the usual lag of a decade or so) in court decisions in the 1980s and 1990s[30] and was carried forward into the *1995 Guidelines* in the three guiding principles that form the core of those *Guidelines*, that: 1) for antitrust purposes, intellectual property is essentially comparable with any other form of property;[31] 2) the antitrust enforcement agencies will not presume the existence of market power from the mere possession of intellectual property rights;[32] and 3) intellectual property licensing allows firms to combine complementary factors of production and is generally procompetitive.[33]

These three principles are, in effect, a direct repudiation of the old approach. If intellectual property is comparable with any other form of property, then there is no invisible magic line, the crossing of which automatically leads to antitrust penalties. For antitrust law to be violated, there must be an anticompetitive effect, determined through the usual tools of *per se* or – more typically in the intellectual property context – rule-of-reason analysis. And under the rule of reason, licensing restraints are not automatically forbidden or permitted in and of themselves, for the competitive effect of a restraint depends on the economic context in which it occurs. If market power in an antitrust sense is not to be presumed, then, as with any other form of property, the existence of such power must be determined by evaluating the availability of close substitutes. And, if intellectual property licensing involves the combination of complements, then it has a substantial vertical component, even in situations that might superficially look horizontal and that would have been treated as such under the old approach.

The last point bears some explanation, because it is such a central feature of the *1995 Guidelines*.[34] Licensing is a way of bringing together complementary inputs such as manufacturing and distribution facilities, workforces, and other complementary or blocking intellectual property;[35] and transactions involving complementary inputs are essentially vertical in nature.[36] Consider, for example, two manufacturers of product X, where manufacturer A has licensed the technology for manufacturing product X to manufacturer B. Suppose that manufacturer A possesses a patent broad enough to cover product X and any likely substitutes, so that, absent the license, manufacturer B could not lawfully produce product X at all. In such a case, where manufacturer B is in the business of manufacturing product X only on the sufferance of manufacturer A, does it make any sense to treat, say, a territorial restriction in the license from A to B in the same way we would treat a market division between two horizontal competitors? Clearly not. The restraint is much more akin to a restriction imposed by a manufacturer upon its distributors. Without some theory of how the restraint creates, maintains, or facilitates the exercise of market power, and without facts to support the theory, the restraint is lawful under normal antitrust principles. It is unnecessary, in such cases, to resort to the patent laws as a "trump" that exempts the licensor's conduct from the antitrust laws.

ILLUSTRATIVE CASES AND POLICY STATEMENTS FROM THE NO-NO YEARS: ANOTHER LOOK

THE CONTRAST BETWEEN THE FORMALISM of the "separate spheres" model and the economics-oriented instrumentalism of the *Guidelines* approach can be seen by looking back at some of the leading cases and policy statements from the "separate spheres" period: *International Salt Co. Inc. v. United States*;[37] *United States v. Line Material Co.*,[38] the "nine no-nos" announced by the Antitrust Division of the Justice Department in the early 1970s,[39] and the cases of patent misuse.[40]

INTERNATIONAL SALT

IN *INTERNATIONAL SALT*, THE DEFENDANT LEASED its patented industrial salt-processing machines on terms that required lessees to purchase from the lessor unpatented salt and salt tablets – the primary inputs for salt-processing – as a condition of the lease.[41] The Supreme Court condemned the requirement as a *per se* unlawful tying arrangement. The Court reasoned that while International Salt had a right to the monopoly power presumed to be conferred by its patents, it stepped outside the protected sphere when it attempted to extend its power to salt and salt tablets:

> The appellant's patents confer a limited monopoly of the invention they reward. From them appellant derives a right to restrain others from making, vending or using the patented machines. But the patents confer no right to restrain use of, or trade in, unpatented salt. By contracting to close this market for salt against competition, International has engaged in a restraint of trade for which its patents afford no immunity from the antitrust laws.[42]

Under the *Guidelines*, the restraint would be analyzed quite differently. First, market power in the tying product would not be presumed from the mere existence of the patent.[43] Second, the fact that defendant's conduct related to unpatented goods would not prove that competition in some relevant market had been harmed. Instead, the enforcement agencies would consider whether "the arrangement has an adverse effect on competition in the relevant market for the tied product."[44] Third, the antitrust enforcement agencies would consider whether there were justifications for the practice on the grounds of efficiency.[45] Instead of focusing on whether the defendant's conduct falls inside or outside the narrow scope of the patent grant, the *Guidelines* approach scrutinizes the actual competitive effects of the practice.

LINE MATERIAL

IN *UNITED STATES V. LINE MATERIAL CO.*,[46] the Supreme Court reviewed a cross-licensing arrangement between two patent owners, Line Material Company and Southern States Equipment Corporation. Southern held a patent covering a dropout fuse with a complicated and expensive mechanism to break electric circuits when the current became excessive.[47] Although Line had patented a simpler and less expensive version of the dropout fuse release mechanism, it could not be used without infringing Southern's patent.[48] To resolve the blocking position, Line and Southern entered into a cross-licensing arrangement and further agreed to sublicense their combined patents to several third-party licensees.[49] Line, Southern, and the parties to the sub-license arrangements agreed to minimum price levels for the sale of products made with the patents Line and Southern had cross-licensed.[50]

The Court held that the parties had engaged in price-fixing in violation of the *Sherman Act*. In the Court's view: "[b]y the patentees' agreement the dominant . . . and the subservient . . . patents were combined to fix prices."[51] The issue, therefore was whether the patent laws provided defendants with immunity from the antitrust laws,[52] for "[i]n the absence of patent or other statutory authorization, a contract to fix or maintain prices in interstate commerce has long been recognized as illegal per se under the Sherman Act."[53] The Court concluded that there was no such immunity, explaining that "the possession of a valid patent or patents does not give the patentee any exemption from the provisions of the Sherman Act *beyond the limits of the patent monopoly*."[54]

Thus, the Court hardly paused over the facts that but for the Line/Southern cross-licensing arrangement, the blocking positions of the relevant patents made it impossible for "the public or the patentees [to] obtain the full benefit of the efficiency and economy of the inventions"[55] or that the patents cross-licensed by Line and Southern were "not commercially competitive."[56] Instead, it stated that since "[t]here is no suggestion in the patent statutes of authority to combine with other patent owners to fix prices on articles covered by the respective patents,"[57] such a practice is "outside the patent monopoly."[58]

Contrast this with the approach to cross-licensing and pooling arrangements under the 1995 *Guidelines*. Under the *Guidelines*, the problem of blocking and complementary patents is explicitly recognized:

> Sometimes the use of one item of intellectual property requires access to another. . . . An item of intellectual property "blocks" another when the second cannot be practiced without using the first. For example, an improvement on a patented machine can be blocked by the patent on the machine. Licensing may promote the coordinated development of technologies that are in a blocking relationship.[59]

The *Guidelines* recognize that cross-licensing and pooling arrangements "may provide pro competitive benefits by integrating complementary technologies, reducing transaction costs, clearing blocking positions, and avoiding costly infringement litigation."[60] In the terminology of the *Guidelines*, these are all vertical relationships – for example, if two parties each possessed patents that would block the other from using its respective technologies, and it was not possible for either party to invent around the other's position, then the parties would not "have been actual or likely potential competitors in a relevant market in the absence of the license."[61] On the other hand, if the parties *are* horizontal competitors – whether because their patents represent competing (i.e., substitutable) technologies, are invalid, or would likely have been invented around – then restraints on price, output, or territories in connection with a cross-licensing or pooling arrangement can harm competition in the same manner as such restraints among competitors can outside the intellectual property context.[62] The analysis thus turns away from merely categorizing the licensing restraint as "within" or "without" the scope of the patent grant, and toward analysing the actual economic circumstances in which the particular practice can either harm or promote competition.

THE NINE "NO-NOS"

IN 1970, THE ANTITRUST DIVISION OF THE JUSTICE DEPARTMENT articulated what came to be known as the "nine no-nos."[63] These were intellectual property licensing practices that would attract the scrutiny of the Division.[64] Although there is some dispute as to whether every "no-no" was understood by the Division to constitute a *per se* violation of the antitrust laws,[65] the licensing practices were described in at least one speech by then-deputy-assistant attorney-general Bruce B. Wilson as practices "which in virtually all cases are going to lead to antitrust trouble because of their adverse effect upon competition."[66] The practices – many of which had antecedents in the case law[67] – were:

- tying of unpatented supplies,[68]
- mandatory grant-backs,[69]
- post-sale restrictions on resale by purchasers of patented products,[70]
- tie-outs,[71]
- giving the licensee veto power over the licensor's grant of further licenses,[72]
- mandatory package licensing,[73]
- compulsory payment of royalties in amounts not reasonably related to the sales of the patented product,[74]
- restrictions on sales of unpatented products made by a patented process,[75] and
- specifying prices licensees could charge upon resale of licensed products.[76]

Like *International Salt* and *Line Material*, the "nine no-nos" are a vivid illustration of the traditional approach to antitrust and intellectual property as separate spheres. Indeed, Wilson introduced the list with these words:

> "[W]hat licensing practices does the Department of Justice consider to be clearly unlawful? I believe that I can identify at least nine. Each of them has an effect on competition which *extends beyond the metes and bounds of the claim of the patent.*"[77]

Tying unpatented supplies, for example, made the list because of the Supreme Court's decision in *International Salt*, which, as discussed above, based its condemnation on the belief that such tying extended the patent monopoly beyond the scope of the congressional grant.[78] Mandatory package licensing likewise was "an unlawful extension of the patent grant."[79]

In the case of compulsory grantbacks, the Department of Justice and the courts disagreed as to the result, but both arguments were largely within the bounds of the "separate spheres" paradigm. In *Transparent-Wrap Machine Corp. v. Stokes & Smith Co.*,[80] the Supreme Court held that a clause obligating the licensee to assign any improvement patents to the licensor was not *per se* invalid,[81] explaining:

> One who uses the patent to acquire another is not *extending his patent monopoly* to articles governed by the general law and as respects which neither monopolies nor restraints of trade are sanctioned. He is indeed using one *legalized monopoly* to acquire another legalized monopoly.[82]

The Department believed otherwise:

> [T]he Department views it as unlawful for a patentee to require a licensee to assign to the patentee any patent which may be issued to the licensee after the licensing arrangement is executed. Quite clearly, the legitimate desire of a patentee to be able to practice later-developed commercial embodiments of his invention which may be patented by his licensee can be adequately satisfied by requiring the licensee to grant back a non-exclusive license under any subsequent improvement patent. Moreover, the logical result of such an assignment grant-back provision is to stifle innovation on the part of the licensee.[83]

In the last two sentences, we see the glimmerings of the modern approach. Although the basic focus is still on whether the conduct is inside or outside the patent grant, the Department expressed interest in how the legitimate desires of a patentee could be satisfied and on the effect of the provision on the incentives for innovation on the part of the licensee. What is missing is any attention to whether a prohibition upon exclusive grantbacks would stifle innovation on the part of the patentee and the relative significance of the two effects in particular circumstances.

The 1995 *Guidelines* approach contrasts with that of the "nine no-nos" in the same way that it contrasts with the "separate spheres" case law. Tying arrangements (including mandatory package licensing) are scrutinized for actual anticompetitive effects and for possible procompetitive justifications.[84] Compulsory grantbacks are analyzed under the rule of reason, with the agencies recognizing that a grantback "may be necessary to ensure that the licensor is not prevented from effectively competing because it is denied access to improvements developed with the aid of its own technology";[85] that even where a grantback provision reduces licensees' incentives to improve the licensed technology, it may have offsetting procompetitive effects;[86] and that permitting such provisions may increase licensors' incentives to innovate in the first place.[87] Exclusive licenses (presumably including their less restrictive cousins – licenses giving the licensee veto power over the licensor's grant of further licenses[88]) – are treated generously, with the *Guidelines* stating that "[g]enerally, an exclusive license may raise antitrust concerns only if the licensees themselves, or the licensor and its licensees, are in a horizontal relationship."[89] Compulsory payment of royalties in amounts not reasonably related to sales of the patented product[90] might be challenged as it was in *United States v. Microsoft Corp.*,[91] but only upon a rule-of-reason showing that the restraints "anticompetitively foreclose access to, or increase competitors' costs of obtaining, important inputs, or facilitate coordination to raise price or reduce output," and that those effects outweigh the procompetitive effects.[92] Thus, in contrast to the "nine no-nos," the approach under the *Guidelines* focuses on the actual effect of a practice in particular market circumstances, rather than attempting to derive broad rules from the supposed nature of a given licensing practice and from notions regarding the practice's inherent relationship to the intellectual property being licensed.

PATENT MISUSE

OUTSIDE THE ANTITRUST FIELD, the closely related intellectual property doctrine of patent misuse exhibited the same separate-spheres perspective of its antitrust analogue. Patent misuse is an equitable doctrine, under which a patent owner that misuses its patent by extending it beyond the term or scope of the grant or by using it to commit an antitrust violation is deemed to have "unclean hands," disqualifying it (until the misuse is "purged") from seeking the aid of a court of equity to enforce its patent right.[93] Had the economics of licensing transactions been better developed at the time, patent misuse – as an equitable rather than legal doctrine – might have been particularly well suited to taking into account the procompetitive justifications for the licensing restrictions claimed to constitute misuse. However, the tool at hand to determine whether the patent owner had behaved inequitably was the metes and bounds approach we have already discussed.[94] Thus, in *Morton Salt*,[95] the owner of a patent for a machine that deposited salt tablets in food cans was held to have committed misuse by making the lease of the machine conditional on the lessee's use of salt tablets made by the patentee's subsidiary.[96] The Supreme Court reasoned that the patentee had attempted to extend its monopoly over the unpatented salt tablets, thus going beyond the scope of what the patent had granted. Similarly, in *Mercoid Corp. v. Minneapolis-Honeywell Regulator Co.*,[97] and in *Mercoid Corp. v. Mid-Continent Investment Co.*,[98] the Court held a patent owner to have engaged in misuse for having granted licenses for patented systems only on the condition that an unpatented component (which was designed for use with the patented system and could be used for no other purpose) be purchased from the patent owner. Numerous other decisions took the same approach.[99] The *Guidelines* do not deal with the misuse doctrine, but a number of recent cases[100] and some recent legislation[101] have led to results in the misuse area that are somewhat analogous to positions taken in the antitrust area by the *Guidelines*.

DOCTRINAL BASES OF THE RESPECTIVE WORLDS

THE TRADITIONAL ANALYSIS OF THE RELATIONSHIP between antitrust and intellectual property restraints did not exist in a vacuum. It was closely related to two other familiar doctrines of traditional antitrust law: the "*per se* rule" and the concept of "express and implied exemptions" from the antitrust laws. First, both of those doctrines, like the "separate spheres" model, rely on formalistic logic and categorization as contrasted with the economics-based instrumentalism of the *Guidelines* approach. Second, one could argue that but for the overbroad application of substantive *per se* rules, it would not have been necessary to treat patent-antitrust cases as falling into a "separate sphere" that was exempted from normal application of the antitrust laws. By the same token, the *Guidelines* approach to the antitrust/intellectual property interface should be understood in the context of broader changes in antitrust analysis, which gave more scope to efficiency considerations, narrowed the application of *per se* rules, and made an exemption approach to patent-antitrust cases unnecessary.

THE PER SE RULE AND THE RULE OF REASON

MOST RESTRAINTS ON COMPETITION ARE ANALYZED under the rule of reason.[102] In applying the rule of reason, a court considers all relevant facts, the nature of the restraint, and the conditions of competition to determine "whether the restraint imposed is such as merely regulates and thereby perhaps promotes competition or whether it is such as may suppress or even destroy competition."[103] There are, however, "certain agreements or practices which because of their pernicious effect on competition and lack of any redeeming virtue are conclusively presumed to be unreasonable and therefore illegal without elaborate inquiry as to the precise harm they have caused or the business excuse for their use."[104] These "*per se*" violations include agreements among competitors to fix prices, allocate markets, reduce output, or – under some circumstances – to boycott collectively actual and potential competitors.[105] "With respect to such arrangements, antitrust plaintiffs need not demonstrate unreasonableness . . . . " nor anticompetitive effects.[106] For a court to condemn a restraint as *per se* unlawful, all that must be established is the existence of the restraint. Thus, just as the nature of the license restraint determined its treatment under the "nine no-nos" without regard to the surrounding circumstances or the possible competitive effects, so the substantive *per se* rule takes a formalistic approach that focuses on the intrinsic nature of certain restraints, eschewing any inquiry into the effects of such restraints on competition.

IMPLIED EXEMPTIONS FOR REGULATED INDUSTRIES

THE IP/ANTITRUST/SEPARATE-SPHERES CONSTRUCT ALSO FINDS an analogue in traditional antitrust analysis of the conduct of regulated industries. Various aspects of insurance[107] and shipping,[108] for example, are exempted by statute from the antitrust laws.[109] In other industries, the courts have inferred various "implied exemptions" from the nature of the regulatory scheme.[110] In either case, the Supreme Court has followed similar approaches. With respect to statutory exemptions, the Court has stated that "exemptions from antitrust laws are strictly construed. . . ."[111] With respect to implied exemptions, it has stated that "[r]epeal [of the antitrust laws] is to be regarded as implied only if necessary to make the [regulatory scheme] work, and even then only to the minimum extent necessary. This is the guiding principle to reconciliation of the two statutory schemes."[112] The cases from the "separate spheres" era employ strikingly similar language with respect to reconciling the two regimes of intellectual property and antitrust law. As the Court declared in the *Masonite* case: "Since patents are privileges restrictive of a free economy, the rights which Congress has attached to them must be strictly construed. . . ."[113]

THE USEFULNESS OF "SEPARATE SPHERES" IN THE FACE OF EXPANSIVE PER SE RULES AND LIMITED TOLERANCE OF LEGITIMATE MONOPOLIES

AT TIMES IN THE HISTORY OF ANTITRUST LAW, *per se* rules have been extended to practices whose "manifestly anticompetitive"[114] character might seriously be questioned. The best known example is the condemnation of vertical territorial and customer restraints in *United States v. Arnold, Schwinn & Co.*[115] Schwinn had assigned specific territories to each of its wholesale distributors and had required them to sell only to franchised Schwinn accounts in their respective territories. The District Court had held the territorial restriction unlawful *per se*, a holding that was not appealed, but had upheld the requirement of selling only to franchisees. The Supreme Court reversed, holding that both restraints were "in the nature of restraints upon alienation which are beyond the power of the manufacturer to impose upon its vendees and which, since the nature of the transaction includes an agreement, combination or understanding, are violations of § 1 of the Sherman Act."[116]

We do not suggest that *Schwinn* was the impetus for treating intellectual property as being in need of an antitrust exemption: that decision came well after the "separate spheres" jurisprudence was well established, and was itself an anomaly that reversed an earlier decision treating vertical territorial restraints under the rule of reason.[117] Yet the usefulness of an antitrust exemption approach becomes readily apparent when the *Schwinn* rule is juxtaposed with a statute that expressly gave the patentee the right to convey an exclusive right under the patent "to the whole or any specified part of the United States."[118] If the antitrust *per se* rule condemned all territorial allocations, whether horizontal or vertical, then the two regimes truly did collide, which implied that repeal of the antitrust laws was "necessary to make the [regulatory scheme] work," but under the traditional doctrine should be granted only "to the minimum extent necessary."[119]

Such an exemptions approach was also a logical response to antitrust law's traditional analysis of monopolization. Although it has long been settled that the mere possession of monopoly power was not unlawful,[120] there was a belief that monopoly is "inherently evil,"[121] and that monopoly acquired through superior skill and hard competition was "tolerated but not cherished."[122] From the (mis)understanding that patents by their very nature conferred monopolies,[123] there followed the conclusion that the two legal regimes were fundamentally at odds – enhancing the appeal of an "antitrust exemption" approach to the perceived conflict.

THE GUIDELINES WORLD

THE WORLDVIEW THAT LEGITIMIZED THE "SEPARATE SPHERES" APPROACH was substantially undermined from the late 1970s through the early 1990s by a series of federal court decisions, legislative changes,[124] and emerging trends in the application of economics to antitrust analysis.[125] These developments profoundly influenced the 1995 IP *Guidelines* and the approach embodied therein.

Several Supreme Court cases – most notably *Sylvania*[126] and *BMI*[127] – introduced significant analytical components of the *Guidelines* world, including: 1) the expansion of rule of reason analysis and a concomitant erosion of the *per se* unlawful category of restraints; and 2) a greater willingness to look beyond the form and legal characterization of restraints and to focus the inquiry on economic substance, i.e., the actual or likely effects of specific arrangements on competition.

The *Sylvania* Case

In *Sylvania*, the Supreme Court reviewed an antitrust challenge to a territorial restraint in a franchise agreement. Under the challenged contract, Continental – the franchisee – agreed to sell Sylvania electronics products subject to the restriction that the Sylvania products could only be sold from specific geographical locations expressly approved by Sylvania – the franchisor. When Continental gave notice that it intended to sell Sylvania products from an unauthorized location, Sylvania dropped Continental as its franchisee. Continental sued Sylvania, claiming that the territorial restraint in the distribution agreement between Sylvania and Continental constituted a *per se* violation of section 1 of the *Sherman Act*.

 Under the then-governing precedent of *United States v. Arnold, Schwinn & Co.*,[128] a territorial restraint imposed by the franchisor in the distribution of a product was *per se* unlawful if the manufacturer parted with title before the product was sold by the distributor. However, the same territorial restraint would receive rule-of-reason treatment if the manufacturer retained title through the chain of distribution to the ultimate purchaser.[129] In reviewing the *Schwinn* distinction, the *Sylvania* Court noted that "[t]he market impact of vertical restrictions is complex because of their potential for a simultaneous reduction of intrabrand competition and stimulation of interbrand competition,"[130] and that "the form of the transaction by which a manufacturer conveys his products . . . to retailers" does not affect the competitive impact of a restraint reducing intrabrand competition.[131] Acknowledging the typically procompetitive effects of vertical restrictions in overcoming "free-rider" problems and other obstacles to efficient distribution,[132] the Court noted further that "[e]conomists have identified a number of ways in which manufacturers can use . . . [vertical non-price restraints] to compete more effectively against other manufacturers."[133] Continuation of the *Schwinn* rule, then, would – in cases where distribution arrangements direct that title to products destined for retail sale pass from manufacturer to distributor – arbitrarily deprive consumers of the net benefits of vertical non-price restraints promoting interbrand competition.[134] The Court overruled *Schwinn* and held that the legality of vertical non-price restraints was to be determined under a rule-of-reason analysis inquiring into the actual economic effects of the challenged restraint.[135]

The *BMI* Case

In *Broadcast Music, Inc. v. Columbia Broadcasting System*,[136] the Supreme Court reviewed an antitrust challenge to the "blanket" licensing of music copyrights. Broadcast Music, Inc. (BMI) and the American Society of Composers, Authors and Publishers (ASCAP) serve as the non-exclusive licensing agents for thousands of composers as well as monitoring usage, prosecuting infringements, and collecting and distributing royalty income.[137] Under the type of blanket licence challenged in the *BMI* case, licensed users such as the CBS television network purchase the rights to broadcast any and all of the works in the repertories of BMI and/or ASCAP, for a fixed period of time, regardless of how many compositions are actually used or how often the works are broadcast. Under the blanket broadcast licenses at issue in the *BMI* case, then, the fee paid by CBS as blanket licensee was not based on charges for specific uses of specific compositions. Rather, in exchange for the right to broadcast any ASCAP and (under a separately negotiated license) any BMI composition at any time during the term of the blanket licenses, CBS agreed to pay ASCAP and BMI a fixed percentage of the network's broadcast advertising revenue.[138] Although CBS and the individual composers whose works were broadcast by the blanket licensee were free to enter into individual per-performance licensing agreements, CBS argued that the BMI and ASCAP blanket licensing arrangements nevertheless amounted to *per se* unlawful price-fixing in violation of the *Sherman Act*.[139] More specifically, CBS contended that BMI and ASCAP were "using the leverage inherent in [their] copyright pool to insist that . . . [blanket licensees] pay royalties on a basis which . . . [did] not bear any relationship to the amount of music performed."[140]

Although the *BMI* case was not a government prosecution, CBS's theory was quite consistent with the "nine no-nos" and with traditional approaches to the antitrust analysis of intellectual property licensing.[141] In essence, CBS accused BMI and ASCAP of violating "no-no" number 6 (mandatory package licensing)[142] and number 7 (compulsory payment of royalties in amounts not reasonably related to sales of the . . . [copyrighted] product).[143] The U.S. Court of Appeals for the Second Circuit, in its opinion finding that the BMI licensing arrangements violated section 1 of the *Sherman Act*, analogized the blanket broadcast licenses to the patent pooling agreement that had been condemned as *per se* unlawful price-fixing in *United States v. Line Material, Inc.*[144]

Looking beyond the form of the arrangement and refusing to accept the price-fixing label as a basis for *per se* condemnation of blanket broadcast licensing, the Supreme Court reversed the Second Circuit, holding that the legality of the licensing arrangement was to be determined under the rule of reason. The Court observed that "ASCAP [and BMI] and the blanket license developed together out of the practical situation in the marketplace,"[145] a marketplace in which the transaction costs of separately negotiating rights with respect to each individual musical composition are, for even the largest customers, very high.[146]

The Court's inquiry into actual market conditions and competitive effects revealed no indication that much, if any, competition that would have existed but for the blanket licenses had been materially restrained. Nothing, moreover, prevented individual customers from licensing compositions directly from individual composers or through other agents on a non-exclusive basis.[147] The actual effect of blanket licensing through ASCAP and BMI was rather to create competition that would otherwise have been stymied because of prohibitively high transaction costs.[148]

The contrast between the *BMI* analysis and the condemnation of the patent pooling arrangement in the *Line Material* case is instructive. Presented with evidence and argument in the earlier case that a patent-pooling arrangement may have resolved a blockage and thereby provided for the diffusion of a superior product at a lower price, the *Line Material* Court subjected the agreement to *per se* condemnation and eschewed any serious inquiry into whether the restraint might have been procompetitive, on balance.[149] As the *BMI* Court noted, a literal approach to the application of *per se* rules is "overly simplistic and often overbroad."[150]

The Impact of *Sylvania* and *BMI* on the *Guidelines*

Both *Sylvania* and *BMI* emphasized substance, i.e., the actual effect on competition, over form, while expanding the scope of the rule of reason. Economic concepts such as "transaction costs" and "free-rider" problems took on a potentially determinative significance in the Court's analysis of licensing restraints. With the evolution of the antitrust doctrine signaled in *BMI*, the courts could turn, by and large, from trying to decide whether a particular practice was within or outside the patent or copyright grant to determining whether the practice advanced or retarded innovation and consumer welfare.

The influence of *BMI* and its progeny on the 1995 *Guidelines* is particularly evident in the articulation of the enforcement agencies' general framework for evaluating licensing restraints.[151] While affirming the applicability of *per se* condemnation to a relatively narrow category of IP licensing restraints,[152] the *Guidelines* adopt the basic *BMI* inquiry into "whether the restraint in question can be expected to contribute to an efficiency-enhancing integration of economic activity."[153] Because, "in general, IP licensing can be expected to "contribute to an efficiency-enhancing integration of economic activity," the rule of reason is articulated as the default setting for the antitrust analysis of IP licensing restraints:

> In the vast majority of cases, restraints in intellectual property licensing arrangements are evaluated under the rule of reason. The Agencies' general approach in analyzing a licensing restraint under the rule of reason is to inquire whether the restraint is reasonably necessary to achieve procompetitive benefits that outweigh those anticompetitive effects.[154]

Similarly, the influence of *Sylvania*'s approach to vertical restraints permeates the *Guidelines*, because they treat intellectual property licensing arrangements as having a significant vertical component. The third principle of the *Guidelines* recognizes the complementary and therefore vertical character of most intellectual property licensing transactions.[155] Given the vertical character of the transaction, *Sylvania*'s recognition of the concerns that a manufacturer may have about one distributor free-riding upon the efforts of others and thereby undermining the entire distribution system takes on a particular salience. To take but one example, section 2.3 of the *Guidelines* observes that:

> Field-of-use, territorial, and other limitations on intellectual property licenses may serve procompetitive ends by allowing the licensor to exploit its property as efficiently and effectively as possible. These various forms of exclusivity can be used to give a licensee an incentive to invest in the commercialization and distribution of products embodying the licensed intellectual property. . . . The restrictions may do so, for example, by protecting the licensee against free-riding on the licensee's investments by other licensees or by the licensor.

COSTS AND BENEFITS OF THE RESPECTIVE APPROACHES

BENEFITS OF THE "SEPARATE SPHERES" APPROACH, COSTS OF THE *GUIDELINES* APPROACH

THE BENEFITS WE MIGHT EXPECT FROM THE "SEPARATE SPHERES" APPROACH to antitrust review of intellectual property restraints are those associated with a well-conceived system of bright-line rules: efficient administration, predictability, and transparency.[156] As the Supreme Court has observed, "*per se* rules tend to provide guidance to the business community and to minimize the burdens on litigants and the judicial system of the more complex rule-of-reason trials. . . ."[157] The traditional inquiry of the "separate spheres" world – whether a given arrangement is within or without the intellectual property holder's "monopoly" – is conceptually straightforward and transparent, at least on the surface. And the "nine no-nos" go even further toward ease of administration, predictability, and transparency. They are concrete, specific, and again, at least on the surface,[158] inflexible and therefore completely predictable.

A system of bright-line prohibitions generally applying *per se* rules embodies two related judgments regarding the antitrust/intellectual property interface: first, that most or all determinations can be made on the basis of prepackaged, specific rules of decision, and second, that the marginal cost of acquiring and considering information beyond that embodied in those rules of decision exceeds the marginal benefit of bringing additional information to bear in deciding cases. If those propositions were true, the "separate spheres" approach would have much to commend it, and the *Guidelines* approach would likely be found wanting. Bereft of more than a very few bright-line rules subjecting substantial classes of restraints to *per se* condemnation, and rejecting the presumption of market power based on the mere possession of a patent or copyright, *Guidelines* analysis generally burdens the agencies with factual inquiry into market conditions and anticompetitive effects. It would follow that *Guidelines* analysis would be slow, resource-intensive, less predictable, less of a deterrent and, perhaps, disproportionately susceptible to what statisticians call "type 2 error."[159] That is to say, enforcement resource constraints, in combination with the vastly expanded ambit for arguments justifying licensing restraints, could allow more anticompetitive conduct to escape investigation or, upon investigation, be erroneously classified as procompetitive or competitively benign.

COSTS OF THE "SEPARATE SPHERES" APPROACH, BENEFITS OF THE *GUIDELINES* APPROACH

THE OTHER SIDE OF THE COST-BENEFIT LEDGER suggests a different story. It is not at all clear, for example, that the "separate spheres" approach is more efficient administratively than the *Guidelines* approach.[160] More significant, the efficiency of a legal regime must be measured not by its administrative costs alone, but by its net effect on the efficiency of the economy as a whole.[161] Possible administrative efficiencies notwithstanding, the "separate spheres" approach and "nine no-nos" analysis almost certainly skew antitrust/IP enforcement toward overdeterrence of efficient conduct and type 1 error in the condemnation of procompetitive licensing arrangements. Because prepackaged bright-line rules of decision can never fully anticipate and account for all circumstances, such rules are likely to be under- and overinclusive.[162] Conduct that falls outside the patent monopoly, for example, may, in some cases, be efficient and, on balance, procompetitive. The same can also be said of some arrangements that are subject to *per se* condemnation in the "separate spheres" world. The Supreme Court's condemnation of a patent- pooling arrangement, regardless of whether the patents are blocking, complementary, or substitutable, is a case in point.[163] The wholesale prohibition of grantbacks and of tying unpatented supplies, regardless of market conditions and competitive effects, are two others.[164] By definition, overdeterrence and legal condemnation of efficient licensing conduct reduces allocative efficiency. Moreover, although no one can predict with confidence whether a given licensing arrangement will foster innovation, overdeterrence of efficient licensing transactions will almost certainly prevent some transactions that would have fostered innovation. Thus the "separate spheres" approach is likely to reduce innovation-driven gains in dynamic efficiency that play a pivotal role in generating economic growth and the rise of living standards.

The 1995 *Guidelines* substantially address the "separate spheres" propensities for overdeterrence and type 1 error by 1) recognizing that intellectual property licensing is generally procompetitive, 2) eschewing, with a few exceptions, bright-line prohibitions and *per se* condemnation of wholesale categories of restraints, and 3) adopting a rule-of-reason analysis that focuses not on the formal characterization of the restraint, but on its competitive effects.

A Third Alternative – *Per Se* Lawfulness

A CONCEIVABLE WAY OF ACHIEVING CERTAINTY AND PREDICTABILITY and at the same time avoiding overdeterrence of efficient conduct would be to simply make all conduct concerning intellectual property, other than sham transactions, *per se* lawful. Such treatment would be analogous to the treatment that Judge Posner has advocated for vertical restraints[165] and, as far as intellectual property licensing transactions – even among competitors – are regarded to a significant extent as vertical,[166] similar arguments apply.

This approach would be particularly attractive if, as conventional wisdom has had it, antitrust furthers static allocative efficiency (the optimal allocation of existing resources) at the expense of dynamic efficiency (the maximization of output over the long run through optimal investments in productive assets and R&D).[167] Although *per se* lawfulness would maximize type 2 error (false negatives), it would minimize type 1 error (false positives). Since harm to dynamic efficiency is vastly more significant to social welfare than harm to static efficiency,[168] *per se* lawfulness might be preferable if false positives often harmed the former and false negatives only harmed the latter.

Unfortunately, the formulation of sensible policy does not seem to be so simple a task. Just as the Posnerian approach to vertical restraints has been undermined by developments in economics suggesting how vertical restraints can, under certain conditions, be used to achieve or exploit market power,[169] so there is reason to believe that restraints on competition can themselves impede innovation. The arguments and evidence to this effect fall into two general categories: 1) that dominant firms have reduced incentives to innovate, and 2) that firms which do have the incentive to innovate can be blocked from doing so by anticompetitive practices that deprive them of complementary assets needed to turn new ideas into commercially viable products. The points are related, because to the extent that potential rival innovators can be prevented from becoming effective competitors, a dominant firm may feel less competitive pressure to innovate, whereas in the absence of such exclusion, the dominant firm may be forced to innovate simply to maintain its position.

The debate over whether monopoly or competition is generally more conducive to innovation began with Joseph Schumpeter, who argued that monopoly encourages innovation because, among other reasons, a monopolist is better able to appropriate the value of its innovations.[170] That is, in a competitive market an innovation can be imitated by the innovator's rivals, who can thereby appropriate much of the value of the innovation. By contrast, a monopolist can reap the full benefit of its invention if there are no other rivals and barriers to entry into the market are high. Some decades later, Kenneth Arrow demonstrated that, under some conditions, a monopolist may have less incentive to innovate than a firm in a competitive market, because the monopolist that brings out a new or superior product may simply cannibalize its own markets, i.e., draw sales away from products on which it is already earning a monopoly profit.[171] The empirical evidence on this subject has been mixed and difficult to interpret.[172] While earlier studies suggested that R&D expenditures increased as industries moved from unconcentrated to moderately concentrated and then fell off again as concentration increased further, that relationship mostly evaporates when researchers control for company- and industry-specific effects, such as the degree of appropriability across industries.[173]

But even if sweeping generalizations cannot be made about what industry structure is best suited to innovation, more targeted arguments and evidence support the view that giving free rein to anticompetitive conduct would dampen innovation. In one provocative article, Jonathan Baker addressed the question of why in some industries leading firms are the most innovative ones, whereas in other industries fringe producers are more innovative.[174] Using the U.S. automobile industry as an example, Baker suggests that four principal factors explain why the Big Three automakers chose to allow fringe producers from Japan to become the most innovative firms, rather than aggressively deterring fringe innovation by making substantial R&D investments of their own.

- If leading firm innovation imposes costs on the leading firms greater than the costs imposed by fringe firm innovation, accommodation is more likely than deterrence.
- If the ability of fringe firms to expand is limited, accommodation will again be more attractive than deterrence.
- Risk aversion may make accommodation more attractive than deterrence.
- If the leading firms are able to engage to some degree in coordinated interaction with each other, accommodation may again be more attractive than deterrence.[175]

All four of these factors can be affected by competitive conditions in the relevant markets, in two principal ways. First, if potential fringe-firm innovators can be deprived of access to important complementary assets (whether those assets are in distribution, manufacturing, or technology), or if the cost of such access can be raised substantially, then their ability to expand can be limited (Baker's second factor). In turn, their impact on the leading firms will be reduced, and their innovation is likely to have less impact on the leading firms than would innovation by one of the leading firms (Baker's first factor).[176] In addition, risk aversion (Baker's third factor) may be a more viable strategy where such barriers to innovation by other firms are substantial, because absent such barriers, a leading firm may be faced with the prospect that "[i]f you don't keep running on the treadmill, you're going to be thrown off."[177] Second, the conditions for oligopolistic coordination (Baker's fourth factor) can be created through mergers, foreclosure, or facilitating practices.

While Baker focused on the factors that determined whether innovation in a particular industry would come principally from the industry leaders or from fringe firms, rather than how the total amount of innovation would be affected, it is readily apparent that depriving fringe-firm innovators of access to important complementary assets can adversely affect both sources of innovation – reducing both fringe firms' ability and leading firms' incentives to innovate.[178]

The evidence for such effects tends to be anecdotal, since quantification of such restricted access to complements is more difficult than measuring concentration (and, as has been noted, the evidence on the relationship between concentration and innovation has itself been exceedingly difficult to interpret).[179] Yet there are certainly a number of examples where innovation seems to have been furthered by a dose of competition. Illustrative is the example of Corning, Inc., after it made its pioneering optical fiber invention in 1970.

> Once the breakthrough was made, the commercial fun began. . . . AT&T, which owned most of the telephone lines in America at the time, said it would be 30 years before its telephone system would be ready for optical fiber. And when it was, AT&T planned to make its own fiber. After all, it was a vertically integrated monopoly. . . . Finally, in 1982, after the MFJ was signed, the commercial breakthrough happened. MCI took the risk and placed a 100,000 kilometer order for a new generation of fiber, single-mode fiber. We took the MCI order, built a full scale plant, and started a technological revolution.[180]

Whatever AT&T's views may be of that particular episode, its officials agree that the AT&T divestiture and the resulting separation of the local "bottleneck" monopoly from the competitive parts of the telephone business has been good for innovation. At the FTC's Global Competition Hearings in 1995, an AT&T representative described the divestiture as "one of the most successful remedies in antitrust history," and noted that "innovation has burgeoned" as a result of the decree.[181] Other business witnesses at the hearings, while not addressing the specific situation in which vertical integration or vertical restraints have been used to deprive potential competitors of the markets or other complements necessary to produce marketable innovations, agreed that competition is an important spur to innovation. An Eastman Kodak representative noted that competition has led Kodak to spend $3 billion over the past 15 years on R&D directed toward electronic imaging.[182] Other witnesses suggested a similar relationship between competition and innovation in automobiles, steel, financial services, and grocery products.[183]

When these general observations are considered along with the circumstances confronted in the specific enforcement actions (discussed below), *per se* lawfulness for transactions involving intellectual property does not seem to be a viable option. Despite the administrative facility, predictability, and transparency of a system of bright-line rules, neither the simple hostility of the "separate spheres" approach nor the simple permissiveness of *per se* lawfulness seems best calculated to promote innovation or consumer welfare over the long run, at least on the present state of the evidence. We are thus left with the overriding general principle of the *Guidelines*: that the same antitrust regime is appropriate for intellectual property as applies to other forms of property.

The Guidelines Approach to Particular Antitrust Issues

THE *GUIDELINES* GO BEYOND GENERAL PRINCIPLES to a discussion of applications to specific practices.[184] Much of that discussion is straightforward and does not require extended exegesis. We focus our discussion here on five issues that we find of particular interest: 1) the distinction between horizontal and vertical restraints, 2) the treatment of tying and exclusive dealing, 3) cross-licensing and pooling, 4) licensing arrangements that should be analyzed as acquisitions, and 5) innovation markets.

Horizontal and Vertical Restraints

THE THIRD *GUIDELINES* PRINCIPLE says that intellectual property licensing is a way of bringing together complementary inputs, such as manufacturing and distribution facilities, workforces, and other complementary or blocking intellectual property.[185] Implicit in that principle is that intellectual property licensing transactions typically have a substantial vertical component, for transactions involving complementary inputs are essentially vertical transactions.[186] As is by now well known, vertical restraints can have numerous efficiency-enhancing characteristics, and the restriction on one party's freedom of action as a result of the restraint does not by itself eliminate any competition.[187] Instead, a vertical restraint is harmful if it facilitates collusion among horizontal competitors[188] or confers on a party power over price by raising the costs of that party's competitors.[189]

An example of a collusion-facilitating arrangement is a sham licensing arrangement. Example 7 of the *Guidelines* is of this type. A manufacturer licenses a technology for the manufacture of product X to all its competitors. The licensor and each licensee agrees to stay within assigned territories, not just for product X produced through the licensed technology, but for all product X, however made. The technology itself is not an advance over existing technologies, and indeed none of the licensees actually use the technology. Under these extreme circumstances, it is easy to see that the licensing arrangement is a sham, designed only to cloak a market division among horizontal competitors. In such a case, one could either ignore the ostensible verticality altogether and simply regard the arrangement as a horizontal market division, or one could treat the arrangement as a series of vertical agreements that facilitate collusion among horizontal competitors. In either case, the anticompetitive effect is clear, as is the absence of redeeming virtue.

An example of an arrangement that forecloses rivals or raises their costs is the *Microsoft* case (discussed in the next section),[190] in which a dominant vendor of computer operating systems used what amounted to exclusive dealing contracts to make it difficult for rival vendors of operating systems to get access to computer manufacturers, through which operating systems are principally distributed.

In both of these situations, the *Guidelines* help define the nature of the competition being restrained by helping determine whether the parties are in a horizontal relationship in some respect or whether there is some other horizontal relationship that is affected by the restraint. The *Guidelines* define a horizontal relationship as one in which the parties "would have been actual or likely potential competitors in a relevant market in the absence of the license."[191] This means, for example, that two manufacturers of a particular product are not treated as being in a horizontal relationship if one manufacturer is in the business only at the sufferance of the other – as would be the case, for example, where the other manufacturer possessed a patent broad enough to cover both the product and any likely substitutes. In such a case, the licensor would be free, for example, to impose territorial or field-of-use restrictions without any fear that such a restriction would be viewed as a *per se* unlawful horizontal market division. Another way of describing this stance is to say that the antitrust laws do "not require the owner of intellectual property to create competition in its own technology."[192]

Examples 5 and 6 of the *Guidelines* illustrate the circumstances under which various relationships might be viewed as horizontal or vertical. As might be expected in guidelines, these examples deal with clear cases in order to make a conceptual point. Harder cases come about under conditions of uncertainty, and especially where enforcers (or courts) and the parties have asymmetric information. (This point is discussed at greater length below in the section entitled "Cross-Licensing and Pooling").

The importance of identifying the horizontal and vertical relationships can be seen in the *Pilkington* case[193] brought by the Department of Justice. In the 1930s, Pilkington, a British company, developed a process for making sheet glass by floating molten glass on a molten metal bath. It was a revolutionary process and eventually became the dominant technology for producing sheet glass. Pilkington licensed its technology by giving its licensees exclusive territories in which they were permitted to compete. Sixty years later, Pilkington's basic patents had long since expired, but the exclusive territories persisted. Although Pilkington still asserted trade secrets, most of the know-how had in fact become publicly known, so Pilkington did not in reality possess any intellectual property rights of significant value. The arrangement was partly vertical, in that the original license transferred a patented technology and associated know-how to licensees whose principal assets were complements, not substitutes (i.e., although the licensees may have been in the glass-making business, what they supplied were complements, such as manufacturing capacity, not substitute technologies capable of competing with Pilkington's technology). If the relationship were entirely vertical, i.e., if the competitors could not be in the glass-making business absent a license from Pilkington, it would be difficult to identify any competition that had been restrained; absent the license, there would be no competition at all. But in this case, the arrangement was also partly horizontal, because even absent the license, there would by now likely be competition among some or all of these firms using their own glass technology or technology that was in the public domain. The territorial restrictions in the license significantly inhibited this competition because Pilkington vigorously attempted to enforce them against all of its competitors' glass-making activities, even if they did not appear to infringe any existing intellectual property rights. Of course the identification of a horizontal element, and therefore of competition that can be restrained, does not necessarily mean that a restraint on that competition is necessarily unlawful. A restraint might be justified if it is reasonably necessary in order to achieve efficiencies.[194] In *Pilkington*, however, there appeared to be no legitimate need for a territorial restriction stretching indefinitely into a future in which the patents had expired and the trade secrets had emerged into the public domain.

TYING AND EXCLUSIVE DEALING

SECTIONS 5.3 AND 5.4 OF THE *GUIDELINES* deal with tying and exclusive dealing. These two types of restraint nominally receive very different treatment under U.S. antitrust law; the former is considered a *per se* violation, while the latter is evaluated under the rule of reason. Nonetheless, both because of the way tying law has evolved in the courts and the way in which the enforcement agencies describe in the *Guidelines* how they will exercise their prosecutorial discretion, analysis of these types of restraints can be very similar, and indeed the two types of restraints can be alternative ways of achieving the same anticompetitive ends in a particular case.

Exclusive Dealing or Tying by a Dominant Firm to Maintain or Enhance Market Power

United States v. Microsoft Corp.[195] is a good example of the last point. In that case, Microsoft employed a variety of practices that locked original equipment manufacturers into dealing with Microsoft and discouraged the use of competing operating system products, such as IBM's OS/2 and Novell's DR-DOS. Specifically, Microsoft used per-processor licences, which charged computer manufacturers (original equipment manufacturers, or OEMs) for every computer they shipped, whether or not MS-DOS, some other operating system, or no operating system shipped with it. That made it harder for competing vendors of operating systems because an OEM, and therefore the ultimate consumer, would have to pay twice: once to Microsoft and once to the competitor. In other words, the per-processor license functioned as a penalty for dealing with any vendor in addition to Microsoft, i.e., it was a form of exclusive-dealing arrangement. The competitive effect of an exclusive-dealing arrangement depends, among other things, on the market power of the party imposing it, the degree of foreclosure, and the duration of the arrangement.[196] In this case Microsoft was a highly dominant firm, and the contracts often locked up OEMs for five years or more – well beyond the product-life cycle of most PC operating system products. In some cases the contracts left OEMs with unused balances on their minimum commitments, balances that Microsoft often allowed to be used if the contract was extended but that were forfeited if the OEM did not extend the contract. This stretched out the effective length of the arrangement even further. Such restraints can have the effect of denying rivals sufficient outlets for exploiting their technologies and thus the ability to be anticompetitive. (This effect is often referred to as "customer foreclosure.") In addition, Microsoft employed unusually restrictive non-disclosure agreements (NDAs) that would have precluded other applications software companies from working on products to be used on competing operating systems for an unreasonably long time. These NDAs thus denied operating system rivals access to complementary products that would have made their operating systems more valuable. (This effect is often referred to as "input foreclosure.")

The settlement the Department of Justice obtained with Microsoft enjoins both the challenged practices and other practices to which Microsoft could turn to achieve the same effect, such as lump-sum royalties and tying arrangements.[197] As the Competitive Impact Statement points out, without a ban on tying arrangements (especially tie-out arrangements that condition the sale of a product on the buyer's promise not to purchase the product of a competitor), Microsoft could achieve the same effect as an exclusive dealing arrangement by licensing its operating system software to OEMs only on the condition that the OEM did not license, sell, or distribute competing operating system software.[198]

Note several things about the *Microsoft* case. First, the focus was on the effect on competition between Microsoft and other operating system vendors – horizontal competition that did not depend on any licensing arrangement among the competitors. Second, the restrictions had to involve enough OEMs, and entry into computer manufacture had to be sufficiently difficult, that operating system competitors actually were disadvantaged.[199] Third, Microsoft had to be sufficiently dominant in operating system software that it could both impose the foreclosure and benefit from it.[200]

The Agencies' Discretionary Rule-of-Reason Approach to Tying

We have already noted that despite the nominally *per se* rule against tying, judicial decisions have already moved the law of tying considerably in the direction of a rule-of-reason analysis.[201] Thus, the courts have required a showing of market power in order to establish a violation under the *per se* rule,[202] and they have been willing to consider justifications in defence of a tying arrangement.[203] A number of lower courts, and the agencies in their exercise of prosecutorial discretion (at least with respect to intellectual property), take the analysis the rest of the way toward the rule of reason by requiring proof of anticompetitive effect in the tied market[204] and declining to infer market power from the mere possession of an intellectual property right.[205]

In the view of earlier cases following a *per se* approach, tying was seen as evil because the seller gained an advantage in the second market that was unrelated to the price or quality of the second product.[206] This belief came under sharp criticism from scholars, who argued that in general there is only a single monopoly rent that the seller could enjoy, and that a tying arrangement could not increase the price a buyer was willing to pay for the second product without forgoing an equal amount of rent the buyer would be willing to pay for the first product.[207] More recent studies have suggested a number of circumstances in which that criticism would be inapt.[208] Among them is the situation in which the products are complements, there are economies of scale in the second market, a tying arrangement is used to gain so large a share of sales in that market that competitors cannot reach minimum efficient scale, the seller gains a monopoly in the second market, and the buyers in that market are not identical to the buyers in the first market (i.e., there is an alternative use for the tied product that does not involve the simultaneous use of the tying product).[209] The courts that rejected the more rigid, *per se* approach have recognized this situation by suggesting that a tying arrangement can be unlawful if there is a "substantial danger that the tying seller will acquire market power in the tied product market."[210]

If the second market is in a network industry, this strategy may be easier than otherwise because of network externalities. Network externalities exist where the value of a product to one purchaser increases with the number of other purchasers of the product.[211] The best-known example is the telephone network, in which the value to a user is zero if no one else is attached to the network and increases as other users become attached and therefore can be reached. Such network externalities can be thought of as demand-side economies of scale.[212] As noted above, economies of scale are one of the conditions for the anticompetitive harm (outlined above) in which the party imposing the tie is able to gain monopoly power in the second market.[213] Of course, if such economies of scale are large and not exhausted throughout the entire relevant range of demand, then the market will be a natural monopoly without the need for the tie. In many cases, however, such economies of scale, although they "point in the direction of [natural monopoly] . . . may not carry the system all the way toward . . . natural monopoly or essential facilities status."[214] In such cases, the effect of very small advantages, such as that conferred by the tie, could be magnified by the network effects and result in substantial harm.[215]

The same anticompetitive effect could occur where the "second market" exists only in a temporal sense rather than in the *Jefferson Parish* sense.[216] If enough of the market agrees to buy only from A for 10 years after expiration of the patent, then it may be impossible for a new player, B, to enter the market even after expiration of the patent, because it may be unable to reach minimum efficient scale. Such a practice has traditionally been dealt with as anticompetitive because it extends the life of the patent past its prescribed term.[217] It has not been altogether clear, however, how to distinguish anticompetitive extensions of the patent grant from benign or even procompetitive actions that may resemble such extensions, such as the spreading out of royalty payments over a longer term than remains in the patent.[218] Whatever one may think of other practices that could be characterized as extensions of the patent grant, however, a tying arrangement that maintains monopoly power by depriving otherwise efficient entrants of the scale necessary to operate should be a cause for antitrust concern.

A tying arrangement can also harm competition in the market for an input or complement. For example, imagine two machines that, in conjunction with various patented processes, can each be used to provide two distinct services (e.g., chemical assays), X and Y. Suppose there is only one process, owned by A, that can be used by either machine to produce service X, but there are two processes, owned by A and B, to produce service Y: A's process in conjunction with A's machine and B's process in conjunction with B's machine. Through a tying arrangement, A could force customers who wished to provide both services to use its process and the complementary machine to produce service Y. If this practice forced the machines complementary to B's process below minimum efficient scale, B's process could be forced from the market, even if it was technologically superior.

The above discussion has focused on instances in which a tying arrangement might be used in an attempt to monopolize the market for the tied product or for a complement to the tied product. There are also cases in which a tying arrangement can be used to maintain or enhance power in the tying product. In *United States v. Electronic Payment Services* (EPS), the Department of Justice challenged such an arrangement.[219] EPS owned the MAC ATM network, the dominant provider of ATM network access in several states. It used that power to force banks that wanted network access services to obtain ATM processing – a distinct service – from EPS as well. According to the complaint and

Competitive Impact Statement, such control over ATM processing gave EPS an additional, critical advantage. A bank's ATM processor controls that bank's access to ATM networks. A bank that used EPS' ATM processing could only connect to a network other than MAC if EPS agreed to establish the connection. The Justice Department charged that EPS generally had not provided connections to the ATM networks that would be its strongest competitors. The tying arrangement thus served to maintain EPS' monopoly in the tying product, network access.[220]

An analogous case – although the analogy may not be obvious at first[221] – is *Dell Computer Corp.*[222] EPS amounted to an agreement to deny a critical complementary input, ATM processing, to competing vendors of ATM network access. The agreement of the banks was secured through the use of EPS's market power in the tying product, network access, hence the tying count. EPS gained a measure of control over access to an important complement through its tying. But control over access to complementary inputs can be secured through other means as well.

In 1992, the Video Electronics Standards Association (VESA) set out to devise a standard for a local bus (a mechanism to transfer instructions between a computer's central processing unit and peripherals such as a video monitor). As is often the case with standard-setting, the adoption of a standard local bus had the potential for substantial efficiencies. Manufacturers of peripheral products would know that their products would work on any computer that used the VL-bus standard. Computer manufacturers would have a larger number of peripheral manufacturers designing products that would work on their machines, thus significantly increasing the size of their potential market. Consumers would benefit by the elimination of wasteful duplication and would have a greater variety of peripheral products that would be compatible with whatever computer they bought. In other words, the standard facilitated each participant's access to complements. In turn, each of these participants, knowing that the other participants would perceive all of these efficiencies, would find it difficult and costly to depart from the standard, and thus control of the standard could confer substantial market power.

At the time that VESA's Local Bus Committee finished its work and approved the standard, all the representatives on the committee, including Dell's, certified in writing that, to the best of their knowledge, "this proposal does not infringe on any trademarks, copyrights, or patents"[223] that each company possessed. Shortly thereafter, as part of adoption of the new standard by VESA as a whole, Dell made an identical certification along with all of the other members of VESA.

The VL-bus design standard became very successful and was installed in 1.4 million computers in only eight months. At that point, Dell informed certain VESA computer manufacturers that it had received a patent in July of 1991 that gave it "exclusive rights to the mechanical slot configuration used on the motherboard to receive the VL-bus card."[224] Dell demanded royalties from those computer manufacturers that used its patent. Dell thus was able to put itself in a position in which it controlled the standard and thereby gained a measure of control over access to complements.

Of course, nothing would be wrong with that if the standard had been adopted with full knowledge of the intellectual property on the part of those adopting the standard, any more than a firm could be faulted for securing all the distributors by offering a better product or lower (but non-predatory) prices. In such a case, one could presume that the innovation protected by the patent was sufficiently valuable that the standard-setters concluded that paying rents to the patent holder made economic sense. Where such a standard is adopted because the intellectual property was intentionally concealed or not disclosed despite an explicit requirement of disclosure adopted by the standard-setting body, no such presumption can be maintained, and obtaining market power in this fashion can violate the antitrust laws.

Dell's actions had the potential to harm competition in two principal ways. If they succeeded in forcing other manufacturers to pay royalties for access to a standard that otherwise would have been accessible without charge, that would raise the competitors' costs and prices and give Dell the power to raise its own prices. If, on the other hand, some manufacturers rescinded adoption of the VL-bus standard and implemented alternative approaches, they would incur the costs of substitution, again giving Dell the power to raise price.[225] The consent order against Dell required the company to refrain from enforcing its patent in any claim of infringement based on the use of the VL-bus standard.

CROSS-LICENSING AND POOLING

THE GUIDELINES RECOGNIZE that cross-licensing and pooling arrangements "may provide procompetitive benefits by integrating complementary technologies, reducing transaction costs, clearing blocking positions, and avoiding costly infringement litigation."[226] In the terminology of the Guidelines, these are all vertical relationships. In the purest case, the relationship would be completely vertical if two parties each possessed patents that would block the other from using its respective technologies, and it was impossible for either party to invent around the other's position or challenge its validity or scope. In such a case, the parties would not "have been actual or likely potential competitors in a relevant market in the absence of the license."[227] At the opposite pole, the parties would be purely horizontal competitors if their intellectual property was a pure substitute and the complementary relationship with the other party's assets was trivial. In that case restraints on price, output, or territory in connection with a cross-licensing or pooling arrangement could harm competition in the same manner as such restraints among competitors can do so outside the intellectual property context.[228]

At the level of the broadest general principle, or in a world of perfect information, these precepts are uncontroversial. If the relationship between the parties is clearly complementary or blocking, then the parties are not in a horizontal relationship and horizontal theories of harm cannot apply. If the items of intellectual property are clearly substitutes, then restraints in connection with the pooling arrangement are horizontal and must be looked at closely. More difficult issues arise in a world of uncertainty or of more complex relationships that are partly complementary and partly horizontal.

Suppose, for example, that there is asymmetric information between the parties and the enforcement agencies or courts. The extreme scenario is that the parties each have patents that they know are pure substitutes. Nonetheless, they each claim that the patents block the other; sue for infringement; and settle on terms that fix high royalty payments for use of the pooled patents, fix the price or output of the downstream good, or divide customers or territories. Perhaps their counsels advise them that their claims have no merit, but when the enforcement agencies investigate, the parties interpose a claim of attorney-client privilege. Less extreme scenarios can be constructed in which, although the claims of infringement are not wholly frivolous, the parties have grave doubts about the merits of their own claims but in the end are simply indifferent to the merits because they are anxious to settle on the joint profit-maximizing terms. It is not at all clear how enforcement policy should deal with this situation. Are there presumptions or burdens of production or persuasion that would help? Should our approach be affected by how unreasonably restrictive the restraints are or how dramatically they raise price? These issues may warrant further exploration by scholars and practitioners.

A related issue is that of the killer patent portfolio, assembled either through acquisition or pooling. In form, the patents are complementary. What harm can come from assembling them? Doesn't such assemblage both reduce transaction costs and avoid the "double marginalization" problem?[229] In a world of uncertainty, the effects are not necessarily so benign. To take a simple example, suppose, prior to the merger, that both the technology claimed by A's patents and the technology claimed by B's patents are required to produce a commercially marketable product. But each set of patents is also associated with a certain probability that either the other patent owner or a third party will be able to invent around the patents or have the necessary claims declared invalid. Thus even without acquisition, pooling, or cross-licensing, the two parties are potentially horizontal competitors, and there is some possibility that a third party will be able to enter by obtaining a license from one and inventing around or challenging the patent claims of the other. The prices for licenses will reflect the perceived probabilities. After the acquisition or pooling, the probability of competition is greatly reduced. A potential entrant will have to invent around or declare invalid a much greater array of patents. This is potentially anticompetitive in the same way that a two-level entry problem is anticompetitive under section 4.21 of the 1984 Merger Guidelines.[230]

ACQUISITIONS

SECTION 5.7 OF THE *GUIDELINES* APPLIES MERGER ANALYSIS to certain transfers
– including sales and exclusive licenses – of intellectual property rights. An
example of facts in which such treatment would be appropriate can be found in
United States v. S.C. Johnson & Son.[231] In that case, Miles Inc., a U.S. subsidiary
of Bayer A.G., developed a new line of household insecticides containing a
potent new active ingredient, cyfluthrin, developed and patented by Bayer.
After Miles had substantially completed its preparations to enter the market,
however, Bayer cancelled the project. Instead, it agreed to sell the product
research and packaging design and to license cyfluthrin on a de facto exclusive
basis to S.C. Johnson, the leading manufacturer of household insecticides in
the United States. The result was to ensure Johnson's continued dominance of
the highly concentrated household insecticides market. The Justice
Department challenged the arrangement and obtained a consent decree that,
among other things, enjoined the parties from entering into exclusive licenses
between them unless approved by the Department, and required Bayer to
license cyfluthrin – under reasonable terms and conditions – to any person that
requested such a license.

The facts in *S.C. Johnson*, as alleged in the complaint and Competitive
Impact Statement, make out a fairly clear case under the potential competition
doctrine. The market was concentrated, entry was difficult, and Bayer had a
considerable entry advantage because of its ownership of cyfluthrin.[232]
Moreover, in light of the substantial preparations Bayer had made to enter the
market, evidence of likely actual entry was particularly strong.[233] The case thus
does not stand for the proposition that an intellectual property owner facing a
make-buy decision (in this case, a decision whether to develop and use the property itself or license it to someone else to use) can never license the property to
the dominant manufacturer. Such a rule would be counterproductive, for in
many cases the leading manufacturer may be the most efficient developer and
user of the innovation. Instead, the case applies the first principle of the
Guidelines, i.e., that the basic analytical tools that antitrust uses with respect to
other forms of property – here the potential competition doctrine – can be
applied to intellectual property.

A similar approach can be used with respect to acquisitions or exclusive
licenses that lack the element of horizontality present in *S.C. Johnson*. In the
absence of horizontality, one would examine whether the traditional vertical
theories of harm applied: whether the vertical acquisition either facilitates
horizontal collusion or raises rivals' costs in such a fashion as to gain power over
price.[234] Instances in which the conditions for these theories of harm are met
are rare. In *Kobe, Inc. v. Dempsey Pump Co.*,[235] for example, the court found that
the defendant had acquired "every important patent" in the field, not to use
them, but simply to exclude competition.[236] Since the defendant did not actu-

ally use the patents, the acquisitions were not for the purpose of reducing its own costs, but simply to raise the costs of potential rivals and thereby exclude them.

INNOVATION MARKETS

IN RAPIDLY CHANGING, HIGH TECH INDUSTRIES, the most important dimension of competition is often not the price of existing goods and services, but the price and – more importantly – the quality of goods and services that may come into being in the future. For example, computer manufacturers may compete to supply more powerful machines with faster processors and greater memory. Drug companies may compete to develop new products and treatments for specific diseases. Communications firms may seek to provide new and innovative multiple media products to households. Defence firms may compete to produce military aircraft with greater ability to elude radar.

The *Guidelines* describe two ways of analyzing such effects: "as a separate competitive effect in relevant goods or technology markets, or as a competitive effect in a separate innovation market."[237] There has been considerable debate about the innovation market concept,[238] some of it revolving around the question of whether the effects in question can be analyzed equally well, with perhaps less risk of misunderstanding, under the potential competition doctrine.[239]

The FTC has had a number of cases in which the potential competition doctrine, with a few adjustments, could be used to model the effects and would reach similar results as analyzing the transaction's current effects in an innovation market. In *Glaxo plc*,[240] for example, Glaxo, the acquiring firm, sold a current product for the treatment of migraine attacks that was approved by the Food and Drug Administration (FDA) in injectable form only. Both Glaxo and Wellcome, the acquired firm, had products in the FDA approval process that would treat migraine with an oral dosage. Hardly any other companies were involved in research and development for such drugs, and barriers to entry were high. The Commission challenged that aspect of the acquisition because it would have eliminated both the competition to develop those drugs and the competition between those drugs once developed and approved. The result was a consent order allowing the transaction as a whole to go through but restoring the competition in that class of drugs. Similarly, in *American Home Products*,[241] the Commission alleged that the acquisition of American Cyanamid by American Home Products would lessen competition in a number of markets. Both firms, along with one other firm, had active R&D programs for a rotavirus vaccine. Both merging parties had products at an advanced stage of the FDA's approval process. The merger eliminated the likelihood that at the end of the FDA approval process the two products would compete with each other. Moreover, the merger gave American Home Products the ability and the incentive to close the American Cyanamid development effort, decreasing the likelihood that two products would exist at all. *Upjohn Co.*[242] and *Hoechst*[243] presented similar sets of facts.

In each of these cases, the approval process established by the *Food, Drug, and Cosmetics Act*[244] created a clear measure of the timing and likelihood of market entry for a particular drug. No new drug can be sold in the U.S. without FDA approval, and the process is highly visible and time-consuming. And the process itself often gives the FTC an indication of the competitive significance of a particular drug. If FDA trials place substantial doubt on the safety or efficacy of a particular drug, the FTC will discount that drug's likely impact. Similarly, the closer a drug is to final approval, the more assured the FTC will be in its assessment of the competitive significance of the drug. In such cases, where the product parameters are clear and the potential competitors can be identified with precision, one could expand the potential competition doctrine to deal with potential entry into future goods markets and thereby capture the price effects of competition among the future products. One might want to make further adjustments in order to capture innovation effects in those markets (i.e., the elimination of competition to develop the drugs, not just competition between the drugs once developed and approved), but one would not need the concept of innovation markets.

Cases involving competition to produce the next-generation product, where the contours of that product are not completely clear, are harder to analyze without the innovation market concept. The FTC dealt with such a situation in *Sensormatic*,[245] in which the Commission alleged a loss of competition for research and development of a next generation of electronic article surveillance (EAS) systems for retail stores. Both Sensormatic and the firm from which the assets were to be acquired, Knogo, manufactured current-generation EAS systems. Current EAS systems involve electronic labels attached by retailers; the next-generation EAS product would allow manufacturers to attach the marker before shipping to retailers. There were only a few companies capable of doing research on this next-generation product. Thus, what was being eliminated was not simply the competition between two products some years hence, but the very incentive to conduct the research that might result in a product. It may be that only one of the two research paths would succeed, so one could not say with assurance that future goods market competition was being eliminated. The current effect on research and development, in contrast, seems much clearer.

The Department of Justice faced a similar situation in its challenge to the proposed acquisition of General Motors' Allison Division by ZF Friedrichshafen, which would have combined the two companies' bus and truck automatic transmission businesses. The two firms competed in certain narrow product and geographic markets, and one could have made a case based on the impact on the relatively small number of consumers in those markets. Such a case, however, would have missed the big picture. As expressed in its complaint, the Department's principal concern was that the combined firm would have controlled most of the assets, worldwide, necessary for innovation in heavy duty truck and bus automatic transmissions.[246] In this industry, the ability to carry out R&D activities was closely associated with the possession of specialized production assets. Innovation required constant feedback between innovative ideas and production experience. Only these two firms possessed the necessary productive capacity. The history of the industry revealed a pattern of the two companies constantly leapfrogging each other with product improvements. Thus, innovation would have been stifled by the merger. Consumers worldwide would have been affected, even in the goods markets in which the two companies did not compete directly, because having adopted a new technology or created a new product for use in the markets in which the companies did compete, the companies would normally implement the change worldwide. The Department's complaint alleged an anticompetitive effect, not just in the specific goods markets that had been the subject of direct sales competition in the past, but in a market for innovation.[247]

The *Guidelines* emphasize that the innovation-market concept will only be used when "the capabilities to engage in the relevant research and development can be associated with specialized assets or characteristics of specific firms."[248]

CONCLUSION

THE *GUIDELINES* REFLECT A MOVEMENT from the "separate spheres" model that prevailed from early in this century to the mid-1970s, to a model of intellectual property as being essentially similar to other forms of property. The *Guidelines* approach comes at the cost of some simplicity of application, but avoids the harmful effects of either excessive hostility to intellectual property or excessive deference to actions by intellectual property owners that could foreclose other innovators and retard efficiency. Although a thorough understanding of some of the specific, practical implications of this approach must await the accumulation of the agencies' experience in all enforcement contexts, both the *Guidelines* and recent enforcement actions by the agencies have explored various ways in which licensing restraints and other conduct can facilitate collusion, create or maintain market power by raising rivals' costs, or promote efficiency. The *Guidelines* will have been successful if they help enforcement agencies in distinguishing one from the other.

NOTES

1   Willard K. Tom is Assistant Director for Policy and Evaluation, Bureau of Competition, Federal Trade Commission. Joshua A. Newberg is Visiting Associate Professor of Legal Studies at the University of Texas at Austin, on leave from the

Federal Trade Commission, where he was Attorney-Advisor to Commissioner Roscoe B. Starek, III.

2   *United States v. Masonite Corp.*, 316 U.S. 265, 280 (1942).

3   U.S. Department of Justice and Federal Trade Commission, *Antitrust Guidelines for the Licensing of Intellectual Property*, Apr. 6, 1995, reprinted in 4 Trade Regulation Report, (CCH) ¶ 13,132 (hereinafter "*Guidelines*," "IP *Guidelines*," or "1995 *Guidelines*").

4   See, e.g., James B. Kobak, Jr., "Running the Gauntlet: Antitrust and Intellectual Property Pitfalls on the Two Sides of the Atlantic," *Antitrust Law Journal*, 64 (1996): 341, 342-52; Norman F. Rosen, "Intellectual Property and the Antitrust Pendulum," *Antitrust Law Journal*, 62 (1994): 669; Stephen A. Stack, Jr., "Recent and Impending Developments in Copyright and Antitrust," *Antitrust Law Journal*, 61 (1993): 331; Charles F. Rule, "Patent-Antitrust Policy: Looking Back and Ahead," *Antitrust Law Journal*, 59 (1991): 729; Gerald Sobel, "The Antitrust Interface with Patents and Innovation," *Antitrust Law Journal*, 53 (1984): 681; Stephen M. Hudspeth, "Recent Developments In The Patent/Antitrust Interface – Response To A New Reality," *Journal of Law and Commerce*, 3 (1983): 1; Joseph P. Griffin, "Special Considerations Concerning International Patent and Know-How Licensing, and Joint Research and Development Activities: Problems Raised by Various Types of Restrictive Clauses," *Antitrust Law Journal*, 50 (1981): 499.

5   *Supra*, note 3. The 1995 *Guidelines* superseded, in relevant part, a previous set of enforcement guidelines, issued by the Justice Department without FTC participation, which had addressed the application of antitrust to intellectual property. Antitrust Division, U.S. Department of Justice, *Antitrust Enforcement Guidelines for International Operations* (1988) at § 3.6, reprinted in 4 Trade Regulation Report (CCH) ¶ 13,109 (hereinafter "1988 *Guidelines*").

6   See, e.g., *E. Bement & Sons v. National Harrow Co.*, 186 U.S. 70 (1902); *National Folding- Box & Paper Co. v. Robertson et al.*, 99 F. 985 (C.C.D.Conn. 1900). Cf. Hans B. Thorelli, *The Federal Antitrust Policy*, 1955, p. 47 ("[T]he common law background [governing restraints of trade] could furnish but little guidance when the courts were to be faced with the problem of drawing a reasonable borderline between the scope of the patent monopoly, on the one hand, and the scope of the antitrust law on the other").

7   See, e.g., *Heaton-Peninsular Button-Fastener Co. v. Eureka Specialty Co.*, 77 F. 288 (6th Cir. 1896) ("The Button Fastener Case"); *Bement*, 186 U.S. 70; *Henry v. A. B. Dick Co.*, 224 U.S. 1 (1912); see also Mark S. Massel, "Antitrust and Patent Laws: Effects on Innovation," *American Economic Review*, 56 (1966): 284, 285 ("the grant of a patent right was regarded merely as a logical extension of conventional rights in industrial property").

8   On the expansive scope and significance of property rights and the freedom of contract during this period, see, e.g., *The Political Economy of the Sherman Act*, edited by E. Thomas Sullivan, 1991; Morton J. Horwitz, *The Transformation of American Law, 1780-1860*, 1977, pp. 31-62, 161-210; Arnold M. Paul, *Conservative Crisis and the Rule of Law: Attitudes of the Bar and Bench, 1887-1895*, 1976; Lawrence M. Friedman, *A History of American Law*, 1973; James Willard Hurst, *Law and the Conditions of Freedom in the Nineteenth-Century United States*, 1956; Herbert Hovenkamp, "The Political Economy of Substantive Due Process," *Stanford Law Review*, 40 (1988): 379.

9   *United States v. Standard Sanitary Mfg. Co.*, 226 U.S. 20 (1912).

10 *Motion Picture Patents Co. v. Universal Film Mfg. Co.*, 243 U.S. 502, 513 (1917).

11   *Id.*

12   226 U.S. at 49.

13   The tension between antitrust and IP is not confined to older judicial opinions. A relatively recent Second Circuit decision notes as follows:

> While the antitrust laws proscribe unreasonable restraints of competition, the patent laws reward the inventor with a temporary monopoly that insulates him from competitive exploitation of his patented art. . . . When . . . the patented product is so successful that it evolves into its own economic market, . . . the patent and antitrust laws necessarily clash.

SCM Corp. v. Xerox Corp., 645 F.2d 1195, 1203 (2d. Cir. 1981), cert. denied, 455 U.S. 1016 (1982); see also *Crucible, Inc. v. Stora Kopparbergs Bergslags AB*, 701 F. Supp. 1157, 1160 (W.D. Pa. 1988) (following SCM analysis of § 7 of the *Clayton Act* and § 2 of the *Sherman Act*).

14   See, e.g., *Zenith Radio Corp. v. Hazeltine Research, Inc.*, 395 U.S. 100, 135 (1969) (referring to patent as "lawful monopoly"); *Crown Dye & Tool Co. v. Nye Tool & Mach. Works*, 261 U.S. 24, 35-36 (1923) ("A patent confers a monopoly"); *Continental Paper Bag Co. v. Eastern Paper Bag Co.*, 210 U.S. 405, 424 (1908) (same). But see *United States v. Dubiher Condenser Corp.*, in which IP is distinguished from monopoly:

> The term 'monopoly' connotes the giving of an exclusive privilege for buying, selling, working, or using a thing which the public freely enjoyed prior to the grant. Thus, a 'monopoly' takes something from the people. An inventor deprives the public of nothing which is enjoyed before his discovery, but gives something of value to the community by adding to the sum of human knowledge.

289 U.S. 178, 186 (1933) (citations omitted).

15   *Bement*, 186 U.S. at 91.

16   *Motion Picture Patents*, 243 U.S. at 510.

17   See, e.g., *United States v. Univis Lens Co.*, 316 U.S. 243, 250 (1942) ("[a patent grants] to the inventor a limited monopoly, the exercise of which enable[s] him to secure the financial rewards for his invention"); *Masonite*, 316 U.S. at 277 (referring to patent as a "limited monopoly"); *Ethyl Gasoline Corp. v. United States*, 309 U.S. 436 (1940) ("The patent law confers a limited monopoly"). The same point is made in some more recent cases. See, e.g., *Int'l Wood Processors v. Power Dry, Inc.*, 792 F.2d 416, 426 (4th Cir. 1986) (noting that courts often refer to the patent holder's rights "as either a limited monopoly or a patent monopoly"); *Glen Mfg., Inc. v. Perfect Fit Indus., Inc.*, 324 F Supp. 1133 (S.D.N.Y. 1971); 299 F. Supp.. 278, 282 (S.D.N.Y. 1969) ("To promote scientific innovations and invention, the patent laws grant a monopoly to the patentee for a limited time, subject to strict limits of the patent.").

18   See generally U.S. Department of Justice and Federal Trade Commission, *Horizontal Merger Guidelines* §0.1 (Apr. 2, 1992) ("Market power to a seller is the ability profitably to maintain prices above competitive levels for a significant period of time."); see also, Warren G. Lavey, "Patents, Copyrights, and Trademarks as Sources of Market Power in Antitrust Cases," *Antitrust Bulletin*, 27 (1982): 433, 435 ("In antitrust economics, a firm has market power if it can profitably price its products above the competitive level.") (citing Robert Landes and Richard A. Posner, "Market Power in

Antitrust Cases," *Harvard Law Review,* 94 (1981): 937; Philip Areeda and Donald Turner, *Antitrust Law* ¶ 322, 1978).

19   We use the term "formalistic" to denote mechanistic, static, theoretically self-contained judging in which an established rule or doctrine is apt to take precedence over concrete facts, where such facts might otherwise suggest the utility of re-examining the putatively applicable rule. On legal formalism, see generally Richard A. Posner, "Legal Formalism, Legal Realism, and the Interpretation of Statutes and the Constitution," *Case Western Res. Law Review,* 37 (1987): 179, 180 ("'Formalist' can mean narrow, conservative, hypocritical, resistant to change, casuistic, descriptively inaccurate . . . , ivory-towered, fallacious, callow, authoritarian — but also rigorous, modest, reasoned, faithful, self-denying, restrained."); Steven M. Quevedo, Comment," Formalist and Instrumentalist Legal Reasoning and Legal Theory," *California Law Review,* 73 (1985): 119; Thomas C. Grey, "Langdell's Orthodoxy," *University of Pittsburg Law Review,* 45 (1983): 1; Morton J. Horwitz, *The Transformation of American Law: 1780-1860,* 1977, pp. 254-55 (characterizing legal formalism as "anti-utilitarian" and giving "common law rules the appearance of being self-contained, apolitical, and inexorable"); Grant Gilmore, *The Ages of American Law,* 1974, pp. 62, 70, 108-10 (legal formalism treats law as a closed logical system of "theoretical formulas assumed to be of universal validity," in which "[d]ecision becomes a mechanistic process in which it is forbidden to look beyond the letter of the statute and the holding of the last case"); H. L. A. Hart, *The Concept of Law,* 1961, p. 249 ("formalism" nearly synonymous with "mechanical" or "automatic" jurisprudence).

20   The analogy between the scope of the intellectual property holder's rights and the physical metes and bounds delineating the boundaries of real property has long been recognized:

> The scope of every patent is limited to the invention described in the claims contained in it. . . . These so mark where the progress claimed by the patent begins and where it ends that they have been aptly likened to the description in a deed, which sets the bounds to the grant which it contains.

Motion Picture Patents, 243 U.S. at 510; accord *Ethyl Gasoline,* 309 U.S. at 456; see also *T.C. Weygandt v. Van Emden,* 40 F.2d 938, 939 (S.D.N.Y. 1930) ("Though the most intangible form of property, [the patent right] still, in many characteristics, is closer in analogy to real than to personal estate."). In the "separate spheres" model, however, these metes and bounds became the boundary, not of the property right, but of antitrust liability: any attempt by the patentee to restrict a licensee's conduct in some respect that went beyond the boundaries of the patent grant became, *ipso facto,* an antitrust violation.

21   See, e.g., *E. Bement & Sons v. National Harrow Co.,* 186 U.S. at 91 ("the general rule is absolute freedom in the use or sale of rights under the patent laws of the United States").

22   See the sections on *"International Salt"* and on "The Nine No-Nos," below.

23   See the section on "Patent Misure," below.

24   See, e.g., *United States v. Line Material Co.,* 333 U.S. 287, 309-310 (1948); *Ethyl,* 309 U.S. at 452; *United States v. Univis Lens Co.,* 316 U.S. 241(1942).

25   See, e.g., *Q-Tips, Inc. v. Johnson & Johnson,* 109 F. Supp. 657, 661 (D.N.J. 1951), modified by, 207 F.2d 509 (3rd Cir. 1953), cert. denied, 347 U.S. 935 (1954).

26 See, e.g., Ward S. Bowman, Jr., *Patent & Antitrust Law: A Legal & Economic Appraisal*, 1973; William F. Baxter, "Legal Restrictions on Exploitation of the Patent Monopoly: An Economic Analysis," *Yale Law Journal*, 76 (1966): 267.

27 *Supra*, note 3.

28 1988 *Guidelines*, *supra*, note 5 at167.

29 Bowman, *supra*, note 26 at 1 (emphasis in original).

30 See, e.g., *Atari Games Corp. v. Nintendo of America, Inc.*, 897 F.2d 1572, 1576 (Fed. Cir. 1990) ("the aims and objectives of patent and antitrust laws may seem, at first glance, wholly at odds. However, the two bodies of law are actually complementary, as both are aimed at encouraging innovation, industry and competition.").

31 This should not be understood to mean that there are no differences at all between intellectual property and other forms of property. For one thing, intellectual property is much easier to misappropriate than the typical item of tangible property. The owner of a factory can prevent others from using that factory, not only by relying on the legal system, as does the intellectual property owner, but also by putting up fences, installing locks, and hiring security guards. Moreover, such a factory owner can hardly help but notice a break-in. By contrast, the intellectual property owner may not even know that it has been robbed until its sales start to plummet. Moreover, the high fixed costs and near-zero marginal costs of intellectual property mean that price discrimination (e.g., Ramsey pricing) may be essential to achieve an efficient result. See generally F. M. Scherer and David Ross, *Industrial Market Structure and Economic Performance*, 3d ed., 1990, pp. 496-98. The principle that intellectual property is like other forms of property for antitrust purposes means only that the normal antitrust principles of the rule of reason already take into account these differences in assessing the competitive benefits and harms of a practice in a particular market circumstance.

32 Compare *Guidelines*, *supra*, note 3, § 2.2 with *Jefferson Parish Hosp. Dist. No. 2 v. Hyde*, 466 U.S. 2, 16 (1984) (stating in dictum that a patented product presumptively has market power).

33 The principles are set out in section 2.0 of the 1995 *Guidelines*.

34 *Id.* §§ 2.3, 3.1, 3.3, 4.1.

35 *Id.* §§ 2.0, 2.3.

36 *Guidelines*, *supra*, note 3, § 3.3; cf. Thomas G. Krattenmaker and Steven C. Salop, "Anticompetitive Exclusion: Raising Rivals' Costs To Achieve Power Over Price," *Yale Law Journal*, 96 (1986): 209, 226 (noting that it is somewhat arbitrary whether to treat a manufacturer's product as an input to downstream distribution or instead to treat distribution as input into the manufacturer's overall process of making the product and getting it into the hands of the ultimate consumer).

37 332 U.S. 392 (1947).

38 333 U.S. 287 (1948).

39 Bruce B. Wilson, "Patent and Know-how License Agreements: Field of Use, Territorial, Price and Quantity Restrictions," Address Before the Fourth New England Antitrust Conference, Nov. 6, 1970 [hereinafter "Wilson, *Nine No-No's*"]. Although the "Nine No-No's" were not announced to the public until 1970, the "Nine No-No's" era dates from 1968 to 1981; the period during which the Antitrust Division's enforcement policy was guided by the "Nine No-No's" view of the IP/antitrust interface.

40 See the section on "Patent Misure," below.

41 *International Salt Co., Inc. v. United States*, 332 U.S. at 394.

42 *Id.* at 395-96.

43 *Guidelines, supra,* note 3, §§ 2.2, 5.3.

44 *Id.* § 5.3.

45 *Id.*

46 333 U.S. 287 (1948).

47 *Line Material,* 333 U.S. at 290 n. 4.

48 After an interference proceeding, the Patent Office had awarded "dominant claims to Southern and subservient claims to Line." *Id.* at 291 and n. 5 ("Only when both patents could be lawfully used by a single maker could the public or the patentees obtain the full benefit of the efficiency and economy of the inventions.").

49 *Id.* at 292-93, 297.

50 *Id.* at 293-297.

51 *Id.* at 307.

52 *Id.* at 309 (citing *Bement,* 186 U.S. at 92) ("The *Sherman Act* was enacted to prevent restraints of commerce but has been interpreted as recognizing that patents were an exception.").

53 *Id.* at 307 (footnotes omitted).

54 *Id.* at 308 (emphasis added).

55 *Id.* at 291, 297. See also George L. Priest, "Cartels and Patent License Arrangements," *Journal of Law and Economics,* 20 (1977): 309, 356-58 (discussing *Line Material* and procompetitive aspects of cross-licensing complementary and blocking patents).

56 *Line Material* at 311.

57 *Id.* at 312.

58 *Id.*

59 1995 *Guidelines, supra,* note 3, § 2.3.

60 *Id.* § 5.5.

61 *Guidelines, supra,* note 3, § 3.3.

62 *Id.* § 5.5.

63 See Wilson, *Nine No-No's, supra,* note 39.

64 *Id.* at 3.

65 See, e.g., Charles F. Rule, "Patent-Antitrust Policy: Looking Back and Ahead," *Antitrust Law Journal,* 59 (1991): 729, 732 ("The Antitrust Division took the position in the early 1970s that nine ["No-No's"] practices were *per se* unlawful"); Griffin, *Antitrust Law Journal,* 50 at 508 n. 38 (same). In the judgment of one Division official, speaking toward the end the "Nine No-No's" period, DOJ typically evaluated IP licensing restraints under the rule of reason. Ky P. Ewing, Jr., "Antitrust Enforcement and the Patent Laws: 'It Is As Craftsman That We Get Our Satisfactions And Our Pay,'" Remarks Before the San Francisco Patent Law Association, in Trade Regulation Report (CCH) ¶ 50,398 at 55,886 (May 5, 1979). In the same speech, Mr. Ewing implied that the core "No-No's" are Nos. 1, 4, 6-8. *Id.* at 55,887; see also Richard H. Stern, "What Ever Happened to the Nine No-No's," Address Before the American Bar Association Section of Patent, Trademark, and Copyright Law at 1-2, 5-6 (Aug. 10, 1993) (maintaining that the Division did not treat most of these practices as necessarily unlawful, but rather regarded the Nine No-No's as a checklist of practices that, if encountered, would lead a prosecutor to consider further investigation); Bruce B. Wilson, "Myth or Reality? Or Straight Talk from 'Alice in Wonderland,'" Remarks before the American Patent Association 11 (Jan. 21, 1975) [hereinafter

"Wilson, *Alice in Wonderland*"] ("Even some of the 'nine no-no's,' . . . are not totally susceptible to a wooden application.").

66   See Wilson, *Alice in Wonderland, supra,* note 65.

67   See *infra* notes 68-76.

68   See Wilson, *Nine No-No's, supra,* note 39 at 3 (citing *International Salt Co., Inc. v. United States,* 332 U.S. 392 (1947); see also Rex Chainbelt, *Inc. v. Harco Products, Inc,* 512 F.2d 993 (9th Cir.), cert. denied, 423 U.S. 831 (1975).

69   See Wilson, *Nine No-No's, supra,* note 39, at 4-5. But see *Transwrap Corp. v. Stokes Co.,*329 U.S. 637, 644 (1947) (compulsory exclusive grantback held to be lawful "use of one legalized monopoly to acquire another legalized monopoly;" not an unlawful extension of the patentee's monopoly) (emphasis in the original).

70   See Wilson, *supra,* note 39 at 5 ("the Department believes it is unlawful to attempt to restrict a purchaser of a patented product in the resale of that product"); cf. *United States v. CIBA GEIGY Corp.,* 508 F. Supp. 1118 (D. N.J. 1976), final judgment, 1980-81 Trade Cases (CCH) ¶ 63,813 (D.N.J. 1981) (license restricting purchasers of bulk form of drug from reselling it in finished dosage form, unless approved by the seller, constitutes *per se* violation of section 1 of the *Sherman Act*); *Hensley Equip. Co. v. Esco Corp.,* 383 F.2d 252, 262-64 (5th Cir.) (license provision restricting the use and sale of patented parts purchased from licensor constitutes *per se* violation of section 1 of the *Sherman Act*), modified *per curiam,* 386 F.2d 442 (5th Cir. 1967).

71   See Wilson, *supra,* note 39 at 5 ("a patentee may not restrict his licensee's freedom to deal in products or services not within the scope of the patent"). If A says "I will license my product to you [B] if you agree not to carry competing products," A is proposing a "tie-out agreement" with B. See, e.g., *McCullough v. Kammerer Corp.,* 166 F.2d 759, 761 (9th Cir. 1948) (where the licensee agreed "not to manufacture or use or rent any device . . . in competition with the . . . devices covered by [the] licens[ing] agreement," Ninth Circuit held that "there [was] no difference in principle between extending the monopoly of the patent by suppressing the manufacture or use of competitive devices, patented or unpatented," and other practices previously held to constitute patent misuse), cert. denied, 335 U.S. 813 (1948); see also *Stewart v. Motrim, Inc,* 1975-2 Trade Cases (CCH) ¶ 60,531 (S.D. Ohio Sept. 11, 1975) (tie-out provision in licensing agreement constitutes patent misuse). According to one commentator, even at the Department of Justice during the mid-1970's, there was little support for this "No-No." See Griffin, *supra,* note 4 at 511 n. 55.

72   See Wilson, *supra,* note 39 at 6 ("the Department believes it to be unlawful for a patentee to agree with his licensee that he will not, without his licensee's consent, grant further licenses to any other person"). See, e.g., *United States v. Krasnov,* 143 F. Supp. 184, 199 (E.D. Pa. 1956), aff'd *per curiam,* 355 U.S. 5 (1957). In Krasnov, two companies, which accounted together for 62 percent of the ready-made furniture slip cover market in the U.S., entered into a cross-licensing arrangement in which they agreed, *inter alia,* to refrain from licensing others without each other's consent. Finding violations of sections 1 and 2 of the *Sherman Act,* the District Court concluded that the terms of the cross-licensing agreement "were well beyond the protection afforded by patent grants" and that "their combined effect was to stifle competition." *Id.* at 199; see also *United States v. Ciba Corp. & CPC International, Inc.,* 1978-1 Trade Cases (CCH) ¶ 62,123 (D.N.J. 1978) (two drug manufacturers barred by consent decree from entering into licensing agreements for the manufacture, use, or sale of drug, where the licensor's grant of a license would require prior approval of a third

drug, where the licensor's grant of a license would require prior approval of a third party other than the prospective licensee).

73 See Wilson, *supra*, note 39 at 6 ("the Department believes that mandatory package licensing is an unlawful extension of the patent grant").

74 See Wilson, *supra*, note 39 at 6 ("the Department believes that it is unlawful for a patentee to insist, as a condition of the license, that his licensee pay royalties in an amount not reasonably related to the licensee's sales of products covered by the patent [e.g., royalties calculated on combined sales of patented and unpatented products]"); cf. *Glen Mfg., Inc. v. Perfect Fit Indus., Inc.*, 324 F. Supp. 1133 (S.D.N.Y. 1971); 299 F. Supp. 278 (S.D.N.Y. 1969). In *Glen Manufacturing*, 299 F. Supp. 278 (S.D.N.Y. 1969), the District Court found patent misuse where royalties were paid by the licensee to the patentee-licensor for toilet tank covers not within the scope of the patent held by the patentee-licensor. Condemning the licensing agreement requiring royalties on all toilet tank covers manufactured or sold by the licensee, regardless of whether the toilet tank covers came within the scope of the patentee-licensor patent, the Court wrote that "[w]here the patentee seeks to use its patent monopoly to suppress the manufacture and sale of non-patented competing items in any manner other than that of free competition, the courts have a duty to protect the public interest and restrain the patentee." *Id.* at 282. See also *La Peyre v. FTC*, 366 F.2d 117 (5th Cir. 1966) (discriminatory royalties held to violate § 5 of the *Federal Trade Commission Act*).

75 See Wilson, *supra*, note 39 at 7 ("it is pretty clearly unlawful for the owner of a process patent to attempt to place restrictions on his licensee's sales of products made by the use of the patented process") (citing *Cummer-Graham Co. v. Straight Side Basket Corp.*, 142 F.2d 646, 647 (5th Cir.), cert. denied, 323 U.S. 726 (1944)).

76 See Wilson, *supra*, note 39 at 7 ("the Department of Justice considers it unlawful for a patentee to require a licensee to adhere to any specified or minimum price with respect to the licensee's sale of the licensed products"). Special Assistant Wilson articulated the "Nine No-No's" view on this licensing practice as follows:

> I do not believe that it has been demonstrated that the dangerous power to control the price at which a licensee may sell *must be added* to the benefits of a patent in order to provide adequate incentive for invention, disclosure or licensing. *The patentee obtains the full value of his patent when he exacts all the traffic will bear in the way of royalties or where he exercises his privilege to be the sole maker or seller.* Royalties, or profits from exclusive exploitation, are the marketplace's impersonal way of evaluating the worth of an invention. To be sure, the patent owner might reap even greater rewards were he able to set the prices charged by his licensees. But those additional rewards would reflect not the value of the invention itself but rather the value of price-fixing.

Id. at 8-9 (emphasis supplied).

77 *Id.* at 3 (emphasis added).

78 See *supra*, notes 41-42 and accompanying text.

79 Wilson, *Nine No-No's*, *supra*, note 39 at 6. The distinction between "mandatory" and voluntary package licensing paralleled the Supreme Court's contrasting holdings in *Automatic Radio Mfg. Co., Inc. v. Hazeltine Research, Inc.*, 339 U.S. 827, 834 (1950), and *Zenith Radio Corp. v. Hazeltine Research, Inc.*, 395 U.S. 100, 135, 139-40 (1969). In the former, the Court rejected a licensee's challenge to a package license that cov-

ered hundreds of radio technology patents owned by HRI, reasoning that the package licensing was a convenience to the parties and "does not create another monopoly." 339 U.S. at 833. In the latter case, the Court condemned mandatory package licensing as patent misuse, holding that "conditioning the grant of a patent license upon payment of royalties on products which do not use the teaching of the patent does amount to patent misuse." 395 U.S. at 135 (emphasis added). Cf. *American Securit Co. v. Shatterproof Glass Corp.*, 268 F.2d 769, 777 (3d Cir.), cert. denied, 361 U.S. 902 (1959) (observing that "[m]andatory package licensing is no more than the exercise of the power created by a particular patent monopoly to condition the licensing of that patent upon the acceptance of another patent. . . . The protection, or monopoly, which is given to the first patent stops where the monopoly of the second begins.").

80   329 U.S. 637 (1947).

81   *Id.* at 639.

82   *Id.* at 644 (emphasis added). When presented with a similar licensee claim some thirty years later, the Ninth Circuit relied on the same Transwrap language cited above to uphold the challenged grantback. See *Santa Fe-Pomeroy, Inc., v. P.& Z Co., Inc.*, 569 F.2d 1084, 1100- 11 (9th Cir. 1978) ("the improvement patents must be viewed as simply a species of property given as consideration for the right to use the basic patent"). Some lower courts, applying the *Transwrap* analysis of grantback provisions, have considered factors such as the duration of the license, scope of the grantback obligation and its effect on competition when assessing the legality of a compulsory grantback provision. See, e.g., *Santa Fe-Pomeroy*, at 1101; *Duplan Corp. v. Deering Milliken, Inc.*, 444 F. Supp. 648, 671 (D. S.C. 1977), aff'd in part and rev'd in part, 594 F.2d 979 (4th Cir. 1979), cert. denied, 444 U.S. 1015 (1980). Carving out a more sharply-defined exception to the *Transwrap* rule, a few lower courts have also held that mandatory grantback provisions may violate the *Sherman Act* when "[s]uch agreements . . . which effect a restraint of trade or create monopolies" have been "designed for that purpose." *Kobe, Inc. v. Dempsey Pump Co.*, 198 F.2d 416, 422 (10th Cir.), cert. denied, 344 U.S. 837 (1952); accord *United States v. Associated Patents, Inc.*, 134 F. Supp. 74 (E.D.Mich. 1955), aff'd *per curiam*, 350 U.S. 960 (1956).

83   Wilson, *Nine No-No's, supra,* note 39 at 4 n. 7 (citing *Transparent Wrap* as contrary authority).

84   See *Guidelines, supra,* note 3, § 5.3.

85   *Id.* § 5.6.

86   *Id.*

87   *Id.*

88   Item five on the "no-no" list. See *supra,* note 72.

89   *Guidelines, supra,* note 3, § 4.1.2.

90   Item seven on the "no-no" list. See *supra,* note 74 and accompanying text.

91   159 F.R.D. 318 (D.D.C. 1995), rev'd, 56 F.3d 1448 (D.C. Cir. 1995).

92   See *Guidelines, supra,* note 3, § 4.1.2.

93   See James B. Kobak, Jr., "The Misuse Doctrine: An Introduction," Address Before the ABA Antitrust Section, Intellectual Property Committee 1-2 (Mar. 28, 1996) (transcript available from ABA Antitrust Section).

94   See *supra,* notes 17-25 and accompanying text.

95   *Morton Salt Co. v. Suppiger,* 314 U.S. 488 (1942).

96   *Id.* at 494.

97   320 U.S. 680 (1944).

98   320 U.S. 661 (1944).

99   See, e.g., *Zenith Radio Corp. v. Hazeltine Research, Inc.*, 395 U.S. 100, 135 (1969) (holding that "conditioning the grant of a patent license upon payment of royalties on products which do not use the teaching of the patent does amount to patent misuse."); *B.B. Chemicals Co. v. Ellis*, 314 U.S. 495, 497 (1942) (following *Morton Salt*, 314 U.S. 488, to find misuse); *American Securit Co. v. Shatterproof Glass Corp.*, 268 F.2d 769, 777 (3d Cir.), cert. denied, 361 U.S. 902 (1959) (owner of several patents barred from claiming infringement after refusing to license any patent, except as part of a package of patents).

100   See, e.g., *Mallinckrodt v. Medipart, Inc.*, 976 F.2d 700, 708 (Fed. Cir. 1992) ("Patent owners should not be in a worse position, by virtue of the patent right to exclude, than owners of other property used in trade."); *Windsurfing Int'l, Inc. v. AMF, Inc.*, 782 F.2d 995, 1001-02 (Fed. Cir.), cert. denied, 477 U.S. 905 (1986) (patent misuse defence will not be sustained absent "a factual determination . . . that the overall effect of the license tends to restrain competition unlawfully in an appropriately defined relevant market"); *USM Corp. v. SPS Technologies, Inc.*, 694 F.2d 505, 511-14 (7th Cir. 1982), cert. denied, 462 U.S. 1107 (1983) (upholding dismissal of misuse claim after evaluating the claim "under antitrust principles" and finding no anticompetitive effect attributable to the alleged misuse).

101   See, e.g., *Patent Misuse Reform Act* of 1988, Pub. L. 100-703, 102 Stat. 4676 (codified at 35 U.S.C. § 271(d)(5) (1994) (claim of misuse will not lie against patent owner who "conditioned the license of any right to the patent or the sale of the patented product on the acquisition of a license to rights in another patent or purchase of a separate product, unless . . . the patent owner has *market power* in the relevant market for the patent or patented product on which the license or sale in conditioned") (emphasis added).

102   *Business Electronics Corp. v. Sharp Electronics Corp.*, 485 U.S. 717, 723, 726 (1988) ("Ordinarily, whether particular concerted action violates § 1 of the *Sherman Act* is determined through case-by-case application of the so-called rule of reason. . . . [T]here is a presumption in favor of a rule-of-reason standard."); *Continental T.V., Inc. v. GTE Sylvania Inc.*, 433 U.S. 36, 49 (1977) ("Since the early years of this century a judicial gloss on this statutory language has established the rule of reason as the prevailing standard of analysis.").

103   *Chicago Board of Trade v. United States*, 246 U.S. 231, 238 (1918).

104   *Northern Pacific Raylway. Co. v. United States*, 356 U.S. 1, 5 (1958).

105   See generally *White Motor Co. v. United States*, 372 U.S. 253, 259-60 (1962) (listing types of *per se* unlawful business arrangements).

106   See generally *Heatransfer Corp. v. Volkswagenwerk, A.G.*, 553 F.2d 964, 977 (5th Cir. 1977), cert. denied, 434 U.S. 1087 (1978).

107   See *McCarran-Ferguson Act*, 59 Stat. 34, 15 U.S.C. § 1012 (1993) (antitrust immunity for "the business of insurance" where regulated by state law).

108   98 Stat. 72, 46 U.S.C. app. § 1706(a) (1994).

109   A number of other industries once enjoyed such exemptions. See, e.g., *Reed-Bulwinkle Act* of 1948, 49 U.S.C. § 5b(9) (1976), partially repealed by Pub. L. No. 95-473, § 4(b), (c), 92 Stat. 1377, 1466-70 (1978) (codified as amended at 49 U.S.C. § 10706 (b) (1988)) (trucking); *Federal Aviation Act* of 1958, 49 U.S.C. § 1394 (1976), partially repealed by *Airline Deregulation* Act of 1978, Pub. L. No. 95-504, 92 Stat. 1705 (1978) (codified at 49 U.S.C. § 1551 (1988)).

110 See, e.g., *Brown v. Pro Football, Inc.*, 116 S. Ct. 2116 (1996) (non-statutory labor exemption); *Gordon v. New York Stock Exchange*, 422 U.S. 659 (1975) (securities).

111 *FMC v. Seatrain Lines*, 411 U.S. 726, 733 (1973).

112 *Silver v. New York Stock Exch.*, 373 U.S. 341, 357 (1963); see also *Otter Tail Power Co. v. United States*, 410 U.S. 366, 372 (1973).

113 316 U.S. 265, 280 (1942).

114 *Id.* at 50.

115 388 U.S. 365 (1967).

116 *Id.* at 377.

117 *White Motor Co. v. United States*, 372 U.S. 253 (1963).

118 35 U.S.C. § 261 (1994).

119 Cf. *Silver v. New York Stock Exch.*, 373 U.S. 341, 357 (1963) (stating standard for implied repeal of antitrust laws).

120 *United States v. Grinnell Corp.*, 384 U.S. 563, 570-71 (1966); *United States v. Aluminum Co. of America*, 148 F.2d 416, 429-30 (2d Cir. 1945).

121 *Berkey Photo, Inc. v. Eastman Kodak Co.*, 603 F.2d 263, 273 (2d Cir. 1979), cert. denied, 444 U.S. 1093 (1980) (quoting *United States v. United Shoe Mach. Corp.*, 110 F. Supp. 295, 345 (D. Mass. 1953), aff'd *per curiam*, 347 U.S. 521 (1954)).

122 *Berkey Photo*, 603 F.2d at 274.

123 See *supra*, notes 14-16 and accompanying text.

124 See, e.g., *National Cooperative Production Amendments* of 1993, Pub. L. 103-42, 107 Stat. 117 (codified at 15 U.S.C. §§ 4301-4305 (1994); *Patent Misuse Reform* Act of 1988, *supra*, note 99; *National Cooperative Research Act* of 1984, Pub. L. 98-462, 98 Stat. 1815 (codified at 15 U.S.C. §§ 4301-4305 (1994).

125 On developments in the economic analysis of antitrust that have contributed to the fall of the "Nine No-No's" world-view and to the rise of the *Guidelines* world, see generally, William G. Shepard, "Theories of Industrial Organization," in *Revitalizing Antitrust in its Second Century* 37, edited by Harry First, Eleanor M. Fox and Robert Pitofsky, 1991; Thomas M. Melsheimer, "Economics and Ideology: Antitrust in the 1980s," *Stanford Law Review*, 42 (1990): 1319 (reviewing Robert J. Larner and James W. Meehan, Jr., *Economics and Antitrust Policy*) (discussing the Chicago School's influence on antitrust merger and vertical restraint law during the 1980s); Herbert Hovenkamp, "The Antitrust Movement and the Rise of Industrial Organization," *Texas Law Review*, 68 (1989): 105 (chronicle of parallel development of antitrust law and the economics of industrial organization); Franklin M. Fisher, "Games Economists Play: A Non-cooperative View," *Rand Journal of Economics*, 20 (1989): 113 (discussing developments in industrial organization; concluding that, since the 1970s and 1980s, "[o]ligopoly theory in particular . . . [has been] totally dominated by the game theoretic approach."); George J. Stigler, "The Economists and the Problem of Monopoly," *American Economic Review*, 72 (1982): 1, 9 ("Competition is now much more vigorously supported than it was in 1890 primarily because we understand it much better today."); Robert H. Bork, *The Antitrust Paradox* 90-91,1993 (influential critique of traditional antitrust advocating economic analysis to achieve allocatively efficient results to be evaluated under a single "enhancement-of-consumer-welfare" standard).

126 *Continental TV, Inc. v. GTE Sylvania, Inc.*, 433 U.S. 36, 58-59 (1977).

127 *Broadcast Music, Inc. v. Columbia Broadcasting Sys., Inc.*, 441 U.S. 1 (1979).

128 See *supra*, notes 115-118 and accompanying text.

129   388 U.S. at 41.

130   *Sylvania*, 433 U.S. at 51.

131   *Id.* at 54.

132   *Id.* at 57-58 ("[t]here is substantial scholarly and judicial authority supporting their [i.e., vertical non-price restraints'] economic utility.") (emphasis added).

133   *Id.* at 54-55.

134   *Id.*

135   *Id.* at 57-59. See also *Bork, supra,* note 125 at 287 ("The great virtue of *Sylvania* is not so much that it preserves a method of distribution valuable to consumers . . . but that it displays a far higher degree of economic sophistication . . . and introduces an approach that, generally applied, is capable of making antitrust a rational, proconsumer policy"). Although the *Sylvania* decision dramatically narrowed the applicability of the *per se* rule to vertical non-price restraints, including vertical non-price restraints in the licensing of intellectual property, subsequent decisions have indicated that *Sylvania* did not abolish *per se* condemnation of some tying arrangements. See generally, *Jefferson Parish Hosp. Dist. No. 2 v. Hyde,* 466 U.S. 2, 9-10, 15-16 (1984) (five-member majority reasserting applicability of the *per se* rule to "certain tying arrangements"); see also *ABA Antitrust Section, Antitrust Law Developments* 134 (3d ed. 1992) ("Although tying arrangements are classified as *per se* violations, the test used to determine whether the *per se* rule should be applied to a particular arrangement is in practice very similar to a rule of reason inquiry, because a number of market related inquiries must be conducted before the *per se* rule is applied.").

136   441 U.S. 1 (1979).

137   *Columbia Broadcasting Sys., Inc. v. American Society of Composers, Authors and Publishers, et al.,* 400 F. Supp. 737, 742 (S.D.N.Y. 1975) ("As a practical matter virtually every domestic copyrighted composition is in the repertory of either ASCAP . . . or BMI"), rev'd, 562 F.2d 130 (2d Cir. 1977), rev'd sub. nom., *Broadcast Music, Inc. v. Columbia Broadcasting Sys., Inc.,* 441 U.S. 1 (1979).

138   400 F. Supp. at 743. Cf. *Automatic Radio, supra,* note 79 and accompanying text.

139   At trial, price-fixing was just one of five of the claims CBS asserted in challenging the blanket licenses. The television network also argued that the blanket licensing arrangements constituted unlawful tying, a concerted refusal to deal, monopolization and copyright misuse. 400 F. Supp. at 745.

140   *Id.* at 745 (quoting from CBS complaint).

141   The DOJ Antitrust Division had challenged ASCAP's licensing practices in 1941, and had brought a similar action against BMI several years later. *Id.* at 743-45. At the time of the CBS lawsuit, both ASCAP and BMI were bound by separate, but substantially similar, consent decrees that had been entered into with the government in 1950 and 1966, respectively. *Id.* A curious aspect of the CBS litigation was that CBS had only to invoke the consent decrees to compel the blanket licensors to license at "reasonable fees" one or more specific ASCAP and/or BMI musical compositions from ASCAP or BMI, directly from composers, through other agents, or through "per-program" licenses. *Id.* The "per-program" licensing option under the 1950 and 1966 consents allowed a broadcast licensee to license the rights to an entire repertory for a given broadcast program, but to pay royalties only for the works that were actually broadcast. *Id.* at 744-45.

142   See *supra,* note 73 and accompanying text.

143   See *supra,* note 74 and accompanying text.

144 *Columbia Broadcasting System, Inc., v. American Soc'y of Composers, Authors and Publishers, et al.*, 562 F.2d at 136 ("There is . . . some analogy to the patent pooling cases which broadly hold that the pooling of competing, and perhaps even non-competing, patents is illegal.") (citing, *inter alia, United States v. Line Material*, 333 U.S. 287 (1948)).

145 *BMI*, 441 U.S. at 20.

146 *Id.* at 20-21.

147 *Columbia Broadcasting Sys., Inc. v. American Soc'y of Composers, Authors and Publishers, et al.*, 400 F. Supp. 744-45 (ASCAP and BMI licensed their repertories on a non-exclusive basis allowing any composer to license performance rights to his works to any other non-exclusive licensee).

148 *BMI*, 441 U.S. at 19.

149 See generally *Line Material*, 333 U.S. 287.

150 *BMI*, 441 U.S. at 8-9.

151 1995 *Guidelines*, § 3.4.

152 *Id.* § 3.4 ("If there is *no* efficiency-enhancing integration of economic activity *and* if the type of restraint is one that has been accorded *per se* treatment, the Agencies will challenge the restraint under the *per se* rule. Otherwise, the agencies will apply a rule of reason analysis.") (emphasis added).

153 *Id.* (citing *BMI*, 441 U.S. at 16-24).

154 *Id.* § 3.4.

155 See *supra*, notes 33-36 and accompanying text.

156 See generally William C. Wood, "Costs and Benefits of *Per Se* Rules in Antitrust Enforcement," *Antitrust Bulletin*, 38 (1993): 887-88 ("In existing justifications of the *per se* rules there is an explicit cost-benefit argument. A *per se* rule, it is argued, is less costly than a rule of reason.") (citing, *inter alia, United States v. Container Corp. of America*, 393 U.S. 333, 341 (1969)); see also Jonathan B. Baker, *per se* "Rules In The Antitrust Analysis of Horizontal Restraints," *Antitrust Bulletin*, 36 (1991):733-37 ("The [Supreme] Court has stated repeatedly that *per se* rules are created in order to reduce litigation costs and increase business certainty about forbidden conduct. . . .") (citing, *inter alia, Arizona v. Maricopa County Medical Society*, 457 U.S. 332, 343-44 (1981)).

157 *Sylvania*, 433 U.S. at 50 n. 16.

158 But see *supra*, note 65 (no-no's "not totally susceptible to a wooden application.").

159 See generally, Daniel L. Rubenfeld, "Econometrics in the Courtroom," *Columbia Law Review*, 85 (1985): 1048, 1051 ("Type 1 errors involve the cost of concluding that an activity was illegal . . . when in fact it was not. Type 2 errors involve the cost of wrongly concluding that an activity was not illegal, when in fact it was.") (citations omitted); R. Hogg and E. Tanis, *Probability and Statistical Inferences*, 1977, p. 254 (distinguishing Type 1 and Type 2 errors); see also R. S. Radford, "Statistical Error and Legal Error: Type One and Type Two Errors and the Law," *Loyola L.A. Law Review*, 21 (1988): 843.

160 See generally Wood, *supra*, note 156 at 891-95 (reviewing empirical data from price-fixing cases tending to show that *per se* cases may be as or more costly than cases decided under the rule of reason); Baker, *supra*, note 156 at 738 ("The fight over characterization [in horizontal restraint cases] – determining whether the conduct is in the appropriate pigeonhole – can involve as much cost, and generate as little business certainty, as a full-blown analysis of reasonableness.").

161   See generally, W. Kip Viscusi, John M. Vernon, and Joseph E. Harrington, Jr., *Economics of Regulation and Antitrust* 1992, pp. 9-10.

162   The cases and enforcement statements during the "separate spheres" period tended to be overinclusive rather than underinclusive.

163   See *Line Material, supra*, notes 46-58 and accompanying text.

164   See the "*Nine No-No's*" discussion, *supra*, notes 78-83 and accompanying text.

165   Richard A. Posner, "The Next Step in the Antitrust Treatment of Restricted Distribution: *Per Se* Legality," *University of Chicago Law Review*, 48 (1981): 6.

166   See *supra*, notes 34-36 and accompanying text.

167   See William J. Baumol and Janusz A. Ordover, "Antitrust: Source of Dynamic and Static Inefficiencies?," in *Antitrust, Innovation, & Competitiveness*, 82, edited by Thomas M. Jorde and David J. Teece, 1992 (hereinafter "Jorde and Teece"):

> If there is any one prevailing view on the merits and demerits of antitrust legislation as a stimulus to economic efficiency it would appear, very roughly, to hold that on the static side, by discouraging the exercise of monopoly, these laws have served unambiguously to promote economic welfare. Nevertheless, there has been a trade-off for social welfare, in that at least in the past antitrust rules have discouraged joint research efforts, have exacerbated the innovator's free-rider problems through restrictions on the scope of the licensing contracts, and may have impeded the attainment of the firm sizes needed to mount the most effective research and innovation efforts.

Baumol and Ordover go on to argue that there is another side to both of those propositions; i.e., that antitrust can undermine static efficiency through rent-seeking by unscrupulous plaintiffs (in private suits) or complainants (to the enforcement agencies), *id.* at 86-88, and can encourage innovation by reducing the profitability of innovation and redirecting entrepreneurs' activities into production-enhancing innovation, id. at 88-91.

168   E.g., Frank H. Easterbrook, "Ignorance and Antitrust," in Jorde and Teece, *supra*, note 165 at 122-23:

> An antitrust policy that reduced prices by 5 percent today at the expense of reducing by 1 percent the annual rate at which innovation lowers the costs of production would be a calamity. In the long run a continuous rate of change, compounded, swamps static losses.

169   See, e.g., Steven C. Salop and David T. Scheffman, "Raising Rivals' Costs," *American Economic Review*, 73 (1983): 267; Steven C. Salop and David T. Scheffman, "Cost-Raising Strategies, " *Journal of Industrial Economics*, 36 (1987): 19 .

170   Joseph A. Schumpeter, *Capitalism, Socialism, and Democracy*, 1942, pp. 81-106.

171   Kenneth J. Arrow, "Economic Welfare and the Allocation of Resources for Innovation," in *Essays in the Theory of Risk-Bearing*, 1976, p.144.

172   See generally Wesley M. Cohen and Richard C. Levin, "Empirical Studies of Innovation and Market Structure," in *Handbook of Industrial Organization*, 2, edited by Richard Schmalensee and Robert D. Willig, 1989, p. 1059 (surveying literature); Baker, *supra*, note 156 at 639-41 (same); Richard J. Gilbert and Steven C. Sunshine, "Incorporating Dynamic Efficiency Concerns in Merger Analysis: The Use of Innovation Markets," *Antitrust Law Journal*, 63 (1995): 569, 579-80 (same).

173   See Federal Trade Commission, *Global and Innovation-Based Competition Hearings* (hereinafter "*Hearings*"), transcript at 1065-66 (testimony of Richard J. Gilbert and of Dennis Carlton); *Hearings*, prepared statement of Dennis Carlton at 8-9; Baker, *supra*, note 156 at 640 and nn. 88-89 (citing, *inter alia*, Richard C. Levin et al., "R&D Appropriability, Opportunity, and Market Structure: New Evidence on Some Schumpeterian Hypotheses," *American Economic Review*, 75 [Papers and Proceedings] (May 1985): 20; John T. Scott, *Purposive Diversification and Economic Performance*, 1993, p. 87). The Hearings transcript, prepared statements of witnesses, and staff report summarizing the hearings can be found at http://www.ftc.gov/opp/global.htm.

174   Baker, *supra*, note 156.

175   *Id.* at 636-39.

176   Cf. Department of Justice and Federal Trade Commission, *Horizontal Merger Guidelines* § 2.22 (Apr. 2, 1992) (where firms are differentiated in their capacity, they differ in their ability to constrain prices), reprinted in 4 Trade Regulation Report (CCH) ¶ 13, 104.

177   Hearings, *supra*, note 173, transcript at 3308 (testimony of F. M. Scherer); cf. *Hearings* (prepared statement of Russell Wayman at 3) ("Clearly, the customer is best served by encouraging a regime within which the best defence of any company is to attempt to run faster than any of its competitors."). In a similar vein, Baumol and Ordover point out that antitrust can affect the relative rewards of entrepreneurship and monopolization and thereby encourage the former: "To the extent [antitrust] prevents or impedes monopolization or reduces its profitability, it can discourage entrepreneurs from embarking on such ventures and cause them to reallocate their talents and efforts into production-enhancing innovation." Baumol and Ordover, in Jorde and Teece, *supra*, note 167 at 91.

178   In some cases, of course, such deprivation could be welfare-enhancing in the long run if it protects the ability of an innovator to appropriate the benefits of its innovation as against imitators. But since there is no necessary connection between the opportunity to deprive competitors of access to complements and situations in which the patent system is inadequate by itself to protect appropriability, the possibility of efficiency benefits flowing from a restraint would seem to be an argument for the rule-of-reason approach of the *Guidelines* rather than for a rule of *per se* lawfulness.

179   See *supra*, note 172 and accompanying text.

180   Testimony of Timothy J. Regan, Division Vice President and Director of Public Policy, Corning, Inc., before the House Judiciary Committee, May 9, 1995.

181   *Hearings*, *supra*, note 173 (prepared statement of Mark Rosenblum at 11, 14) (quoted in 1 FTC Staff, *Anticipating the 21st Century: Competition Policy in the New High-Tech, Global Marketplace*, ch. 6, 1996, p. 13, [hereinafter "*Hearings Report*"]).

182   *Hearings*, *supra*, note 173, transcript at 510 (testimony of Terence W. Faulkner) (cited in *Hearings Report*, *supra*, note 181 ch. 6, p. 14).

183   *Hearings Report*, *supra*, note 181, ch. 6, p. 14 nn. 66-67.

184   *Guidelines*, *supra*, note 3, § 5.

185   *Guidelines*, *supra*, note 3, §§ 2.0, 2.3.

186   See discussion *supra*, note 36 and accompanying text. Prof. Baxter would reverse the direction of the statement in text, and recommends that the terms "horizontal" and "vertical" should be banned from antitrust parlance altogether in favor of "substitutes" and "complements." Comments of Prof. William F. Baxter at the Author's "Symposium on Competition Policy, Intellectual Property Rights and International

Economic Integration," Aylmer, Quebec (May 13, 1996). There is a great deal to commend this view, but in this paper we emphasize the verticality of relationships among complements rather than the reverse, in order to connect the analysis of the complementary relationships that abound in intellectual property with the extensive literature on vertical restraints.

187   See generally Posner, *supra*, note 165; Bowman, *supra*, note 26.

188   *Guidelines*, *supra*, note 3, § 4.1.1.

189   *Guidelines*, *supra*, note 36, § 4.1.1; see also Krattenmaker and Salop, *supra*, note 35 at 242-48.

190   See the section on "Tying and Exclusive Dealing," below.

191   *Guidelines*, § 3.3.

192   *Guidelines*, § 3.1.

193   *United States v. Pilkington plc*, Civ. No. 94-345 (D.Ariz, filed May 25, 1994); see also Robert P. Taylor, "Microsoft and S.C. Johnson Signal a Policy Shift at DOJ," *Antitrust*, 23 (Fall 1994).

194   See *Guidelines*, *supra*, note 3, § 4.2.

195   1995-2 Trade Cases (CCH) ¶ 71,096 (consent decree); see also 59 Fed. Reg. 42,845 (Aug. 19, 1994) (competitive impact statement).

196   See *Antitrust Law Developments*, *supra*, note 135 at 171-79. A refinement that may not be fully reflected in the case law is that these factors are relevant because they cast light on whether the arrangements reduce rivals' ability to constrain prices and thereby augment the defendant's market power. See *infra* notes 199-200 and accompanying text.

197   *United States v. Microsoft Corp.*, 1995-2 Trade Cases ¶ 71,096 at 75,244-46 (D.D.C. 1995) (part IV of consent order).

198   Competitive Impact Statement, at 11, reprinted at 59 Fed. Reg. 42,845 at 42,852 (August 19, 1994).

199   Cf. Krattenmaker and Salop, *supra*, note 36 at 242-46.

200   Thus, if there were a large number of operating system competitors not subject to the foreclosure, or entry into the operating system business by parties not subject to the foreclosure were easy, then Microsoft could not profit by the foreclosure. See Krattenmaker and Salop, *supra*, note 34 at 236-38. In a network industry in which small advantages can result in large consequences (e.g., Michael L. Katz and Carl Shapiro, "Systems Competition and Network Effects," *Journal of Economic Perspectives*, 8 (1994): 93, 105-07), profiting from an exclusion may be less difficult than otherwise.

201   *Supra*, note 194.

202   See, e.g., *Jefferson Parish Hospital District No. 2 v. Hyde*, 466 U.S. 2, 13-14 (1984) (requiring "some special ability – usually called 'market power' – to force a purchaser to do something that he would not do in a competitive market.").

203   See, e.g., *United States v. Jerrold Electronics Corp.*, 187 F. Supp. 545 (E.D. Pa. 1960), aff'd *per curiam*, 365 U.S. 567 (1961); cf. *International Salt Co. v. United States*, 322 U.S. 392, 398 (1947) (considering an asserted justification but rejecting it on the facts).

204   See, e.g., *Will v. Comprehensive Accounting Corp.*, 776 F.2d 665, 674 (7th Cir. 1985) (alternative holding), cert. denied, 475 U.S. 1129 (1986); *Guidelines*, § 5.3; cf. *Jefferson Parish*, 466 U.S. at 32 (four-justice concurrence, taking position at variance with majority).

205 See, e.g., *A.I. Root Co. v. Computer/Dynamics, Inc.*, 806 F.2d 673, 676-77 (6th Cir 1986); *Guidelines*, § 5.3; cf. *Jefferson Parish*, 466 U.S. at 32.

206 See *Northern Pac. Ry. v. United States*, 356 U.S. 1, 6 (1958); see also, e.g., *United States v. Loew's, Inc.*, 371 U.S. 38, 49 (1962).

207 See Bowman, *supra*, note 26 at 53-119, 140-82; Bork, *supra*, note 125 at 365-81; Richard A. Posner and Frank H. Easterbrook, *Antitrust: Cases, Economic Notes, and Other Materials*, 2d ed., 1981, pp. 777-856.

208 See, e.g., Michael D. Whinston, "Tying, Foreclosure, and Exclusion," *American Economic Review*, 80 (1990): 837; Louis Kaplow, "Extension of Monopoly Power Through Leverage," *Columbia Law Review*, 85 (1985): 515.

209 Whinston, *supra*, note 208 at 854-55; cf. *Hearings*, *supra*, note 173 at 3549-50 (testimony of William F. Baxter) ("The only time I recognize the existence of a problem is when an independent base of market power is being established in the adjacent market that will be able to collect monopoly rents from people who have no demand in the first market.").

210 *Will v. Comprehensive Accounting Corp.*, 776 F.2d at 674.

211 See, e.g., Katz and Shapiro, *supra*, note 200 at 94; Michael L. Katz and Carl Shapiro, "Network Externalities, Competition, and Compatibility," *American Economic Review*, 75 (1985): 424.

212 *Hearings Report*, *supra*, note 181, ch. 9 p. 1.

213 *Supra*, note 209 and accompanying text.

214 See *Hearings*, *supra*, note 173, transcript at 3732 (testimony of Richard Schmalensee).

215 Cf. Deputy Assistant Attorney General Carl Shapiro, "Antitrust in Network Industries," Address before the American Law Institute and American Bar Ass'n, San Francisco, CA 27-31 (text released March 7, 1996) (available from the Department of Justice, Antitrust Division, Legal Procedures Unit) (leveraging may permit today's standard-bearer to extend its control into the next generation of technology).

216 For a tying arrangement to be *per se* unlawful, there must be two separate products. In *Jefferson Parish Hosp. Dist. No. 2 v. Hyde*, 466 U.S. 2, 19-21 (1984), the Supreme Court held that whether there are separate products depends on whether the arrangement links two distinct products that are "distinguishable in the eyes of buyers."

217 See *Brulotte v. Thys*, 379 U.S. 29 (1964); *American Securit Co. v. Shatterproof Glass Corp.*, 268 F.2d 769,777 (3d Cir. 1959).

218 See Baxter, *supra*, note 26 at 327.

219 *United States v. Electronic Payment Servs., Inc.*, 1994-2 Trade Cases (CCH) ¶ 70,796 (consent decree).

220 Competitive Impact Statement, *United States v. Electronic Payment Servs., Inc.*, 59 Fed. Reg. 24,711 (May 12, 1994).

221 Indeed, in an earlier draft of this article, we classified it, with equal justification, with *Walker Process* claims as cases in which anticompetitive consequences result, not from licensing restrictions but from the circumstances surrounding the creation or enforcement of intellectual property rights.

222 5 Trade Regulation Report (CCH) ¶ 24,054 (May 20, 1996 (final acceptance of consent order).

223 *Dell*, Dkt. C-3658, Complaint ¶ 7.

224 *Dell*, Complaint ¶ 6.

225 In addition, to the extent that Dell's actions led to fragmentation of the standard, consumers of both Dell's and competitors' products would likely face a reduced array

of complementary products, thus reducing the attractiveness of both Dell's and competitors' products. Presumably, Dell's share of that cost was not great enough to outweigh the prospect of gaining some rents from control of the standard.

226   *Guidelines*, § 5.5.

227   *Guidelines*, § 3.3; see also discussion *supra*, note 34 and accompanying text.

228   *Guidelines*, § 5.5.

229   See F. M. Scherer and David Ross, *Industrial Market Structure and Economic Performance*, 3d ed., 1990, p. 489.

230   U.S. Department of Justice, *Merger Guidelines* (1984) [hereinafter "1984 *Merger Guidelines*"], reprinted in 4 Trade Regulation Report (CCH) ¶ 13,103. As with a two-level entry problem, there are limiting principles involving the degree to which the transaction increases the need for multiple-level entry, the extent to which such entry is more difficult than single-level entry, and the degree to which the affected markets are susceptible to monopolization or collusion. And one might also have to consider the possibility of efficiencies that could not readily be achieved through less restrictive means.

231   Civ. No. 94-C-50249, (N.D. Ill., filed Aug. 4, 1994).

232   See *supra*, note 213, 1984 *Merger Guidelines*, § 4.13.

233   *Id.* § 4.133.

234   See Michael H. Riordan and Steven C. Salop, "Evaluating Vertical Mergers: A Post-Chicago Approach," *Antitrust Law Journal*, 63 (1995): 513, 519-20.

235   198 F.2d 416 (10th Cir.), cert. denied, 344 U.S. 837 (1952).

236   *Id.* at 423-24.

237   *Guidelines*, § 3.2.3.

238   See, e.g., Commissioner Roscoe B. Starek, III, "Innovation Markets in Merger Review Analysis: The FTC Perspective," Address Before the Florida Bar (Feb. 23, 1996); Richard J. Gilbert and Steven C. Sunshine, "Incorporating Dynamic Efficiency Concerns in Merger Analysis: The Use of Innovation Markets," *Antitrust Law Journal*, 63 (1995): 569; "Symposium: A Critical Appraisal of the 'Innovation Market Approach," *Antitrust Law Journal*, 64 (1995): 1.

239   See *Hearings Report, supra*, note 181, ch. 7; Richard T. Rapp, "The Misapplication of the Innovation Market Approach to Merger Analysis," *Antitrust Law Journal*, 64 (1995): 19, 37-46.

240   5 Trade Regulation Report (CCH) ¶ 23,784 (June 14, 1995).

241   5 Trade Regulation Report (CCH) ¶ 23,712 (February 14, 1995), reopened and modified, *Trade Regulation Report*, 5 (CCH) ¶ 23,966 (January 16, 1996).

242   5 Trade Regulation Report (CCH) ¶ 23,914 (February 8, 1996).

243   *Hoechst AG*, 5 Trade Regulation Report (CCH) ¶ 23,895 (December 5, 1995).

244   *Food, Drug and Cosmetic Act* § 505, 21 U.S.C. § 355 (1988 and 1993 Supp.)

245   *Sensormatic Elecs Corp.*, 5 Trade Regulation Report (CCH) ¶ 23,742 (December 5, 1995).

246   *United States v. General Motors Corp*, Civ. No. 93-530 (D. Del. filed Nov. 16, 1993), summarized at 6 Trade Regulation Report (CCH) ¶ 45,093 (Case 4027).

247   *Id.*, Complaint ¶ ¶ 35-45.

248   *Guidelines, supra*, note 3, ¶ 3.2.3.

ACKNOWLEDGMENT

THE AUTHORS GRATEFULLY ACKNOWLEDGE the research assistance of Ramsen Betfarhad and the helpful comments of Prof. William F. Baxter and Timothy P. Daniel on an earlier draft of this article. The views expressed herein are solely those of the authors and do not necessarily represent the views of the Federal Trade Commission or any individual commissioner.

Comment

William F. Baxter
Law School
Stanford University

THIS PAPER IS NICELY WRITTEN AND HAS VERY FEW VULNERABILITIES. I was, however, surprised by the emphasis placed on the early cases and on the reasoning behind the decisions. I disagree with the suggestion that economics was an important element in those decisions. The fact is the courts did not always get it right. There is nothing in the briefs, opinions, or the speeches of the justices to suggest that they were based on economics.

Rather, the reasoning process was one of metaphysics, of converting abstract concepts into pseudo-tangible pieces of turf that could be thought about in physical rather than intellectual terms. This is true of the best of them: I read several of Louis Brandeis' opinions, because he had a reputation as a great thinker in this area. His opinions are no better than those of most of the others. I refer you, for example, to the *Chicago Board of Trade*, which is utter nonsense from beginning to end. In another, less well known case, Brandeis talks about the cost of capital in the process of rate-making in public utilities, – the *Southwest* case. His confusion over debt and equity markets and the behaviour of interest rates under various circumstances is truly painful.

The statute said every contract that restrains trade is unlawful, and in the very earliest cases the courts tended to take it literally. Sooner or later they realized this was misguided: since the role of every contract is to restrict the freedom of the parties to exercise their discretion, every contract would be an illegal restraint of trade under a literal interpretation. It took them a number of years to get out of that particular intellectual box. The paper is somewhat misleading in suggesting that the judges were busy reading J. B. Clark in the evening, but had not quite got things straight.

An important feature of intellectual property that has been insufficiently remarked relates to price discrimination. In information dependent industries the great preponderance of all costs is sunk when a product finally becomes available; the incremental cost of another use and the marginal cost are essentially zero. The average cost is still quite substantial because the large up-front costs have to be collected somewhere. We are thus confronted with the question: what should a pricing structure look like under those circumstances? Of course, the answer is Ramsey pricing.

Everyone who values an intellectual property should use it, because the social cost associated with its incremental use is zero. Therefore, the optimum structure involves features that can appropriately be called price discrimination; yet it is price discrimination that is optimal in these circumstances. Prohibiting price discrimination in the intellectual property context would be sorely misguided.

Finally, I would like to comment on a procedural feature that I hoped to find some mention of in this paper. I think most of us would agree that the effort to decide antitrust cases in ways that achieve global efficiency or global optimality is totally beyond our reasonable aspirations. In fact, we are arguing about what should be the elements of causes of action or claims, what should be the elements of the defences that can be raised, what should be the elements of the justifications that plaintiffs can then advance in response to the defences, and how many different elements we are going to try and take into account before we say: enough. This is a very expensive business.

Not only do we have to decide when to stop allowing additional justifications and additional theories, we have to distinguish between probabilities and mere possibilities. For example, it might just happen that whenever a producer changes a product the marginal customer is pleased by the change but the average customer is indifferent or even hostile to change. But while such things can happen, we need to be able to prove whether they are probable. The mere fact that they can happen is not a justification for restricting producers' freedom to make product changes in response to their perceptions of demand.

I would like to see the judge in antitrust cases select at his discretion one or two issues to be resolved in the initial trial segment. After resolving one set of issues, if the case as a whole is not yet resolved, the trial can proceed to the next set of issues. In other words, I would introduce what I call "trial by interlude": a couple of weeks in court, a couple of weeks preparing for the next two weeks of trial, and so on.

We tried some administrative law cases in this way in the United States, in particular, the Civil Aeronautics Board hearings to pass out new route authority to a group of carriers. The solutions are intensely interdependent. For example, you cannot give Delta the route from Charlotte to Miami without taking into account that TWA already flies from Orlando to Richmond. You must resolve one part of the puzzle before you can even think usefully about the next part. Trial by interlude evolved as a solution to a problem, and it worked reasonably well. I think it would also work well in antitrust cases.

Another worthwhile though politically difficult aspiration is to get rid of jury trials in antitrust cases. They make no sense whatsoever. Juries become less and less clear what the case is about after each successive week of trial.

Finally, Tom and Newberg discuss a genuine difficulty that arises in attempts to settle certain intellectual property cases – particularly those turning on priority of invention – the question of whether the technologies are independent or whether there is only one technology. The difficulty arises when the parties come in arm-in-arm and say: "Well, we finally worked it out, your Honour: The nature of the settlement is that everybody has a legitimate claim to some protection and everybody will get a piece of the action." Such a settlement would look very much like a cartel. It is almost impossible to tell the parties: "No, you can't settle, you must go on litigating." Perhaps it would be useful to have a statute providing that the government should be notified of all such settlements and may, if it wishes, step into the plaintiff's shoes and continue litigating, even if the private plaintiff wishes to settle. This would take advantage of the litigation that has occurred so far and may be the best way to proceed in these cases.

Robert D. Anderson,   Paul M. Feuer,   Brian A. Rivard   & Mark F. Ronayne   11
Competition Bureau   Competition Bureau   Competition Bureau   Competition Bureau
Industry Canada   Industry Canada   Industry Canada   Industry Canada

Intellectual Property Rights and International Market Segmentation in the North American Free Trade Area

INTRODUCTION

IT IS INCREASINGLY RECOGNIZED that intellectual property rights (IPRs) and competition policy have implications for international trade and economic integration. IPRs are an important factor impinging on business strategies regarding R&D, trade, domestic production, and international investment.[1] Competition policy bears directly on decisions regarding national and transnational mergers and strategic alliances, production, distribution and marketing channels, and technology transfer arrangements. The roles of intellectual property (IP) and competition policy as factors affecting international trade and investment are reflected in both the North American Free Trade Agreement[2] and in recent and ongoing deliberations at the multilateral level.[3]

An important aspect of the debate on IP, competition, and international trade concerns the use of intellectual property rights to segment international markets. To varying degrees, the IP statutes of most countries allow rights holders to exclude competing foreign versions of their products, even when such versions are legitimately made under the foreign countries' IP legislation.[4] The ability to segment markets may, in some instances, help to prevent free-riding and facilitate the establishment of efficient distribution systems.[5] It can also facilitate international price discrimination.[6] Market segmentation under IP legislation may also have implications for other variables such as the degree of competition in particular industries and incentives for the rapid introduction of new products and production processes in particular countries.

The rationale for import protection under IP rights appears to differ, to an extent, across the various types of rights. For example, concerns regarding the preservation of goodwill in a brand name are most directly applicable to trademarked goods, although they may also be a consideration in regard to patented or other types of IP-protected goods in some cases. Import-control rights under patent legislation may serve as an incentive for domestic manufacturing of patented products. The role of import-control rights in enabling firms to engage in international price discrimination appears to cut across all types of IP.

Some ability to exclude competing foreign versions may be essential to the maintenance of desirable standards of protection, particularly for patents. For example, in the absence of other means of segmenting international markets, goods made under regimes embodying shorter patent terms could flow freely into countries that want to maintain higher standards. As a result, the effective patent protection term would tend toward the shortest prevailing internationally for a particular good. The need to maintain nationally acceptable standards of protection probably precludes the sweeping elimination of import-control rights under patent legislation in a multilateral context, at least given current disparities in basic standards (particularly between developed and less developed countries).[7]

These considerations may not, however, justify the ability to exclude legitimate foreign products in all circumstances. For example, in the context of regional free trade or economic integration initiatives, it could be welfare enhancing for countries to eliminate the ability to exclude IP-protected products made in other countries in the region, while adopting uniform standards of IP protection. While this is not (at least at present) contemplated under the North American Free Trade Agreement, it is reflected in the policy of "exhaustion" of IP rights that applies across the European Community. Under this policy, legitimately made articles embodying IPRs that are placed on the market in any member state may move freely throughout the community.[8] It is worth considering whether such a policy would be desirable in the context of NAFTA.[9]

In contemplating this possibility, it is worth noting that concerns about charging discriminatory prices for IP-protected products have surfaced in Canadian economic policy debates on various occasions. For example, in the 1960s, an extensive inquiry by the Restrictive Trade Practices Commission found that the prices of patented drugs in Canada were higher than those prevailing in other major industrialized countries.[10] This report was instrumental in the subsequent enactment of legislation to expand the availability of compulsory licenses to manufacture and import patented drugs.[11] More recently, concerns have been expressed regarding the use of trademark rights to bar the importation of lower priced versions of brand name consumer products (e.g., Heinz ketchup) from the United States into Canada.[12] On the other hand, at least with regard to patented goods, the ability to segment markets may ensure the availability of some products that would not otherwise be offered in Canada.[13]

In thinking about these issues, it is helpful to consider the application of competition laws to licensing and other contractual arrangements that restrain international trade. Depending on jurisdictional and other factors, competition law may be directly applicable to restrictive licensing arrangements that go beyond rights that are explicitly conferred under IP statutes. For example, the consent decree issued by the U.S. courts in the 1994 *Pilkington* matter dealt specifically with restrictive conditions, including territorial restrictions in patent licences, for float glass technology.[14] As well, the treatment of contractual restrictions has specific implications for the implementation of exhaustion. To the extent that IPR owners can readily substitute contractual restrictions for import-control rights arising under IP legislation, the impact of exhaustion would be reduced. The application of competition law to such restrictions has a bearing on this possibility.[15]

This paper examines various theoretical, empirical, and policy considerations relating to the issue of market segmentation under intellectual property legislation. This includes a discussion of the treatment of licensing and other contractual restraints on international trade under Canadian and U.S. competition laws. The paper also discusses the pros and cons of possible policy responses to market segmentation, including adopting the principle of exhaustion of IP rights across the North American free trade area. The focus is principally on market segmentation and exhaustion in the context of patents and trademarked goods, and does not consider the case of copyright.

More specifically, the remainder of the paper is structured as follows. In the first section we examine the economic effects of market segmentation under IP laws. We then evaluate the degree of import protection that is currently available under IP laws in Canada and the United States.

In the next section, we examine the application of competition policy to contractual restraints on international trade in licensing and other interfirm agreements, in the United States and Canada. Follows a discussion of the concept of exhaustion, as it is applied in the European Union (EU), and related aspects of EU competition law. In the penultimate section we discuss a range of practical considerations that would be entailed by a policy of exhaustion of IP rights within the NAFTA. In the final section we provide concluding remarks.

ECONOMIC IMPLICATIONS OF INTERNATIONAL MARKET SEGMENTATION THROUGH IPRs

IN THIS SECTION, WE REVIEW VARIOUS RATIONALES FOR, and welfare implications of, international market segmentation as they are discussed in the economic literature.[16] We examine possible private incentives for international market segmentation and the implications of these rationales for economic welfare. Such incentives include international price discrimination, the prevention of free-riding on location-specific investment, and facilitating tacit collusion. We also review empirical studies that examine various explanations for parallel imports. Finally, we discuss the implications of international market segmentation through IPRs for the gains from trade, and the extent to which contractual provisions can provide an acceptable substitute for IPRs in ensuring an efficient degree of control over trade in IP-protected goods.

Private Incentives for International Market Segmentation and Their Welfare Implications

International Price Discrimination

The ability of an original IPR owner to segment international markets by means of IPR licensing provides the original IPR owner with an opportunity to practice third-degree price discrimination.[17] In general, three conditions must be present in order for a firm to practice third-degree price discrimination.[18] First, a firm must possess market power. Without it, the firm could not charge consumers more than the competitive price. Second, consumers must differ in their willingness to pay (as measured by demand elasticities) for the firm's product, and the firm must be able to sort consumers into different markets according to demand elasticities. Finally, the firm must be able to prevent or limit resale from lower to higher price markets. A free flow of goods between markets would act to arbitrage any price differences that might exist.

These three conditions will often be present for IPR-embodying goods. First, patents (and copyrights) by definition confer exclusive rights to supply particular goods.[19] Most branded products that are covered under trademark laws, by their nature, have at least a modest degree of market power.[20] Second, the price elasticities of consumers for IPR-embodying goods commonly vary from country to country. In general, relatively high income countries have more inelastic demands for luxury goods such as cosmetics and fragrances and electronic goods. Finally, IPRs and other instruments may provide a manufacturer with a legal tool for segmenting international markets by excluding parallel imports.

Optimal pricing under third-degree price discrimination implies that the manufacturer (IPR owner) will charge more in markets in which the elasticity of demand is low relative to other markets. Conversely, if a manufacturer is forced to charge a uniform price in all markets (as would tend to be the case with the implementation of exhaustion), this uniform price will be greater than the price charged to the consumers in the high elasticity market under discrimination, but no greater than that charged to the consumers in the low elasticity market.

The implications of third-degree price discrimination for economic welfare can be considered from at least two viewpoints: a) in terms of who benefits and who is harmed by allowing discrimination, and b) from the perspective of its effects on total economic welfare.

With regard to the matter of gains and losses, manufacturers are clearly better off with the ability to practice price discrimination, relative to uniform pricing, since, at worst they can always charge the uniform price in each market. Countries with low-elasticity markets are adversely affected by discrimination (they must pay a higher price for the good) and would benefit from uniform pricing. Countries with high-elasticity markets will generally pay lower prices and therefore will prefer discrimination.

Of course, the effects of price discrimination in IPR-embodying goods on individual countries may depend on other factors such as the ownership of IPRs. If a particular country is home to a significant number of IPR owners, it may still prefer price discrimination over exhaustion, since the higher profits of IPR owners may compensate for the higher consumer prices.

In general, the effects of third-degree price discrimination on total economic welfare are ambiguous.[21] Nonetheless, there are reasons for believing that in some circumstances the ability to discriminate in the prices charged in individual country markets may yield significant benefits. For example, it can encourage firms to supply entire markets that otherwise would not be served.[22]

Malueg and Schwartz analyse how the total welfare effects of price discrimination are influenced by the degree of demand dispersion between international markets (i.e., the degree to which demand elasticities differ across the relevant countries).[23] If international demand dispersion is sufficiently low, uniform pricing results in a higher level of total welfare relative to discrimination.[24] Conversely, if international demand dispersion is sufficiently high, total welfare is higher under price discrimination than it is under uniform pricing. This reflects the fact that under uniform pricing, as the degree of international demand dispersion increases, some markets (i.e., those with the highest demand elasticities) are not served. For sufficiently high levels of demand dispersion, the loss in efficiency due to the decrease in total output outweighs the gain due to the misallocation of output (i.e., total welfare is higher under discrimination).[25]

Malueg and Schwartz also consider the total welfare implications of what they refer to as "mixed systems" of international market segmentation. In a mixed system, countries are segmented into designated groups (such as trading blocks) with different prices allowed among but not within them. In other words, exhaustion would be implemented within trading blocks but manufacturers could use their IPRs to facilitate price discrimination among trading blocks. Such mixed systems maintain the benefits of discrimination by serving all countries, while at the same time limit the welfare loss resulting from the misallocation of resources. This carries a clear implication that the gains from implementing exhaustion are likely to be greatest in the context of regional trading blocks with relatively similar demand elasticities.[26]

Location-Specific Investments and the Prevention of Free-Riding

Another important rationale for international market segmentation relates to encouraging domestic distributors to invest in location-specific assets that enhance the value of a manufacturer's product and preventing free-riding on such investments. (These may include investments in product/firm reputation or goodwill, product quality, and new product development.)

A domestic distributor may have a cost or informational advantage in making location-specific investments. For instance, that distributor may incur a lower cost when collecting information on local market conditions, and be better at interpreting and assessing their implications for the sale of the manufacturer's product in that local market. In these circumstances, it may be more efficient for the manufacturer to license the IPR to domestic distributors than to have one organization distribute the relevant goods in all countries.

When a domestic distributor makes location-specific investments, opportunities may be created for authorized foreign distributors or parallel importers to free-ride on these investments.[27] Moreover, an authorized foreign distributor may not incur the same expense as the domestic distributor in making such investments.[28] The foreign distributor may, therefore, have an incentive to divert some of its production to the domestic producer's market, price its product above marginal cost but below the price set by the domestic distributor, and capture some of the domestic producer's market.

More generally, free-riding is a problem when domestic distributors are not compensated separately for their location-specific investments, but are compensated for their investments only when they sell the product. If a distributor cannot realize the full benefits of its investment (because of parallel imports, for example), it has an incentive to reduce its investment, and the value of the manufacturer's product is not enhanced. Therefore, if there is free-riding, the manufacturer earns less profit.

In terms of consumer welfare, preventing free-riding through international market segmentation will normally benefit consumers. Without market segmentation, there would be little or no investment in location-specific assets by domestic distributors. As a result, the domestic consumer would not receive the same level of product quality and variety, service, and information that would prevail under market segmentation. Since both consumers and producers are better off under market segmentation, total welfare is higher.

Tailoring Products for Specific Country Markets and the Issue of Passing-Off

Preferences for product quality and variety often vary across countries. When preferences are different across countries, a domestic producer may have better information about domestic consumers' preferences for quality and variety than would the IPR owner. A domestic producer may also be able to alter the product more quickly in response to changes in preferences than could a centralized manufacturer. When the domestic producer has these advantages, the IPR owner may find it more efficient to license the production rights to the domestic producer and have it make specific investments relating to the proper mix of product quality and variety.

When the original IPR product differs across countries to reflect each country's preferences, a further opportunity for free-riding can arise. A price differential may exist between countries reflecting consumers' willingness to pay for the specialized products. With different prices in different countries, parallel importers may have an incentive to import a foreign country's authorized product into the domestic country and pass it off as the local product. Such "passing-off" can create customer confusion regarding the characteristics of the product and undermine the reputation of the domestic producer's products. The domestic producer may respond to the passing-off by cutting back on its investments in quality and variety. If all distributors were to respond in this manner, eventually there would be only one product of constant quality.

Facilitating Tacit Collusion

Market segmentation through IPRs does not normally involve collusion in the sense of a horizontal arrangement to limit competition among otherwise independent parties. Rather, in most cases the holders of rights to particular inventions or other forms of intellectual property will be part of a single corporate enterprise or will be assignees of a common enterprise. In this sense, arguments for prohibiting market segmentation through IPRs on the ground that it is intrinsically anticompetitive are misplaced. In contrast, licensing agreements that are merely a sham to provide cover for a horizontal market allocation arrangement may well constitute criminal conspiracies.[29]

The ability to segment international markets through IPRs may also provide a means of facilitating tacit collusion. When there is interbrand competition between IPR owners with similar products, the competing IPR owners may have an incentive to segment international markets in a way that softens interbrand competition and maintains their supracompetitive returns.

An example of this type of arrangement is where a company developing a new technology to compete with an existing one is induced to enter instead into a licensing arrangement involving the existing technology. This could have the effect of suppressing the use of a new competing technology. However, since the technology has not yet been developed, there will be no explicit exchange of IPRs to clearly bring the practice under competition legislation.[30]

Another potential concern may arise where collusion involves licensees or distributors and not IP owners. In other words, the licensees and distributors as well as the IP owner may hold some degree of market power. It might be argued that this market power could be used to extract exclusive territories from the IP owner even though the owner might want to encourage intrabrand competition.

Other ways in which such conspiracies can be facilitated might include separating fields of use for an IPR or rent-sharing arrangements. As a matter of policy, such arrangements should be subject to effective sanctions under competition law.

Empirical Evidence on the Causes of Parallel Imports

The empirical evidence does not indicate unambiguously whether parallel imports are a response to free-riding opportunities or to arbitrage opportunities precipitated by international price discrimination. For example, there is some evidence that "incomplete pass-through" is a common occurrence.[31] Incomplete pass-through offers scope for international arbitrage that occurs when import prices, measured in terms of the destination currency, do not decline proportionately with the appreciation of that currency. The occurrence of incomplete pass-through would seem to provide support for the view that international price discrimination is the cause of parallel imports. However, a correlation between parallel imports and exchange rate movements in the importing country's currency could also be explained by the free-rider hypothesis. In particular, an appreciation in the destination country's currency could lead to cost-based differences between the importing manufacturer's price and the destination country's price. This could increase the opportunities for free-riding.[32] Similarly, there is evidence that parallel import goods primarily consist of brand name consumer goods (i.e., goods that require large promotional investments).[33] This would provide support for the free-riding explanation. However, this evidence may also be consistent with the price discrimination explanation. Brand name consumer goods tend to be highly differentiated, so their manufacturers generally possess some market power. This market power provides an opportunity for international price discrimination.

While the empirical evidence on the general causes of parallel imports is inconclusive, there is nonetheless a large body of evidence to suggest that manufacturers practice international price discrimination.[34] In his study of parallel imports in the U.S. economy, Hilke concluded that price discrimination as an explanation for parallel imports was more consistent with the existing evidence than were others such as free-riding.[35]

Only a handful of studies have tested for general price differences within North America among IPR protected goods. These studies have generally found average Canadian prices across a broad range of products to be similar to average U.S. prices. For example, Globerman, in a 1987 study of Canadian and U.S. list prices of industrial chemicals, found Canadian prices to be lower in most cases where there was a difference between the two countries' prices. However, the average Canadian price across all the products examined was slightly higher than the average U.S. price.[36] A 1976 study of Canadian versus U.S. prices for 79 patented consumer products found that, while Canadian prices were on average between 2 and 3 percent higher, the price difference was statistically insignificant.[37]

Blomqvist and Lim, in a 1981 study, found a significant difference between Canadian and U.S. prices for books.[38] The study found that the ratio of average Canadian to U.S. list prices across a broad range of books was 1.06 to 1.08. It should be noted, however, that in earlier work that compared

Canadian and U.S. record prices, Blomqvist and Lim found that the average Canadian list price was less than 90 percent of the U.S. list price.[39]

In sum, the empirical evidence as to whether parallel imports are a response to free-riding opportunities or to arbitrage opportunities triggered by international price discrimination is inconclusive. Furthermore, price differences on IPR goods within North America appear to be insignificant when measured across the entire class of IPR goods.

INTERNATIONAL MARKET SEGMENTATION THROUGH IPRS AND THE GAINS FROM TRADE

IN EVALUATING THE OVERALL WELFARE EFFECTS of market segmentation under IPRs, it is also important to consider possible implications for the gains accruing from trade. As Anderson et al. point out, while the right or ability to prevent imports under intellectual property legislation is often referred to as having effects similar to tariff and traditional non-tariff barriers,[40] the comparison is misleading. In particular, traditional tariff and nontariff barriers are nondiscretionary instruments that normally apply to all imports, regardless of the identity of the importer. They cannot, therefore, be applied differentially (or waived) in respect of trade involving firms that enjoy contractual or other commercial links.[41]

In contrast, the application of IP-based import control rights is subject to the discretion of the rights holder. Consequently, the rights holder remains free to engage in unimpeded trade himself or to structure his licensing or other arrangements in a manner that prohibits its licensees from exporting the product. For example, unlike a manufacturer whose products are subject to significant tariffs, an IPR holder is free to rationalize production activities by manufacturing its products in one country while distributing them in many countries through its licensees without economic penalty. In fact, it retains a clear incentive to undertake such rationalization where there are cost advantages or economies of scale to be exploited.[42]

The general conclusion that IP-based import control rights are unlikely to impede the realization of gains from trade does not imply that there is no basis for concern regarding the impact of IPRs in international trade. For example, it is sometimes suggested that border remedies for IPR infringement can be employed to harass and thereby deter legitimate trade in IPR-embodying goods.[43] More specifically, critics have argued that provisions such as section 337 of the *U.S. Tariff Act of 1930* provide domestic manufacturers with stronger protection against infringement by foreign-produced than domestic-produced goods.[44] Under it, domestic manufacturers with registered IPRs in the United States can petition the International Trade Commission (ITC) for action against infringing importers. If the ITC rules that there is an infringement, it can issue a general exclusion order instructing U.S. Customs officials to preclude the importation of a designated product class. This class would include importers other than the individual infringer for which the petition was filed. In this sense, the general exclusion order represents a traditional non-tariff barrier to trade, since it provides a domestic IPR owner with an import prevention instrument that applies to all imports (within the general class), regardless of the identity of the importer. However, it should be stressed that in such a case, the special nature of the remedy (i.e., the fact that it is a border measure), rather than the principle of IP-based import control rights, is the underlying source of concern.

THE SUBSTITUTABILITY OF CONTRACTS AND IPRS FOR SEGMENTING INTERNATIONAL MARKETS

IMPORTANT TO ASSESSING THE IMPLICATIONS of exhaustion of IP rights is the potential substitutability of voluntary contractual restrictions for IP-based import control rights. In this sense, it is useful to note the blurring which may occur between purely contractual restrictions and those restrictions which form part of an IPR licensing agreement, as both are contractual in nature, although the latter may be exempt from antitrust consideration if such restrictions are legitimately within the scope of the IPR. It is worth emphasizing that, in the domestic markets of most developed countries, contracts are widely used to address concerns about the promotion of location-specific investments and prevention of free-riding (i.e., the rationales for market segmentation). In principle, it seems reasonable to suppose that contracts can also serve this function in transitional markets, where there are well-developed institutions for enforcing complex contracts.

Compared with IPR-based import restraints, contractual import restraints are likely to be a particularly effective tool for segmenting markets under a range of circumstances. An IPR is an exclusive right that provides protection against any and all infringements, since the legal authority to enforce IPR-based restraints is unaffected when the relevant goods change hands. IPR holders can enforce their right directly against any infringing imports, whether or not the importer had notice or was aware that importation of the relevant goods would constitute an infringement.[45]

By contrast, contracts containing territorial restrictions to protect against parallel imports may be enforceable only where subsequent purchasers of the relevant goods have been informed that the goods are not for resale in the importing country. Even if such notice is given, however, the ability to prevent parallel imports under contract law does not rest with the authorized distributor of the goods in the importing country.[46] Rather, direct responsibility for ensuring that restrictions against parallel trade are notified to subsequent purchasers and that unauthorized exports do not occur rests with the original supplier and subsequent purchasers of the goods in the exporting country.

A second potential advantage in using IPRs for market segmentation is the specialized forms of legal remedies that may be invoked against parallel imports. Canadian remedies for patent, trademark, and copyright infringements allow for injunctions to prevent further imports, damages or an accounting of the infringer's profits derived from the infringement (both damages and an accounting may be sought in the case of copyright infringement), destruction or delivery up of the infringing goods to the IPR holder, and court and legal costs. Furthermore, infringers may also be criminally liable and expose themselves to a fine and imprisonment.

SUMMARY OF ECONOMIC IMPLICATIONS OF INTERNATIONAL MARKET SEGMENTATION THROUGH IPRs

IN SUM, THE ECONOMIC LITERATURE IDENTIFIES three distinct private incentives for segmenting international markets through intellectual property rights. It also indicates that the welfare implications depend on the incentives underlying the segmentation. More specifically, the segmentation of international markets has positive implications for welfare when its purpose is to prevent free-riding. In this instance, it leads to higher levels of product quality, increased product variety and customer service and less product confusion for consumers. Market segmentation may also have positive welfare implications when the underlying incentive is the practice of price discrimination. International price discrimination will increase global economic welfare when there is a large dispersion in demand elasticities across countries. In fact, as Malueg and Schwartz imply, welfare may well be optimized by preventing market segmentation within regional trading areas with broadly similar demand characteristics, while allowing it among different regional areas. On the other hand, price discrimination through international market segmentation will have negative welfare implications globally when the countries involved have broadly similar demand characteristics. Moreover, if international markets are segmented to facilitate collusion, welfare will be adversely affected.

Second, available empirical studies do not provide conclusive guidance on the causes of parallel imports. The very nature of the subject, unauthorized trade in IP products, makes empirical investigation inherently difficult. Furthermore, the available evidence is consistent with both the price discrimination and free-riding explanations. Nonetheless, there is evidence to suggest that manufacturers do practice international price discrimination and that price discrimination is a more consistent explanation for parallel imports than other explanations such as free-riding. Additionally, the existing evidence indicates that price differences between Canada and the United States are, in general, insignificant even in spite of international price discrimination. Arguably, this would indicate a general similarity in demand characteristics between the two countries.

Finally, a good argument can be made that market segmentation under IP rights does not necessarily impede the realization of gains from trade in the same way that tariff or conventional non-tariff barriers do, in that such rights can, in principle, be waived where it is desirable to do so. Nonetheless, the border remedies currently associated with IPRs in many countries may indeed constitute a genuine barrier to trade.

THE SCOPE FOR EXCLUDING PARALLEL IMPORTS UNDER CANADIAN AND U.S. IP LAWS

THIS SECTION EXAMINES existing intellectual property legislation and jurisprudence to determine the scope of IPR holders' ability to unilaterally exclude legitimately manufactured parallel imports using infringement actions.[47] We focus on two main types of intellectual property: patents and trademarks. We also comment in passing on the IP regime applicable to integrated circuit topographies (semiconductor chips), a *sui generis* type of IP that incorporates the exhaustion principle in a limited form.

PATENTS

A PATENT IS A STATUTORY RIGHT, granted by each nation, which provides an innovator with exclusive rights to make, use, and sell the patented "process, machine, manufacture, or composition of matter" within the national territory of the country granting the patent.[48] Patent rights are therefore entirely territory-based. In exchange for full disclosure of the invention, the patentee is rewarded with a statutory monopoly lasting 20 years for any invention that is new, useful, and involves an "inventive step".[49] During this period the patent owner alone may decide how to exploit the invention. Following the expiry of this statutory period, anyone may use and exploit the discovery.

From a policy perspective, there are two reasons for granting exclusive patent rights on inventions.[50] First, exclusive patent rights encourage innovation by rewarding the inventor with the full stream of monopoly profits associated with the invention. If other individuals could obtain the information at no cost and benefit from the inventor's efforts, the inventor would have less incentive to produce it than if everyone had to pay for using the information. Second, patent laws encourage disclosure of new discoveries. This accelerates the diffusion of new technologies.

When a patent holder sells a patented product in Canada without any restrictions, the patentee's rights are exhausted in that the patentee has no further control over the buyer's use or resale of the product. However, it is possible to use patent rights to block parallel imports for the purpose of segregating domestic from foreign markets. While these issues have not been extensively considered by Canadian courts, U.K. case law is generally considered to govern the situation in Canada.[51]

In the 1883 U.K. case *Société Anonyme Manufactures des Glaces v. Tilghman*,[52] the Court held that a licence to manufacture only in Belgium did not imply permission to sell in England and distinguished parallel imports of products sold abroad by a U.K. patentee without restrictions from products made under a foreign licence.[53] In essence, the Court confirmed that the grant of rights under one country's patent laws does not confer rights under any other country's patent laws. The scope to prevent parallel imports by foreign licensees not authorized to sell in the IP owner's domestic market has also been considered in a line of Commonwealth cases outside Canada.[54] These cases indicate that an IP owner/licensor may exercise the IPR to prevent the importation of goods by a parallel importer who purchased them from a licensee, even if the parallel importer did not have express notice of existing limits on the resale of the goods.

The 1871 U.K. case of *Betts v. Wilmott* indicated certain limits on the scope of a patentee's right to prevent parallel imports.[55] The Court held that a U.K. patent holder could not block imports of products that were sold abroad directly by the patentee or his agents without restriction.[56]

Prior to 1993, protection against import competition could also arise in the context of compulsory licences granted due to patent abuse in situations where a patent was not being worked on a commercial scale or where such working in Canada was being prevented by imports of the patented article from abroad.[57] Such licences could have included provisions prohibiting any importation of the relevant products to Canada.[58] These provisions were not compatible either with article 28 of the TRIPs Agreement or the NAFTA.

In summary, the violation of a territorial restriction contained in a licence pertaining to patented products will normally constitute an infringement. In addition, territorial restrictions notified to successive purchasers run with patented products, and in the case of parallel imports may run even without notice. Consequently, the resale or use of patented products outside allotted territories may be held to infringe the Canadian patent.[59] In this sense, it may be said that the doctrine of exhaustion does not presently apply to Canadian domestic trade in patent-embodying goods.

In the United States, the principle of exhaustion applies in the domestic context under the "first sale" doctrine, which states that the first sale of a product without restriction by a patentee or licensee exhausts the ability of that rightholder to control any further resale of the product anywhere within the United States, the rationale being that the first payment released the patentee's exclusive rights over the good by giving the benefit intended by statute.[60] This also applies to first sales abroad by a patentee or licensee who also has the right to sell in the United States.[61]

By contrast, contractual restrictions, including territorial restrictions such as may be found in a patent licence which are within the scope of a patent and do not offend U.S. antitrust laws, are binding on the patent-embodying good. However, the concept of "patent misuse" has developed in the United States to address practices which draw anticompetitive strength from the statutory right and may be used to extract market benefits beyond those which properly inhere in that right.[62]

In general, U.S. courts have declined to apply the exhaustion principle to parallel imports from foreign countries, usually on one of two grounds: a) the U.S. patentee or licensee did not receive any benefit from the foreign purchase (this rationale is in keeping with the domestic "first sale" doctrine, which is predicated on the holder of an exclusive right being entitled to receive a benefit in return for a release from that right);[63] and b) imports of U.S. goods sold abroad – either by a patentee subject to restrictions prohibiting their subsequent sale in the United States or by a licensee subject to territorial restrictions – to a purchaser with notice of these restrictions, have been held to infringe U.S. product patents.[64] Conversely, if the foreign sale of U.S.- patented and manufactured products is not subject to the condition that the goods not be re-exported to the United States, the foreign sale may exhaust U.S. patent rights.

The principle of exhaustion does not apply to foreign parallel imports: in effect, the U.S. patentee may impose an import ban through mere reliance on the territorial rights inherent in the U.S. patent, as long as this does not lead to a breach of antitrust principles (this aspect is dealt with in the section entitled "Competition Policy and the Treatment of Contractual Restraints on International Trade in the United States and Canada").[65]

With respect to process patents, the *Process Patent Amendments Act of 1988* provides that the unauthorized importation of goods made by a process patented in the United States may also constitute an infringement.[66] The main question is whether the importation takes place with the authorization of the U.S. patentee. Prior to 1988, the importation of products manufactured abroad by processes patented in the United States was not considered an infringement on the basis that it did not involve the actual manufacture, use, or sale of the invention in the United States.[67]

Section 261 of the U.S. *Patent Code* expressly allows patentees to segment markets through contractual territorial restrictions defined in licensing agreements, which amounts to a form of import ban to prevent parallel imports.[68] In *Dunlop Company, Ltd. v. Kelsey-Hayes Co.*, the Court held that licensing restraints on the importation of products manufactured by foreign licensees were merely territorial licenses as permitted under section 261, and not horizontal agreements to divide markets.[69] The Court basically treated foreign licenses with domestic implications as if they were domestic licensees. In *Becton, Dickson & Co. v. Eisele & Co.*, a contractual import ban preventing foreign licensees from importing their products into the United States was upheld as merely being in support of a U.S. patentee's exclusive right to sell within the United States and hence within the scope of the patent monopoly.[70]

Regarding export bans, the U.S. courts have generally upheld the right of patentees to impose territorial restrictions on exports from the United States by their licensees. The basis of this doctrine is the pre-*Sherman Act* case of *Dorsey Revolving Harvester Rake Co. v. Bradley Mfg. Co.*[71] It should be noted, however, that this decision has been criticized as being inconsistent with other Supreme Court doctrine, which holds that the U.S. patent system has no extraterritorial effect.[72]

TRADEMARKS

A TRADEMARK IS A WORD, NAME, SYMBOL, MARK, OR OTHER IDENTIFIER used by a firm or person to distinguish its goods or services from those of its competitors. It provides its owner with rights of exclusive use in relation to the products associated with the trademark.[73] The rationale for trademark rights is twofold. First, trademark laws prevent consumer confusion by providing an efficient means of enabling consumers to recognize products with certain desired attributes. If the trademark could be affixed on the label of more than one brand, consumers might not be able to distinguish the product they want from other products. This confusion would lead to increased search costs for consumers. Second, trademark protection encourages the trademark owner to maintain a higher level of product quality and thus maintain goodwill in the trademark. Without trademark protection, consumers would become confused by lower-quality products passed off as the genuine product.

Trademarks may exist under common law and under a statutory registration scheme. In common law, a trademark right arises from the moment the mark is actually used, while under a statutory registration scheme an application may be made without prior use. In both cases, a trademark provides the owner with the ability to enforce the mark against use that is unauthorized or involves a confusingly similar mark.[74] Registration under a statutory regime provides several benefits, including a statutory cause of action for infringement.[75] The period of protection of a registered mark is limitless as it may be renewed indefinitely.[76]

In Canada, a registered trademark owner can attempt to prevent parallel imports or an infringement under the common law tort of passing-off or the *Trade Marks Act*.[77] The difference between the statutory and common law actions is that, in common law, the plaintiff does not need to have an exclusive right to the mark. The tort of passing-off is based on a test of whether there is a likelihood that the public will be deceived with resulting injury to the plaintiff, while the statutory action is founded on the invasion of a registered owner's right to exclusive use of the mark.[78] To succeed in a common law action, there must be an intentional misrepresentation by the grey marketer. However, in the *Seiko* case the Supreme Court of Canada limited the utility of the common law tort of passing-off to prevent parallel imports in holding that there is no passing-off when a genuine good is sold in Canada, as long as there is no significant element of consumer misrepresentation.[79] In that case, it was held that a disclaimer, to the effect that the international warranty on Seiko watches sold by the grey marketer did not apply, was sufficient to avoid misrepresentation. While this decision seems to favour a form of exhaustion under the common law tort, other cases indicate that an action for infringement of a registered trademark will still provide a measure of protection from parallel imports under the *Trade Marks Act*.[80]

A distributor is not entitled to protection under the *Trade Marks Act*, but may ask the owner to bring a case on its behalf under the Act. A licensee has the right to enforce the license under the Act if the owner will not do so.[81] A licensee or distributor may also have recourse to contract law if the licensing or distribution contract contains exclusive territorial rights.[82] As yet, there have been no parallel import cases in which the Canadian distributor has been the originator of the trademark who licenses foreign firms to manufacture and sell in foreign markets.

If a Canadian trademark owner was the originator of the product and directly sold the product abroad, where it was purchased and then re-imported into Canada, the exhaustion principle would likely apply since there is no possibility for deception – the owner who markets these goods gives with them an implied licence to resell.[83] In *Wilkinson Sword (Canada) Ltd. v. Juda and Breck's Sporting Goods Co. v. Magder*, the Courts held that a parallel importer can challenge the validity of a Canadian assignee's trademark (to prevent the use of the implied licence to resell defence) if the assignee does not take sufficient action to distinguish any local goodwill from that of the original trademark owner, as the public would continue to believe that the source of the product was the original trademark owner.[84]

The more recent case of *Mattel Canada Inc. v. GTS Acquisitions Ltd.* seems to have introduced a new consideration: instead of deciding the case on the sole basis of whether there was a likelihood of consumer deception, the Court considered the economic investment of the rightholder as a factor in granting an interlocutory injunction to exclude the parallel imports.[85] However, in *Smith & Nephew Inc. v. Glen Oak Inc. et al.*, the Federal Court of Appeal rejected the reasoning in *Mattel* on the ground that it was based on an unconstitutional provision of the *Trade Marks Act* prohibiting business practices "contrary to honest industrial or commercial usage in Canada."[86] In doing so, the Court reaffirmed that the test for trademark infringement in Canada was the likelihood of consumer deception. It held that a licensee of a Canadian registered trademark could not prevent the parallel import of goods bearing the same trademark, which originates with the licensor. It reasoned that there can be no deception as to the origin of the goods where both the licensee's and the parallel importer's goods are manufactured by or under licence from the same trademark owner who controls the quality and character of those goods. The Court did, however, leave open the possibility that a Canadian subsidiary that owns the trademark rights, as opposed to being a mere licensee, might be able to sufficiently distance itself from its parent and exercise its Canadian trademark rights to prevent the importation of its parent's goods.[87]

In addition to the usual remedies available under the *Trade Marks Act*, which include injunctions against infringing goods, recent legislative amendments (not yet in force) specifically provide Canadian registered trademark owners with the ability to block infringing importations. Section 53.1 provides that a Canadian registered trademark owner may apply to a court for an order requiring the Minister to detain wares associated with the mark that are about to be imported or have been imported but not yet released, where the distribution of the wares would contravene the *Trade Marks Act*. If the court's final determination is that the importation would be contrary to the Act, the court may order that the goods be destroyed, exported, or delivered up to the Canadian registered trademark owner as that owner's property.[88] Where the goods are imported contrary to the Act, and the use of the mark was unauthorized and done with the intent to counterfeit or imitate the mark or deceive the public, the court may not order the exportation of the goods in an unaltered state.[89]

In the United States, there is strong statutory justifications for preventing grey imports without the consent of the U.S. trademark holder that are based on two sections of the *Lanham Act*, three sections of the *Tariff Act of 1930*, and one section of the *Copyright Act*. A U.S. licensee who is not a trademark owner is not entitled to protection under the *Lanham Act*, or section 526 of the *Tariff Act of 1930*, but may still have recourse to contract law or the tort of unfair competition or unlawful interference with contractual relations.[90]

Section 32 of the *Lanham Act* provides a general prohibition against the use of any "reproduction, counterfeit, copy or colorable imitation" of a registered trademark that is likely to cause confusion, mistake or deception of any kind.[91] Section 42 of the Act permits a registered trademark owner to have imported goods that "copy or simulate" their registered trademark seized at the border by the Customs service.[92] Section 526 of the *Tariff Act of 1930* applies to domestic owners of registered marks only and is not limited to "copies or simulations," but more broadly prohibits any merchandise of foreign manufacture bearing a trademark owned by a U.S. trademark owner, including imported goods bearing a genuine foreign trademark ("genuine goods") identical to that owned by the U.S. trademark owner.[93] Customs regulations implementing section 526 state that if the domestic and foreign marks are owned by the same person or parent-subsidiary, then there can be no protection against imports under section 526.[94] This regulation was upheld as valid by the U.S. Supreme Court in *K-Mart v. Cartier*.[95] In that case, the Supreme Court also held that a related regulation allowing importation of foreign-made goods authorized by the U.S. trademark owner was invalid, since it was in direct conflict with the language of section 526. For example, this regulation would have allowed parallel importation of goods by a foreign manufacturer or a third party where a

U.S. trademark owner had authorized that independent foreign manufacturer to use the trademark in a particular foreign location, contrary to section 526.

Although the case law is unsettled, at least two things seem clear: first, there is entitlement to block imports where a trademark owner proves that the goodwill is factually distinct and is owned independently from a foreign trademark; and second, if the domestic and foreign trademark owners are the same or affiliated, section 526 cannot be used to automatically exclude imports.

In addition to the prohibitions listed above and contractual restrictions, U.S. trademark, patent, and copyright owners can seek relief from the United States International Trade Commission under section 337(a) of the *Tariff Act of 1930*.[96] At the time it was enacted, section 337 was not aimed specifically at infringing imports but rather at a broad range of import practices that were viewed as unfair.[97] It has been broadly construed to include trademark infringement, unfair competition, and violations of section 43 of the *Lanham Act*,[98] and has evolved into an important remedy against infringing imports.[99] In fact, section 337 appears to have become the remedy of choice for domestic IPR owners, in part because it is faster and less expensive than an infringement action, it may be applied to multiple parties simultaneously, and the remedy is a broad general exclusion order of a designated product class.[100] Amendments made to the legislation in 1988 have eliminated the need for intellectual property holders to show injury in section 337 actions.[101]

Concerns about the scope and nature of section 337 have been addressed in the context of the GATT. In 1990, a GATT panel ruled that aspects of section 337 were incompatible with GATT principles respecting non-discrimination and national treatment.[102] Subsequently, section 337 was amended to allow importers to file counterclaims and to provide that proceedings may only continue in one of two possible forums (the International Trade Commission or the district court) instead of both concurrently.[103] However, the discriminatory aspects of section 337 remain largely intact, and the section continues to be a bone of contention with major trading partners.[104]

INTEGRATED CIRCUIT TOPOGRAPHIES

INTEGRATED CIRCUIT TOPOGRAPHIES (SEMICONDUCTOR CHIPS) are the subject of a *sui generis* form of intellectual property protection in both Canada and the United States. The principles underlying this protection are enshrined in the Treaty on Intellectual Property in Respect of Integrated Circuits, signed in 1989.[105] Article 6(6) provides for the exhaustion of rights where the protected layout design (topography) has been put on the market with the consent of the rightholder. This approach recognizes that the creation of a new importation right without qualification "could readily be abused to impede international trade in items such as television sets or computers simply because one of the many dozens of chips involved ... might be a parallel import as opposed to an authorized import."[106] Canada has incorporated exhaustion in its legislation to the extent that the owner of the registered topography has already consented to its commercial exploitation in Canada or exploited it himself.[107]

In sum, IP laws in Canada and the United States clearly provide broad scope for segmenting markets, although the ability to segment markets varies depending on the particular type of IPR. Patent rights provide the broadest scope to prevent unauthorized imports of goods manufactured legitimately under the patent in a foreign country due to their inherently territorial nature. Trademark protection does not embody as strong a territoriality principle, focusing instead on the issue of consumer deception. The Supreme Court of Canada's decision in the *Seiko* case has limited the ability of a trademark owner to use the common law tort of passing-off to prevent parallel imports. However, statutory protection against parallel importers may be available under the *Trade Marks Act*, as suggested by the recent *Heinz* and *Mattel* cases. These decisions suggest that courts are aware of economic concerns such as free-riding and local investments in their treatment of IPRs (discussed in "Economic Implications of International Market Segmentation through IPRs," above) and that the legal treatment of parallel goods will take into account the economic impact of parallel importation. The inclusion of the exhaustion principle in semi-conductor chip legislation, unlike other IPRs addressed in this discussion, represents a conscious attempt by its developers to limit the potential use of related rights for market segmentation purposes.

COMPETITION POLICY AND THE TREATMENT OF CONTRACTUAL RESTRAINTS IN INTERNATIONAL TRADE IN THE UNITED STATES AND CANADA

THIS SECTION OF THE PAPER EXAMINES THE APPLICATION of U.S. and Canadian competition laws to licensing and other contractual arrangements that restrain international trade. This topic is of interest for two reasons. First, depending on jurisdictional factors, competition law may be directly applicable to restrictive territorial arrangements that go beyond the rights conferred by the IP statutes. Second, the competition law treatment of contractual restrictions has implications for the implementation of exhaustion. To the extent that IPR owners can readily substitute contractual restrictions for import-control rights that exist under IP legislation, the effects of exhaustion would be limited. The competition policy treatment of territorial market restraints is one factor that may affect the substitutability of contracts for IPR-based import-control rights.

The availability of contractual restraints to prevent parallel trade depends on the extent to which such restraints are tolerated by each country's competition laws. Both Canadian and U.S. competition laws take a relatively permissive approach toward the use of territorial restrictions and exclusive territories, and provide broad scope for allowing efficient vertical licensing practices and related arrangements. In the United States, the antitrust framework for intellectual property licensing has recently been extensively clarified by the 1995 *Antitrust Guidelines for the Licensing of Intellectual Property*.[108] These guidelines clarify the policy framework for licensing arrangements in the United States, which has evolved through distinct phases from the *per se* prohibition of many standard licensing practices in the 1960s and 1970s, including territorial restrictions, to the comparative laissez-faire of the mid to late 1980s.[109] The Canadian approach paralleled developments in the United States and, according to the sceptical view, the role of IPRs in a competitive economy gave way to an understanding that IPRs promote dynamic competition and that restrictive licensing practices may have efficiency benefits.[110] The United States has also indicated a willingness to pursue extraterritorial enforcement of U.S. competition laws in the 1995 *Antitrust Enforcement Guidelines for International Operations*, which is a change from the more limited approach taken in the 1988 version of these guidelines.

In the United States, the cornerstone antitrust prohibitions aimed at territorial restrictions are contained in sections 1 and 2 of the *Sherman Act*,[111] which would apply where a restraint is related to an IPR. However, U.S. courts have taken a permissive attitude toward contractual restraints on parallel trade in IPR-embodying goods, finding that such restrictions in licensing agreements generally do not contravene antitrust law unless they are unreasonably broad and anticompetitive. In general, territorial restrictions regarding importation from abroad in a patent license have been justified as being "within the scope of the patent" (see the section "Patents" above), although domestic territorial restrictions are subject to exhaustion under the first-sale doctrine.

However, the courts have held that patents cannot shield certain territorial restrictions from the application of antitrust laws. Restrictions that benefit only the licensee and not the patent owner are subject to antitrust laws, as the restrictions would not be shielded under section 261 of the *Patent Code*.[112] Restrictions that operate outside the United States are not technically within the ambit of the first-sale doctrine set out in section 261, although courts have supported export bans on this basis.[113]

Another important exception to the permissive treatment of contractual restraints on trade in IPR-embodying goods is when import restrictions go beyond what is necessary to legally exploit the IPR and in reality constitute a cartel. In the "cartel cases" of the 1940s and early 1950s, import restrictions were inserted within the patent as part of broader arrangements to limit interbrand competition or divide up world markets among firms that would otherwise be in competition.[114] The cartel cases indicate that, in such circumstances, contractual import restrictions are indeed subject to the antitrust laws and may be struck down. Both represent significant limitations on the ability of IPR owners to segment international markets.

The 1992 case of *Mallinckrodt Inc. v. Mediport, Inc.* reinforced a patentee's ability to impose contractual restrictions under a patent licence.[115] In this case, the patentee's medical devices were marked "single use only," but the defendant recycled them for resale to the customer hospitals. The Federal Court Ninth Circuit rejected the argument that the single-use condition was illegal simply by virtue of being a restriction. The Court held that "[u]nless the condition violates some other law or policy (in the patent field, notably misuse or antitrust law. . .), private parties retain the freedom to contract concerning conditions of sale", and stated that anticompetitive restrictions that are not *per se* violations are to be reviewed in accordance with the rule of reason.[116] The *per se* violations discussed in *Mallinckrodt* include price-fixing and tying; vertical territorial restrictions would generally be reviewed under the rule of reason.

The U.S. approach to antitrust enforcement concerning contractual IP licensing restraints is clarified in the 1995 *Antitrust Guidelines for the Licensing of Intellectual Property* ("IP Guidelines") of the U.S. Department of Justice and the Federal Trade Commission (FTC),[117] which indicate that most licensing arrangements will be evaluated under the rule of reason rather than under *per se* rules. In particular, the Department of Justice and the FTC will apply a rule of reason analysis *unless* (a) the restraint in question does not contribute to efficiency-enhancing integration of economic activity; and (b) the restraint is of a type which has been accorded *per se* treatment in the jurisprudence.[118] The IP *Guidelines* recognize that many "restrictive" licensing practices such as field-of-use, territorial, and other limitations serve legitimate procompetitive purposes, for example by reinforcing incentives for the commercialization of products and preventing free-riding. Antitrust issues are more likely to arise when a licensing arrangement harms competition among entities that would have been actual or likely competitors in a relevant market in the absence of the license (i.e., in the context of horizontal as opposed to vertical relationships). For example, a restraint in a licence may harm competition if it facilitates market division, and a restriction with respect to one market may anticompetitively foreclose access to an input in another market. The IP *Guidelines* also note the potential economic benefits of cross-licensing and pooling arrangements, where two or more owners of different IPRs agree to license one another or third parties. However, it is further noted that such practices may be mechanisms to accomplish market division, in which case they will be challenged under the *per se* rule.

In addition to the jurisprudence and guidelines applicable to trade in IPR-embodying goods noted above, it is also relevant to consider more general antitrust doctrines involving territorial restraints in non-IPR embodying goods. Unlike the Canadian experience, the U.S. approach to such restrictions has undergone a significant evolution due to changing antitrust approaches related to vertical restraints. Before 1967, the courts tended to take a permissive attitude toward the use of such restraints. This was subsequently put in doubt by the decision in the 1967 case of *U.S. v. Arnold, Schwinn & Co.*[119] In that case, the U.S. Supreme Court ruled that territorial restrictions and similar vertical non-price restraints applying to goods after their title has passed to others were so "obviously destructive of competition" as to constitute a *per se* violation of section 1 of the *Sherman Act.* In a landmark decision that heralded judicial acceptance of new thinking regarding the potential procompetitive aspects of vertical restraints, the Supreme Court reversed itself ten years later in *Continental T.V., Inc. v. GTE Sylvania, Inc.*[120] The Court held that such restraints should instead be examined under a rule of reason, noting that vertical restraints, although inherently restrictive of intrabrand competition, often have the effect of promoting beneficial competition among alternative brands.[121]

The enforcement of U.S. antitrust law with respect to territorial restrictions that affect international trade can be determined to some extent from the 1995 *Antitrust Enforcement Guidelines for International Operations.* These guidelines clarify the threshold for international application of U.S. antitrust laws – including foreign import commerce that would include parallel imports – and mark a significant willingness to enforce U.S. antitrust laws extraterritorially compared with the 1988 version of the same guidelines. Pursuant to the *Foreign Trade Antitrust Improvements Act of 1982* (Title IV), the U.S. Department of Justice is empowered to bring antitrust suits against foreign companies whose licensing conduct adversely affects U.S. domestic commerce and export trade.[122]

The increased willingness to enforce U.S. antitrust law abroad was exemplified in the 1994 *Pilkington* consent decree, which involved restrictive conditions – including territorial restrictions in patent licenses – for float glass technology.[123] The complaint filed by the Department of Justice asserted that these restrictions were unjustifiable restraints of trade in light of the fact that the patents had long ago expired and also because the restrictions prevented U.S. licensees from using and exporting the technology to build float glass plants outside the United States.

In Canada, the ability of IPR holders to block parallel trade through infringement suits in particular circumstances does not, by itself, provide a broader exemption from Canadian competition law.[124] The imposition of vertical contractual market restrictions (i.e., those relating to a particular product brand or technology owned by a single corporate enterprise) is not explicitly sanctioned by the relevant intellectual property statutes, and in many cases such restrictions may be viewed as incidents of the contract rather than the intellectual property right.[125] On this basis, the use of vertical contractual restraints on international trade in IPR-embodying products would also remain subject to the *Competition Act,*[126] although Canadian competition policy has traditionally provided broad scope for efficient vertical licensing practices and related arrangements.

Sections 32, 61 and 79 of the *Competition Act* expressly address the exercise of intellectual property rights. Section 32 is a civil provision that permits the Federal Court of Canada to issue orders to remedy abuses of patents, copyrights, trademarks, or registered industrial designs. The remedies available include orders declaring void restrictive provisions in licensing agreements, which would apply to territorial restrictions, or restraining any persons from carrying out such objectionable provisions.[127] Section 32 has not been applied in any recent cases.

Section 61, the price maintenance provision, prohibits the use of the exclusive rights conferred by patents, trademarks, copyrights or registered industrial designs to influence prices upward or discourage their reduction, or to refuse to supply someone due to their low pricing policy. A recent case under section 61 is relevant to the concept of market segmentation using contractual terms in Canada although it does not expressly involve an IPR. In *Polaroid Canada Inc. v. Continent-Wide Enterprises Ltd.*, the Court held that a contractual term providing for a separate, prohibitively high price for goods destined for export compared with the usual price for goods to be sold in Canada did not offend the provision.[128] The refusal was not due to the distributor's low pricing policy, but rather because of the intended destination. The Court reasoned that although the export price policy was in restraint of trade, it was in Polaroid's legitimate interest to ensure adequate supply for Canadian customers.

The abuse-of-dominance provisions found in sections 78 and 79 provide for a case-by-case evaluation of restrictive practices engaged in by dominant firms. Subsection 79(5) stipulates that acts that are engaged in "pursuant only to the exercise of any right or the enjoyment of any interest" derived under intellectual property statutes do not constitute anticompetitive acts for the purposes of the abuse provisions. This exception limits the ability to take enforcement action against transfers of IPRs to Canadian subsidiaries for the purpose of excluding parallel imports and segregating the Canadian market from other markets.

Section 78 of the Act provides a non-exhaustive list of possible anticompetitive acts that may be dealt with under section 79. The list includes acts such as requiring or inducing a supplier to sell primarily to certain customers or refrain from selling to a competitor, with the objective of preventing a competitor's entry into, or expansion in, a market. The list of anticompetitive acts was deliberately left open-ended by Parliament. Accordingly, the abuse provisions are potentially applicable to a broad range of licensing practices, including territorial restrictions.

An example of an abuse case involving IP rights is *NutraSweet*. In this instance, the NutraSweet Company had employed contractual restrictions as part of the marketing strategy for its sweetener to artificially extend its exclusive rights once its patent had expired.[129] The Competition Tribunal rejected NutraSweet's argument that its various exclusivity clauses were necessary to prevent free-riding and to enable the company to recoup the costs of regulatory approvals and market development, stating that it "does not accept that NutraSweet is entitled to any more protection against competition than it was able to obtain through patent grants that provided it with a considerable head start on potential competitors."[130]

Several other sections of the *Competition Act* do not refer specifically to intellectual property rights, but are nevertheless potentially applicable to territorial restrictions that result in market segmentation. For example, an attempt by Chrysler Canada Inc. to segment international markets for Chrysler auto parts by refusing to supply a distributor who exported its parts for sale outside Canada was found to contravene section 75 of the Act concerning refusal to supply.[131] Chrysler had argued that a term of its sale was that products supplied were not to be exported, but the Tribunal did not find this on the evidence and ordered Chrysler to supply the distributor. In its decision, the Tribunal noted that it is not compelled under section 75 to order the supply of products in every case where the elements of the section are met, and that it might refuse to issue such an order where there are legitimate economic and business interests to protect. Other examples of potentially relevant provisions include the practices of tied selling, exclusive dealing, and territorial market restriction found in section 77. These civil offences are reviewed under a rule of reason analysis and are only illegal where the practices are likely to result in a substantial lessening of competition and meet other statutory conditions.

In sum, the competition policy treatment of international market segmentation also has specific implications for the potential impact of exhaustion. It suggests that, under an international exhaustion regime, contractual or licensing restrictions would be available in many cases as potential substitutes for IPR-based import-control rights in regard to parallel trade among developed countries.

EXHAUSTION OF IPRS IN THE EUROPEAN UNION

THE EUROPEAN UNION PROVIDES A PARADIGM ILLUSTRATION of how the exhaustion principle has been adopted for the explicit purpose of fostering economic and political integration. Prior to the Treaty of Rome, national competition laws allowed for market segmentation using IPRs in much the same way as the national laws of the NAFTA countries do today. Under the Treaty, the scope for using intellectual property rights to restrain parallel imports of IPR-related products into member states of the EU is limited by two separate sets of provisions. First, the freedom-of-movement provisions provide the basis for community-wide exhaustion of IPRs between members. Second, the competition provisions of the Treaty have been applied so as to impose strict limitations on territorial market restrictions in licensing agreements. This policy is based directly on the fundamental goals of the Treaty, which emphasize the economic integration of member states.

With respect to the free movement of goods, the implications of the Treaty for import-control rights under national intellectual property statutes depend on whether the imports originate in an EU member or non-member country. Where the goods have not been brought into commerce in an EU member state, the relevant jurisprudence indicates that patents, trademarks, and copyrights can, in many circumstances, be used to block parallel imports into the EU.[132] Thus, IP rights continue to provide significant scope for control of trade between EU member and non-member states.

On the other hand, if the goods have been brought into commerce within the common market with the consent of the IPR owner, any rights to restrain EU imports provided under the national intellectual property laws of individual EU member states are superseded by the Treaty. In general, such goods are subject to a community-wide doctrine of exhaustion. Under this doctrine, the first sale of IPR-protected products with the IPR owner's consent normally exhausts the owner's right to control further movement within the EU.[133]

The exhaustion doctrine is a compromise between the principle of free movement of goods and exceptions involving several provisions of the Treaty. Article 30 prohibits all quantitative restrictions on imports and all measures with equivalent effect between member states. This has been interpreted widely as "all trading rules enacted by member states which are capable of hindering intra-community trade."[134] For instance, the use of a trademark in Germany to exclude a British product that has the same legal trademark would be prohibited. However, article 36 provides an exception to the effect that certain restrictions may be justified on various grounds including "industrial and commercial property," but any such restrictions must not be arbitrary discrimination or disguised restriction on trade between member states.[135] This leaves the determination of what is or is not justified to the courts. Moreover, article 222 provides that the Treaty shall in no way prejudice the rules in member states dealing with the system of property ownership. In simpler terms, article 30 sets out the basis for the free movement of goods and the exhaustion principle, while articles 36 and 222 validate to some extent the contrary ability of national IP laws to segment markets.

The doctrine of exhaustion was applied in the 1974 patent case of *Centrafarm B.V. v. Sterling Drug*.[136] In this case, a Dutch patentee attempted to prevent parallel imports by a third party of goods placed on the U.K. market by a licensee. In response to a request for a ruling by the Dutch Supreme Court in accordance with article 177 of the Treaty, the European Court of Justice declared that the broad scope of the Dutch patent law to prevent parallel imports was inconsistent with the freedom of movement provisions, and the patentee was not permitted to prevent parallel importation.[137]

The doctrine of exhaustion does not completely eliminate the scope to prevent imports on the basis of intellectual property rights. In the 1985 case of *Pharmon B.V. v. Hoechst*, for example, the Court did not apply exhaustion to imports of goods produced in another EU member state under a statutory compulsory licence.[138] This holding was based primarily on the view that the granting of a compulsory licence did not constitute consent on the part of the patentee.[139]

In *Centrafarm v. Winthrop*,[140] the Court held that exhaustion applies to trademarks as well, although in *Hoffman LaRoche v. Centrafarm*[141] the Court held that the trademark owner could keep out the parallel imports on the basis that the repackaging or relabelling would likely cause confusion as to the origin of the product, contrary to the purpose of a trademark.

Two central themes have dominated the market integration approach in the EU: first, the need for EU-wide IPR laws to avoid the tensions caused by differences among national laws; and second – in recognition that an EU-wide law may not be forthcoming in the short term – attempts to further harmonize national laws to reduce these tensions.[142] An example of such tensions caused by the principle of exhaustion is that a shorter patent period in one member jurisdiction means that producers consent to enter that market at their peril; once the shorter period expires, third parties may produce in that market and export anywhere in the EU regardless of unexpired patents in other countries.

The EU approach to exhaustion is closely related to the treatment of territorial market restraints under the competition provisions of the Treaty of Rome. Restraints of parallel trade between EU member states are subject to the competition provisions of the Treaty, particularly article 85(1).[143] This article generally prohibits agreements having "as their objective or effect the prevention, restriction or distortion of competition within the EU." Article 85(3) permits exemptions where the agreement "contributes to improving the production or economic progress, while allowing consumers a fair share of the benefit." The European Commission and Court of Justice have generally taken a strict approach to the application of this provision to territorial market restrictions.

The strict approach to the treatment of territorial market restraints involving IPR-embodying goods under article 85 is illustrated by the 1982 case of *Nungesser v. Commission (Maize Seed)*.[144] In this case, a French intellectual property holder granted a German assignee the exclusive right to distribute the protected product within Germany and agreed to take steps to impede importation into Germany by third parties.[145] Further territorial protection for the German assignee was provided by an agreement between the assignee and a third party importer, sanctioned by the German Court, that prohibited imports into Germany without the consent of the assignee.

The European Court of Justice held that the arrangements under consideration fell under the general prohibition of article 85(1) and were not exempted under the provisions of article 85(3). In reaching this conclusion, the Court relied on a distinction between "open" and "closed" exclusive licences.[146] The Court indicated that open exclusive licences may, in certain circumstances, be permitted. It found that an open exclusive licence, whereby the parties agree that the owner will not grant other licences in respect of a territory or to compete itself with the licensee in that territory, could be an acceptable limit on competition in order to encourage licensees to accept the investment risks necessary to develop the market for a product. However, any exclusive licence that amounted to an absolute territorial restriction was held to be contrary to article 85(1) and could not be exempted from the application of the provision. The Court defined an absolute territorial protection as being a contract by which the parties propose to eliminate all competition from third parties, including parallel importers or licensees, from other territories.

The importance of the availability of parallel imports to maintain competition is made clear in this decision, although it is arguable that subsequent decisions of this Court display a growing acceptance of contract terms that prevent parallel imports on the basis of a need to encourage investment.[147] The arrangements in this case were, however, considered to be closed exclusive licences since they provided the German assignee with absolute territorial protection (i.e., territorial protection with respect to parallel importers as well as the licensor). This decision was an extension of earlier findings of the European Court of Justice holding absolute territorial protection to be contrary to the Treaty.[148]

The *Block Exemption for Patent Licenses*, released by the EC Commission in 1984 to provide licensing guidelines, follows the approach adopted by the Court in *Maize Seed*.[149] Article 1 of these guidelines lists a number of licensing provisions, including open exclusive licenses, which qualify for an automatic exemption from article 85 of the Treaty. However, article 3 of these guidelines sets out a "black list" of licensing provisions that preclude the application of the block exemption to a licensing agreement. The black-listed licensing provisions include, among others, measures designed to impede parallel trade within the common market. This has been superseded by a new-technology-transfer block exemption which came into force on April 1, 1996 and incorporates a similar approach with respect to patent and know-how licensing.[150] The new exemption also provides that any arrangement that might otherwise be exempted may still be challenged by the Commission where the licensee's market share in the licensed territory exceeds 40 percent.

Finally, it should be noted that in the EU, as in Canada and the United States, intellectual property rights do not sanction parallel trade restraints in situations where they are undertaken in connection with horizontal arrangements to restrain competition with respect to competing innovations. Such arrangements, where they have the requisite effects on trade between EU member states, are not protected from the application of article 85 of the EU Treaty on the basis that they represent invalid attempts to extend intellectual property rights.[151]

In sum, the experience of the European Union exemplifies the use of exhaustion to foster economic integration within a regional economic association. The relevant case decisions indicate that it has been applied in this way. However, the fact that exhaustion of IPRs in the EU is based on political and not necessarily economic rationales may limit the application of the European experience to other situations. The principle of exhaustion has resulted in a movement towards harmonization of EU member countries' IP laws, with the benefit that parallel importers cannot take advantage of the weak laws of one EU member country to undermine the rights of IP holders in other member countries. While exhaustion promotes a base-level of effective IPR protection among member countries, to some extent there is accommodation of differences in the scope of rights that may vary under each member's national laws.

POLICY OPTIONS: THE POSSIBLE
APPLICATION OF THE EXHAUSTION PRINCIPLE

THIS SECTION DRAWS UPON THE ECONOMIC AND LEGAL ANALYSIS of the previous two sections to provide a normative analysis of the implications of implementing the principle of exhaustion of intellectual property rights in international trade, with principal reference to patents and trademarks. The discussion has four main elements. First, we discuss some misplaced arguments that are sometimes made in support of applying the principle of exhaustion. Next we consider the practicality of two alternative policies of exhaustion: i) a unilateral policy of exhaustion and ii) a worldwide or global policy of exhaustion.[152] Finally, we consider the implications of adopting exhaustion within the North American free trade area.

MISPLACED ARGUMENTS IN FAVOR OF EXHAUSTION

TWO ARGUMENTS THAT MIGHT BE PUT FORWARD in support of adopting a general policy of exhaustion (either unilaterally, globally or among a certain group of countries) are that international market segmentation through IPRs: i) is intrinsically anticompetitive; and ii) represents a traditional barrier to trade that results in an inefficient use of society's productive resources. Each of these arguments is discussed below.

The Argument That Market Segmentation
Is Intrinsically Anticompetitive

It could be argued that countries should prohibit market segmentation (by applying the principle of exhaustion) on the ground that it is intrinsically anticompetitive.

However, this argument is misleading for two reasons. First, it omits that in most cases, the parties holding IPRs will be members or assignees of a common enterprise. In these instances, the effects of market brand are more analogous to intrabrand territorial market limitations than to an interbrand conspiracy or cartel. On the other hand, where intellectual property rights are used to reinforce what is essentially a cartel, involving firms that would otherwise be in competition with each other, the parties' conduct can potentially be attacked under competition law provisions relating to horizontal market restraints.[153]

Second, this argument fails to recognize that segmenting international markets through IPR licensing can, in many instances, have procompetitive effects. For example, as noted earlier, market segmentation through IPR licensing leads to a higher level of economic welfare when its purpose is to prevent free-riding. A practice that can have procompetitive effects as well as anticompetitive effects should not be considered strictly or intrinsically anticompetitive.

The Argument That Market Segmentation Through IPRs is Equivalent to a Traditional Barrier to Trade

It could also be argued that countries should prohibit international market segmentation because it has effects that are similar to tariff and traditional non-tariff barriers. This argument is also misleading. As mentioned previously, the application of IP-based import control rights, unlike traditional tariff and non-tariff barriers, is subject to the discretion of the rights holder. Consequently, the rights holder remains free to engage in unimpeded trade itself or to structure its licensing or other arrangements in a manner that prohibits its licensees from exporting products. Furthermore, the rights holder retains a clear incentive to locate its production activity where there are cost advantages or economies of scale to exploit. This is in contrast to the situation of traditional tariff and non-tariff barriers, which create an artificial incentive for production of commodities in countries that lack a comparative advantage in these goods. In this instance, society's productive resources are employed inefficiently and economic welfare loss occurs.

Despite this general conclusion, we caution that countries should try to avoid imposing *additional* border remedies for the enforcement of territorial rights under IP legislation, since these can have the effect of restraining efficient trans-border trade. The reason is that such remedies tend to be less discriminating and may not incorporate the same procedural safeguards as are generally present in respect of non-border remedies enforced by a rights holder.

THE ADOPTION OF A UNILATERAL POLICY OF EXHAUSTION

ON THE SURFACE, COUNTRIES MIGHT APPEAR TO HAVE AN INTEREST in implementing a unilateral exhaustion policy that eliminates the use of their national IP legislation to prevent parallel trade. Such a policy would facilitate importation of low-priced products from outside the country. At the same time, it would not directly affect cases where domestic prices are already low relative to foreign prices. There are, however, a number of situations in which low-priced imports occurring as a result of a general exhaustion principle would actually decrease the welfare of countries implementing such a policy. This might be the case, for example, where the relevant imports reflect free-riding on investments in local goodwill, product differentiation, or manufacturing. A key consideration regarding these situations is that, even though the application of unilateral exhaustion could lead to lower overall domestic prices, the benefits of these low prices could be more than offset by the loss of economic welfare associated with reduced levels of investment in local goodwill, product differentiation, or manufacturing. In our view, adopting a unilateral policy of exhaustion without recognition of the potential economic benefits of market segmentation would be unwise.

Furthermore, a unilateral policy of exhaustion with rules designed for allowing IPR-based market segmentation to capture only the situations with procompetitive effects (i.e., free-riding) would be impractical. First, as was argued earlier, it is difficult to distinguish precisely the cause of parallel imports; whether parallel imports are a response to price discrimination or free-riding opportunities. Therefore, product, industry or origin specific exemption rules designed to permit only welfare increasing market segmentation would be arbitrary at best. Second, the unilateral implementation of exhaustion would run the risk of eliciting adverse reactions, and potential retaliatory policies, on the part of other countries. The reason is that IPR owners located abroad would see their returns reduced in countries implementing exhaustion, without compensating advantages.[154]

Third, general rules for allowing the use of IPRs to prevent parallel imports could encourage market segmentation in circumstances where this is welfare reducing as well as where it is beneficial. For example, a general exception based on investments in goodwill could promote inefficient investments in goodwill basically for the purpose of facilitating price discrimination. Similarly, rules relaxing the application of exhaustion to IPRs being worked in Canada could lead to inefficient Canadian production of the relevant goods.[155] For these reasons, under this type of policy, one could not guarantee that economic welfare would be higher than it would be with the status quo.

A GLOBAL POLICY OF EXHAUSTION

UNDER A GLOBAL POLICY OF EXHAUSTION, the level of IP protection in a country would tend towards the standards of the country applying the lowest level of protection. As patent protection expired in the country with the lowest level of protection, new manufacturers in this country would begin to produce goods that could replace the original invention. Under exhaustion, these goods would then be free to flow into other countries where the IPR standards are higher and compete away the returns granted to the IPR holders of these countries. This would undermine the objectives of the IP laws in these countries.

Furthermore, a global policy of exhaustion would not recognize the need for manufacturers to prevent free-riding. In many countries such as Canada, contract law and competition law could help protect the manufacturers' ability to segment markets in procompetitive instances. In other countries, however, contract law and competition law would not be a sufficient substitute for IPR-based protection. The benefits of a global policy of exhaustion are limited unless there is some similarity in the standards of competition and contractual laws.

THE IMPLICATIONS OF ADOPTING EXHAUSTION WITHIN NORTH AMERICA

SUPPORT FOR A NAFTA EXHAUSTION PRINCIPLE has been expressed by various commentators.[156] To a large extent, this has been based on the view that the application of exhaustion within the EU has shown it to be a desirable policy within a free trade area. Thus, Knopf notes that the "European Community has been a laboratory for experimentation on this (exhaustion) and related issues for 30 years and the experiment has apparently succeeded."[157]

Caution should be exercised in basing North American policy toward exhaustion solely on the EU experience. As indicated in the section "Exhaustion of IPRs in the European Union," the use of exhaustion in the EU is based, in part, on the Union's social and political objectives to promote and ensure more open and harmonious relations between its member states. From this perspective, the removal of perceived private or government impediments to internal trade is considered to be beneficial in and of itself. To date, the goal of promoting market integration *per se* has been given less emphasis in the context of NAFTA. Nonetheless, as NAFTA evolves over time and the degree of integration among the participating countries deepens, it will become increasingly reasonable to consider the potential advantages of adopting exhaustion within the NAFTA area from an economic point of view.

In reflecting on the potential benefits and costs of adopting exhaustion in the context of NAFTA, it is important to keep in mind the incentives behind market segmentation and the economic effects of prohibiting segmentation in each case. First, adopting a policy of exhaustion will tend to prohibit certain practices that would have otherwise increased the economic welfare of the participating countries. Specifically, it will reduce the IPR holders' ability to prevent free-riding. However, as the analysis in this paper has spelled out, contractual provisions in licensing agreements could represent a good substitute for the IPR holders in this instance. In particular, the existence of appropriate legal regimes governing contracts in each of the participating countries could permit market segmentation for the purposes of preventing free-riding on investments.

Second, adopting a policy of exhaustion will reduce the opportunity for practices that would have otherwise decreased the economic welfare of the participating countries. Specifically, it would be increasingly difficult to use IPR licensing to facilitate collusion. Of course, strong competition laws should generally be available to capture any remaining opportunities for collusive behavior.

The remaining incentive behind the segmentation of markets is international price discrimination. A policy of exhaustion would limit the opportunity of IPR holders to practice international price discrimination. However, it is not clear that limiting international price discrimination would increase or decrease the economic welfare of the participating countries; the economic effects of third degree price discrimination are ambiguous. However, as Malueg and Schwartz indicate, if demand dispersion between the countries is small, eliminating price discrimination between them would likely increase their economic welfare. In assessing the effects of an adoption policy between countries, a key factor to consider is the relative differences in demand characteristics.

A further matter to consider when assessing the economic effects of exhaustion is the relative level of IPR protection in each participating country. As was mentioned earlier, under exhaustion, the effective standard of protection for IPRs will tend toward the lowest standard among the participating countries. Consequently, in practice, exhaustion is only viable where countries enforce similar standards of protection of IP rights.

This framework can be used to assess the effects of applying a policy of exhaustion covering Canada and the United States, and NAFTA more generally. In our view, it appears likely that applying exhaustion between Canada and the United States would have positive effects for the economic welfare of both countries. First, in general, Canada and the United States have similar well-developed contract law regimes that could be used by IPR holders to segment markets for the purpose of preventing free-riding. Second, both Canada and the United States have strong competition laws that could be used to address concerns about anticompetitive behavior between the countries and promote overall competitive behavior. Third, general demand characteristics in Canada and the United States are similar. As indicated in the review of empirical studies, differences in prices of IPR goods across the two countries are insignificant. Because demand characteristics are similar, applying exhaustion to prevent international price discrimination is likely to improve economic welfare in the two countries. Finally, IPR standards in the two countries are very similar. Under a bilateral policy of exhaustion, there would be little opportunity for the erosion of IPR standards in either country. In sum, a policy of exhaustion across Canada and the United States is likely to improve the economic well-being of both countries.

In terms of a NAFTA-wide policy of exhaustion, the inclusion of Mexico complicates the assessment of the economic effects. In this paper, it has not been possible to assess Mexican competition and IP laws relating to international market segmentation as was done with the laws of the United States and Canada. However, it seems reasonable to observe that Mexico has only recently updated its competition and IP legislation, and is still gaining experience in these areas. Furthermore, there is generally a large dispersion in demand between Mexico and the rest of North America. Consequently, it is less certain that a policy of exhaustion across North America (including Mexico) would eliminate welfare-reducing price discrimination.

CONCLUDING REMARKS

AN IMPORTANT ASPECT OF THE DEBATE ON IP, competition, and international trade is the use of intellectual property rights to segment international markets. To varying degrees, the IP statutes of most countries allow rights holders to exclude competing foreign versions of their products, even when such versions are legitimately made under the foreign countries' IP legislation.

In this paper, we have shown that the economic effects of market segmentation through IPRs are complex and difficult to predict. Determining the economic implications of the principle in any situation is likely to require careful consideration of a wide range of factors such as the private motivations for market segmentation, alternative means for segmenting markets, differences among the IP systems of countries adopting exhaustion, and the ability to unilaterally apply exhaustion. Given the range of issues to be considered in relation to exhaustion policy, determining whether it is likely to be in the interests of a particular country is difficult *a priori*. Moreover, the nature of the subject, unauthorized trade in IP products, makes empirical investigation inherently difficult.

With respect to trademarks, we would suggest that the specific circumstances in which trademark rights are available for preventing parallel imports into Canada should be examined carefully. Recent Canadian cases suggest that these circumstances may go beyond traditional "passing-off" concerns to include protecting investments in local goodwill or manufacturing. While this may be viewed as moving trademark law closer to the economic analysis of market segmentation to protect local investments, it raises concerns that inefficient local investments will be made merely to support profitable price discrimination.

With regard to exhaustion in NAFTA, as we have stressed throughout this paper, its implementation requires effective convergence of IP and competition policies. While this has broadly been achieved between Canada and the United States, we have not attempted to evaluate whether Mexico has also implemented similar standards for the protection of IP rights and for the application of competition law. Nonetheless, as competition and IP enforcement policies continue to converge, and economic integration in the NAFTA countries deepens naturally, at some point in the future consideration should be given to implementing a policy of exhaustion across the NAFTA zone. An alternative would be for Canada and the United States to commence exploring implementation of exhaustion between the two countries over a shorter time horizon.

NOTES

1   Consumer and Corporate Affairs Canada, *Intellectual Property and Canada's Commercial Interests: A Summary Report*, Ottawa, 1990.

2   See the North American Free Trade Agreement, chapter 15, "Competition and Antitrust, State Enterprises," and chapter 17, "Intellectual Property."

3   A key outcome of the Uruguay Round of Multilateral Trade Negotiations was the new Agreement on Trade-Related Intellectual Property Rights (TRIPs). In addition, while the Uruguay Round agreements do not contain general provisions relating to competition policy, a number of existing agreements do incorporate provisions dealing with anti-competitive practices by firms. These include the General Agreement on Trade in Services (the GATS), the Agreement on Trade-Related Intellectual Property Rights and the Agreement on Trade-Related Investment Measures (TRIMs). For a survey of relevant provisions, see Peter Lloyd and Gary Sampson, "Competition and Trade Policy: Identifying the Issues After the Uruguay Round," *The World Economy*, 18, 5 (September 1995): 681-705. In December 1996, the Singapore Ministerial Conference of WTO Members established a WTO Working Group to examine issues relating to the interaction between trade and competition policy.

4   The ability to exclude legitimately produced foreign versions (referred to as "grey goods" in the context of trademark goods), or parallel imports, should be distinguished from the exclusion of truly pirated versions (i.e., goods that are illegitimate even in their country of origin).

5   David A. Malueg and Marius Schwartz, "Parallel Imports, Demand Dispersion and International Price Discrimination," *Journal of International Economics*, 37, 3 (November 1994): 167-95; and Nancy T. Gallini, *An Economic Analysis of Grey Market Imports in Canada*, Ottawa: Bureau of Competition Policy, November 1992.

6   See Malueg and Schwartz, *id.*, and R. D. Anderson, P. J. Hughes, S. D. Khosla, and M. F. Ronayne, *Intellectual Property Rights and International Market Segmentation: Implications of the Exhaustion Principle*, Ottawa: Bureau of Competition Policy, Working Paper, October 1990.

7   Anderson et al., *supra*, note 6.

8   For further background on the EC policy of exhaustion of IPRs, see section entitled "Exhaustion of IPRs in the European Community," in this chapter.

9   See discussion in section entitled "Policy Options: The Possible Application of the Exhaustion Principle," in this chapter.

10   Restrictive Trade Practices Commission, *Report Concerning the Manufacture, Distribution and Sale of Drugs*, Ottawa: Queen's Printer, 1963.

11   See R. D. Anderson, S. D. Khosla and M. F. Ronayne, "The Competition Policy Treatment of Intellectual Property Rights in Canada: Retrospect and Prospect," in *Canadian Competition Law and Policy at the Centenary*, edited by R. S. Khemani and W. T. Stanbury, Halifax: Institute for Research on Public Policy, 1991, chapter 23, pp. 497-538, 508-9.

12   For a thoughtful analysis, see Howard P. Knopf, "Trade-Marks Law and the Free Flow of Goods in Canada," in *Trade-Marks Law of Canada*, edited by Gordon F. Henderson, Scarborough: Carswell, 1993, chapter 13, pp. 333-76.

13   See section entitled "Private Incentives for International Market Segmentation and their Welfare Implications," in this chapter.

14 *United States v. Pilkington plc and Pilkington Holdings Inc.* (CCH 1994-2 Trade Cases 70,842).

15 Of course, the substitutability of contractual for IPR-based territorial restraints is limited by certain other factors, such as the non-enforceability, in general, of contractual rights against third parties (i.e., the doctrine of privity of contract). For further discussion, see section entitled "The Substitutability of Contracts and IPRs for Segmenting International Markets," in this chapter.

16 In particular, this section draws on the analysis of Gallini, *supra*, note 5; Malueg and Schwartz, *supra*, note 5; and Anderson et al., *supra*, note 6. P. Rey and R. Winter, "Exclusivity Restrictions and Intellectual Property," in this volume, also discuss some of these issues in relation to exclusive territories.

17 Third-degree price discrimination involves the charging of differing prices to different groups of consumers based on their exogenous characteristics. For a discussion of third-degree price discrimination, see Hal R. Varian, "Price Discrimination," in *The Handbook of Industrial Organization*, edited by Richard Schmalensee and Robert Willig Amsterdam: North Holland, 1989, chapter 10, pp. 617-24.

18 See Varian, *id.*

19 It should be noted, however, that patents (and copyrights) do not always involve the creation of significant market power, in that the product space covered by a particular IP right is likely to be smaller than a relevant antitrust market. See J. Paul McGrath, "Patent Licensing: A Fresh Look at Antitrust Principles in a Changing Economic Environment," *Patent and Trademark Review*, 82, 9 (September 1984): 355-65.

20 In practice, firms typically require only a limited degree of market power to engage in price discrimination. See Severin Borenstein, "Selling Costs and Switching Costs: Explaining Retail Gasoline Margins," *Rand Journal of Economics*, 22 (Autumn 1991): 354-69.

21 See Varian, *supra*, note 17. In the context of international market segmentation, total welfare is measured as the sum of consumers' surplus and profit across all markets. This measure may be referred to as "global" welfare.

22 See Jerry Hausman and Jeffrey MacKie-Mason, "Price Discrimination and Patent Policy," *Rand Journal of Economics*, 19 (Summer 1988): 253-65. The authors present a model in which a monopolist, with non-increasing marginal cost, supplies output to two separate and distinct markets. In their examples, the monopolist, when constrained to setting a uniform price, serves only the high demand market. In contrast, when the monopolist is free to discriminate, it serves both markets and does not raise the price in the high demand market.

23 Malueg and Schwartz, *supra*, note 5.

24 When there is little difference between the elasticities of demand across countries, under uniform pricing the monopolist sets a price for which all countries purchase the product (all markets are served). Therefore, in this case, and given linear demands, total output does not increase with discrimination (a necessary condition for total welfare to improve under discrimination) so that total welfare must be higher with uniform pricing.

25 Malueg and Schwartz, *supra*, note 5, identify an additional impact on welfare under uniform pricing which differentiates their results from those of Hausman and MacKie-Mason, *supra*, note 22. They point out that, when there are more than two markets, as low-priced markets are dropped, the monopolist reoptimizes its uniform

price upwards providing a further fall in output. Accordingly, "increased dispersion eventually makes uniform pricing inferior to discrimination not because of the impact effect of dropping markets, but because dropping markets leads the monopolist to reoptimize and raise price."

26   Malueg and Schwartz point out that "Interestingly, the bulk of the welfare gain is achieved with a very small number of groups. Thus, one could imagine dividing countries into a few blocks based on per capita income – e.g., low, middle and high – and allowing discrimination only between blocks." Malueg and Schwartz, *supra*, note 5.

27   Another possible incentive for international market segmentation that can occur independent of the free-riding hypothesis, namely the prevention of "destructive competition," is noted in Gallini, *supra*, note 5. In particular, suppose an IPR owner must charge a fixed fee to license its IPR. Suppose it also wishes to license to different distributors in different countries for reasons similar to those listed above. Once a licensee has incurred the (sunk) cost of the fixed license fee, it will have an incentive to sell some of its goods in the foreign countries at prices below the foreign distributors' prices. This will reduce the return to the foreign distributors, potentially to the point where they cannot even cover the fixed licensing fee. International market segmentation may help to prevent this from occurring.

28   Free-riding may actually occur in both directions. For instance, if a domestic distributor and a foreign distributor face similar market conditions and are investing in promotional activity to the same degree, each distributor may try to sell some of its products in the other distributor's territory. In this instance, each distributor would not capture all the rents of its own investments and would therefore reduce its promotional activity.

29   See section entitled "Competition Policy and the Treatment of Contractual Restraints on International Trade in the United States and Canada," in this chapter, for a discussion of cases in which international market allocation arrangements involving patent licenses have been treated as conspiracies in restraint of trade.

30   Gallini suggests another way in which exclusive territories might facilitate tacit collusion by softening competition. Gallini, *supra*, note 5.

31   For example, see R. C. Marston, "Pricing to Market in Japanese Manufacturing," *Journal of International Economics*, 29 (1990): 217-36; or K. Kasa, "Adjustment Costs and Pricing to Market: Theory and Evidence," *Journal of International Economics*, 32 (1992): 1-30.

32   See D. G. Tarr, "An Economic Analysis of Gray Market Imports," Federal Trade Commission, September 1985.

33   See J. S. Chard and C. J. Mellor, "Intellectual Property Rights and Parallel Imports," *World Economy*, 12 (1989): 69-83.

34   See, e.g., M. M. Knetter, "Price Discrimination by U.S. and German Exporters," *American Economic Review*, 79 (1989): 198-210.

35   J. C. Hilke, "Free Trading or free-riding: An Examination of the Theories and Available Empirical Evidence on Gray Market Imports," *World Competition*, 79 (1988): 244-50.

36   See Steven Globerman, *Canada's Interest in Two Way Exhaustion of Intellectual Property Rights in Trade with the United States*, Ottawa: Consumer and Corporate Affairs Canada, 1987, p. 10.

37   J. Kushner and I. Masse, "Patents as a Basis for International Price Discrimination," *Antitrust Bulletin*, 21, 4 (Winter 1976): 639-56.

38　Ake Blomqvist and Chin Lim, *Copyright, Competition and Canadian Culture: The Impact of Alternative Copyright Provisions on the Book Publishing and Sound Recording Industries*, Ottawa: Consumer and Corporate Affairs Canada, 1981.

39　Ake Blomqvist and Chin Lim, *Copyright Act Import Provisions: Effects on the Book and Record Trades*, Interdepartmental Committee on Copyright Law Revision, mimeo, June 1979, Part B, p. 20.

40　See, e.g., Economic Council of Canada, *Report on Intellectual and Industrial Property* Ottawa: Information Canada, 1971.

41　Anderson et al., *supra*, note 6.

42　The scope for an intellectual property holder to engage in trade to minimize costs and therefore capture available gains from trade was also considered in Demaret, *Patents, Territorial Restrictions and EEC Law*, Munich: Max-Planck Institute for Foreign and International Patent, Copyright and Competition Law, 1978, p. 835. In this regard, Demaret states:

> When the cost of production is lower in one territory than in another or when economies of scale require that production be concentrated in a single plant, one may expect the patentee to set up manufacturing facilities in only one territory . . . and export to other territories . . . . If, on the other hand, shipment costs and tariff duties make exports unprofitable, the patentee's interest is to build plants in both territories . . . .

43　See also Anderson et al., *supra*, note 6. For background, see Peter C. Ward, *"The Tariff Act of 1930*, Section 337: An Antitrust Ugly Duckling," *Antitrust Bulletin*, XXVII, 2 (Summer 1982): 355-88.

44　For a more detailed discussion of the use of section 337 as a trade barrier and the economic implications of this barrier, see M. Schwartz, "Patent Protection Through Discriminatory Exclusion of Imports," *Review of Industrial Organization*, 6 (1991): 231-46.

45　In Canada, U.K. and Commonwealth cases to this effect would presumably apply. See section entitled "Trademarks," in this chapter. In the U.S. patent case of *Dickerson v. Tinling*, 84 F. 192 (8th Cir. 1897), imports of U.S. goods sold abroad, either by a patentee subject to restrictions prohibiting their subsequent sale in the United States or by a territorially restricted licensee, to a purchaser with notice of these restrictions were held to infringe U.S. product patents. The Court noted that notice to the purchaser could be "immediate or remote," which implies that express notice is not required to prevent the third-party purchaser from importing the patent-embodying goods.

46　The legal doctrine applied here is privity of contract where only parties to a contract may sue on it with certain exceptions.

47　While Mexican law and jurisprudence is not canvassed here, it should be noted that Mexican law conforms to chapter 17 of NAFTA, which requires the NAFTA parties to adhere to basic levels of IPR protection.

48　The above-noted subject matter of a patent describes acceptable U.S. subject matter. U.S. *Patent Act*, 35 U.S.C. §101. In Canada, acceptable subject matter also includes an "art." *Patent Act*, R.S.C. c. P-4, s. 2. Pursuant to the Paris Convention for the Protection of Industrial Property as last revised at Stockholm (1967), article 4bis recognizes that a patent granted in one country is independent of a patent for the same invention in another country.

49 Canada *Patent Act*, R.S.C. P-4, s. 44, and 35 U.S.C. 154, as am.; article 33 of TRIPs mandates a period of 20 years from the date of filing a patent application.

50 For a discussion, see F. M. Scherer and David Ross, *Industrial Market Structure and Economic Performance*, Chicago: Rand-McNally, 1984, 2nd ed., pp. 440-50.

51 Harold G. Fox, *Canadian Patent Law & Practice*, Toronto: The Carswell Company Ltd., 1969, 4th ed., p. 6.

52 (1883), 25 Ch. D. 1 (C.A.). See also David Gladwell, "The Exhaustion of Intellectual Property Rights," *European Intellectual Property Review*, 12 (1986): 367-68.

53 *Id.* at 8.

54 Kenya: *Beecham Group v. International Products*, [1968] R.P.C. 129 (H.C.), Hong Kong: *Beecham Group v. Shewan Tomes* (Traders), [1968] R.P.C. 268, Singapore: *Sime Darby Singapore v. Beecham Group*, [1968] 2 M.L.J. 161, as discussed in W. A. Rothnie, *Parallel Imports*, London: Sweet & Maxwell, 1993, pp. 134 *et seq.*

55 (1871), 5 Ch. App. 239. For a discussion of this case, see also Harold G. Fox, *supra*, note 51, p. 385.

56 The Court observed that, had the patentee assigned his U.K. patent to another party but continued to manufacture the product abroad, the product could not be sold in the United Kingdom in violation of the assignee's rights. *Id.* at 245. For a discussion of this case, see Gladwell, *supra*, note 52, pp. 367-68.

57 Under sections 65(a) and (b) and 66 of the *Patent Act*.

58 *Patent Act*, section 66(1)(a). The cases also indicate that section 67 is applicable even where the working of patented inventions in Canada on a commercial basis is more costly than serving the Canadian market from foreign sources. For discussion, see Fox, *supra*, note 51, p. 547.

59 The leading Canadian case in this regard is *Hatton et al. v. Copeland-Chatterson Co.* (1906), 37 S.C.R. 651. It should be noted that the ability for territorial restraints to run with patented products when notified to successive buyers is an exception to the general principle that the conditions attached by producers to the resale of their products may be binding only in regard to the first purchaser of these products. See *Taddy & Co. v. Sterious & Co.*, [1904] 1 Ch. 358 and *McGruther v. Pitcher*, [1904] 2 Ch. 306.

60 *Keeler v. Standard Folding Bed Company*, 157 U.S. 659 (U.S.S.C. 1895).

61 *Holiday v. Matheson*, 24 F. 185 (S.D.N.Y. 1885) and *Dickerson v. Matheson*, 57 F. 524 (2nd Cir. 1893).

62 See the discussion *infra* regarding *Mallinckrodt Inc. v. Mediport, Inc.*, 976 F. 2d 700 (1992) at 708 in which the 9th Circuit overturned the District Court, 15 U.S.P.Q. (2d) 1113 (1990), which had held that no condition or restriction may be placed upon the resale of a patented article, and at 704*ff* regarding patent misuse.

63 *Dickerson v. Matheson, supra*, note 61.

64 *Dickerson v. Tinling*, 84 F. 192 (8th Cir. 1897). For a discussion of these issues see Peter D. Rosenberg, *Patent Law Fundamentals*, New York: Clark Boardman, 1980, 2nd ed., pp. 18-25. The Court held that the notice could be "immediate or remote" and that the patent monopoly would remain intact, which at least one commentator has suggested as meaning a) that the notice need not be by contract but could be by any means, and b) that liability rested as if it was a patent infringement and was not contractual in nature. See also W. A. Rothnie, *supra*, note 54, at pp. 174-75.

65 *United States v. Westinghouse Elec. Corp.*, 471 F. Supp. 532 (N.D. Cal. 1978), affirmed 648 F.2d 642 (9th Cir. 1981).

66 The 1988 legislation amended section 271 to provide that anyone who, "without authority imports into the United States or sells or uses in the United States a product which is made by a process patented in the United States shall be liable as an infringer . . ." See Title IX of the *Omnibus Trade and Competitiveness Act* of 1988, P.L. 100-48.

67 For example, see *Cummer-Graham Co. v. Straight Side Basket Corp.*, 1944-45 U.S. Trade Cases (CCH) ¶57,241 (F. 2d 1944); cert. denied 65 S. Ct. 60. Because they were not protected as of right under the U.S. *Patent Code*, restraints of such imports were subject to the U.S. antitrust laws. See Barry E. Hawk, *United States, Common Market and International Antitrust: A Comparative Guide*, vol. I, Frederick, MD: Aspen Law and Business, 1996, pp. 383-84.

68 35 U.S.C. § 261. Section 261 of the U.S. *Patent Code* expressly grants the patentee, his assigns or legal representatives the power to transfer exclusive rights under a patent "to the whole or any specified part of the United States."

69 484 F.2d 407 (6th Cir. 1973) cert. denied 415 U.S. 917 (1974). See also *Brownell v. Ketcham Wire Mfg. Co.*, 211 F.2d 121 (9th Cir. 1954).

70 86 F.2d 267 (6th Cir. 1936). The case involved the grant of an exclusive licence for the entire United States, which the Court held to be within the patent holder's rights and not contrary to the antitrust laws. The use of section 261 to support the blanket validation of import bans under antitrust law has been criticized for not considering the differences in market factors between the domestic and foreign context, such as differences in barriers to entry and the fact that market effects of section 261 are mitigated by the "first sale" rule in the United States which exhausts the ability to impose territorial restrictions within the United States after the first sale of the goods. It has also been criticized as not addressing economic considerations of the contractual practices. Hawk, *supra*, note 67, vol. I, pp. 392-93, and Anderson et al., *supra*, note 6.

71 7 F.Cas. 946 (N.D.N.Y. 1874).

72 See, in this regard, Hawk, *supra*, note 67, vol. I, p. 395.

73 In the United States, marks used to distinguish services are referred to specifically as service marks. 15 U.S.C § 1127 as am.

74 Canadian trademark owners can invoke the tort of passing-off; U.S. trademark owners can pursue an action for unfair competition involving trademark infringement.

75 Registration also provides constructive notice of the person's ownership of the mark nationwide and details of the registrant's rights with respect to the use of the mark. W. C. Holmes, *Intellectual Property and Antitrust Law,* New York: Clark, Boardman, Callaghan, 1995, at § 3.02. In Canada, statutory infringement actions take place under the federal *Trade Marks Act*, R.S.C. T-13. In the United States, such action may take place for federally registered trademarks under the *Lanham Act*, which also protects unregistered marks that are used in interstate commerce (15 U.S.C. §§ 1114 and 1125(a), respectively).

76 Article 18, TRIPs. Indefinite renewal has been provided for in the Canadian *Patent Act*, R.S.C. T-13, and in the U.S., 15 U.S.C. §§ 1058(a), 1059 as am.

77 R.S.C., c. T-13.

78 W. L. Hayhurst, "Importation of Gray Goods into Canada," *Intellectual Property Journal*, 1985.

79 *Consumers Distributing Co. v. Seiko Time Canada Ltd.* (1984), 1 C.P.R. (3d) 1.

80 The right to exclusive use of a registered trademark is found in section 19 of the Act. Sections 20 and 7 of the Act describe the conditions under which that exclusive right

is violated by a competitor. Section 20 provides that a person or firm "not entitled to its use" is found to infringe the said trademark if he "sells, distributes or advertises wares or services in association with a confusing trademark." Section 7 prohibits "unfair competition," and in particular subsection (e) provides that "no person shall adopt any business practice contrary to honest industrial or commercial usage in Canada." However, subsection (e) has been held unconstitutional. *Bosquet v. Barmish Inc.* (1993), 46 C.P.R. (3d) 510 (Federal C.A.). See discussion *infra*, *Mattel Canada Inc. v. GTS Acquisitions Ltd.*, [1990] 1 F.C. 462 (T.D.) and *H.J. Heinz of Canada v. Edan Food Sales.*(1991), 35 C.P.R. (3d) (F.C.T.D.).

81 Subsection 50(3).

82 Gallini, *supra*, note 5, p. 73.

83 This would not likely amount to infringement under section 20, as there is no "confusing mark" - the owner has marketed these goods directly himself. For reasons, see Gallini, *id.* p. 8, note 12 and Gordon F. Henderson, *Trade-Marks Law of Canada* Thomson: Scarborough, 1993, p. 171.

84 [1968] 2 Ex. C.R. 137 and (1971), 1 C.P.R. (2d) 177 (Ex. Ct.), rev'd [1973] F.C. 360 (C.A.) which was aff'd [1976] 1 S.C.R. 527.

85 [1990] 1 F.C. 462 (T.D.). Mattel held both of the Canadian trademark rights and was the exclusive distributor in Canada of Nintendo videogames which GTS was importing from the United States without permission from Mattel. The Court held that the products were identical but that deception of the public was not a deciding factor compared to the unfair competition element of GTS's free-riding off Mattel's goodwill in terms of its marketing efforts.

86 *Smith & Nephew Inc. v. Glen Oak Inc. et al.* (June 4, 1996), A-683-94 (Federal Court of Appeal). The Supreme Court declared section 7(e) to be unconstitutional in *McDonald v. Vapour Canada Ltd.* (1976), 22 C.P.R. (2d) 1, [1977] 2 S.C.R. 134.

87 The Court also noted that a difference in the quality and character of the parallel importers' product from that of the Canadian licensee was an issue to be taken up with the trademark owner who controls the quality and characteristics of the product, and did not amount to a justification to exclude the importation of these goods. Indeed, in *Smith & Nephew*, the Court mentions *H.J. Heinz of Canada v. Edan Food Sales* as an example of a case that, while perhaps open to question in its reasons, turned on the fact that a Canadian subsidiary owned the Canadian trademark. In that case, the Canadian trademark owner was granted an injunction to prevent parallel imports of ketchup being sourced from its U.S. parent. The injunction granted in the *Heinz* decision was at least partially justified by the Court on the basis of economic factors such as the Canadian subsidiary's large investment in Canada and the fact that Canadian employment would suffer if Heinz Canada was forced to seek out cheaper tomatoes from foreign sources. (1991), 35 C.P.R. (3d) 213 (F.C.T.D.).

88 Section 53.1(7).

89 Except in limited circumstances. Section 53.3.

90 Gallini, *supra*, note 5, p. 73.

91 15 U.S.C. § 1114.

92 Section 43(a) of the *Lanham Act* authorizes civil action by registered or unregistered trademark owners where there is false advertising or false representations of origin concerning a product. Section 43(b) prohibits the importation of such products. 15 U.S.C. § 1124.

93 19 U.S.C. § 526. This was enacted to protect the rights of U.S. trademark holders from genuine goods produced then imported under a valid foreign trademark, in response to the Second Circuit Court decision in *Bourjois v. Katzel* 275 F. 539 (2d Cir. 1921) which held at p. 543 that "If the goods sold are the genuine goods covered by the trademark, the rights of the owner of the trademark are not infringed."

94 19 C.F.R. 133.21(C)(1)-(2). See also *Yamaha Corp. of America v. ABC International Traders* 745 F. Supp 1938 (C.D. Cal. 1988) in which the Court held that the importation of genuine grey market goods did not violate s. 526 of the *Tariff Act of 1930* nor did it violate s. 42 of the *Lanham Act*, finding in this case a parent-subsidiary relationship between the domestic and foreign trademark owners.

95 486 U.S. 281 (1988).

96 19 U.S.C. § 1337(a). See Hawk, *supra*, note 67, vol. I, p. 384. Section 337 actions may proceed concurrently with infringement proceedings in a U.S. court, in respect of the same goods, and without *res judicata* or collateral estoppel effect. See W. L. Hayhurst "Some Background to Intellectual Property Rights in Relation to Trade Between the United States and Canada," *Patent and Trademark Institute of Canada Bulletin*, 4, 2 (May 1988): 204.

97 See Andrew S. Newman, "The Amendments to Section 337: Increased Protection for Intellectual Property Rights," *Law & Policy in International Business*, 20 (1989): 572.

98 See Hawk, *supra*, note 67, vol. I, p. 452.1.

99 This is reflected in the proportion of section 337 actions that involved intellectual property rights. In this regard, a Government Accounting Office study noted that between 1974 and 1986, 95 percent of section 337 investigations involved IPRs. See Newman, *supra*, note 97, p. 572.

100 See Hayhurst, *supra*, note 78.

101 See, generally, Newman, *supra*, note 97.

102 See Ronald A. Brand, "Private Parties and GATT Dispute Resolution: Implications of the Panel Report on Section 337 of the U.S. *Tariff Act of 1930*," *Journal of World Trade*, 24, 3 (June 1990): 5-30. See also "GATT's New Hot Topic: Rules of Origin," *Canadian Competition Policy Record*, 10, 4 (December 1989): 36-39. It should be noted that changes to the U.S. patent enforcement system have been proposed by the U.S. trade representative in response to the GATT panel's finding. See Bureau of National Affairs Inc., "USTR Proposes Changes to Patent Enforcement System Under S.337," *World Intellectual Property Report*, 4, 3 (March 1990): 57.

103 BNA's *Patent, Trademark and Copyright Journal*, 49, December 8, 1994, pp. 129-30.

104 It is worth noting that the European Union, through its internal exhaustion principle, similarly provides importation disadvantages for foreign owners trying to import into the EU.

105 Canada is a signatory to this treaty.

106 See Knopf, *supra*, note 12, at p. 340 note 15.

107 *Integrated Circuit Topography Act*, R.S.C. I-14.6, section 11(1).

108 See U.S. Department of Justice and Federal Trade Commission, *Antitrust Guidelines for the Licensing of Intellectual Property*, April 6, 1995. For a useful exposition, see Richard J. Gilbert, "The 1995 Antitrust Guidelines for the Licensing of Intellectual Property: New Signposts for the Intersection of Intellectual Property and the Antitrust Laws," paper prepared for the Spring meeting of the American Bar Association Section of Antitrust Law, April 6, 1995.

109 Arguably, the policy swing was, to some extent, rhetorical rather than substantive. See Willard K. Tom, Special Assistant to the Assistant Attorney-General, U.S. Department of Justice, "Antitrust and Intellectual Property," paper prepared for Copyright in Transition: Enforcement, Fair Dealing and Digital Developments, Ottawa, Ontario, October 13, 1994.

110 See R. D. Anderson, S. D. Khosla, and M. F. Ronayne, "The Competition Policy Treatment of Intellectual Property Rights in Canada: Retrospect and Prospect," in *Canadian Competition Law and Policy at the Centenary*, edited by R. S. Khemani and W. T. Stanbury, Halifax: Institute for Research on Public Policy, 1991, chapter 23, pp. 497-538, 537.

111 15 U.S.C. §§ 1 and 2. Section 1 prohibits agreements which unreasonably restrict trade such as territorial agreements while section 2 prohibits monopolization over a particular product or service.

112 See William C. Holmes, *Intellectual Property and Antitrust Law*, New York: Clark, Boardman, Callaghan, 1995 pp. 17-5.

113 *Brownell v. Ketcham Wire and Mfg. Co.*, 211 F. 2d 121 (9th Cir. 1954).

114 For example, the parties in *United States v. Crown Zellerbach Corp.*, 141 F. Supp. 118 (N.D. Ill. 1956) dominated the market for hand towel dispensers and were found to have conspired, contrary to section 1 of the *Sherman Act*, to horizontally allocate territories using patent license restrictions. See also e.g. *United States v. National Lead Co.*, 332 U.S. 319 (1947). An excellent discussion is provided in George L. Priest, "Cartels and Patent Licence Arrangements," *The Journal of Law and Economics*, 2 (October 1977) : 309-77.

115 976 F. 2d 700. The Court reviews past jurisprudence on the issue in some detail.

116 *Id.*, at 708. The Court set out the proper test to determine the validity of a restriction:

> "Should the restriction be found to be reasonably within the patent grant, i.e., that it relates to subject matter within the scope of the patent claims, that ends the inquiry. However, should such inquiry lead to the conclusion that there are anticompetitive effects extending beyond the patentee's statutory right to exclude, these effects do not automatically impeach the restriction. Anticompetitive effects that are not *per se* violations of law are reviewed in accordance with the rule of reason. Patent owners should not be in a worse position, by virtue of the patent right to exclude, than owners of other property used in trade."

117 The IP *Guidelines* focus on technology transfer and innovation issues, and are specifically applicable to the licensing of patents, copyrights, trade secrets, and know-how. They do not apply to trademarks that involve product differentiation issues, although they indicate that treatment of trademarks would be broadly similar.

118 *Id.*, at p. 16.

119 388 U.S. 365.

120 433 U.S. 36.

121 In this regard, the Court stated: "Economists have identified a number of ways in which manufacturers can use such restrictions . . . to compete more effectively against other manufacturers . . . there is substantial scholarly and judicial authority supporting their economic utility. There is relatively little authority to the contrary." 1977-1 Trade Cases (CCH) ¶ 61,488, pp. 71,900-901. Vertical export restraints have been found to be reasonable to protect a manufacturer's goodwill by controlling distribution in foreign markets by allowing it to respond to language differences, variations of med-

ical practice, and differences in government regulations. *Bruce Drug, Inc. v. Hollister Inc.*, 1982-2 Trade Cases (CCH) ¶ 64,941, pp. 72,790-791. A vertical import restriction was similarly upheld on the basis of a rule of reason analysis in the 1981 case of *Copy-Data Systems, Inc. v. Toshiba America, Inc.* 1981-2 Trade Cases (CCH) ¶ 64,343 (CA-2:1981). It should be noted, however, that the case of *Eiberger v. Sony Corp. of America*, 1980-2 Trade Cases (CCH) ¶ 63,328 (CA-2:1980) indicates that harm to intrabrand competition without evidence of benefits to interbrand competition may lead to a vertical restriction being found illegal.

122   The International Guidelines incorporate the "effects" doctrine set out by the Supreme Court in *Hartford Fire Insurance v. California*, 113 S. Ct. 2891 at 2909 (1993), which stated that the *Sherman Act* would apply to foreign anticompetitive conduct that was meant to and did in fact produce a "substantial effect" in the United States. Parallel imports will, by definition, affect the U.S. domestic market directly and will therefore satisfy the intent part of this test, although whether they produce the requisite substantial effects depends on the facts of each case.

123   *United States v. Pilkington plc and Pilkington Holdings Inc.* (CCH 1994-2 Trade Cases ¶ 70,842).

124   In this regard, Henderson states: "The applicable industrial property statute creates, at the highest, property status for industrial property ... they cannot elevate such property to the high level of exemptions from specific anti-competitive regulation." See Gordon F. Henderson, Q.C., "The Control of Abuse of Intellectual Property Rights," *Patent and Trademark Institute of Canada Bulletin*, series 8, vol. 13, April 1982, p. 835.

125   Henderson, *id.*, p. 835, states:

> If the contract of sale [of a patented product] imposes conditions upon the purchaser either in the contract or by notice, ... the Combines [*Competition Act*] considerations arise from the contract or notice; the fact that the contract relates to a patent is neutral. Similarly, where a patentee grants a licence and imposes limitations and conditions, the limitations and conditions are incidents of the contractual right rather than the patent. Again, the patent is neutral.

126   R.S.C., c. C-34, as am.

127   However, the requirement that remedies taken under this section may not violate Canada's international obligations with respect to the protection of intellectual property may exclude the possible use of this provision.

128   59 C.P.R. (3d) 257 (Ont. Ct. Gen. Div.). This decision is currently under appeal.

129   *Canada (Director of Investigation and Research) v. The NutraSweet Co.* (1990), 32 C.P.R. (3d) 1 (Comp. Trib.).

130   *Id.* at p. 52.

131   *Canada (Director of Investigation and Research) v. Chrysler Canada Ltd.* (1989), 27 C.P.R. (3d) 1 (Comp. Trib.).

132   "The Court's reasoning in *E.M.I. v. CBS*, [1976] E.C.R. 811 suggests that member state patents may be exercised to prevent infringing imports from non-community countries." Barry E. Hawk, *United States, Common Market and International Antitrust: A Comparative Guide*, vol. II, Frederick, MD: Aspen Law and Business, 1996, p. 465.

133   For general background on the exhaustion doctrine in the EU, see Hawk, *ibid.*, p. 433. Regarding the basis of the doctrine, Hawk (p. 464.1), states: "Although the Court judgments are not entirely consistent, it appears that consent of the patentee is the predominant basis of the patent exhaustion doctrine."

134 Weatherill and Beaumont, *EC Law*, London: Penguin, 1993, p. 727, interpreting *Procureur du Roi v. Benoit et Dassonville*, [1974] E.C.R. 837.

135 Articles 59 and 60 provide for the free movement of services. Although there is no counterpart to article 36, in *Coditel S.A. v. Cinévog Films*, [1980] E.C.R. 881 ("Coditel I"), the ECJ found that similar freedom of movement principles apply to services by analogy. See Hawk, *supra*, note 132, vol. II, p. 579.

136 [1974] E.C.R. 1147.

137 Hawk, *supra*, note 132, vol. II, p. 460.1.

138 [1985] E.C.R. 2281.

139 Hawk, *supra*, note 132, vol. II, p. 464.

140 [1974] 2 C.M.L.R. 480.

141 [1978] 3 C.M.L.R. 217. See Weatherill and Beaumont, *supra*, note 134, p. 741.

142 Such as the 1975 Convention for a Community Patent (still not ratified in many countries), which provides for the granting of a community-wide patent. In the area of trademarks there is similarly the Commission Directive 89/104 which continues to be debated. See *ibid.*, at 750 *et seq.*

143 *Id.* It should be noted that articles 30-36, 59-60 and 86 may also be relevant to contractual restraints of parallel trade.

144 *Nungesser v. Commission*, [1982] E.C.R. 2015.

145 While this case did not directly involve patent rights, the Court's reasoning appears to be relevant to patent licenses. In this regard, see Brian Cheffins, "Exclusive Territorial Rights in Patent Licenses and article 85 of the EEC Treaty: An Evaluation of Recent Developments in the Law," *Boston College International and Competition Law Review*, 10 (1987): 89-91; and Hawk *supra*, note 132, vol. II, p. 472.3.

146 For a definition of open and closed licences see *Commission (EEC), Twelfth Report on Competition Policy*, ¶ 44, (1983).

147 See, e.g., *Coditel S.A. v. Cinévog Films SA (No.2)*, [1982] E.C.R. 3361, and *Pronuptia de Paris GmbH v. Pronuptia de Paris Irmgard Schillgalis*, [1986] E.C.R. 353.

148 See *Nungesser v. Commission*, *supra*, note 144, and the cases cited therein.

149 *Commission Regulation (EEC) 2349/84.*

150 C(95) 2353.

151 *Nungesser v. Commission*, *supra*, note 144, in which the E.C.J. held that justification under article 36 does not preclude application of article 85.

152 A unilateral policy of exhaustion refers to a policy in which a country, independent of the policies of other countries, prohibits domestic IPR holders from restricting legitimately produced parallel imports into the country through their IPRs. A global policy of exhaustion refers to an international agreement amongst all countries to prohibit market segmentation through IPRs.

153 Recall the discussion of the competition policy treatment of contractual restraints on international trade, *supra*.

154 This would be analogous to the extensive concerns voiced by U.S. IPR owners regarding the previous Canadian policy of compulsory licensing for the manufacture or importation of patented drugs. For a discussion, see the paper by McFetridge, in this volume.

155 Related concerns are expressed in Knopf, *supra*, note 12, who states:

> "Even if some leeway with respect to exhaustion is left at the end of the day, businesses will doubtless rearrange their affairs to come within the narrower rules (i.e.,

by assigning trade-marks to their subsidiaries and creating slight differences in the "Canadian" product) and hence attempt to achieve market segmentation" (p. 366).

156   See, e.g., Anderson, Khosla and Ronayne, *supra*, note 11 at pp. 536-37, and Knopf, *supra*, note 12 at pp. 338-40; Globerman, *supra*, note 36 and Malueg and Schwartz, *supra*, note 5, could also be viewed as supporting consideration of a separate NAFTA exhaustion principle in that it demonstrates that the application of exhaustion within trading blocks may yield different results than among trading blocks.

157   Knopf, *id.*, p. 337.

ACKNOWLEDGEMENTS

HELPFUL COMMENTS BY MARIUS SCHWARTZ, and past discussions and collaboration with Patrick Hughes, Nancy Gallini and Dev Khosla, are gratefully acknowledged. The views expressed belong to the authors and do not necessarily reflect those of any organizations with which they are affiliated.

Comment

Marius Schwartz
U.S. Council of Economic Advisers, and
Georgetown University

BOTH THE ECONOMIC AND LEGAL TREATMENTS OF THIS PAPER provide a useful review and a thoughtful, balanced discussion. The paper resists making simple-minded characterizations such as "any restrictions on parallel imports are tantamount to violating free trade," a trap I have heard even good economists fall into.

The paper identifies the relevant economic trade-offs from restricting parallel imports. These tradeoffs depend on what is driving the parallel imports – free-rider behaviour or arbitrage of international price discrimination (whether of systematic price discrimination or of transitory price differences). In fact, both free-rider behaviour and international price discrimination play a role. For the types of goods in which parallel imports are concentrated – name-brand consumer goods like cameras, electronics, perfumes, luxury automobiles, and pharmaceuticals – there is a pretty strong free-rideable advertising and marketing component. Also interesting is the type of outlet where parallel imports are found – discounters – which suggests that one purpose of the parallel imports is to circumvent restrictions imposed by licensors or producers in their distribution chain. They may want to sell only through full service stores, so parallel imports are a way to undermine that and get the product into the hands of discounters, again suggesting a free-rider component. This point could have been developed further in the authors' paper.

Another reason Anderson et al. give to explain why parallel imports may be undesirable is that they cause consumer confusion. One should not exaggerate this point, but it is interesting. Products do get tailored to consumer tastes of different countries. There is an amusing story of Cabbage Patch dolls that were imported into the United States from Mexico. The manufacturer complained that consumers had the right to have the dolls' birth certificates in English, rather than in Spanish.

A good way to look at this issue is to say that if parallel imports are driven by free-rider motivations, then it is usually all right to prevent them. And price discrimination − although it may not be an airtight case − is the best case for allowing parallel imports. The question here is: which is more desirable, third-degree price discrimination (different prices in different countries) or uniformity of prices ? The answer depends on whether you look at it from a national or a global perspective. A lot of the complaints about grey market imports come from countries that think that they are paying high prices. Even within these countries, there is sometimes tension between consumers and intellectual property owners. Often, it is the consumers in "high-price countries" who are the winners from allowing parallel imports that curb price discrimination. This is a somewhat schizophrenic situation, at least in the United States, because we do not like low prices when they result from "dumping," nor do we like high prices because they hurt consumers. So what exactly do we want?

David Malueg and myself wrote a paper (*Journal of International Economics*, 1994) in which we looked at the issue from the perspective of world welfare. If there is movement from a regime of discrimination to uniform pricing, while high prices may fall, some low prices may rise. Both need to be taken into account in a calculation of global welfare.

We translated this problem into one that economists have thought about: what is better from an overall welfare standpoint: third-degree discrimination or uniform pricing? It depends on the degree of demand dispersion. The trade-off is simple: the best way to allocate a given quantity is through uniform pricing, through which marginal values are equated. On the other hand, discrimination may let you serve more markets than otherwise might be the case and thus increase total output. To illustrate the fact that welfare can go either way, consider the case of two markets. If the demand dispersion between them is small, then a monopolist who is forced to charge a uniform price will serve both and, at least in the case of linear demands, the total quantity will be the same as it would be under price discrimination. Therefore, welfare is higher under uniform pricing than it is under price discrimination, because quantity has been allocated optimally.

However, if we extend this analysis to more than two countries – we consider a continuum of countries – and increase the dispersion between countries, then a new effect arises that is not captured in the two-market case. If the dispersion becomes sufficiently large and uniform pricing is required, then the monopolist will simply choose to drop some markets. As before, that causes a reduction in output, which is bad. On the other hand, in markets that are still being served, because uniform pricing is used, output is allocated optimally, which conveys an advantage to uniform pricing. The greater the demand dispersion in the markets still being served, the larger the misallocation that is avoided by requiring uniform pricing. (This effect cannot be captured in the two-market case, because if dispersion is sufficiently increased, the bottom market is not being served under uniform pricing, whereas optimal allocation occurs trivially in the single top market also under price discrimination.) In a model with demand dispersion and a continuum of countries, we nevertheless show that the conventional intuition is validated. Where dispersion is low, allowing discrimination decreases welfare, but where it is sufficiently high, discrimination is good, since under uniform pricing too many markets would be lost. The welfare loss from a reduction in output eventually outweighs the misallocation effect of price discrimination.

Another question that Malueg and I raised in our paper ties into the Anderson et al.'s point about NAFTA and regional trading blocks. Are there better alternatives than uniform pricing versus a different price in each country (which we refer to in our paper as "complete discrimination")? (Under complete discrimination, as opposed to perfect discrimination, within each country you are charging a linear monopoly price.) To answer this question, consider a case in which the monopolist – assumed to have constant marginal cost – who is constrained to charge a uniform price would choose to serve only countries where per capita income is above some threshold, say $10,000. As the world dictator, one might say: "In those markets (with per capita income above $10,000), designated as trading block A, only one price must be charged." Then society is no worse off under the trading block system with respect to that top group of countries (block A) than it would have been under uniform pricing. But for the remaining, unserved countries, suppose the monopolist is allowed to charge a lower price. What will that price be? Suppose it is the price at which countries with a per capita income ranging between $5,000 and $10,000 would buy. Then the world dictator designates those countries as trading block B and in trading block B permits only one price to be charged. If that partition of countries into blocks continues recursively by income, every country will be served. This outcome is an actual Pareto improvement over uniform pricing.

This recursive system that dominates uniform pricing does not, in fact, maximize global welfare. An even better outcome is possible if a small number of high income countries joined the low-income-country block. The result would be an improved allocation, since those high demand countries, instead of paying the very high price, would enjoy the low price and therefore buy more. Too much of this grouping, however, would result in a higher price in the poor countries and a loss of markets and thus a decrease in total output.

This brings us to Anderson et al.'s point about NAFTA exhaustion of IPRs: Is it a good idea to require one price in a North America trading block? It is true that in the story just described, some rich and poor are combined together. The problem is that if you lump Mexico in with the United States, however, the Mexican price will not stay near the low level but will instead rise substantially toward the U.S. level, in which case we would lose much of the Mexican market.

Anderson et al. identify another problem with uniform prices that does not hinge on differences in per capita income (or other non-policy differences in demand). Suppose that government policies differ with regard to intellectual property standards, forced licensing, or the presence of governmental monopsony (for pharmaceuticals, for example). Requiring a uniform price may inefficiently dilute the rights of the intellectual property rights holders. This potential problem requires more research and some empirical examples.

I'm not quite sure I agree with the authors' characterization of the world as fairly permissive towards attempts to control grey market imports; I believe there is some hostility out there. For example, in the United States, in the 1988 case of K-Mart v. Cartier, the Supreme Court decided that the Customs service need not block parallel imports in cases where the U.S. entity is affiliated with the foreign supplier. This decision is somewhat of a retreat from protection of the trademark holder's exclusion rights. (On the other hand, I am not sure I agree with the authors' claim that exhaustion exists within the United States. It is true with respect to the first-sale doctrine; but it is also true that firms can give exclusive geographic territories contractually and prevent distributor A from selling to territory B.)

Japan is particularly hostile to the prevention of parallel imports. The JFTC issued guidelines in 1991 that preclude action against parallel imports, not only on Japanese soil, but also on foreign soil. For example, Japanese manufacturers may not trace the product code to determine which exporter from Hong Kong is supplying the parallel goods so as to terminate relationship with the supplying distributor.

Finally, the authors made the very good point that in the European Union (EU), exhaustion is driven by market integration goals. The EU may well be putting the cart before the horse by prohibiting restrictions on parallel imports in order to promote integration, instead of letting integration reduce the differences that promote price discrimination and thus spur parallel imports. That is, greater integration would reduce the need to protect parallel imports for purposes of reducing price discrimination.

444

Part IV
Roundtable Discussion and
Conclusions

Roundtable Discussion on Competition Policy, Intellectual Property and Innovation Markets

NANCY GALLINI: Should competition policy be used to "fine-tune" intellectual property (IP) policy; that is, should competition policy attempt to correct for possible excesses or shortcomings of IP policy? Two basic points of view have been presented today. The first view, expressed by several authors, is that competition policy *should* be used to fine-tune IP policy. In this view, IP policy is a blunt instrument and may not always provide the correct incentives for research: if the level of protection is too weak, competition policy should be more permissive; if it is too broad, as some have argued is the case for copyright and patent protection in network industries, then competition policy should intervene. The alternative view is that competition policy should *not* intervene for purposes of correcting deficiencies or excesses in the incentives for innovation; rather, competition policy should take IP policy as given and focus on the efficiency of contracts and technology transfer.

I would like to open up the discussion to see if we can reach some general consensus on this question.

DEREK IRELAND: I think you are saying that we should render unto Caesar what is Caesar's (i.e., the domain of IP policy) and then render unto God those things that are God's, and, of course, most of us would agree that the latter is the domain of competition policy. There are problems with this. Sometimes Caesar doesn't get it right and sometimes, God forbid, God doesn't get it right, and we have had numerous examples of that. I think that to the extent that Canada, an importer of intellectual property, would be uncomfortable with a particular intellectual property standard, we may have to consider using competition policy to redress the balance in the Canadian context. In the late 1960s, we brought in compulsory licensing for brand name drugs under patent law. One reason it was done was that competition law in Canada was in considerable disarray and could not take on that issue.

So when one side gets it wrong, there has to be a response from the other. And when a problem occurs in the marketplace, politicians, the media, and the general public do not care which law is applied. They just want it to get solved.

In other words, there has to be flexibility to respond to problems that emerge, regardless of whether or not we would like a nice mapping of "render unto Caesar," et cetera.

MICHAEL SCHERER: I would vote for using competition policy to fine-tune intellectual property policy. What concerns me most is Robert Merges' killer patent portfolios, and in particular, the extension over time of patent monopolies. Let me illustrate with the case of the Federal Trade Commission's actions on Xerox. For various reasons concerning the way the Commission is organized, that one landed on my desk and I had to decide it. I was never so scared about anything in my life as accepting a decree providing for compulsory licensing of all of Xerox's patents. Xerox was one of the great technological triumphs of the 20th century. It was a major innovation. It was a very difficult innovation and they carried it off brilliantly. Why should one intervene in such a situation? Why should one tamper with their patent rights? They had somewhere between 1,000 and 2,000 patents in the mid-1970s. They were adding to their portfolio at a rate of several hundred patents a year. They had the technology completely encircled, and a consideration that prompted our decision to intervene with compulsory licensing was that the 914 Copier was introduced in 1959. The case came for a decision in 1975. They had enjoyed 16 years of a spectacular patent monopoly. How long should a monopoly last?

We intervened because we thought essentially that 17 years was what the law had in mind, 17 years was enough. As I said, I was very, very apprehensive about doing this to what I considered a technological marvel but, in hindsight, I think our action was well justified because it turns out that Xerox was resting on its technological laurels. In his book, David Kearns, former CEO of Xerox, admits that. We expected IBM and Kodak to come in and create the technological competition for Xerox. What we did not anticipate was the Japanese coming in with smaller, much more reliable copiers, and I think the whole thing was a Pareto improvement in the sense that Xerox was shaken out of the lethargy into which it had fallen after a 16-year run. They intensified their R&D efforts. They built bigger and better machines. Consumers had more choice. It's hard to see how anybody would be hurt by this kind of action.

NANCY GALLINI: This example raises a monopoly versus monopolization issue of applying competition law to IP. Are you saying that antitrust authorities should be concerned about firms that grow by accumulating patents, even if this follows simply from a technological advantage? Or should only those cases in which patents are accumulated through some exclusionary practice be subject to antitrust scrutiny; for example, if an innovator is pre-emptive in covering a field or uses exclusive arrangements to foreclose rivals from the market? Are you suggesting that firms that exceed some threshold size should be stopped, even if their dominance resulted from the legal collection of patents?

MICHAEL SCHERER: That was the essence of our case. There were all sorts of peripheral practices that, at least I thought, were entirely peripheral. We used them for fighting purposes. But the essence of the case was, frankly, social engineering. It was time to break open this monopoly and create competition. It was a task that was going to be very difficult to achieve just through the market, without intervention, and that was the essential rationale. The theory about acquisition and some of the price discrimination practices, and so forth, was fluff. The centre of the case was the extension over time of the monopoly through patent accumulation.

NANCY GALLINI: How far would you extend this policy? Would you extend it to non-IP methods of acquiring a monopoly, for example, buying up all the coal mines in a particular region from less-efficient firms or expanding one's market through successful advertising? That is, should we be concerned about large firms simply because they are large?

MICHAEL SCHERER: Well, the magic 17 years, I think, was essential in the Xerox case. I don't believe in just going in willy-nilly and knocking down any monopoly, because I think monopolies frequently arise in response to superior skill, insight, hard work, and so on. The question is, how long is enough? How long is sufficient reward to maintain incentive, on the one hand, and to be just, on the other?

WILLIAM BAXTER: I cannot leave an argument for intervention unanswered. You had a very favourable climate for success, in a sense, because there was no anticipation of your intervention. Anticipation would have led to different behaviour on the part of Xerox and a whole array of unknown entrants – the Japanese, for example. So the question that has to be answered is not the one to which you have given us an answer, but this one: If it were pre-announced that the government would march in after 17 years, without regard to the value of follow-on improvements, without regard to the ingenuity of the trade secrets that were employed in the manufacturing process and continue to be trade secrets 25 years later, what would be the effect on incentives for innovation and efficient behaviour? I think it would have a very depressing effect on R&D investment in about the 12th year. On the other hand, it might stimulate outside firms. So it's hard to say. But I certainly couldn't work up any enthusiasm or conviction for the view that we would be better off as a result of such intervention.

MICHAEL SCHERER: Let me reply by citing the case that I think is an example of how not to do it, and that is *United Shoe Machinery*. The first United Shoe Machinery decree was in 1953, when the court declared licensing of patents compulsory and said to USM: "We're going to come back and look at you in a few years and we're going to see whether you still have a monopoly, and if you do, we're going to intervene and do some more stuff to you." I happened to interview United Shoe Machinery in 1958, and it was clear that they were directing their research and development away from the shoe machinery industry to diversify into avenues that, in the end, turned out to be failures. Meanwhile, the quality of their machinery declined. They did lose some market share, but not enough to satisfy Judge Wyzanski, so he moved in again and required some divestiture of assets. The quality of their technology declined. By 1970, USM was very nearly dead. The Italians, who by that time were making far superior shoe making machinery, essentially took over the industry. So United Shoe Machinery was bled to a slow death.

I think to announce in advance, as Bill is suggesting, that we're going to watch you for a while and if you retain that monopoly we're going to clobber you, is in fact detrimental to incentives. You must spring out somehow from behind the tree, and how many times can you do that before people anticipate that you're going to spring? That is the dilemma.

MARIUS SCHWARTZ: As a general matter, I'm concerned about altering competition policy in order to correct for possible excesses or shortcomings of some other body of law. I think it was a tremendous struggle to get antitrust policy into a reasonably good state; the prospect of having to find some other principle to keep it on track, while it is also meddling around in another body of law, is a bit troublesome. Although I worry about issues like very long extensions of the patent monopoly, I think they can be dealt with through traditional antitrust principles and doctrines without distorting antitrust law.

There is also the example that Robert Merges raised yesterday of Hewlett Packard acquiring patents that it had no intention of using itself, but was acquiring solely for the purpose of driving another competitor out of business. Here, again, there are antitrust doctrines (somewhat controversial, in the nature of vertical foreclosure theories) that have built-in limiting principles that I think make them workable for addressing such foreclosure problems. We ought to apply them. I am at a little bit of a loss as to how to operationalize the idea of going beyond that in any way to deal with the problems in intellectual property law.

NEIL CAMPBELL: I find this a slightly strange way to be talking about IP and competition policy issues. It became most clear to me yesterday when Michael Trebilcock suggested that we might find ourselves in a world where we all thought that, as economists, we would accept the principle about total welfare maximization, being sensitive to both static allocative issues and the long-term dynamic issues. We all agreed that is socially where we wanted to be. Hopefully that was an informed start at getting the dynamic side right. To then suggest that competition law as it interfaces with intellectual property should somehow not pay attention to an overall, long-term welfare standard, if that's what I think I heard Michael saying, seems inconsistent to me. I would have thought that we certainly would want to continue to use competition law and the enforcement of it in an informed way, to try to achieve total welfare, both in the short and long terms. If, for whatever reason, we have situations like the killer patent portfolio, why wouldn't we say that it is perfectly appropriate for the competition laws to come in and try to move us towards total welfare?

NANCY GALLINI: I think Michael Trebilcock, myself and others who say that competition law should not be used to fine-tune patent policy *are* taking a dynamic view of competition policy. While both institutions need to coordinate to achieve dynamic efficiency, we are suggesting that patent policy may be more effective at providing the right incentives for R&D, with competition policy respecting those rights. Competition policy should concern itself with the diffusion of innovation and the maintenance of competition down the road. In other words, competition policy should not allow restrictions for the purpose of getting firms to do more R&D because patent policy has already addressed the incentive problem. However, if there is something anticompetitive about the use of a right, then clearly, that is a competition issue.

ROBERT MERGES: Could I add on to that, taking the killer patent portfolio again as the example. As I understand it, the killer patent portfolio is made possible by the intellectual property regime. You can go out and create such a portfolio and spend a lot of time doing it. I wouldn't mind living in a system where everybody *ex ante* had some signals that if you take that to a level of abuse – the killer patent portfolio used in a way to entrench market power excessively or artificially or unreasonably –, whatever standard we might want under a rule of reason approach in competition law, they are not going to get away with it. That's not part of the incentive to innovate. You can have your reasonable patent protection for innovation, but we're not going to promise you the sort of unmitigated right to create a killer patent portfolio and abuse it.

JEFFREY CHURCH: I just want to clarify a few things about what we are talking about when we talk about fine-tuning. I think what I have in mind was maybe not the same as what Nancy has in mind. When I talk about competition policy intervention, what I'm thinking about is that competition policy should take action against restrictions associated with the use of intellectual property rights in cases where there is a clear abuse of dominance. We live in a world where there are many industries (network externality industries are a good example) for which a little bit of intellectual property rights can be translated into a huge advantage for the firm(s) involved. There are also all kinds of anticompetitive practices that can be used to sustain that dominant position, deter entry and maintain market power. I don't think that intellectual property rights should be an excuse for competition authorities not to go after a dominant position, and particularly an abuse of dominant position. If that's fine-tuning, then I'm for it.

I will give you a good example, a situation that we are going to face in Canada. We used to have a policy of compulsory licensing for patented drugs, and we stopped that. The brand-name companies are now attempting to deter entry by trying to get trademark protection for the appearance of their pills. So they are trying to get the size, shape, and colour of their pharmaceutical preparations trademarkable, and then if a generic company were to enter and produce the exact same pill, it would be infringing on their trademark.

Let's assume that after 17 years of patent protection in which consumers have learned and adapted to the information in that field, there is a significant switching cost: that consumers, if faced with the choice between two pills, go with the one that they have been using for 17 years and not the other one. Then I would say that if drug companies were, in fact, able to get protection for the size, shape and colour of their pill, competition policy should step in and say "no"; from a competition perspective, this is wrong. The generic company should be allowed to produce the same size, shape and colour of the pill.

ROBERT ANDERSON: Are you saying that competition should step in by prosecuting people under the law or just by getting involved in the policy debate? The latter is another possible approach that should be considered. A lot of our discussion over the past day and a half has focused on whether we should be applying the law to prosecute firms engaging in anticompetitive conduct, but the other way is to fine-tune how IP rights are defined in legislation and policies, and perhaps that is what competition authorities should be doing more of: namely, getting involved at the policy level.

We used to do it this way in Canada quite effectively. People may not know this, but the compulsory licensing regime we had for pharmaceutical products actually came about originally through enquiries and then policy advocacy efforts that originated with the Competition Bureau or its predecessor. There are different ways to fine-tune IP policy, and sometimes pursuing the policy debate may be the preferable tool.

JEFFREY CHURCH: I agree, but would just point out that these two approaches are not mutually exclusive. We should be doing our best on the policy front, but then when an abuse of dominance situation arises, where a dominant firm engages in anticompetitive practices to maintain or extend its market power, we should use the provisions of the *Competition Act* to step in and say no, regardless of what is going on in the policy dialogue. I can imagine Chicago types saying that any restrictions that you place on the use of my intellectual property right cycles back into my incentive on R&D, so don't put any restrictions on my intellectual property right.

MICHAEL SCHERER: Let me amend my testimony in one respect, following up the dialogue with William Baxter. Suppose we had said to Xerox in 1959, "All right Xerox, we think the 914 and related machines are wonderful, so we're going to give you a 17-year exclusive run with these machines. At the end of 17 years, we're not going to ask you what your market share is, but we're going to expect you to open up your patent portfolio and license any of your remaining patents at 1.5 percent." How would Xerox have reacted to this situation? I don't think they would, under the circumstances, have diminished their R&D investment. I think, given the position from which they began, they would have said at about year 13 or so "My God, we're going to have to face open competition in four years, let us make ourselves as lean and tough and technologically advanced as we can possibly be." I suspect they would actually have done more, and they would have been in a better position to repel the Japanese threat than they were when we essentially jumped out from behind the tree in the middle of the 1970s.

DONALD MCFETRIDGE: First, I would like to go on record as being against fine-tuning. It's a bit presumptuous, I think, to be talking about fine-tuning when we barely have the motor running at all. But we want to be thinking ahead, and we certainly are. On a broader level, I think competition policy and intellectual property policy are inextricably linked. Again, this goes back to the early Nordhaus-style models on the optimal patent term or, in the more recent literature, the questions of breadth and novelty. It's all contingent on what the government is promising in terms of how much of the surplus created by the invention the patentee is able to extract. If he is able to get it all, it implies a different term and breadth solution than if you're only able to get part of it. I don't think you can detach them. At a conceptual level, they have to be dealt with simultaneously. So if you're promising a simple monopoly, as in the case of the Nordhaus model, that's very different from promising the right to discriminate, or bundle, or tie, or do any number of other things.

Second, I would like to address an issue that was brought up very cogently: suppose we're looking at something like tying or bundling. Such practices may be either good or bad in a static sense. We know quite well that the evidence required to distinguish the good cases from the bad in the static sense is very hard to come by, so we're not likely to get it right very often. We may say we're moving from rule of reason to *per se* legality, but we're not there yet. We can all think of cases where these practices might be harmful, and we would hate to tie our hands in those kinds of circumstances.

Then you add the dynamic considerations. Yes, a practice could be harmful statically, but good dynamically. That moves you further again – if you were just on the verge of *per se* legality, dynamic considerations might tip you over the edge. I'm not saying that would be the case, but those kinds of considerations can and should influence competition policy.

One possibility is to treat such matters on a case-by-case basis. You can go back to something like *NutraSweet*, which focused on abuse. The question is: What is the bargain? Is it that a firm invents something and receives the right to collect simple monopoly profits for 17 years? Or is the firm promised the ability to make use of that intellectual property to see what could be made of it, either with a trademark, as in the *NutraSweet* case, or with whatever legal means are at hand. Of course, the question still remains: What is legal? The whole notion that the bargain doesn't include any action that would lead to collection of rents beyond year 17 is a bit hard to take.

MARIUS SCHWARTZ: What I think we learned most from the conference is the point asserted about networks: if you believe that you have the rewards right in other industries, then the rewards are likely to be excessive in network industries. This notion is intellectually provocative. I would worry about what you do about it, especially with the idea of forcing open interfaces. I really worry about implementation, and I will come back to this point.

Suppose you force somebody to open up his or her interfaces and make sure the product is compatible with somebody else's. What happens if that somebody else's product doesn't work? Who is to blame? Then there is all kinds of fingerpointing, and in a technologically complex industry, that can get us – whether it's the competition authorities or someone else – into a regulatory mess. I don't think you should underestimate the practical problems that such actions can create.

In general, the closer you are to something, the more aware you are of its limitations. I hear regulators and IP practitioners saying: "Let antitrust solve the problem," as if competition law administrators were deities with crystal balls. The fact is that sometimes, we grossly overestimate how much we can contribute to decisions, which is why I found Michael Trebilcock's and William Baxter's points to be well taken. How much of this stuff can you really implement, taking into account the transaction costs and the adversarial process? Academic economists try to subsume that issue when they write down the model and then at the end, say: "Well, of course, there are other things to worry about." This is a very incomplete approach to policy.

I think some of Bill's suggestions about how one might change the litigation process are quite interesting possibilities to address this. I also liked Michael Scherer's point that sometimes private litigants have an incentive to settle in ways that don't solve the problem from a social perspective. I think that's a point worth pursuing and that maybe in cases like that the government should step in.

RALPH WINTER: I think both sides of the fine-tuning debate are persuasive and I find myself agreeing with whoever was the last speaker. Marius Schwartz has really articulated the point I wanted to make, which is that when I think about fine-tuning, I cannot personally articulate rules of reason that would apply in cases like the pharmaceuticals industry or even in cases of killer patents. I'm worried about the uncertainty that this would create in the incentives for firms to invest in the first place, especially in the light of changing political parties and changing competition law regimes. They have to predict far ahead what the rules are going to be and the extent of fine-tuning, compared with cases where the rules of law are either statutes or firmly established principles in common law.

DENNIS YAO: Following the tradition of agreeing with the previous speaker, I was thinking along the same lines as Ralph Winter. On the issue of fine-tuning, it would be nice to have a sense of how much fine-tuning affects, *ex ante*, the incentives to innovate. Some kinds of fine-tuning may be irrelevant for *ex ante* incentives, and so, we're on reasonably firm ground. But it could be that for other types of fine-tuning, and in particular, the type that people are really concerned about (for example, networks), there is a tipping phenomenon. If tipping exists and allows a firm to get control of an industry, that's a big deal that may affect the *ex ante* incentives.

Ralph Winter's point suggests to me that it is very important to be predictable. You don't want to get into a position in which the analysis changes, either because of the name of the staff person or even the name of the political party involved. One thing we can be sure about is that uncertainty is bad for business planning. If we think this is a real problem, it is probably worth doing some gradual experimentation. It's not that you have to shift from one regime to another regime, it's something that you can learn as you go. Economic theory doesn't have a lot to offer about whether or not there is enough R&D in particular circumstances. The empirical work isn't very convincing either. But perhaps on a case-by-case basis we can learn something that will guide us, as long as we go in a gradual, relatively predictable way. If we catch problems with an evolving fine-tuning policy early, before the problems become really big, then policy adjustments are easier. But, then again, I'm not sure we know in general how big a problem most types of fine-tuning pose to *ex ante* incentives to innovate.

WILLIAM BAXTER: I think the question of whether we should try to fine-tune intellectual property through the application of competition law is really a false question. To a large extent, we're talking about the breadth of judges' discretion. To take U.S. law just as an example, it is totally unimaginable to me that a judge might one day say: "You know, 17 years is beginning to look from the literature like a long time, so I think I will just cut it down to 13, or make comparable changes." On the other hand, our statutes also say that if something has been for sale for two years, it can't be patented, and then there is the experimental exception to that.

It seems to me not only permissible, but fairly likely that in interpreting the way those statutory pieces fit together a judge will take into account the effect it is likely to have on the strength of innovation incentives. The facts that judges are not going to reduce the 17-year period and that they are going to take incentives to innovate into account in doing the statutory interpretation together represent the inevitable answer to the question of whether each of the systems should take the other into account. Of course, they should take the other into account, but at the same time, they should tend primarily to their own knitting.

Returning to the argument that I have been having with Michael Scherer, I think it is quite permissible to say at the beginning of the period, "you only have 17 years of protection," but I don't like the idea of cutting back on reward structures because a company has in the past been successful. I believe you have to have done something wrong before we cut back on the reward structure, and that is where I see the major problem with Michael Scherer's comments.

ROBERT MERGES: I certainly didn't mean to imply that my goal was to perform some sort of optimal social engineering. It is not a subterfuge to ruin the hard-fought legitimacy of the competition law system. The reason I was calling for fine-tuning from the antitrust side is because we don't do it much in patent law. The lack of expertise about economic issues in patent law, at least in the United States, can be disturbing. What I really would like is for us to import some of the economic expertise about effects on competition into the debate about intellectual property policy.

What leads me to propose this is that at least antitrust people are asking the right questions. Sometimes in patent law we seem to be stuck at the stage of metaphysics. In a perfect world, we could import some of the expertise that has been built up on the antitrust side and have a better informed intellectual property policy. I think there is hope that we're heading toward a better world. I think the U.S. antitrust authorities have finally realized that a lot of the policy issues and legislative issues on the intellectual property side have a very significant impact on competition. So there are some heartening signs.

Another sign of hope is the fact that in their *amicus* (i.e., competition advocacy) practice, the U.S. antitrust authorities are starting to pay more attention to cases that are under the IP side of the ledger. These are the grant of rights side, not the abuse side. They understand that it is quite possible to have an abusive grant of rights, and they are beginning to get a sense that we need to enter into the discussions right at the point where the rights are going to be expanded, which is to say legislatively, and in some cases, in the appellate courts. This is a very hopeful sign.

Let me just suggest one thing about network industries, because it's directly relevant to my point. One possible way to solve the problem is to give a property right to people who are doing, for example, an application program that fits into the interface, but also to maintain the property rights in the person who owns the interface and essentially say: "You guys have to work it out yourselves. We don't want to get into the regulatory game." We do that with blocking patents. In some sense, every improver who holds a blocking patent is put into a bilateral monopoly relationship with the pioneer, and they have to work it out. Strangely enough, more often than not, it works. It's actually kind of an elegant solution stumbled upon in the 19th century. This is a logical structure that you might propose for the problem of network externalities.

I think ideally we would fine-tune intellectual property rights at the original, policy level (i.e., in legislation or judicial decisions). But I'm not sure we're going to be able to import the expertise quickly enough, given the institutional barriers, to do it "in time" to save ourselves from some trouble.

It is definitely an example of what Marius Schwartz was talking about. The closer you are to something, the more defects you see in it. It may be true that economists are sort of one-eyed men with very bad vision, but let me tell you, I'm in the land of the blind and one-eyed vision looks pretty good from here.

JEFFREY CHURCH: My point, which is very similar to Robert Merges', is that if a dominant firm has intellectual property rights on a standard that is an essential facility for competition, and the dominant firm refuses to deal or refuses to license, I think the competition authority should treat this as a potentially viable case. We should investigate it and decide whether or not there is an abuse. The abuse of dominant position provision of the Canadian *Competition Act* is well-suited to the task.

In terms of remedies, it seemed from Michael Scherer's remarks yesterday that in compulsory licensing cases pricing had not been a major issue. To the extent that problems arise, perhaps they can be addressed through cooperative standard-setting institutions. One last thing for Don McFetridge. When we give these people a patent, we do say, or we should say, that their right to use that patent is subject to the competition law. That is something that they know in advance, and they cannot claim we are changing the environment for their investment. They know the abuse of dominance provisions are there.

NANCY GALLINI: By way of summary, I would like to go around the table and ask everyone to identify which issue he/she considers to be most important in the IP competition debate.

WILLIAM BAXTER: I'm moved, once again, to say that as soon as you start telling people they must deal with one another, that is to say, mandating open interfaces or compulsory licensing, you must be prepared to tell them all of the terms on which they must deal from then on. Unless you're prepared to undertake that regulatory role, and it is an intensely interventionist role, then you should think of something else to do, because that is part of the job.

NEIL CAMPBELL: I think that paying attention to rights at the grant stage, be it by legislative policy or be it by the judicial decisions that get made about intellectual property rights, is very important. It seems to me that it is important for competition authorities to think about the extent to which you want to participate in the review of intellectual property legislation, as well as cases where interventions may be useful for network system-type issues.

Beyond that, I think about it from the point of view of what does a Canadian lawyer have to have in mind vis-à-vis his clients in this day and age. I leave this symposium basically feeling that in Canada, we have a pretty good set of competition laws. They're not perfect, we can always do better, but our abuse of dominance provision is broad and fairly sophisticated. It was used in *NutraSweet* and it has been used to address some complex types of abuse. Not much is likely to change dramatically. We probably have a better sense of the possibilities for extension and abuse of monopoly power through intellectual property rights, but it doesn't call for a whole new system.

DON MERCER: I would just like to remind everybody here, picking up on a comment made earlier, that there are institutions in place, we have a jurisprudential legal system and that the analysis and conclusions of this kind of meeting between scholars and enforcement officials will eventually find their way, to an extent, into our enforcement policies and jurisprudence. That will happen on both the criminal and civil law sides, as it has over time, and that is the immense value of these exchanges.

MARK RONAYNE: An undertone here, which wasn't really developed, is how different types of intellectual property relate to each other. We have seen some of that in *NutraSweet* where there was an attempt, I believe, to bring patent protection into the world of trademarks, which has a longer life if you keep using it. Related to this is the issue of trade secrets and how they interact with other forms of intellectual property law.

WILLARD TOM: On the enforcement side, I don't think we have fully explored or exhausted the application of traditional doctrines in the antitrust field to the problems that are posed in industries where intellectual property is important. We need to figure out how to deal with particular practices in particular market settings and industries. We may make more progress on the enforcement side in that way than in trying to provide cosmic solutions to the problem.

On the advocacy side, I think that Robert Merges and Robert Anderson are right. There are many competition implications to the way intellectual property protections are interpreted, created, and enforced, and industrial organization economics, perhaps as opposed to antitrust law, may have a lot to say on those issues.

I also agree that there are many institutional and political barriers that may impede quick success on that front. There is going to be an inherent assumption that the Patent and Trademark Office has the expertise or the Intellectual Property Bar has the expertise, and who are we as the Federal Trade Commission, the Department of Justice, or the Canadian Competition Bureau to tell them how to run their business? That is just something we are going to have to deal with.

But I think there are hopeful signs, at least in the U.S. federal judiciary. If you look at Judge Newman's concurrence in the *Hilton Davis* case or the First Circuit decision in *Lotus v. Borland*, judges are finally saying: "Well, gosh, what does the economic literature have to say about this problem and does it cast any light on the specific issue that we have to deal with in this case?" I regard that, at least, as a hopeful sign.

MARIUS SCHWARTZ: I gave you my main comments earlier, so I will just make a comment and pose a question to Rob Merges. I like the idea of using competition policy for advocacy purposes with regard to intellectual property and elsewhere. We do that as a routine matter in lots of different contexts. One thing, Rob, that concerns me is that if the intellectual property community is as powerful as you suggest, isn't there the danger that if we start meddling too much in their affairs, they are going to drop the boom on us, they could lobby Congress.

MICHAEL SCHERER: First of all, given the difficulties, I think that rather than talking about fine-tuning, we should be using words like "rough hewing." Second, I'm concerned that we haven't talked at all about something Richard Gilbert mentioned last night in about two sentences, and that is the dangers when a large well-established, well-financed firm uses its patent portfolio to bludgeon small newcomers. As U.S. doctrine has developed, you have to engage in some pretty egregious behaviour before you get into trouble under the precedent in *Columbia Pictures* and that, I think, is a very serious problem.

RICHARD GILBERT: I think we need to understand a lot more about how intellectual property contributes to economic growth and to the economy, and I would certainly be cautious about moving aggressively in any area of intellectual property, for that matter in any area of antitrust, without being confident about what the effects are going to be. The kind of thinking that goes on in a conference like this helps a great deal to define our interests and understanding and to focus the questions. The answers are going to come very gradually. Like competition advocacy, it's chipping away at a mountain, but mountains eventually erode.

DEREK IRELAND: I have had a sense for a long time that these are two very important policy instruments (competition policy and intellectual property). I'm concerned that very few people know how important they are and that, in a sense, both instruments are being monopolized by certain very limited interests. I think that mechanisms must be found to open up both involvement and understanding in competition policy and intellectual property rights, from the policy side, but also from the dispute resolution side. We're talking a lot about the abuse of dominance provisions of the *Competition Act*, and at the present time only the Director can take an abuse of dominance case to the Competition

Tribunal. I think that is something that might need to be addressed from the point of view of opening up the Act. Another thing I have learned is to think a lot more about working with what we already have rather than proposing any sort of hare-brained "this is the way we ought to do it" and "in the ideal world" sort of proposal. So when people like Willard Tom tell me there are some tools we can use and there are some institutions that are in place, it makes me think I have to learn more about those and integrate my thinking a little more with what is there. I think some of the foreclosing vertical competition and raising rivals costs analysis is going to be helpful and important for some of these issues we've been discussing.

ROBERT MERGES: To answer the question that Marius Schwartz posed a few moments ago, I think the first defence against a political onslaught, not to be too idealistic, is intellectual coherence. Some of us have been around Washington long enough to know that, just when you least expect it, an appeal to a rigorous intellectual argument can save the day or turn the tide. It certainly isn't irrelevant. So working backwards from that, if we have good ideas about how intellectual property affects competition and how competition policy thinking – applied microeconomics – can help us think about intellectual property, we then have a line of defence for the day when the Intellectual Property Bar tries to run us out of town on a rail.

The second line of defence is much more practical and that is to recruit some lobbying assistance. There are some groups finally taking shape. I will just mention one: the American Committee for Interoperable Systems is one group, aside from the generic drug producers, who are self-identified weak protectionists. Given the historical trends, it's a sign of how strong rights are becoming in some domains when lobbies for weak protection emerge. To have an intellectual focal point and a policy focal point for these groups would be a good thing.

The last thing I learned is really something I remember, which is how pleasant it is to talk with rational, measured people. When I come to Canada, this tends to be the norm. So, I will end with a joke that Canadians all know, but some of the U.S. people present might not. There was a contest, I think in the Toronto paper. It's a fill-in-the-blank in the statement: "As Canadian as . . ." I think you will all appreciate that the winning entry was "As Canadian as is reasonably possible under the circumstances."

DONALD MCFETRIDGE: Something that Derek Ireland brought up this morning deserves some response. It's that the goals of competition policy should be broadened again to include various consumer protection goals. The ability of the Competition Bureau in the last few years to narrow its goals and to focus on competition issues and efficiency of resource allocation and be able to ignore industrial policy goals and other regional development and other pressures has been one of its most important achievements. It would be very unfortunate, I think, to open the door to broader goals. That would be harmful to enforcement and may be straying too far into fine-tuning with respect to intellectual property.

A question you asked, which I don't know if anybody has really addressed is: Is compulsory licensing a good remedy if you decide that you want to, for whatever reason, cut short the intellectual property right? What I have learned from the Canadian experience is that quite often, compulsory licensing is like pushing on a string. You can get access, but that is really all you are getting, and to the extent that something else is required from the licensor, you may have to go a long way with a lot of regulatory intervention to get it. In some cases, it may not be a very good solution.

VAL TRAVERSY: As Director General responsible for Economics and International Affairs in the Competition Bureau, it falls to me to thank the participants in this Symposium, and particularly the organizers, Nancy Gallini and Rob Anderson, for their efforts and input. This has been a remarkable event. The subject matter of the Symposium – the role of competition policy as it relates to intellectual property and the knowledge-based economy – could not be more timely. You, the participants, comprise an exceptionally impressive group of academicians, current and former senior government officials and private sector practitioners of the law and economics of competition policy from across Canada and the United States. The range of intellectual contributions has spanned the realms of theory, empirical analysis, policy design and implementation. Even the weather has cooperated by being truly terrible – thereby ensuring that everyone has been happy to remain inside.

As many of you have pointed out over the past day and a half, the pace of events and the pressures of work in government and private practice these days are such that it is exceptionally difficult to take time out of one's everyday duties to mingle with informed observers, to take on fresh perspectives and to reflect analytically on the design and application of the policies that we are charged with administering. Yet nothing is more important to ensuring a smooth adaptation to the forces of change.

On the academic side, I also appreciate the time and effort that is involved in refining your analyses to the point where they are both theoretically and empirically rigorous and yet accessible to policy practitioners.

This Symposium has been a singular success in both respects. To all of you for your diverse contributions, and to the team of Rob and Nancy for their organizational efforts and initiative in making the event happen, I extend the Bureau's thanks.

NANCY GALLINI: Thank you, Val, for your comments and for the Bureau's support, and to all the participants for your contributions. The Symposium is now concluded.

Robert D. Anderson   &   *Nancy T. Gallini*
Competition Bureau   *Department of Economics*
Industry Canada, and   *University of Toronto*
World Trade Organization

13

Summary and Conclusions

A BROAD SET OF ISSUES RELATED TO THE INTERACTION between competition policy and intellectual property rights (IPRs) has been analyzed in this volume, with particular focus on patents and licensing practices. As pointed out in the Introduction to the volume, IPRs provide important incentives for innovation and can also facilitate the diffusion of new technologies in the economy. Occasionally, they also give rise to concerns about the accumulation or abuse of market power. Competition policy is another important instrument that guards against the abuse of market power, by limiting the set of practices and contractual arrangements that may be used by firms. This affects both a patentee's *ex ante* incentive to innovate and its *ex post* incentive to diffuse new technologies. In general, the wider the set of practices that are legally permitted, the greater the flexibility that the innovator has to increase the return from its investment in R&D and to restrict imitation and other potential rent-dissipating activities of licensees. On the other hand, such restrictions may have the welfare-reducing effect of excessively limiting access to new technologies and suppressing incentives to develop improvements or substitutes. The challenge for policy makers and competition authorities is to balance these various effects so as to achieve an efficient allocation of resources in dynamic markets.

In this final chapter, we identify some of the main conclusions and lessons to be drawn from the papers contained in the volume. Although the various papers present a great diversity of views on issues related to the competition policy treatment of IP, a number of insights and guiding principles emerge from them. We discuss these findings below. First, we consider general principles for competition policy as presented in the introductory papers of Part I; second, we outline guiding principles for the competition treatment of particular licensing practices; and third, we identify competition approaches, especially within NAFTA countries, that might have a favourable impact on innovation and diffusion in international markets.

GENERAL OBSERVATIONS

THE PAPERS IN PART I EXAMINE GENERAL QUESTIONS relating to the interface between competition policy and intellectual property rights. In chapter 2, Gallini and Trebilcock present three alternative approaches to the competition policy treatment of IP. The approach supported by the authors is that competition authorities should focus primarily on the allocative effects of a contract on diffusion and pricing, and not attempt to "counter-balance" perceived excesses or deficiencies of intellectual property protection. Where innovation concerns arise, as in joint ventures or in the suppression of a rival's incentive to conduct research, they argue that applying the potential-competition approach to technology and product markets may be sufficient to analyze the impact of a licence on innovation, diffusion, and prices. Gallini and Trebilcock also highlight two basic principles that are common to all papers in the volume:

1. **Competition policy should not presume that an intellectual property right confers market power.**

This principle, which is also emphasized in the U.S. Department of Justice and the Federal Trade Commission's *Antitrust Guidelines for the Licensing of Intellectual Property*, is critical to the sound application of competition policy to IP rights. It reflects the fact that, in most instances, good substitutes are available for patented products and processes.

2. **Competition policy should recognize that licensing restrictions may be welfare-increasing if they encourage the efficient diffusion of intellectual property.**

This point is also basic to the appropriate application of competition policy towards licensing practices. It reflects the fact that licensing restrictions generally increase the incentive for patent holders to make their technology available to users.

In contrast to the Gallini and Trebilcock paper, which focuses on the impact of competition policy on the diffusion of innovations, the paper by Merges emphasizes the importance of intellectual property rights to the diffusion of innovations. The author's key message is that stronger patent rights may lead to greater diffusion. Providing a positive analysis of the impact of patent rights on the organization of the production and diffusion of innovation, he argues that stronger patent rights encourage firms to enter into licensing arrangements rather than to vertically integrate production. An implication of this reorganization response to increased patent protection is that the traditional strategy of "killer portfolios" by large, vertically integrated firms may be of diminishing concern to antitrust authorities. However, he warns that new patent-acquisition strategies have emerged, requiring vigilance by competition authorities. Thus, Merges identifies an important interaction between patent protection and antitrust issues:

> 3. **Stronger patent protection gives rise to less-integrated organizations and more arm's-length licensing arrangements. Hence, the accumulation of "killer portfolios" is less likely to occur under strong patent protection. However, competition authorities must remain vigilant against abusive acquisition strategies and licensing arrangements that thwart competition.**

McFetridge also emphasizes the importance of IPRs to the diffusion of innovation in his paper, with particular attention being paid to the Canadian experience with compulsory licensing. He asks whether compulsory licensing (a weakening of patent rights) has in fact resulted in greater production and use of innovations in Canada. While he recognizes that compulsory licensing may provide on-the-job experience that generates spillovers for facilitating subsequent innovations, he argues that it has not been an effective solution for encouraging R&D and diffusion in Canada. In contrast to the situation in the United States, compulsory licensing in Canada has not been used primarily as a remedy to counter the anticompetitive exploitation of patents. While the U.S. and Canadian policies differ in several regards, Canada's accession to the NAFTA and the TRIPs agreements resulted in amendments to the *Patent Act* that have reduced the potential for conflict with U.S. policies. McFetridge concludes that:

> 4. **In general, compulsory licensing is not an effective mechanism for encouraging local working of a patent since it provides access without the transfer of knowledge necessary for commercial use of the innovation.**

THE TREATMENT OF PARTICULAR LICENSING PRACTICES

THE FOUR PAPERS IN PART II EXAMINE COMPETITION POLICY towards particular licensing practices and arrangements. The Baxter and Kessler paper introduces the topic with an analysis of the economics of tying in the context of IP, contrasting the Canadian and U.S. legal approaches. The authors note that the Canadian approach is more consistent with general economic principles in that it avoids the *per se* nomenclature of the U.S. approach and enables the appropriate balancing of beneficial and adverse welfare implications of tying in particular cases. They also argue that a justification for tying is to enhance the return from R&D investment, although they caution that such a policy may only alter the type, not the quantity, of R&D undertaken. The main recommendation drawn from their paper is as follows:

5. The competition policy treatment of tying in the area of intellectual property licensing should be subject to a rule-of-reason analysis.
The Canadian approach is better designed than the U.S. approach
in this regard, although the U.S. approach has moved closer to that
of Canada in recent years.

This recommendation is also made in the Rey and Winter paper, which focuses on exclusivity provisions in licensing contracts, including contracts to a single licensee, exclusive dealing, and territorial restrictions. The authors note the contrasting approaches that are found in competition policy towards these practices, especially between North America and the European Union. As in the treatment of non-IP goods, they recommend that competition policy follow a rule-of-reason approach towards these restrictions for IP, but that it be mindful of the fact that exclusivity restrictions can reduce incentives for future innovation. Hence, they propose that the competition authorities be prepared to intervene in cases where IPRs foreclose markets from potential innovators. To the extent that potential-competition analysis can be used to assess the social costs associated with the suppression of future innovation by rival firms, this recommendation is consistent with that advocated by Gallini and Trebilcock, which leads to the next recommendation:

6. Competition authorities should be prepared to challenge exclusivity
restrictions in the area of intellectual property licensing in so far
as they impact on future potential competition in technology and
product markets.

The paper by Scotchmer examines the efficiency and anticompetitive implications of research joint ventures and related horizontal arrangements. Recognizing that both Canadian and U.S. competition policies are more suspicious of horizontal than vertical arrangements, the author nonetheless points out that there may be redeeming efficiency benefits to both types of arrangements. She contrasts *ex ante* and *ex post* licensing, noting that while both facilitate the diffusion of innovations, the former is more effective at reducing inefficiencies from wasteful R&D. Although joint ventures have the undesirable potential of facilitating monopolization and reducing R&D spending, she cautions against overemphasizing this concern. Scotchmer's recommendations regarding competition policy towards joint ventures are as follows:

7. Horizontal arrangements involving intellectual property should be
evaluated under a rule-of-reason standard.

8. *Ex ante* alliances should be permitted unless they facilitate practices that would be prohibited *ex post* had they been implemented
through an anticompetitive licensing restriction.

Finally, the Church-Ware paper considers the interaction between competition policy and IPRs in the context of network industries, where issues of standardization and compatibility are important. They encourage competition authorities to recognize that the degree of market power conferred by IPRs may sometimes be excessive in those industries, where the normal effects of IPRs are often reinforced by network externalities and particularly heavy first mover advantages. They note that, contrary to their own views on appropriate levels of protection, the level of IP protection in network industries – including protection provided by patents, copyrights, and legislation pertaining to integrated circuit topographies – has been getting progressively stronger. Licensing restrictions, including refusal to license, horizontal agreements, exclusive dealing, and the tying of software with copyrighted operating systems, compound this market power. To the extent that IP protection is excessive, they argue that competition policy can play an important role in mitigating the market power conferred by IPRs. In summary, their observations and recommendations for both competition and patent policies are:

9. **Intellectual property rights and externalities in network industries often work together to create market power that may impede future innovation as well as create static inefficiencies.**

10. **In network industries, competition policy should be used to counteract the impact of intellectual property protection by constraining the exercise of market power through licensing restrictions.**

COMPARATIVE ISSUES AND POLICY PERSPECTIVES

THE THIRD PART OF THE VOLUME provides a comparative analysis of competition policy towards IP in Canada, the United States, and (to a lesser extent) the European Union. The potential benefits of guidelines in directing the production and diffusion of innovation both domestically and in the international arena are addressed in this part. Ireland's paper discusses various aspects of the Canadian policy environment and highlights specific aspects of consumer behaviour relevant to the application of both IP and competition policies. The author stresses that consumers' concerns are not always accounted for under these policies. For example, he warns of the dangers of providing strong IP protection in response to the rent-seeking behaviour of producers, especially for technologies that are relatively unknown and have potentially harmful consequences for consumers. Ireland's message is more cautionary than prescriptive in noting that competition policy may have a role to play in balancing these components of the welfare calculations, especially for technologies or products in which innovators have asymmetric information.

The competition treatment of IPRs in the United States is the focus of the Tom-Newberg paper. The authors provide a historical treatment of the rich assortment of laws, guidelines, and cases from the early days of the *Sherman Act* up to the current DOJ-FTC *Guidelines*. In contrast to the legal doctrine that was applied in preceding decades, the 1995 *Guidelines* view IP as being essentially similar to other forms of property rights. This approach avoids the harmful effects of both excessive hostility towards the monopoly rights granted on the innovation or excessive deference towards licensing practices based on their potential effects on innovation. The authors argue that providing certainty about the parameters around which innovators can operate is critical to a healthy and active research environment in which new innovations are developed and diffused widely. Accordingly, they conclude that:

11. **Guidelines for the competition treatment of intellectual property will promote the discovery and diffusion of innovations by providing a more certain policy environment in which firms can operate.**

12. **A separate legal regime is not required to address competition policy concerns relating to intellectual property. Rather, the application of existing competition law can be tailored to satisfy the special considerations of intellectual property and the rights conferred under patent law.**

The last paper in this part, by Anderson, Feuer, Rivard and Ronayne, explores the welfare and policy implications of using patents to segment markets internationally. As the authors point out, a good argument can be made that patents and other IPRs that are national in scope may be efficient and practical in many circumstances. Indeed, in the multilateral context, a certain degree of territorial divisibility of rights may be needed to prevent an undesirable lowering of standards of protection. Nonetheless, the authors suggest that at some point in the future, consideration be given to implementing a policy of "exhaustion" of IP rights across the North American free-trade area on the grounds that it would foster competition and the free movement of goods and services. This would be comparable to the policy applicable in the European Union, where legitimately made patented articles that are placed on the market in any member state may move freely throughout the Union. The implementation of exhaustion requires effective convergence of IP and competition policies. Accordingly, say the authors,

13. **As competition and intellectual property enforcement policies converge and economic integration deepens, consideration should be given to adopting a policy of "exhaustion" of intellectual property rights across the North American free-trade area, or at least between Canada and the United States.**

THE ROUNDTABLE DISCUSSION

THE VOLUME CONCLUDES WITH AN EDITED SUMMARY of the roundtable discussion that took place at the Authors' Symposium. Several important issues raised in the papers were revisited for further analysis during this discussion. While consensus was not achieved on all of them, a lively exchange took place on a wide range of questions. For example, participants examined the following questions: What role should competition policy play when patent protection is either too weak or overreaching? Should competition policy challenge the growth of a firm if its size is attributed to the accumulation of patents, even when the patents are legally acquired? Should the level of intervention by competition authorities to constrain contentious IP practices vary across industries? Does compulsory licensing reduce the incentive to innovate? Should the refusal to deal or license an essential facility be treated as an abuse of dominant position under the *Competition Act*?

Several important lessons emerged from the Symposium:

- Both competition policy and intellectual property rights play vital roles in fostering innovation and the diffusion of new technology.

- Particularly in technologically complex industries such as network industries, IP rights can sometimes facilitate the undue exercise of market power. While an active competition policy may serve to check this tendency, it is important that clear and predictable rules of reason be formulated to deal with cases in which IPRs are abusive or simply too broad. Uncertainty in the policy could impede technological progress in these industries.

- Policy makers should move cautiously when imposing open interfaces or compulsory licensing, since such interventions have the potential to turn the competition authority into a regulatory body. While such action by competition authorities or courts may nonetheless be appropriate in some contexts (particularly those of network industries), where possible it should be implemented in ways that require a minimum of ongoing regulatory supervision.

- Ensuring an appropriate balance between competition and IP policies, especially as they apply to complex technologies, may best be served by the participation of the competition authorities in reviews of the relevant legislation.

- In designing enforcement policies towards IP, competition authorities should be mindful of the important contribution of IP to economic growth, as well as the potential for adverse market power effects.

The purpose of this volume was to present our understanding of the relationship between intellectual property and competition policy, from both economic and legal perspectives, and then to identify and explore the remaining unanswered questions in this area. The complexity and rapid growth of new technologies, the expansion of markets internationally, and the multitude of recent trade agreements require further analysis of the way in which intellectual property is and should be treated under competition law. The volume offers a framework for such an analysis as well as a guide for the sound application of competition policy in the knowledge-based economy.

About the Contributors

Robert D. Anderson is Counsellor, Intellectual Property and Investment Division, at the World Trade Organization (WTO) in Geneva, where he is assigned to work on emerging issues relating to the interface between trade and competition policy. Recently, he contributed to a Special Study on Trade and Competition Policy for publication in the 1997 Annual Report of the WTO. Prior to joining the WTO in May 1997, he was on the staff of the Competition Bureau, Industry Canada, where he held the positions of: (i) Chief, Economic Policy, and (ii) Acting Director, International Affairs. Mr. Anderson received his B.A. (Hons.) in Economics from the University of British Columbia and his LL.B. from Osgoode Hall Law School, York University, and has also completed graduate courses in economics and international affairs at York and Carleton Universities. He is the author or coauthor of numerous articles and monographs on topics in competition policy and economic regulation, including the interface between competition policy and intellectual property rights.

William F. Baxter, B.A., J.D., Stanford, joined Stanford Law faculty immediately upon graduation, taught several years, then practiced with Covington & Burling in Washington D.C. He returned to Stanford in 1960. He subsequently taught at Yale; and then in 1968 and 1969 served on the President's Task Force on Antitrust Policy and on the President's Task Force on International Telecommunications. In 1971, he represented a group of retailers before the United States Price Commission, then spent a year at the Centre for Advanced Study in the Behavioral Sciences. He served as Assistant Attorney General of the United States for the years 1981 through 1983. During this period, he dismissed the government's suit against IBM, brought to conclusion its suit against AT&T, negotiated AT&T's reorganization and supervised the drafting of the 1982 merger guidelines. He returned to Stanford in 1984 and also became Counsel to Shearman & Sterling.

Neil Campbell is a partner in McMillan Binch, a major Toronto business law firm. His practice is devoted primarily to competition law, marketing and distribution matters, foreign investment and international trade. Mr. Campbell was the gold medalist in his H.B.A (University of Western Ontario, 1982), LL.B. (Osgoode Hall, 1989) and M.B.A. (York University, 1989) studies and is also a Certified Management Accountant. He completed a doctorate in competition law at the University of Toronto in 1993 and his thesis on the Canadian merger review system won the Alan Marks Medal for the best graduate thesis in the Faculty of Law. Mr. Campbell is the author of *Merger Law and Practice: The Regulation of Mergers Under the Competition Act* (Carswell, forthcoming) and has published numerous articles on competition law and corporate governance topics. Mr. Campbell has taught at the University of Western Ontario School of Business Administration, York University and the University of Toronto Faculty of Law, and is the past Chair of the International Competition and Trade Committee of the Canadian Bar Association Competition Law Section.

Jeffrey Church has a Ph.D. in economics from the University of California at Berkeley and is presently an Associate Professor in the Department of Economics at the University of Calgary. His fields of specialization are industrial organization, regulatory economics, and competition policy. His published research includes articles on network externalities, strategic competition, entry deterrence, and the law and economics of abuse of dominant position. He is the coauthor with Roger Ware of *Industrial Organization: A Strategic Approach* (forthcoming). He was the 1995-1996 T. D. MacDonald Chair in Industrial Economics at the Canadian Competition Bureau.

Joseph Farrell is Professor of Economics, affiliated Professor of Business, and Academic Affiliate in the Center for Law and Technology, at the University of California, Berkeley. Much of his research has focused on network effects and lock-in. Mr. Farrell is North American editor of the *Journal of Industrial Economics*, and a former President of the Industrial Organization Society. At the time of the conference, he was on leave from his Berkeley position and serving as Chief Economist at the U.S. Federal Communications Commission.

Paul M. Feuer is a lawyer within the Economics and International Affairs Branch, Competition Bureau. He joined the Bureau in 1995 and has since coauthored or contributed to works on competition, trade policy and intellectual property. He has a B.A. from the University of Ottawa and an LL.B. from the University of Manitoba.

Nancy T. Gallini is Professor of Economics and currently serves as Chair of the Department of Economics at the University of Toronto. She received her Ph.D. from the University of California, Berkeley, in 1980 and has held visiting positions at the University of California, Berkeley, at Yale University and at the Centre de Recherche en Économie et Statistique, Paris. Her published research includes articles in the field of industrial organization with focus on resource economics, technology licensing, competition policy and intellectual property law, in leading academic journals. Currently, she serves on the editorial boards of the *American Economic Review*, the *International Journal of Industrial Organization* and the *Journal of Industrial Economics*.

Richard Gilbert is Professor of Economics and Business Administration at the University of California, Berkeley. From 1993 to 1995 he was Deputy Assistant Attorney General for Economics in the Antitrust Division of the U.S. Department of Justice, the highest-ranking economics position in the Antitrust Division. While in that capacity, he led a task force that produced the joint Department of Justice and Federal Trade Commission *Antitrust Guidelines for the Licensing of Intellectual Property*. Professor Gilbert's research focuses on antitrust policy, regulation, intellectual property and energy economics.

Derek Ireland has thirty years of experience as an economist in the Canadian public and private sectors. He has held several senior positions with the federal and Saskatchewan governments and worked for ten years as a private consultant with the DPA Group in Vancouver. Mr. Ireland returned to the federal government in 1988 as Senior Economist with the Department of Consumer and Corporate Affairs with responsibilities for intellectual property, bankruptcy and corporate law reform; he then became Director of Economics and International Affairs in the Competition Bureau from 1990 to 1994. During this period, Mr. Ireland contributed to OECD work on international competition law and the links between competition and trade policies. Since August 1995, Mr. Ireland has held the position of Director of Consumer Research and Analysis, Office of Consumer Affairs, at Industry Canada. In both his government and private sector work, Mr. Ireland has directed international aid projects and provided technical assistance on competition, consumer and other policies in a large number of emerging market economies, ranging from Russia, Malaysia and Brazil to Sri Lanka, Pakistan and the Yemen Arab Republic.

Daniel P. Kessler is Assistant Professor of economics, law and policy at Stanford University's Graduate School of Business and a faculty research fellow at the National Bureau of Economic Research. He holds a J.D. from Stanford Law School and a Ph.D. in economics from M.I.T. He has published articles in political science, law, and economics journals. His research interests are in the economic analysis of the causes and effects of law and regulation. In particular, his research investigates the determinants of legal reforms, particularly reforms to the tort liability system; how tort laws affect outcomes of the system such as delay in the courts and in settlement; and how tort and antitrust policy affect innovation and efficiency, especially in the health care sector.

Donald G. McFetridge is currently Professor and Chair of the Department of Economics at Carleton University in Ottawa. Professor McFetridge has published numerous articles and books and supervised doctoral research on various aspects of industrial economics, the economics of innovation, science policy and competition policy. He held the T. D. MacDonald Chair in Industrial Economics at the Competition Bureau in Ottawa during the 1992-93 academic year. Professor McFetridge is presently serving as Chair of the Economics and Law Committee of the National Competition Law Section of the Canadian Bar Association and is a member of the editorial board of the *Canadian Competition Record*.

Robert P. Merges received a B.S. degree from Carnegie-Mellon University, a J.D. from Yale University and an LL.M. from Columbia University. Prior to joining the faculty at Boalt Hall at the University of California, Berkeley, Professor Merges was a faculty member at Boston University School of Law and served as a visiting professor at Harvard Law School. Professor Merges has authored or coauthored four books: *Patent Law and Policy: Cases and Materials* (now in its second edition); *Intellectual Property in the New Technological Age, Cases and Materials; Legal Protection for Computer Technology;* and *Outer Space: Problems of Law and Policy* (2nd ed, 1997). In addition, he has published numerous articles on the subject of intellectual property and new technologies including, most recently, "Contracting into Liability Rules: Intellectual Property Rights and Collective Rights Organizations," *California Law Review*, 1997. He also serves as the editor-in-chief of *Intellectual Property Abstracts*, the leading online abstracting service in the intellectual property field. Professor Merges was recently named as the inaugural holder of the Wilson Sonsini Goodrich & Rosati Chair in Law and Technology/Intellectual Property. He is co-director of the Berkeley Centre for Law and Technology, which studies the role that legal institutions play in technological development.

Joshua A. Newberg is an attorney with the Bureau of Competition at the U.S. Federal Trade Commission, where he has also served as attorney-advisor to Commissioner Roscoe B. Starek, III. He earned his Bachelor of Arts (B.A., 1981), Master of Arts (M.A., 1982), and Juris Doctor (J.D., 1989) degrees from the University of Pensylvania. Before joining the Federal Trade Commission in 1994, he was a judicial clerk for Hon. William J. Holloway, Jr., Chief Judge of the United States Court of Appeals for the Tenth Circuit (1989-90), and an associate attorney in the New York and Washington offices of the Shearman & Sterling law firm (1990-94). During the 1996-97 academic year, he served as Visiting Associate Professor at the University of Texas Business School, at Austin.

Patrick Rey earned diplomas from École Polytechnique and ENSAE and a Ph.D. in economics from the University of Toulouse. He has been Assistant Professor at ENSAE and economist at INSEE (Bureau of Economic Forecasts and Research Unit), Visiting Professor at MIT, and Director of the Laboratoire d'Économie Industrielle (LEI-CREST). He is currently Professor of Economics at the University of Toulouse, Research Director at the Institut d'Économie Industrielle (IDEI), and Associate Professor at École Polytechnique.

Brian A. Rivard is an economist within the Economics and International Affairs Branch of the Competition Bureau. He joined the Competition Bureau as an economist in 1993. He has an M.A. and a Ph.D. from the University of Western Ontario.

Mark F. Ronayne is a senior economist within the Civil Matters Branch of the Competition Bureau. He joined the Competition Bureau as an economist in 1983. He is the coauthor of several papers on the interface between competition law and intellectual property rights, and other aspects of competition law. Mr. Ronayne has a B.A. and an M.A. in economics from Carleton University.

F. Michael Scherer is Larsen Professor of Public Policy and Management at the John F. Kennedy School of Government, Harvard University. He has also taught at Princeton University, the University of Michigan, Northwestern University, and Swarthmore College. In 1974-76, he was chief economist at the U.S. Federal Trade Commission. His research interests are industrial economics and the economics of technological change. He has published books on *Industrial Market Structure and Economic Performance* (third edition, with David Ross), *The Economics of Multi-Plant Operation: An International Comparisons Study* (with three coauthors), *International High-Technology Competition*, *Competition Policies for an Integrated World Economy*, *Mergers, Sell-offs, and Economic Efficiency* (with David J. Ravenscraft), *Innovation and Growth: Schumpeterian Perspectives*, *The Weapons Acquisition Process* (two volumes, one with M. J. Peck), and a new textbook, *Industry Structures, Strategy, and Public Policy*.

Marius Schwartz is Professor of Economics at Georgetown University. He obtained his B.Sc. with first-class honours from the London School of Economics in 1976 and his Ph.D. in economics from the University of California at Los Angeles in 1982. He has published and presented work extensively on subjects such as vertical restraints, price discrimination, intellectual property, exclusionary practices, potential competition, and regulatory reform. From April 1995 to June 1996, he served as Senior Economist at the President's Council of Economic Advisers, responsible for industrial organization issues including antitrust and regulation, where he worked especially on the *Telecommunications Act*, competition in international satellite services, and restructuring of the electric utility industry. Since 1980 he has consulted for the Antitrust Division of the U.S. Department of Justice and for international organizations on a wide variety of competition matters, and has taught microeconomics and competition policy to executives and government officials in the U.S. and abroad.

Suzanne Scotchmer is Professor of Economics and Public Policy at the University of California, Berkeley, and previously taught at Harvard University. Her graduate degrees are in economics and statistics. She has held visiting appointments at Tel Aviv University, University of Paris I (Sorbonne), Boalt School of Law, the University of Toronto Law School, Yale University, Stanford University, and the New School of Economics, Moscow. She has published on intellectual property law, rules of evidence, tax enforcement, cooperative game theory, club theory, and evolutionary game theory. She currently serves on the editorial boards of the *Journal of Economic Perspectives* and the *Journal of Public Economics*.

Willard K. Tom is Assistant Director in charge of the Office of Policy and Evaluation in the U.S. Federal Trade Commission's Bureau of Competition. Prior to joining the FTC, Mr. Tom was counsellor to the Assistant Attorney General in the Antitrust Division, U.S. Department of Justice. There he served as a member of the task force that drafted the Department of Justice and the Federal Trade Commission *Antitrust Guidelines for the Licensing of Intellectual Property*. Mr. Tom was Chair of the editorial board for the American Bar Association's treatise, *Antitrust Law Developments* (3d ed., 1992), and has spoken and written on a variety of antitrust topics. Mr. Tom is a graduate of Harvard College (A.B. *cum laude*, 1975) and Harvard Law School (J.D. *cum laude*, 1979).

Michael J. Trebilcock is Professor of Law and Director of the Law and Economics Programme at the University of Toronto Law School. He has authored *The Common Law of Restraint of Trade* (1986), *The Limits of Freedom of Contract* (Harvard University Press, 1993), and *Exploring the Domain of Accident Law: Taking the Facts Seriously* (Oxford University Press, 1995), and has coauthored *Canadian Competition Policy* (1987), *Trade and Transitions: A Comparative Analysis of Adjustment Policies* (1990), and *International Trade Regulation* (Routledge, London, 1995). The first book was awarded the Walter Owen Prize in 1988 for best legal text in English published in Canada during the previous two years. He has also participated in various studies on Canadian competition policy, public enterprise in Canada, business bail-outs in Canada, misleading advertising and unfair business practice laws, regulatory reform and the choice of governing instruments, "reinventing" government, regulation of the professions, trade-related adjustment assistance policies, trade remedy laws, tort reform and the liability insurance crisis, traffic safety regulation, and liability for medical malpractice. He teaches contract law, competition law, international trade law, and public goals – private means, at the University of Toronto Law School. He was a member of the Competition Tribunal from 1987-89 and a visiting scholar at the University of Chicago Law School (1976) and Yale Law School (1985). In 1986, he was elected a Fellow of the Royal Society of Canada and in May of 1991, he was named a University Professor at the University of Toronto.

Roger Ware is Professor of Economics at Queen's University. He holds degrees from Cambridge University, the University of Sussex and Queen's University. He has taught previously at the University of Toronto and the University of California at Berkeley. He specializes in industrial organization issues and competition policy and has published extensively in academic and policy journals. In 1993-94, he held the T. D. MacDonald Chair in Industrial Economics at the Canadian Competition Bureau.

Ralph A. Winter is Professor at the University of Toronto where he teaches in the Department of Economics, the Faculty of Management and the Faculty of Law. Professor Winter received his B.Sc. in mathematics and economics from the University of British Columbia, and an M.A. in statistics and a Ph.D. in economics from the University of California at Berkeley. As well as teaching at the University of Toronto, he has held positions as a National Fellow at the Hoover Institution at Stanford, and as Olin Fellow in Law and Economics at Yale Law School. Professor Winter's research areas include the application of contract theory to issues in competition policy and the interaction between tort law and the liability insurance markets.

Dennis A. Yao is Associate Professor of Public Policy and Management at the Wharton School, University of Pennsylvania. He has a Ph.D. from the Graduate School of Business, Stanford University. From 1991-94 Professor Yao served as one of the five commissioners of the U.S. Federal Trade Commission. His research is largely in the area of industrial organization economics and business-government relations, and he has published a number of papers on antitrust, procurement contracting, and innovation and intellectual property.

PRINTED AND BOUND
IN BOUCHERVILLE, QUÉBEC, CANADA
BY MARC VEILLEUX IMPRIMEUR INC.
IN JULY, 1998